William Crolly, Archbishop of Armagh, 1835–49

WILLIAM CROLLY

ARCHBISHOP OF ARMAGH, 1835–49

AMBROSE MACAULAY

FOUR COURTS PRESS

This book was typeset
in 11 on 13 Ehrhardt by
Koinonia Ltd, Manchester for
FOUR COURTS PRESS,
Kill Lane, Blackrock, Co. Dublin, Ireland.

A catalogue record for this book
is available from the British Library.

ISBN 1-85182-1473

Publication of this book has been grant-aided by First Trust Bank.

Printed in Ireland by
Beta Print Ltd, Dublin

I learn from that Bible, which we all regard as the common foundation of our faith, that no one can serve the God of peace without exerting himself to promote peace, and kindness, and harmony, and charity, in the world; and it is only by thus acting that I can ever make you a return for your kindness. . . . It is not necessary that we should sacrifice or compromise our conscientious convictions; but it is necessary that we should carry our prejudices to the Communion Table of Charity, and there consume them on the altar of our common country.

William Crolly, thanking the Protestants of Belfast who had entertained him after his episcopal ordination.

I feel much pleased to be this night instructed by the Bishop of a Church from which I differ in matters of faith. He has demeaned himself in society, and regulated his conduct in the ministry, so well, that we find here assembled men of all religious persuasions, to congratulate him on his advancement in his Church. This testifies best, how differences in creed make no distinction in the discharge of the common and social duties of life.

Henry Montgomery, on the same occasion.

Oh, faithful sainted Plunkett! you who confronted the bloody persecutors of our holy principles, and yielded up your life for your faith; how must your spirit be troubled to behold one of your successors in the see of Armagh cajoled and deceived into the adoption of a course of conduct fraught with such dangerous consequence to that faith for which you endured the tortures of martyrdom.

Patrick Mallon, at a meeting of protest in Eglish, Co. Tyrone against the Charitable Bequests Act.

CONTENTS

LIST OF ILLUSTRATIONS

PREFACE

William Crolly was born in 1780 and died in 1849. His life coincided with the resurgence of Irish Catholicism in the late eighteenth and first half of the nineteenth century. His birth just preceded the dismantling of much of the penal code – the Crolly family lost its ancestral lands in 1784, when its head took advantage of 'the Act to prevent the further growth of popery' to claim and then sell the entire estate – and his death occurred at the end of the great Famine, which devastated the country and decimated its population. He was one of the first students educated at Maynooth who was appointed to its staff, and later one of its first ex-alumni to be appointed a bishop. He was parish priest for thirteen years and bishop for ten years in Belfast, and for much of that time enjoyed warm, personal and pastoral relationships with leading clergy and laity of that predominantly Presbyterian town.

Archbishop of Armagh from 1835 to 1849, he played a major role in Irish ecclesiastical and political life, especially in the decade 1839-49. In those years the Catholic Church was riven by three serious controversies. The first of these, which concerned the system of national education, was fought out among the bishops, but the other two, which were provoked by the Charitable Bequests Act and the Colleges (Ireland) Act, engaged the general public in an intense and impassioned way. Crolly headed the victorious party in the dispute over the national schools, but several of his colleagues deserted him on the other two issues, and his following was reduced to less than a third of the entire episcopate. His support among the priests and their congregations was even smaller, and reflected his forfeiture of public sympathy by his refusal to endorse the popular campaign for the Repeal of the Union.

A short account of the archbishop's life was published by his nephew, George Crolly, in 1851. George had defended his uncle's educational policies in an exchange of letters with a Carlow priest in the *Dublin Evening*

ix

Post, and then printed some of them as an appendix to a brief outline of the primate's career. He omitted all mention of several pastoral and political problems with which the archbishop was concerned and was rather sparing with details of the Crolly family. William Crolly deserves a fuller study, and it is hoped that the present biography will fill some of the more frustrating gaps left by the loyal, if slight, work of George Crolly.

I am grateful to all those who have helped me in the preparation of this book. For permission to use archival material I should like to acknowledge my indebtedness to the following: Cardinal Sodano, Secretary of State; Cardinal Stickler, former Librarian of the Holy Roman Church; Cardinal Tomko, Prefect of the Congregation for the Evangelization of Peoples; Cardinal Daly, Archbishop of Armagh; Archbishop Connell of Dublin; Archbishop Couve de Murville of Birmingham; Bishop Francis G. Brooks of Dromore; Bishop Patrick J. Walsh of Down and Connor; Bishop James McLoughlin of Galway; Bishop David Konstant of Leeds; Monsignor John Hanly and Monsignor Sean Brady, former Rectors of the Pontifical Irish College, Rome; Revd John McGrane, Parochial House, Cooley, Co. Louth.

I wish to thank the librarians and staffs at the Bodleian Library, the British Library, the British Library Newspaper Library, the Linen Hall Library (Belfast), the Liverpool Public Library, the National Archives (Dublin), the National Library of Ireland, the Public Record Office (London), and the Public Record Office of Northern Ireland.

I am especially indebted to Fr Joseph Metzler, Prefect of the Vatican Archives; to Monsignor Charles Burns, Archivist at the Vatican Archives; to Monsignor Marcello Camisassa, Archivist at the Secretariat of State, Vatican City; to Fr Sarkis Tabar, Archivist of the Congregation for the Evangelization of Peoples; to Dr Herman H. Schwedt, Archivist of the diocese of Limburg; to Mr David Sheehy, Director of the Dublin Diocesan Archives.

For their kindness in reading my typescript and giving me much valuable advice I am happy to record my thanks to Bishop Michael Dallat, Monsignor Patrick J. Corish, Dr Brian Trainor, Professor Vincent Comerford, Fr Joseph Gunn and the late Jack Magee. Finally, I should like to express my gratitude to the First Trust Bank for its very generous sponsorship of this publication.

Ambrose Macaulay,
Belfast,
1 February 1994

ABBREVIATIONS

AA.EE.SS.	Archives of the Second Section (Relations with States) of the Secretariat of State (formerly the Congregation of Extraordinary Ecclesiastical Affairs).
ADA.	Armagh Diocesan Archives
A.G.	*Armagh Guardian*
AICR	Archives of the Pontifical Irish College, Rome
APF	Archives of the Sacred Congregation for the Evangelization of Peoples (formerly Propaganda Fide), Rome.
ASV	Vatican Archives
BDA	Birmingham Diocesan Archives
B.L.	British Library
B.M.M.	*Belfast Monthly Magazine*
B.N.L.	*Belfast News Letter*
D.A.	*Drogheda Argus*
DCDA	Down and Connor Diocesan Archives
DDA	Dublin Diocesan Archives
D.E.P.	*Dublin Evening Post*
DrDA	Dromore Diocesan Archives
F.J.	*Freeman's Journal*
GDA	Galway Diocesan Archives
H.C.	House of Commons
Ir.	*Irishman*
LDA	Leeds Diocesan Archives
N.	*Nation*
N.Ex.	*Newry Examiner, (Newry Examiner and Louth Advertiser)*
N.H.	*Northern Herald*

N.H.I.	*A New History of Ireland* V, ed. W.E. Vaughan (Oxford, 1989).
N.T.	*Newry Telegraph*
N.W.	*Northern Whig*
P.	*Pilot*
V.	*Vindicator*
W.V.	*Weekly Vindicator*
G. Crolly, *Crolly*	*The Life of the Most Rev. Doctor Crolly, Archbishop of Armagh, and Primate of Ireland, which are appended some letters in defence of his character* (Dublin, 1851).
O'Laverty, *Down and Connor*	J. O'Laverty, *An Historical Account of the Diocese of Down and Connor, ancient and modern*, 5 vols. (Dublin 1878-95).
O'Reilly, *MacHale*	B. O'Reilly, *John MacHale, Archbishop of Tuam; his Life, Times and Correspondence*, 2 vols. (New York and Cincinnati, 1890).

STUDENT, SEMINARIAN
AND PROFESSOR

The townland of Ballykilbeg, which is situated about four miles from Downpatrick, acquired fame in the second half of the nineteenth century through its association with the militant Orange leader, William Johnston. His controversial political career, which brought him into open and successful confrontation with a government that had prohibited Orange marches, ensured for his little fief a notoriety which it would otherwise never have achieved. However, Ballykilbeg had earlier given birth to another son, who, if his career was less shrill and flamboyant, brought at least as much distinction to the place of his birth.

The Swordes family, which was of Anglo-Norman origin, held extensive property in the vicinity of Downpatrick for centuries as barons of the palatinate of Ulster. According to the Ulster Inquisitions of 1586 a Robert Swordes—or Crolly according to the Gaelic version of the name—stood possessed of Ballykilbeg, and of a group of neighbouring townlands, all of which were forfeited in the early seventeenth century to Theophilus Buckworth, the Protestant bishop of Dromore.[1] The family, which was regarded as one of the leading Catholic families of Co. Down, succeeded in retaining possession of Ballykilbeg throughout that turbulent century. But in the following century, either due to bad luck or bad management, it was forced to mortgage the lands heavily. When John Crolly, the owner of the estate, died intestate in 1773, he left substantial debts against it. In the following year, George, his eldest son, read his recantation from the Church of Rome in St Mary's Parish Church, Dublin, obtained the bishop's certificate that he was a Protestant, filed it in the Rolls office, received the Sacrament and took the oaths of Allegiance and Supremacy. According to the terms of the 'popery act' of 1704, which was designed 'to prevent the further growth of popery', he was thereby entitled to claim sole possession of Ballykilbeg.

[1] O'Laverty, *Down and Connor*, V, 583.

In 1778 he advertised the sale of the estate but his stepmother, sister and nephew published notices in the press to warn potential purchasers that they were entitled to shares in it. The sister, widow and children of his late brother, Daniel, then filed a bill in chancery charging that George had relapsed into popery and claiming their portions of John Crolly's property. George denied that he had reverted to his former religion and again put Ballykilbeg on the market. Though it was sold in 1780, legal disputes prevented the deal from being finalized, and it was not till 1784 that Ballykilbeg was bought for £4,140 by William Johnstone (the name was later abbreviated to Johnston). By then George Crolly, the last Baron Crolly of Swordes, had died.[2]

The estate consisted of two hundred and eighty eight acres, and, according to the advertisements offering it for sale, about four fifths of it was good arable land and meadow, and one fifth was turf bog. About one hundred and thirty acres were leased to tenants and nearly forty to tenants-at-will. Among the leaseholders was a junior branch of the family to which John Crolly, a cousin of George's, belonged.

Though documentary evidence about this line is scanty—even the headstones in the cemetery in Downpatrick have disappeared—it seems likely that John's wife, Mary Maxwell, was a Protestant. An oral tradition to that effect survives, and both the name and the fact that Protestant Maxwells owned the adjoining townland of Ballyrolly lend some support to it. Moreover, John subsequently farmed in Ballyrolly, and, perhaps, his son's sensitivity to Protestant feeling and his deep desire for peaceful community relations may owe something to his mother's background.

This son, William, was born at Ballykilbeg on 8 June 1780. He had at least one brother, John, who later farmed in Ballyrolly, and a sister, Ann, who married and lived near Downpatrick, and may have had others whose names do not appear in the few references to the family that exist. According to the life of his uncle written by George Crolly in 1851, which is tantalizingly brief about the family background and early years of its subject, William Crolly attended a local preparatory school, which had Catholic staff but which also numbered some Protestant pupils on its rolls. In his fourteenth year he transferred to a classical school in Downpatrick, which was conducted by Dr James Neilson, the Presbyterian minister of the town, with the aid of an usher or assistant named Doran, who was a Catholic. Such schools, which specialized in teaching their pupils Latin and Greek, and preparing them if necessary for higher

---

[2] PRONI D880/1/12D, B.N.L., 8, 18, 22 Sept. 1778, 1 Oct. 1779, 14 Oct. 1783, McClelland, *Johnston of Ballykilbeg*, 2–3.

education were springing up in many Irish towns. Their existence was often brief and precarious and their standards ranged from the competent to the haphazard. Neilson, a graduate of the University of Glasgow, seems to have kept one of the best schools of its kind and among his pupils he numbered two other future bishops and several priests of the diocese of Down and Connor. When Doran withdrew his services from Neilson and set up his own school, Crolly was sent to it. But he retained the highest regard for his former teacher and, when bishop of Down and Connor, wrote to the parish priest of Dromore warmly recommending Neilson's son, William, who had been appointed to the charge of the Presbyterian congregation of that town, and describing James Neilson as 'one of the most liberal and respectable clergymen in County Down'.[3]

Crolly's studies were disrupted by the rebellion of 1798 when Doran was arrested for seditious political views and lodged in Downpatrick jail. An accommodating governor of the prison, however, permitted him to continue giving lessons and Crolly was among the pupils who pursued his secondary studies in this unlikely and uncongenial environment. During this troubled time the young student experienced at first hand the consequences of rebellious opposition to the forces of the crown. Chancing to break the curfew imposed under martial law, he was riding home from Downpatrick when he was pursued by six or seven dragoons. He narrowly escaped capture when a large mastiff sprang at a dragoon's horse and caused them both to fall. The dragoons continued their pursuit, entered the family home and on finding a large family bible may have concluded that the occupants were Protestant, for they abruptly ended their search.[4] Crolly later testified that politics did not impinge on him at this stage of his life, so the teacher had obviously not tried to indoctrinate his pupils with his own political views. And whether or not the escapade with the dragoons had any lasting effects, the nationalism of the adult was subsequently of a very muted and decidedly non-violent nature.

As a boy he had read a life of St Patrick and, inspired by it and by the Patrician associations of the Downpatrick area, had turned his thoughts towards the priesthood. A meeting with three priests from the staff of Maynooth confirmed him in his intention, and though his father would have preferred the choice of a different career, his mother was pleased by his decision.[5] Consequently, completing his classical studies at Down-patrick, he entered the newly-established seminary at Maynooth. He was then aged twenty-one, a somewhat advanced age for entry to Irish

---

[3] Crolly to Revd H. McConville, 11 Mar. 1825, DrDA [4] G. Crolly, *Crolly*, xi–xiv.
[5] Ibid., viii, xiv.

seminaries by the standards obtaining later in the century, but not unusual at a time when seminarians often went off to the continent to pursue their theological studies after ordination at home.

II

The Royal College of St Patrick at Maynooth was one of the beneficial, if indirect, consequences of the French Revolution. The Irish colleges in France had quickly attracted the anti-religious ire of the revolutionaries and, though some managed to survive for a time, others had ceased to function by 1791. When Britain declared war on France their position became impossible and they were quickly closed. A similar fate soon overtook those in the Low Countries. The Irish bishops decided to appeal to parliament for permission and for financial support to erect a seminary in Ireland. The law against seeking education abroad had been repealed, and in 1793 Catholics were enfranchised on the same terms as Protestants, though they were still not permitted to stand for parliament. The government acceded to their request, and in April 1795 a bill establishing a college was introduced and an annual endowment of £8,000 was later agreed. A site was acquired at Maynooth and the college opened its doors to about forty students and four professors in October 1795.

Among the first ten appointments to the staff were those of two French emigrés who became professors of mathematics and natural philosophy, and of logic, metaphysics and ethics: Peter Delort and Andrew Darré. Three years later another Frenchman, the aristocrat, Louis Delahogue, a Fellow of the Sorbonne, was named professor of moral theology; in 1801 he transferred to the principal chair in the college, that of dogmatic theology, which he held till 1820 and from which he was destined to exercise a powerful influence over the Irish priesthood for many years. In 1802 another exiled French scholar and former professor at the Sorbonne, Francis Anglade, joined the staff as professor of logic, metaphysics and ethics in succession to Darré, who moved to the chair of mathematics and natural philosophy. Stripped of office by the revolution, Anglade had spent several years gardening in Wales until rescued by Delahogue for the chair in Maynooth.[6]

By 1799 the first set of buildings, to house two hundred students, was completed. Meanwhile, the college had become embroiled, however tenuously, in the rebellion of 1798. The trustees, who viewed with equal

[6] Healy, *Maynooth College*, 148–9, 160, 190–200.

detestation the state of political excitement which Ireland had reached in the spring of 1798 and the French source of inspiration to which it was traced as both disloyal and irreligious, empowered the president to expel any student who held political views 'tending to subvert a due regard to the established authorities'. Ten students were charged with having taken the oath of the United Irishmen and were sent down. Seven extern students who were attending the junior classes suffered the same punishment, though eventually only one of those who were dismissed took part in the rebellion.[7]

William Crolly entered the humanity, or junior class in classics in November 1801. He did not read the rhetoric course, probably because his bishop felt, as did some of the staff, that the pressing pastoral needs of the country necessitated the limitation of seminary training, but passed into the class of logic, metaphysics and ethics. At Christmas 1802 he became seriously ill and moved to Dublin for medical care. He wrote to his brother, John, about his condition remarking that he had 'a disease which is very seldom cured', expressing resignation to God's will and inviting his brother to stay with him during his illness. He was forced to remain in Dublin for sixteen weeks, but on his return to Maynooth he studied 'with more than ordinary attention' and, despite his lengthy absence, obtained very favourable results at the end of the year. On his way home for vacation in the summer he heard at Dundalk that Robert Emmet's rebellion had broken out. He was told to travel on quickly lest he might be apprehended, as he was not known in that part of the country. He hastened to Newry where he had acquaintances who could testify to his identity. When he reached home illness again struck him and he was unable to return to Maynooth until February in 1804. It was then too late for him to join the class of mathematics and natural philosophy and he had to content himself with reading that course privately after ordination.[8] He spent a further two years studying theology, and in 1806 achieved the distinction of winning first place in dogma, the most coveted prize in the college.

Twenty years later at a commission of inquiry into Maynooth, he commented on the facilities which the college offered in his student days. He noted that the opportunities for the study of sacred scripture were limited. In his first year, Peter Flood, the president, obliged the students to commit to memory a certain portion of the New Testament every week. They were examined on it each Saturday and the president explained

[7] Ibid., 242-3.   [8] G. Crolly, Crolly, xv–xvii.

difficult passages. Flood became ill in 1802, before he had had a chance to complete his course, and his successor, Andrew Dunne, either because he was not 'so deeply conversant with theological matters' or because he was 'not equal to Doctor Flood in his explanations', seems to have dropped the classes in scripture. Consequently, Crolly received no instruction on the Old Testament.

He was also to regret later the lack of proper training in elocution. As president, Flood had been accustomed to listen to a student's sermon almost every Sunday evening, to criticize it and to invite other students to do the same. His successors were not capable of continuing this practice with the same facility. And little opportunity was afforded the students for the study of English, apart from preparing pieces of composition, which were then publicly examined, but Crolly devoted much time to reading the English classics.[9]

The fledgling college was also handicapped by a lack of textbooks in theology and philosophy. The destruction of ecclesiastical life in France and the prolonged Anglo-French wars prevented the staff from acquiring books at their normal source. The students were compelled to rely almost entirely on their class notes, and it was to remedy this situation that Delahogue and Anglade subsequently compiled their valuable manuals. On the completion of his second year of theology, which, because of illness, meant in effect that his studies had been limited to four years, Crolly was ordained priest on the feast of Pentecost, 24 May 1806. A month later he was appointed assistant to Francis Anglade as lecturer in logic, ethics and metaphysics. On the same day Patrick McNicholas was promoted to a junior lectureship in classics. They were the second batch of alumni of Maynooth to join the staff; in 1801 Thomas Coen, the first registered student of the college, had become dean of discipline and Michael Montague had been named a lecturer in mathematics and natural philosophy. Crolly's bishop had not been consulted about this development and was none too pleased, as the pastoral needs of the diocese required the services of all available clergy. But when Crolly assured him that, far from seeking to join the staff, he had been surprised by the decision of the trustees and held himself in readiness to go to Down and Connor when required, the episcopal displeasure was assuaged.[10]

The college was a mere decade in existence when Crolly's teaching career commenced. That decade had been hectic and difficult. Accommodation problems had eased with the completion of the first set of

---

[9] *Eighth report of the commissioners of Irish education inquiry*, pp. 373–8, H.C. 1826–7 (509), xiii.
[10] G. Crolly, *Crolly*, xvii–xviii.

buildings, in 1799. But it took time to develop a smooth daily horarium, and work out a satisfactory set of disciplinary regulations to accommodate the needs both of those who had already been ordained in anticipation of completing their studies abroad and of those who were beginning their full course. The system of government which, because of the state grant permitted the participation of Protestant laymen, prevented the Irish bishops from exercising the immediate control that was customary in seminaries. The brief tenures of office enjoyed by the first superiors contributed to a sense of uncertainty and unrest. Thomas Hussey, the first president, was eased out of office in 1798 when his pastoral letter protesting about the restrictions on the religious practice of Catholic soldiers in the army provoked the government's displeasure. Andrew Flood, Hussey's successor, who had been rector of the Lombard College, the seminary for Irish student priests in Paris, and whose academic work was appreciated by the students took ill in 1802 and died in the following year after less than five years in command. The next two presidents resigned after each had given a mere three years service, and in both cases under a cloud. Patrick Everard, who left his school at Ulverstone in Lancashire in 1810 to assume the office of presidency, met at first with some success but health reasons forced him to return to Lancashire after a short time and he resigned in 1812. The gravity of the situation was highlighted by the decision of the coadjutor archbishop of Dublin, Daniel Murray, to take over the presidency in 1812 and to bring with him Peter Kenny, a distinguished Jesuit, as his vice-president.

The problems that troubled the college in its early years derived from a variety of sources—complaints about food, disciplinary regulations, lack of text books and lack of general facilities. The French and Irish members of staff did not always work harmoniously together. In fact, the first serious crisis occurred in 1803, when the aristocratic Delahogue disdain-fully commented about the behaviour of the peasant body. The students, stung by what they regarded as an insult, revolted. The trustees took firm action and ordered the expulsion of the five leaders, one of whom was William MacMullan, the nephew of the bishop of Down and Connor.

Edward Ferris, the professor of moral theology, who had been dean of discipline, disapproved of this decision, and together with the librarian gave MacMullan a testimonial which sought to exonerate him.[11] As a result of the students' action, the food and fabric of the buildings were improved, the rules were better observed and the ringleaders were toasted

[11] Ferris and A.C. McCormick to MacMullan, 4 Mar. 1803, DCDA.

for their courage on St Patrick's Day.[12] However, complaints about indiscipline among the students and disharmony among the staff persisted. Archbishop Murray's appointment was a serious bid to set a new course, which he and his successor successfully did.

Crolly, as a lecturer, had no responsibility other than to his classes. Edward Ferris reported to William MacMullan in 1807 that the young lecturer in logic, ethics and metaphysics was 'doing perfectly well',[13] and, more than a year later, again commended him and singled him out as the only lecturer who gave repetitions in his class.[14]

In 1810 Anglade was transferred to the chair of moral theology and Crolly succeeded him as professor. He later testified that he followed closely his predecessor's system, which, apart from 'some little differences on some questions respecting ideas', was to be found in Anglade's published work. In fact they both covered the essential elements of philosophy as taught in continental seminaries. The medium for teaching both philosophy and theology in Maynooth was Latin, though the professors gave occasional explanations in English, a facility which Crolly appreciated and which he regarded as highly beneficial to the students.[15] In his 'observations on the state of studies in the R.C. College of Maynooth', which he submitted to Archbishop Troy in 1818, Delahogue described the Maynooth course in logic, metaphysics and ethics as 'the curriculum which has been imperturbably followed for centuries in the University of Paris'. And he went on to say that no 'professor would ever be allowed to introduce into his lectures any French work, not even the Logic of Port Royal (the best ever composed)', and he favoured the exclusion of English works 'both because the most celebrated works of this kind contain principles of scepticism and invective against what their authors call the prejudices and superstitions of Popery; and because it is essential that the young logicians get used to speaking Latin, and to this scholastic form so necessary for the study of Theology'.[16]

For six years Crolly taught unobtrusively in Maynooth. He could scarcely have been known in his native diocese except by contemporaries, and his family, friends and acquaintances in Downpatrick. Yet when the aged and ailing pastor of Derriaghy and Belfast, Hugh O'Donnell, decided finally in 1812 to retire, he and his parishioners sent a deputation to Bishop MacMullan in Downpatrick requesting that he confer the parish on Crolly, when Richard Curoe, one of the two curates serving in

---

[12] John Hurley to MacMullan, 12 Apr. 1803, Ibid.   [13] Ferris to MacMullan, 19 Feb. 1807, Ibid.
[14] Ibid., 18 Nov. 1808.   [15] *Eighth report of the commissioners of Irish education inquiry*, pp. 373–8.
[16] Delahogue to Troy, Jan. 1818 in *Clogher Record*, vi (1968), 485.

it had expressed a preference to go to Kilkeel. There were, of course, few candidates available because of the scarcity of priests; but the application of the congregation to the bishop may have indicated that it felt it was offering a suitable field of labour to a scholarly young man by inviting him to a flourishing town with commercial potential and literary scope.

MacMullan, who may have already intended to appoint Crolly to the vacant parish, invited the deputation to wait on their candidate at his home and inform him of the episcopal wish that he should become parish priest of Belfast.[17] Despite the strong persuasions of Archbishop Troy to remain in Maynooth, Crolly accepted MacMullan's invitation in August 1812 and took up office in Belfast at the beginning of September. He had been given little opportunity to get to know the new president of the college, Archbishop Murray, who had only been appointed at the end of June, but the favourable opinion formed of him by Murray was destined to have important ramifications later.

[17] G. Crolly, *Crolly*, xxxi–xxxii. In response to Bishop MacMullan's account of his diocese in 1814 the congregation of Propaganda expressed surprise that in some parishes the people should arrogate to themselves the right to elect parish priests, and reminded him that that right belonged to the bishop. (Propaganda to MacMullan, 17 June 1815, APF, *Lett.*, 296, ff 110r–111r.)

2

PARISH PRIEST OF BELFAST

Belfast had formed part of a united parish with Derriaghy until Crolly's appointment. But by 1812, with a Catholic population of more than 4,000 it had become much larger than Derriaghy.[1] The parish boundaries, like those of the town, did not cross the Lagan, but extended to the north some twelve or fifteen miles, though few Catholics then lived in places like Whiteabbey, Ligoniel and Glengormley. St Mary's Church, built in 1784, had become too small to accommodate the parishioners comfortably at the Sunday Masses. Crolly brought with him as curate Bernard McAuley, a young Glenarm man, who had just been ordained in Maynooth, to replace Richard Curoe. Peter Cassidy, the other curate, whose health was failing, died in 1815. Charles Hendren, who was ordained in 1816, served in the parish until the end of 1824, and the pattern of two assistants to the parish priest remained unchanged during Crolly's association with the town.

For some years St Mary's had had an active committee of some twenty laymen who were elected by the congregation and managed its finances. This committee met regularly, organized collections for the upkeep of the church, took charge of repairs, paid the sexton and cleaner and occasionally made donations from its funds to some charity such as that of providing coffins for the poor. It financed the services of a catechist who taught catechism to the children each Sunday, and from time to time gave donations to the choir or special artists. One of the priests usually attended and chaired its meetings, but the committee elected its own officials. It was this committee which took steps in 1808 to obtain a site from the marquis of Donegall for a second church, and let his agent know that it was prepared to spend £1,500 on its construction and to build a house for the clergy. When the landlord agreed to lease a site in Donegall

---

[1] This estimate for the year 1808 is taken from Rogers, 'Fr Hugh O'Donnell' in *Essays in British and Irish History in honour of J.E.Todd*, 233

Street, the committee appointed a treasurer to control the funds for the new church, made preliminary preparations by walling in the property, chose the architects and decided on the dimensions of the building. After the construction had begun, it appointed foremen, arranged for the collection and payment of instalments and kept a close check on the progress of the work.

By 1812 the building was nearly completed. Described by an historian of architecture as 'plainish', but boasting 'a rudimentary pediment topped by pinacles and battlements in a vaguely Gothic style',[2] its appearance had given rise to heated controversy and its 'embattled pediment' had been angrily denounced as 'an improper termination for a place of worship dedicated to the religion of a Meek Jesus'.[3] Several years elapsed before the committee was able to complete the second part of its plan—a house for the clergy—but on this occasion the choice of design escaped the hostility of the critics. This house in Donegall Street, to which Crolly moved after ten years residence in Castle Street, was described by the same historian as 'a handsome box-like three storey brick house in the country rectory tradition'.[4]

The first use to which the new church was put was not religious but political. Catholics in Ireland, when campaigning for Emancipation, were forced to use their churches as meeting places since they had no other available venues. On 11 October 1811 the Catholics of Co. Antrim planned to meet in the Exchange Rooms in Belfast to make their contribution to the cause of Emancipation, but the numbers who turned up were so large that they had to move to the unfinished church. The Lord Lieutenant had issued an order in February 1811 prohibiting the election of delegates to the Catholic Committee in Dublin, and, when arrangements were made for the Catholics of each county to appoint members to a central committee to draw up petitions to parliament, the government again declared this step illegal. This heavy-handed intervention galvanized the Catholics of each county into holding meetings to prepare petitions for parliament calling for the repeal of all penal statutes. At the Antrim meeting Edmund McGildowney, a Catholic landlord from Ballycastle, presided, and nine other prominent Catholics were commissioned with him to prepare a petition calling for the repeal of all laws which excluded them from the full enjoyment of all the rights and privileges of the British constitution. Resolutions were passed proclaiming their right to assemble for the purpose of petitioning for the redress of

² Brett, *Buildings of Belfast*, 14.   ³ B.M.M., Mar. 1811, VI, 183-5 and July 1811, VII, 21-2.
⁴ Brett, *Buildings of Belfast*, 20.

their grievances and thanking all the leaders in Dublin and London who campaigned on their behalf. Profound gratitude was expressed to Protestant participants, the most distinguished of whom, the veteran liberal, William Drennan, proclaimed the need for all who cherished the good order and tranquillity of their country to support the Catholic claims. He declared, to great applause, that he ascribed the progressive union and concord of his fellow-countrymen chiefly, if not solely, 'to one cause—to the rashness, the precipitance, and the infatuation of an administration, which have overleaped all the bounds of sage and sound discretion, and by standing in the way of a right of Nature, the right of Petitioning, have acted in direct contradiction and contempt of common sense and the common feelings of humanity—and in doing so, by a sort of *providential fatuity*, have not only roused all that is man within the Catholic bosom, but have awakened a social sympathy, a general fellow-feeling with the case of the Catholics in the breasts of every other rank and order in the community'. He predicted that the resulting friendly coalition of Catholic and Protestant would accomplish the good purposes of the legislative union and would be a great step towards the reform of the House of Commons, without which mere Emancipation would be useless. Other speakers made reference to the loyalty of Catholics to the throne and to their invaluable contribution to the British forces fighting Napoleon.[5]

Two years later a similar meeting was held in the new church. Crolly, who was by then parish priest of Belfast, may have attended, but, if so, he did not play an important part and was not one of the principal speakers. Henry Grattan had introduced a bill in parliament which contained what most Catholics, both clerical and lay, had come to find intolerable, namely, securities for the state in return for Emancipation: a commission of Catholic peers was to be empowered to examine all material from Rome in connection with episcopal appointments and to testify to the loyalty of the candidates for office. The Irish bishops rejected these concessions and the bill provoked the Catholic laity throughout the country to protest at any government interference in their internal ecclesiastical affairs.

Resolutions were passed at the Belfast meeting adopting the petition to parliament which had been recently accepted by the Catholic Board in Dublin, asserting the congruence of their faith and discipline with the allegiance due to their sovereign and expressing their gratitude for the advocacy of their cause by the General Assembly of the Church of Scotland, the Synod of Ulster, by various other prominent supporters and

[5] B.M.M., Sept.-Oct. 1811, VII, 324-336.

by the Protestant and Presbyterian brethren who had attended the meeting, among whom William Drennan and John Hancock were given special mention. The leading Catholic speakers, James McGuckin, Hugh Magill and Peter McGouran, vigorously denounced the terms of Grattan's bill. McGouran, claiming that the proposed cure was worse than the disease, maintained that the bill held forth 'a kind of visionary relief to the oppressed laity, while it insidiously provided fresh penal enactments for our clergy'. Drennan drew a wry conclusion from the defeat of the bill at Westminster: it was the will of the House of Commons that the Catholics and Protestants of Ireland should assemble annually 'for the purpose of promoting public peace and national concord, not to commemorate hatred and hostility . . . an association of amity and good neighbourhood, prospective of political liberty'. He advised them to ensure that their movement obeyed strictly the moral law, the Christian law and the law of the land. Hancock congratulated the Catholics on the defeat of the bill which he regarded as a third governmental attempt to fetter the liberties of the Irish people in line with the established church and the *Regium Donum*.[6]

As many Irish churches had few, if any, seats and congregations were accustomed to standing at religious services, the poor facilities afforded by this uncompleted structure would have been readily accepted and understood by those who attended these meetings. In fact, poverty often forced parishes to make do with the most basic furnishings in their chapels.

When Crolly arrived in Belfast he would not have been surprised by the delay in completing the new church. The parish committee, though active and energetic, found the problem of fund-raising difficult and frustrating. He attended his first meeting of it on 18 September 1812, and in the following month was invited to take the chair. In February 1813 he was asked to join three other members in collecting subscriptions from Protestants.[7] His relations with the committee, however, were not always smooth and harmonious. Realizing that the congregation was growing so fast that it would soon outstrip the available accommodation in the church, Crolly decided that a gallery should be added and proposed that pews in it should be sold to those who could afford them, and that the ground floor should be left to the poor. But the members, who were mainly middle-class and represented those rich enough to own pews, objected to being assigned to the remoteness of the gallery and insisted on having their seats on the ground floor. Crolly stipulated that a large space

[6] Ibid., Nov. 1813, XI, 403-11.   [7] *Minute book of the Belfast Chapel Committee, 1804-13*, DCDA.

around the altar be left for the poor and this proposal also met resistance. He finally insisted on adding the gallery at a cost of £1,500 and hoped to cover the outlay by selling pews in it. Though some of the richer families still resisted, they succumbed when several of their members broke ranks and began to buy the pews. Apart from two benches close to the altar the ground floor was left for a standing congregation.[8]

The completion of the building took longer than expected but the church, dedicated to St Patrick, was finally blessed and opened by Bishop Patrick McMullan on 5 March 1815. After the ceremony of consecration, Crolly preached the special sermon. Taking as his text Luke 2,14, he expressed particular thanks to his Protestant and Dissenting brethren, who, through their generous support, had made possible the erection of the church. According to the *Belfast News Letter*

he characterised it as the dawn of a brighter day than had yet visited Ireland, when good will and rational ideas of tolerant benevolence should take the place of more inhospitable feelings, and Christians of every religious denomination would hence-forward live with each other in harmony and the bond of peace . . . He remarked that he had been in different parts of Ireland, but had never seen such benevolence and liberality manifested as in Belfast, where he had now the happiness to reside, and where he hoped to have the honour to spend the remainder of his days. This liberality had done more than anything that had occurred for a length of time to produce unanimity and cordiality among the people. In fact, it had quite emancipated the Catholics; and if the Protestants throughout Ireland would follow the example, Catholic emancipation would be but a name.

The preacher then went on to exhort all Christians to fulfil their duty by attending public worship and reminded those of exalted rank of the power of their example in encouraging the poor to imitate their behaviour. He disclosed that the Protestants and Dissenters of the town had contributed £1,300 and the Catholics £2,800 to the cost of the building, which was upwards of £5,000. The collection on the occasion realized £450 and the collectors, all of whom were Protestant, included not only the leading figures in the commercial life of the town but also the marquis of Donegall, the earl of Londonderry, the earl of Massereene, Lord Belfast and the sovereign and high sheriff. The *News Letter* remarked that the chapel was the finest in the province, noted that some beautiful pieces of sacred music were performed by eminent professionals, including an Italian couple, and summed up the sermon by remarking that 'the whole seemed well calculated to gratify every person present, by exhibiting on the one hand, generosity and enlightened sentiment, and on the other a

---

[8] G. Crolly, *Crolly*, xxxvii–xxxviii.

grateful and affectionate sense of the protection and favour extended to the Catholic, and which cannot fail of having the best effects'.[9]

At a meeting of the Catholic congregation held on 8 March resolutions of gratitude were passed to the noblemen and gentlemen, who had collected at the dedication ceremony, to Protestants who had subscribed to the church, and to Crolly:

Resolved—that we felt it a duty which we owe to our much esteemed Protestant and Dissenting Brethren of Belfast, and its vicinity, to express publicly our grateful acknowledgements for the disinterested generosity which they manifested at the Consecration of the New Chapel; on which occasion the sum collected, together with donations since received, amounts to £530.16.7.

In calling the attention of our countrymen to this unparalleled example of liberality, we are anxious to convince the people of Ireland, that social affection and mutual confidence exist amongst Christians of every communion in this enlightened part of the kingdom.

Resolved—that the Rev. William Crolly is entitled to our most sincere thanks, for his liberal, enlightened, and conciliating discourse—a discourse which must succeed in vindicating the Catholic Religion against its calumniators, and in establishing that honest and ingenuous confidence, which all denominations of Christians shall ever repose in the conscientious convictions of one another.[10]

The church, which continued to be called the New Chapel in contradistinction to the Old Chapel (St Mary's), may have been of little significance architecturally, but proved a great boon to the expanding Catholic population. It has been suggested that the architect was Patrick Davis,[11] a glazier and prominent member of the Catholic committee, and that perhaps he and the committee improvised overmuch as the building progressed. No other Catholic church was built in the town for thirty years and St Patrick's, though less historic than St Mary's, was used for all important liturgical and ceremonial occasions.

Crolly himself celebrated Mass daily in St Mary's at eight o'clock. He began hearing confessions soon after seven o'clock each morning and resumed after Mass was over. And during Lent and Advent and before the major holydays he spent a large part of each day in the confessional. He only broke this routine when called away on ecclesiastical business, and during his entire pastorate in Belfast and Armagh he never allowed himself the luxury of a holiday.[12]

With the opening of St Patrick's, an active parochial committee and a

[9] B.N.L., 7 Mar. 1815.   [10] Ibid., 10 Mar. 1815.
[11] Brett, *Buildings of Belfast*, 14.   [12] G. Crolly, *Crolly*, xxxiii–xxxiv.

population moving towards 5,000 and likely to keep on increasing, Belfast
had become the best equipped parish in the diocese. In his report to Rome
on the state of his diocese in 1814, Bishop McMullan noted that there
were about 34 parish priests, excluding his own parish of Downpatrick,
and that 'some, but very few of the parish priests keep curates or
assistants'. This would suggest a total of about 50 priests. He did not
submit estimates of the total population of the diocese or of individual
parishes, limiting himself to the statement that in some parishes there
were between 400 and 500 Catholic families; in others between 500 and
600; in others again about 300 and in a few others considerably less.[13]
These estimates would indicate a maximum population of about 4,000 for
a few parishes. The income of Belfast was also the largest in the diocese.
Even in 1801, when Lord Castlereagh requested the bishops to furnish
him with returns of the incomes of their clergy, Belfast, with £100,
though this sum had to cover the upkeep of three priests, was the highest
in the diocese.[14] Whether or not the figure given in 1800 was too small, it
had risen eight years later to £240. For the first two years of his pastorate,
Crolly had to pay his predecessor £70 annually.[15] After Hugh O'Donnell's
death the parish priest's income must have been about £150.

Taking advantage of the goodwill evidenced by the generosity of
Protestants to St Patrick's, Crolly decided that he would hold a series of
lectures on the Catholic faith, which would be open to all Christians. His
purpose was to dispel ignorance and misunderstanding rather than seek
converts, and the talks were pitched at an explanatory and 'ecumenical'
rather than argumentative or polemical level. He doubtless also wanted to
dispel the religious misunderstandings or ill-feelings that he feared might
contribute to communal violence.

Belfast had, as yet, been spared most of the politico-religious tensions
associated with the Orange order and its parades, which had led to
violence in parts of the Ulster countryside, especially in Co. Armagh. But
on 12 July 1813 a riot occurred as Orangemen returned to the town after
a demonstration at Lisburn. As they approached a bar in North Street, a
crowd gathered to jeer, and some mud and brickbats were thrown at
them. Windows in the public house were broken and then some Orangemen emerged and fired several musket shots into the crowd killing two
men (who were Protestants) and injuring four others (who were Catholics). The *News Letter* regretting the occurrence of such occasions that

[13] Bishop McMullan to John Connolly (copy), 12 Oct. 1814, DCDA.
[14] *Memoirs and Correspondence of Viscount Castlereagh*, iv, 116-7.
[15] O'Laverty, *Down and Connor* II, 418.

could lead to the revival of party spirit, recalled a recent debate in the House of Commons, when 'the illegality of such associations was declared and admitted by the most distinguished characters in the British Senate', and expressed its fears about the hostile reactions in London, when the news of the disturbance reached the capital. The magistrates in Belfast unlike some of their colleagues in the countryside took swift action and had arrests made, and this vigorous response probably helped prevent a repetition of such events in the town for several years.[16]

Crolly, who was always very conscious of his Christian duty to combat sectarian discord and to ensure that migrants from the troubled parts of the countryside did not display their old antagonisms, doubtless regarded his talks as a contribution to that end. And perhaps it was because of the positive and 'ecumenical' approach that he adopted that some Protestants felt encouraged to join the Catholic church. Writing to Rome thirty years later, Bernard McAuley, claimed that during Crolly's pastorate in Belfast some three hundred people were converted to Catholicism each year, (though in George Crolly's life of his uncle he is quoted as saying the converts numbered upwards of a thousand over seven years). He did not make clear, however, whether any of these were preparing for marriage to Catholics, and, since this statement was elicited in defence of Crolly's memory in the course of a public controversy, it can be confidently asserted that this number, if not greatly exaggerated, was certainly as large a figure as the writer could with impunity suggest.[17] Had there been large-scale movement to the Catholic church, there would surely have been controversies in the newspapers about it and their silence on the subject probably indicates that the numbers changing their allegiance were not extensive.

II

Crolly, on his arrival in Belfast, decided to participate as widely as possible in the general social and literary life of the town; and his urbane and affable manner and conciliatory approach greatly eased his way into a society that was predominantly Presbyterian. In December 1812 his name

[16] B.N.L., 13 July 1813, and Budge and O'Leary, *Belfast: approach to crisis*, 24-5.
[17] McAuley to Propaganda, APF, SC (Irlanda), 29, ff 381r and 388rv. References to this aspect of Crolly's work were made by Archbishop Curtis and the priests of Down and Connor when advocating his appointment as coadjutor bishop. And Döllinger, the church historian at Munich, noted that Charles William Russell of Maynooth had told him that the great increase in Catholic numbers was due to Crolly's zeal and great talent. (Friedrich, *Ignaz von Döllinger*, II, 525.)

was proposed for membership of the Belfast Society for Promoting Knowledge (later known as the Linen Hall Library). In January 1813 he was elected and in the following month was chosen to sit on the governing committee. In the following year he was invited, with two other members of the committee, to supervise the relocation and cataloguing of the books after they had been displaced because of repairs to the Linen Hall.[18]

He promptly subscribed to the funds for the erection of the Belfast Academical Institution, which had been launched by the liberals of Belfast and neighbourhood in 1810 to provide tertiary education in arts and theology and secondary education for boys who wished to pursue their studies further or who aspired to a career in business or commerce. In the early nineteenth century the conservative and liberal were defined by attitudes towards the United Irishmen and Catholic Emancipation: the conservative had opposed the rebellion of 1798 and either opposed Catholic Emancipation or reluctantly conceded that it should come about gradually; the liberal had either been a United Irishman or favoured the movement, and wanted Catholic Emancipation as soon as possible. The 'conservative party' had established and supported the Belfast Academy since 1785; from 1792 to 1822 its president was Dr William Bruce, a Presbyterian clergyman, who had exchanged the uniform of a volunteer for that of a yeoman. Dr William Drennan, the former United Irishman, Dr James McDonnell and other 'liberals' led the campaign for the establishment of the Academical Institution.

Crolly as a subscriber of five guineas was entitled to vote for the governors or managers of the Institution and he regarded this right as giving him an important and valuable connection with the school. He was present at a St Patrick's Day dinner in 1816, which was attended by some of those prominently associated with the Institution, when some of the toasts proved too 'radical' for the government's taste led to the cancellation of the annual grant. But he had left before the celebrations had reached the state of warmth that produced the toasts. Supporters of the Institution made repeated efforts to get the grant restored and eventually the government allowed it to be included among the educational establishments which were to be investigated by a royal commission. Questioned at the commission in 1825 about the attendance of Catholic boys, Crolly replied that he believed the teachers encouraged them to pay particular attention to their religious and moral duties. While he thought it probable that boys might insult one another about religion on their way to and from

---

[18] *Minutes of the General & Committee Meetings of the Belfast Society for Promoting Knowledge* (Linen Hall Library), 6–9, 54–55.

school, he felt that there was no cause for complaint about conduct in the Institution. An aspirant to the priesthood was studying there, and he had no objection to other seminarians doing likewise, though he 'might find it, perhaps, desirable to establish a diocesan seminary; and in that case . . . would in all probability, give the preference to it'. The Catholic students at the Institution attended 'at the explanation of the catechism and public worship regularly' in his Sunday School. At the request of some of the professors, who were Presbyterian clergy, and who paid 'a proper and respectful attention to the religious principles of their Catholic scholars', he had supplied these pupils with Catholic versions of the scriptures.

Crolly's general opinion of the Institution was very favourable. He was happy with the good conduct and progress of the students he knew, and looked forward to even greater advantages for persons of every religious communion mixing together for education if it 'were guarded against any preponderating influence'. He suggested that Protestants and Catholics would not attend with sufficient confidence as long as it was regarded, more or less, as a sectarian establishment; the removal of theological teaching would leave it an exclusive 'scientific Institution', in which candidates for the university from both the Protestant and Catholic churches might receive their scientific education; and in which future teachers of parochial (primary) schools could be trained and from which they would go out 'to diffuse the spirit of virtue, learning and liberality among the pupils intrusted to their care'. That kind of united education tended to extinguish party animosities and to generate kindly feelings. Consequently, he was at pains to exonerate the Institution from its association with the 'offensive' toasts and emphasize the fruitful results that would flow from a restoration of the grant.[19]

At the primary level there were two schools in the town: the Lancasterian school in Frederick Street, founded by Joseph Lancaster in 1811, in which the pupils were taught by a male and female teacher with the assistance of monitors, or senior students, specially selected for that purpose. By 1815 there were seven hundred pupils drawn from all denominations on the rolls, but, as attendance was voluntary, the numbers present in the classrooms varied greatly according to the season of the year, parental interest and the students' state of health. On 8 July 1815 some three hundred prizes, consisting of 'bibles, testaments and useful books' for the boys, and dresses for the girls, were distributed, and Crolly gave the address. Paying tribute to Lancaster for creating such an

[19] *Fourth report of the commissioners of Irish education inquiry*, pp. 180-3, H.C. 1826-7 (89), xiii.

excellent system of education and to the people of Belfast for founding the schools, which were free and open to all without distinction of means, and who were thereby rescued from the misery associated with idleness and ignorance, he called upon the children to appreciate the opportunities they enjoyed. Predicting that the system would produce a most beneficial effect on society, he noted with satisfaction that in the schools 'the speculative differences of religious opinion were entirely lost sight of, and Protestant, Presbyterian and Catholic went hand in hand in the benevolent endeavour to be useful', and he expressed the hope that 'this liberal and tolerant feeling . . . would be still more widely disseminated and Belfast would thereby be improved and benefited in an inconceivable degree.' Warning the children to avoid every kind of unlawful association as not only injurious to society but hostile to their own peace, he concluded by praising Maurice Cross, the headmaster, for his skill and proficiency, and for the order and regularity obtaining in the school.[20]

Crolly continued to subscribe to and patronize the Lancasterian school as long as he remained in Belfast. Four years later Henry Montgomery, the Presbyterian minister of Derriaghy, noted at the prize-giving ceremony that the majority of the children were Catholics, and, exonerating the Catholic clergy from the imputation occasionally cast upon them of desiring to keep their flocks in ignorance so that they could govern them more tyranically, described their parish priest 'as one of the most active and useful members of the committee, anxious not only for the education of the rising generation, but for the most peaceful and conciliating exercise of their religion'.[21] The Lancasterian school never swerved from its policy of non-interference with the religious tenets of its pupils. In 1822 the *Irishman* referred to the 'enlightened sentiment of religious liberality' that seemed to animate the members of the school committee, which included the leading clergy of all the denominations of the town, and described the sentiments expressed at the school meeting by the clergy, including Crolly, as 'a fine exemplification of the pure spirit of Christian charity, and in every way worthy of the pure spirit of religious liberty which characterized the town of Belfast'.[22] This comment could with equal, if not greater, justice also have been applied to the Belfast Auxiliary Society for the education of deaf and dumb children, of which he was also a member. His association, however, with the other large non-denominational school, that of Brown Street, was destined to come to an abrupt and unhappy end.

[20] B.N.L., 11 July 1815.   [21] Ibid., 20 July 1819.   [22] Ir., 20 Apr. 1822.

Philanthropically-minded laymen as well as clergy had been conducting Sunday schools in Belfast since the late eighteenth century. Though generally, but not always, geared ultimately to the study of the bible, they afforded children the initial opportunity of learning to read and write, and so, apart from their religious dimension, they made a valuable contribution to the spread of literacy. In 1802 a few of the leading liberals of the town, including former United Irishmen, established a Sunday school in Ferguson's Entry. Anxious conservatives, unwilling to be out-manoeuvred by their opponents, set up the Sunday School Society in 1809 and opened their own school in the House of Industry in Smithfield in 1811. Another school, which was opened in the same year, in Union Street, was called on later to take the overflow from Smithfield, and its founder, William Booth, then joined the Sunday School Society.[23] The large numbers in attendance prompted the society to build a new schoolhouse in Brown Square, which would afford ampler accommodation and relieve it of the burden of paying an annual rent for the premises they had until then been using. From those savings it was hoped to pay the salary of a teacher on the Lancasterian principle.[24] With the help of a grant from the Sunday School Society for Ireland, and with local subscriptions, work began on a school-house capable of holding one thousand children. Blown down by a storm on 16 December 1814, it was rebuilt in 1815 and formally opened on 5 May 1816.

The Sunday School Society for Ireland, which began in 1809, had a none too savoury reputation as a proselytizing body. The recipient of grants from other proselytizing societies, it initially gave financial help to local schools but then limited its aid to school books and books for general religious instruction. Unlike the Kildare Place Society, which permitted the use of Catholic versions of the bible as long as they had no notes or comments, the Sunday School Society of Ireland did not make this concession.

Two clergymen were invited by the committee of management to address the parents, children and teachers when the school was being reopened: Samuel Hanna, a Presbyterian and professor at the Academical Institution, and Crolly.[25] The new school, which enjoyed the patronage of the leading citizens of the town, soon attracted nearly 1,000 students. The Sunday School Society continued to provide support by gifts of books and money to purchase bibles, and proposals were approved for fitting up a separate room for the instruction of adults.[26] Crolly attended the annual

---

[23] McClelland, 'The Early History of Brown Street School' in *Ulster Folklife*, 17, 52-9.
[24] B.N.L. 19 Aug. 1814. [25] Ibid., 7 May 1816. [26] Ibid., 4 Sept. 1818.

meetings of the subscribers, was elected to the committee, and expressed satisfaction with the progress and success of the undertaking. He obviously hoped that the scripture study in the school would be generally acceptable to all Christians and that the Catholic children would ultimately be permitted to use their own version of the bible. In the meantime he was anxious that they make use of facilities that were not otherwise available. In 1819 a decision was taken to establish a free day school in the same buildings and this was realized in 1821. In the meantime the Sunday school had combined with others to form a union for the Belfast area.

At the general meeting of the Sunday School Society in Brown Street on the 26 March 1822, it was reported that 696 boys had been enrolled in the day school during the year 5 March 1821 to 5 March 1822, though 395 had subsequently withdrawn to be apprenticed to trades, and during the same period 404 girls had been in attendance, of whom 158 remained. Some of these children paid one penny per week and the others received free education; some of the teachers also gave their services gratuitously. Resolutions were passed expressive of keen satisfaction at the progress reported, of encouragement for the Female Local Sunday School Association and of gratitude to Revd William Carr for his charity sermon preached on behalf of the schools, which had brought in £40.[27] That sermon had, however, provoked newspaper controversy. The *Irishman* accused Carr of declaring that the fields of the South of Ireland were ensanguined by the blood of innocent inhabitants, shed by a peasantry destitute of the first elements of religious knowledge.[28] While insisting that the mass of the poor classes in some of the southern counties were both uneducated and depraved, Carr had argued that he did not accuse the Catholic clergy of sloth or indifference, believing as he did that 'the deluded beings, who agitate their native land, attach no importance to any system of religion'.[29] The subscribers did not pursue the subject of the sermon at their meeting but, significantly, they did discuss proselytism or the dangers of proselytism, if the appointments of teachers were not seen to be fair.

Two prominent clergymen who had recently been elected to the committee—A.C. Macartney, who had become vicar of Belfast in 1820, and Thomas Dix Hincks, a Presbyterian, who had been appointed to the staff of the Academical Institution in 1820—joined Professor Young in strongly repudiating any attempts at tampering with the religion of the

---

[27] Ibid., 29 Mar. 1822.   [28] Ir., 1 Mar. 1822.   [29] B.N.L. 26 Feb. 1822.

young, and seemed to win general approval for their views.[30] But when it came to voting for membership of the new committee, Crolly and three others, who had taken a 'liberal' line, failed to be elected. The press at the time did not assign any reason for his rejection, but, in a letter dated 13 January 1828, the pseudonymous author, *Veritas*, claimed that the representatives of the Catholic congregation were excluded 'by a low and illiberal combination of anti-Catholic subscribers'. He explained that Crolly had proposed at his own expense to provide a Douay version of the New Testament for the Catholic children, and had won the approval of the marquis of Downshire, who chaired the meeting, but had not won the approval of a majority of his colleagues.[31]

Religious divisions in Ireland had been accentuated since the turn of the century by the proliferation of Protestant religious societies, several of which aimed at rescuing benighted Catholic peasants from ignorance and superstition by the diffusion of scriptural knowledge. Their missionary activity and the spread of anti-Catholic tracts helped to sharpen the general religious perceptions of many Protestant people, both clerical and lay. William Bruce's comments at a meeting of the Hibernian Bible Society in Belfast reflected the attitudes produced by such societies and explain the worried reaction of the Catholic clergy to them. Bruce, remarking that many Catholics evinced a great desire to hear the bible read by their children, suggested that 'the dissemination of the scriptures might produce a renovation of true religion among them, and, in the process of time, might break the shackles of the Roman Pontiff, and that they might thereby return to the true religion which they professed before being conquered by England and sold by the pope'.[32] Crolly's repudiation by the subscribers was ultimately due to this worsening atmosphere. The immediate consequences of the decision by the subscribers of the Brown Street School was the establishment of a Sunday school for·Catholic children at St Patrick's Church in 1822. Two years later the Catholic children of the Brown Street school were withdrawn and transferred to it, and it soon numbered 1,500 pupils on its rolls.

In an editorial on this development the *Northern Whig* praised Crolly for having 'invariably devoted his time and his money to the welfare of every institution in this town, conducted on liberal principles, which had for its object the illumination of the human mind, and the progression of moral improvement' and thereby offering 'a palpable contradiction to the charge made against his clerical brethren of the Roman Catholic faith, in

[30] Ir., 12 Apr. 1822.   [31] N.W., 17 Jan. 1828.   [32] B.N.L., 11 Apr. 1817.

other parts of Ireland, that of wishing to perpetuate the ignorance of the poor'. While regretting the foundation 'of Sabbath schools for the *exclusive* benefit of any particular body of Christians, . . . as a measure unfavourable to unity of affection', it claimed that the decision was 'hastened, if not altogether caused, by the impolicy of the system pursued by the "Sunday School Society for Ireland" and imitated by the local seminaries connected with that body'. Suggesting that if the many working members of the Sunday School Society for Ireland had manifested a spirit of concession to Roman Catholics and given permission for the use of the Douay or Rhemish version of the Testament, there would have been no need for exclusively Catholic schools, it went on to maintain that the distrust felt by many Catholics for that body arose from 'the narrow and ill-advised system of policy' adopted by the Institution.[33] This interpretation was undoubtedly correct for Crolly continued to support the Lancasterian school which permitted the use of Catholic-approved versions of Scripture. He did not comment in public on the reasons for withdrawing the children from the Brown Street school until 1832, and his explanation then sparked off a controversy that revealed the tension that had existed among the managers and subscribers of the school.

The occasion that brought forth his comments was the report of a meeting in defence of scriptural education at which clergy associated with the Brown Street school, in particular, R.W. Bland, Tobias and George Bellis, Henry Cooke, John Edgar, Thomas Hincks and James Morgan, took up the cudgels against the national system of education. In a vehement protest against the system in Belfast on 17 January 1832, Morgan laid bare his concept of the purpose of education and declared that 'his object was to proselytize' and that 'he would endeavour to convert every Catholic in the kingdom'. Stung by this public avowal of a policy which he believed had been applied surreptitiously to the detriment of Catholic children, Crolly wrote to Lord Donegall, who had presided at the meeting, to object to the slurs cast on the Catholic Church in general and the priests of Belfast in particular at the meeting. He recalled his sad experience in the Brown Street school:

I was, for some time, a member of a committee, in a school which has been rendered almost useless, by the folly of fanatics, who could not be contented without the perversion of the Catholic children. As soon as I detected their schemes, I disconcerted their plans, by using my Chapels as seminaries of education for the poor, until I could build a convenient schoolhouse for that purpose. When first I discovered the dark designs of these illiberal men, they positively denied that they had made the

33 Ibid., 22 July 1824.

slightest attempts at proselytism; but now they have been obliged to lay aside the hypocritical mask; their former assertions are now refuted by their own concessions; they cannot conceal their intentions of entrapping innocent infants; and some of them on last Tuesday declared, in your Lordship's presence, that they will not be satisfied with any system of Scriptural instruction, unless they shall have an opportunity of kidnapping the consciences of unsuspecting children. The man who is capable of such cowardly and iniquitous conduct is an object of my pity and commiseration but I cannot conceive how such behaviour can be reconciled with the common principles of honour and honesty.[34]

Thomas Hincks, the chairman of the Brown Street committee, who was professor of Latin in the Academical Institution, replied to Crolly.[35] He attempted to refute Crolly's charge that the school had been 'rendered almost useless by the folly of fanatics' by showing that it had an attendance of 380 pupils in 1831, only three less than when Crolly's membership of the committee ceased and 34 less than in its peak period six months before that time. He claimed that the Brown Street school committee was in no way responsible for the proceedings of the meeting of the friends of scriptural education and he called on Crolly to reveal the evidence on which the charges of illiberality and proselytism were based, or by acknowledging his error to offer reparation to 'offended truth and injured character'.[36]

In his defence, which was addressed to Lord Donegall, Crolly wrote that the demand of the Brown Street school committee that he produce evidence of his claims was reasonable, but he did not retract or conceal his hostile attitude to the illiberal system of education which the school had maintained for the previous decade. He recalled his participation in the establishment of the school and his offer in 1819 to provide at his own expense, copies of the Douay Testament for the Catholic children. The offer was rejected and Catholic versions of the scriptures were never permitted. Then in 1822 a proposal was made to establish local schools in various parts of the town under some ladies who expected to receive assistance from the Brown Street institution. Fearing that the religion of Catholic children might be endangered in such schools, he suggested at

[34] N.W., 23 Jan. 1832.
[35] John Edgar, a Presbyterian minister, also replied to Crolly to clarify a story about exorcism which he had recounted at the public meeting. He alleged that a woman had told him that she had seen a priest pull the devil out of a man's throat in Pipe Lane, lay it on a plate, and that it resembled a great long eel. Crolly, taking exception to this tasteless anecdote, had remarked that he would dispense with the priest's services, if he could find him, though he might permit him to try his power 'in banishing the demon of falsehood' from the soul of his clerical colleagues. Edgar riposted: 'I am accountable for the fact of this story having been told me in seriousness and for the propriety of giving it as an illustration of the powers attributed by the lower orders of Roman Catholics to their spiritual guides but I am in no way accountable for its truth or falsehood'. (N.W., 2 Feb. 1832)
[36] Ibid., 6 Feb. 1832.

the meeting of the committee that teachers of all denominations should be appointed to these schools, provided they had satisfactory testimonials of their moral character. Four members, including William McEwen, minister of the second Presbyterian congregation, supported this proposal. But some members 'resisted the admission of Catholic teachers with such illiberality and obstinacy' that McEwen and he were obliged to charge them with wishing to proselytize. Though he obtained enough support to carry this proposal, he and his four supporters paid the price of their opposition: they were dropped from the committee and their proviso about the teachers was never acted upon. To illustrate his claim that the management of the school was still as biased and intolerant as in 1822, he pointed out that seven clerical members of the committee had been present at the recent meeting, ostensibly in support of scriptural education, and quoted a few of the extreme comments made by some of them. He concluded by challenging his opponents to show that the presence of 380 Protestant children alone at a school which had once been attended by 300 Catholics as well was a triumphant refutation of his case.[37]

Thomas Hincks, the chairman of the Brown Street committee, again replied—this time adopting a much more aggressive stance and claiming to substantiate his case by evidence lest 'the sophistry and assumed plausibility so ingenuously interwoven with dates, names, and apparently official authority, should deceive the superficial observer'. He maintained that he could find no trace in the records of the school of Crolly's offer of free copies of the Douay Testament to Catholic children, but admitted that the acceptance of it would have been a violation of one of the fundamental rules of the Sunday School Society of Ireland. Hincks maintained that not a single Catholic child was removed from the school until 1824, and asked, querulously, if the withdrawal of children at that time represented the 'promptitude of a watchful shepherd' who had discovered proselytism in 1819 or 1822? He argued further that the founding of Crolly's Sunday school in 1824 was part of a general response to a public criticism made at that time, that the Catholic clergy were culpably neglectful of the education of their youth—a criticism which stimulated priests throughout Ireland to establish schools. He further denied Crolly's statement that a proposal was made at the Brown Street school committee to establish local schools: some respectable ladies had formed a Local School Association and sought the patronage of the committee to which Crolly raised no objection. And to rebut the charge of

[37] Ibid., 6 Feb. 1832.

proselytism in their schools, he defied Crolly to point to a single attempt having ever been made to induce a Catholic child to join another communion. Insisting that no objection was ever raised to the use of the Douay bibles in the daily school, Hincks promised that, if Crolly supplied them, they would certainly be made available to Catholic children.[38]

Crolly countered by interpreting the appeal to the rules of the Sunday School Society as an excuse for an act of intolerance. He insisted that he brought the children to St Patrick's Church in March 1822 and not in 1824; that his references to the meetings of 1822 were accurate and supported by the memory of William Ritchie, a member of the committee whom he had consulted; repudiated the transfer of responsibility for his non-appointment to the committee from the managers of the school to the subscribers, and enthusiastically expressed his satisfaction on hearing that no proselytes had ever been made in the schools. He attributed this failure to the heartfelt attachment of poor Catholics to their religion, to the vigilance of their clergy and to the bond of charitable affection between them, and he accepted the offer to supply free copies of the Douay Testament to the remaining Catholic pupils. He again made reference to the speeches delivered at the protest meeting, lamenting their deficiency, 'in charity, truth, honesty, and common decency', and repeated his remarks about the 'illiberal mismanagement' of the school.[39]

The Brown Street school committee hit back in a sharper tone at Crolly's 'reckless reiteration of refuted charges' and singled out, from the accusations he had made 'under irritating, vindictive epithets' and 'with such virulence', as deserving of notice the one about the offer of the Douay version of the scriptures to the Catholic children. By his own admission this could not have been made to the early school, which did not then exist, and would not have been tolerated by the rules of the Sunday School. Repeating its claims about the time lag in the opening of his Sunday School, it proclaimed its conviction that 'no ingenuous or discerning mind will view with any other feeling than sorrow, the melancholy exhibitions of levity' which disgraced many parts of Crolly's last letters, particularly the quibbling about the use of the term 'proselyte'. Proselytism understood as an underhand exertion to effect the transfer of people from one denomination to another was never practiced; but if proselytism were defined as 'zealous exertions to teach how to read the Word of God, and to understand and reduce to practice what is read from the Word of God, then the Brown St. Society is a most decided and

---

[38] Ibid., 20 Feb. 1832.   [39] Ibid., 23 Feb. 1832.

incorrigible proselytizing Society'. Crolly had misinterpreted the assertion that no attempt had been made to withdraw a single child from his communion to mean that not a single proselyte had been made by the society; and his failure to produce any evidence of attempted proselytism demonstrated the utter falsehood of the charges. The letter ended on a threatening note: asking rhetorically if the bishop ought not to be 'considered as standing convicted of the foulest calumny, and the basest slander', the committee warned that if he persevered in such conduct, it might be tempted to go further.[40] Crolly, however, did not pursue the dispute.

Education was one of the most difficult and demanding problems facing the Catholic Church in Ireland in the first half of the nineteenth century. In the first two decades a wave of missionary and proselytizing societies established, or grant-aided, schools which the bishops and clergy considered unsafe for Catholic children. Consequently, the clergy had either to establish their own—which their limited financial resources often forbade—or try to work with schools, whether under Protestant management or not, which did not interfere with the religious allegiance of their pupils.

In 1819, in response to the anxieties and complaints revealed in their reports to Rome, Cardinal Fontana, prefect of Propaganda, (the congregation which had charge of Ireland) issued a stern warning to the bishops about the dangers inherent in schools funded by these evangelical socieites, and exhorted them to counteract the enemy that sowed tares among the wheat, by establishing Catholic schools throughout their dioceses:

For, information, has reached the ears of the Sacred Congregation, that 'Bible schools', supported by the funds of the heterodox, have been established in almost every part of Ireland, in which, under the pretence of charity, the inexperienced of both sexes, but particularly peasants and paupers, are allured by the blandishments and even gifts of the masters, and infected with the fatal poison of depraved doctrines. This further stated that the directors of these schools are, generally speaking, Methodists, who introduce Bibles translated into English by 'the Bible Society'. and abounding in errors,—with the sole view of seducing the youth, and entirely eradicating from their minds the truths of the orthodox faith.

Fontana demanded that every exertion should be made to keep youth away from those destructive schools and parents should be warned never to suffer their children to be led into error.[41]

---

[40] Ibid., 8 Mar. 1832.
[41] Propaganda to Archbishops, 18 Sept. 1819, APF, *Lett*, 300, ff 642r-643r, and B.N.L., 4 Jan. 1820.

Archbishop Curtis of Armagh, enclosing a copy of this letter to Bishop McMullan of Down and Connor, informed him that he had assured Rome in his reply that 'the Prelates had long since, and would continue to exert themselves, and apply effectual remedies to preclude all such evils'.[42] McMullan himself was keen to conform to Fontana's advice and subsequently bequeathed £50 in his will to the parish of Downpatrick and £60 to the parish of Loughinisland for the promotion of Catholic education.[43]

Little evidence of the success or failure of parishes throughout the diocese in setting up schools exists for this decade, but one may presume that several priests, at least, established Sunday schools in the same manner as Crolly did in his parish, and thereby sought to counter any dangers that might have arisen in the local schools founded by landlords or subsidized by the evangelical societies. Since Crolly's parishioners were, for the most part, confined to the town, the compactness of his community facilitated his educational and, indeed, general pastoral activities, though by the 1820s Belfast had become a magnet, attracting the rural unemployed in search of work, which often was not available.

The size of the Catholic population of Belfast was disputed at the time and it is impossible to estimate it accurately. When the Catholic rent was launched in 1824 to forward O'Connell's campaign for Catholic Emancipation, John Lawless, the editor of the *Irishman*, a pro-Emancipation paper, reported to Dublin about the first meeting that had been held in Belfast and remarked that there were 12,000 Catholics in the congregation of the town.[44] The *News Letter* challenged this figure, quoting the returns of the census of 1821, which showed that Belfast had a total population of 37,800, and claiming that the ratio of Romanists to Protestants was 1:7. It argued that the two churches in the town could not accommodate 6,000 let alone 12,000 and were, in fact, attended by about 5,000.[45] It later explained that the Catholics from the town who worshipped at Hannahstown were more than counterbalanced by those from Ballymacarrett who came to St Mary's and St Patrick's. Assuming that those 'detained at home by sickness, infirmity, old age, infancy, and accidental causes' on Sundays numbered 1,500, the whole community would amount to 6,500.[46] The *Irishman* countered by maintaining that Crolly could have informed the *News Letter* that 5,000 out of the 8,250 adults had one child each 'in nurses' arms'. The *Irishman* concluded that the four Masses were attended by

[42] Curtis to McMullan, 10 Dec. 1819, DCDA.
[43] Ir., 7 Jan. 1825. In Belfast the Rosarian Society, a religious confraternity, established in 1794, taught religion to children.
[44] Ir., 30 July 1824.   [45] B.N.L., 30 July 1824.   [46] Ibid., 3 Aug. 1824.

7,000 adults, and 1,200 children, and, by adding a further 5,000 infants, who could not be brought to church, reached a figure of 13,200. Moreover, it referred to the testimony of a curate in the town, who pointed out that he had baptized between 700 and 800 children in one year.[47] The *News Letter*, however, was not convinced, and characterized the *Irishman*'s response as vulgar abuse (which it regarded with gratitude since 'slander' was 'the most exquisite eulogy'). It interpreted the publication of inflated figures as an attempt to produce alarm and hold Protestants *in terrorem*.[48]

III

Apart from the Brown Street schools, Crolly's association with the voluntary bodies dedicated to the public welfare of Belfast was happy and fruitful. In 1815 he attended the first meeting that was called to launch the Belfast Savings Bank, which was established specifically to encourage the poor to be thrifty, and which undertook to accept the small sums of money that commercial banks would not handle, provided they exceeded ten pence. Interest was to be paid at the rate of five per cent on sums exceeding ten shillings. A committee of fifty, of whom six were clergy-men, was appointed to oversee the affairs of the bank, and, at its last quarterly meeting each year, to nominate a board of management for the forthcoming year, to consist of a treasurer, secretary, cashier, two accountants and four directors. Crolly was honoured by being chosen as one of the first directors.[49] In 1816 he was elected, at a public meeting, to a seven-member committee, which was commissioned to draw up a petition to parliament in protest at changes made in the taxation of property and payment of rates in the Belfast Police Bill, which had been recently introduced.[50]

Another aspect of social welfare in which he took a deep interest was in helping the unemployed. The House of Industry was an establishment which tried to find work for the unemployed poor and to provide outdoor, and, if necessary, a little indoor relief for those who could not for any reason be employed. The clergy took turns preaching charity sermons for institutions like the House of Industry or the Poor House. Outlining the

[47] Ir., 6 Aug. 1824. The baptismal registers of the parish do not support this claim. 447 baptisms are listed for 1824 and 519 for 1825. These registers, which began in 1798, are incomplete and unreliable for this period. No baptisms are registered for 1812, 1813 and 1819, and for some years those of several months are omitted. However, from 1822 until 1833 the registers show a steady increase in baptisms from 223 to 1,140, which may indicate that they were kept accurately during that decade.
[48] B.N.L., 13 Aug. 1824.   [49] B.N.L. 26 Dec. 1815.   [50] Ibid., 26 Apr. 1816.

great benefits which the poor derived from the House of Industry, Crolly, at a charity sermon in 1817, remarked that it was 'particularly pleasant to observe that in the management of this charity, Christians of every denomination were to be found making one joint effort for the general good—the Protestant, Dissenter and Catholic were associated in order to promote the benevolent object which all had in view'. In Belfast where the poor had experienced the liberality of the rich, they had responded by behaving in a peaceful and orderly manner, but, in other parts of the country, 'hunger had broken through stone walls'.[51]

In 1817 the Dispensary and Fever Hospital moved from its cramped and inadequate quarters in Berry Street to larger new buildings in Frederick Street. Subscribers of £5 yearly were entitled to choose the management committee. Crolly promptly became a subscriber and his interest was rewarded by being elected to the committee of management in its first year of office. That year was particularly difficult and distressing. Not only was Ireland suffering from the slump that followed the ending of the Napoleonic wars, but typhus fever hit Belfast, and the wards were quickly filled with victims of this epidemic. He served continuously for five years but lost his place in 1822.

When the same fate befell Dr William Tennent, a prominent liberal, friends of both blamed a conservative caucus for their defeat. Dr James McDonnell, a distinguished physician on the hospital staff for many years, and an active member of the committee, did not conceal his displeasure at this development, and he was rewarded in the following year by being excluded from the committee. A reaction in favour of Crolly among the subscribers swept him back to office in 1824, and he was re-elected annually as long as he remained in Belfast. He was also appointed to collect for the hospital in the district of the town in which he lived, and for the following ten years was selected annually with ten or twelve others for this task. He chaired the yearly meetings of the subscribers in 1831 and 1832.

The statistics of the services provided by the charities of the town tell their own tale of the suffering and desolation affecting a considerable proportion of Belfast's residents. Crolly himself suffered some distress—though of a different nature—during 1817, when he found out that he was accused of taking part in a religious controversy under a pseudonym. Both participants in an early manifestation of what later became a widely accepted practice in the Belfast press, wrote under *noms de plume*.

[51] B.N.L. 17 June 1817. In the advertisement for this sermon it was stated that 1,000 families were receiving rations from the House of Industry. The post-war slump had caused severe destitution.

The correspondence was occasioned by the comments of William Bruce, minister of the First Presbyterian Congregation in Rosemary Street, and principal of Belfast Academy. Bruce, who played a prominent part in the civic and literary affairs of the town, was well known to people of all religious denominations. In an address to the Hibernian Bible Society, he had expressed his hope that the differences between the Catholic Church in Ireland and Rome,[52] aided by a dissemination of the scriptures, might lead to a reformation among Catholics.[53]

This aspiration was promptly challenged in the *Ulster Recorder* by the pseudonymous *Pastor*, who insisted that Catholics did read the scriptures in the vernacular and repudiated the charge that the authorities of the church excluded the laity from access to them. This sparked off a correspondence in the *Belfast News Letter*, where someone adopting the name of the Swiss reformer Zuinglius, claimed that the Council of Trent and subsequent popes 'prohibited the use of the Bible in any vulgar tongue'.[54] *Pastor* retorted that the Catholic church simply put 'the reading of the Scriptures under such restraints as were necessary to render it safe and useful', and explained that in different places these rules were left to the judgement and enforcement of the local bishop with the result that the Douay version was generally distributed in Ireland.[55] Several letters in a similar vein were exchanged, suitably garnished with hostile comments about the practices obtaining in the Protestant and Catholic churches, and in particular about their understanding of penance and repentance.

In his third letter, which contained some hard-hitting remarks about 'the spiritual and anti-Christian tyranny' of Rome, Zuinglius quoted propositions about scripture, tradition and papal authority, of the kind which excited the strongest prejudices against Catholics, and observed that they were published, 'while the Parish Priest of Belfast was distributing an English Testament among his parishioners and denying, at least "in any discussion with Protestants", the infallibility of the Pope, if he was the author of *Pastor*'. In a postscript to this letter he disclaimed all intentions of lessening his adversary's influence within the Catholic church and trusted 'that what has passed may neither interrupt our amicable intercourse, nor prevent its increase, as far as cooperation in promoting charity to the poor and general goodwill may be concerned'.[56]

---

[52] This was a reference to the veto on candidates for episcopal office which the Holy See had shown itself willing to concede to the king, but to which both Irish churchmen and laity were inexorably opposed.
[53] B.N.L., 11 Apr. 1817.   [54] Ibid., 25 Apr. 1817.   [55] Ibid., 6 May 1817.   [56] Ibid., 23 May 1817.

Crolly, who was obviously hurt by the implicit charge of authorship of the *Pastor* letters, promptly and vigorously denied it. Insisting that he had nothing to do with the letters and only knew their author by hearsay, he undertook to afford Zuinglius the gratification of religious controversy 'on condition, that he shall lay aside the mask and appear in his own real character—for it is my opinion, that a clergyman should always act with that candour and openness which naturally flow from a conscientious rectitude'. He then went on to deal with Zuinglius' charge that the Catholic church locked up the Scriptures to keep the laity ignorant concerning matters of religion by revealing that in 1816 he had got 4,000 copies of the New Testament printed at very moderate rates and circulated throughout Ulster. Sardonically referring to Zuinglius complimenting himself on gaining a glorious victory over popery by his exposure of 'the absurd doctrines of penance and purgatory', he offered to engage the champion of Protestantism as soon as that gentleman was 'disposed to come to action under true colours'. He concluded by admitting to the vanity of hoping that before their debate ended he would have repaired the breaches that had been made in 'the pillars and outworks of the Catholic church' and begged his opponent not to put him to the trouble of refuting the uncharitable assertion that Catholics worshipped stocks and stones.[57]

Zuinglius, in his next rejoinder, confessed that he, with many others, had wrongly assumed that Crolly was *Pastor*, but was not conscious of being guilty, even unintentionally, of any personal disrespect or unkindness. He refused Crolly's challenge on the grounds that 'to descend into the wide field of indiscriminate controversy, and carry on an interminable war of words, would be a fruitless waste of time, and disproportionate to the limits of a newspaper'. Nonetheless, he went on to point out that 'every intelligent Protestant must know, that this infallible and immaculate guide which assumes the title of THE CHURCH, is tainted with errors, superstitions and corruptions greater and more numerous than the most ignorant and fanatical Protestant sect, or than all our sects together'. He did allow Crolly, however, 'all the credit which he can claim for disseminating the New Testament through the north of Ireland; and particularly for the omission of some very pernicious annotations which disgraced the earlier editions of the Rhemish or Douay version'. Crolly, true to his pledge not to engage in controversy with anyone sheltering behind a *nom de plume*, kept his silence. Zuinglius, his supporter, a

Layman, and *Pastor,* either tired of the controversy or the editor called a halt after the publication of Zuinglius' fifth letter on 10 June.[58]

Crolly must have suspected that it was Bruce who was masquerading behind the name of Zuinglius. Bruce was well known as an able and formidable controversialist and, since he had made the initial statement that led to the exchange and then virtually identified himself as a minister in Belfast, the likelihood that it was he was very strong. However, the correspondence led to no breach between them. They continued to meet on amicable terms as officials of various charitable societies, and Crolly was present along with Bruce and other clergy at the examination of the pupils of the Belfast Academy in 1823, a year after Bruce had resigned the principalship of that school.[59] Bruce, in turn, attended Crolly's episcopal ordination and at the dinner on the following day replied to the toast which was proposed to himself and the presbytery of Antrim.

IV

Between 1766 and 1829 there was no precise canonical procedure for the appointment of bishops in Ireland. In 1766, on the death of James, the Old Pretender, the Holy See refused to confer on his son, Charles, the Young Pretender, the privilege, which his father and grandfather had enjoyed, of nominating to Irish sees. In 1829 the congregation of Propaganda issued a rescript detailing the exact arrangements to be followed when a vacancy occurred or a coadjutor was required in a diocese. Between 1766 and 1829 the Holy See usually relied on the recommendations of the bishops of the province or country at large. But the clergy of the see to which appointments were to be made were usually determined, if possible, to influence the final decision, and various factions within the dioceses often held caucuses to advance the causes of their candidates both by influencing the bishops of their ecclesiastical province and the congregation of Propaganda in Rome, which made the final recommendation to the pope. The rules which were drawn up in 1829 were designed to put an end to improper clerical politicking and unseemly canvassing.

---

[58] In a note in a copy of the *Belfast News Letter* in the Linen Hall Library, Zuinglius is identified as Dr Bruce and *Pastor* as Daniel Jennings, the parish priest of Moira. Jennings' authorship of the *Pastor* letters was revealed in an obituary notice in the *News Letter* on 12 Aug. 1817. Internal evidence supports the likelihood of Bruce's authorship of Zuinglius. When the Belfast Academical Institution was being established, an anonymous article strongly opposing it appeared in the B.N.L., and the founders of the Institution believed that Bruce, who did not want a rival to his academy, was the author of it. (Jamieson, *Royal Belfast Academical Institution*, 1810-1960, 6-7.)

[59] Stewart, *Belfast Royal Academy, The First Hundred Years*, 43.

Patrick McMullan, bishop of Down and Connor, long troubled by ill-health and feeling the weight of old age—he was then in his seventy-third year—decided in 1824 that he needed the assistance of a coadjutor bishop. He wrote to his metropolitan, Archbishop Patrick Curtis of Armagh, on 20 July, signifying his intention of calling his priests together to select a suitable candidate for the coadjutorship, and inviting Curtis to confirm the result for the benefit of Rome. Curtis was not pleased by the proposal. He informed McMullan that the officially approved practice seemed to be that 'during the lifetime of any Bishop filling a See, no Coadjutor, or eventual Successor (both of which now always go together) can be legitimately called, or, as it is commonly said, postulated for (tho' the term of postulation, in this sense, had been rejected, and reprehended, as improper, by the Propaganda) without the previous consent, and express order, of the Holy See'. He thought, however, that Rome might accept the excuse that time did not permit rigid adherence to that requirement. He, therefore, could neither sanction nor confirm the selection made by the clergy, but could only declare that after due examination he had found that the bishop and his priests had conducted their meeting in a canonical manner, free of any irregular influences or pressures. Consequently, he advised McMullan to ensure that his priests were summoned by circular to meet and ballot for the candidate whom they conscientiously deemed to be the most suitable, and to accept, from those who could not attend, a sealed envelope containing their votes. An account of the proceedings was then to be drawn up in Latin and the document authenticated by the bishop or a notary apostolic.[60]

What was worrying Curtis, as he made clear to his former pupil and close friend, Archbishop Murray of Dublin, was the possibility of McMullan's nephew, William McMullan, the parish priest of Loughinisland, emerging as successor. He thought William McMullan and Crolly, whom he had recently met and 'who appeared . . . a man of considerable merit', were the two candidates most likely to go forward. But he feared that the McMullan influence would preponderate (he believed—wrongly—that the diocese had been handed down from uncle to nephew by the McMullans for the last half century) and that McMullan relatives controlled 'the greater number of the parishes', even though Crolly would obtain a good number of votes, 'indeed all, or nearly all, such as are free and unbiassed'. So strong were Curtis' apprehensions, however, that he wondered if Murray would join him and be prepared to

[60] Curtis to McMullan, 23 July 1824, DCDA.

rally the other archbishops to support Crolly, 'in case it should appear that he had been unjustly overpowered by nepotism'. The archbishop of Armagh was not sure about the wisdom of his own involvement in this Down and Connor affair, for he concluded by asking Murray whether he should avoid having anything to do with it.[61] Nonetheless, he was convinced of the necessity and expediency of appointing a coadjutor to Down and Connor. When approached by Bishop MacLaughlin of Derry, whom McMullan had obviously asked to preside at the forthcoming assembly, about the propriety of doing so, he readily gave his consent and approval, explaining the advantages of an episcopal authentication of the proceedings for Rome.[62]

Once given the green light McMullan lost little time in initiating proceedings. He summoned the clergy to meet in St Patrick's Church in Belfast on 4 August 1824. Since he himself was too ill to attend, Bishop McLaughlin presided in his place. Fifty seven priests were present and forty four of them recommended Crolly for the appointment. The other two candidates, whose names went forward to Rome, were John Fitzsimons, the parish priest of Ballyclug and Kirkinriola (Ballymena) and Bernard McAuley, the parish priest of Drummaul (Randalstown and Antrim), who had been Crolly's curate from 1812 to 1819. It is not known how many votes each received, or if any other candidates obtained votes; perhaps the overwhelming preponderance of support for Crolly disposed the clergy to regard the distribution of the remaining thirteen suffrages as unimportant.

The size of the majority accorded to the parish priest of Belfast was a well-deserved tribute from his fellow-clergy and reflected the reputation he enjoyed for devoted pastoral service, academic ability and administrative talent. He himself stated, at a royal commission of inquiry into Irish education in 1825, that he had not been absent from the town for more than a month at any time during the previous thirteen years.[63] The clergy doubtless believed that he had the strong health and youthful energy required for the leadership of the diocese after the long episcopate of a bishop who had been ailing for several years.

The result of the ballot was published in the local press, and Crolly's convincing lead was enthusiastically greeted by the *Irishman*, which anticipated a favourable reception of the clergy's opinions in Rome. Proclaiming that the election had given very unmixed satisfaction to every man of every denomination in Belfast, the editor, John Lawless, stated

[61] Curtis to Murray, 28 July 1826, DDA.   [62] Curtis to McMullan, 29 July 1824, DCDA.
[63] *Fourth report of the commissioners of Irish education inquiry*, p. 181

that he had had the pleasure of witnessing the labours of the leading candidate for the previous nine years—labours which, he added, were 'not more distinguished by zeal than talent—unbendingly asserting the pre-eminence of his own doctrines without letting fall *a single expression* which could by possibility (sic) offend the members of any other denomination'. Reflecting on the difficulty facing a conscientious man of enforcing his own convictions without giving offence to the consciences of others, he observed that Crolly had 'with great address defended his own doctrines without offering the most distant insult to the doctrines of other men—a rare and valuable merit and worthy of every Minister of the Gospel'.[64] The *Northern Whig* also commented favourably on the outcome and remarked that the result would find general satisfaction, as Crolly's conduct had been 'ever marked by an ardent desire to conciliate the affections of his fellow townsmen, and to assist, on all occasions in every work of benevolence and charity'.[65]

As Curtis had proposed, a Latin document, dated 7 August, was drawn up for submission to Rome detailing McMullan's illness as the reason for his seeking an assistant, and explaining that he had called together his clergy to petition the pope to nominate the priest whom they judged to be most worthy. It then pointed out that the great majority of them thought Crolly was the most worthy candidate, and went on to add that he was in his forty fourth year, had taught moral philosophy and, on occasion, theology with distinction at Maynooth, was conspicuous for zeal, virtue and learning, had made many converts to the church and would be most acceptable to the whole people. There then followed the signatures of thirty nine priests.

The archbishop of Armagh, highly pleased with the result of the clerical poll in Belfast, wrote enthusiastically to Rome in Crolly's favour. Reinforcing the comments of the Down and Connor clergy, he claimed that Crolly possessed all the right qualities, was the popular choice of both priests and people and was far superior to the other two candidates, whose names were included merely to conform to custom.[66] This letter also included postscripts from both Archbishop Murray of Dublin and Archbishop Kelly of Tuam: they limited themselves to remarking that Crolly was most suited for episcopal office.[67]

The congregation of Propaganda was annoyed by what it considered

---

[64] Ir., 6 Aug. 1824.
[65] N.W., 5 Aug. 1824. The *Whig* mentioned that McMullan's name was 'put in nomination' but no evidence is available of the number of votes he received.
[66] ponuntur pro more.   [67] Curtis to Propaganda, 21 Aug. 1814, APF, *Acta*, 188, ff 9v-10r.

the irregularity of these proceedings. Curtis, in his letter, had described the forty four priests who gave their votes to Crolly as electors, and neither he nor his two colleagues had bothered to dilate on the merits or demerits of the other two priests, whose names they had sent forward. Propaganda concluded that they were treating the appointment as an election by the clergy and thereby restricting the pope's exclusive right to appoint to episcopal office. Rejecting any claim by such assemblies of clergy to enjoy electoral rights and the suggestion that two other names could be forwarded merely to satisfy a formal obligation, Propaganda wrote to Murray and Kelly on 25 September seeking their views as to whether or not the other two priests possessed the requisite qualities for episcopal office. Murray explained in reply that he had simply been asked by Curtis to submit his testimony on behalf of Crolly, whom he had known at Maynooth. But he also knew the other two candidates and judged them to be men of zeal, piety, integrity and considerable merit; Crolly, however, far surpassed them in learning, eloquence and prudence, and enjoyed much more respect from both clergy and laity; and in terms of the other qualities mentioned he was in no way second to them. While the choice of either Fitzsimons or McAuley would not be unacceptable, the clergy and people of Down and Connor seemed to have placed their hopes on Crolly. Kelly disclaimed all knowledge of both of them.[68]

If Bishop McMullan was disappointed by his nephew's failure to obtain clerical support for the coadjutorship, he was determined to offer him some compensation while still able to do so. In the previous year he had sought to detach a part of his mensal parish of Downpatrick and join it to Loughinisland, to which it had formerly belonged, and also to obtain the deanship of Down for his nephew. An irregularity in his application had afforded Rome the opportunity of stalling. He now revived the application to Curtis and apparently indicated some dissatisfaction with the conduct or outcome of the clerical meeting in August. Curtis reassured him in reply about the likelihood of Rome's appointing his nephew dean and notary apostolic, and even of altering his parochial boundaries, but went on to express disquiet about whatever feelings of dissatisfaction McMullan had conveyed to him: 'I am very sorry that there should be any such feeling there, as it is now totally unreasonable, and useless. For, if at all founded, it should have been publickly brought forward, at the proper time, or forever buried in silence, at least, it should not be produced on *ex parte* testimony.'[69]

[68] Ibid., ff 2r-4r, 10v-11r.   [69] Curtis to McMullan, 29 Sept. 1824, DCDA.

The situation was somewhat altered by Bishop McMullan's death on 25 October. On 3 November the clergy met to elect a vicar-capitular to take charge of the diocese until a successor would be appointed. Crolly was unanimously chosen, having obtained the votes not only of those who were present but also of some who were unable to attend, but submitted their suffrages. The new vicar-capitular promptly informed the archbishop of Armagh of what had taken place, inviting him to confirm the result or, if he questioned the validity of the proceedings, to name a vicar-capitular himself. Curtis, realizing that the Down and Connor clergy had acted *ultra vires* since they, as a body, did not enjoy the rights and privileges of a non-existent chapter, exercised his authority as metropolitan and appointed Crolly vicar-capitular. William McMullan, who had been acting as the late bishop's secretary-cum-counsellor, if not *éminence grise*, when notifying the archbishop of Armagh of his uncle's demise, apparently took advantage of the occasion to raise again the question of the deanship of Down and of the extension to his parish in Loughinisland. Curtis declined to intervene on these requests, but promised McMullan that he would lend him his support, if a petition were to be presented through the new bishop, who would be happy to procure in that way what he might 'be offended to see snatched, as it were, underhand, against his will'.[70]

Informing Crolly of this answer, the archbishop observed that he had been pleased with the professions of peace and docility which McMullan had made in his letter. And in a postscript he referred briefly to a comment Crolly had made about the archbishop's letter to Rome, presumably connected with the suggestion of adding the other two priests' names as a mere formality. Explaining that he was not surprised at Crolly's 'appearing a little hurt', he assured him that the remarks were made 'by a true friend, anxious for you'.[71]

Crolly, himself, writing to his lifelong friend, Cornelius Denvir, professor of natural philosophy at Maynooth, referred to the forty one votes cast at a meeting, (presumably the one to choose the vicar-capitular) and noted that his former competitor—McMullan—and most of his friends had given their votes to him. On the wider issue of succession to the bishopric, he remarked that 'although there is still a possibility of a failure, yet I can scarcely suppose that the sacred Congregation will appoint any other but the person whom they have reason to consider best qualified'. Placing the matter in God's hands, he went on to express his

[70] Curtis to William McMullan, 5 Nov. 1824, DCDA.   [71] Curtis to Crolly, 11 Nov. 1824, DCDA.

gratitude to Curtis, Murray and Denvir for their support of his candidacy for an office which he was clearly not unwilling to assume:

Let our Business terminate as it may I shall never forget my obligations to the Most Revd Doctor Murray, and even if a failure should take place I am still deeply indebted to the Primate, who was perhaps too anxious for my success. He is still confident there can be no obstacle to my appointment, but his letters to me latterly shewed that he had been mortified in some manner which I now understand, from your explanation.[72]

Very shortly after Bishop McMullan's death, another letter of support for Crolly reached Rome. Patrick McNicholas, bishop of Achonry, who was writing on business relating to his own diocese took advantage of the opportunity to offer support for his former colleague on the Maynooth staff. Remarking that he had known Crolly for almost twenty years and paying tribute to all his priestly gifts, McNicholas concluded with the bold claim that there was no one in the diocese or even in the province comparable to him.[73]

With McMullan's death the diocese required not a coadjutor, but a bishop possessing full jurisdiction, but neither Curtis nor Crolly thought it necessary to convene the clergy of Down and Connor again to test their views on the succession. The likelihood of any significant change of opinion since the meeting of 4 August was extremely slight; if anything, Crolly's appointment as vicar-capitular had strengthened his position and had left Rome in no doubt that he enjoyed the confidence of the clergy to a remarkable degree.

Consequently, when the cardinals of Propaganda met on 31 January 1825 to recommend a candidate to the pope for appointment, they had no documentation before them that related to the actual vacancy of the see, apart from McNicholas' letter. Cardinal della Somaglia, in summarizing the situation for them, drew particular attention to the impropriety of Curtis' use of the term 'electors' for the clergy who assembled on 4 August and to the reference to the names of Fitzsimons and McAuley being included as a mere formality. To prevent a recurrence of such an infringement of the rights of the Holy See, the cardinals decided to apprise the archbishop of Armagh of their determination not to accept any letters or petitions in which reference was made to the election or postulation of bishops by clergy. However, their chagrin at the irregularity of which Curtis was guilty did not prevent them from accepting the clear

[72] Crolly to Denvir, 6 Nov. 1824, Ibid.
[73] McNicholas to Propaganda, 8 Nov. 1824, APF, *Acta*, 188, f 12v.

and convincing preference of three archbishops and the great majority of the clergy of Down and Connor; they recommended Crolly to the pope and Leo XII formally appointed him on 6 February.[74]

The ceremony of episcopal ordination was performed by Archbishop Curtis, assisted by Bishop MacLaughlin of Derry and Bishop McGettigan of Raphoe in St Patrick's Church on 1 May 1825. The sermon was preached by Peter Kenny, a Jesuit, who had been vice-president of Maynooth during Crolly's last weeks on the staff. Taking his text from Psalm 89, 35 he dealt with the unchangeable nature of the church, its divine authority and the continuity of Petrine jurisdiction within it. The tickets of admission to the ceremony cost seven shillings and sixpence, and the money raised on the occasion was devoted to the liquidation of the debt on St Patrick's. And such was the demand for a place at the ceremony that some of the congregation had begun arriving two hours before it began.

On Monday, 2 May, the new bishop entertained to dinner in Ward's Hotel some two hundred and fifty guests,[75] including the sovereign, John Agnew, clergy of all denominations and the leading citizens of the town, most of whom had been at the ordination the previous day. The majority were Protestants, and the whole occasion was wrapped in a haze of genial benevolence and 'ecumenical' goodwill. A staggering number of toasts was drunk and, not surprisingly, the celebrations lasted more than six hours.

Archbishop Curtis, replying to the first set of toasts, which linked his name and that of the hierarchy of Ireland with the royal family, the Lord Lieutenant and prosperity to the country, expressed the pleasure he felt on hearing about 'the uniform liberality of the people of Belfast' from the newly-consecrated prelate and remarked that the general harmony which he himself had witnessed evidenced that true spirit of Christianity which ordered every man to love his friend. Toasts were drunk to Richard Mant, the bishop of Down and Connor in the established church, and to his clergy; to William McEwen, the Presbyterian minister of the second Congregation of Belfast and to the Presbyterian clergy of Antrim and Down. Samuel Hanna, the professor of divinity in the Academical Institution, was temporarily absent and could not respond to the toast to himself and the Synod of Ulster, but, in his place, Henry Montgomery, his colleague on the staff and in the ministry, drew enthusiastic cheers when he referred to the fidelity of the Synod to the principles of civil and

---

[74] Ibid., ff 6r-9v.
[75] The *Irishman* which copied the report of the occasion from the *Northern Whig* changed the venue to the Assembly Rooms of the Commercial Building.

religious liberty and alluded to its recent repudiation of Henry Cooke's claim that the majority of its members did not favour Catholic Emancipation. William Bruce in response to a toast to himself and the Presbytery of Antrim expressed the hope that 'no triumph or mortification would be shown on either side', when parliament reached its decision on the measure then being debated for Catholic Emancipation. William Carr, in giving thanks for the good wishes expressed to the Seceding Synod, disabused the guests of any beliefs they or others might have about the Seceders being hostile to Catholic Emancipation; on the contrary, he insisted that 'the present evening proved that the Catholic religion also, however calumniated, was such as to cherish the purest feelings of benevolence'.

When the sovereign of the town, John Agnew, replied to his own toast, he proposed the health of the host and

Dr Crolly declared that this was not the first time for him to feel the kind partiality of the people of Belfast. When he first came among them, he was friendless and unknown, without even an introduction to any inhabitant. But he had not breathed the air of Belfast for many days, when the clergymen of different denominations stepped forward to extend the right hand of fellowship and welcome; nor were the laity slow in following the example. He rejoiced that his present elevation would afford him more opportunity of proving his gratitude. It shall be my constant endeavour, said he, to diffuse universal benevolence through the diocese committed to my care; nor shall I cease, while one illiberal member of our Church is to be found, from the mountains of Mourne to the caverns of the Causeway. If there should be any Priest tainted by narrow and gross prejudice, I shall send him for his cure to inhale the liberal atmosphere of Belfast. He was proud to be able to convince Dr Curtis, and his other brethren, that Belfast might well be counted the most liberal and charitable town in any part of Europe. Of this there was a standing testimony in the New Chapel, which was built by the generous contribution of every class of Christians— and, I trust, said the worthy prelate, that under my care the voice of bigotry has never profaned its walls. . . . He concluded with hoping, that he would never give his townsmen cause to change their favourable opinion of him.

Toasts were drunk to Lords Donegall, Downshire and Londonderry and to Professor Young and the Belfast Academical Institution, to the Belfast Academy and its principal, to George Canning and the liberal and enlightened members of the government, to the high sheriff of Down and to Charles Brownlow, the Honourable convert to the cause of civil and religious liberty. Young observed that universal joy had been manifested at Crolly's elevation, alluded to the former illiberality of Scotland, which had almost died away, and boasted that no attempts were made to gain proselytes to any sect among the students of the Academical Institution, all the offices of which were open to all who possessed the right qualifications, irrespective of creed.

Crolly himself gave a toast to Thomas Moore, the bard of Erin, and to the memory of Robert Burns, and, after his own health had been proposed a second time, he remarked that he anticipated many such happy social occasions; and noting that the suffrages of his brethren had raised him to the episcopal dignity, he promised to remember 'that their good opinion had been in a great measure gained by the kind feeling of his Protestant friends towards him, and those feelings he should always be most anxious to cherish and cultivate'.

The *Northern Whig* concluded its report of the ceremony and celebrations with an enthusiastic description of the genuine concord so evident at the dinner and a forecast of a halcyon future.

It was not one of those meetings, whose intercourse is confined to the mere pressure of the hand, or the cold exchange of formal civility—it was a meeting of Irish men and of brothers . . . It was an anticipation of what may be expected, when Catholic and Protestant are placed upon the same footing and when they learn everywhere to look upon each other—not with the sullen or exasperated glare of party feud—but with the kindly beam of brotherly affection. When the apple of discord shall have been for ever removed from our island, and faction shall have ceased to embroil its inhabitants, such meetings as this will be no longer contemplated with surprise, and the Irish heart will be permitted to shew itself in its true light, warm, generous and sincere.[76]

On 18 May some one hundred and seventy 'of the most respectable Protestant Inhabitants' of Belfast 'with a liberality highly creditable to them as Patriots and as Christians' reciprocated Crolly's hospitality by entertaining him to dinner, in what, according to the *Northern Whig*, was a 'genuine tribute of the heart, to a man, whose talents and liberality as a minister, and benevolence as a citizen, had endeared him to his fellow-townsmen'. The two prominent liberals, John McCance and John Sinclaire, acted as chairman and croupier. Many of the toasts drunk were to the same people and bodies as at the previous dinner. Newcomers to the list included the vicar of Belfast, A.C. Macartney, the Chancellor of the Exchequer, Frederick Robinson, the Attorney General for Ireland, William Plunket, the agricultural societies of Ireland, Professor Stevely and the Belfast Mechanics Institute, the mining companies of Ireland, William Tennent and the bankers of Belfast, Bernard McAuley and the other priests who were present, and—a chivalrous, if light-hearted touch—'the ladies of Belfast' and 'all honest men, and bonnie lasses'.

[76] N.W., 5 May; Ir., 6 May 1825.

The chairman proposed Crolly's health, saluting 'a most benevolent divine', who, since coming to Belfast, had displayed in all his actions the true spirit of Christian liberality. Returning thanks for the gesture of friendship he was then enjoying, Crolly declared:

After thirteen years residence among you, during which I have been your unprofitable steward in society, you have thus generously come forward to offer this high mark of your regard and approbation. I prize it more than anything this world can offer. You lately did me the honour to meet me on my advancement in the Church, and that honour I looked on as sufficient. But there was still a higher species of consecration reserved for me—a consecration which was to stamp my character as an unprejudiced and liberal man . . . I feel it impossible that I can ever discharge my Episcopal duties without promoting goodwill among men to the utmost of my power. I learn from that Bible, which we all regard as the common foundation of our faith, that no one can serve the God of peace without exerting himself to promote peace, and kindness, and harmony, and charity, in the world; and it is only by thus acting that I can ever make you a return for your kindness. I trust that your patriotic example will be followed by every person of influence and talents in every part of Ireland. . . It is not necessary that we should sacrifice or compromise our conscientious convictions; but it is necessary that we should carry our prejudices to the Communion Table of Charity, and there consume them on the altar of our common country.

The applause which greeted these sentiments lasted for nearly ten minutes. Another speaker who was heartily cheered was Henry Montgomery. He vigorously defended the record of the Synod of Ulster, whose members, in consistently advocating Catholic Emancipation, were but supporting 'this great national act of common justice'. He revealed that he felt himself growing more catholic with the passing years, as he came to view the creeds of other sects in a more charitable light, and, while there would always be differences of opinion on speculative points, he was more anxious to discover points of agreement among Christians. He believed that all were travelling to the same great happy land and he trusted they would all arrive together in peace and be hailed with joy by the spirits of their Catholic ancestors, who might gladly welcome the thousands of the wise and good of all sects into which their descendants were divided. William Smith, the curate of St Anne's, responding to the toast to the vicar of Belfast and 'the Established Church of this Diocese', paid tribute to the dignified silence his church had maintained during the debates in parliament on Emancipation and pledged a cheerful submission to the decisions of Westminster. Like other speakers he lauded Crolly's 'liberal and benevolent character', and commented favourably on their cooperation in works of charity, irrespective of the religious or political opinions they held. Bernard McAuley asked rhetorically where had liberality been so conspicuous or philanthropy so truly displayed; loud cheers greeted his answer to these and other questions that elicited similar compliments—'Belfast'.

The *Whig* summed up the balmy atmosphere of camaraderie and bonhomie of the occasion by declaring that 'there were no features to distinguish the members of one Christian Church from those of another; but, Catholic and Protestant all mingled like brothers, and vied in promoting the happiness of the evening'.[77]

Crolly could not have hoped for a more auspicious start to his episcopate, and the goodwill of these Protestant friends was to stand him in good stead as a more sectarian tone developed in the attitudes of some of their co-religionists.

[77] N.W., 19 May; Ir., 20 May 1825.

3

THE STRUGGLE FOR
CATHOLIC EMANCIPATION

During the first years of his priesthood, which he spent on the staff at Maynooth, Crolly became familiar with the political arguments for Catholic relief and the controversies surrounding the price which the goverment threatened to exact for it—the power to veto candidates for the episcopacy whom it deemed politically unsuitable. Like the vast majority of priests, he did not take part in the public discussions concerning these issues: they were conducted by the Catholic gentry, landowners, merchants, barristers and professional men, among whom Daniel O'Connell quickly came to the fore, and the bishops. Disagreements among the activists about both goals and means and the unrelenting opposition of the British government ensured that no progress was made.

Crolly's appointment to the pastorate of Belfast in 1812 placed him in the forefront of what was then the second largest urban community of Catholics in Ulster and which a few years later bypassed that of Newry to become the largest. In the area covered by the diocese of Down and Connor, Catholics probably accounted for about a quarter of the population,[1] but, both in Belfast and in the country parishes, only a few had attained the status of moderately well-off shopkeepers and farmers and only a tiny proportion had entered the professions. Unlike their co-religionists in Dublin they did not have a prosperous middle class or gentry that could devote spare energies to politics. The northern rebellion of 1798 had occurred in Counties Antrim and Down, and, though by the end of the first decade of the nineteenth century political allegiance had swung back to the crown, liberal sentiments survived among many of the Presbyterians. In 1813 at the annual meeting of the Synod of Ulster in Cookstown one hundred and thirty nine ministers and elders 'fully

---

[1] According to the census taken by the Commissioners of Public Instruction in 1834, Catholics represented 30% of the population of the diocese of Down and 26% of that of Connor. The dioceses of the established church, to which the census figures refer, were almost conterminous with those of the Catholic church.

representing the wealth, intelligence and feelings of the great mass of the Presbyterian population of Ulster' reaffirmed their attachment to the principles of the British constitution and then felt obliged to declare 'that, from the abolition of political distinctions, on account of religious profession, so far as may be consistent with the principles of the Constitution, we anticipate the happiest consequences'.[2] But Grattan's bill of that year, which would have subjected episcopal correspondence with Rome and the loyalty of candidates for bishoprics to the scrutiny of a committee appointed by the government, was defeated. In the following year intense excitement was provoked by the rescript of Monsignor Quarantotti, an official of the Roman curia, who, in the absence of the pope, declared that the government might be empowered to prevent the appointment of those candidates whom it considered politically unaccept-able. Though Quarantotti broke no new ground by this concession— continental rulers enjoyed wider privileges in the nomination of bishops— the advocates of Emancipation scented an ecclesiastical surrender which could lead to the political subjugation of the Irish church to the British state, and mounted a determined resistance to it. On his return to Rome, Pius VII insisted on his right to make this arrangement, but with the defeat of Napoleon and the need of the papacy to cooperate with Britain in redrawing the map of Europe, the pressure on the government to yield to Catholic claims diminished.

The cause of Emancipation received a fillip in Belfast and, to a lesser extent, in the counties nearby with the establishment of a newspaper, the *Irishman*, in the town in 1819. Its managing editor, John Lawless, was a Dublin-born lawyer who had published a political and literary magazine, the *Ulster Register*, at Newry from 1816 to 1818, and, from what was then the strongest Catholic base in the province, had striven to alert his readers to the issues involved in Emancipation, the veto and the other securities which were demanded as a *quid pro quo*. An ardent and uncompromising political reformer, Lawless sought to galvanize opposition to the injus-tices, political, social, religious and economic, which he considered required urgent redress. And he vigorously encouraged and praised those who, irrespective of creed, had indicated their support for Catholic Emancipation, and, with equal vigour, he excoriated the factious bigotry that led to clashes between Orangemen and Ribbonmen[3] (a Catholic

---

[2] *Records of the General Synod of Ulster from 1691 to 1820*, iii, 397 and N.W., 21 Apr. 1825.
[3] The Ribbonmen were one of the secret agrarian societies that sought by violence and intimidation to obtain redress of grievances about rents. They occasionally paraded as nationalists and engaged the Orangemen in street battles.

agrarian secret society, which existed in pockets of Ulster) and demanded that all party processions, which were known to be illegal, should be banned.

The *Irishman* resisted and denounced all attempts to diminish the value of Catholic Emancipation by conceding a veto on episcopal appointments to the government, and the trimmers or vetoists were sharply rebuked for demanding a freedom that benefitted the gentry or professional classes and left the others virtually untouched. And, as if to prove Lawless' point about illegal societies, the Grand Master of the Orangemen of Armagh (the county where the order was strongest) and the Grand Chairman of the Ribbon Association of Counties Down, Antrim, Armagh and Fermanagh issued addresses to their supporters in December 1819 calculated to exacerbate the divisions which they had already helped to harden and sustain: the Orange leader denounced those who campaigned publicly for reform, but who had robbery and plunder in their hearts and who schemed to seduce the people from their loyalty to their king and religion. The Ribbon leader reminded his brethren that they were the offspring of persecution and that the law of self-defence was the first law of nature, but promised to unite with the Orangemen in adhering to Christianity and encouraged loyalty to the king and fidelity to religion and to Ireland.[4]

The advocacy of the *Irishman* doubtless helped concentrate the minds of the Belfast liberals again on Emancipation. A requisition signed by some hundred leading members of this group—including John Barnett, William Drennan, James McDonnell, William Tennent, Robert McDowell, James Munfoad and Robert Grimshaw—appeared in the *Belfast News Letter*, of 1 December 1818 calling for a meeting in the Linen Hall on the following day to take into consideration the propriety of presenting a petition to parliament for the total repeal of the penal code that had so long disqualified Catholic fellow-subjects from participating in all the advantages of the British constitution. The Linen Hall was too small for the crowd that turned up and the meeting had to be postponed and held in the Lancasterian school a few days later. As he opened the proceedings, Robert Getty, the chairman, remarked that those present constituted 'the most respectable in station and in property' of which Belfast could boast and expressed the hope that the example of that 'enlightened town would call forth such a feeling throughout the Protestant community of Ireland, as would demonstrate to the Imperial Legislature that the party interested in the continuance of Catholic

---

4 Ir., 17 Dec. 1819.

disqualification was small, poor and contemptible'. There were a few voices raised in opposition to the resolution calling for the immediate repeal of the penal code affecting Catholics, when it was put to the floor, but when the same occurred with a further resolution expressing sympathy with Catholics and declaring that their emancipation was the best means of promoting the interests of the empire, Adam McClean, who seconded it, explained that the opposition was not directed to the justice or policy of the measure, but came from those who were concerned about the timing and manner of the removal of the restrictions on Catholics.

The petition to the House of Commons, which was presented to the meeting, and was generous and comprehensive, received unanimous support. The petitioners pointed out that as Christians they wished to see done to others what in like circumstances they would wish to have done to themselves, and called for a total and unqualified repeal of the penal laws which kept the Catholics a distinct people in the empire, so that every relique of a bad and barbarous policy would disappear and that the pledges given, or understood to have been given, at the period of the legislative union should be redeemed and faithfully performed. Lawless concluded the meeting by thanking the chairman and commending all present for their liberal and enlightened sentiments.[5]

In Dublin O'Connell had begun again to organize Protestant support for a similar petition and influential Protestants added their names to it. But to so low an ebb had enthusiasm for the struggle sunk that by 1819 even O'Connell was prepared to contemplate the surrender of some ground on the veto issue. And it must have been with some sadness that Drennan told him that he would have to balance 'the *much* you may receive against the *comparatively* little you lose', and had gone on to predict that 'the Catholic *regium donum*' will follow 'the Presbyterian *regium donum*'. But, as Grattan's motion for a committee to inquire into Catholic disabilities was defeated, the issue was not then pursued any further. Grattan died in the following year before he could present further petitions to the House of Commons.[6]

William Drennan, the lifelong reformer and United Irishman, also died in 1820. In the *Irishman* Lawless extolled his 'inflexible integrity' and claimed that support for equal rights and equal duties was the star by which he had guided his political life since 1778.[7] Drennan's death coincided with the change in attitudes of many Presbyterians towards Emancipation. In the first two decades of the century Presbyterians and

[5] B.N.L., 1, 8, Dec. 1818.
[6] MacDonagh, *The Hereditary Bondsman: Daniel O'Connell 1775-1829*, 108.

some members of the established church either supported Emancipation
or kept silent about it. But as the third decade dawned opposition to a
change in the law became more vocal, and the Protestants of Ulster who
favoured Emancipation came to be greatly outnumbered by those who
opposed it. Political factors—the fear of losing privilege and pre-eminence, the fear of a reversal of the Williamite constitutional settlements
with all the upheavals in land ownership which that might entail—
accounted for some of this change of heart, but among the mass of the
Protestant population the exacerbation of sectarian feeling consequent
upon the work of the evangelical societies, who were spearheading the
'new Reformation' in Ireland, played a highly significant role.

II

While Presbyterianism in Ulster had been vivified from time to time by
outstanding preachers, the visits by John Wesley to the province in the
second half of the eighteenth century were destined to affect Protestants
of various denominations far beyond the Anglican church to which he
belonged. Wesley's brand of popular evangelicalism found a powerful
resonance in the last quarter of the century in the northern parts of
Ireland. Itinerant Methodist preachers, with their outdoor sermons, hymn
singing, simple and popular religious expressions and sharp sectarian
edge, attracted increasing bands of followers, especially in areas where
competition for work or land had already created some strife among
Catholic and Protestant. The growth of Methodist societies in the area
around Lough Erne and in the 'linen triangle' (an area stretching from
Newry to beyond Lisburn on the east side and somewhat beyond
Dungannon to the west) had gathered momentum in the wake of the 1798
rebellion and again in the harsh economic climate of the slump following
the Napoleonic wars. In 1799 the Methodist mission stipulated that its
itinerant missioners should be able to speak Irish so that they could
preach more effectively to Irish-speaking Catholics.[8] Catching this evangelical atmosphere, ministers of the Seceding Presbyterian Synod established the Evangelical Society of Ulster in 1798 and, though they did not
enjoy the favour of their synod, attracted support from other Presbyterian
bodies and the help of fiery English preachers from the London Missionary Society.[9]

[7] Ir., 11 Feb. 1819.   [8] Hempton and Hill, *Evangelical Protestantism in Ulster Society*, 1740-1890, 37.
[9] Ibid., 39.

It was reports from Methodist revivalists and appeals for help to like-minded groups in London that sparked off a wave of interest in Ireland among English evangelical societies. Soon men and money were poured into the country to wean the benighted peasantry from the superstitious practices to which their priests subjected them, to inject them with a powerful strain of evangelical religion, to equip them with bibles and bring them to a higher state of civilization. To the tried and proven techniques of the Methodists was added the apostolate of education: schools were established and teachers paid to draw Catholic children through scriptural study to an understanding and acceptance of Protestantism, and in some cases the Irish language was used as the medium through which this work of conversion was to be effected.

In 1800, the Association for Discountenancing Vice and Promoting the Knowledge and the Practice of the Christian Religion, which had been founded in Ireland by members of the established church eight years earlier, received its first grant from parliament—a modest sum of £300. Twenty years later this grant had been increased thirty-fold and the Association which had started off distributing bibles and tracts had control of a whole network of schools. None but clergy of the established church were allowed to manage these schools and they were obliged to ensure that the Catholic children in attendance read the authorized version of the bible. As this society grew in strength its proselytizing zeal grew in proportion. An even more vigorously proselytizing body was the London Hibernian Society, which placed strong emphasis on bible reading in its schools, and which directly and indirectly received government funding for its work. The Baptist Society for Promoting the Gospel in Ireland, founded in 1814, and the Irish Society for Promoting the Education of the Native Irish through the Medium of their Own Language, founded in 1818, established schools where they employed Irish as the vernacular to reach Catholic children. The Sunday School Society for Ireland, founded in 1809, obtained funds from other proselytizing agencies and supplied local Sunday schools with tracts and catechisms.[10] Not surprisingly Catholic priests, who had taken for granted that they would serve the Catholic people unchallenged, as the Protestant and Presbyterian clergy served theirs, soon came to see the activities of these various societies as an assault on their church and responded by trying to withdraw children from the most energetically proselytizing of the schools and to warn their people against giving credence to the itinerant missionaries.

[10] Akenson, *The Irish Education Experiment*, 80–5.

Though the majority of the clergy of the established and Presbyterian churches did not encourage and in many cases resented and opposed the evangelicals, both clerical and lay, who flooded into the country, they could not prevent their own denominations from assuming some of the fervour and passion which the adherents of the new religious societies exuded. Since these qualities were laced with hostility to Catholicism, both in theological terms and in its practical expression in Ireland, the progress of the new Reformation was accompanied by increased sectarian antagonisms. While millenarianism was characteristic of some revivalist preaching on the Protestant side, the prophecies of Pastorini (a commentary by the English vicar- apostolic, Charles Warmsley, on the book of the Apocalypse which, using the symbolism of three hundred years, predicted the overthrow of Lutheranism and therefore of Protestantism in general by 1825) led to an excited millenarian mood among Catholics. But this seems to have been confined mainly to Munster and Leinster and was severely repudiated by Bishop Doyle of Kildare and Leighlin. While Catholics came to see themselves as defending a faith that was under seige and as campaigners for equality of political rights, members of other denominations came to regard them as aggressors who were attacking the constitution of the state. The Orange order and the Ribbon societies exploited and magnified sectarian tension by their illegal marches and displays.

One such display at a fair at Crebilly near Ballymena in the summer of 1819 led to serious strife. A party of Ribbonmen from the Portglenone district with musical accompaniment arrived at the fair and, though some heeded the advice of the parish priest to withdraw, others remained and were attacked by Orangemen. The Ribbonmen who had left returned to assist their friends and drove the Orangemen back to Ballymena 'where a furious conflict took place with sticks, whips, swords etc'. The *Irishman*, voicing a widely-felt anger over this unseemly violence, demanded to know why these desperate factions were tolerated. And it then supplied the answer which both Catholics and liberal Presbyterians were to give throughout the next decade: the Orange faction was allowed to parade illegally as the magistrates looked on 'with an indifference bordering on patronage'. The magistrates, it insisted, had a duty to suppress both the Orangemen and Ribbonmen with even-handed equality and impartial justice.[11] Despite these warnings nothing happened and Lawless was again forced to express his indignation that the magistrates of mid-Antrim did

11 Ir., 4, 9, July 1819.

not prevent parades of Orangemen and Ribbonmen at fairs at Connor and Crebilly in August 1819.[12]

Developments within the main Protestant churches also had repercussions which intensified religious differences between Protestants and Catholics. In 1822 William Magee, the archbishop of Dublin, set his church on a collision course with the two other largest Christian denominations in the country by his famous charge, in which he described Catholicism as a church without a religion and Presbyterianism as a religion without a church. This call to his clergy to evangelize the members of both bodies and bring them to that church which had a religion obliged some at least of his co-religionists to be more determined and combative in their relations with their Christian neighbours. Some landlords took their spiritual responsibilities so seriously that they even appointed 'moral agents' to look after their estates; and the agents generally believed that their moral supervision of the tenants included a duty to direct them towards Protestantism. Theological disputes within the Synod of Ulster were also of great importance in giving that body a stamp that was politically more conservative and therefore less sympathetic to Catholicism, even though political and theological conservatism were by no means conterminous.

III

In the eighteenth century rigid adherence to official professions of faith was not required of Presbyterian clergy. The atmosphere of the Enlightenment was not conducive to the acceptance of the element of mystery in religious creeds, and some clergy tended to play down the divinity of Christ and his full equality with God the Father, limiting him, as Arius had done in the fourth century, to the role of an exceptional agent in God's plan of redemption. Though the clergy of the Synod of Ulster were obliged to conform to the Westminster Confession of Faith, which excluded such views and required belief in the Trinity, they could be licensed by the Presbytery of Antrim which did not impose such obligations, and, in fact, clergy could move fairly easily from one jurisdiction to the other. That some clergy did not accept Christ's divinity is not in dispute, though the objection to abiding by confessions of faith did not necessarily imply support for Arianism, as several of those who were opposed to the imposition of creeds argued that the truth of the

[12] Ibid., 10 Sept. 1819.

gospel could not and should not be encapsulated in man-made formulae. A visit to Ulster in 1821 by an English Unitarian activist, Revd John Smethurst, who preached in Belfast and in twenty other places, set alarm bells ringing among the traditional Calvinist-minded clergy. Henry Cooke, the young minister of Killyleagh, picked up the gauntlet, followed Smethurst around in his own district challenging his claims, and thereby discovered an ability and taste for public controversy that he was to develop and exploit for the remainder of his life.[13] A conservative in politics as in theology, Cooke soon realized that his views found welcome acceptance in influential political circles, and a weakness for the favour of the great encouraged him to persevere in his anti-Unitarian campaign.

The next round in the fight against Unitarianism came in 1821. A vacancy occurred in the chair of Hebrew and Greek at the Belfast Academical Institution and the candidates William Bruce (junior) and R.J. Bryce, both Presbyterian clergymen, represented the liberal and conservative or evangelical wings of the church, or were 'new-light' or 'old-light' in theological terms. When it became known that Bruce's appointment would be favourably received in government circles and, perhaps, encourage the government to restore the annual grant that it had withdrawn from the Institution after a couple of professors had participated in an allegedly radical toast in 1816—a toast to America, the land of freedom— even Cooke's theological hostility was to no avail. But, nothing daunted, Cooke kept up the pressure against Arians and Arianism in the Institution and the church, and annually raised issues at the meeting of the Synod of Ulster to restrict the influence of Arian-minded clergy. In 1824 the Synod decreed that presbyteries, before licensing candidates to preach, should require them to subscribe to the Westminster Confession of Faith, a document that expressly proclaimed belief in the Trinity, or oblige them to submit to an examination to test the soundness of their faith.

Henry Montgomery, the minister of Dunmurry and the head of the English School in the Academical Institution, emerged as Cooke's chief antagonist, and the two locked horns with increasing force until Montgomery and his supporters were driven out of the Synod of Ulster. Montgomery was about the same age as Cooke but his position in the Institution, where he was also in charge of one of the two boarding houses, gave him an initial advantage in status over Cooke, and, furthermore, he became Moderator of the Synod of Ulster in 1818, a post Cooke did not obtain until 1824. Montgomery maintained that no church had the

[13] Holmes, *Henry Cooke*, 21.

right to compel its members to submit to man-made creeds, and argued that a clergyman ought only to be responsible to his own congregation; if it tolerated his theological views, no synod was entitled to impose further obligations. In 1828 the Synod decided to appoint a committee to examine candidates for the ministry on their views on the Trinity, justification by faith and other doctrines, and Montgomery's supporters drew up a remonstrance threatening withdrawal unless the Synod rescinded this decree. Montgomery's political opinions matched his theological credo, for by the touchstone of the time—the issue of Catholic Emancipation— he was unhesitatingly liberal. Cooke, on the other hand, was prepared to tolerate a limited concession and was always fearful of Catholics making political and social progress at the expense of Protestants.

The struggle between Cooke and Montgomery was dour and uncompromising. But from 1824, when he became Moderator of the Synod, Cooke and his party gained the upper hand and nothing but the complete rout of Montgomery's party would satisfy him. Indirectly the issue of Catholic relief was adversely affected by the passions generated by these theological arguments, for Cooke's supporters, who were in the main hostile to Catholic claims, came to enjoy much more public power and influence than their opponents, who were generally more liberal.

IV

In 1821 O'Connell recommended that petitions for Catholic Emancipation be dropped in favour of parliamentary reform. Lawless in the *Irishman* expressed agreement with this policy. He held that an unreformed parliament would never grant Emancipation and believed that justice demanded a democratic system based on a wide suffrage and frequent parliaments.[14] But attempts, however emollient, to win Emancipation continued to prove illusory. In 1821 William Conyingham Plunket introduced a bill which purported to offer Catholics a way of taking the oath of supremacy without violating their religious beliefs. It contained other 'securities' as well: a commission appointed by the government would examine and report on the loyalty of candidates being proposed for bishoprics and another commission would oversee the correspondence of the Irish bishops with Rome. The bill, which was defeated in the Lords, pleased the vetoists both in Ireland and England but was vigorously denounced by O'Connell in Dublin and Lawless in Belfast. The *Irishman*

[14] Ir., 12 Jan 1821.

declared that the measure would have made slaves of the Catholic laity
and corrupt, ministerial agents of the clergy, and remarked that its terms
could have provoked Archbishop Troy and the clergy to institute a
prosecution for libel against the publisher![15]

Political disaffection in Ireland, resulting from the failures of all
attempts to achieve Emancipation, was intensified by the famine of 1821-
2 and the upsurge in agrarian crime which it provoked. The Whiteboys in
the South of Ireland and the Ribbonmen in parts of the North became
more active, and Orangeism, which enjoyed the advantage of being able to
claim the sympathy of magistrates, because the brethren sought to
maintain and defend the status quo, was in turn stimulated by their
violent acts.

Despite the disheartening failures at Westminster and the refusal of
Wellesley, the Lord Lieutenant, who was credited with Catholic sympathies, to come to grips with the Orangemen (who paraded openly in
several towns in Ulster in July 1821), the continuing agrarian violence in
the south encouraged O'Connell and his friends to make another effort.
The upshot was the foundation in May 1823 of the Catholic Association,
which was committed to strive for Emancipation, but in the short term to
contribute towards the amelioration of Catholic grievances. Membership
of the Association cost one guinea annually and in 1824 was extended to
all who could pay one penny per month. The aim was to amass a yearly
rent of £50,000 and to use three fifths of such funds for helping Catholics
fight cases in court, especially where Orange magistrates were involved,
and the remainder was to be divided among the papers favourable to the
cause, the education of the Catholic poor, the provision of priests for
America, the building of churches and schools and parliamentary expenses. O'Connell soon attached the priests to the Association by giving
them honorary membership. He also invited them to suggest the names of
rent collectors, and to transmit the collections that had been taken up at
their churches to Dublin. So effective was this scheme for raising money
that by the last quarter of 1824 the rent was averaging £600 weekly.[16]

On 19 July 1824 a meeting was held in Belfast to launch the rent.
Lawless explained that the main object of their contributions was to
provide a fund on which their underprivileged fellow-countrymen might

[15] Ibid., 16 Mar. 1821. The Catholic prelates of Leinster and clergy of Dublin met on 26 March and pointed out that attempts to regulate their contact with Rome would impede the exercise of their ministry, questioned the justice of confidential communications with Rome being submitted to people of a different faith and suggested that an unlimited right of rejecting candidates for the episcopacy amounted to a right of positive nomination. (Ir., 30 Mar. 1821)

[16] MacDonagh, *The Hereditary Bondsman*, 206-13.

draw for protection against injustice and which would enable them to proceed from the tainted court of the local magistrate 'to the purity and talent' of the courts of King's Bench. A branch of the Catholic Association was then established and officials appointed. Lawless, who was chosen as secretary, reported to headquarters in Dublin that the resolutions in support of the Catholic rent were passed with unanimous enthusiasm and went on to pay tribute to the liberality and generosity of the Presbyterian body, pointing out that the first contribution received was from a Presbyterian who promised ten shillings yearly and that a co-religionist at Saintfield had promised a third of that sum.[17]

However, Presbyterian enthusiasm for the Catholic Association was a lot more muted than Lawless' letter would suggest. Indeed, the *Northern Whig*, a newspaper which had begun publication at the beginning of the year and which represented the views of the more liberal-minded of the Presbyterians (in contrast to the *Belfast News Letter*, which catered for the Anglicans and conservative Presbyterians) had consistently derided the aims of the Association. The *Whig* stood for constitutional and parliamentary reform and true to the tradition of the Enlightenment, from which Belfast liberalism ultimately derived, campaigned for civil and religious liberty for all citizens. In repudiating Lawless' claims it explained:

The Presbyterians here are not favourable either to the ASSOCIATION, or the system of raising funds under the name of Rentes. They are staunch advocates for the most extensive enjoyment of civil and religious freedom, by all men; and as such, favourable to Catholic Emancipation, to be obtained in a legal and constitutional manner; but not through intimidating measures, or threatening words, such as the orators of Capel-street have most injudiciously put forth.

The paper proceeded to explain how one of the two Presbyterians whose 'incautious act' had been made 'a sounding trumpet, through which the sentiments of the Presbyterians of the North' were to be spoken was cajoled into subscribing. It then went on to make an even more potentially damaging claim:

We assert that the measure of establishing a Rente committee in Belfast, was entered into in defiance of the inclinations and against the judgements of the highly respectable Parish Priest, and the most reputable of the Roman Catholic community here. The former used his influence to put a stop to it; and we have the opinions of numbers of the latter, reprobating it as injudicious.[18]

Significantly, neither Crolly nor Lawless commented on this claim.

[17] Ir., 30 July 1824.   [18] N.W., 29 July 1824.

Had it been untrue, both would doubtless have said so. In the following
year Crolly was quick to challenge an incorrect report about himself in the
press,[19] and Lawless, being a professional communicator, would not have
allowed a statement that might have discouraged numerous Catholics
from subscribing to the rent to pass uncorrected, had he known it be false.
The *Whig* had always opposed the Catholic Association; it had singled out
the Association and the Orange Order as the two greatest nuisances
confronting the sober-minded and well-intentioned people of Ireland;[20]
and it would continue to pour scorn on the objects of the rent, asking why
Presbyterians should pay for the education of priests for America, or help
'to influence (we love a soft name) the public press', and to demand that
oppression by the law be first proved before it was combated.[21] Crolly was
aware of the views that his natural allies among the Presbyterians in the
struggle for Emancipation held, and must have concluded that the
establishment of the rent would do more harm than good by antagonizing
those very friends whom he hoped to have by his side. Though bishops
and priests elsewhere encouraged their people to back the Association, he
obviously felt that the special circumstances obtaining in Belfast and in
those parts of Ulster where Catholics were in a minority called for a
different policy and approach.

When the rent campaign did not live up to its sponsors' expectations,
the *Whig* could not refrain from indulging in *Schadenfreude*. It congratulated the Catholics of Belfast on 'the wisdom and discernment' which they
had shown in resisting 'the unpopular and unwise measure of raising
funds for the Association in Dublin by unworthy subscriptions', and
begged their leaders to discontinue the collection or risk making themselves 'more ridiculous' than they already were.[22] And it repeated the
charge that Crolly held aloof: 'the enlightened and liberal Roman Catholic
pastor of Belfast stirs not a step—moves not a finger, to facilitate the
collection of the Rentes. His silence is golden—his indifference porten-
tous'.[23] The *Irishman* fought back however, and insisted that 'a considerable number of the most respectable among the Catholic Clergy of Down
and Connor' with whom it had been recently in communication favoured
the rent.[24] The increase in the rent was taken as a mark of its approval by
the 'enlightened Presbyterian' and the 'oppressed Catholic'.[25]

But when speakers at the Catholic Association in Dublin denounced
the Kildare Place Society for its policy of insisting on the study of the
bible without note or comment in its schools, a further line of division was

[19] Ibid., 20 Jan. 1825.   [20] Ibid., 22 Jan. 1824.   [21] Ibid., 5 Aug. 1824.   [22] Ibid.
[23] Ibid., 12 Aug. 1824.   [24] Ir., 6 Aug. 1824.   [25] Ibid., 20 Aug. 1824.

opened up between the *Whig* and its supporters and the Catholics. This alleged insult to the bible was regarded as very offensive:

We say, that the connexion avowedly established between the advocates of the Roman Catholic Rente and the opponents of Scriptural instruction, has strengthened the suspicions which we entertained, of the prudence or policy of countenancing the impost. We find in the political, the self-same individuals, whose inveterate rancour and insidious sophistry disgust us in the religious arena. We cannot conceive, that any Protestant in the land should be invited to make common cause with those who seek to suppress that volume, in which to use the language of Stillingfleet, is the religion of Protestants.[26]

Before the end of 1824 O'Connell had driven a further wedge between the Catholics and the *Whig* by one of those intemperate and injudicious remarks to which he was so unfortunately prone. O'Connell had commented to the *Morning Register* that Belfast had never failed to betray 'the secret of affectation of liberty' when elections were held. Lawless wrote to R.L. Sheil, a promiment member of the Catholic Association, explaining that Belfast was a close borough, which meant that Lord Donegall was the sole elector, and in his paper regretted that O'Connell should have confounded the liberal, enlightened mind of the Presbyterian layman with the cold sectarian bigotry which distinguished some of the clergy, and maintained that the Presbyterians of Belfast had never given their support to an illiberal sentiment or an illiberal measure.[27] The *Whig* asked in reply to O'Connell if Belfast was hostile or silent when petitions for Emancipation were being presented to parliament, and went on to recall the generosity of Protestants and Presbyterians to the building funds of the two Catholic churches in Belfast. Rejoicing that so little rent was forwarded from Belfast, it called on Catholics to declare publicly whether Belfast deserved the obloquy cast upon it and whether they had found Presbyterians liberal or illiberal in their conduct and conversation.[28]

A pastoral of the Irish bishops admonishing their people to avoid using the tracts and unauthorized translations of the scriptures distributed by the bible societies provoked further annoyance among well-disposed Protestants. The bishops advised their readers to return or destroy the tracts and, if they did not give back the bibles, to deposit them with the priests, and

---

[26] N.W., 18 Nov. 1824. Edward Stillingfleet (1635-99), bishop of Worcester, was an advocate of union between Anglicans and Presbyterians, and a controversialist who wrote in defence of the divine authority of scripture and of the Protestant religion. On 9 Dec. 1824 the *Whig* claimed that the Presbyterians of Ulster had learned more of 'the polemic theology and spiritual acerbity of the Roman Catholic Church from the proceedings of the Association, during the last three months . . . than from the history of any former period of the same length, since the accession of the House of Hanover'.
[27] Ir., 17 Dec. 1824.   [28] N.W., 23 Dec. 1824.

pointed out that it was 'not without reason . . . that we thus exhort and enjoin you to exclude from your houses these pernicious books. . .'

The *Whig* duly carried the pastoral and commented extensively on it,
pointing out that by the strangest confusion of language, if unintentional,
and the most appalling, if intended, St Augustine was represented as
including the scriptures among those books from which he said that much
evil and nothing good could be learned. The paper concluded its scathing
analysis of the pastoral by quoting the phrase from it that God spoke by
his pastors, whom when you hear, you hear him, and asking if he spoke
'equally authoritatively', when the use of the Douay version without
notes, was permitted in Belfast, by a 'pastor of the Church'.[29]

A week later Crolly wrote to the editor and explained that such severe
animadversions had been made on the pastoral charge in general, and such
pointed allusions to himself in particular, that readers would be expecting
a reply from him. Declining to argue from the authority and obligation
claimed by Catholic prelates to rule their church, he stated that he would
vindicate the views of his colleagues from arguments acknowledged by the
religious principles of Protestants and Presbyterians. Maintaining that
Christians of every denomination held that their clergy had a right to
advise, instruct and admonish their laity, and as a consequence Protestants
had proscribed Catholic doctrines as dangerous to salvation, so Catholics
had retained the bible, which they had received from their predecessors.
As in their preaching they gave explanations of the inspired writings, so
they claimed the same toleration when they put the scriptures, which
contained things difficult to understand, into the 'hands of the illiterate'.
He then asked rhetorically why there should be surprise when the bishops
branded 'with deserved infamy those books, which contain gross and
detestable calumnies concerning our divine worship, our sacraments etc'.
Would Protestants, he wondered, suffer their children to read pamphlets
designed to turn their religion into ridicule and contempt, if Catholics
were to disseminate such works among them? He promised to continue to
allow the Catholic children in the Lancasterian School, 'that distinguished
monument of unaffected liberality', to read the Douay version of the
scriptures, if the managers continued to cooperate with him. He ended by
implicitly complimenting the *Whig* for not allowing the cowardly and
contemptible enemies of the Catholic religion to contaminate the paper by
scurrilous and calumnious accusations, and expressed the hope that he
had not used any language which could cause the slightest offence.[30]

---

[29] Ibid., 13 Jan. 1825.   [30] Ibid., 20 Jan. 1825.

His letter was, in fact, uncontroversial and conciliatory. He even anticipated the ecumenical movement by using the phrase, 'our separated Brethren' to describe his fellow-Christians. By defusing the anger of the *Whig* he contributed to that inter-denominational goodwill that he wanted Catholic Emancipation to enhance. The *Whig* was grateful for his clarification of the pastoral, and while not prepared to admit the claims to infallibility of any church, declared that it was happy to learn that the young might still read the scriptures without appendages, even though 'the generality of the Roman Catholic priesthood insist on the necessity of such appendages to the Book of God'. The compliments paid to Crolly were generous and unreserved:

We know of no individual in the Roman Catholic Church, for whom we entertain a more sincere respect, than the writer to whose communication we have given insertion. Distinguished by energy and activity, the acquirements of the scholar and the urbanity of the gentleman, he has long and deservedly possessed the respect of the public. We find in his letter much which even increases our respect.[31]

And indeed Catholics in Belfast could then not afford to antagonize potential Presbyterian friends. Anti-Catholic and Orange elements had grown stronger and more active in the surrounding districts. In April 1823 two petitions against the Catholic claims—one from Co. Antrim bearing nearly 19,000 signatures, and one from the nobles and gentlemen of Lisburn—were presented to parliament. Catholics were charged with providing no evidence of conciliation, and of being leagued together to overturn the entire Protestant establishment of the country and to extirpate its Protestant inhabitants. In view of the dangers involved in acceding to the exorbitant demands of the Catholics, the House of Commons was begged to pause before investing them with privilege and power, and instead to protect and preserve the constitution of Britain and Ireland.[32]

V

The suppression of the Association in February 1825 removed this bone of contention from the advocates of Emancipation in Belfast. But the bill introduced by Sir Francis Burdett in April soon created bewilderment and anger among them. O'Connell, who was visiting London to give evidence on the state of Ireland before a parliamentary commission,

[31] Ibid., 20 Jan. 1825.   [32] B.N.L., 22 Apr. 1823; Ir., 27 June 1823.

helped Burdett draw up the details of the bill, and stunned friends and supporters by accepting 'two major securities' to assuage Protestant fears—state payment of the Catholic clergy and disfranchisement of the 40s freeholders. A board was to be formed which would exclude foreigners from the prelacy of Ireland, and would report to the government on the characters of candidates for the episcopacy. The two principal concessions seemed such a volte-face for one who had so bitterly resisted the veto and who must have known, that the 40s freeholders were not mere voting fodder in the hands of landlords, that even the most loyal of his followers were astounded. John Lawless was not convinced by O'Connell's explanation of his conduct. He wrote a furious letter denouncing the bill as a betrayal of a generous people with the sanction of principles degrading to the character of the Catholics of Ireland—most injurious of the political and civil rights of the Irish peasantry, and destructive of the hopes of men who had laboured to enlarge the political power of the people. And in an editorial the Irishman claimed that in his sermon on St Patrick's day, Crolly, who had recently become bishop-elect of Down and Connor, 'distinctly declared his hostility to the provisions of the intended Bill'.[33] The bill succeeded in passing the Commons but in May was rejected by the Lords.

Before the excitement generated by Burdett's bill had caught hold in Ireland, Belfast had its own share of excitement deriving from petitions for and against Emancipation. In February a petition asking for an investigation into the wisdom, nature and operation of the disqualifying laws was prepared by the liberal Presbyterians and made available for signatures. Some five hundred people duly signed. Not to be outdone their Tory opponents drew up a petition opposing any change and got sixteen hundred signatures. The value of the two petitions was then debated by the journals representing both camps, in terms of the influence and respectability of the signatories. As the *Whig* and the *Irishman* pointed out, the advocates of Emancipation included the prominent merchants, bankers and manufacturers of Belfast as well as a host of shopkeepers, publicans, professional men and craftsmen. The *Belfast News Letter* countered this claim by insisting that many men of honourable and lucrative mercantile pursuits signed the other petition.

Burdett's bill was not the only source of excitement in Ireland in the spring of 1825. At the parliamentary commission of inquiry into the state of Ireland, prominent political and religious figures were questioned.

---

[33] Ir., 25 Mar. 1825.

Among them were O'Connell, five Catholic bishops and Henry Cooke. Cooke's evidence produced quite a stir in the north of Ireland. While he himself was prepared to accept Emancipation, albeit in a grudging and half-hearted way, he provoked considerable anger by his analysis of the attitudes of Presbyterians to Catholic relief.

Recalling various attempts by Catholics during the previous two hundred years to overthrow the Protestant constitution, he went on to divide his co-religionists who favoured Emancipation into three groups: a radical element which wanted to 'new-model the State' by using the votes of the 40s freeholders to elect men by mere popular desire; a considerable class which regarded the Catholics as dangerous tinder in the hands of the Catholic Association and the priests, and which would tolerate a limited admission of the leading Catholics to office 'as a kind of safety valve'; a class which trusted both government and opposition and would acquiesce in anything parliament would decide. But on the other hand a large proportion of the Protestant population was opposed to Emancipation; some of them were opposed because they did not understand what was involved, but a more important class was hostile to the proposal because of the violence perpetrated on their ancestors in 1641, the violation of their liberties under James II and the efforts made to restore the Stuarts. The largest party of all, however, was opposed to Emancipation for purely religious reasons; this group maintained that those who believed that most frightful and uncharitable of all doctrines 'that a Protestant could not be saved and the even more dreaded one that a man who could pardon the sins of another could not be entrusted with the power of legislating for a Protestant state'. Among Protestant farmers very few, he declared, were prepared to countenance Catholic relief.

Cooke himself favoured a limited concession—Catholic Emancipation with the disfranchisement of the 40s freeholders—and maintained that to assuage Protestant fears Catholics should not be admitted to the highest offices of the state—the Lord Lieutenancy, the Chief Secretaryship, the Lord Chancellorship and some of the principal secretaryships in England. He also supported the state payment of the Catholic clergy as an effective means of muzzling them politically.[34]

The publication of Cooke's evidence in the newspapers drew a prompt and angry riposte from a group of Presbyterian clergy and elders of Belfast and district. They included Montgomery, William Bruce of the first Congregation, W.D.H. McEwen of the second Congregation, and the

---

[34] *Third report from the select sommittee on the State of Ireland*, pp. 341-80, H.C. 1825 (129), viii.

ministers of Moneyrea, Dundonald and Holywood; the elders included some of the leading businessmen and liberals of the town. In their letter, which was addressed to Thomas Spring Rice, a persistent supporter of Catholic Emancipation in parliament, they explained that the office of Moderator, which Cooke then held, was extremely limited both in duration and in its representative capacity of the views of members of the synod 'except by the special appointment and instruction of his brethren' and, having made clear that Cooke's opinions were merely those of a respectable Presbyterian minister, went on to contend that 'he labours under the greatest misconception with regard to the feelings and views of the Presbyterians of Ulster'. Quoting the decision taken by the Synod of Ulster in 1813 in favour of Emancipation, they admitted that religious animosity had lately been increased by public contests at Bible Associations and by a confusion of civil rights and religious opinions, but they insisted that the reverse of Cooke's allegations was true, namely, that 'very many respectable and influential individuals', who had formerly been hostile to Emancipation, had come to favour it from the conviction that it was right in principle and essential to the peace and prosperity of the country. They concluded by maintaining that thousands of respectable signatures could have been obtained, had a general declaration on the subject been entertained, for 'we have never known any occasion, on which a more unanimous feeling of chagrin and disappointment was manifested by Protestants of all denominations, and especially by Presbyterians, than on the reading of Mr Cooke's reported evidence.'[35]

Cooke defended himself in a letter to the *Belfast News Letter*. Pointing out that he had said that the less politically informed of Presbyterians almost entirely disapproved of Emancipation, he insisted that he knew 'the state of mind of the common people among orthodox Presbyterians' better than any other man in Ulster, and he stood by his original assertion. Repeating his view that there had been an increase of feeling amongst Protestants against Emancipation, he argued that the threats of the Catholic Association to defy any legislation interfering with its activities had alienated Protestant sympathy in the north of Ireland. He was prepared to admit that opinion had swung back in favour of Emancipation in the wake of O'Connell's and his colleagues' conversion 'to English feelings' and the extinction and submission of the Association. He further maintained that he was reflecting majority Protestant opinion when he suggested that the throne, and the offices of Lord Chancellor, Lord

[35] N.W., 21 Apr. 1825.

Lieutenant and Chief Secretaryships should be limited to Protestants, and declared that he knew very few Protestants who favoured unlimited concessions.[36]

The dispute could not have been settled by a head-count but, had it been, Cooke's interpretation of the mind of the lower orders, as he called them, would certainly have been proved to be nearer the truth than that of his more liberal opponents. Subsequent events were to reveal religious fears and antipathies among the Presbyterian body which their more liberal spokesmen would have preferred did not exist and would cheerfully have wished away.

Burdett's bill had not been defeated when Crolly entertained a distinguished body of guests of all denominations after his episcopal ordination. On that occasion Henry Montgomery seized the opportunity afforded by a reply to the toast of the Synod of Ulster to repudiate again the sentiments expressed by Cooke in London. Remarking that the Synod had always advocated the principles of civil and religious liberty, he argued that if his brethren were present they would have unanimously echoed his views. Without specifically referring to Cooke, he contented himself with observing that some late circumstances had rendered that declaration necessary. The representative of the Seceding Synod also threw in his assurances that the creed of that body was not calculated to produce 'feelings inimical to Emancipation'.[37]

At the return dinner given to Crolly by the leading Protestants of Belfast, Montgomery in responding to the toast of the Synod claimed that there was scarcely a member of it who would not be found on the side of toleration and liberality. Acknowledging the blemishes that might be detected in that body, he insisted, nonetheless, that its members 'had been uniform and consistent friends of Roman Catholic Emancipation, and in doing so, they only preserved their character for liberality and consistency'. To deny that they were friendly 'to this great national act of common justice' was a libel on their professions and on their principles. On behalf of the vicar of Belfast, W.St.J. Smith referred to the uniform dignity the established church had preserved in its 'silence and pledged that they would cheerfully submit to the decisions of parliament'.[38]

These cheering sentiments may have been still ringing in Crolly's ears when he attended the consecration ceremonies of the Pro-Cathedral in Dublin on 14 November 1825. Called upon to respond to the toast to Archbishop Curtis at the dinner afterwards, he claimed that the people of

[36] B.N.L., 29 Apr. 1825.   [37] N.W., 5 May 1825.   [38] Ibid., 19 May 1825.

his part of the country were more devoted to liberty than in any other part of Ireland. 'They there entertained no feelings but as Irishmen' and he added that 'Protestant, Presbyterian and Catholic went hand in hand in promoting the common interests of their fellow countrymen'. The participation of Protestants at the celebrations in Dublin on that occasion indicated that the liberal feelings existing in Belfast were extending southwards.[39]

VI

The suppression of the Catholic Association which allegedly had produced salutary effects among Northern Presbyterians was of short duration. Soon after his return to Ireland O'Connell encouraged the resumption of general meetings to appeal for Emancipation. The *Whig*, questioning the prudence of this policy, firmly repudiated the other activities of the former Association. It hoped that the rent would never again be collected and, commenting on its use to aid the liberal papers, remarked that 'the very idea of a stipendiary press did more to excite public disapprobation than any measure adopted within the memory of man'. However, it reserved its severest strictures for the Orangemen:

If the surviving dregs of the Orangemen should presume to celebrate their revolting orgies, let those who hold sacred the principle but despise the outward and visible sign, by which that party is distinguished, openly discountenance, and endeavour to bring to punishment those ignorant and deluded disturbers of the peace.[40]

In the course of the July celebrations pitched battles occurred in the town when the Belfast Orangemen returned from Carrickfergus. The *Whig* praised the Catholics for their forbearance and good sense under circumstances of the most peculiar delicacy and the most irritating provocation, and commended the clergy in Antrim, Derry, Tyrone and Donegal who had urged their flocks to stay away from flash-points on that day.[41] It also expressed reservations about the plans of the new Catholic Association which O'Connell had formed, particularly the possibility of collecting rent but also the taking of a census of the Catholic population.[42] As the new Association sponsored numerous general meetings in the south of Ireland, the Protestant advocates of Emancipation felt that Belfast should not hold back. They called on their Catholic friends to

[39] B.N.L., 18 Nov. 1825.   [40] N.W., 7 July 1825.   [41] Ibid., 21 July 1825.
[42] Ibid., 21 July 1825.

assemble and solicit their support, assuring them that Belfast would uphold 'that high character for unshaken independence which she has so long enjoyed'.[43]

The bishops sought to improve the politico-religious atmosphere, and thereby remove obstacles to Emancipation, by correcting some of the views put about by the missionaries of the 'new reformation'. Accordingly they issued a pastoral address in January 1826. It laid down the conditions for cooperation between Protestant and Catholic in the conduct of schools and then sought to correct the mistaken views about the doctrinal tenets of the church regarding the role of the Blessed Virgin Mary and the saints, the importance of scripture, the requirements for salvation and the forgiveness of sins. That misapprehensions on these matters had a significant bearing on attitudes to Emancipation had been revealed not least by Henry Cooke's evidence before the commission of the House of Lords. But the bishops also dealt with questions that had a more direct bearing on the political attitudes of their people: they pointed out that Catholics did not believe that it was lawful to murder heretics, or not to keep faith with heretics; that Catholics pledged their loyalty to George IV and repudiated any temporal authority allegedly enjoyed by the pope; and rejected on behalf of their people any desire to reclaim forfeited lands or subvert the Protestant establishment.[44] The forthright denial of a divided allegiance in the Catholic body drew praise from those disposed to grant Emancipation.[45]

The transfer of the *Irishman* to Dublin and the departure of John Lawless from Belfast provided an occasion for the reiteration of pro-Emancipation sentiments by the Belfast liberals. They held a dinner in his honour, rededicated themselves to the struggle for Emancipation, unqualified and unconditional, and commended their friend for his unswerving commitment to civil rights and parliamentary reform. John Barnett, the chairman, proposed a toast to Crolly which included the wish that 'the kindly sentiments' existing between Roman Catholics and Protestants in the north of Ireland would last for ever. Crolly in reply disclaimed any title to a place in the ranks of patriots and explained where the obligations of the Christian ministry lay:

He laid no claim to be estimated as a distinguished character in the list of patriots—although patriotism could never sully the clerical character. But the duties of a Christian minister consisted more in studying, in practising, and in inculcating the great principles of Faith, Hope and Charity. It is the duty of the Divine to study and

[43] Ibid., 3 Nov. 1825.   [44] B.N.L., 21, 24 Feb. 1826.   [45] N.W., 2 Mar. 1826.

to teach that charity which carries the hearts of all men to the throne of their great and all-merciful Creator; and which binds us to regard all professing Christians with affection and good will . . . Indeed, he always found the Protestant, the Presbyterian and the Roman Catholic Clergy, ready to join with him in the performance of works of charity and mercy. He (Dr C.) felt himself bound to continue in the same course, and to use his best exertions to promote mutual good-will amongst men of every class and of every persuasion, without reference to their name, or their creed.[46]

Within a few months those who had been hoping for some movement on the Emancipation issue were heartened by the results of the election. The most symbolic of these was in Waterford where the clergy helped mobilize the Catholic 40s freeholders to oust the candidate of the Beresford family, which had dominated the county constituency for years, in favour of Emancipationists. Similar, if less publicized, results were obtained in Louth, Westmeath, Monaghan and in Armagh where Charles Brownlow, a liberal-minded landlord, beat the Orange standard bearer. Both supporters and opponents of Emancipation realized that a highly significant, and perhaps decisive, element had been introduced into the whole system of elections. The *Belfast News Letter* complained of the 'open and injudicious interference of the Roman Catholic clergy, with the freeholders of the south of Ireland' and predicted that such interference would have an injurious effect, as the priests had been shown to exercise power that was not merely spiritual. It feared that an increase in the franchise would bring about an increase in their temporal power.[47]

The Belfast liberals met to celebrate Brownlow's victory in September and also to salute a fellow guest, James Caulfield, a descendant of the volunteer leader, the earl of Charlemont. In their speeches John Barnett and Henry Montgomery stressed the political consequences of the Protestant right of private judgement. And Montgomery, in a stirring repudiation of expediency and cautious neutrality in politics, demanded that the great cause of national and Christian equity should go forward, and dismissed contemptuously the threat of Catholic ascendancy, which he interpreted either 'as a bugbear to frighten the weak, or . . . a spirit raised by an evil conscience to appal the wicked'. Crolly, who hailed Brownlow as 'the representative of the liberality of Ulster—the promoter of his Catholic countrymen's interests, and the asserter of their wrongs', concluded his speech by appealing for the exclusion of discord and party rage and the triumph of charity without ostentation and religion without bigotry.[48]

When calling for the rejection of discord Crolly probably had in mind

[46] Ibid., 6 Apr. 1826.   [47] B.N.L., 30 June 1826.   [48] Ibid., 12 Sept. 1826.

the bloody affray that had occurred earlier in the summer at a fair in Crebilly, near Ballymena. Orangemen and Ribbonmen had apparently arranged to renew hostilities in a trial of strength at the fair, and rumours of their plans had leaked out. Though the clergy of Ballymena made frantic efforts to persuade both parties to desist and contacted the local magistrate to have a police force in readiness, their requests were ignored. The magistrate did not accompany a police unit to Crebilly until violence had broken out and the contestants were already 'cut, bloody, and dangerously wounded'. He took little action then or later in the evening when the strife had transferred to Ballymena and, according to the *Northern Whig*, the Orange party was allowed to wreck the homes of Catholics.[49]

However limited these outbreaks of violence were, they contributed, in association with the verbal conflicts of the debates between the clerical champions of Protestantism and Catholicism, to a deterioration in inter-denominational relations and to an increase in Protestant hostility to Catholic Emancipation. The consequence was a spate of petitions from both lay and clerical Protestants to both Lords and Commons pointing out the dangers involved in granting Catholics the right to sit in parliament. The *Belfast News Letter* noted that Presbyterians were the most numerous signatories of these petitions and instanced Bangor as an example: of the 1,450 male Presbyterians in the town 1,100 had signed, and a correspondent had indicated that nine tenths had done so.[50] Yet in 1825 the ministers and elders of the presbytery of Bangor had signed a petition in favour of Emancipation.[51]

A local landlord reporting enthusiastically to a friend about the stiffening Presbyterian opposition to Emancipation, explained that their colleague, Robert Nicholson, had promised Crolly he would not sign the Bangor petition: he kept his promise, but all his tenants signed![52] The *News Letter* was soon claiming on the authority of one of its ministers that no member of the Secession Synod of the Presbyterians would venture to propose to that body that it should support Emancipation. To illustrate that claim the paper was able to carry the petition of the members and elders of the presbytery of Donegal to the House of Lords against Emancipation. The language was tough and uncompromising; the petitioners declared that they were 'indignant at the repeated assertions of the

[49] N.W., 6 July 1826.   [50] B.N.L., 2 Jan. 1827.   [51] Ibid., 12 Jan. 1827.

[52] Cleland to Maxwell, 28 Feb. 1827, PRONI, D3444/G/1/48. Cleland concluded: 'Indeed, all the Presbyterians are decidedly against Catholic Emancipation, and this you may boldly assert as being the actual fact, although circumstances prevent their petitions.'

Roman C. Association and others, that the Presbyterians of Ireland are friendly to their claims, when your petitioners know that of the many thousands under our pastoral care, not one individual is favourable to them—that the ministers and people belonging to the Secession Church in Ireland are almost to a man averse to them—and that all the Dissenters we reside amongst, belonging to the ministers of other denominations are, in general, utterly dissatisfied with them'. Maintaining that any further concession to Catholics would endanger the security of the Protestant Establishment in church and state, the Donegal Seceders proceeded to analyse the origin and exercise of political power, declaring that it did not 'belong to the class of natural rights; that it originates in the will of the community, and in every well-regulated state is defined and regulated by social compact; and, therefore, that our Roman Catholic countrymen have no just and legitimate claim to it as their birthright'. Turning to the clerical side of Catholic influence, the Seceders insisted that Roman priests possessed an authority extending to civil and political affairs, which, by absolution and excommunication, became a powerful political engine capable of producing any result.[53]

This combination of political and religious suspicions fuelled the production of numerous petitions against Emancipation. General O'Neill presented a petition to parliament from Co. Antrim signed by more than 31,000 people, the majority of whom were said to be Dissenters.[54] Smaller numbers from districts in other northern counties also made their views known. The bishops of the established church, by far the most influential clergy in Ireland, resolutely opposed all concessions. The archbishop of Armagh and his clergy told the House of Commons 'that men professing a determined hostility to that branch of the United Church which is established in Ireland, and transferring an important part of the undoubted jurisdiction of the Crown to a foreign Bishop, cannot, on any just principles of political prudence, be admitted to legislate in matters affecting the stability of a Constitution essentially Protestant, or be entrusted with the most confidential exercise of its power'.[55] Richard Mant, an Englishman, who was bishop of Down and Connor, and an opponent of both Catholics and Dissenters, joined with his clergy in imputing to the Catholics a disposition to establish, if possible, 'the ascendancy of the Romish Church, and to humiliate and depress the Protestant Church of England and Ireland'.[56] Archbishop Magee of Dublin, who, in a pastoral letter in the previous year, had described

[53] Ibid., 2 Feb. 1827.   [54] Ibid., 2 Mar. 1827.   [55] Ibid., 13 Feb. 1827.   [56] F.J., 22 Sept. 1827.

Catholics as their 'cruel and bloodthirsty enemies'[57] now accused them of being eager 'to confederate themselves with a foreign enemy' against the very existence of the realm, both in Church and state.[58]

Anti-Catholic polemics on theological differences helped create an atmosphere more favourable to the reception of dire fears about the political dangers which Emancipation would produce. The established church which had earlier frowned on the swordsmen of the bible societies had come by the late 1820s to countenance them and give them a helping hand against Catholic priests. The Catholic bishops did not want their clergy to engage in public debates with the self-appointed champions of Protestantism but were occasionally forced to yield when the Catholic laity argued that a refusal to accept a challenge would mean a loss of face. Presbyterians generally held aloof from these theological jousts, but the temptation not to do so proved too strong for some of them. In Belfast, Samuel Hanna, the minister of the third congregation, joined a group of clergy of different denominations in preaching 'a Series of Discourses on the points controverted between the Reformed Churches and Roman Catholics', and in Ballymena, Robert Stewart, the redoubtable minister of Broughshane, who was the friend and mentor of Henry Cooke, and a vigilant opponent of what he regarded as Catholic errors in theology and excesses in political demands, engaged the local parish priest in a three day contest.

The advertisement for the series of sermons to be introduced by Samuel Hanna prompted the liberal Robert Tennent to challenge the motivation and purpose of the preachers. Tennent, who questioned the wisdom of initiating a discussion of topics of so subtle and inflammatory a nature, in apparent imitation of the Methodists, who, with many honourable exceptions were 'seldom behind in the race of intolerance', suggested that the person who was sincere in wishing to convert the Catholics should be equally anxious that they enjoyed the same civil and political privileges as others.[59] Hanna replied that his only motive in preaching such sermons was 'an imperative sense of duty and a desire to promote the cause of truth and righteousness'. And he wondered why Tennent had not cautioned Crolly for preaching in his church in explanation and in defence of his religions system.[60] Tennent effectively justified Crolly's right to preach his sermons, since they were not

---

[57] N.W., 24 May 1827.   [58] F.J., 22 Sept. 1827.   [59] B.N.L., 30 Mar. 1827.
[60] Ibid., 3 Apr. 1827. On the day on which this letter was published the *Belfast News Letter* carried a report of a sermon on the previous Sunday by A.C. Macartney, the vicar of Belfast, on the papal claim to authority through the Petrine succession.

publicized as controversial, and were not designed to proselytize but merely to confirm the beliefs of his own people. He insisted that at least some of the preachers were, perhaps unconsciously, actuated by some urge to attack Catholicism, and he dismissed religious controversies as worse than unprofitable because of the party feeling that then existed. However, the *News Letter* remained convinced that Hanna and his friends had 'embarked in an undertaking of general utility' and could not be given too much publicity in their defence of gospel truth and 'Reformation principles'.[61]

In defence of that truth and those principles, Robert Stewart of Broughshane preached a sermon in Ballymena against papal supremacy. He then accused Bernard McAuley, the parish priest of Ballymena, of surreptitiously obtaining a copy of it from the printer before it was published and railing against it in his pulpit on two Sundays. Claiming that any book could be made to seem ridiculous by quoting garbled extracts from it and making sarcastic comments on them, he then challenged McAuley to make his accusations in public in the courthouse in Ballymena.[62] To McAuley's reply that he had bought the book from the printer,[63] Stewart retorted that he had charged his critic 'not with a pecuniary but with a literary or theological fraud'.[64] More heated exchanges followed and eventually a formal confrontation was arranged. Crolly must have followed these skirmishes with increasing anxiety. He was probably reluctant to forbid his former curate from taking part in the inevitable debate and yet he must have been pained by the prospect of an ecclesiastical clash that was bound to cause at least some damage to interchurch relations. Terms were duly arranged for a public discussion and on 24, 25 and 26 July 1827 Stewart and McAuley debated whether or not Christ had invested St Peter and his successors with supreme authority over the whole Christian church. In the course of their encounter they adhered fairly closely to the central issue, paid each other conventional compliments[65] and doubtless satisfied their respective supporters with their intellectual prowess. The *Northern Whig* had predicted that 'not an auditor will leave the assembly who will not be more strongly convinced of his own belief being the right, and his brothers, of an opposite faith, the wrong one',[66] and from the four hundred present the paper subsequently

---

[61] Ibid., 6 Apr. 1827.   [62] Ibid., 10 Apr. 1827.   [63] Ibid., 1 May 1827.   [64] Ibid., 18 May 1827.

[65] In *An authentic report of the Discussion which took place at Ballymena* Stewart claimed that McAuley had recently been 'a promising candidate for the mitre' and to McAuley's dissent replied 'you cannot deny that when you were the present bishop's assistant in the Northern metropolis you were by much the more popular preacher of the two'.

[66] N.W., 19 July 1827.

reported that no converts had been made. Crolly would probably have agreed whole-heartedly with the implicit judgement of the *Whig* that the only beneficiary from this theological battle was the Mendicity Association to which the profits were allocated[67] and he would not have begrudged Stewart the service of plate and valuable edition of the bible which his grateful friends and admirers subsequently presented to him.[68]

VII

The death in Febuary 1827 of the long-serving prime minister, Lord Liverpool, who had been opposed to the Catholic cause, and the likelihood of George Canning, who had been regarded as favourably disposed to it, succeeding him gave some hope to the pro-Emancipationists. But the defeat of Burdett's motion for Emancipation in March tempered their expectations. Canning did succeed in April but died in August and was in turn succeeded by Goderich whose tenure of the office was also brief. In January 1828 Wellington, a strong upholder of the Protestant constitution (O'Connell regarded him as a villain without heart or head) took office, with Peel, his like-minded friend, in charge of the Home Office.

Towards the end of 1827, O'Connell, in an effort to increase the rent from which both evicted tenants and needy schools were receiving subventions, arranged for the appointment of two church wardens in each parish. One was to be selected by the priests and the other by the parishioners, and they were assigned the duties of choosing collectors for the rent, ensuring that a census of the Catholic population was made, and reporting on evictions and other improper activities, such as proselytism. The Catholic Association further decided that in January 1828 as many meetings as possible should be held on the same day to petition for Emancipation and impress the government by their keenness and determination.

---

[67] Ibid., 26 July 1827.

[68] B.N.L., 20 Nov. 1827. On that occasion Stewart in an eloquent description of 'the darkened and degraded state' of Catholics in the south of Ireland revealed the robust contempt in which he held their religion: 'To see upon every Lord's day, and upon their numerous holidays, the multitudes that in all parts of Munster crowd to mass-houses without a Bible in their hand or the trace of an idea in their countenance—to witness their ardent anxiety to be sprinkled with what they superstitiously imagine to be holy water—to see their numerous genuflexions or abject prostrations before a picture, an image, or a wafer, in direct opposition to the second commandment . . . to see how, after having prostituted their understandings in such idle mummeries . . . the heart must be indeed callous and the soul insensible that does not bleed and feel for their degradation'. McAuley challenged these sentiments and a further correspondence ensued.

In accordance with this policy the Catholics of Co. Antrim announced
that they would meet in St Patrick's Church, Belfast on 10 January 1828.
The announcement elicited a curmudgeonly comment from the *Belfast
News Letter*. Objecting to the very use of the word 'Emancipation' as
implying that Catholics were held in a state of slavery, it went on to argue
that the right of self-preservation entitled any state to prevent a body of
men within it from doing mischief until assured that the disposition to do
so had ceased. And since Roman Catholics had professed and practised
principles at variance with the safety of those who religiously differed
from them, an assurance, which was not forthcoming, was required, that
the persecuting spirit of other days would not be resuscitated. The
demand for Emancipation was a demand for power, and Protestants had
been given no guarantee that such power would not be used against them.
Consequently, if Catholics would 'give no securities, consent to no terms,
and at the same time insist on an unqualified admission to the highest
offices in the state' the paper trusted that *'Protestants* of the County
Antrim, and of every county in Ireland, will show themselves equally
zealous in support of privileges which their ancestors dearly purchased'.[69]

The *Northern Whig* on the other hand was so enthusiastic that it
published a special supplement about the proceedings to ensure that its
readers did not have to wait a full week for a report. It estimated that
between two and three thousand people were present in the church,
among whom were many Protestants and Presbyterians. Crolly helped
organize the occasion in association with the leading Catholics of the
town—Hugh Magill (a linen merchant), James O'Neill Falls (a solicitor),
Henry Murray (a general merchant), James Murray (a doctor) and
Bernard McAuley, his former curate.

The bishop was invited to take the chair at the meeting and after
explaining the purpose for which they had assembled, expressed his hope
that their proper and constitutional conduct on that occasion would be a
further proof to their enemies of the injustice and cruelty of witholding
from the Roman Catholics of Great Britain and Ireland a fair participation
in the honours and privileges of the state. Returning thanks for the
support which their cause had already received from the liberal and
enlightened Protestants of the north, he instanced, as proof of this
assertion, the testimony of respect which had been given to Charles
Brownlow, the M.P. for Armagh County, 'on an occasion when the
property, influence and talent of Belfast were gathered around the

[69] Ibid., 8 Jan. 1828.

standard of civil and religious liberty'. He denied the accusation that Catholics sought political power rather than equal rights and defended the participation of the Catholic clergy in the movement for liberty as an integral part of their service to their people. In conclusion he advised:

As your claims are just, let them be supported by temperance and reason. As we have one common cause, let us be united; and I feel confident that the day is not far distant, when we shall enjoy a full participation in the blessings of the British Constitution.

Before the petition was read resolutions were passed stigmatizing all penalties imposed on account of religious affiliation as unjust, and pledging a renewal of the application to parliament for the total and unconditional repeal of the 'insulting, penal and degrading laws by which the Catholics of Ireland are grievously oppressed'. Bernard McAuley and Murray emphasized the loyalty of the Catholics to their king, and McAuley indignantly repudiated Peel's prediction that the Catholics would endeavour to strip the established church of its political supremacy and restore their own lost former splendours. Murray, who read the petition, complained of the refusal of the marquis of Donegall to lend his name to their campaign, and praised the marquis of Downshire, an 'inestimable friend of his country and of man', who had joined sixty eight other peers in demanding Emancipation; Downshire would present their petition to the Lords and Brownlow would present it to the Commons. Calling for the repeal of all statutes which infringed their liberty of conscience, the petition did so on two grounds: the 'statutes which imposed disabilities on the exercise of the Catholic religion infringed the inalienable right of every man to worship God according to the dictates of his conscience', and they were enacted 'in gross and palpable violation of a solemn national compact, the Treaty of Limerick'.

Resolutions were also passed thanking the king for choosing an enlightened administration; praising the bishops of Ireland for their vigilant defence of their religion; regretting the deflection to proselytizing activities of large sums of money voted by parliament for the education of the poor; promising cooperation with other counties in setting up a provincial meeting to further the cause of Emancipation; encouraging the promotion of pro-Emancipation meetings at parish level; praising the contribution of a free press to the cause of freedom; and recognizing in particular the beneficial advocacy of their movement by the *Northern Whig* and conveying their affectionate esteem to the liberal Protestants and Presbyterians who had been their constant friends. John Morgan, the editor of the *Whig*, gratefully acknowledged the tribute paid to his paper, and John Barnett acknowledged the tributes paid to Protestants. He went on to dismiss the objections that had been raised about Emancipation possibly paving the way for a Catholic to succeed to the throne as silly; about the danger of Catholics coming to achieve too much power as a cloak for wishing not to divide the emoluments of office; and about the need for Catholics to offer securities, as an insult to a Catholic's sense of honour in executing the terms of an oath.[70]

A dinner was held that evening in Kerns' Hotel. Crolly again presided and beside him sat the leading liberal Presbyterians of the town—John Ferguson, Henry Montgomery, Adam and James McClean, Dr Patrick, W.D.H. McEwen, John Barnett and Dr Tennent. Having toasted the king, members of the royal family and a speedy and unrestricted Emancipation, the bishop then declared that there was not

a Catholic in the North of Ireland who has not often experienced, amidst his night of political degradation, the cheering support of Presbyterian comfort and consolation. (Loud cheers). The conduct of the Presbyterians this day is not a new or novel instance of their kindly feelings towards their Catholic countrymen (Cheers). It is but a renewal of that mingling of their feelings with ours as IRISHMEN, which we are proud and happy to acknowledge (Cheers). But they have acted but a consistent part in pursuing this line of conduct: there are heavy chains which are most galling on the limbs of the unfortunate Catholic; and there are lighter ones irritating the still fettered footsteps of the Protestant Dissenter; as our duty to ourselves must be, to effect by every legal means the speediest emancipation from our fetters, so our next desire is, that not a link may remain to fetter the free and unrestricted operations of our Presbyterian brethren. In fact, we must all feel and acknowledge, that if PRESBYTE-RIANISM be a name, LIBERALITY must be its surname.

Dr Patrick, a prominent elder from Ballymena, in reply to this toast pointed out that the same accusations of seeking and using political power which were being brought against the Catholics had once been brought against the Presbyterians; they were as groundless in one case as in the other. He concluded by quoting Drennan's repudiation of both Protestant and Catholic ascendancy and his plea for 'one equal law of liberty, one powerful empire, one free constitution'. Crolly in proposing the toasts of the bishop of Norwich (a consistent supporter of Emancipation, who was virtually alone among Anglican dignitaries in expressing such views) the marquisses of Downshire and Londonderry, and John S. Ferguson (the high sheriff of Co. Antrim) paid generous tributes to them. And he paid enthusiastically 'ecumenical' tributes to the Presbyterian ministers, Henry

70 N.W., 10 Jan. 1828.

Montgomery and W.D.H. McEwen. Remarking that 'the liberality of the Presbyterian ministers is interwoven with the records of their religion', he hailed 'one of the many excellent ministers belonging to the Synod of Ulster'—Montgomery. Montgomery in responding to the toast deprecated the violence exhibited by some of the leaders of the Catholic people, though he admitted that in proportion to the treatment they had received, Catholics had behaved with remarkable temperance and patience. Recommending perseverance and patience, he, in turn, proposed a toast to Crolly, and the bishop in reply praised the cooperation of his clergy and trusted that they would stand by their people in any future attempts that might be made by legal and constitutional means to bring about the restitution of long lost privileges. He then saluted W.D.H. McEwen 'a reverend gentleman, whose simpleness of heart and kindness of disposition, could only be equalled by his principles of unbounded liberality and universal charity'.

After greeting the liberal Presbyterians and Protestants who were present, Crolly toasted the Belfast Academical Institution. Observing that the serpent was often found coiling around the tree of knowledge, he claimed that in Belfast they had a tree of knowledge 'near unto which, no serpent of bigotry or intolerance dare intrude' and described the Institution as, 'a perfect model of education without bigotry'. Montgomery in reply spoke at length on the great advantages of an education at home, and in an allusion to Cooke's anti-Arian inquisitorial campaign, predicted that that 'admirable seminary' would triumph over all its difficulties. Among other speakers were John Barnett and the editor of the *Northern Whig*. And that paper concluded its report by remarking wryly that the Catholics of Belfast could not be accused of intemperance as the company separated at an early hour![71]

The generous support of the liberal Presbyterians obviously touched the Catholics deeply. The drift of the majority of Belfast Protestants into the other camp ensured that those who stood out against the tide were more cordially appreciated. Crolly was grateful not only for the moral assistance given to his people's political aspirations but also for the general inter-denominational goodwill which it reflected. He was fully aware of the counter-effects of the Emancipation campaign and before long was obliged to meet them both in Belfast and in other towns in his diocese.

Several parishes throughout the diocese held meetings to petition for Emancipation and show their solidarity with the Catholic Association. But

[71] Ibid., 17 Jan. 1828.

Crolly, whose antennae were finely tuned to Protestant sensitivities, feared that some elements of the policy of the Association would antagonize the friends and potential friends of Emancipation in Down and Connor.

On 20 February 1828 O'Connell wrote to him enclosing letters for distribution to his parish priests and exhorting him to encourage them to arrange for a rent to be collected by church wardens. Crolly replied on 5 March and his letter was read out at the meeting of the Catholic Association three days later. He first informed O'Connell that he had distributed the letters as requested for he believed that his clergy should act as prudence dictated after taking into consideration the circumstances of their flocks. He himself was averse to this procedure:

After consulting with some of the most influential and best informed Catholics in this part of the country, I find that it would be a dangerous experiment to appoint churchwardens to make a general collection of the Catholic Rent amongst the poor or to take the census desired by the Catholic Association. In my opinion you should not urge the adoption of those measures in this part of the United Kingdom, where they might be attended with a dangerous reaction, which would be extremely detrimental to the present condition of the Catholics in the lower classes of society.[72]

The need for such sensitivity was soon proved. The *Whig* reported shortly that 'notwithstanding the indefatigable and personal exertions of Crolly to discountenance the progress of Ribbonism' in his diocese and prevent processions on St Patrick's Day, a serious affray had occurred near Portglenone between Ribbonmen marching from Rasharkin and Orangemen. One man was killed and many seriously injured.[73] On Easter Monday, 7 April an Orange lodge with a scarlet-clad leader bearing a musket and fixed bayonet marched out from Belfast to Cave Hill, where crowds had gone to relax for the day. The Orangemen positioned themselves below the crowd, played party tunes and 'called with blasphemy for the face of papists'. Crolly had been forewarned of this dangerous possibility and on the previous day had begged the members of his congregation who usually went to Cave Hill not to do so. On Easter Monday he, along with the police magistrate, tried to persuade Catholics who had joined the crowds to go home. The *Northern Whig* opined that

---

[72] Ibid., 13 Mar. 1828. Five months later the *Whig*, commenting on the unpopularity of the rent with the great body of Protestants and Presbyterians and with 'many of the most respectable and influential Roman Catholics', claimed that its own hostile attitude was vindicated by Crolly's sensitivity to the feelings of his Protestant brethren, 'in whose estimation he deservedly maintains so high a place'. The reasons it assigned for his opposition to the rent were 'the manner in which the Protestant and Catholic population is intermixed, the violent party feeling which exists, and the deadly collisions which sometimes take place between the lowest classes of both sects'. (N.W., 14 Aug. 1828.)

[73] Ibid., 27 Mar. 1828.

Crolly's lively admonition and personal exertions had prevented the calamitous consequences that otherwise would have ensued. Coincidentally, that paper along with its denunciations of inflated harangues by itinerant fanatics, the inflammatory appeals of an incendiary press and the ravings of political madmen like Sir Harcourt Lees, published on the same day a report that a petition against Catholic Emancipation had been got up in Belfast and was being circulated secretly for signatures.[74]

Not long afterwards politico-religious tensions boiled over in Co. Antrim. A scuffle broke out in Randalstown as Orangemen, wearing full regalia and playing party tunes, were returning from the funeral of a colleague. Several Catholics sustained severe wounds. To avenge the attack a crowd of Orangemen entered Antrim on a fair day, took control of the town and the fair was suspended. A liberal Protestant, mistaken for an Orangeman was murdered. A few Orangemen later assembled before the home of Daniel Curoe, the parish priest, to mock Catholic ceremonies. Ironically, Curoe had heard of a proposal by the Ribbonmen to march on the previous St Patrick's Day, and having apprised Crolly of these plans, they had both toured the district begging their co-religionists to desist, and their pleas had been heard.[75]

Catholics and liberal Protestants, however, were able to chalk up a success against deteriorating relations in Downpatrick, though at a price they would have preferred not to pay. A group of itinerant missionaries from the British Reformation Society arrived in the town and arranged for a conversion meeting to be held in the courthouse. Some of the more prominent gentry from the district got control of the meeting and spoke sternly against the estabishment of a branch of the Reformation Society in their midst, which, they averred, would inflame party passions among people who were living on good terms with each other. Two clergymen of the established church, Edward Hincks and Robert Kyle, moved that all who believed in the principles of the Reformation were obliged to promote them, and their views were forcefully supported by Robert Stewart of Broughshane. Three Catholic clergy—Cornelius Denvir, the parish priest, Bernard McAuley and Daniel Curoe opposed the introduction of the society. The plan to set up the Reformation Society was defeated but, partly as a compromise and partly to elaborate on theological issues that had been raised, the clergy of the established and Catholic churches agreed to hold a public discussion. The five clergy present and H.S. Cumming of Ballymena duly held a six day debate in Downpatrick

[74] Ibid., 10 Apr. 1828.   [75] Ibid., 29 May 1828.

between 22 and 30 April and ranged widely over controverted theological questions.[76] The Catholic participants later expressed their wholehearted agreement with the views relayed to them by their co-religionists who declared that 'in common with many of our enlightened Protestant brethren, we deprecate those polemical disputations, which have been forced upon you by the misguided zeal of itinerant Gospellers, who, perambulating the country, have induced some clergymen of the Established Church to join in proceedings calculated to engender bad feelings among persons of different Creeds and to dissipate the few remaining charities which the political condition of our country has left us'.[77]

Such local hiccups, however, did not halt the momentum of the campaign for Emancipation. O'Connell's victory in the Clare election in July transformed the political situation completely. In consequence, Wellington and Peel were threatened with numerous Catholic candidacies and would either have to outlaw them at the risk of serious civil strife or come to some accommodation. To the stern upholder of the Protestant constitution O'Connell's success was an outrage, a provocation and a disgrace and called for tough counter-measures to prevent a collapse of all he believed in. The trouble was that he did not know what effective counter-measures to take.

One response was the foundation of the Brunswick Constitution Club of Ireland to fight for the maintenance of the constitution. Brunswick Clubs spread rapidly and they not only deepened sectarian tensions but encouraged a display of Orange power which was presageful, menacing and intimidatory. Parades led by aristocrats or gentry with the tacit support or connivance of magistrates often threatened to spill over into violence.

It was to cool passions and retain the favour of the liberal Presbyterians that Crolly made a further effort to prevent the establishment of a formal organization to collect the Catholic rent. On 14 August the *Whig* again referred to the hostility of many zealous Protestant friends of the Catholic cause to the rent. On 17 August a meeting of Catholics was held in St Patrick's Church, Belfast to decide on arrangements for collecting the rent that would suit their own circumstances rather than have one imposed on them by the Catholic Association from Dublin. Though it was reported that Crolly, who had been known to subscribe generously to the Catholic Association, had endeavoured to defer systematic fund-raising for some time, lest it might interfere with his own fund-raising for the new

[76] *An authentic report of the discussion which took place at Downpatrick,* 1828.
[77] N.W., 8 May 1828.

Catholic schools which were then being built, he was also undoubtedly paying attention to the warnings of a friendly press about the antipathy which the appointment of church wardens and the taking of a census would arouse among Protestants who were favourable to Emancipation.[78]

The mission of John Lawless to the north further threatened to provoke the darkest sectarian fears and animosities. Lawless was commissioned by the Catholic Association to 'animate the Northern counties to the payment of the Catholic Rente, to expound its objects, to explain the principles it was calculated to support; to inculcate brotherly love among all denominations; and to demonstrate that this feeling could never be realised in Ireland, but by the establishment of equal and impartial justice—common privileges, or a national constitution'. However, he soon encountered determined Protestants of the Orange variety who were sturdily immune to the seductiveness of brotherly love and heartily opposed to the establishment of equal and impartial justice, which they interpreted as a diminution of their own status. Lawless' advance quickly took on the character of a triumphal procession, as great crowds followed him. But the threat of Orange violence at Ballybay in Co. Monaghan prevented him from going further north to Armagh and more Protestant parts, even though he did collect the rent in Monaghan and Castleblaney.[79] The whole tragi-comic escapade revealed the deep layers of sectarian tension and the real dangers of strife in those districts of Ulster where Protestant and Catholic numbers were fairly evenly balanced. The *Whig*, which had warned Catholics not to be driven into acts of violence by the exasperating conduct of their adversaries,[80] and had castigated Lawless' triumphalistic behaviour, though admitting ruefully that the collapse of his plan showed that in Ireland there was one law for the Catholic and another for the Protestant,[81] went on to accept the painful state of sectarian feeling: the great majority of the Protestants of Ulster were opposed to the concession of the Catholic claims.[82]

However, the paper insisted that the majority of the wealthy and intelligent Protestants of Ulster favoured Emancipation, and that 'a great portion of the middle ranks of Protestants, particularly the Presbyterian body, though prejudiced against the Catholic religion, are not inclined to make any overt opposition to Emancipation'.[83] A Protestant declaration stressing the deleterious effects of the disqualifying laws on Catholics and calling for a final and conciliatory adjustment of the relations of Catholics with the state was prepared in Dublin, sponsored in Belfast by the *Whig*

[78] Ibid., 21 Aug. 1828.   [79] Ibid., 30 Oct. 1828.   [80] Ibid., 25 Sept. 1828.   [81] Ibid., 2 Oct. 1828.
[82] Ibid., 30 Oct. 1828.   [83] Ibid., 1 Jan. 1829.

and in November 1828 extensively signed by the wealthier Presbyterians, who had been well disposed to the Catholic claims.

VIII

Catholic hopes were raised in the following month, when a letter from the duke of Wellington to Archbishop Curtis of Armagh declaring his interest in finding a solution to the Catholic problem was published in the press. Curtis, who as rector of the Irish College in Salamanca had become friendly with the duke during the peninsular war and had allowed his students to act as guides for the British forces, wrote to him on 4 December pressing the Catholic case. The duke replied that he was sincerely anxious to witness the settlement of the Catholic question, which, by benefitting the state, would benefit every member of it. But he then added rather gloomily that he saw no prospect of such a settlement while the issue was associated with party politics, and then, tortuously twisting both logic and politics, suggested that 'if we could bury it in oblivion and employ that time diligently in the consideration of its difficulties on all sides (for they are very great), I should not despair of seeing a satisfactory remedy'.[84] Wellington, as Curtis subsequently explained, franked the letter himself and must have been aware that the news of its arrival would quickly spread through Drogheda. So, to kill false rumours about its contents, the archbishop showed it to a few friends, sent a copy to the archbishop of Dublin, and the newspapers got hold of it and published it. The Lord Lieutenant, Lord Anglesey, then inquired if the published version was authentic, whereupon Curtis sent the original to him, and he responded by repudiating Wellington's suggestion for a lull in the agitation, advising that all constitutional means should be adopted to further the cause and that no violence, physical or verbal, be allowed to sully or delay it. Anglesey was dismissed for stepping out of line by proffering what Curtis regarded as the most perfectly satisfactory declaration in favour of the Catholic cause.

Curtis' reply to Wellington was very deferential, nonetheless he pressed the premier for movement. Suggesting that the opponents of Catholic Emancipation would 'instantly fly and appear no more', if Wellington took up the case against them, he insisted that the proposal to bury the Catholic question in oblivion for a time would be 'totally

[84] F.J., 2 Jan. 1829.

inadmissible, and would exasperate in the highest degree those who are already too much excited, and would only consider that measure as a repetition of the same old pretext so often employed to elude and disappoint their hopes of redress'.[85] Privately, some of the bishops began to worry about the price they might have to pay for the concession. A rumour in Rome that the pope might be forced to grant the same rights to the king as he had given to the king of the Netherlands in the appointment of bishops alerted Archbishop Curtis to advise his colleagues that they should protest at Rome against such a possibility. Curtis also detected, among both clergy and laity in the north, much alarm at the prospect of 'wings and securities' being tied to an Emancipation bill.

Pro-Emancipation Protestants counselled their Catholic friends not to succumb to Wellington's advice, but to pursue their aims by holding county meetings to petition, in a 'temperate and respectful fashion for the equalization of civil rights'.[86] Tyrone was the first county to take up this advice. Antrim followed suit on 27 January 1829 when a numerous meeting, which would have been larger had the weather not been so inhospitable, took place in St Patrick's Church, Belfast. Crolly, who presided, introduced the subject by pledging to continue the struggle for civil and religious liberty. Praising the late viceroy for his statesmanlike advice and adverting to Wellington's admission that a settlement of the question would be beneficial to the whole empire, he rejected the duke's assertion that the issue was surrounded by difficulties, maintaining on the contrary that

our allegiance is unimpeached; our faithful attachment to the throne and the constitution cannot be disputed; our services to the country are established by incontrovertible facts. In return for these, we ask for no remuneration but a fair and equitable enjoyment of our civil rights, together with our fellow subjects of every denomination. What unprejudiced mind can see any difficulties in a case such as ours? There is not a court of equity on earth, where our question would not be disposed of in five minutes. The Premier pretends that we would render our cause an important service, by burying it for some time in oblivion. This proposal appears to us incompatible with honour, with reason, and with justice. Our detestation of oppression, and our love of freedom, are blended with our nature, and rooted in our very soul.

A great outburst of cheering greeted this last declaration. He then proceeded to question the reasons for burying the agitation in oblivion, and suggested that Wellington may have felt that he needed time to

[85] Curtis to Wellington, 19 Dec. 1828 in N.W. of 8 Jan. 1829.   [86] N.W., 1 Jan. 1829.

negotiate a concordat with the pope. Such an application to Rome would be 'most impolitic and unconstitutional', for the pope had no right to be consulted on a subject connected with the civil rights or temporal concerns of Catholics. Their object was a full participation in the privileges to which British subjects were entitled and they took heart from the recent removal of restrictions on the liberties of their dissenting brethren in England.[87]

Twelve resolutions demanding Emancipation without 'wings' or 'securities', a veto or the disfranchisment of the 40s freeholders were passed and lengthy, repetitive speeches excoriating maltreatment of Catholics from the breach of the Treaty of Limerick to the penal laws, and emphasizing the right of Catholics to full citizenship, were made. Peter McGouran regretted that many of their former friends in the province had joined the ranks of their adversaries, allegedly because of the intemperance of the Catholic Association or the violence of O'Connell, Sheil or Lawless; he did not rule out their retracting and returning to the standard of civil and religious liberty. Praising the Association for its many valuable services, its integrity and unifying capacity, he nonetheless insisted that the Catholics of Belfast did not seek political advice from it: they never went further than to their liberal Protestant and dissenting neighbours who were not only willing to give them good advice at all times but also to render them more substantial services.

Much stress was laid on the Catholics' determination to disclaim all ascendancy and seek only equality, and on their fidelity to the British connexion; the contribution of Catholics to the success of British arms, particularly in the struggles against Napoleon, were adduced as evidence of their loyalty. Gratitude was expressed for the contribution of the *Northern Whig* to the Catholic cause and the editor, in response, promised renewed and increased support for Catholic Emancipation as a measure of justice and expediency.

The speaker who received by far the most enthusiastic welcome was Henry Montgomery. When he rose to approach the altar he was greeted with a standing ovation. This gesture undoubtedly acknowledged his consistent defence of civil and religious liberty, but probably reflected the

---

[87] The *Belfast News Letter* which had been calling on Protestants to meet in defence of their political ascendancy and had on 16 January assured them that if such a meeting were called in Belfast 'an aggregate of respectability and numbers will be presented greater than the popish meeting', commented on Crolly's and subsequent speeches: 'we had expected from the temperate, and we may add, dignified introductory observations of Dr Crolly that moderation would have been the order of the day; but instead of that, we had a series of harangues calculated to work upon the passions of a credulous and susceptible populace, who are often too ignorant to be able to make allowance for "rhetorical flourishes"'. (B.N.L., 30 Jan. 1829)

indebtedness the audience felt to him for his recent advocacy of their cause in England.

At the beginning of January, Montgomery had paid a visit to Manchester, where, as a representative of Unitarianism and as an advocate of freedom of conscience in relation to man-made creeds, he was welcomed by the Unitarians of that city. When he had completed his tour of the churches he was entertained to dinner and there spoke warmly to some 180 members and friends of the Manchester congregation on the justice of Catholic Emancipation. In the Cross Street chapel he informed the congregation that in Ireland multitudes of miserable Roman Catholics were 'tolerated to worship the God of their fathers before shapeless altars of stone, with no other covering than the blue canopy of heaven above them; or in a dripping hovel, dignified by the name of a chapel, in which you would think it inhuman to house your domestic animals'. He further explained that they were so allowed to worship 'on the penal condition of largely contributing to the erection of splendid temples for the accommodation of a few scattered worshippers and a form of religion which they believe to be destructive'.

At the dinner, Montgomery proposed a toast to Catholic Emancipation and the universal acknowledgement that civil and religious liberty were the solid foundations of a nation's happiness. Claiming that the people of Ireland were as 'well disposed, as kindly affectioned as any people on the face of the earth', he insisted that the melancholy picture, which the country presented, of dark and jarring passions arose from a perversion of religion into a sword of persecution, a source of hatred and contention. Regretting that some few of the apostles of intolerance were clergymen, he quoted one as hoping that in the next conflict Catholics would not be left the alternative of Connaught as a refuge. Far from concessions to Catholics trenching on the integrity of the Protestant church, the continuance of those restrictions obstructed the progress of Protestantism. The Catholic could not believe that a church which was interested in his salvation could deny him the rights of man. The way to advance the Protestant religion was to remove Catholic disabilities. If these were removed, the Catholics might in time merge in the Protestant churches; he wished to see them so converted, but the first step towards their conversion was the conferment of full civil rights. While he could not justify every particular act done or every phrase used by Catholic campaigners, he admitted that if he were deprived of his rights he would be as violent, if not more so, as any member of the Catholic Association. He explained to his English hosts that the Unitarians of Ireland, like their

English confrères were favourable to Emancipation but that the evangelical party in his church were not so.[88]

This 'propaganda' on behalf of Emancipation was reported in the Belfast papers and raised Montgomery's standing even higher in the Catholic community. At the beginning of his speech in St Patrick's Church he advèrted to the rarity of the occasion when a Presbyterian minister could stand beside his friend, a Catholic bishop, and speak on Catholic grievances. It led him to muse how

I, who differ so widely from you in my religious sentiments, should be received by you with such testimonies of cordiality and affection, while those who agree most with you in theological opinions, are the bitterest enemies of your rights? Is it because the old saying holds good in this as in other cases, that in family feuds, the nearer the relationship, the more bitter is the enmity; or does it arise from the intermingling a portion of that charity which Christianity inculcates, and which is calculated to diffuse principles of peace, and harmony, and brotherhood, among all sects and denominations?

Reporting on his trip to England he brought good news of increasing support from all Christian denominations, but he confessed with regret that some presbyteries in Scotland had protested against Emancipation. Declaring that he had spoken and acted according to the dictates of his conscience, he concluded with a salvo calculated to stir the blood of his audience:

I would not, to inherit the wealthiest living of the wealthiest church in Christendom, forego the cheer with which I was greeted, and the feelings it excited, when I approached this altar today. I have spoken and acted as my conscience dictated. Whether I have consulted my interest by what I have done, I neither know nor care. I have only one consideration—to do my duty faithfully—and in the name of truth, of justice and of liberty to 'cry aloud and spare not'.

In the evening Crolly presided at a dinner in the Royal Hotel, which was attended by many of those present in the church, and 'by his urbanity and liberality, diffused a feeling of delight and pleasure over the entire company'. Toasts were drunk to the king, the royal family, the Lord Lieutenant, the marquis of Anglesey, the duke of Leinster and Protestant advocates of civil and religious liberty, and the Anglican bishop of Norwich (whom the chairman described as 'an honour to the age, and a redeeming feature in the body to which he belongs'). In introducing the toast to Henry Montgomery, Crolly referred to their indebtedness to

[88] Crozier, *The Life of the Rev. Henry Montgomery, LL.D., Dunmurry, Belfast*, 237-8; N.W., 15 Jan. 1829.

many Protestant friends in every part of the empire, and, remarking that gratitude like charity should begin at home, went on to salute their local champion:

He has stood in the midst of trials like a pillar of patriotism; and he has lately assumed the appearance of a pillar of light, diffusing the beams of liberality wherever he passed. It was lately the intention of some of our brethren to send a deputation to England, for the purpose of making the people of that country better acquainted with the feelings and situation of Ireland; but we have here a single gentleman who has done more service to our cause, in his late visit to the sister country, than the whole deputation from the Catholic body could have effected. He has long engaged our esteem; now he merits our love and affection.

When the lengthy applause had died down, Montgomery in turn proposed Crolly's health and paid a warm tribute to him. Crolly commented in response that his religion obliged him to exercise charity and added that he had been fortunate in being placed 'in a portion of the empire, where I daily see the principles of that charity admirably dispensed'. Claiming that the pope protected the rights of Protestants, both civil and religious, in the papal states, he looked forward to a time when

more liberal principles will soon pervade every denomination in these countries; the principles which direct us 'to love God above all things and our neighbour as ourselves'. And I should be glad to know where any man would get a good argument against this principle. I should be glad to know what injury the Established or the Presbyterian Church would receive, if it possessed more members like those to my right and left? *Good Christians*, of every denomination hold pretty nearly the same views on all matters of a moral nature; and I should never wish to see speculative points interfere with the principles of Christian benevolence.

Crolly went on to pay handsome compliments to Lords Donegall, Downshire, Londonderry, Charles Brownlow MP, Robert Grimshaw, John McCance and John Sinclaire. In his speech Grimshaw vigorously denied that the majority of persons of 'worth or excellence in this neighbourhood were favourable to intolerant principles'. He dismissed their noisy opponents in the Brunswick Clubs in Carrickfergus, Ballymena, Lisburn and Belfast as 'the retainers and hangers-on of bigoted landlords and intolerant rectors and curates'. Francis Finlay, the proprietor of the *Northern Whig*, assured them that every journal of worth and talent was with them and, opposed to them, was the renegade in religion and the apostate in politics. He sardonically interpreted the slogan, 'the church in danger', which the opponents of Emancipation in the established church had used to exploit Protestant fears, as 'the tithes are in danger'. Other liberal Protestants also spoke. Crolly then proposed the health of the absent John Lawless and significantly complimented him on the stand he had taken against the proposal to disfranchise the 40s freeholders and to pension the Catholic clergy.[89] The meeting and dinner were further demonstrations of the genuine support of the liberals of Belfast for Catholic Emancipation and of the close and friendly relations which the bishop had forged with prominent Presbyterians in the town.

Henry Montgomery, however, later admitted that he had been disappointed by the response of the Presbyterians on that occasion. Replying two years later to O'Connell's abrasive dismissal of him as 'a fawning, cringing sycophant' and incidentally revealing that he 'suffered greater pecuniary loss than any other Protestant in Ireland' by his uncompromising advocacy of Catholic Emancipation, he described his feelings at the beginning of the meeting:

I looked around for the crowds of Presbyterians, who had formerly cheered such assemblies; I saw a few honoured and venerable faces, but there was a melancholy defalcation; and the spirit of despondency brooded over the meeting. Did I too, sail away upon the ebbing tide of desertion? . . . No, Unitarian and Presbyterian though I am, I ascended the steps of a Catholic Altar . . . I poured forth my whole heart and spirit in their cause, and drove away the demon of despondency that had frowned upon their assembly.[90]

The enthusiasm of Montgomery and the faithful Presbyterian reformers seems to have atoned for the absence of former supporters.

Crolly and some of his priests took part in the meeting organized by the Catholics of Co. Down at Newry on 18 February at which similar motions were passed. In thanking the chairman, Nicholas Whyte, he remarked on the suitability of his co-religionists of Co. Down playing a prominent part in the attainment of civil and religious liberty, for it was in that county that the 'standard of that religion had been first raised, which, when well understood, afforded the best protection to true liberty'.[91]

By then George IV had given permission for the Catholic question to be discussed in the cabinet and in parliament. And the Catholic Association with the approval of twenty two of the twenty six bishops—of whom Crolly, who always believed in minimizing the possible sources of friction, was one—had dissolved itself. Though the king later changed his mind, he was forced to retract, as no alternative government was available. In March 1829 Wellington and Peel with Whig assistance comfortably overrode the opposition of the diehards, and the Emancipation bill passed

[89] N.W., 29 Jan. 1829.   [90] Ibid., 14 Feb. 1831.   [91] Ibid., 26 Feb. 1829.

through both houses and became law in April. The oath required of Catholics to enter parliament no longer contained clauses compelling them to abjure belief in transubstantiation and other doctrines, but did require acceptance of the Protestant succession, the existing land settlement and the established church. Religious orders were excluded from entering the United Kingdom and Catholic bishops were forbidden to use the titles of their sees—measures which O'Connell believed were derisory, unenforceable and self-defeating. A separate act disfranchised the 40s freeholders by limiting the vote to those with property valued at £10 or more. All offices were thrown open to Catholics except those of Regent, Lord Chancellor of Britain or Ireland, and Lord Lieutenant.

Psychologically, Emancipation was a tremendous victory affording to Catholics a liberty and nominal equality that they had dreamt about for decades. Though the translation of nominal into real equality involved struggles and setbacks for more than half a century, the concession of 1829 was the essential step without which other basic civil rights would have been worthless. But satisfaction with the concession was tinged with disappointment. The gesture was neither graciously nor generously made. The withdrawal of the franchise from the 40s freeholders, the threat of which Crolly had strongly deprecated, was a mean blow to those whose courage and selflessness had forced king and parliament to surrender. The restrictions imposed on the religious orders were offensive but meaningless. Some orders were already beginning to reorganize and reconstitute themselves, and few thought there was much likelihood of the exclusion threats being taken at face value. The gratitude that the measure could have called forth was therefore diminished and sullied by the grudging means by which it was enacted.

The liberal Protestants who had consistently defended the entitlement of Catholics to full civil rights were pleased with the enactment. But the Orangemen, the supporters of the Brunswick Clubs and the increasingly large numbers of Presbyterians who fell for their propaganda, interpreted civil equality for Catholics as a defeat for themselves. They were left an easy prey to those who sought to pander to their worst fears and prejudices. Even before the Emancipation bill was passed into law Henry Cooke had begun to scaremonger and manipulate the passions of his followers with ominous implications for the future peace of Ulster. With a colleague from Downpatrick he signed a requisition requiring the Moderator of the Dromore presbytery to convene a meeting of that body to discuss the government's plans to abrogate penal legislation against Catholics, and, when it was called, explained that he had done so for three reasons: because the government was about to vote a large sum of money to Maynooth College and should therefore be asked for grants for newly erected Presbyterian congregations; because Presbyterians were going to be robbed of their birthright by the grant of political privileges to one part of the king's subjects; because a new election committee should be chosen to oversee the appointment to the chair of moral philosophy in the Belfast Academical Institution. Though he did not use the word Emancipation he professed to contemplate the policy 'with horror, disapprobation and dismay'. Warming to his theme, he made bold to declare that there was not one out of a hundred Presbyterians who was not opposed to the proposed legislation. Conjuring up the picture of a Protestant king and a Catholic premier, and a Protestant Lord Chancellor and a Catholic council for England, and a Protestant viceroy and a Catholic council for Ireland, he predicted that this scenario would be realized in a few years and that they would then find themselves enduring the misery and persecution which their forefathers suffered under Charles II and James II. He demanded a bill of rights, complained that four fifths of the British army was required to keep the Catholic parts of Ireland in control, and claimed that Presbyterians would be deprived of their birthright by losing the right to vote in vestries and by having Catholics placed on the same footing as themselves.

Cooke's motion was lost by thirteen votes to three; nine ministers and four elders voted against it, and only two clergymen joined him in voting for it.[92] Attempts in other congregations to link the Presbyterians who supported the resolutions in 1813 in favour of Emancipation with heterodoxy and thereby smear their successors were similarly unsuccessful; the successful exception occurred in the congregation of Ballymena, where Robert Stewart of Broughshane, Cooke's zealous ally, had long 'drawn the sword against the Roman Catholics' and had 'converted the peaceful town of Ballymena into an arena of theological gladiatorship and party animosity'.[93] Whatever about the views of the average man in the pew, the influential Presbyterians who manned the positions of authority in the church felt that resistance to the decisions of parliament or attempts to rewrite their own history were pointless.

Some one hundred and twenty five of the notable liberals of Belfast who had long campaigned for civil and religious liberty celebrated the passing of the Relief Act by dining together at the Commercial Buildings. John Barnett struck the predominant note on the occasion when he

---

[92] Ibid., 2 Apr. 1829.   [93] Ibid., 16 Apr. 1829.

pointed out that they had met not to hail the triumph of party but rather of liberality, justice and sound policy. In response to calls for a speech Crolly rose and expressed his gratitude to God, and to his assembled friends for making him a freeman in the land of his birth. He owed a very special debt to Belfast, and he trusted the good example shown by that town would be widely followed:

Yet, I am bound to say, that despite of penal enactments, I have been a freeman by the practical benevolence of my fellow-townsmen for the last seventeen years. It has long been the general characteristic of your town, that no one can live in Belfast, without feeling himself at perfect liberty to worship his God according to the dictates of his conscience . . . I trust that Irishmen of every communion will recollect, and that Catholics in particular, will never forget that when the balance was doubtful, the inhabitants of Belfast stepped forward and threw eleven millions of property into the scale of freedom. This act of generosity demands the most ardent feelings on our part . . . I trust yet to see the day when all men in this country will remember that they are brethren partaking of the same feeling and frailties—breathing the same air—all needing forgiveness from the same God—acknowledging the same monarch, and the children of one common country; and that Irishmen of every communion will stretch out the hand of peace and good will to each other. It was in this town that the struggle for freedom first commenced; and I have no hesitation in saying that in its efforts to emancipate the country, Belfast has emancipated itself. Had Belfast been a nest of illiberality, it would still have been a village, whereas it is now one of the first commercial towns in the Empire.

The usual felicitations were exchanged and many of the same speakers as on similar occasions in the past took part. Crolly was again called to reply to the toast that the clergy of Belfast should ever teach their people to love one another. He explained that he did so with enthusiasm as he went on to praise his clerical brethren in the town. He singled out A.C. Macartney, the vicar of Belfast, for special praise, and added that the Presbyterian clergy inculcated the same Christian sentiments from their pulpits. Then, reflecting on the parable of the Good Samaritan, he remarked that no man could be a servant of God or a faithful minister of the gospel who did not enforce by precept and example the Saviour's doctrine of mutual love without distinction of creed or country, colour or clime. And he trusted that the good example set by well-educated men uniting in the expression of such sentiments would 'have a happy effect upon those persons, whom ignorance and prejudice have so long arrayed against each other'.[94]

This celebration was a happy note on which to bring the Emancipation chapter to a close. That struggle had produced evidence of a genuine desire among the liberal Protestants of Belfast and its neighbourhood that

[94] Ibid., 30 Apr. 1829.

the Catholics also should enjoy that civil and religious liberty which they so prized for themselves. For their part, the Catholics, conscious of their weakness and minority status, responded to the Dublin leadership and its decisions with more caution and circumspection than their co-religionists in the south of Ireland. As the movement gained momentum a very different Protestant response also became evident: the perception of equality as a diminution of 'Protestant rights', a natural response in the case of the established church, which enjoyed special privileges and power. Such a response might seem at first sight remarkable among Presbyterians but, significantly, it emerged more strongly among the poorer members of that church who felt threatened by their real or imagined loss of a somewhat higher status than Catholics in the pecking order among classes and denominations. And at the spiritual level anti-Catholic attitudes had been hardened by the evangelicalism that was increasingly animating Protestantism. The theological victory won by Henry Cooke in the Synod of Ulster over Henry Montgomery and the exponents of non-subscription to Christian creeds represented a defeat for the liberally-minded Presbyterians in politics as well. The 'New Light' clergy were generally more liberal than their evangelical, Calvinistic 'Old Light' brethren and their withdrawal from the Synod of Ulster in 1829 severely weakened liberal influences in that body. Crolly's hope of living to see the day when Irishmen of every communion would stretch out the hand of peace and good will to each other was destined to remain in the realm of dreams.

4

PASTORAL CARE AND ECCLESIASTICAL PROBLEMS, 1825–35

Shortly after his episcopal ordination Crolly set out on a pastoral visitation of his diocese, which, because of the age and ill-health of his predecessor, was the first of its kind for several years. On his return to Belfast he wrote a formal letter to Rome to notify the pope of his ordination. He also took advantage of the opportunity afforded by this customary courtesy to ask permission to transfer his mensal parish from Downpatrick to Belfast. Hitherto, bishops had lived in and depended upon Downpatrick for their sustenance and income. He explained that his clergy would find it more convenient if the bishop were to live in the geographical centre of the diocese, and went on to add that no part of Down and Connor required the more constant presence of the bishop than Belfast, a mainly Protestant town, and one where continuous vigilance was required to check the machinations of a biblical society against their religion.[1] In fact, he was so confident of the success of this petition that he asked that Cornelius Denvir, a professor in Maynooth, be appointed to Downpatrick. Both requests were promptly granted.

Belfast was undoubtedly the most suitable centre for the bishop's residence and by making it his parish Crolly ensured that he had immediate pastoral supervision of the largest and most important town in the diocese. According to the census returns of 1821 and 1831—which are not regarded as wholly trustworthy—the population of the town increased from 37,000 to 53,000 during that decade. By 1825 it must have comfortably passed 40,000 and little foresight was required to see that it was destined then to become much larger. Crolly already enjoyed the advantage of knowing the town intimately for the previous thirteen years

---

[1] Crolly to Pope Leo XII, 7 Sept. 1825, APF, SC (Irlanda), 24, ff 500v-501v. In this letter he also apologized for being unable to contribute to the rebuilding of St Paul's Basilica, for which a world-wide appeal was then being made, as his coffers were empty because of expenses incurred at his episcopal ordination and subsequent celebrations.

and was better equipped than any other priest to guide the destinies of its Catholic population, which must have numbered at least one quarter of the whole.

This central location also facilitated Crolly's visitation, and enabled him to be present at functions in Co. Antrim which his predecessors would not have attended. The improvements in the roads which took place in the 1820s and 1830s, together with his own youthful vigour and robust health, also facilitated his travels around the diocese. These more frequent visits throughout Down and Connor permitted the bishop to see the needs of parishes and to persuade his priests to attend to them. The example of Crolly's own energetic application to, and dedicated concern for, the pastoral requirements of Belfast gave his clergy an example on which to model themselves in their own parishes.

The provision of new churches and the repair and enlargement of existing buildings were his first priorities. In Lecale or East Down, where the better-off Catholics—mainly tenant farmers but also shopkeepers and a few merchants—lived, churches had been built from the last quarter of the eighteenth century. They were simple architecturally, unimpressive and frequently poorly constructed and finished, but they were much appreciated by a mainly poor and grateful people. Some of them needed to be repaired and extended. In other parts where the Catholic population was thin and scattered, few and, in some places, no churches existed. During the ten years of Crolly's episcopate a truly impressive feat of church building occurred. In June 1834 he informed the pope that he had consecrated twenty three churches, which were either entirely new or rebuilt and enlarged; a further ten were then being built or renovated.[2] Churches were erected or extended at Clanvaraghan (1825), Castlewellan (1827), Glenshesk (1827), Hannahstown (1827), Ballymena (1828), Ardglass (1828), Killough (1828), Feystown (1828), Cargan (1829), The Rock (1830), Holywood (1830), Bryansford (1830), Ballymacarrett (1831), Portaferry (1831), Larne (1831), Tannaghmore (1831), Greencastle (1832), Ballyclare (1832), Glasdrumman (1832), Killyleagh (1832), Kilkeel (1833), Ballygowan (1833), Ballymoney (1834).[3] Moneyglass and Culfeightrin were opened in November 1835 after Crolly had been appointed to Armagh. Some of these—Holywood, Ballymacarrett, Ballymena, Greencastle, Ballyclare, Killyleagh—were located in mainly Protestant

---

[2] Crolly to Gregory XVI, 29 June 1834, APF, SOCG, 950, ff 212r-214v.

[3] Many of these dates are taken from newspaper reports and the rest are from O'Laverty, *Down and Connor*. The *Ordnance Survey Memoirs* state that Castlewellan was built in 1825, Ardglass in 1830, Kilcoo in 1832, and that Clanvaraghan was rebuilt in 1831 and that Glenravel was enlarged in 1834.

districts and facilitated local Catholics, who had previously travelled long distances to Mass. Others replaced ecclesiastical structures that had existed in that locality or nearby. Most were barely furnished and had enough pews to accommodate only part of the congregation; the rest would have been obliged to stand.

Parish boundaries were also rearranged to ensure better pastoral service for those who had previously lived far from the parochial church or priest's house. North-west Antrim, partly because of the paucity and the poverty of the Catholics there and partly because of its distance from Downpatrick, which led to a certain ignorance of its needs by successive bishops, had suffered from a dearth of clergy. The parish of Rasharkin before 1825 embraced the areas which later became the parishes of Ballymoney, Portrush, Coleraine and Dunloy. Crolly had been present at a conference of priests in Antrim in 1820 when a deputation from the Catholics of Ballymoney approached Bishop McMullan to ask for better pastoral care. McMullan had taken no steps to meet this request when he died four years later, but Crolly on succeeding him promptly did so. On 1 August 1825 he appointed Henry McLaughlin parish priest of Ballymoney, which included the districts of Bushmills and Portrush, and McLaughlin erected a new church in Ballymoney. In 1834 McLaughlin was transferred to Loughguile and a further division was made: a parish priest was appointed to the Bushmills—Portrush part of the parish and instructed to reclaim the district of Coleraine east of the Bann, which had been under the pastoral care of priests of the diocese of Derry.[4]

Crolly, on his first visitation to North Antrim, also responded favourably to a plea for the creation of a parish at Ballycastle by separating the Ballycastle—Glenshesk area from Armoy. And in 1833 he detached the Braid district from Ballymena and attached it to Glenravel.[5]

Though he erected churches at Greencastle and Ballyclare, he did not form parishes around them. They continued to be served by the clergy of Belfast, probably because the numbers would not have been able to support a parish priest. But to the other side of Belfast he did make parochial adjustments. A single parish extending from Bangor to the outskirts of Belfast at Ballymacarrett served the Catholics of North Down. He cut off the Holywood and Ballymacarrett parts of this parish in 1828 and kept them under his own care until he could erect churches in both places. When the second one was completed in Ballymacarrett, he appointed a parish priest to this new parish.[6]

[4] O'Laverty, *Down and Connor,* IV, 137-9 and V, 593.   [5] Ibid., V, 590 and III, 452.
[6] Ibid., II, 208-9.

Crolly frequently took advantage of the opportunities afforded by the opening of churches to preach on charity and to stress the obligations of Christians of all traditions to practice that virtue towards each other. On such occasions Presbyterians and Anglicans were always present, always contributed to the collections and often supplied many of the collectors. The *Northern Whig* invariably commended the bishop for his exhortations to inter-denominational goodwill and fellowship. Its comment on his sermon at the opening of the church in Ballymena may be taken as typical:

We candidly confess that we can only give an imperfect outline of this useful, impressive and eloquent sermon;—the great perspicuity with which the liberal and esteemed divine arranged and enforced this argument, was evidently entitled to the admiration of all who had the pleasure of hearing him; but we believe that the entire auditory were mostly deeply affected with his reasoning regarding the love which we owe to our neighbours of every communion, especially when he described the absurdity and impiety of the man, who, with bitterness and malice in his breast, dares to insult the eternal Father of the human race, by repeating that petition of the Lord's prayer 'Father forgive us our trespasses, as we forgive them that trespass against us'. With a tenderness of feeling, and a strength of expression which we will not attempt to describe, he depicted the impious conduct and unnatural attitude of a Christian who raises his right hand to the throne of divine mercy, whilst his left hand is directed against the life of his fellow-creature, and contaminated with the blood of his Christian brother.

The *Whig* noted that the Protestant gentlemen who were present invited him to publish that sermon.[7] It was even more enthusiastic about his call for reconciliation four years later at the opening of the church at Ballyclare. Commenting that it had often borne willing testimony 'to the talented, Christian and charitable discourses pronounced by him', it claimed that, since his elevation to the episcopacy, he had never made a more powerful or deeper impression on his hearers.[8]

II

The provision of more and better churches obviously enabled people to cultivate their spiritual lives more easily and fruitfully. Crolly was anxious to encourage and empower them to do so. Before he became bishop Catholics had been put on their mettle by the proliferation of proseltyzing societies and schools. Resistance to the activities of these societies, and the exclusion of Catholic children from their schools, had engaged the concerns of the clergy for several years. This resistance strengthened

[7] N.W., 13 Nov. 1828.   [8] Ibid., 22 Nov. 1832.

Catholic denominational loyalty, and the attacks of such Protestant zealots as Sir Harcourt Lees and Tresham Gregg increased this denominational solidarity further. The main contention of the Evangelical missionaries, who were prepared to compete with the priests for the allegiance of Catholics, was that they were freeing the benighted poor from the bondage to which their clergy had subjected them by denying them access to the liberating power and truth of God's word. The Catholic clergy were taunted with cowardice in refusing their ignorant and credulous people access to the bible lest they might lose control of them.

In his early years as parish priest, Crolly did not have to confront evangelical militancy to any great extent, but in the years after he became bishop, evangelical enthusiasm with a sharper anti-Catholic edge gathered force in Belfast, Antrim and Down. He also encountered it at first hand in Cavan in December 1826. Lord Farnham, one of the great landlords of that county, was a most perfervid patron of evangelical missionaries and a generous sponsor of gifts to tempt the poor on his estates into embracing Protestantism. He helped set up an 'Association for Promoting the Second Reformation' and the effective diffusion of propaganda about the success of this enterprise brought English interest and aid to the Cavan mission.[9] Fearing that there was some truth behind the reports of numerous conversions, and anxious to lend their support to the aged and ailing bishop of Kilmore in his quest for a coadjutor, the hierarchy decided at a meeting in Dublin to send representatives to investigate the situation. Crolly was chosen to accompany Archbishop Curtis of Armagh, the bishops of Kilmore and Ardagh and the coadjutor bishop of Killala in conducting an inquiry into the allegations of widespread lapsing from Catholicism.

The bishops soon encountered missionary zeal at close quarters: five itinerant preachers had collected a crowd at the gates of the church, where they were due to meet the clergy of Kilmore, and, failing to provoke any excitement by this action, sent a letter to the prelates calling for a public discussion on the subject of religious controversy. The bishops, in a public statement issued after their proceedings ended, declared that, from an examination of the clergy and laity there assembled, they had established 'that money, salaries, situations in the Hibernian schools, profitable employment, clothing, and other species of bribery, were proffered to the poor Catholics, for the purpose of betraying them into a temporary and hypocritical abandonment of their faith'. They further claimed that those

⁹ Bowen, *The Protestant Crusade in Ireland*, 94.

who yielded to these persuasions were the very poor, abandoned vagrants and unemployed labourers, and that every enlightened and liberal Protestant was disgusted with such tactics 'by which party spirit is excited, good will amongst Christians diminished, and the peace of society deplorably endangered'. When the bishops had established the truth of these facts by sworn witnesses and by those who had repented and returned to their former faith, they hoped the magistrates would take sworn statements from the deponents and, if necessary, examine them. But as the magistrates refused to do so they appended some of the affidavits to their statement. On Sunday, 17 December Curtis, Crolly and MacHale preached at different hours in the church, and were convinced by the 'immense multitude that attended from morning until evening' that the new reformation was 'not much relished by the Catholics in that part of the country'.[10] Curtis in a subsequent letter to Rome claimed that in the presence of 5,000 Catholics and many Protestants, a great number of those who had lapsed renounced their defection and sought pardon with tears of repentance.[11] A hostile source, however, maintained that when the prelates were speaking in the church no less than forty nine people renounced the Catholic faith a few yards away.[12]

To counter such threats the bishops realized that polemics alone were insufficient. Positive action and prayerful vigilance were required. And some help in this direction was fortuitously provided by the jubilee indulgence of 1825 and the richer interior devotional life which this engendered and encouraged. In 1826 a new pope, Leo XII, extended to Catholics throughout the world the holy year indulgences, if they carried out certain prescribed religious and penitential exercises. An example of the effect of this measure is provided by a comment on the response of the Catholic community at Ballymoney: Mass was celebrated each morning at 5.00 a.m. 'and it was nothing short of miraculous to see the old chapel crammed to the door at that early hour, by as earnest a congregation as could be found in the kingdom'. Before that time some had been careless and indifferent but then 'a wholesome change took place which showed clearly what a zealous and faithful pastor can accomplish'.[13]

Crolly was fortunate that the beginning of his episcopate concided with this fillip to the devotional life of the church in Ireland. He himself gave encouragement and leadership to the clergy, who were introducing their people to a more varied liturgy than had been possible until the

---

[10] B.N.L., 26 Dec. 1826.   [11] Curtis to Propaganda, 10 Sept. 1827, APF, *Acta*, 190, f 162rv.
[12] B.N.L., 26 Dec. 1826.
[13] McErlain, *A Statement of Accounts and a few facts concerning Ballymoney and Derrykeighan*, 16.

nineteenth century, by celebrating High Masses at the opening of churches throughout the diocese and in his own parish in Belfast. Even the *Belfast News Letter*, which rarely bothered to comment on or enthuse about Catholic religious practices, could write in 1830:

> To Protestants the most singular part of the service was the ceremony of high Mass, in which Dr Crolly, R.C. Bishop of Down, and two other clergymen, officiated in the gorgeous canonicals of their order, with crosier [*sic*] incense etc. etc. Some five passages were admirably executed by a select choir, the whole having a splendid and imposing effect.[14]

Later jubilees, extended to the whole church by the new popes, Pius VIII and Gregory XVI, after their accessions in 1829 and 1831, further encouraged the diffusion of new kinds of spiritual exercises, of Italian or French origin, that had begun to spread throughout the church. The enthusiasms generated in the parishes by the construction or extension of churches also increased this religious spirit. And it was partly to develop this spirit that the bishops at the instigation of Bishop Doyle of Kildare and Leighlin founded the Catholic Book Society in 1827.

Their primary aims, however, were to educate their people doctrinally, to supply them with 'satisfactory Refutations of the prevailing Errors and Heresies of the present age' and to provide their children, especially the poor, in the parochial schools not only with catechisms but also with books of general knowledge. This plan was put into effect at a meeting of the clergy of Dublin at which Archbishop Murray was appointed vice-president and treasurer, the primate was appointed president, the other archbishops vice-presidents and the bench of bishops guardians. The managing committee and secretary were drawn extensively from the priests of Dublin and were empowered to examine and report on books suitable for circulation. Their goal was to circulate 100,000 religious books throughout the country within three months, and to continue doing so till every poor family had a 'select library of religious and other useful books'. The bishops opened the fund by subscribing £5 each and promised a further £5. Those who subscribed £1 became members of the society and larger subscriptions entitled the donors to further privileges. Each parish in Dublin, Cork, Limerick, Waterford and Galway, and rural deaneries in every diocese in Ireland, were to be supplied in proportion to the Catholic population of the district with a number of books for the cost of which the bishops were to be responsible. Books or tracts to the value of five

---

[14] B.N.L., 18 May 1830. The *Whig* had looked forward on that occasion to the contribution of the choir and soloist, and was highly pleased with their performances. (N.W., 13 and 17 May 1830.)

shillings were to be circulated for every thousand people and the bishop of the diocese was responsible for forwarding the costs to the treasurer in Dublin. Crolly promptly forwarded the circular announcing the establishment of the society to his clergy and advised them to encourage the project.[15]

The society got off to an enthusiastic start. Matthew Flanagan, the secretary, declaring extravagantly that the church in Ireland was not inferior in suffering, patience, fortitude and charity to the church of the apostolic times, wrote that the society aspired to introduce the poor man and his family to feast with the rich man on the common gift of God, to become the friend and assistant of every instructor of youth and to preserve true religion from the deadly effects of heresy and error.[16] Thousands of copies of catechisms, expositions of Catholic doctrine and books of piety were soon printed and, in its half-yearly report in November, the society was able to announce that it had collected more than £1,000. The bishops subscribed £165 and the lion's share came from the Dublin clergy who subscribed £235. Kildare and Limerick contributed £184 and £126, four dioceses around £50 and a few others ranged from £17 to £1. Down and Connor contributed something over £5, and so found itself in the same league as Armagh, Clonfert and Clogher.[17] By the following year subscriptions from Down and Connor had picked up, and in February the diocese was listed as contributing £12.

Heavy financial commitments seem to have prevented the priests of Down and Connor from observing fully the regulations of the society. In 1830 the bishop was obliged to apologize to Archbishop Murray, the treasurer, for the failure of his clergy to forward their subscriptions to that 'laudable Institution'. His priests had told him at a clerical conference that they were reluctant to call on their people for assistance because of the debts so many of them had incurred in church building. The society had also been inefficient. Some of the priests had complained that their orders had not been satisfactorily delivered. He himself was unable to get the books he required for his own school and was compelled to have recourse to the stocks of the Kildare Place Society. While pledging his own support, Crolly expressed the hope that his bank society in Belfast would settle the difficulties with the Catholic Book Society.[18] In 1835, another society, the Catholic Book Society of Ireland, was established to equip parochial libraries and to facilitate the work of those engaged in teaching religion through the various confraternities.

[15] Circular in DCDA and F.J., 22 May 1827.   [16] F.J., 30 June 1827.   [17] Ibid., 15 Nov. 1827.
[18] Crolly to Murray, 8 Dec. 1830, DDA.

In 1822, after Crolly had set up a Sunday school in St Patrick's Church, when the committee of the Brown Street school refused to allow the Catholic children to use the Douay version of the bible, he invited a Protestant publisher to produce a small book entitled the *Grounds of the Catholic Doctrine, contained in the Profession of Faith*, published by Pope Pius IV. This was a general catechism which was subsequently sold or distributed freely to the children who attended his Sunday school. His principal contribution, however, to the intellectual and devotional life of Catholics in the north was the publication of many cheap editions both of the whole bible and of the new testament in the Douay version. The first of these publications, by Belfast Protestant firms, was made in 1817, and thereafter at regular intervals new editions were made available. Many of the clergy of the diocese were quick to take advantage of the reduced costs to try to circulate the scriptures among their people. Arthur O'Neill, the parish priest of Larne, writing to the *Irishman* in 1820 to add his protest to those of other clergy against the policy of the Kildare Place Society in allowing only the Protestant versions as a daily school book, asked rhetorically if every priest in the diocese of Connor had not subscribed to reduce the approved version of the new testament to a price within reach of the poorest, and to circulate copies from their churches. He himself, 'in the very poorest part of Ulster, in respect of Catholicity' had given out a hundred copies of the new testament and the same number of the *Abridgement of Christian Doctrine* from his altars, and had found the demand for them increasing. Conscious of the happy results of this enterprise he advised every pastor in Ireland to place those two volumes in every cabin where either a parent or child could read and assured them, from experience, that they could then 'bid defiance to the fanatical zeal of the chartered calumniator or the itinerant proselytizer'. Moreover, widespread use of the new testament in that way would reduce the price very significantly.[19]

At the commission of inquiry into the Belfast Academical Institution Crolly himself revealed that he had disposed of 8,000 copies of the scriptures in cheap editions and complete with notes.[20] He continued to patronize Belfast printing firms, and ten years later, could claim that he had circulated more copies of the old and new testaments than anyone else in Ireland. He had got an edition printed entirely at his own expense, had recently paid his printers £1,000 and the bible, which had formerly cost

[19] Ir., 24 Mar. 1820.
[20] *Fourth report of the commissioners of Irish education inquiry*, pp. 180-3, H.C. 1826-7 (89), xiii.

eighteen shillings, was then being sold at six.[21] In fact there was scarcely a Catholic family in the diocese without a bible, and he had found 'religion to be much improved by it'.[22] Bishop Denvir of Down and Connor subsequently claimed that by 1839 Crolly had got 39,000 copies of the bible printed in Belfast and that between 1817 and 1852 308,600 bibles and testaments had been printed for Crolly, Bishop Blake of Dromore and himself.[23]

However, despite these continuous attempts to provide literate Catholic households with the scriptures at the cheapest possible rates, Crolly was often exposed to the accusation that his church discouraged or forbade the distribution of the bible. At the great meeting in Belfast to protest against the national system of education in January 1832, John Edgar, the professor of theology for the Remonstrant Presbyterians in the Belfast Academical Institution, touted this hoary canard in its most extreme form. Claiming that the government had been 'grossly imposed upon as to the feelings of the R. Catholic laity', he insisted that lay Catholics far from being opposed to scriptural education were sending their children to the schools of the Kildare Place Society 'in despite of curses, anathemas, and persecutions from their clergy'. According to him the commissioners of education had found that the scriptures, with or without comment, were not read in any school under Catholic control, and in the Catholic school in Belfast, even though the notes were retained, the scriptures were never read.[24]

In his letter to Lord Donegall challenging some of the statements made at that meeting, Crolly related how at the beginning of his pastoral work he had undertaken to make available many thousands of copies of the new testament among the Catholics of Belfast and its vicinity. He also assisted Joseph Smyth, the Belfast publisher, in circulating copies throughout Ulster and the whole British empire. When he became bishop, he decided to try to provide a copy of both the old and new testament for every family in his diocese, and consequently wrote to and obtained the cooperation and financial assistance of every bishop in Ireland to enable him to have many copies printed. He added that he had supposed that those facts were not unknown to his clerical brethren in Belfast.[25]

Edgar was not prepared to surrender his argument, however strongly it was contradicted by such facts. Replying to Crolly he proceeded to quibble about the meaning of Pope Pius VI's introduction to an Italian translation of the bible. The pope had said that the translation and

[21] N.W., 9 July 1835.   [22] Ibid., 26 Oct. 1835.   [23] Denvir papers, DCDA.
[24] B.N.L., 20 Jan. 1832.   [25] N.W., 23 Jan. 1832.

circulation of the bible was 'a good work' but the addition of explanatory notes from the Fathers made it still better. In an extremely curious non-sequitur, Edgar wanted to know whether the Catholics claimed that the translation and free circulation of the scriptures 'for the use of all, was not a good work'. Furthermore, Edgar maintained that a synod at Toulouse in 1829 had decreed that the laity should not be permitted the use of the bible.[26] There was little Crolly could do to counter such obstinate persistence in accusing his church of hostility to scriptural faith, and as opposition to the system of national education among Protestants grew, remarks like those of Edgar's became more common.

III

In 1824 Crolly established on a permanent footing the Sunday school in St Patrick's Church, which he had first launched two years earlier, for the Catholic children whom he had withdrawn from the Brown Street schools. He and his assistants taught religion to the assembled children on Saturdays and Sunday afternoons. As numbers grew this arrangement became more difficult and unsatisfactory, and he turned his thoughts to the establishment of a day school, which would cater for the increasing numbers of Catholic children who could not find places in the Lancasterian school, and in which religion could be taught daily alongside other subjects. Bishops and priests in the more affluent parts of the country set up many such schools in the 1820s, partly in response to the activities of the proselytizing societies and of the Kildare Place Society and partly as a social and pastoral service to their people. In July 1828 Crolly laid the foundation stone for male and female schools beside St Patrick's Church in Donegall Street. A year later the schools were opened and by 1830, when a charity sermon was preached by Bishop Kelly of Dromore, to pay off the debts, some 700 pupils were on the rolls. On that occasion prominent Protestants headed by the marquis of Donegall acted as collectors and £150 was raised.[27] When the schools applied for aid from the commissioners of national education in 1832—with almost as many Protestants as Catholics signing the application form—there were 430 boys and 325 girls on their rolls for weekday classes and some hundred extra pupils on Saturdays. The children who could afford to do so paid

[26] B.N.L., 27 Jan. 1832.
[27] B.N.L., 18 May 1830. Encouraging the Protestants to contribute liberally to the collection, the *Whig* (13 May 1830) pointed out that Catholics contributed generously to public charities 'and in the management of their own concerns they taxed themselves voluntarily more than any other class in the community'.

one penny per week, but many of them were unable to do so, and their annual payments did not amount to £20. This fell far short of paying the teachers salaries, (£60 for the male-teacher and £30 for the female) and the parish was obliged to make up the shortfall and to provide the equipment.[28] St Patrick's schools were among the first to join the national system, and thereby to obtain from the commissioners the payment of the teachers' salaries.[29]

A few Protestant children attended these schools and were permitted to use their own version of the bible when the Catholics were using the Douay version. After the schools were connected with the national system, the *Ulster Guardian* charged the teachers with discrimination against Protestants by using a Catholic textbook, the *Grounds of Catholic Doctrine*, during school hours. Crolly wrote to the *Northern Whig* deploring public controversy on education as being of little benefit to the country and enclosing sworn statements from both teachers listing the books they used, including both a Protestant and Catholic version of the bible, and insisting that they taught the catechism only to the Catholic children on Saturdays.[30]

This was the first substantial Catholic parochial school to be built and opened in the diocese. Unlike some of the better-off dioceses in the south of Ireland, Down and Connor did not have any day schools funded by parishes at which children received free tuition. Consequently, the Catholic children attended schools subsidized by various Protestant societies or pay schools conducted by individual teachers. According to the returns of the commissioners of Irish Education Inquiry nearly 4,000 Catholic pupils in Co. Antrim and more than 6,000 in Co. Down attended such schools in 1824.[31]

Probably the only form of education which many Catholic children received was in the Sunday schools which the clergy, throughout the 1820s, were striving to establish. In some cases these were conducted by teachers who taught in local schools during the week and in other cases the clergy and parishioners who were believed to have a competent knowledge of their faith taught the catechisms and prayers to the pupils. Catholic Sunday schools are included among most of the Sunday schools

---

[28] PRONI, ED/1/1/3.

[29] In the second report of the commissioners of national education for the year ending 31 December 1834 the enrolment of the pupils is given as 571 boys and 512 girls. The two teachers received £70 salary and a grant was made for the school requisites which amounted to £17.5s.5d. (*Second report of the commissioners of national education*, p. 46, H.C. 1835 (300), xxxv.)

[30] N.W., 9 Apr. 1832.

[31] *Second report of the commissioners of Irish education inquiry*, pp. 28-9, 36-7, H.C. 1826-7 (12), xii.

listed by the ordnance surveyors for Co. Antrim. They noted that a Sunday school was established in Lisburn in 1795, had twenty teachers and five hundred pupils, used bibles and spelling books and met each Sunday for three hours in the afternoon except during the winter months from December to April. Glenravel was credited with two hundred and fifty pupils but no enrolment figure was given for Larne or Loughguile.[32] In some Protestant districts a few Catholic children attended Sunday school in Protestant churches, where, apart from bible study, they would have learned to spell and read. Little evidence of the financial details of these Sunday schools survives; an exception, however, is the parish of Drummaul (Randalstown and Antrim) where it is known that the parish committee set aside £10 in 1827 to pay the Sunday school teachers in the parish and arranged for two collections to be held to raise that sum. In the following year the payment was increased to £15 but by 1831 it had dropped to £8 as the collections had not been as large as expected.[33]

Crolly, unlike his parish clergy, could not limit his educational apostolate to primary schools. He had indicated in 1825 at the inquiry into the Belfast Academical Institution that, while aspirants to the priesthood could receive their secondary education there in preparation for their higher studies at Maynooth, he might establish his own seminary for that purpose. Diocesan colleges as feeders for the major seminaries had been established in Kilkenny, Carlow, Navan, Tuam and Newry and the Jesuits had founded Clongowes Wood College in 1814. In November 1832 Crolly leased Vicinage Mansion House, a country house set in eleven acres of land in the immediate suburbs of the town, for an annual rent of £60. Preparations for the reception of students were made during 1833 but little publicity attached to the plan until the announcement of a charity sermon for 13 October 1833.[34] To emphasize the significance of the occasion Crolly had invited the archbishop of Armagh and five other bishops of the northern province to attend and Bishop Michael Blake of Dromore to preach. The *Northern Herald* reported that in the course of the sermon Blake spoke of 'the character of Belfast; of its commerce, its literature and its liberality' and 'passed a high eulogium on the distinguished Prelate who governs the Diocese—distinguished by his unwearied

---

[32] *O.S. Memoirs*, viii, 83; xiii, 16; x, 126; xiii, 65.

[33] *Minute book of the parish committee of Drummaul* (copy). DCDA. On 28 Feb. 1828 the N.W. reported that nearly 800 Catholic children were attending the Sunday schools in the parish. Crolly pointed out that he had confirmed 1,651 persons in the parish during his last visit.

[34] The N.W. trusted that 'from the known liberality of the people of Belfast and from the kindly and affectionate manner in which the liberal Protestants and Catholics intermix in all the social and political duties of life' the response would be generous. (10 Oct. 1833.)

efforts in the cause of knowledge and religion, and the spirit of conciliation which has marked every part of his career'. The collection, which was indeed generous, amounted to £150.[35]

A little later an advertisement informed the public that boarding fees in the new school would be £12 annually, with £2 extra for washing, and that tuition fees would be £1 quarterly for classics, £1 for mathematics, geography and the use of globes, £1 for classics and mathematics, and English, arithmetic and book keeping were to vary from seven shillings and sixpence to fifteen shillings, depending on the age and advancement of the pupils.[36] Cornelius Denvir, the parish priest of Downpatrick, who had been professor of natural philosophy at Maynooth until 1826, was appointed to teach classics and mathematics, while commuting to his parish for weekends, and John Lynch, a curate in Belfast, was assigned to assist him with the lower classes. The English and Mercantile Master was a layman. Eight boarders and ten day pupils were enrolled on 4 November as St Malachy's College was finally inaugurated. Before the end of the first academic year the number of students had risen to sixty nine, fifty of whom were boarders. A few Protestant boys attended, both as boarders and day pupils, in the first few years. Vicinage House was the residential part of the new college; tuition was given in classrooms beside St Patrick's schools in Donegall Street, whither the boarders walked daily.[37] Apart from candidates for the priesthood, St Malachy's College catered for boys who hoped to engage in professional or commmercial occupations.[38] It duly became and has since remained one of the great secondary boys' schools in Ulster, and can claim to be one of Crolly's most enduring contributions to the north of Ireland.

While St Malachy's College could accommodate all the Belfast Catholic boys whose parents wanted them to have secondary education and could afford the fees, St Patrick's could not accommodate all the Catholic children of both sexes who wanted primary education. Crolly continued to give active support to the Lancasterian school which served all religious denominations and remained on its committee of management. When the Lord Lieutenant, Lord Mulgrave, visited the school in October 1835, he returned to Belfast for the occasion and in his speech recalled how during his twenty three years association with that 'laudable institution' the various clerical members of its committee 'did not retard the progress of

[35] N.H., 19 Oct. 1833.   [36] N.W., 31 Oct. 1833.

[37] Rogers, 'St Malachy's College, Belfast 1833-1933' in *The Collegian* (1933), 13-29, and Dallat, 'In the Beginning' in *St Malachy's College Sesquicentennial* (1984), 36-40.

[38] At the examinations in 1834 Crolly praised the proficiency of the pupils and congratulated the town and the north 'on the additional nursery of enlightenment'. (N.W., 23 June 1834.)

education by comparing their creeds, or engaging in controversial conflicts concerning disputed points of speculative Theology' but rather
'agreed in recognizing the principles that "peace on earth to men of good
will" is the proper means of giving glory to God in the highest'.[39] And
because of this support and his comments about the scope afforded by
combining children of different denominations for softening animosities
he has been claimed as an advocate of 'mixed' or 'integrated' education.

But to depict Crolly either as a supporter of 'integrated' or 'Catholic'
education is anachronistic. In fact, to pose the question in these terms is to
suggest that he had a choice between these different forms of education,
and that was a luxury which he simply did not have. He was faced with
the problem of trying to ensure that a large and mainly impoverished
people, who were very desirous that their children should enjoy the
benefits of education, would be enabled to do so, but, above all, would do
so without having to contend with any form of proselytism, covert or
avowed. Until the advent of the national system, the struggle to protect
Catholic children from systems of education that were at least suspected,
if not convicted, of proselytizing tendencies, had been hard and persistent.
Had the national system not come into existence, he would probably have
tried to establish other schools like St Patrick's on the fringes of his
parish, despite the paucity of his financial resources. But that system
relieved him of what would have been a heavy burden. Throughout the
subsequent disputes among the bishops about national education and the
Queen's Colleges, he constantly emphasized the inability of the Catholic
people to fund fully denominational schemes of education. Rigid adherence to the principle of exclusively Catholic education would have
deprived many Catholic children in Ulster of any opportunity for school
learning. Far from being free to choose between Catholic and mixed
schooling, Crolly was obliged to make use of whatever kind was possible
or available, provided the faith of the children was safeguarded. His
options were extremely limited.

IV

Education was but one of the many problems facing the bishops of Ireland
in the first half of the nineteenth century. The restoration of the church to
a state of full canonical normality was another.

[39] N.H., 24 Oct. 1835.

It was for this reason that the bishops of the Armagh province met at Navan in August 1834 to draw up statutes for their dioceses. The bishops of the provinces of Cashel, Tuam and Dublin had legislated for their dioceses in 1808, 1817 and 1831, respectively. In Navan the metropolitan of Armagh and his suffragans compiled the decrees and then each prelate issued them officially to his own diocese to take effect a few months later. As the bishops subsequently explained, they had imposed scarcely any new regulations: they had faithfully followed the canons of the church and had added nothing apart from what they deemed necessary for the integrity of ecclesiastical discipline, priestly decorum and the increase of religion. In effect, they applied the legislation and spirit of the Council of Trent, and as Trent sought reform through energetic and committed bishops empowered to enforce their jurisdiction, the authority of the bishops in Ireland was enhanced by the more effective application of Trent. The statutes in Down and Connor took effect on 6 January 1835 and supserseded all previous laws and decrees.

The statutes contained much material which was exhortatory rather than preceptive, and which was extracted from various church canons and statements of the popes. The clergy were encouraged to lead lives of exemplary piety, sobriety and selflessness, to wear black clerical dress, to prepare their people for, and to administer, the sacraments with extreme care, zeal and devotion. The general suspensions, reservations, and censures of canon law were declared applicable in the diocese. Important particular laws were also enacted. The office of vicar forane was instituted; the diocese was divided into vicariates, or groups of parishes, which were placed under the supervision of the vicar forane, who was commissioned to watch over clerical discipline, ensure that there was no neglect of duty by the priests of his vicariate and report to the bishop every three months. The vicars were commissioned especially to note whether the clergy of their districts had given proper religious instruction on Sundays and holydays (to list the backsliders and the number of their offences); whether catechism had been properly taught in all the chapels on Sundays and holydays, and whether the clergy of the area had appointed qualified persons to teach, in each village of the parish, the aged and infirm who could not attend the instruction in the chapel; whether clergy or laity had given any public scandal and, if so, the circumstances and the means taken to repair it; which priests had applied for and had been given leave of absence, and for what length of time since the previous report; whether the statutes had been observed and what was the state of religion; whether there had been any conversions to the Catholic faith or whether public sinners had been reclaimed; and any other observation beneficial to the spread of religion. Vicars forane for Down and Connor were not listed in the Catholic Directory until the 1860s when the names of ten parish priests were given, most of whom were in charge of the larger parishes. Most of the vicariates probably date back to Crolly's time.

Parish priests were also supplied with formularies to be completed before each episcopal visitation of the parish. In addition to questions about the number and equipment of churches, each pastor was asked to list the number and kind of religious confraternities, the number of daily, weekly and monthly communicants, the number of adults who did not fulfill their Easter duty and the number of children preparing for first communion; the number of schools according to denomination, the names of the teachers and the number on the rolls; the number of public Masses, the time when the catechism was taught in the church and the names of the teachers; and, if vespers were celebrated, by whom and with what attendance. Both curates and parish priests were obliged to sign this statement and, furthermore, the parish priest was required to give the names of the most obstinate absentees from their Easter duty, the names of the public sinners and some account of their misdeeds, as well as other crimes such as illegal combinations, quarrelling, violation of the Lord's day, misbehaviour at wakes or Sunday dances, of which the bishop ought to have knowledge.

Careful regulations were made concerning matters about which there had been disputes within the dioceses, which sought to prevent dissension or bad example. Personal stipends were to be divided between parish priests and curates in the proportion of two to one; if there was one curate he obtained a third, and, if two curates, they received one quarter each. Priests were to form committees to help them when building churches and to deposit money collected for constructing or refurbishing churches with a trustworthy parishioner rather than retain it themselves. To avoid hurt or insensitivity it was suggested that dues should be collected not at the 'stations' but rather by two trustworthy parishioners appointed by the parish priest. Priests were also ordered not to engage in business and not to farm more than fifteen acres of land without the bishop's permission. They were also encouraged to make wills to avoid any disputes about legacies, and to distribute their superfluous goods to charitable purposes.

The 'stations' or visits of the clergy to certain parish houses to celebrate Mass and hear confessions from 29 September till the octave of the Epiphany were commended, but, to avoid burdening the hosts with the expense of large entertainment, priests were permitted to take only a snack after the completion of their services. Apart from confessions during the 'stations' certain days each week, especially the vigils of Sundays and holydays, were to be set aside when opportunities for penance would be available.

Clergy were exhorted to study, especially material of ecclesiastical interest, and were obliged to attend the clerical conferences at which theological problems were discussed. Penalties were imposed for those who missed two such without permission. Priests who violated marriage laws by officiating without permission at the weddings of couples from other parishes, or without publishing banns, were automatically suspended. And the threat of suspension was hung over the heads of parish priests who did not keep a register of baptisms and marriages; of clergy who allowed, through neglect, any parishioner to die without the last rites; of priests who demanded money for the administration of the sacraments; of priests who were absent for more than five days from their duties without permission; of priests who took part in hunting, horse racing or attended the theatre, dances, or without necessity drank in taverns; and of priests who aided or abetted lay people in shutting the doors of churches against the parish priest or curate or incited the laity not to pay their customary stipends.

Those who contracted clandestine marriages, together with the minister and witnesses, were excommunicated and the bishop's permission was required for the celebration of a 'mixed' marriage. Among the censures listed from general church law were those for apostasy, duelling and membership of the Freemasons. And among the usual sins the forgiveness of which was reserved to the bishop were membership of illegal societies and cooperation in any way in closing the doors of churches against the clergy of the parish. Down and Connor had been spared these particular problems but other dioceses had encountered them to their cost.

The last chapter of the statutes concerned abuses at wakes. The custom of the deceased's relatives giving alcohol as part of the hospitality traditional on these occasions, and especially the bawdy language and obscene behaviour of some of the publicity-seeking spongers who invariably frequented such gatherings had worried the bishops throughout Ireland for some time. Parish priests were exhorted to ensure that there should be prayers and spiritual exercises for the deceased during wakes, that no young unmarried people apart from relatives should keep vigil during night-time and that the episcopal prohibition on the use of alcohol be made known to their parishioners. This decree was an attempt to control the cadgers and exhibitionists who exploited the vulnerability of relatives of the deceased under the guise of offering sympathy but in reality to get free alcohol and win cheap plaudits for their antics from those present.

Most of the material in the statutes would have been found in the diocesan decrees of any of the Catholic countries of the world. The new regulations related to situations that had arisen as the church renewed and expanded its structures in the wake of the abrogation of the penal laws. The rules about financial matters, the keeping of registers, the celebration of marriages and other disciplinary matters only became enforceable when the church began to enjoy greater stability in society; in the eighteenth century, with a paucity of churches and clergy, the few priests there were in parts of Down and Connor had simply to make the best of the situations they found themselves in, and bishops could give them little guidance or exercise much control over them. The creation of the office of vicar forane enabled the bishop to keep in much closer contact with his clergy, thereby furthered centralized control and ensured that ecclesiastical discipline was more strictly observed. The one persistent abuse among the laity which the bishops addressed was that associated with wakes, and the eradication of misbehaviour associated with them was difficult and protracted.

Significantly, the statutes made no mention of Mass-attendance by the laity (apart from asking priests to list the names of those who did not make their Easter duty and thereby implying that neglect of this obligation was not extensive) and in view of the use made by historians of statistics collected in 1834 by the Commissioners for Public Instruction to claim that the practice rate of Catholics in the poorer parts of Ireland (or as in Down and Connor where the church was weak) was low, the absence of all reference to the fulfilment or non-fulfilment by lay people of their obligation to participate at Mass on Sundays is most noteworthy. Had the bishops believed that there was serious neglect by their people in this regard, they would surely have admonished their clergy to counter it as effectively as possible.[40]

V

By the time of Crolly's succession to Down and Connor many of the abuses that had crept into expressions of popular religion under penal

[40] *Statuta Dioecesana in Episcopo* [sic] *Dunensi et Connoriensi* [sic] *observanda, et a RRmo. Guilielmo Crolly, episcopo Dunensi et Connoriensi, in sua Synodo diocesana edita et promulgata.*

times had been eradicated in the diocese. Pilgrimages to places particularly connected with the lives of the saints had always been a feature of
Catholic devotion; in Ireland these exercises generally took the form of
celebrating 'patterns' or patrons' feastdays, often at holy wells, which
some local saint had blessed, either to eliminate pagan powers hitherto
associated with them or to attach curative powers to the waters for the
benefit of the sick and infirm. In the seventeenth and eighteenth centuries
these holy places, because of the absence of churches, drew crowds of
devotees either on the saint's feast day, May Day or St John's Day. As the
concourses increased in line with a larger population, the social and
recreational element attached to the visits to the shrines took on a greater
importance, so that pilgrims were offered not only the opportunity of
performing penitential exercises but also of singing, dancing and drinking
alcohol. Gradually the entertainment got out of control and pilgrim
gatherings ended with noisy and often quarrelsome behaviour. In 1781 the
bishops of the Armagh province decreed that all such pilgrimages with the
exception of Lough Derg should cease.[41]

By the 1830s, when the ordnance survey of Antrim and Down was
being carried out, this prohibition had for the most part taken effect. The
surveyors in Co. Antrim mentioned a well at Toberbilly in the parish of
Kilraghts 'round which the superstitious Catholics were accustomed to go
on stated days on bare knees and do such other penance as their church
enjoins but the better sense of the Scotch and English settlers had caused
the practice to fall into disuse'.[42] The wells at Struell, near Downpatrick,
had proved more durably attractive. The surveyors remarked that they
were allegedly endowed by St Patrick himself with extraordinary properties including that of restoring sight and noted that great numbers had
undergone the difficult penance on St John's Eve. Then after walking on
bare knees over stones they went to a bathing house nearby where thirty
or forty people of both sexes would bathe naked in the healing waters.
Whiskey was available in tents specially erected for that purpose in the
vicinity. However, the pilgrimage was in rapid decline as a result of
clerical determination to end it.[43]

Elsewhere in Antrim and Down the surveyors commented on the abuse
of 'patterns' or celebrations of saints' days, with the exception of St
Patrick's and St John's, and observed that the Catholic clergy had been
successful in some places in ending dancing, especially in public places
and on public occasions. The main public assemblages which attracted

[41] Moran, ed. *Spicilegium Ossoriense*, iii, 393-4.   [42] *O.S. Memoirs*, xvi, 125.
[43] Ibid., xvii, 50.

their attention were the parades of Freemasons on St John's Day and of Orangemen on 12 July. Cock-fighting and card-playing seem to have lasted longer as local forms of amusement. The only references in the diocese of Down and Connor to impropriety at wakes related to the parishes of Loughguile and Ahoghill where, it was reported, that 'wakes (in the mountainous parts) are generally, but not quite so much as formerly, resorted to as places of amusement, and various low plays and tricks are performed at them'; in Ahoghill the participants were also said to play trumps or Jews harps.[44] But the behaviour at wakes that drew this adverse comment was not confined to these parishes or the bishop and his successors would not have denounced it at a diocesan level.

The surveyors commented adversely on the degree of superstition they encountered in Co. Antrim (those responsible for Co. Down seldom took such matters into consideration). They claimed to find widespread belief in fairies, ghosts, witchcraft, enchantments and charms. Ailments of cattle and the production of milk could be affected by the application of spells. Bad luck or good luck followed the adoption of certain practices or the use of particular plants or trees. The removal of mounds or forts and the cutting down of hawthorn trees brought ill luck. These superstitions transcended denominational allegiance. Staunch Presbyterians of Scottish descent were accused of being as superstitious as their Catholic neighbours. The parish of Carnmoney, which was predominantly Presbyterian, was awarded top marks: 'in no part of Ireland does a more implicit belief in witchcraft, sorcery or the blackout, as also in fairies, brownies and enchantments [exist]'.[45] Some of the customs and practices that gained this encomium for Carnmoney originally derived from Scotland, and some ultimately derived from a common Celtic past.

It is very difficult to know how serious and sincerely held such beliefs were. When the surveyors reported that the parish of Carncastle and Killyglen was free from superstition, while it was so rife in neighbouring parishes, the likelihood must be taken into account that the eloquence of respondents, whether genuine or assumed, played an important part in creating impressions that could not be verified otherwise. Assuming that respondents were fully truthful and not exaggerating to 'cod the strangers', the question arises as to how such superstitions and Christian faith could coexist. The starting point must be that people in all ages are often inconsistent in matters of belief, as witness the modern atheist who believes in luck and the stars. And some of these beliefs, especially those

[44] Ibid., xiii, 65 and xxiii, 17.   [45] Ibid., ii, 63.

connected with cures for animals, probably originated in some primitive form of folk medicine. But that still left an area where official religion had to compete against usuages and observances that were deep-rooted and defiant. Episcopal decrees or clerical admonitions could not easily change attitudes which were not regarded by those who held them as antipathetic to religion. All the churches continued to fight against these tendencies and in two or three decades the tide turned against them.

VI

In 1834 the Whig government set up a comission to gather statistical information about Ireland to enable it to promote policies of an ameliorative nature, and in particular its plan of national education. The commissioners re-employed the enumerators who had taken the census of 1831 and asked them to return to the districts they had already covered to find out and enter in their lists the religious denomination of the inhabitants. They were also invited to consult with the local clergy, and the returns, when completed, were left open for public inspection in a central place in each census area. A commissioner came along later to verify them by oath and to solicit the help of clergy of all denominations in checking on the religious affiliation of all those whose names were listed. Clergy of the established church, who already had careful censuses of their parishes, were asked to submit them to the commissioners. Efforts were made to correct errors or omissions in the returns of 1831, and the figures obtained in that year were altered by the same percentage of growth or diminution as had occurred between the censuses of 1821 and 1831 to arrive at a reliable estimate for the population and its religious components in 1834.

Clergy of all denominations were also requested to give details of the services held in their churches and an estimate of the numbers attending them. The commissioners were required to note the principal service and the attendance at it but could add further details, if they thought fit.[46] Since priests were not allowed to celebrate more than two Masses and since many of them served two churches, it is often possible to work out whether or not more than one Mass was celebrated in a particular church, when such details are not given.

The response to queries of this nature probably varied widely accord-

[46] The statistics for Mass attendance for Down and Connor are to be found in the *First report of the commissioners of public instruction Ireland*, with appendix, pp. 192-235, 1835[45] xxxiii.1. 244-87. See also Miller, 'Irish Catholicism and the great famine', in *Journal of Social History*, IX (1975), 81-93 and Corish, *The Irish Catholic Experience*, 166-9.

ing to the interest of the priest and the value he attached to statistical information. The rounded figures given as attending most services point to general estimates rather than to any careful headcount. The commissioners in their report noted the difficulties of taking a census in towns where there was a large and fluctuating poor population often living in houses where each room was a separate tenement and who were frequently unknown to their neighbours and fellow-lodgers. This problem led to disputes about the figures produced for parts of Belfast.

When the enumerator for the Rosemary Street district of the town was being sworn before the commissioner, Thomas Drew, the minister of Christchurch, accused him and his colleagues of negligence or at least of having been incorrect. He pointed out several entries, which he knew were inexact, and claimed that some of those entered as Catholics were Episcopalians. Drew argued that a correct statement could not be made to the government, suggested that a new census be taken and added that an amicable arrangement had been made by the clergy of the town to do so. Crolly, who was also present, admitted that inaccuracies had occurred in the returns but claimed that such mistakes afforded no grounds for impugning the motives of the enumerators. He pointed out that he had proposed to the other clergy 'an amicable method of ascertaining the correct numbers of each denomination, but, somehow, the thing was not followed up'. Had this been done, he maintained, much trouble, expense and disagreeable observations would have been avoided. Drew went on to show that two houses had been mistakenly listed as containing twenty six Catholics and charged that Episcopalians were under-represented and other denominations over-represented in the returns. His colleague, A.C. Macartney, the vicar of Belfast, suggested that in some lanes wrong information had been deliberately given to the enumerators. Crolly did not complain about Catholic numbers erring on either side, and explained that most of the poor children not listed in the Donegall Street district were the children of parents who had been carried off by death, and who could not have provided the required information. He also pointed out that he had then the assistance of four curates, though this would not seem to have been a permanent arrangement.[47] And he added that services were generally not held in St Patrick's on weekdays but were held at St Mary's daily and sometimes three or four times each day.[48] Though the kind of service was not specified, presumably Masses were celebrated once or twice each morning and devotions were conducted in the evenings.

[47] N.W., 11 Dec. 1834.   [48] N.H., 13 Dec. 1834.

Despite its shortcomings, the census produced returns of denominational allegiance and attendance at service which, if lacking the accuracy of later and more scientific techniques, give a valuable picture of the church in the 1830s. It also revealed that the diocese was served by fifty four priests (in addition to the bishop) and as the population was 152,337 this means that there was one priest for every 2,821 Catholics. The ratio of priests to people in the Armagh province was 1: 2,805 and in Ireland as a whole 1:2,991. Down and Connor was somewhat better than the national average and considerably better than the average in the provinces of Cashel (1:3,188) and Tuam (1:3,675).[49]

Before considering the percentage attendances at Sunday Mass it is opportune to recall the law which obliged Catholics to attend and the generally accepted interpretations of it by theologians. Children who had reached the use of reason, usually assumed to be at about the age of seven years, and adults who were not impeded from doing so were required to keep holy the sabbath by hearing Mass. Theologians accepted that the obligation did not bind those who could not physically attend church, such as sailors, prisoners, the sick who were unable to do so, those who had to remain at home to look after the sick or children (and even servants who were bound to do housework). Two other reasons for justifying absence from church on Sundays have particular relevance in the Irish context: the want of decent clothing appropriate to one's station, and a distance of three miles or more from one's home to the church.[50]

Questioned in 1824 before the commission inquiring into the state of Ireland, a priest from Co. Clare said that his people were so poor, and a large proportion of them were in such a state of 'perfect nudity' that adults and parents could not attend church on Sundays together, but had to alternate because of the need to share their clothes.[51] As a county, Clare would have had much more extensive poverty than Antrim or Down, but many Catholic peasants and their landless and unemployed children experienced the kind of severe poverty which would have prevented them

---

[49] Connolly, *Priests and people in pre-famine Ireland*, 36

[50] St Alphonsus de Liguori, who systematized the moral teaching of the church in the eighteenth century, rejected the views of theologians who put the distance at two miles or even one. St Alphonsus claimed that the condition of the roads, the weather and other relevant circumstances, and the sex of the person were also to be taken into consideration when making a decision. See *Opera Moralia Sancti Alphonsi Mariae de Ligorio, Theologia Moralis*, Tomus Primus cura et studio P. Leonardi Gandé, 591-9.

[51] Malachi Duggan, *Report of the select committee on disturbances in Ireland*, p. 207, H.C. 1825 (20), vii. The crushing poverty of Killala forced the clergy of the diocese to petition parliament for grants to finish their cathedral and build a seminary. They pointed out in their petition that 30,000 souls were obliged each Sunday 'to hear Mass under the canopy of heaven', explained that of those who attended the second Mass in the towns the greatest number had borrowed the clothes of those who had been at the first. (F.J., 20 Jan 1834.)

from attending church regularly. Though it is impossible to estimate the proportion of Catholics in Down and Connor who lived three miles or more from a church, there is no doubt that it was significantly large, as the pressures of population growth forced families on to marginal land on remote hilltops and mountain sides. Improvements were being made to the principal roads in the 1830s, but the side roads were still rough and unfinished and the network of communication, apart from that linking the main towns, was still poor. For the great majority of Catholics the only mode of transport was by foot, and this was virtually impossible for women and children in wet and stormy weather, particularly if they had to negotiate boggy lanes and cross streams over which there were no bridges. Only a small proportion of country people could have afforded to travel to Mass by trap or horseback. The attendance figures of the 1834 census can only be understood against this background.

The parish of Shankill in the established church, which embraced Hannahstown and Greencastle, as well as Belfast, was credited with 22,078 Catholics. In the Catholic church Hannahstown was a separate parish, and since Greencastle was a few miles outside Belfast, the town was in effect a parochial unit with a population of about 21,000. There were four Sunday Masses with a total attendance rate of 9,000. If one assumes that children under five years of age and the sick and old were not included in this figure—a minimum of twenty one per cent of the total—the attendance rate would be of the order of fifty five per cent. However, in 1824 when a controversy broke out between the *Irishman* and the *Belfast News Letter* about the Catholic population of the town, John Lawless, the editor of the *Irishman*, an able and respected journalist, implied that the church-going population was in the ten to seventy year old bracket, and calculated that about 8,250 attended Mass out of a total Catholic population of 13,200. If there was a local rule which discouraged those under ten years of age from attending Mass (perhaps catechism classes on Sunday afternoons was regarded as sufficient for them) because of shortage of space, then the proportion attending would rise from about fifty five per cent to about sixty four per cent.[52] Very few could have been excused because of distance but some would not have had adequate clothing, and others would have been obliged to remain at home to take care of the young, the aged and the infirm.

A probable contributing factor to absenteeism from Sunday Mass in Belfast was the lack of sufficient accommodation in the two churches. The

[52] Ir., 6 Aug. 1824.

Catholic population had expanded enormously since St Patrick's was opened in 1815 and by 1830 a third church was greatly needed. The town had grown as a port and centre for industries such as brewing, distilling and tanning, and as a commercial base for the linen trade. The cotton industry which had also flourished around the turn of the century had experienced a slump after the ending of the Napoleonic wars and again in the late 1820s. But the establishment of mills where flax could be spun by machines, which dated from 1828, led to great urban expansion and the provision of more employment.[53] Belfast became a magnet attracting thousands of migrants in search of work, of whom about a third were Catholic. Shortage of funds must be the explanation of Crolly's inability to provide a third church. On a visit to the town in 1839 he spoke of a plan to build two further churches, and almost certainly he had something like that in mind since the late 1820s. But in 1829 and 1833 he had to undertake the heavy financial burdens of St Patrick's Schools, St Malachy's College and the extension of Friar's Bush cemetery, and during those years he was also heavily involved in the construction of the surburban churches of Ballymacarrett, Holywood, Greencastle and Ballyclare. Belfast must have had to wait its turn in the queue for the limited funds that the Catholic community of the town and surrounding districts could afford.

There is no way of estimating the numbers in the country parishes who would not have been bound to participate in Mass because of distance, because of the duty to look after children, the sick or incapacitated, or because of the want of decent clothing. Those aged seven years and less constituted about twenty per cent of the population; the aged and the bedridden must have constituted at least a further five per cent. At the very least a quarter of the total Catholic population, perhaps a third, could not have been present at Mass. If one takes this minimal figure of twenty five per cent as excused, and ignores those exempted for other reasons, the rate of attendance (based on the higher figures where two sets are given) in the parishes of Lecale (Downpatrick, Saul, Ballee, Kilclief, Bright and Dunsford) was forty seven per cent; in the Mourne group of parishes (Kilkeel, Lower Mourne, Newcastle, Kilcoo and Castlewellan), sixty four per cent; in Loughinisland, Drumaroad and Tyrella fifty per cent; in Ballymacarrett and Holywood thirty per cent. In Co. Antrim similar curious discrepancies occur. Rathlin Island had an attendance rate of seventy one per cent while Ballycastle on the opposite shore was as low

[53] Beckett and Glasscock, *Belfast, the origin and growth of an industrial city*, 84-6.

as thirty five per cent. The united parish of Culfeightrin and Cushendun had a rate of forty eight per cent while in Cushendall (Layde and Ardclinis) it was thirty seven per cent. The parishes to the north of Lough Neagh, Duneane and Drummaul, (Moneyglass, Randalstown and Antrim) had a rate of fifty per cent, but the parish to the east, Glenavy and Killead, had a thirty seven per cent rate. Ballymena (Ballyclug and Kirkinriola) had an attendance rate of fifty three per cent, but in Ahoghill and Portglenone, it was as low as thirty three per cent.

Records of stations are, unfortunately, virtually non-existent and so it is impossible to calculate what percentages of parishioners might have attended the occasional Masses in their local townlands. From the registers of William McMullan, the parish priest of Loughinisland, it is clear that during the months of March to June he held forty stations, but as his parish was associated with Downpatrick, Ballykinlar and Drumaroad in the returns, it is not possible to calculate what percentage of his parishioners is represented by the attendance figures at the stations.[54]

Is one to conclude from these figures that a substantial number of those listed as Catholics were *non-pratiquants*, or even *sans religion*? Had such been the case there would surely have been references to this problem in the correspondence of bishops of other dioceses where similar figures were to be found, and the *cris de coeur* of Archbishop Dixon about the situation in Belfast in the 1850s, when the shortage of priests and churches was regarded as a contributory factor to a low practising rate, proves that the state of religion at that time in the town was exceptional; had a majority been accepted as *non-pratiquants* in many of the country parishes of Armagh or Down and Connor, Dixon would scarcely have bewailed the failure in Belfast as forcefully and persistently as he did. It seems more likely that the great majority of those who were not included in the attendance figures were *pratiquants occasionels*, in that they would have been present at 'station' Masses in their own neighbourhoods a few times each year, been to confession during the 'station' season (which lasted about four months) and been to the church on some Sundays and for special feasts, and for occasions such as funerals.

When account is taken of some members of families wearing in turns the only respectable clothing they possessed to go to Mass or looking after the young, ill or housebound, the number of *pratiquants* is considerably increased. That would explain the comments of Bishop Plunket of Meath

54 McMullan Papers, DCDA.

who noted in his visitation register that in a few parishes the paschal obligation of receiving the sacraments of penance and communion once a year at the Easter season was being neglected, but for 1822 (the last year for which details are given) mentioned only one parish where some parishioners did not attend Mass.[55] And Bishop Michael Blake, who visited each parish of his small diocese every year and thoroughly examined the children preparing for communion and confirmation, had no comment to make about absenteeism from churches, even though the figures of the census might suggest it.

And the bishops who in their reports to Rome commented on the great crowds who attended the services of the jubilee in 1832, even in the poorest parts of the country, do not give the impression of dealing with a people, a large part of whom did not practice their religion seriously. The diocese of Down and Connor under Crolly was, in fact experiencing its 'neo-Tridentine devotional evolution'.[56] Structures were being re-established and Tridentine patterns introduced. Some of the rural migrants to Belfast may well have succumbed to the pressures of a hostile or indifferent environment and ceased to practise as their co-religionists from similar backgrounds were doing in the great cities of the continent. The likelihood is that for a variety of justifiable reasons people in country parishes could not attend Mass regularly. And the higher practice rate of later decades probably reflects the greater availability of churches, transport and dress. If those not included among the church-going were merely careless or unconcerned, it seems unlikely that such large numbers would have been sent forward for confirmation, or that the clergy would have received the support which they got to build churches and open schools.

VI

In May 1834 Crolly took advantage of a vacancy in Ballymoney parish caused by the transfer of its pastor to Loughguile to subdivide its extensive territory. John Green was appointed parish priest of Bushmills and the adjacent districts of Portrush and Portstewart and instructed to celebrate Mass in the town of Coleraine. Crolly was well aware that this order would provoke trouble with the bishop and clergy of the diocese of Derry. Priests of that diocese had ministered in that part of Coleraine

[55] Cogan, *The Diocese of Meath, Ancient and Modern*, iii, 440-3.
[56] This term is taken from Corish, *The Irish Religious Experience*, 232 and describes the restoration of ecclesiastical life and religious structures which he dates from the first quarter of the nineteenth century rather than from a post-famine 'devotional revolution'.

which lay east of the Bann for many years and regarded it as part of their parish of Killowen, which was based on the west side of the river. When Green indicated his intention of celebrating Mass for the Catholics of Coleraine on the following Sunday, he promptly drew down on his head an interdict from Bishop McLaughlin of Derry forbidding him to officiate in what he claimed was part of his diocese.

The clash of jurisdictions did not occur as suddenly as this measure might suggest: both bishops had seemingly discussed their rights and interests on different occasions and both had concluded that they were not free to alienate the possessions of their dioceses. So after McLaughlin issued his interdict both appealed to Rome to settle the controverted claims.

McLaughlin argued that Crolly had invaded his rights by having one of his priests minister in Coleraine, thereby creating scandal, subverting the legitimate authority of the parish priest and causing harm to the faithful. Crolly, after referring to the historical background to his claims, pointed out that the Catholics of Coleraine, not long after his appointment as bishop, had begged him to provide them with a pastor and not to allow the parish to be separated from the diocese of Connor to which it undoubtedly belonged. Accordingly, he laid these facts before Bishop McLaughlin of Derry but McLaughlin refused to make any change in the status quo. Then at a meeting of the provincial bishops he had suggested to the bishop of Derry that they should submit their claims either to the primate or to two of the other bishops who were present. But all attempts to get a local solution failed.[57] He also transmitted sworn statements from several priests supporting his case.

The congregation of Propaganda on receipt of these letters contacted Archbishop Thomas Kelly of Armagh and invited him to submit a statement on the dispute. To avoid complaints from any of the clergy involved and to act in a way respected by both sides, Kelly asked Bishop James Browne of Kilmore and Bishop William Higgins of Ardagh, both of whom were acceptable to the contestants, to accompany him to Coleraine to hear the evidence and inspect the boundaries. Their inquiry began on 9 October 1834.

The central problem facing the investigators was to determine whether the bishop of Derry was entitled by historical right or custom to exercise jurisdiction over Coleraine. After the plantation of Ulster very few Catholics were left in the lands near the town and with the scarcity of

---

[57] McLaughlin to Pope Gregory, 15 June 1834 and Crolly to Pope Gregory, 29 June 1834. APF, SOCG, 950, ff 209rv and 212r-214v.

priests and the restrictions on their ministry in much of the seventeenth
and eighteenth centuries there were obvious gaps in the pastoral care of
that part of Counties Antrim and Derry. Evidence of the jurisdiction to
which Coleraine belonged in pre-Reformation times was therefore of vital
importance. While the synods of Rathbreasail and Kells in the twelfth
century generally followed the natural and political boundaries then
obtaining in their demarcation of dioceses, there could be no guarantee
that all the land east of the Bann belonged to Connor and, in fact, the
district of Ballyscullion which adjoined the parish of Duneane, belonged
to the diocese of Derry, even though it lay east of the Bann.

However, at the beginning of the nineteenth century rolls containing
the returns of the taxes on the ecclesiastical properties of Ireland, which
had been originally imposed by Pope Nicholas IV and confirmed and
extended by his successor Clement V in 1306, were found in Westminster.
The vicar of Rathmullan, who had used the evidence of the taxation rolls
to justify a right of presentation in the established church, drew Crolly's
attention to their value in vindicating his claims to Coleraine. They
showed beyond doubt that the disputed territory was part of Connor in
1306. Crolly got an official copy made in London and authenticated by
the Italian chaplain of the Sardinian embassy, and John Green was
thereby enabled to identify most of the parishes which were listed in the
Coleraine area.[58]

Convincing as this evidence was, the Down and Connor advocates were
also anxious to prove that their bishop had never surrendered his rights to
Coleraine and that the Derry priests had ministered there only with his
leave and authorization. Richard Curoe, the aged pastor of Crossgar,
testified that Bishop Hugh McMullan of Down and Connor met Bishop
Philip MacDevitt of Derry in 1779 and that McMullan agreed to
MacDevitt's request that priests of Derry administer Coleraine but on
condition that his jurisdiction there remained intact. Furthermore,
McMullan had expressed the hope on that occasion that the Ballymoney–
Coleraine district would soon be able to support a priest. He also
maintained that Bishop Hugh McMullan's successor, and namesake,
Patrick, had often said that he would claim Coleraine, had his health been
better and were he not averse to law suits; Curoe also stated that Patrick
McMullan knew of Hugh's agreement and thought that Bishop
Theophilus McCartan, Hugh's predeccessor, had also given permission
for the Derry priests to exercise pastoral care in Coleraine at an earlier

[58] The taxation rolls for three of the dioceses with extensive explanatory notes were published by William
Reeves in 1847 as *Ecclesiastical Antiquities of Down, Connor, and Dromore*.

date. William McMullan, the parish priest of Loughinisland and nephew of Patrick McMullan, recalled a discussion with his uncle in 1814, when the bishop told him that he would not like to quarrel with Bishop O'Donnell of Derry but that his conscience troubled him about not claiming Coleraine. The bishop had also asserted that Coleraine came to be served by Derry clergy because of a shortage of priests in Down and Connor.

Peter McMullan, the parish priest of Rasharkin, maintained that he had carried out pastoral work in Ballymoney, Rasharkin, Dunluce and Finvoy from 1796 to 1826, when another priest was appointed to Ballymoney and Dunluce. He had often heard old parishioners say that the districts around Coleraine had belonged to Down and Connor, and that they had attended Mass celebrated by clergy of that diocese at Spittal Hill near the town. He himself and his assistants had also officiated at station Masses near the liberties. A layman gave evidence that the Protestant church in the disputed area belonged to the diocese of Connor and pre-dated the Reformation. Other laymen confirmed the assertion that Down and Connor clergy had offered Mass within the liberties in the eighteenth century.

Bernard McAuley, parish priest of Ballymena, recalled being present when Crolly asked Patrick Brennan, the aged parish priest of Culfeightrin, to which diocese Coleraine belonged, and Brennan had replied that his uncle, who was parish priest of Rasharkin from 1755 to 1795, had ministered there. John Green explained how he had prepared to celebrate Mass in Coleraine on the Sunday after his arrival in Portrush but had desisted when the interdict was issued. On the following Sunday he officiated in a hayloft, and later in his own room, and informed the congregation that he was to be their pastor.

The Derry priests strove to prove the continuity of their jurisdiction on both sides of the Bann. John Rogers, the parish priest of Kilrea, then aged seventy six years, recalled that his uncle was parish priest of Coleraine, and listed his successors there, all of whom he believed exercised jurisdiction on both sides of the Bann; he had never heard that they had been merely delegated to do so. Charles McCaffrey, the parish priest of Coleraine from 1802 to 1808, had heard with astonishment in 1807 from Bishop O'Donnell of Derry that Bishop McMullan claimed jurisdiction over the area east of the Bann. O'Donnell had asked him to investigate this claim, and accordingly he had interrogated the oldest parishioners but found no evidence that clergy from Down and Connor had officiated in the disputed places. He had never heard of delegated jurisdiction until recently. Patrick Bradley, the parish priest of Coleraine who was attached to the church at Killowen, explained how he had obtained and publicized the interdict, which was meant to extend to Portrush and Portstewart as well. He argued that Derry priests had officiated in these places from time immemorial. Lay people certified that they knew of marriages and baptisms performed by Derry clergy east of the Bann for a long time and about people who lived there attending Mass at Killowen in the west of the town. In all thirteen priests and seventeen lay people gave evidence.[59]

Bishop Browne was obliged by diocesan business to leave the inquiry after three days but Archbishop Kelly and Bishop Higgins spent eight days investigating the case and examining the boundaries. Before the end of the month they forwarded their conclusions to Rome. Kelly's was an admirably succinct summary of the controversy. Dealing with the historical background he pointed out that, when James I in 1613 granted the town of Coleraine to the Incorporated Society of London, he had extended its municipal privileges to a distance of about three miles, and explained that this rural district of the liberties was the centre of the dispute. The district had once embraced four parishes but because of the paucity of Catholics was then administered as one parish. The issue could be resolved by deciding whether or not Coleraine and that district ever belonged to Connor, and if so, whether or not the rights of the bishop of that see had been abrogated or lost by prescription or by the prolonged possession of the bishop of Derry. He then recapitulated the evidence from the taxation of Nicholas IV which he accepted as proving that the parishes of Coleraine and district formed part of the diocese of Connor.

He quoted the evidence of Curoe, Brennan and William McMullan of Down and Connor and of Charles McCaffrey of Derry, and accepted that Bishop O'Donnell knew nothing about the claims of Down and Connor. He also referred to various documents that he had seen from Protestant sources which indicated that Coleraine belonged to the diocese of Connor in the established church, and noted that this was valuable evidence since the Protestants had probably retained the ancient borders. The Bann was the acknowledged boundary between the two dioceses and Derry had no possessions to the east of it apart from Ballyscullion; this was the exception which proved the rule, for Ballyscullion had probably belonged to a monastery which was situated on an island in the middle of the river, and so came to be assigned to Derry. The liberties, which constituted the disputed area, were a mere civil division of James I. Authorities on canon

---

[59] The evidence is to be found in the Coleraine papers, DCDA, in O'Laverty, *Down and Connor*, iv, 237-249; and Crolly in APF, SOCG, 950, ff 216r-236r.

law were then adduced to show that the boundaries of a diocese, once delineated by legitimate authority, could not be altered by prescription.

Kelly characterized the argument of the Derry clergy that they had never heard of Connor clergy ministering in Coleraine as a merely negative one. In his opinion, when priests were few and distant during penal times, the people of Coleraine, with the tacit consent of the clergy of Connor, who were unable to look after them, attended the church of Killowen. Recounting the appointment of Green and the interdict, Kelly added that on receiving his commission from Rome he had written to Crolly to recall Green until the Holy See had resolved the controversy.[60] Both Higgins and Browne concurred with Kelly's verdict.[61]

After the investigation had ended Crolly wrote a long letter to Rome detailing the evidence he had brought forward, which, in addition to what was already known, included the views of distinguished Protestant historians that Coleraine belonged to Connor, and the fact that not only did the Protestant clergy of Connor receive tithes from the disputed area, but also that the wills of those who died in that district were probated in the Protestant episcopal curia at Lisburn. Moreover, before 1611 no bridge existed at Coleraine so the river of necessity divided the parishes. He also showed that the Derry priest had changed the interdict, at his bishop's request, from a personal to a local one, which extended to all priests ministering in the parts of Co. Antrim claimed by Derry, and that the bishop of Derry had admitted that he had made various efforts to settle the issue between them.[62]

When the cardinals of Propaganda met to consider the dispute on 26 January 1835, they unhesitatingly endorsed the conclusions of Archbishop Kelly and his two colleagues.[63] The pope ratified the decision a few days later.

The Roman verdict allowed Crolly to complete his rearrangement of parishes in North West Antrim. He engaged in the contest over Coleraine not out of a spirit of litigiousness nor as an exercise in empire-building. From the beginning of his episcopal ministry he wanted to ensure that the Catholics of North Antrim were adequately supplied with priests— something that had not previously been feasible because of the shortage of both clergy and financial resources—and this desire entailed the division of old and the creation of new parishes. The decision of Propaganda

---

[60] Kelly to Propaganda, 29 Oct. 1834, APF, *Acta*, 198, ff 68r-71r.
[61] Ibid., 22 and 25 Oct. 1834, f 71v.
[62] Crolly to Propaganda, 10 Nov. 1834. Ibid., SOCG, 950, ff 237r-240v.
[63] Ibid., *Acta*, 198, ff 65r-66r.

enabled the bishop of Down and Connor and the parish priest of Portrush to provide churches for the scattered communities of that district. Before 1834 there was a small church in Bushmills. New churches were opened at Coleraine in 1840, at Bushmills in 1846 and at Portrush in 1851.

VII

Crolly himself had experienced the difficulties of settling ecclesiastical disputes some four years earlier, when he was invited to accompany Thomas Kelly, then the coadjutor of Armagh, on a mission to Galway. Kelly was commissioned by Rome to act as peacemaker and conciliator among the bickering factions in the city of the tribes and to attempt to persuade them to accept normal episcopal jurisdiction.

For centuries Galway had enjoyed an anomalous form of ecclesiastical government.[64] The Anglo-Norman merchants and citizens who had obtained enhanced status for their borough from Richard III in 1484 also wanted a measure of ecclesiastical independence from the mere Irishry and this they obtained in a bull of Pope Innocent VIII in the following year. By virtue of this provision the citizens of Galway were exempted from the ordinary jurisdiction of the archbishop of Tuam and given a quasi-independent form of church government under a warden and eight vicars. The warden and vicars were to be elected by the mayor and corporation each year, and the warden would then institute the vicars and vice versa. The archbishop of Tuam was to retain some rights of visitation, but as the precise canonical relationship of the wardenship to the archbishopric was not carefully defined, abundant opportunities for strife lay ahead, and they were further increased by the expansion of the wardenship to include parishes outside the city, and later by the religious settlement of the Reformation.

When the corporation of Galway became Protestant, the Catholics, the great majority of the citizens, decided to maintain their privileges and met annually to elect their warden and vicars. The shaky authority of the religious leaders during penal times opened the way to internecine disputes and in the early eighteenth century conflicts arose between the secular and regular clergy over the revenues deriving from funeral services and 'Remembrance' Masses. A settlement was reached which was accepted for some years and some clarification of the archbishop's entitlements was given in 1733: his right to a triennial visitation and to hearing

[64] See Coen, *The Wardenship of Galway*.

appeals from Galway was recognized, and the election of the warden also became triennial. However, other controversies soon arose. Not only did the elections lead to turmoil, canvassing and charges about deals being done between the supporters of rival candidates, but strong antagonisms arose over the rights of electors. Members of the thirteen or fourteen ancient families or 'tribes' claimed the exclusive right of election, a right which the 'non-tribal' families challenged with mounting vehemence. Towards the end of the eighteenth century the secular-regular hostility flared up again and, though temporarily settled, always threatened to erupt. Rome was bombarded with petitions from the opposing parties, and the congregation of Propaganda was forced to devote a disproportion-ate amount of time to the dispute. In addition to the accounts which the congregation heard about the unseemly aspects of the elections it was also perturbed by the practice of the vicars transferring from parish to parish according to seniority rather than by any form of merit. Further complications arose with the election of Edmund French, a Dominican, as warden in 1812 and his appointment to the bishopric of Kilmacduagh and Kilfenora in 1824. Various commissions were appointed to visit Galway and report on the situation.

By the 1820s, as the disputes worsened, the solution that seemed most likely to achieve lasting success was the re-establishment of episcopal governance either in the shape of an independent diocese for Galway or in a union of the wardenship with a contiguous diocese. This resolution was canvassed at a meeting of the Irish bishops in February 1829 when four bishops of the Tuam province were joined by the warden of Galway and fifteen other bishops (including Crolly) in submitting it to Rome.[65] Finally, after repeated attempts at settlement, the congregation of Propa-ganda decided on 13 July 1830 to send Thomas Kelly, the bishop of Dromore, to Galway to try to put an end to the strife and confusion. Kelly was urged to seek to obtain the agreement of the various parties to the establishment of a diocese in Galway, or to join it to a neighbouring diocese, but, if that were not possible, to get the warden elected for life and to widen the voting rights to include the non-tribes.

Kelly was not told to bring another bishop with him but he obviously decided that it would be safer to have a counsellor in support, when moving into such a hornet's nest. He and Crolly arrived in Galway on 28 September and spent fifteen days in the city. They started to take evidence under oath immediately from all interested parties, questioning

[65] APF, *Acta* 192, ff 282v-283r.

both the secular and regular clergy and the leaders of the 'tribal' and 'non-tribal' factions. The clergy had by then concluded that only normal diocesan administration would settle their problems. Kelly and Crolly met the 'tribal' leaders on 10 October and put to them the damage being done to religion by the prolonged disputes; Crolly backed up this plea 'by a most powerful and energetic appeal' for a complete change in the system of ecclesiastical governance.[66] The 'tribal' leaders bowed to the inevitable, admitted that their ancient privileges no longer corresponded to any political reality and asked for a bishopric for themselves. Edmund French, the warden, who was also bishop of the neighbouring diocese, resigned the wardenship and also petitioned for a bishop for Galway. Kelly forwarded his report to Rome before leaving the city, pointing out that all parties had agreed to the establishment of a diocese. When he reached home he sent a further letter giving more details of the disputes that had rent the church in Galway and again recommending that the wardenship be made an independent diocese rather than form part of a union with a neighbouring diocese or with Kilmacduagh and Kilfenora.[67] Crolly also wrote to Rome to confirm Kelly's statements, pointing out that he, too, had heard all the evidence of the conflicting parties and had carefully examined all the documents which the bishop of Dromore had transmitted.[68] The congregation happily accepted all Kelly's recommendations and the cardinal who prepared the documentation gave warm praise to Kelly and Crolly.[69]

Kelly also advised that a non-Galway priest be appointed bishop and that he, Crolly and the bishops of the Tuam province should recommend candidates for the vacancy to the pope. Rome accepted all Kelly's proposals and on 12 January 1831 he and Crolly travelled to Tuam to discuss with their western colleagues likely candidates for the new see. They put forward three candidates and when the first one was appointed and refused, the Holy See appointed the third on the list.[70] With his assumption of office the peculiar problems of Galway came to an end.

Crolly's involvement in this tangled web of historical claims and clerical and lay intrigues was his first experience of dealing with a difficult issue pertaining to another diocese. His contribution to the success of Kelly's mission may have helped turn Rome's attention to him when an even more tortuous and byzantine situation arose in the west a few years later.

[66] Coen, The Wardenship of Galway, 166.
[67] Kelly to Propaganda, 13 and 22 Oct. 1830, APF, Acta 193, ff 563r-565r and ff 567v-570v.
[68] Crolly to Propaganda, Ibid., 22 Oct. 1830, f 570v.   [69] Ibid., ff 555r-558v.
[70] Coen, The Wardenship of Galway, 173.

The campaign for Catholic Emancipation had provoked strong sectarian feelings among some Protestants, both in the established and Presbyterian Churches. Opponents professed to fear the replacement of a Protestant by a Catholic Ascendancy, and Catholics, to defuse this hostility, insisted that they had no further designs on the constitution other than their demand for their rightful place in parliament. O'Connell and his followers were to spend their first years in the House of Commons endeavouring to translate the gains of Emancipation into reality by seeking to remove the grievances felt by their co-religionists, and, in particular, their forced financial support of the established church.

But before O'Connell tackled seriously any of the social problems pressing on the Catholic community he turned back to his first political love—repeal of the union. Though he set up a Society of the Friends of Ireland of all Religious Persuasions, which called for the abolition of duties on some household goods, as well as Repeal, it was the national political issue which he emphasized when occasion offered, as it did, with the celebration of the French and Belgian revolutions. But Repeal was an unpopular measure even with the Whigs who returned to power in November 1830, and O'Connell himself was later arrested and jailed for a short time for infringing the orders of the Whig Lord Lieutenant, who proclaimed his policy.[71] By 1830 Protestants of all denominations in Ireland had come to regard the union as the sheet anchor of their security and any attempt to break it was viewed with alarm and anger.

When O'Connell first made comments favourable to Repeal, after Emancipation, the *Northern Whig* remarked that, though Ireland looked with pride on his former services, she would not readily follow his suggestions in opposition to the benefits obviously flowing from her present condition.[72] The paper regretted the appeal, made by John Lawless at a meeting of the Friends of Ireland, for every county and city to petition for Repeal and predicted that it would weaken the work of the Society without providing the anticipated movement.[73] With the fall of Wellington's government the *Whig*, believing that the party taking office should not be deflected from a programme of reforms by demands for a measure that would be harmful economically, grew stronger in its strictures against a policy which, it maintained, was opposed by the wealth and intellect of the country. Moreover, it claimed that the Catholics of

[71] MacDonagh, *The Emancipist*, 34-9. [72] N.W., 23 Nov. 1829. [73] Ibid., 15 Apr. 1830.

Ulster, who had been expected to support Repeal, had not done so because they refused 'to foster a state of public feeling that would neutralize the blessings of Emancipation and involve the country in renewed scenes of distress and discord'. It then went on to declare (and emphasized the point by placing it in italics) that

the Rt. Rev. Dr. Crolly disapproves of the present anti-Union agitation; and we are authorized by the most influential R.C. Clergyman in this part of the country, to state, that he and his brethren in the North of Ireland entirely disapprove of the means now adopting to urge a repeal of the Union.

This was followed by an expression of satisfaction at being able to make that claim and of the hope that contemporary newspapers in Dublin would balance it against the illiberal and intemperate declamations of "the Irish Volunteers".[74]

Whether Crolly wanted to have his views publicized in this way may be open to question but there is no doubt that the *Whig* accurately described them. He always remained aloof from the campaign for Repeal even when that movement in the 1840s drew the enthusiastic support of the great majority of his colleagues and friends. His politics were and always remained Whiggish. He believed in obtaining redress for Catholics by cooperating if possible with the party that was disposed to ameliorate their conditions of life rather than antagonize it by supporting policies of which it disapproved.

The *Whig* also warned its readers of the danger of sectarianism. Describing Repeal as a preposterous scheme, it referred to the 'grossest attacks' being made on Catholic families by Protestants 'in this part of Ulster', and while not claiming that 'these outrages spring from the Union question' pointed out that 'the Orangemen may attempt to hinge their infamous proceedings on that measure'.[75] Orangemen had not been inactive since Emancipation. In Belfast in June 1829 a boxing match took place between a Protestant and a Catholic and, when the Catholic's supporters were returning home through Sandy Row, Orangemen fired at them and several were wounded.[76] Shortly afterwards Orangemen were accused of trying 'by every means of insult to excite the Roman Catholics to acts of insubordination' as 12 July neared, but the bishop and clergy were 'incessant in their exhortations and visits to those persons whom they considered likely to offer opposition'. The magistrates requested the Orange masters to refrain from parading, and though unsuccessful, the

---

[74] Ibid., 1 Nov. 1830.   [75] Ibid., 20 Dec. 1830.   [76] Ibid., 18 June 1829.

day passed off without serious violence.[77] At night some rioting occurred. The *Belfast Chronicle* commended Crolly for issuing 'the most pressing directions to all his flock, on no account to notice these processions, not to be offended at them but to keep within doors', and declared that 'had it not been for this salutary recommendation, it is believed that much more mischief would have happened'.[78] In the following year despite the Lord Lieutenant's ban Orangemen again marched but no trouble ensued.

The potential of the Repeal agitation for creating sharp division where goodwill had existed was further illustrated by the tough exchange between O'Connell and Henry Montgomery. The reformers of Belfast— liberal Presbyterians who had supported Emancipation—held a meeting at the end of 1830 but, while advocating some Whiggish measures, refused to endorse Repeal. O'Connell, succumbing to his weakness for heaping scurrilous abuse on those who disagreed with him, promptly denounced them as hypocrites and deluders of the people.[79] And when the Unitarians who had left the Synod of Ulster presented an address of welcome to the new Lord Lieutenant, Lord Anglesey, O'Connell, against whom a case was pending in accordance with the viceroy's proclamation, attacked them and, in particular, their leader, Henry Montgomery, whom he had lavishly praised a month earlier but whom he then described as 'a paltry and pitiful slave' and a 'fawning, cringing sycophant'. Montgomery in a lengthy response lambasted O'Connell's irresponsibility in forsaking the cause of reform, which 'wisdom, patriotism, Christian charity, nay, even well-considered selfishness would have pointed out' to excite 'a turbulent and insurrectionary spirit amongst the ignorant portion' of his country-men in order to aid him in 'propping up a scheme of agitation, equally bankrupt in principle and character'. In a hard-hitting personal attack on O'Connell for base insinuations against himself and his fellow Unitarians, Montgomery counselled him to give up his 'wild and impracticable projects', which could not succeed, as 'the virtue, the intelligence, the moral power of the country' were all arrayed against him.[80]

O'Connell's criticism of Montgomery did not deter priests and their parishioners from welcoming Anglesey and thanking him for his sympa-thy for their cause during his previous sojourn in Ireland as viceroy. Addresses were presented to him from the parishes of Antrim and Randalstown, Ballymena, Ahoghill and Portglenone, Duneane and Culfeightrin. The people of Culfeightrin declared that they could not refrain from expressing their decided disapprobation of those who, when

---

[77] Ibid., 13 July 1829.   [78] Quoted in N.W., 16 July 1829.   [79] N.W., 10 Jan. 1831.
[80] Ibid., 14 Feb. 1831.

ministers were pledged to promote peace, retrenchment and reform
'would by agitation, impede the progress of those salutary measures; and,
for a theoretic good, risk the existing peace and permanent tranquillity of
the country'.[81] The fear that Crolly and some of his clergy entertained of
the strife which a campaign for Repeal might provoke must have been
greatly strengthened by the reactions of Henry Montgomery to
O'Connell's attack. If someone who had persistently supported them at
great personal inconvenience could feel so strongly about threats to the
union, it required little imagination to picture the attitudes of the great
majority of Protestants.

As religious tensions increased in Belfast during the 1830s, Crolly
strove to reduce them by cooperating as effectively as he could with the
clergy and laity of all denominations in the organization of public
charities. He was very conscious of the value of ecclesiastical gestures of
goodwill and took every available opportunity to establish links with other
churches. In 1832 John Scott Porter was installed as minister of the First
Presbyterian Congregation in succession to William Bruce (senior) and as
a colleague of William Bruce (junior). Crolly joined representatives of all
denominations at the service, and at the celebration afterwards was placed
on the chairman's left. In reply to his toast, the bishop paid a fervent
tribute to the new minister's father, who was always foremost in the ranks
to protect the oppressed and 'to throw the shield of his advocacy over the
miseries and misfortunes of the injured and degraded Irish Catholic',
when the Catholic most needed it. Expressing satisfaction at the coming
of the son among them, Crolly then looked forward to a continuation of
that same spirit of friendship:

My Church commands me to love in my heart every man who has been received by
his Saviour; and to do my utmost to spread the works of charity, love, and mercy.
With these feelings, in my endeavours to extinguish the unhappy flame of party
discord, in my native country, I have always found the First Presbyterian Congregation most ready to cooperate with me in everything for the good of society. As it is
first in name, so it is *first* in the honourable and useful work of spreading abroad the
seeds of knowledge and liberality, and, if proof were wanting, of what I state, you
have it here, in the man who this day you have had installed over you, at your
unanimous request, as your guide and teacher in spiritual concerns. With him I
expect long to live in the closest bonds of amity and friendship; and I thank God for
the opportunity I now have of offering him my hand as the pledge of my love and
affection.

The bishop and minister then shook hands 'amidst the loudest cheers'.[82]

[81] Ibid., 17 Feb. 1831.   [82] Ibid., 6 Feb. 1832.

Unfortunately, this friendship and harmony did not percolate down to some of those in the pews and to some others who rarely, if ever, sat in the pews. Sectarian skirmishes at times with fatal results continued to take place throughout Ulster. In the summer of 1830 South Derry was the scene of much party violence. In July 1831 five Catholics lost their lives after an Orange attack at Katesbridge. Within Crolly's ecclesiastical jurisdiction violence began to occur more frequently. In February 1832 a Catholic was killed in a fracas at a fair in Crossgar, and in the following month a Protestant lost his life in a similar affray at Portglenone. In Belfast an Orangeman was murdered on 17 April and four days later a Catholic suffered the same fate. The Orangeman's funeral was turned into a political occasion by the presence of a large crowd of his brethren headed by Sir Robert Bateson, a magistrate and member of parliament. And Bateson and other magistrates subsequently caused offence to local Catholics and reformers by offering a reward of £200 for the apprehension of the Orangeman's murderers and £20 for that of the Catholic. The Catholic's funeral was also extensively attended, though the mourners wore white scarves, as was customary for members of trades groups, rather than party insignia. After the interment Crolly, who was present with his curates, addressed the crowd and begged all present to return home in an orderly and inoffensive manner. But several young men from Sandy Row attacked the rear of the returning procession and then those at the front rushed back to join in the mêlée. However, Crolly and the clergy, aided by the police and others, succeeded in restoring peace, though one man was severely injured.[83]

The parades on 12 July 1832 passed off quietly. Orange processions were made illegal by an act passed in August, but violence claimed four lives before the year ended. On 22 December the supporters of the Conservative victors in the general election playing party songs chaired the successful candidates around the centre of Belfast. A riot broke out when the procession moved into Hercules Street, where many Catholic butchers lived, and the police opened fire, killing four people. The *Whig* reported that the conduct of the victorious mob was most reckless and insulting, and claimed that the police in firing into a crowded street without the orders of a magistrate acted with 'a most unwarrantable degree of rashness'.[84]

Some of this violence may have originated in the tough camaraderie and macho ostentation that in other towns led to urban thuggery without

[83] Ibid., 26, 30 Apr. 1832.   [84] Ibid., 24, 27, Dec. 1832.

a religious dimension, and may have assumed politico-religious forms in Belfast because political divisions mostly coincided with religious affiliation. That may explain the attacks on Catholic funerals which reached such a state that the *Whig* complained that a deceased Catholic could not be carried to Friar's Bush cemetery except under police guard,[85] and which prompted the commissioners who investigated the state of the municipal corporations in Ireland in 1835 to refer to the 'melancholy particulars of the "Sandy-row riots" arising out of the unchristian practice of hooting at, insulting and attacking persons attending the funerals of deceased Roman Catholics'.[86] In January 1833 a funeral procession was approaching the Malone turnpike, when, according to the *Whig*, it was attacked by ' a number of the low blackguards belonging to Sandy Row' ('that infamous nest of ruffianism and party spirit'). Crolly joined a group that went off to seek help from Sir Stephen May, the sovereign (mayor) of the town, and succeeded in obtaining military protection for the funeral cortège.[87] Orangemen also occasionally damaged Catholic property. In April 1833 they burst open the doors of the church at Newtownards and kicked the doors of Catholic-owned houses. Crolly's own house, and the adjoining church and schools were attacked more than once and had some of their windows broken. He himself was struck by stones on more than one occasion, when he tried to put an end to riotous behaviour, and was once seriously hurt but concealed the blow till he got home lest the Catholics would be incited to further violence by the news of such an incident.[88]

A further indication of the increasing sectarianism in Belfast was the refusal to invite Catholics to conduct services at the Ulster Female House of Refuge, which was inaugurated in 1833. Arrangements were made for clergy of the established and Presbyterian churches to act as official chaplains, but inmates of other persuasions, who requested a visit from their minister of religion, were obliged to meet him in the presence of the matron. The vicar of Belfast, one of his curates and the prominent Presbyterian clergy, Henry Cooke, John Edgar, Samuel Hanna, and others were associated with this venture. In response to complaints that this development was contrary to the liberal traditions of the charitable institutions of the town, the secretary replied that the society was based on Trinitarian principles and that only clergy who held the same essential

---

[85] Ibid., 25 July 1833.
[86] *Appendix to the first report of the commissioners appointed to inquire into the municipal corporations in Ireland*, p 703, H.C. 1835, xxviii, pt i, 259.
[87] N.W., 21 Jan. 1833.   [88] G. Crolly, *Crolly*, lxxi.

doctrines in common would be permitted to officiate in the House of Refuge.[89]

Some of this antagonism may have derived from Crolly's activity during the serious cholera epidemic which claimed more than 400 lives in Belfast in 1832. Crolly, both in his pastoral capacity and as a member of the Board of Health, visited the hospitals daily and often remained for up to four hours, even attending to the temporal needs of the patients. Assisted by his curates who 'alone were not afraid to breathe the air of pestilence' in order to comfort the dying, they also received into the church some members of other denominations. Samuel Hanna, a professor of divinity in the Academical Institution, complained of the custom of giving conditional baptism to these converts but the bishop explained the Catholic belief and practice that obtained in such situations.[90] The numbers involved were probably small, but the story was subsequently exaggerated and a version, according to which Crolly and his curates pushed their way past Protestant clergy at the doors of the hospital to respond to the request of Protestants for their ministrations was subsequently publicized.[91] Had there been any element of proselytism involved, some of the Belfast newspapers would not have failed to milk the story for all it was worth, and their silence on the subject points to the inaccuracy of the subsequent account.

The sectarian feeling which was displayed at working class level often in street brawls was given vicarious approval and encouragement by the great Protestant rally which was held at Hillsborough on 30 October 1834. Though O'Connell had achieved little from his association with the Whigs before the Lichfield House Compact of 1835, apart from the reduction of the Protestant hierarchy by the suppression of ten bishoprics—the House of Lords had rejected a bill reducing the rent charge of the tithe composition to sixty per cent—these concessions were too much for the Protestant *verkrampte* of the north. So the Tory aristocrats of Co. Down joined the Orange leaders, second-level dignitaries of the established church and Henry Cooke in a public defence of Protestant interests, property and the union. Resolutions were passed declaring that peaceable subjects had been filled with anxiety and alarm at the state of the country, the doctrines propagated about property, and the way in which the laws could be resisted or evaded. The expectations that had been raised about severing Ireland from the government of Great Britain and the influence which dangerous and seditious leaders exercised over the government

[89] N.W., 17, 24 Jan 1833.   [90] G. Crolly, *Crolly*, lxxi-lxxii.   [91] W.V., 14 Apr. 1849.

were denounced, and the conservative tenet, that every concession that was made tended to advance the ultimate triumph of the enemies of the constitution, was endorsed. O'Connell, the arch agitator, and his Whig allies were savaged and firm resistance to agitation and terror was promised. The aristocrats pandered to the most atavistic Protestant fears of their tenants and labourers: Lord Londonderry declared himself ready, if necessary, to shed his last drop of blood in defence of Protestantism in Ireland. Sir Robert Bateson, having congratulated the sheriff on the splendid display of the rank, property and intelligence of the county, declared that they had assembled in the cause of liberty, truth and Protestantism—the Protestantism of all who protested against the errors of the Church of Rome. Londonderry explained that the union had been effected to give Catholics Emancipation but instead of being grateful for that boon they had raised the cry of Repeal, and as their first act in a domestic parliament would be to examine the claims of Protestants to their property, he asked whether Protestant tenantry would be prepared to surrender their lands. Bateson assured his audience that Popish Ascendancy and Popish domination had arrived. Both these speakers and others condemned the national system of education for its exclusion of the bible from its schools.

Henry Cooke, describing himself as a sample of Presbyterianism, predicted that, if the aristocracy were robbed of its property, the rest of them would be robbed of their liberties, if not of their lives. He rejected as false and foul the claim that Presbyterians were advocates of Repeal. Praising his brethren of the estabished church he expressed his hope that the banns of marriage, which he had proclaimed, between it and Presbyterianism would create an indissoluble union.[92]

Though opponents of this exhibition of Orange power were to charge that bailiffs and agents of the landlords had intimidated many tenants into attending, and though little sympathy was shown for the maintenance of tithes at the meeting, nonetheless, some ten or twelve thousand people attended, and thereby sent a clear and forceful message throughout Ulster about their determination to resist Repeal and concessions to Catholics.[93]

A group of 'Protestant magistrates, freeholders and inhabitants' of Co. Down, the majority of whom were Presbyterian and included the leading middle class liberals of the Belfast area, publicized their objections to the meeting in advance, highlighting the religiously exclusive nature of the

---

[92] N.W., 3 Nov. 1834.
[93] Ibid., 6 Nov. 1834, The *Belfast News Letter* claimed that not less than 30,000 people were present at the meeting.

summons to attend and maintaining that such meetings increased rather than diminished whatever dangers were deemed to exist. But the liberal Presbyterian element had become a small, if persistent minority, singing against the choir which had committed itself to other tunes. And those tunes were but a musical adaptation of Henry Cooke's dictum that every Catholic advance meant a Protestant retreat. Crolly, throughout his twenty three years in Belfast, had made every effort to get its people to march to other tunes, to those of Christian brotherhood and fraternal love, but when he came to leave Belfast, stronger and more discordant notes, reeking of suspicion, division and enmity were ringing in his ears alongside those coming from his well-wishers among the liberal Presbyterians.

IX

In January 1835 the see of Armagh became vacant by the premature death of Archbishop Thomas Kelly at forty one years of age. Kelly, who had been appointed bishop of Dromore in 1826 and coadjutor of Armagh in 1828 held office from 1832 to 1835. As he had not been appointed directly to the see, Armagh had not experienced a vacancy since the death of Richard O'Reilly in 1818. At that time there had been a long and complex struggle for the succession. The clergy did not want a priest from outside the archdiocese appointed but among themselves there was a sharp division between those from Co. Louth and those from the Ulster part, especially Tyrone.[94] Rome solved the difficulty in 1819 by appointing Patrick Curtis, the former rector of the Irish College in Salamanca, who was not a native of Armagh.

Since that time the regulations issued by Propaganda in 1829 limited the attempts of clerical factions to influence the decision by forwarding petitions to Rome in favour of their candidate. The parish priests of the diocese that required a bishop or coadjutor were authorized to meet and select three names in order of preference to be submitted to the Holy See. The bishops of the province were then obliged to comment on the three names but did not have to recommend any of them. The pope, however, remained free to appoint someone whose name was not on the list.

The parish priests duly met on 18 February 1835 in the church in Armagh. The senior suffragan of the province, Peter McLaughlin of Derry, presided and was assisted by James Browne, the bishop of

---

[94] Patrick Curtis, who became archbishop in 1819, identified three groups: Louth, Armagh and Tyrone. The Armagh group was, however, small and generally went along with the Tyrone group.

Kilmore, as secretary. Forty nine votes were cast: Crolly obtained twenty nine, Browne eleven and Matthew McCann, the parish priest of Dundalk, who was vicar-capitular, six. The other three votes did not count as only the first three names were passed on to Rome.

The eight bishops of the province would ordinarily have sent a letter to Rome commenting on the three candidates selected by the clergy, but they did not do so. Crolly, presumably because he came first on the *terna*, took no further part in the proceedings and did not forward any explanation of his reasons for doing so. But the second candidate, James Browne, joined the bishops of Ardagh, Meath and Dromore in forwarding their views on the other two. They ruled out McCann for reasons of age, health and ability. Maintaining that Armagh because of its divisions required a prelate of tireless zeal, great discretion and firm determination to propagate the Catholic faith and defend it against Protestants, they explained that the other bishops of the province held the same views of McCann as they did.

They then declared that Crolly was to be preferred to the other bishop because he knew intimately the divisions among the clergy of Armagh and—what was of great importance—the character of those who were encouraging that unfortunate disharmony. The great majority of votes he had obtained furnished a strong argument for the belief that the voters had judged him capable of uniting dissident factions and disposing them to fraternal charity. The bishops then proceeded to list the qualities and achievements which were recognized by their colleagues and the clergy of Ireland as equipping him for the burdens and honour of the primacy: strength of will; indefatigable zeal in preaching and converting Protestants, and in building churches; suavity of manner, prudence and learning; and they remarked that he had given many proofs of possessing these virtues in his own diocese. They then pointed out that after their discussion at the meeting the other three bishops had openly declared that Crolly was worthy of the archiepiscopal office but had not joined their brethren in writing a letter to that effect. The bishop of Derry had explained that he was engaged in litigation with the bishop of Down and Connor about jurisdiction over Coleraine and that, consequently, it would be improper to vote for a bishop with whom he was in dispute. No explanation was offered for the conduct of the other two dissidents, the bishops of Clogher and Raphoe.

These three bishops sent an extremely short letter to Rome, in which they made no reference either to Crolly or McCann. They simply stated that, they believed that James Browne, who had successfully and with widespread approval governed the diocese of Kilmore for many years was, given the peculiar circumstances of Armagh, a suitable and worthy candidate for the archbishopric.[95]

The letters, in fact, of both groups of bishops are tantalizingly brief. However, they certainly indicate that the divisions among the clergy of Armagh had again surfaced, though they do not specify how this affected the outcome of the voting. It can be safely presumed that McCann's six votes came from priests in Co. Louth; he was the Louth candidate for the office of coadjutor and then of archbishop from 1817 to 1819. A loyal coterie from the county again advanced his name when Kelly was appointed coadjutor in 1828. It seems likely that Crolly obtained the votes of most of the clergy from Armagh and Tyrone and that Browne obtained his from the Louth clergy. Each would have been better known by the parish priests of their neighbouring districts than the other, but as the split between the two sections of the diocese was approximately fifty-fifty, Crolly must have picked up a few votes in Louth. That Crolly was troubled by these clerical divisions is clear from a comment he subsequently made after his visitation of the archdiocese when he remarked that 'the Clergy are disposed to forgive and forget their past dissensions for the purpose of cooperating cordially in the important labours of the Christian Ministry'.[96] These dissensions were not as susceptible to oblivion as Crolly hoped, but, since neither party had its own local candidate in 1835, it had less reason to feel aggrieved at the eventual appointment.

As the submissions from the bishops did not conform to the decree of 1829 which governed the system of recommending candidates for Irish bishoprics, the congregation of Propaganda did not follow its usual procedure of preparing and presenting to the cardinals a *ponenza*, or case, for deciding which name to suggest to the pope for appointment. Instead a summary was prepared and read to the pope at an audience on 12 April and he decided to appoint the bishop of Down and Connor. The brief confirming this decision was sent to Crolly on 23 May 1835.[97] It arrived on 9 June and a week later the priests of Down and Connor elected a vicar capitular to take charge of the diocese until a successor was appointed.

It was probably on this occasion that the clergy of the diocese drew up a petition to the pope asking that Crolly be allowed to remain with them. Bishop Cornelius Denvir, his successor, subsequently explained that they had implored Crolly to stay as 'they feared religion might be injured by his departure'. This declaration of loyalty was 'universal' and 'unanimous'

[95] Bishops to Propaganda, 18 and 21 Feb. 1835, APF, SOCG, 950, ff 299r-303r.
[96] Crolly to Cullen, 18 Nov. 1835, AICR.   [97] APF, *Acta*, 198, ff 111r-112v.

and the resolution to embody it in a plea to the pope would have been carried out, had not Archbishop Murray, Bishop Blake and others prevailed on Crolly to request that the whole matter would be left to the pope's judgement.

Denvir's testimony that he did not believe 'there exists a more zealous, just and mild Bishop subject to the Holy See than Doctor Crolly, nor one who possessed more the cordial affection of his clergy than he possessed the love and veneration of the clergy of the Diocese from which he has been translated'[98] obviously reflected a widespread feeling. Otherwise the priests of Down and Connor would have been content with paying conventional tributes to the departing prelate.

The Catholic laity of Belfast also expressed their esteem for their former bishop. On 8 September a deputation waited on him at St Patrick's Church and presented him with a carriage, horses and a service of plate. In the accompanying address, which was couched in the customary grandiloquent language of the time, they paid tribute to his zeal and energy, his gentle rule and mild, conciliatory disposition. Maintaining that his life had been a perpetual rebuke to the calumniators of his religion, they praised him for ever looking 'with Christian charity and love upon those who conscientiously dissented' from him. In thanking them for their gifts and sentiments, the archbishop referred to their great generosity and explained that 'it would be difficult to conceive the sorrow which oppressed my soul when I reluctantly consented to be separated from my virtuous, loving and respectable flock'. However, 'yielding to the repeated request of my esteemed Brethren in the Prelacy, and obeying the directions of my Superior in the Church' he had suffered himself to be divorced from his native diocese.[99] This was not just a traditional compliment. Crolly did experience pain in leaving the parish and diocese where he had spent twenty three fruitful years. Writing later to Paul Cullen in Rome, he apologized for his delay in returning thanks for the good wishes on his appointment to Armagh and justified his remissness by explaining that 'if you knew the difficulties which I had to overcome before I was divorced from the Clergy of Down and Connor, you would not wonder that I abstained from expressing my thanks to those who congratulated me on that occasion'.[100]

Catholics were not alone in wishing the primate well in his new mission. The *Northern Whig* paid him a kind tribute:

[98] Denvir to Cullen, 28 June 1836, AICR.   [99] N.H., 12 Sept. 1835.
[100] Crolly to Cullen, 18 Nov, 1835, AICR.

It is almost superfluous to say, that he deservedly carries with him from Belfast the respect and esteem of all denominations . . . we can only express our general opinion when we say, that as a citizen of Belfast, his conduct for a long series of years, was eminently calculated to command admiration and regard. His uniform demeanour and exertions were well fitted to foster and promote good feeling among the different denominations; and his unwearying zeal in the encouragement and direction of our charitable institutions was as praiseworthy as it was beneficial to the town.[101]

Crolly left Belfast with the goodwill and appreciation of the Catholics and liberal Protestants of the town. His personality and 'ecumenical' activity had won him a host of friends and many of them remained faithful to him in the difficult years ahead, when political, politico-religious and educational questions opened up wide divisions in the Catholic community.

[101] N.W., 14 Sept. 1835.

5

THE NATIONAL SYSTEM OF
EDUCATION

The first relief act permitting Catholics in Ireland to establish schools was passed in 1782. Within a few years subsequent legislation removed the restrictions imposed by this act. But fresh difficulties for the Catholic clergy arose with the spread of Protestant evangelical societies at the beginning of the nineteenth century. They feared that the schools founded by these societies were proselytizing the Catholic children who attended them to obtain the practical advantages which their enthusiastic parents believed education offered.

In 1811 a religious society which was not so obviously proselytizing as its predecessors came into existence. The Kildare Place Society, which undertook to set up schools and grant aid others, and insisted on the use of the bible without note or comment, gradually established an impressive network of schools, appointed its own inspectors, compiled its own books and trained its teachers in a college in Dublin. In 1816 it obtained a grant of £6,000 from parliament and this sum rose annually until it reached £30,000 by 1831. At first many of the Catholic clergy availed of the funds offered by the Kildare Place Society but by 1820, when it started to give financial support to the other more aggressively proselytizing societies, the clergy grew more restive and hostile. Daniel O'Connell withdrew from its committee of management and some Catholic publicists, most notably Bishop Doyle of Kildare and John MacHale, a professor at Maynooth, began to denounce it vigorously in the press.

Faced with an increasing demand for education by their people, an inability to provide it on the scale required and the danger of proselytizing schools making further inroads among the children, the bishops petitioned parliament for a share in the funds which the Lord Lieutenant had been doling out to the evangelical societies. They pointed out that the Catholic Church did not regard as acceptable any system of education which separated literary and religious instruction and explained that the reading of the scriptures was an inadequate method of conveying religious knowledge and had to be accompanied by catechetical study and prayer.

The government responded to this request by setting up a commission to investigate the entire field of education. This commission, which for the first time had a Catholic among its (five) members, sat from 1824 to 1827 and produced, in all, nine reports, the fruit of its inquiries into schools of every kind, even including Maynooth College and the Academical Institution at Belfast. The commissioners circularized the clergy of both the Catholic and established churches about the kind and number of schools in their parishes, and consequently assembled a valuable dossier of information on the state of education then available in Ireland.

Archbishop Murray was invited to give his views to the commissioners on 16 December 1824 about the possibility of a Protestant teacher giving literary instruction to Catholic children, a Catholic teacher giving religious instruction separately to Catholic children and the extent to which use could be made of the scriptures in combined instruction. He offered no objection to a Protestant giving literary instruction to Catholic children, was enthusiastic about Catholic laymen teaching religion to their co-religionists, but stated that serious difficulties would arise from the proposal to make use of the bible in combined instruction. Instead he suggested that 'no objection would be made to a harmony of the Gospels being used in the general education which the children should receive in common, nor to a volume containing the history of the Creation, of the Deluge, of the Patriarchs, of Joseph, and of the deliverance of the Israelites, extracted from the Old Testament, and that he was satisfied no difficulties in arranging the details of such works would arise on the part of the Roman Catholic Clergy'.

The first report was published in 1825. It recommended the establishment of a government board, which would receive public funds to help found new schools and aid those that applied for assistance. Public money was not to be given to the Incorporated Society; the Association for Discountenancing Vice was to transfer its schools to the new board; and the Kildare Place Society was to stop adding new schools to its lists. Children were to be religiously mixed in schools under the new board, to receive literary instruction together and to separate for one or two days weekly for religious instruction. Two teachers were to be in charge of each school, one of whom was to be a Catholic in schools attended by a large number of Catholics. Arrangements were proposed for the training of teachers, the appointment of inspectors and the title and ownership of school houses. Accepting Murray's concession on scriptural reading for combined study, the commissioners called for the compilation of such a volume.[1]

When the bishops of Ireland assembled in Dublin for their annual meeting in January 1826, they discussed more fully the issue of education and submitted six resolutions, through the archbishop of Dublin, to the commissioners. These represented the fullest and most careful statement of Catholic demands that had yet been made, and probably reflected the principles which the more cautious of the prelates regarded as fundamental and indispensable. The bishops resolved, first that Protestants and Catholics could share literary instruction in the same schools, provided the religion of the Catholic children was protected and adequate means of religious instruction were offered to them. Second, to secure this adequate protection, they asked that the master or mistress of each school in which the majority of the children were Catholic should be a Catholic; where Catholics were in a minority a permanent Catholic assistant was to be employed, and both master and assistant (or mistress and assistant in a girls' school) were to be appointed on the recommendation or with the approval of the bishop of the diocese in which they were employed, and removed if necessary, by that bishop's representation. Third, they requested the establishment and public financing of a male and female model school in each province, as they considered it improper that masters and mistresses who were destined to teach Catholic youth should be trained by persons professing a different religion. Fourth, they requested that the books for the religious instruction of Catholic children should be selected or approved by the Catholic bishops, and that no book or tract intended for the combined instruction of the children, to which the Catholic bishop of the diocese in which the school was situated took objection, would be admitted into that school. Fifth, they expressed their view that any rule which required a transfer of the property of existing schools as a necessary condition for receiving parliamentary support would exclude the participation of many useful schools in a government-financed scheme. Sixth, they pledged themselves to withhold their 'concurrence and support from any system of Education which will not fully accord with the principles expressed in the foregoing Resolutions'.[2] The commissioners in reply pointed out that they were debarred from commenting on the resolutions, as they were obliged to report only to the king.[3]

[1] *First report of the commissioners of Irish education inquiry*, pp 1-102, H.C. 1825 (400), xii.
[2] Murray to the Commissioners, 23 Jan. 1826, *Ninth report of the commissioners of Irish education inquiry*, pp. 8-9, H.C. 1826-7 (516), xiii.
[3] Commissioners to Murray, 26 Jan. 1826, Ibid., 9.

Nonetheless, they pressed on with their attempts to provide an agreed reading book with a scriptural basis for the periods of general instruction. They planned to establish a few schools which would put their principles into practice and serve as an example for the rest of the country. To do this they believed that some form of non-denominational moral and religious instruction was essential for the general syllabus. The widely held Protestant belief that education without a biblical background would be at best secular and stunted and at worst pagan and corrupting, unfitting its recipients for the obligations of citizenship, was so strong and pervasive that they could not envisage proceeding without a book of scripture stories that would give satisfaction to all denominations.

Accordingly, the chairman of the commissioners corresponded with the Protestant archbishop of Armagh and Archbishop Murray of Dublin throughout 1826 in an effort to obtain an acceptable volume of scripture. The established church submitted a booklet derived from the Protestant version of the new testament; Murray objected to its exclusive and verbatim quotations from the authorized version.[4] He was invited to so modify it as to remove the objections of his colleagues to it, but replied that they were opposed to placing in the hands of Catholic children 'as Scripture, any book which is not conformable to their own authorized translation'; and he neatly supported his argument by quoting the similar views expressed in his evidence by his Anglican brother of Dublin. One of the commissioners himself then compiled in historical form a booklet from the new testament entitled *Christian Lessons*, and, though Murray approved of it after making what he called 'some trifling alterations', the Anglican bishops were in no mood for compromise. Arguing that should the Catholic prelates continue to reject every selection from the scriptures that did not conform to their own approved translations, all hope of accommodation would be lost, they declared that *Christian Lessons* was 'unfit to be adopted as the book of Scripture instruction' and dismissed it as 'meagre and incomplete in its exposition of scriptural facts, precepts and doctrines' and 'compiled with a manifest want of that fairness of selection which we are fully persuaded characterizes our compilation'. Bleak as was this response to a particular question they did not sign off without firing a shot across the bows of the Catholic bishops on the wider issue of establishing a national system of education: they claimed that the six resolutions of the bishops precluded all hope of agreement unless it was based on the bishops' 'own pretensions' and, if carried into effect,

---

[4] Murray to T. Frankland Lewis, 17 July 1826, Ibid., 12.

would transfer the 'superintendence of National Education', which was legally committed to the established church, to the Catholic clergy; and though the established church might 'be cast down from the station of preeminence' to which she had been raised by the wisdom and piety of her ancestors, still her clergy would not consent, by acquiescing in those resolutions, to become the instruments of her degradation.[5]

Confronted with the question which the prelates of the established church had posed about the willingness of the Catholic bishops to accept their compilation, if agreement on modifications could be reached, Murray reaffirmed more explicitly than previously the unwillingness of his colleagues to comply. He then made bold to question the policy of the commissioners in designing a plan for scriptural study during common instruction and suggested they desist from pursuing such a dubious and hazardous objective:

the Board has created for itself a very needless difficulty, by requiring as a matter of necessity, any scriptural compilation to be used in Schools for the purpose of general instruction. Were the religious instruction of the children confided wholly to the care of their respective pastors, what appears to be the only remaining ground of disagreement would be removed; and the rest of the plan suggested by the Commissioners might, without any difficulty, be carried into immediate and extensive operation.[6]

Had this simple yet sage advice been followed much of the controversy that was to dog a later scheme of national education would have been averted. Murray himself was fated to become the victim of bitter strife, much of which was provoked by books designed to convey moral and religious information during the time assigned to combined literary instruction.

A further effort to find a solution to the problems of Irish education was made by Thomas Spring Rice, the M.P. for Limerick, who succeeded in persuading the House of Commons to take an interest in the subject. The House appointed a commission to make a further study of the subject, which duly reported in terms that were subsequently translated into action. Unlike its predecessor it did not get bogged down in controversy about the provision of scriptural education during the periods of combined study; it ignored this question completely. It envisaged a national system, which would be run by a board appointed by the government and which would allocate the money made available by

---

[5] Archbishop John G. Beresford to T. Frankland Lewis, 22 Feb. 1827, Ibid., 22-4.
[6] Murray to T. Frankland Lewis, 19 Apr. 1827, Ibid., 26.

parliament. The board would print all books for combined instruction as well as those books, which had been recommended by the bishops of both churches for separate religious instruction, if it approved of them. It spelt out in detail how public money should be spent, teachers trained and appointed, and how time should be divided and allotted for separate religious education. It also recommended, as the Catholic bishops wished, that grants from the state to the various religious societies should cease.[7] But this brought down the wrath of the established church on the heads of the commissioners. The Tory government was naturally reluctant to grasp another nettle after Catholic Emancipation, and the issue hung fire until the Tories lost power. Inevitably, the Whigs, the party favourable to reform and the redress of Catholic grievances, would tackle the long-standing problem and in their second year of office they established the national system of education in Ireland.

II

The system, which 'crystallized into administrative form the ideas of an Irish educational consensus that had been forming for almost fifty years'[8] and was designed to banish even the suspicion of proselytism was not enshrined in an act of parliament but in a letter from Lord Stanley, the Chief Secretary, to the duke of Leinster appointing him chairman of a national board, to which was assigned control of the new scheme. Seven commissioners—Leinster, the recently-appointed archbishop of Dublin in the established church, Richard Whately, the Catholic archbishop of Dublin, Daniel Murray, the provost of Trinity College, Francis Sadleir, the minister of the Presbyterian Church of Mary's Abbey in Dublin, James Carlile, a Treasury official, A.R. Blake, and a Dublin barrister, Robert Holmes—were chosen as the first commissioners and were authorized to disburse an annual grant from the Lord Lieutenant to help existing schools and found new ones. Leinster, Whately and Sadleir were members of the established church, Murray and Blake were Catholics, Carlile was a Presbyterian and Holmes a Unitarian. The board was endowed with full control over the system but local bodies which applied for aid were allowed to retain important rights and duties.

The schools were to be non-denominational, but not secular. Four or

---

[7] *Report from the select committee to whom the reports on the subject of education in Ireland were referred*, pp 1-6, H.C. 1829 (80) iv, 443-9.

[8] Akenson, *Irish Education Experiment*, 59.

five days each week were to be set aside for combined moral and literary instruction, and the remaining one or two days, or a suitable time before or after combined instruction, for separate religious instruction. Responsibility for religious education was committed to the clergy of the various denominations, who were permitted to hold classes for that purpose in the schools at the appropriate periods and who would have control of the books used for that purpose.

The patron or manager was empowered to appoint and, if necessary, dismiss teachers, though in exceptional circumstances, the board could also call for a teacher's removal. The patron could also select the books for combined instruction, though the commissioners retained control over all books, in that none could be used for combined instruction without their sanction or for religious instruction without the sanction of the members who belonged to the same religious denomination as those for whose use they were intended. Gradually the board made available at reduced prices and (for new schools), free, sets of readers geared to the comprehension of various levels in the schools and both the price and quality of these texts ensured their widespread use.

To promote mixed education as effectively as possible, Stanley's letter laid down that the board would probably look 'with peculiar favour' on applications from the Protestant and Catholic clergy of the parish, from the clergy of one denomination and members of another or from parishioners of both denominations. An application bearing the signatures of representatives of only one denomination would be scrutinized to discover why the other religious persuasion was not represented. The commissioners were to require a register to be kept in each school in which would be entered the attendance or non-attendance of each child at divine worship on Sundays. And either by themselves or by their inspectors they were to visit and examine each school and report back their observations.

Stanley's letter was not made public until agreement had been reached with the future commissioners about its terms. In fact two copies of it were printed in the early years[9] and though the substance of both is the same there were significant differences on a few important matters. The first version to appear carried a proviso permitting the use of books containing 'such portions of sacred history or of religious and moral teaching' as met with the board's approval during the time set aside for

---

[9] The first version was printed in the *Dublin Gazette*, in the parliamentary papers of 1831-2 and in the report of the select committee on the national system. The second version was published in the annual reports of the commissioners from 1834 to 1841. (Ibid., 119-20)

combined instruction. Stanley had included no such provision in his original draft but was forced to add it, and at the same time compelled to drop the proposal, to which the Catholic members had agreed, that the Catholic edition of the new testament would be made available to Catholic children for use in separate religious instruction.[10] In view of the stalemate which the commissioners of 1824-27 reached in their fruitless and frustrating search for an elusive harmony of the gospels, one can only conclude that the Protestant clerical commissioners virtually forced Stanley to make this contentious addition to his plan as the price for their support and Murray was later to bear this out when he admitted that he felt obliged to tolerate the publication of scripture extracts for literary instruction rather than see his church deprived of the benefits of the system. It was a concession pregnant with misunderstanding and controversy and it undercut at one stroke the high-sounding guarantees about avoiding any suspicion of proselytism; theoretically, at least, scope was provided for evilly-disposed teachers to tamper with the beliefs of their pupils.

Other differences between the copies with less far-reaching consequences related to the visiting of school houses, the training of teachers and the supply of books for separate religious education at cost price. The commissioners were committed to refusing aid where local applicants could not guarantee a fund sufficient for the annual repairs of the school house and furniture, a permanent salary for the teacher, and a sum sufficient to purchase books and school requisites at half-price. Where aid was sought for building a new school, the site and at least a third of the cost were to be provided locally; in the first version of the letter it was laid down that the finished school was then to be vested in trustees of whom the board approved, but in the other version the vesting was to be done in the board itself. Schools for which only teachers' salaries and books were sought did not have to be vested. The first version made reference to the teachers for the new system being trained in a model school in Dublin; the second gave the board authority to determine the fitness of teachers for appointment before the training school came into operation.

With the establishment of the national system all state assistance to other societies ceased. In 1831 the first grant of £30,000 was made to the new commissioners and in the following year they began receiving applications for aid. Significantly, the third application for Co. Antrim

---

[10] Akenson, *Irish Education Experiment*, 119.

came from St Patrick's Schools in Donegall Street, Belfast, and it was signed by Crolly, John Scott Porter, the Presbyterian minister of the first Belfast congregation, seventeen Catholic and fourteen Protestant laymen.[11] These schools had been opened in 1829 and by 1832 had enrolments of 571 male and 512 female pupils.

The first two applications listed for the county came for schools of which Bernard McAuley, the parish priest of Ballymena, and Daniel Curoe, the parish priest of Drummaul (Randalstown and Antrim) were the correspondents. Together with John Lynch, parish priest of Ahoghill, they were quick to connect their schools with the board. In Co. Down the first applicant was Thomas Kelly, the bishop of Dromore, and within the first two years applications came from schools in the parishes of Lower Mourne, Bright, Kilcoo, Castlewellan, Loughinisland and Saintfield. These bore the signatures of Protestants as well, and Catholic priests and laymen were soon found adding their names to applications for schools in districts which were predominantly Protestant. Crolly himself joined Protestant clergy in soliciting aid for schools at Comber, Greyabbey, Donaghadee, Belfast, Ballymacarrett and Holywood during the first two years of the system's operation.

Crolly encouraged his clergy both by word and example to avail of the opportunities afforded by Stanley's plan to ensure that Catholic children, wherever possible, could receive the benefits of education. Though St Patrick's Schools remained overwhelmingly Catholic, the Frederick Street Lancasterian school was genuinely mixed, and Crolly had no anxieties about the spiritual welfare of the Catholic pupils in it or indeed in the schools of North Down or South Antrim where Catholic children were perforce a small minority.

When the committee of the Lancasterian School discussed the advisability of affiliation to the national system, Crolly was among the most ardent advocates of applying for aid to the board. He expressed his satisfaction with a plan of education that 'was based upon principles of impartiality, and calculated to include the children of persons of all denominations, without encroaching on the religious tenets of any'. The government, he argued, had now applied the principles on which the Lancasterian school was founded to the whole country and he observed that it would be indeed strange, if the school were not placed under a

---

[11] PRONI, ED 1/1/3. The commissioners responded favourably and gave a grant of £70 towards the teachers' salaries.

board that was 'so completely in unison with the plan' which had already been so successfully pursued.[12]

A year later, Crolly at the meeting of the subscribers of the school, in moving that their report be received and printed, expressed his satisfaction that the Lancasterian principle of respecting the liberty of conscience of all pupils had been maintained under the national system, declared that

the presence of the clergy of the Established Church, different Presbyterian Churches, and the Catholic Church at that meeting, was a proof that liberty of conscience had been fully protected, and that the system was calculated to afford satisfaction to all. He trusted that, by thus training up the youth of Ireland together as far as they could go, and then leaving them to separate peaceably, where they differed, a kindly and tolerant spirit would be awakened into them; and that the disputes and strifes that so much and so unfortunately prevailed in their country would be forever banished.[13]

And when Carlile was entertained in Belfast by the friends of the Lancasterian School, and gave an able defence of the system and of his decision to become a commissioner, Crolly approved of these sentiments and referred to the futility of contending about things on which there could be no agreement. Recalling his long association with the Lancasterian School, he observed that he had never felt greater pleasure, than in joining, hand in hand, with the Protestant minister, in binding the laurels round the brows of the young aspirants to educational honours and distinction. Carlile's public conduct was a token of the determination to establish in Ireland a system of education free from sectarian distinctions or political influence. When this would be achieved, bigotry would be 'obliged to hide its face, and superstition and darkness to fly the land'.[14]

Crolly's response seems to have typified that of the Catholic bishops. They were so happy to see public funds withdrawn from the Kildare Place Society and a scheme put into effect that approximated to their demands of 1826 that they were prepared to accept a fulfilment of their

[12] This school was established in 1811. In 1821 it applied for assistance to the Kildare Place Society and Crolly agreed that Catholic pupils, who had hitherto read the Douay version of the bible with notes attached, should use a Douay version without any notes or comments. When the school was connected with the national board, the Catholic pupils with Crolly's permission continued to read a Douay version without notes when Protestant pupils read the authorized version during time set aside for separate religious instruction. All pupils were led in this exercise by a teacher who was a Baptist and then all received separate instruction in their churches from their own clergy on a Saturday and Sunday. In 1837 there were 193 Catholics in attendance out of a total of 520 when a count was taken. (M. Cross, *Report of the select committee of the House of Lords on the plan of education in Ireland*, pp. 1152-66, H.C. 1837 (543-II), viii, pt ii, 414-28 and N.W., 30 July 1832.)

[13] N.W., 22 July 1833. A few months later Crolly joined a committee which was set up to raise money to help Joseph Lancaster, who was then living in poverty in Montreal.

[14] Ibid., 9 July 1835.

resolutions in the spirit rather than in the letter. Their most prominent spokesman on political and educational matters, James Doyle of Kildare and Leighlin, advised his priests to work the scheme, even though it did not fully realize their hopes, and warned that if bad men succeeded the present commissioners and tried to exploit their powers for evil purposes

we are not dumb dogs who know not how to bark; we can guard our flocks, and do so easily by the simple process of excluding the Commissioners and their books and agents from our schools. We might by doing so forfeit the aid which they would, if the supposition were realised, be entitled to withhold, but in withholding it they would be answerable to parliament—to which we also would have access.[15]

The commissioners gradually created an embryonic civil service through which they handled many of the administrative chores of the system—the approval of applications for schools, the distribution of grants and replies to queries about the regulations of the system. They also sponsored the compilation and publication of school books, supposedly geared to the varying stages of intellectual development of the children, and made them available at cheap rates or cost price to the schools. More controversially they published four volumes of *Scripture Lessons*, two from the old testament in 1832 and two from the new testament in 1834, which were designed for use during combined instruction, and 'earnestly and unanimously' recommended them to all schools receiving aid from the Board. The moving force behind this policy was James Carlile. It was he who first raised the question before the board was finally constituted and Stanley agreed to accept whatever the board recommended unanimously to him. A decision was then taken that the entire board would have to approve of the selections made. Carlile himself compiled the greater part of the *Lessons* but also received some help from Thomas Arnold of Rugby, from Whately and Whately's friend, Charles Dickinson. In preparing the drafts Carlile made translations from the original texts of scripture and consulted both the authorized and Catholic versions. He then sent the proofs to Whately and Murray, took their suggestions on board and then sent the revised version to all the commissioners.

In 1835 the commissioners decided to supply free stocks of the *Scripture Lessons* and from 1835 to 1837 most of those which found their way into the schools were provided free of charge. This generosity encouraged managers and teachers to use them more extensively and by 1837 some four fifths of the schools had availed of the free offers. The

[15] Fitzpatrick, *Life, Times and Correspondence of the Right Rev. Dr. Doyle*, ii, 346

Lessons formed part of the course for teachers in training where, as Carlile explained, they were given verbal but not doctrinal explanations of the texts and encouraged to teach as they had been taught, by confining themselves to non-doctrinal explanations to their pupils.[16] Some inspectors sought to persuade the teachers to use the *Lessons;* one of them reported that he used to state in the schools that they had been recommended by all the commissioners, who represented all the religious denominations in the country.

Both Anglican and Presbyterian clergy greeted the *Lessons*, on their first appearance with hostility, despite their authorship. Charles Elrington, the professor of theology at Trinity College, Dublin, took exception to their use of versions other than the authorized, and not only found the notes objectionable but also regarded the translation of many passages as incorrect.[17] Charles Boyton, a former professor in the College, maintained that the extracts contrived 'to put a leg under the Roman-catholic doctrine on almost every contested point, and the tendency . . . is to assert the Roman-catholic doctrine.[18] The Presbyterian delegation that went to London in 1833 to negotiate about the national system told Lord Grey, the prime minister, that the *Lessons* 'formed a most objectionable school book, and were more obnoxious to Protestants than any other part of the System'. They explained that their objection was not to the use of passages honestly extracted from scripture but rather to the notes attached to these particular extracts.[19]

Though the select committee of the House of Lords later reported that Archbishop Murray was keen to have a series of scripture stories compiled, provided they were taken from both Protestant and Catholic versions, presented in the form of lessons rather than in the question and answer form of a catechism and that they were equipped with notes not of a theological but of an historical, chronological, or geographical nature, Murray himself put a very different gloss on the origin of the *Lessons*. Far from wanting to have such scripture extracts adopted in the schools, he felt forced to tolerate them for the sake of preventing more harmful publications being foisted upon the Catholics. He explained privately to Paul Cullen that the *Lessons* were 'not what we would prefer but what we could not refuse . . . this being the only means within our reach of

---

[16] *Report of select committee of the House of Lords on the plan of education in Ireland*, pp. 16-18, 41, 186, H.C. 1837 (543-1), viii, pt i. 20-22, 45, 190.

[17] Ibid., p. 589 (595).

[18] *Report from select committee on the new plan of education in Ireland*, pp. 545-61, H.C. 1837 (485), 551-67, ix.

[19] Porter, *Life and Times of Henry Cooke*, 250.

displacing the Bible from schools, which had been hitherto inaccessible to Catholics unless the indiscriminate use of the *Sacred Volume* was submitted to'. So certain was he that Protestants would not settle for any system of education which did not contain some such compromise, that he believed that a formal condemnation of the extracts by Rome would 'render abortive all my endeavours to keep the education grants out of the hands of the enemies of our faith'.[20]

Though the silence of Catholics on the system was not publicly broken by any significant criticism, there was one exception, which, though then of little importance, had ominous implications for the future. John MacHale, bishop of Killala, who as a professor in Maynooth had lambasted the proselytizing societies, wrote to his clergy from Rome in 1832 giving it very lukewarm acceptance. He was disheartened by what he regarded as the disproportionately small number of Catholic commissioners and the control which the board seemed to enjoy over the books, which were to be used for religious instruction. Curiously, the feature that buoyed him up was its negative one: 'the disapprobation of some of the most rancorous foes of the religion of the people of Ireland'.[21] And indeed the opposition of the Presbyterians and to a lesser extent of the established church—for years it could afford to ignore the system—was undoubtedly rancorous, but was also well orchestrated and ultimately successful in bending the rules of the system to make it effectively denominational.

III

The Presbyterians launched an assault on the system on two fronts: its maltreatment of the bible and its discrimination in favour of popery. Most of the comment about the place assigned to the bible in the system was at best mischievous and at worst untrue.

The bluntest and most obviously false accusation was that the bible was excluded from the schools. The limitation of religious instruction to hours before and after general study, where the bible could be freely used, was often glossed over; and the exclusion of the bible from the combined instruction was at times presented as a general exclusion from the whole

[20] Murray to Cullen, 24 Dec. 1838, AICR. Walter Meyler, one of Murray's vicar generals agreed with this interpretation of the provenance of the Lessons . . . 'it seems to have been got up to silence the bigotted Protestants who are opposed to the system and who would say if such a book were not put forth, that scripture instruction was altogether banished from the schools and even as it is the book is a great cause of discontent to the greater part of them as being too Catholic and not given according to the Protestant version.' (Meyler to Cullen, 15 June 1838, AICR.)

[21] MacHale to the clergy of Killala, 9 May 1832, quoted in Akenson, *Irish Education Experiment*, 206-7.

system. Some Presbyterians, of course, wanted to use the bible as it had been used in their Sunday schools, both as a literary text and as a grammar, reading and spelling book. But the impression was given by some opponents of the system that the bible itself could not be used in the national schools—an impression that was as damaging and outrageous as it was inaccurate. 'The enemies of the Bible' declared John Morgan of the second Presbyterian congregation at the first great protest meeting in Belfast 'had shown a little indiscretion in their present course, for, by endeavouring abruptly to put it down, they had roused the public against them, and prevented that consummation which would otherwise have come about silently, but surely'. Not content with this inflammatory half-truth he added that 'he would tremble to send his child to a place, from which the bible was excluded, on principle'. Defining his philosophy of education as one based essentially on the bible, he insisted that 'to educate is to communicate religious principle: wherever this is not proposed as the object of education, that is not the object of education for my child'.[22]

If the claim about exclusion was too extreme for some opponents to pursue, the charge that the bible was being mutilated carried equally powerful emotive and atavistic force. The provision in Stanley's letter for the use of scripture extracts during combined instruction aroused Henry Cooke's most virulent ire:

Must worms of the earth *approve* of the Word of God, before my child will be permitted to peruse it? Must we be contented to take just what portions of it they will please to dole out to us? If we concede this to them, and they assume the power, then they make themselves the God of God. The moment a man *approves* of one part of Scripture and *disapproves* of another, that moment he constitutes himself God of God, and becomes an awful dictator to the Holy Ghost.[23]

When the *Scripture Lessons* were published Cooke presented them as a deliberate distortion of the contents of scripture engineered by the board to please the Catholics. Key passages were omitted, Catholic translations were used and selections were in general made to avoid giving offence to those who were opposed to the bible! In consequence, Protestants who desired to have only the word of God in its purity and entirety were deprived of their rightful share of their religious inheritance.

In an attack on Carlile, Cooke asked indignantly who it was that leagued himself with popery, and pointed to the Presbyterian commis-

---

[22] The N.W. editorialized: 'we may as well at once expose this nonsense. Mr Morgan attempts by confounding a religious with a literary education, to break down the distinction between them, and thus to impose on the public'. (19 Jan. 1832.)

[23] N.W., 19 Jan. 1832.

sioner 'as the man who puts forth the popish sentiment, making the woman, the "all hail Mary" bruise the head of the serpent by her son'.[24] The gospel of St Matthew had not been published because it contained the words, 'drink ye all of it' which referred to the cup in the Lord's Supper. St Luke was not published in its entirety, parts of it being altered or mutilated to suit the prejudices of the Roman Catholics. The *Lessons* as a whole were finely adapted for fostering popery in its worst form. By 1836 Cooke could declare that he hated the national system with a perfect hatred and felt obliged to enjoin his brethren in the Synod of Ulster 'to wash their hands of the whole unclean thing'.[25]

Moreover, the system not only tolerated, but actually forced them to encourage priests to teach religion to their children. That consequently made them guilty of countenancing the abominable doctrines of Rome to which they could never be accessory. Cooke, who himself had been taught classics by a priest and an ex-seminarian,[26] found this requirement of the system so evil that murder of the body paled beside it: 'it would not be so bad to encourage the commission of murder'.

Cooke and his friends also took exception to the control which the board exercised over books and teachers, condemning it for possessing a power and authority which it did not have: 'they will choose our teachers for us; and they will expel them at pleasure'. The days set aside for separate religious instruction were likened to the holy days observed in the Catholic church and vehemently condemned in consequence of this caricature of the truth. 'Among Catholics' Cooke believed 'such holidays were devoted to idleness and the contracting of evil habits' and the government, he concluded, had decided 'to give the Protestant youth a vast number of holidays with a view to the demoralizing of our children equally with the Catholics'.[27]

A couple of enemies of the board duly made the transition from verbal to physical militancy. In September 1834 the presbytery of Connor passed a series of resolutions against the board and ordered its clergy to read

---

[24] Ibid., 4 July 1833.
[25] Ibid., 17 Sept. 1836. At the meeting of the Synod of Ulster at which Cooke made these remarks, he related how a Presbyterian minister in Co. Armagh made several unsuccessful applications to the commissioners for aid for a school until he did so 'through the Roman Catholic Primate', when the application was immediately granted. Cooke affected incomprehension as he asked: 'Now, was it really come to this, that a Presbyterian Minister was spurned from the Board, until introduced by the Roman Catholic Primate?' On the same occasion Josias Wilson referred to a report he had heard about a friend being seen walking with Crolly in Belfast and described the incident as deplorable: 'Dr Crolly was a designing and dangerous man, and in his heart, an enemy to the Bible; to be seen walking with him, was an unseemly act, on the part of a minister of the Synod of Ulster.' However, the next two speakers deprecated these views.
[26] Holmes, *Henry Cooke*, 5. [27] N.W., 19 Jan. 1832.

them in their churches. According to one of these resolutions teachers were enjoined to oblige their pupils to hold fast even to 'damnable heresy', if they were convinced it was the truth, and children of Protestants could be dismissed from the school house, if Roman Catholic parents required it, so that the priest could inculcate the dogmas of the Church of Rome. Before the presbytery of Ballymena met, at about the same time, posters were put up calling for the adoption of a plan to prevent any schools in the district from being connected with the board 'which forbids prayer, and the reading the Word of God'.[28] George McClelland, the minister of Ahoghill, whom the *Northern Whig* called the 'Agitator of the Synod of Ulster', went on a tour denouncing schools and invading the pulpits of clergy who were favourably disposed to the system. His circuit of denunciation of the 'demi-Pagan Board' brought him through Carnmoney in Co. Antrim and Banbridge in Co. Down, to pulpits where he was not welcome in Grange, Ballymena and Belfast. Assisted at times by his friend, William K. McKay of Portglenone, they not only preached rabidly against the popish system but sought to intimidate fellow clergy by organizing marches with bands and leading processions of children who had been 'emancipated from the prayerless and unscriptual system' to bring pressure to bear on clergy whose schools had joined the system. At meetings of the Ballymena Presbytery McClelland and McKay denounced their opponents as 'liars', 'Jesuits' and 'deceivers of the people'. Mobs demolished or forced the closure of several schools in Counties Antrim, Down and Tyrone. Crosses and Ps for popery were painted on the doors of one school and the teacher of Tannybrake school in Co. Antrim was assaulted as part of the general campaign of intimidation.[29]

This campaign claimed other silent victims apart from those reported in the press. Carlile admitted that many Presbyterian ministers wrote to him expressing their approval of the system but explaining that they could not adopt it because they did not wish to subject themselves to unpleasantness from their congregations. Consequently, more laymen in Ulster than in the other provinces applied for grants from the commissioners. Protestant children were disproportionally represented on the rolls of schools in Ulster for which reports on religious affiliation were made in 1836: they numbered 15,760 as against 131,712 Catholic children.[30]

At an official level the Presbyterian church publicized its reservations

[28] Ibid., 8 Sept. 1834.
[29] Ibid., 25 Sept. 1834 and *Report of the select committee of the House of Lords on the plan of education in Ireland*, pp. 94, 681-2, H.C. 1837 (543-1), viii, pt i, 98, 687-8.
[30] Ibid., pp. 4-6, (8-10).

and set out to negotiate with the government and the commissioners to have the system adapted and adjusted to meet its requirements. At the meeting of the synod in Cookstown in 1832 resolutions were passed against restrictions on the use of the bible, against one Presbyterian member of the commission having control over books for the religious instruction of their children, and against the encouragement which the system called on them to give to teachers of erroneous doctrines to inculcate their faith.[31] In response to this the commissioners published a document specifying their authority in these disputed areas. They pointed out that they did not claim any control over books for religious instruction when a commissioner of a particular denomination checked those in use for the children of his co-religionists: they did not seek to interfere with standard works or catechisms but merely to exclude books that might contain matter that could be offensive or unjust to pupils of other religions. They reiterated the regulations about the appointment and dismissal of teachers and they pointed out that in non-vested schools (those towards which they only gave grants for teachers salaries and supplies of books) they required submission to their regulations only as long as these subsidies lasted. Permanent submission to the rules of the board was required in the case of vested schools (those to which the board had paid a substantial part of their construction costs). These clarifications did not induce the Presbyterians to accept the system. They made further approaches to Lord Stanley, particularly about freedom to use the bible at all times during the school day, and they then sent a deputation to the prime minister, Earl Grey, to seek this privilege as well as to divest themselves of the obligation of having to obtain the signatures of representatives of other denominations when seeking aid from the board. When the moderator of the Synod of Ulster was examined by the committee of the House of Lords in March 1837, and was asked if the principle that no conscientious Protestant could be a party to giving facilities to Roman Catholic pastors to teach religion to their children would not exclude any joint system of education completely, he replied affirmatively. He then added that he had always held the view that from 'the *heterogeneous* materials of society, religiously viewed in Ireland' it was virtually impracticable to bring all parties together in a combined system.[32]

---

[31] *Royal commission of inquiry into primary education (Ireland)*, I, pt i, pp. 47-57, [C6], H.C.1870, xxviii, pt i.

[32] *Report of the select committee of the House of Lords on the plan of education in Ireland*, p 215, H.C. 1837 (543-1), viii, pt i, 219.

Tortuous and byzantine negotiations followed with the commissioners and the representatives of the Synod interpreting each others' stand differently. The Synod decided to build its own schools but resources were insufficient to create a network of bible schools for all the Presbyterian parishes. In 1838 the commissioners made another gesture to the Presbyterians: managers of schools were permitted to arrange that religious instruction could be given at any time during the school day, provided this was publicly announced so that only children of parents who wished them to be present would receive the instruction. Negotiations were reopened with the Lord Lieutenant and the Presbyterians emerged with a substantial victory.

They were relieved of the burden of subscribing to the query sheet used by the board which asked questions about applicants from other denominations and access for clergy to the schools. Religious instruction, the Lord Lieutenant told them, could be given during school hours and no children whose parents objected were obliged to attend it; this interpretation placed the onus of excluding the children not on the manager or teachers but on the parent. A test case was submitted for Correen school at Broughshane, in the parish of Cooke's friend and mentor, Robert Stewart. It was non-vested, religious instruction was not limited to hours before or after general instruction and no child whose parents objected was required to take it. A grant towards the teachers salary and a supply of books were given on these terms.[33]

So by 1840 Presbyterians had in effect turned non-vested schools into denominational schools. As long as they could find the money to build the schools they could take advantage of the system to obtain teachers' salaries and supplies of books for schools where religious instruction could be given at any hour and to which priests *ex officio* had no right of access.

IV

The established church reacted to the system with the same passionate anger and determined hostility as the Presbyterians. A further ingredient in its mix of bitter feelings was a sense of betrayal. As the official church

[33] Correen School, founded in 1818, was built by private subscriptions and a grant from the Kildare Place Society. The school was open to the public at all times and anyone was free to inspect the registers and check if the regulations were being properly observed, but no one, apart from members of the committee and officers of the board, was permitted, ex officio, to interfere in the business or management of the school. This meant that if Catholic children attended they were free to leave during the time set aside for religious instruction and receive it elsewhere; no priest had a right to teach them in the school. *Copies of any applications made by clergymen of the synod of Ulster*, pp. 371-2 H.C. 1840 (110), xl.

of the country it had been entrusted with responsibility for education at all levels for the past three hundred years. It assumed that it was being deprived of its rights and to make matters worse this cruel attack came in the wake of Catholic Emancipation and amidst rumours and predictions of further restrictions on its influence and income. The presence of Archbishop Whately on the board of commissioners did not assuage the hostility of the clergy towards a plan of education which they regarded as unjust and harmful

At a large public meeting held in Dublin on 10 January 1832, the dean of Ardagh declared that the system would endow the bishop of Rome with jurisdiction in Britain and Ireland in direct contradiction of the thirty nine articles, and so he entered his protest 'against the moral and literary education of the rising generation of Protestants being placed under the Bishop of Rome, or that he should have a legal claim to interfere in that education'. As a conspiracy against the bible, and a blasphemy against the Word of God, no words were adequate to describe the evils of the national system. Yet Joseph Singer, a fellow of Trinity College, made a brilliant and colourful effort to do justice to the iniquity foisted upon them:

Is it not too true, written in characters of blood that the Roman Catholic priesthood are opposed to scriptural education? . . . Who has not heard of the denunciation in the chapel, of the curse from the altar, of the refusal of the rites of the Church, of the nameless, shapeless terrors directed against the unhappy victims of superstition and Priestly influence, who may have offended by seeking to introduce their offspring to a knowledge of their Saviour? . . . in many parts of the country the peasantry know not that there is such a book as the New Testament, and others have thought that the Bible was a Protestant book and written by Luther. Nay, in one instance, in the language of a late Popish Bull, the Bible was declared to have been written by the Devil.[34]

Other opponents of the system pointed out that it limited their right and duty to bring the light of truth to Catholic peasants, and forced them to cooperate in the management of schools with those who purveyed superstition and idolatry. The most serious attack was launched by seventeen of the twenty two bishops, headed by Archbishop Beresford of Armagh. They declared that they were willing to forego the advantage of state support for education rather than approve a plan which 'in rigidly excluding the Scriptures from the common schools, would introduce in their place books of religious and literary instruction, in the choice of which they are permitted to exercise neither judgment nor control'. They explained that 'the measure, in the same proposition that it lends to

[34] N.W., 16 Jan. 1832.

remove the clergy of the Established Church from the high position in which they now stand, virtually transfers to the Roman Catholic Priesthood that preference and that preponderating influence, which have been hitherto assigned to the purity and authority of religious truth'. And they encouraged their clergy to support their own schools.[35]

Landlords, who were almost exclusively Anglican, refused in many cases to sell sites for the establishment of schools, and in some cases combined to prevent their tenants from sending their children to the national schools.

Church of Ireland spokesmen also matched the vehemence of Presbyterian criticisms of the power enjoyed by the board over books, teachers and inspectors. Archbishop Whately was left in lonely isolation to fight the commissioners' battle within his church and, saddled with the twin handicaps of being a Whig and an Englishman, his contribution was less than impressive. Whately's episcopal brethren sponsored petitions to parliament against the system and summoned to their aid the anti-papist evangelical zealots associated with Exeter Hall in London.

Though the irreconcilables did not force the government to restore the primacy in educational matters to the established church, they did succeed in discouraging Anglicans from making use of the system and in distancing the church, already sore at the reduction of its sees and tithes as a result of Whig legislation in 1833 and 1838, from the government. The anger of Tories and Orangemen at the interference with grand juries by Thomas Drummond, the under-secretary at Dublin Castle, who insisted on property fulfilling its duties as well as claiming its rights, assured the church of a staunch and sturdy ally in its struggle. But the very extent of the Anglicans' demand precluded agreement without the overthrow of the entire system. Consequently, the church, forced back into a corner, decided to found its own educational system and in 1839 the Church Education Society was launched. Patronized by the majority of church dignitaries and by some of the most prominent and influential aristocrats, the society set about collecting funds and establishing its own schools. These schools were open to children of all faiths, and, though only those of the established church studied the catechisms and doctrinal textbooks, all were obliged to read the scriptures in the authorized version. By the end of the first decade of its existence the Church Education Society had about a quarter of the number of pupils of the national system on its rolls, and of these about a third were Catholics.[36]

[35] B.N.L., 16 Mar. 1832.   [36] Akenson, *Irish Education Experiment*, 198-9.

V

During the first six years of its existence the national system seemed to be giving every satisfaction to the bishops and clergy of the Catholic church. Throughout the country there was a steady and fairly uniform rise in applications for aid and the general expansion of the network of national schools in Catholic parishes could have been safely predicted. Then, suddenly and unexpectedly, the clouds burst as the formidable archbishop of Tuam, John MacHale, launched a massive assault on the operation of the system and the motivation of the government in funding it. For almost twenty years MacHale had fought his corner in the press against perceived injustices to Catholics with powerful eloquence and matching vigour. A convinced Anglophobe, he suspected perfidy behind virtually all the measures proposed by the British government for Ireland and was always ready to lead uncomprising resistance to them. Never one to understate his case or cramp his style by scrupulous attention to details that could upset the broad sweep of his canvas, MacHale's deep distrust of any policy or proposal that threatened to curtail his jurisdiction found an ideal outlet in the national system. He opened his campaign on 1 January 1838 with a broadside to Lord John Russell, the prime minister, in which he complained bitterly that the government, through the agency of its board of education, was usurping the right to select the books, even for religious instruction, of the Irish people, and denounced this interference as an invasion of the right which belonged only to the pope and himself—the right to determine which books the children of his diocese would use for their religious education.[37]

The next skirmish took place at the annual general meeting of the bishops on 3 February. Archbishop Murray was ill and could not attend. Though Bishop Higgins of Ardagh, who was to remain MacHale's most doughty and loyal lieutenant throughout several campaigns in the 1840s, privately claimed the credit for alerting his colleagues to the danger that the system, unless well watched, could undermine the authority of the clergy and ultimately introduce either positive errors or indifferentism,[38] it was MacHale's onslaught on the system that made most impact on the

[37] D.E.P., 1 Jan. 1838.
[38] Higgins to Cullen, 10 Mar. 1838, AICR, Higgins later claimed that he had written to Archbishop Curtis of Armagh setting out his objections to the national system soon after it was established. Experience had since vindicated his fears. Presumably his objections in 1839 were the same as in 1831: episcopal authority was being usurped by laymen and heretics; the distinctive dogmas of Catholicism were omitted from the school books and latitudinarianism was being treacherously instilled into the minds of the children. (Higgins to Cullen, 3 Jan. 1839, AICR.)

assembled prelates, as they had much more reason to fear the reverberations of his opposition. Apart from Higgins, no other bishop seems to
have supported his line, but nothing daunted, he decided to carry his
campaign to the highest level.

Before doing so he launched a series of strongly denunciatory letters to
Lord John Russell in the press. A few days after the first of these was
published Crolly attempted to mend the church's diplomatic fences with
Lord Mulgrave, the Lord Lieutenant, by disowning MacHale's campaign.
Mulgrave later explained to Lord John Russell that Crolly had dined with
him and had 'volunteered his entire disapprobation of it'. The primate
further insisted that MacHale, whom he described as '*our* bishop of
Exeter', was expressing only personal opinions which were not representative of the views of the Irish bishops.[39] On 24 February MacHale wrote to
the pope and, having referred to the confidence with which the people of
Killala diocese looked to the Holy See for a remedy for the evils that
afflicted them, declared that it was with no less confidence that he trusted
to the pope's protection from the duplicity with which the British
government was trying to destroy the faith in Ireland. He explained that,
though government ministers proclaimed their friendly intentions, they
refused to allocate money for separate education but gave it for mixed
education, in which each denomination read the scriptures separately, but
all were recommended to read together scripture extracts which were
taken partly from a Catholic version and partly from an heretical one,
especially on matters of doctrinal dispute. Allegedly for reasons of honour
and justice but in reality for purposes of deception, a few Catholics were
placed on the mainly Protestant commission which selected all books,
including religious ones for the schools, and only the bishops chosen by
the government for the commission and not those appointed by the Holy
See were entrusted with choosing books for use in religious education.
Teachers were required to train in a normal school, where both Catholic
and Protestant came under the influence of a Calvinist rector who, though
obliged to keep silent on questions of dogma, had been found to corrupt
their minds by interpretations of scripture harmful to faith and morals.
The atrocious persecutions of the past had ended but by these perfidious
means the enemies of the faith were striving to subvert the Catholic

---

[39] Henry Philpotts, the Anglican bishop of Exeter, was an extreme Protestant evangelical. (Mulgrave to
Lord John Russell, 18 Feb. 1838, PRO 30/22/3A, ff 130-1.)

John Hamilton, Archbishop Murray's part-time secretary, also made a critical comment on MacHale's
letter: 'The Bishops are quite displeased at its being thought to embrace their sentiments which are far
different from it' . . . (Hamilton to Cullen, 20 Feb. 1838, AICR.)

church.[40] The bishops had been too credulous and had permitted the system to continue, fearing that no grants would be made available for separate schools, but if all Catholics, both clerical and lay, were to oppose the corrupting influences of mixed education, the British government would undoubtedly grant money for separate education.[41]

Considering the gravity of the charges this letter was remarkably short. But if it lacked detail it compensated for such omissions by the simplicity and force of the accusations made about the *Scripture Lessons* and the dangers involved in teacher training. Nothing was more likely to set off alarm bells in Rome than a report of yet further inroads being made on the education of Catholic youth by schools that were purportedly neutral to, or indifferent about, religion. Forms of state or mixed education in Germany, France and Holland were then being widely blamed for producing not only an irreligious but also an anti-religious and revolutionary class.[42] Enclosing this letter in one to Paul Cullen, the rector of the Irish College in Rome and agent for the Irish bishops at the Holy See, MacHale merely recalled his disapprobation of the system in 1831, remarked that it had since become more obnoxious and expressed his belief that Archbishop Murray did not see the extent of its danger though many other bishops, and especially Higgins, were 'now alive to its mischief'.[43]

Confronted with such a serious accusation of religious hostility on the part of 'perfidious Albion' and, by implication, of negligence on the part of other bishops, especially the archbishop of Dublin, the pope ordered the congregation of Propaganda to write to both MacHale and Murray for more detailed information. MacHale sent three letters in reply to Propaganda, in which he repeated his general objections to the system, but which were mainly devoted to the *Scripture Lessons*, copies of which he

---

[40] Privately, MacHale confided to Cullen that the national system posed greater danger to the faith than past persecutions: 'It is my solemn belief that we have now more to fear for the purity of our faith than in former periods of more bitter persecution. The government is labouring to effect by fraud and wiles what past ones could not achieve by force and to supersede the authority of the local pastors and to place, the entire education of the people in bodies over which they may exercise absolute control'. (MacHale to Cullen, 19 Apr. 1838. AICR.)

[41] MacHale to Pope Gregory XVI, 24 Feb. 1838. APF, SOCG, 956, ff 90r-93v.

[42] Pope Gregory XVI himself expressed these views strongly in an audience which he later gave to the Dublin priest, William Meagher. Meagher reported that the pope opened the conversation by deploring the efforts being made by the enemies of the faith, especially in Germany, to found schools in which they could instil into the minds of children the poison of infidelity. He then went on to say that, though Catholic children in the national schools in Ireland might be in no danger of perversion from the instruction they received in class, still the 'very familiarity contracted by Catholic children with their heretical school-fellows would gradually weaken the attachment of the former for our holy religion & lighten their horror of protestantism'. (Meagher to Hamilton, 7 Dec. 1839, DDA.)

[43] MacHale to Cullen, 24 Feb. 1838, AICR.

forwarded to Rome. He enlarged on his previous criticisms to claim that the system was formed in imitation of the evil systems of Germany and maintained that it threatened to reproduce the same evil effects. In the whole process of setting up the system the archbishop of Dublin had shown the simplicity of the dove and not the cunning of the serpent, and deceived by the craft of others did not understand the deceit they practised to the detriment of religion. Commenting on the composition of the board, he described Whately and Carlile as most determined enemies of Catholicism who had not hesitated to attack it with most calumnious writings. The board enjoyed full power over both books and teachers; without consulting the local bishop it could remove any religious books from the schools and dismiss the teachers. Twelve years previously when discussion was taking place about a new scheme of education, the bishops unanimously submitted their views to the government through the archbishop of Dublin; among these was the principle that each bishop was to retain full authority in his diocese to choose suitable and dismiss unsuitable teachers and select the books to be used in the schools. For the benefit of Roman officials unfamiliar with the religious geography of Ireland the archbishop then explained that in his province—Connaught— they had schools that were Catholic where no Protestant ever entered, not as in the northern province, where the archbishop of Armagh lived and where Protestants were so numerous that bishops had perforce to tolerate what, in all conscience, they would not suffer where religion could be freely practised. In the north Catholic children were taught scriptures by Protestant teachers from a Protestant version of the bible, and, accustomed to such a system naturally found the present one less odious.[44] The skulduggery of Protestants in promoting the system was daily becoming more apparent. Though knowing that he would not entrust the children of his diocese to Protestant teachers or officials, they sent Protestants to live in his diocese so that their children could attend schools. This was deliberately done so that they could show that, regardless of the faith of the people or the authority of the bishop, they would place teachers and inspectors in the schools according to their judgement.[45]

---

[44] When Bishop James Doyle of Kildare was asked at the Inquiry on Irish Education in 1825 if he was prepared to believe that scarcely any Catholic child had been withdrawn from the schools in Ulster conducted by the Kildare Place Society, the London Hibernian Society and other societies from which he and bishops had withdrawn Catholic children because of attempted proselytism, he replied: 'From the depressed state of the Catholics in the north, and their inability to have schools wherein their own children can be educated in the manner they would wish, I should think that they might suffer, to a certain extent, abuses which in other countries we would not look at silently for a single day'. (*First report of the commissioners of Irish education inquiry*, p. 775, H.C. 1825, (400), xii.)

[45] MacHale to Propaganda, 1 July, 3 Nov. and 7 Dec. 1838., APF, Acta, 202, ff 209r-212v.

This picture of the national system was, of course, much too sweeping and unfair. To claim that the commissioners exercised full control over books and teachers was just not true; only in exceptional circumstances could they dismiss teachers or withdraw books. While he was certainly entitled to express his reservations about Whately or Carlile, the claim that Protestants were colonizing his diocese to extend their power in the schools was completely fanciful. Indeed, it had not gone unnoticed in Archbishop Murray's camp that the Protestant archbishop of Tuam was as vigorously opposed to the system as MacHale.[46]

Archbishop Murray was bewildered and distressed by MacHale's public onslaught on the system. He did not complain of the personal pain he must have felt at being lampooned as a commissioner but he was deeply perturbed about the threat which MacHale's opposition posed to Catholics continuing to enjoy a share in the state funds and feared that that money would again become the perquisite of Protestant societies, who could then use it to the detriment of the Catholic religion. Other bishops, and Crolly in particular, were annoyed by MacHale's implicit slight on Murray, who, as coadjutor and archbishop of Dublin for thirty years, had come to command the respect and esteem of the vast majority of his colleagues. The archbishops of Dublin, residing in the capital city, close to the seat of government and with quicker postal access to Rome than that available in provincial towns, had, as a consequence, long enjoyed a special kind of authority among their colleagues, which was independent of the strictly ecclesiastical terms of the primacy. Courteous, patient and tolerant, Murray was entirely unsuited to rough and rugged public controversy, and his every instinct led him to disarm opposition by reasoned argument and quiet dialogue, and to avoid unseemly and inurbane contestation. Understandably, his friends regretted his subjection to the truncheon blows that MacHale had dealt him.

When he received the invitation from Rome to submit a report on the national system, he did not know what MacHale's precise charges were, but he could assume that they were similar to the criticisms which had appeared in the press. He sought Crolly's advice and help and the archbishop of Armagh, further alarmed by MacHale's bringing his charges to Rome, suggested that a meeting of all the bishops might be held to discuss the objections that had been raised. He himself was prepared to write to Rome to defend the system but he was confident Murray would do all that was necessary:

---

[46] Hamilton to Cullen, 18 Aug. 1838, AICR.

The arguments which Your Grace will offer to the Holy Father in reply to His Grace of Tuam will probably settle this unpleasant business. But as Dr MacHale seems to set very little value on the opinions of his Brethren in the Prelacy of our National Church, I think, that we are fairly called on to support our authority. I should not hesitate to state my sentiments on this subject to the S. Congregation if I could believe, that it was in my power to add anything to the arguments, which Your Grace can supply; but the subject is so important, that I think a general Meeting of all the Prelates should be called to investigate the charges made by His Grace of Tuam, and then to forward to the H. See the result of their deliberations on this interesting subject. There can be little apprehension that a serious division might take place on this point, as Your Grace has already ascertained the sentiments of all the Prelates. We might meet at Maynooth in the course of the next month, and we could then have all the *Reports* and other *Books* which have given occasion to Dr McHale's complaints. I feel that this is a serious business and that we must proceed in it with great prudence.[47]

MacHale had levelled a further serious and quite unjust charge at the commissioners in a public letter before Murray replied to Rome. The board in response to pressure from the Presbyterians had given permission to managers of schools to allow separate religious instruction to take place at any hour of the day provided the same safeguards as protected it before and after school were maintained. The archbishop of Tuam, knowing that Protestant children would then study the bible during the school hours that had been hitherto reserved for religious instruction had, without any semblance of justification interpreted this change as a permission to make the bible a school book. What was allowed as a concession to Presbyterians was converted into a nefarious transformation of the principles of the system. In private Murray was still patient enough to describe this accusation as merely unfair, though he hastened to add that MacHale could not have believed it.[48]

Publicly he replied to MacHale's assaults on the system after having held his fire for eight months. He pointed out that clergy throughout the entire country, including Tuam, were taking advantage of the funds available to establish and conduct schools, and he quoted letters from Crolly and Denvir testifying to their happy experiences with the national schools in their dioceses. He examined in detail the arrangement and safeguards for religious teaching and the constitution of the national board and claimed that they were satisfactory.[49] But within a few days of this letter being published MacHale returned to the attack and explained in a pastoral letter to the clergy and people of Tuam that from a feeling of respect for Archbishop Murray he had 'suffered much to pass over in

47 Crolly to Murray, 31 May 1838, DDA.   48 Murray to Cullen, 28 July 1838.
49 F.J. 24 Oct. 1838.

silence which would have called forth our earlier animadversion and remonstrance'. When he saw, however, that the 'vicious system teemed with evils which no zeal or piety on the part of any individual member of that body could correct', he was forced to raise his voice in protest.[50] Murray replied directly to MacHale's comments, took him to task for the effects of the 'studied ambiguity' of his language and reminded him that he had signed an application for aid for a school at Hollymount in Co. Mayo as late as May 1837.[51]

In private he dismissed the possibility of a grant for separate education as being 'so utterly visionary that no rational person could entertain it for a moment'. In fact he later revealed that he suspected MacHale's entire motivation in the whole controversy, and attributed it to a rather unworthy reaction to their differing attitudes to a disputed episcopal succession in Killala:

The fact is, I never attributed Dor. McHale's opposition to them [the *Scripture Lessons*] and the National System to any other motive than mere personal pique towards me, on account of some secret information which he was supposed to have received from some of his acquaintances in Propaganda that I was less adverse than he would wish to poor Dor. O'Finan.[52]

Naturally, Murray did not suggest this interpretation of MacHale's behaviour in his letter to Rome. In fact, in his lengthy reply, which he sent off promptly on receiving the request for information, he contented himself with declaring that he was nonplussed by MacHale's opposition; he could not even suspect what provoked it. He began by explaining the background to the national system. The Kildare Place Society would not permit the use of any catechisms or books for religious instructions in its schools, apart from the bible without notes attached to it. Though the bishops resisted these rules and tried earnestly to withdraw their children, they found it very difficult to do so; the poor were very keen on education and landlords often compelled their impoverished tenants and servants to send their children to these schools and very often punished those who resisted with expulsion from their wretched homes. Consequently, to remedy this terrible situation, the government at the request of himself and others decreed that public money should no longer be given to that society and that a new scheme of education, which was acceptable to Catholics, should be established. Having explained the arrangements for separate religious education in the national schools, and the supervisory

[50] Ibid., 2 Nov. 1838.   [51] Ibid., 12 Nov. 1838.   [52] Murray to Cullen, 4 Apr. 1839, AICR.

role of the commissioners, he added that he joined the board and devoted much time and labour to it, to ensure that Catholic youth would have access to education and that religion would not thereby suffer.

Since the commissioners, he went on, could not inspect all schools to ensure justice was done to all, they appointed twenty five inspectors, of whom thirteen were Catholic and twelve Protestant. Among the first duties of the commissioners had been that of preparing books of general moral precepts, which would not give offence from a religious angle, and they also edited works from the historical books of the old testament and the history of Christ from St Luke's gospel and the Acts of the Apostles. He had inspected each sheet before it was submitted to the printer in case any error against faith or morals had crept in. A few notes were added to these excerpts to explain the sacred text in matters of common belief but they contained nothing opposed to Catholic or Protestant doctrine. All these books were recommended to the patrons of the schools but no obligation was imposed on the pupils to use them, if the patrons wished to provide other useful and proven texts.

One could scarcely describe the joy with which the great majority of Catholics greeted the system; it gave their children a safe way of acquiring knowledge without injury to their religion, and their pastors were free to teach doctrinal matters within the schools, if they wished. On the other hand, seventeen Protestant bishops, a large number of clergy and members of parliament denounced it as favouring Catholicism and damaging Protestantism.

After MacHale had sharply attacked the commissioners at the meeting of the bishops and then published bitter letters in the press denouncing the board for not giving money towards the education of Catholics in his diocese (which it could not do) and charged that the system was dangerous to Catholic faith, Murray wrote to all the bishops asking them if there was anything so harmful to the Catholic religion in it that a bishop could not sanction it. The archbishop of Armagh replied that he had found nothing in it to force him to retract the full and sincere support he had given to it,[53] and the bishops of the northern province, where a larger number of Protestants lived than in the other provinces and where danger, if it existed, ought to have been found, all responded favourably, except the bishop of Ardagh, who, though he refused to approve it, added that he had never spoken publicly against it and would not do so unless he

---

[53] Crolly wrote 'after an impartial examination of the arguments which have been urged against the System of National Education, I have discovered no fair, reasonable, or religious grounds, on which I could withdraw from it my sincere support and unaltered approbation'. (Crolly to Murray, 9 Mar. 1838, DDA.)

found something against faith or morals in it.[54] The bishop of Kilmore, while approving of the system, complained about the commissioners editing the gospel of St Luke, or the greater part of it, for use in the schools.[55] All the bishops from the Dublin and Cashel provinces approved, with the exception of the bishop of Ferns, who feared everything that came from a Protestant government,[56] and all the bishops of the Tuam province approved of it, with the exception of the bishop of Elphin, who, nonetheless, saw no reason for Murray to withdraw from the board;[57] he hoped, however, for money for separate Catholic education, something that no one of sane mind, in the present situation in Ireland, would dare hope.

Murray felt, with the other bishops, that there was no danger facing the Catholic religion unless the pastors neglected their duty of teaching it either personally or with the help of others. With a vigilant hierarchy and clergy, if abuses arose, they would be eagerly removed. More than 120,000 Catholics were receiving education in the national schools and in the town of Tuam there was a school with 300 pupils and nearby one with 84 pupils; with the archbishop's permission the priests of Tuam sought public money to erect or support such schools. Consequently, it would certainly not be opportune to deprive poor Catholics of such a great boon without a very grave reason.[58]

---

[54] William Higgins described the system as 'wrong in principle and in many instances very capricious, and perhaps unjust, in its operation'. However, Murray's membership of the board was a safeguard, which if removed, would compel him to cause the clergy and people of Ardagh to break off all connexion with the system. Murray evidently replied lamenting 'the partial and ill-advised clamour' against it, and Higgins in response deprecating any part in this agitation, agreed that 'public and precipitate censure' of the system would give a dangerous handle to their enemies. (Higgins to Murray, 9, 11 Mar. 1838, DDA.)

[55] Another bishop, who strongly approved of the system but complained that the *Scripture Lessons* contained 'many objectionable passages' was Patrick McGettigan of Raphoe. (McGettigan to Cullen, 18 Aug. 1838, AICR.)

[56] James Keating of Ferns, arguing from the theoretical possibilities or what he termed the principles of the system, maintained that the board assumed to itself episcopal rights over the selection and rejection of books for religious instruction, and over the appointment and removal of teachers and added that the scripture extracts had not been sanctioned by any bishop and were not in accordance with the Latin vulgate. Murray's explanation of the very limited power over books and teachers which the board enjoyed confirmed rather than corrected his view that the system made 'an attempt to supersede Episcopal authority and to endanger the purity and integrity of the Faith'. (Keating to Murray, 13, 16 Mar. 1838, DDA.) John Cantwell, the bishop of Meath, thought legislation should be sought as a protection against innovations or concessions to 'biblicals' such as the permission to have religious instruction at any time of the day. Murray's reply removed his apprehensions, though he still feared that the permitted change of time for religious instruction could be inconvenient for Catholic clergy and that a heterodox teacher or fanatical visitor might abuse the time to the detriment of Catholic children. (Cantwell to Murray, 9, 11 Mar. 1838, DDA.)

[57] Burke to Murray, 20 Mar. 1838, DDA.

[58] Murray to Propaganda, 11 June 1838. APF, Acta, 202, ff 214v – 216v. Murray subsequently asked Cullen to explain the arrangements for training teachers in the model school in Dublin, which he had omitted from his letter. He stressed that John Miley, a priest well-known in Rome, assembled both the teachers and the pupils of the school each Saturday for religious instruction and that another priest had been appointed professor of natural philosophy. (Murray to Cullen, 3 July 1838, AICR.) Murray also pointed

Murray's response was characteristically fair, measured and accurate. Eschewing the highly moral theoretical principles on which MacHale chose to base his case, he defended the system for the most part on practical and pragmatic grounds. He also sent the rules of the system to Paul Cullen to be translated into Italian. But while he recounted the origin of the *Scripture Lessons* and scrupulously explained the freedom enjoyed by the patrons of the schools to use them or not as they wished, his defence would scarcely have removed the bad impression created by the quotations from them which MacHale had made. Though the *Lessons* might or might not be used in the schools, still their content was a valuable indicator of the goodwill or fairness of the board that commissioned them. If they contained material bordering on heresy, they raised serious questions about a system in which they were recommended. From the Roman point of view they had one great advantage: they could be examined on the spot by independent consultors, whose verdict would be a helpful pointer to the essence and tendency of the national system.

VI

MacHale devoted part of his second letter to Rome and all of his third to the *Scripture Lessons* and in them he made two telling points: they omitted the customary language of the Douay version because they wanted to exclude the use of certain words associated with Catholic doctrinal beliefs, and the questions attached to the lessons offered opportunities to ill-disposed teachers and inspectors for infecting the minds of the children with poisonous views. These criticisms were effective because they could be neither proved nor disproved. They left the more fundamental questions untouched, for ill-disposed teachers could not find posts in most of the schools, unless appointed by Catholic patrons, and, if patrons sensed that Protestant inspectors were abusing their positions to foist unwelcome interpretations on Catholic children, they could checkmate the inspectors by not using the extracts.

MacHale illustrated his claims about theological terminology by observing that in the *Scripture Lessons* no reference was ever made to priests

out the crudely inaccurate over-simplification of the charge made by MacHale in his public letter to Russell that the bible had become a school book. The commissioners had in their fourth report made provision for separate religious instruction to be given during school hours as well as before or after them. And during that separate instruction Protestants used the bible as a text. MacHale then unfairly accused the commissioners of making the bible a school book. (Murray to Cullen, 28 July, 1838, AICR.)

of the new law, but the word 'presbyter', which was associated with a Protestant sect, was used. From St Luke the angelic salutation was omitted because the Protestants did not want to translate the words 'full of grace'; the Calvinist who compiled the extracts said they were unwilling to have the children discuss material which was discussed in the chapter on the Incarnation, but the real reason was that the Protestant members of the commission did not want to translate the words lest they might savour of reverence for the Blessed Virgin Mary.

Then he went on to claim that expert theologians believed that the *Lessons* insinuated erroneous views on the doctrines of grace, penance, good works, free will and justification. These were the central issues of theological dispute at the Reformation, and if this charge were true, the *Lessons* would certainly be condemned at Rome. Quoting an explanation of an extract from the old testament that 'nothing could purge the soul from the effects of evil works or give peace to the conscience but the sense of the pardoning mercy of God through Jesus Christ obtained through repentance and faith in him' he pointed out that the word 'repentance' that was found in the text was the English word used by Protestants, and signified mere sorrow, whereas the word 'penance' in the Catholic sense involved works of satisfaction.[59] In the *Lessons* the word was used only in the Protestant sense of sadness without reference to works of satisfaction and never in the Catholic sense which included both compunction and chastisement of the body. This note therefore smacked of the heresy condemned at Trent in the decree anathematizing anyone who said that justification has nothing more than trust in the divine mercy forgiving sins on account of Christ. Among the other examples to which he drew attention was the note declaring that human nature produced sin as a poisoned tree produced poisoned fruit: he argued that this comment did not differ much from a proposition of the theologian Baius, which had been condemned, namely that all the works of non-believers were sinful and the virtues of philosophers were vices. Maintaining that many similar errors were included in the *Lessons*, he asked if the Jansenist heresy was so carefully spread over the Augustinus[60] that it permeated the whole work, would it be surprising if the Protestant who compiled the extracts and

[59] Ironically, the extract on penance gave offence to Protestants for the opposite reason. Charles Elrington, the professor of divinity at Trinity College, Dublin described the note on penance as most objectionable because 'the clear construction' of the note was that the Roman Catholic doctrine of doing penance was the right one. The note excluded the part of the Roman Catholic doctrine – satisfaction for sin – to which Protestants objected. (*Report of the select committee of the House of Lords on the plan of education in Ireland*, pp. 592-3, H.C. 1837 (543-1), viii, pt i, 598-9.)

[60] The 'Augustinus' was a book on grace and human nature by Cornelius Jansen. It was published in 1640 after the author's death and condemned as heretical by Pope Innocent X in 1653.

notes sought to conceal the poison by a fallacious form of words? He summed up by declaring that the extracts were put together with the intention of removing the guiding light of the Catholic church and presenting a monstrous and shapeless mass.

By forwarding copies of the extracts to Rome, MacHale made it easy for Propaganda to carry out an independent examination of them. The congregation accordingly passed them on to one of its consultors, Thomas Glover, an English Jesuit. The choice of an Englishman offered the advantage of having an unbiassed judgement from one who understood the political situation, out of which the national system had emerged, as well as being able to detect any erroneous opinions behind the nuances of the English language. Glover produced an exhaustive analysis of the extracts, singling out many passages for special examination and, though much of his criticism was pedantic and jejune, he gave a powerful boost to MacHale's case by listing passages which he claimed illustrated the heretical views of the Protestant authors on the great themes of the Reformation—justification by faith, grace and forgiveness. And he supported MacHale's complaints about the use of English translations unfamiliar to Catholics[61] as well as the scope afforded by the questions to unscrupulous teachers to suggest answers that were either heretical or bordering on heresy. And all teachers were obliged to train in a model school, the principal of which was reputedly a Socinian and the author of the *Lessons*.

Among the notes which he regarded as bearing a heretical complexion was one explaining that 'justice indicated the condition of a man who is just, or is justified before God, through the satisfying sacrifice of Our Lord Jesus Christ'. Strictly interpreted this excluded the sacraments and the acts of penance, apart from faith. Its intent emerged from the words attached to the lesson from the Epistle to the Galatians, where Abraham's faith was praised as the faith from which the just man lived so that all might receive the promise of the spirit through faith. In that chapter he felt the principal error of Protestantism was suggested and would undoubtedly be taught by Protestant teachers. He detected the same error in the extract, which MacHale had already condemned, about the soul being purified from the effects of evil works by a sense of the mercy of God in terms Christ acquired by repentance and faith in him.

For the same reasons as MacHale, he deplored the omission of the

---

[61] Glover noted that there was scarcely a page of the Lessons which did not contain many discrepancies from the vulgate. (The Council of Trent had decreed that the vulgate, the Latin edition of the bible compiled by St Jerome, was the official text of the scriptures for use in the Catholic church.)

angelic salutation from St Luke, deprecated the use of the English words 'repentance' and 'repent' which the vulgate had translated as 'penance' and 'do penance'. Similarly, he rejected as pure Calvinism, the explanation that sin was produced as naturally as a bad tree produced bad fruits.

Furthermore, Glover found the compilers of the *Scripture Lessons* guilty of suspicious omissions. On the comment that Christ imposed silence on the Scribes and Pharisees when they asked him how he could be the messiah and the son and lord of David at the same time, he made the observation that this reference called for an acknowledgement of Christ's divine nature. A similarly disingenuous silence was to be found about Peter's primacy, on the occasions when his denial was mentioned, and he detected indifferentism in the scholium which claimed that different opinions, from which discussions and divisions, but not inveterate or implacable hatreds, might arise, could be found among true Christians. The omissions of particular Catholic doctrines were blameworthy; there was no mention of the Trinity, the nature of Christ, the nature and efficacy of the sacraments, the real presence of Christ in the Eucharist, the sacrifice of the Mass, confession, free will, good works, purgatory, the Catholic church, the primacy of the Roman pontiff, and the invocation of saints.

From Archbishop Murray's claim that he had overseen the compilation of the extracts, Glover drew the opposite conclusion to the one intended: if such material could escape the vigilance of an archbishop, there was great danger that teachers in the privacy of the schools could spread even more pestilential ideas. Glover's ultimate verdict might have come directly from Tuam: there was no justification for a system in which a mainly Protestant board trained and appointed teachers, prescribed books, and drew up the regulations while the bishops enjoyed no right of visiting the schools, approving the books, correcting and, if necessary, dismissing teachers; and, moreover, the hope that the bishops, if they unanimously sought it, might obtain money from the government for separate schools in which the faith would be firmly preserved, was not in vain.[62]

When Archbishop Murray first heard a rumour that theologians at Rome were inclined to judge the *Scripture Lessons* unfavourably, he was both surprised and apprehensive of the consequences for the national system in general. He feared the embarrassment for Catholics that would

---

[62] *Annotazioni del P. Glover della compagnia di Gesù circa i libri ad uso dell'Istituto Nazionale delle Scuole in Irlanda.* APF, *Acta*, 202, ff 216v-219v. Glover's views were not altered by Murray's defence. He continued to regard the national system as totally unacceptable. (Glover to Propaganda, n.d., Ibid., SOCG, 936, ff 105r-106r and 113r-114r.)

arise from a condemnation that would 'give the enemies of our faith a plausible pretext for holding us up to our poor people and their own as Persons who are afraid to let one particle of Scripture reach our deluded followers, lest it should open their eyes to the errors and corruptions of the Church of Rome'.[63] When Propaganda sent Glover's analysis of the *Lessons* to him, he would not accept that they were the fruits of a theologian's independent investigation: he assumed they were the *ex parte* comments of MacHale,[64] and explaining that he was forced to answer them at great length, since it was much easier to make a foolish objection than to answer it satisfactorily, he observed that he 'was obliged to answer in strong language but hardly any language can be strong enough to mark, as it deserved, the dishonesty which pervaded them'.[65]

Murray began by carefully detailing the rules for religious education, the opportunities afforded to the clergy to visit the schools and select the texts for religious instruction, the power vested in the board to dismiss teachers or exclude books from the schools, the utter impossibility of obtaining grants for Catholic schools and the freedom of managers to use, or not, as they wished the *Scripture Lessons*.

Discussing the contents of the *Lessons*, he began by pointing out the legitimacy of using translations from the Greek and Hebrew texts as well as from the vulgate. Noting that the critic of the extracts had admitted that it was possible to give a Catholic answer to the questions at the end of the lessons, he went on to say that teachers were restricted to explaining the grammatical sense of the text; if they strayed into doctrinal issues contrary to either Catholicism or Protestantism during combined instruction, they would be dismissed from office. He further explained that the normal school in Dublin consisted of three sections—national schools for boys and girls, of which the principals were Catholics, and a department where country teachers were trained by two professors, one of whom was a priest of good standing and the other a Protestant but not a Socinian. And, of the fifty three teachers in training in the previous year, nearly fifty were Catholics. Apart from the professor, another priest taught both pupils and teachers each week and encouraged them to frequent the sacraments of penance and the Eucharist. To Glover's sweeping and inaccurate comment that the bishops had come openly or tacitly to disapprove of the system, Murray responded by pointing out

---

[63] Murray to Cullen, 24 Dec. 1838, AICR.   [64] Murray to Cullen, 21 Mar. 1839, AICR.
[65] Murray to Cullen, 13 Mar. 1839, AICR. Murray told Slattery that some of MacHale's objections to the Lessons were 'captious, some of them exceedingly futile, most of them utterly dishonest'. (Murray to Slattery, 16 Feb. 1839, Slattery Papers.)

that it had been established in every diocese and that no bishop had prevented new schools from being erected.[66]

In his second lengthy letter Murray dealt with the particular criticisms which Glover had made. He strove to prove that they did not contain any heretical interpretations, and he insisted that, as long as they were not directly opposed to Catholic dogma, Catholic teachers could elucidate them safely and satisfactorily during separate religious instruction.

To the complaint that the note about justice indicating the condition of man who was just or was justified before God by the satisfying sacrifice of Christ, Murray replied that what the note read was that justice signified sometimes the virtue of justice or equity and sometimes the condition of man who was just or justified before God by the propitiatory sacrifice of Christ. And he argued that neither the principal error of Protestantism nor anything approaching an error was contained in it. To the charge that the scholium about nothing purifying the soul from the effects of sin and giving peace to the conscience but a sense of the mercy of God through Jesus Christ acquired by penance and faith in him also contained the principal error of Protestantism, Murray returned a firm negative and argued that the context from which it was lifted—the story in the book of Genesis about Joseph's brothers painfully recalling their crime twenty years later—provided no ground for reading the Protestant doctrine into that passage. Dealing with Glover's strictures against the use of the English words 'repentance' and 'repent' to translate the vulgate terms 'penance' and 'do penance', he insisted that the word 'repentance' included the internal act and also all that pertained to the virtue of penance in the Catholic sense, and pointed out that the note in the extracts made this clear. And he illustrated his arguments by appealing to the translation of the vulgate by a distinguished English priest who always used the reprobated words 'repentance' and 'repent'. By doing so, this translator rightly conveyed the meaning of the whole virtue of penance and removed all ambiguity from the word. The note in the *Lessons* also explained that the word 'repentance' meant true sorrow for sin, and a desire of amendment and of making reparation for past sins by works of satisfaction.

To the objection about the omission of the angelic salutation in St Luke, which was supposedly done to prevent children learning 'hail Mary, full of grace', Murray responded by admitting that it was he who had been responsible, because the Protestant version of the words 'full of

[66] Murray to Propaganda, 25 Feb. 1839, ff 219v – 223r.

grace' differed from the vulgate and he did not want anything in the *Lessons* that could be a distraction from the usual way of reciting the angelus.

The archbishop concluded his defence by making abundantly clear the purpose of the *Lessons* and seeking to extricate them from a condemnation of not doing what they were never intended to do—to provide an explanation of Catholic beliefs. They were drawn up to exclude the whole bible, which had previously been read in the schools, and which many influential Protestants contended should be read by all pupils in schools which received grants from public funds.[67]

VII

Before these replies had gone to Rome the controversy had developed into a clear split among the bishops of Ireland. The prelates held their annual meeting on 22 January 1839 and what publicly had seemed to be a difference between two archbishops became a fissure in the whole hierarchy. All were present except the bishops of Derry and Cloyne. The issue was bound to occupy a central place on the agenda, for the system impinged on the pastoral care of every bishop in the country, and they were all aware that MacHale's public attacks on it demanded an unequivocal response from them.

Crolly who, if anything, was even a stronger advocate of the system than Murray, since he feared the ravages of proselytism among the poorer Catholics of the north, took the lead at the meeting, as primate, in asking every bishop whether or not he detected anything in the national schools contrary to the Catholic faith or inconsistent with Christian morality. Only MacHale and Higgins expressed reservations. MacHale mentioned a couple of incidents which he regarded as very damaging: a teacher in his diocese had become a Protestant and the board had rejected a request to have him dismissed. Murray retorted by pointing out that the board had no such power and added that the exercise of such power would be detrimental to the Catholic church in many cases, as the conversion of Protestants to Catholicism was very common in the British Empire. MacHale then objected to the *Scripture Lessons*, was reminded that he was free to exclude them from the schools, and to allay his anxieties a suggestion was made that a committee of bishops should be appointed to examine not only the *Lessons*, but to check, the orthodoxy of all the school

[67] Ibid., 12 Mar. 1839. ff 223r – 228v.

books. As Crolly sadly observed, MacHale 'rejected this amicable proposal and seemed unwilling to adopt any terms of conciliation'. Three resolutions, proposed by John Ryan, bishop of Limerick, and seconded by James Browne, bishop of Kilmore, were then passed. These declared that the national system had not damaged the faith or morals of Catholic children, that the board of commissioners merited the confidence of the prelates and that they would continue to watch the system carefully lest any deleterious change might be made in it. MacHale tried to obstruct the resolutions and prevailed on his suffragans and three other bishops to refuse assent, by arguing that the question should first be examined by Propaganda.[68] Nonetheless, sixteen prelates supported the resolutions and decided to communicate their views to Rome. The bishop of Cloyne, who was absent, subsequently supported the majority which consisted of all the bishops of the three provinces of Armagh, Dublin and Cashel with the exceptions of Ardagh, Meath and Ferns. These three joined the archbishop and bishops of the Tuam province in opposition.[69]

Crolly also sent a lengthy account of the meeting to Cullen, which was intended for use in the appropriate quarters in Rome. This considered statement reveals not only his firm commitment to the national system and sympathy for the poor whom it was benefitting but also his grim apprehensions of the consequences of its overthrow and replacement by some such body as the Kildare Place Society:

With painful feelings, I have to acquaint you, for the information of the Holy See, that an unfortunate misunderstanding among the Prelates of this Kingdom has been lately occasioned by the unwise and obstinate conduct of the Most Revd Dr McHale Archbishop of Tuam, who has determined to use every means in his power for the purpose of destroying the liberal and impartial system of National Education, which has been prepared by our paternal Government, sanctioned by all the Prelates of the Country including Dr McHale himself, and the many advantages of which have been enjoyed by the children of poor Catholics in every part of Ireland during the last seven years.

I need not tell you, that throughout all Ireland, for the two last centuries, the children of the poor of every religious denomination have been educated together in the same Schools, and that owing to the fidelity of the people and the prudent zeal of their pious pastors, this mixed system of education was attended with no injury to Religion; but on the contrary, that the more knowledge the Catholics in general acquired, the more capable they were to assist their pastors in converting those who were separated from the true Church.

The bigotted Protestants plainly perceived, that they were constantly losing some

---

68 Crolly to Cullen, 4 Feb. 1839, AICR.
69 There were then 27 dioceses in Ireland. Thomas Feeny, the apostolic administrator of Killala, is listed among the minority and John McLaughlin, the coadjutor bishop of Derry, among the majority. The bishop of Derry was incapacitated.

members of their communion, and that they could never make proselytes of the poor Catholics, unless they could obtain such a system of Education as would enable them to pervert the tender hearts and unsuspecting minds of the poor children. For this impious purpose they obtained from the Tory Government a large grant of money, to enable them to build schools, from which they excluded the Catholic Catechism, and introduced their version of the Bible, which they put into the hands of the pupils, and pointed out many passages of what they called the Word of God, as evidences of the errors of the Catholic Religion. In opposition to this infamous Association of intolerant Protestants, commonly called the Kildare Street Society, the Catholic Prelates, the Clergy and the people made a determined and successful resistance, the children of the faithful were withdrawn from the schools of corruption, and the Kildare Street Society soon sunk into a state of insignificance and contempt. This may afford to the Holy See a satisfactory proof of our unalterable determination to watch over the faithful flocks entrusted to our care, and to guard them from the insidious attacks of their irreligious and inveterate enemies . . .

This laudable system of National Education has been and still is assailed by all the Bigotted Protestants,[70] whilst it has been received with feelings of inexpressible joy by the Catholic Prelates, who together with their Clergy and their faithful flocks have adopted it in every part of Ireland. By the joint exertions of the Board of Education and the Catholic Clergy, commodious Schoolhouses have been erected in every Province, and almost in every parish throughout Ireland, wherein upwards of two hundred thousand children,[71] who with few exceptions are of the Catholic Communion, are receiving at present such literary knowledge as will make them understand the duties which they should perform as members of Society, and at the same time, they are properly instructed in all the articles of Catholic faith, and all their obligations as members of the Church of Christ. . . You will have the goodness to state to His Holiness that the children of the poor in this Country and their indigent parents will be in a miserable and dangerous condition if they be obliged to abandon the national schools, and be once more exposed to the snares of the Kildare Street Society, which would lose no time in renewing their attempts to seduce the Catholic Children from their faith. I fear also that the Catholic Clergy will be deeply mortified and discontented, if they be ordered to abandon the Schools which they have generously and zealously erected at great expense, and under many difficulties. And I cannot conceal from you, that many prudent Prelates are under disagreeable apprehensions, lest this unpleasant business may be attended with a misunderstanding between the Holy See and the British Government which would be injurious to the progress of our holy Religion not only in the British Empire, but also in all the British Colonies.[72]

The minority was also anxious to brief the national agent in the hope that he would use his influence in their favour. William Higgins, the bishop of Ardagh, who seconded MacHale's amendment at the meeting, and whose aversion to the system was to rival even MacHale's, hastened

[70] A distinction is being made here between liberal and extreme Protestants. All Protestants are not being accused of bigotry.
[71] According to the fifth report of the commissioners for the year ending 31 March 1838, there were 1,384 national schools in operation and 169,548 children on the rolls. (pp 68-9. [160] H.C. 1839, xvi, 412-3)
[72] Crolly to Cullen, 4 Feb. 1839, AICR.

to present the other side of the picture. Though Higgins never lost an opportunity to embroider his version of a dispute, his account reveals the depth of the division and the tenseness of feelings provoked by it:

I say with affliction that nothing could surpass the secular views and want of candour on the part of our opponents. Could you ever imagine that an Irish Bishop would stubbornly and not very respectfully refuse to consult the successor of Peter in his doubts & difficulties—yet sixteen have acted in this manner!!! We have Maynooth and all the Catholic feeling of Ireland on our side, and I dare say that we shall have the horror of being persecuted by the Castle, and misrepresented—If the others write; their communications shd. be received with caution, particularly any books, or Regulations, of the Board of Commissioners, as heretic like, they change or modify these things *ad captandum*.[73]

Higgins, like MacHale, distrusted virtually every British initiative in Ireland. Keating, the bishop of Ferns, according to Archbishop Murray, suspected everything that came from a Protestant government and Cantwell of Meath, who was the third of the opponents from outside the province of Tuam, later showed that he was prone to the same conspiracy theory. MacHale seems to have intimidated his six suffragans into agreeing with him. Only one of them had previously shown any signs of querying the value of the system.

Shortly after the bishops' meeting, which lasted for seven days, Crolly, as primate, on his own behalf and on that of the other fifteen who signed, sent a statememt of their case to the pope asking him to interpose his authority to restore the peace and harmony that had reigned among them until sadly disturbed by MacHale's letters on the national system and its board of commissioners. These writings caused not inconsiderable scandal to clergy and people, since the system had been often recommended by almost all the bishops of Ireland. They then repeated the background to the national scheme and the safeguards built into it, noting that the two Catholic lay commissioners, Blake and Bellew, were excellent and zealous Catholics.[74] MacHale had not only not complained about the system and commissioners for almost six years but had erected or permitted the erection of many national schools in his diocese. Then when he raised his objections at their meeting and was barely able to get one or two others to support him, they hoped that he would do nothing to rupture the harmony of their body. But he started writing specious letters to the

---

[73] Higgins to Cullen, 23 Jan. 1839, AICR.
[74] Three commissioners were appointed in May 1838 in addition to the original seven. One of these, Sir Patrick Bellew, was a Catholic. Three more commissioners were appointed in June 1838, one of whom, John R. Corballis, was a Catholic.

newspapers in which he sought to win support partly by distorting and partly by suppressing the facts. Having given an account of their late meeting, they claimed that by the artifice of suggesting an appeal to the Holy See MacHale won over six or seven bishops to his side, who, though they did not fully approve of the system, did not think it should be rejected. Quoting the three resolutions passed on 23 January 1839, the signatories concluded their letter with an assurance of their submission to the pope's authority.[75]

The minority also lost no time in forwarding its appeal to the pope. This contained little fresh material but it pulled no punches in designating the system as fundamentally evil, and it claimed that apart from the archbishop of Dublin the commissioners kept extolling the systems of education in Holland, Prussia and other parts of Germany from which one could conclude that at the opportune time they planned to perpetrate against the Catholic faith and ecclesiastical discipline the same things that had been done in those countries. It reiterated the sweeping statements about the extensive powers possessed by the commissioners to select the books and control the teachers in the schools. Though priests enjoyed the right of visiting the schools, they could rarely exercise it because of pressing pastoral commitments. The *Scripture Lessons* were vehemently denounced.[76]

Apart from these official submissions bishops from both sides continued to put their case forcefully to their agent, Paul Cullen, hoping to convince him and win his influential support at Propaganda. Because of his ready access to the congregation and the respect in which he was held by it, his interpretation of the situation in Ireland was bound to carry great weight. Higgins moved into top gear as he sought to minimize the chances of his opponents. Denouncing the books recommended by the commissioners as 'replete with the abominable principles of "indifferentism" or Arianism', he singled out a recent publication of Archbishop Whately, which was destined to figure prominently in controversies for many years. This was the *Lessons on the Truth of Christianity* which, according to the bishop of Ardagh, called 'everything into doubt—talks of nothing but "Christianity" in the vague or rather Arian sense of the word, incessantly insinuates the Redeemer to be nothing more than the adopted son of God & & &'. The danger of Arianism finding its way into the schools and homes of the poor was far

[75] Crolly and fifteen other bishops to Pope Gregory XVI, 30 Jan, 1839. ff 228v – 231r.
[76] MacHale and nine other prelates to Pope Gregory XVI, 29 Jan. 1839, ff 213r – 214v.

greater than that caused by the Kildare Place Society dropping tracts along the highways. His fears had grown darker:

In my conscience I believe, and this belief is shared by all the Prelates who signed our reference to Rome, that the English Government hope to accomplish by this System what fire and sword could not do—the extinction of the Catholic Faith in Ireland. . . Whatever may result from our application, we have the consolation to feel that we have not been 'dumb dogs' and that we have with us the Catholic feeling of Ireland, and the honour of counting among our opponents, all the bad priests, lukewarm and Castle-hack Catholics, as well as the heretical or Voltairean Liberals of the Empire.[77]

MacHale too became, if anything, even more apocalyptic:

It is my solemn belief that we have now more to fear for the purity of our faith than in former periods of more bitter persecution. The government is labouring to effect by fraud and wiles what past ones could not achieve by force. Perhaps, I may be visionary in my fears, but I never entertained a conviction so strong or so slowly and deliberately formed as that a more disastrous blow was never aimed at the Catholic religion in Ireland than that which is meditated by the establishment of the National Schools.[78]

Murray on the other hand was despondent at the prospect of a bitter struggle against the system. Not only would that entail a loss of the educational advantages and opportunities which the system brought, but an attempt to overturn it would fail and would inflict a wound on religion from which it would not recover for a long time.[79]

The minority, however, was not satisfied with presenting its case in writing. Two of its stalwarts, Higgins (who had spent several years as a student in Rome) and Cantwell, set off for the eternal city, ostensibly to attend a canonization ceremony, but more likely to bring their personal influence to bear on the decision. In London they met Patrick McGettigan of Raphoe, a member of the majority, who was also en route to Rome. Higgins was alarmed at the prospect of the majority views also being aired in Rome and invited Cullen to try to prevent McGettigan from obtaining a hearing before Cantwell and he arrived.[80] Evidence of the impact made by these prelates at Propaganda does not survive, but it is

---

[77] Higgins to Cullen, 1 Feb. 1839, DDA. He also complained of the bishops (presumably he had those of the majority especially in mind) who refused to support a resolution he had proposed to express their admiration for the pope's stand in defence of the archbishop of Cologne. The archbishop had been imprisoned by the Prussian government for enforcing canon law on mixed marriages in the Rhineland.
[78] MacHale to Cullen, 26 Mar. 1839. AICR.   [79] Murray to Cullen, 13 Mar. 1839. AICR.
[80] Higgins to Cullen, 2 May 1839. 'His Lordship entertains very strange ideas about education – the Irish College – Paris etc. and would it not be well so to manage matters that he shall have no opportunity of delivering his sentiments on these subjects, or that of the calumny against Dr McHale etc. before our arrival. You know already that I look upon him to be a well-meaning prelate, and you will not, I trust be disedified at the hints just thrown out.'

not unreasonable to assume that Higgins' extremism proved counter-productive.

Before their arrival in Rome the congregation had submitted the relevant material to one of its consultors, Giovanni Perrone, who was a professor at the Collegio Romano, and sought his judgement on the whole issue. Perrone's verdict came down in favour of the time-honoured Roman policy of compromise. Remarking that the system contained both good and bad elements, he drew up a balance sheet of the virtues and defects delineated by both sets of disputants, and concluded that the preponderance of good and evil depended to a great extent on the state of the provinces where the schools were situated; in the southern provinces good seemed to prevail while in the northern ones, possibly, evil prevailed, and the differing views of the bishops could be understood accordingly. Though his knowledge of the geography of Ireland was obviously wobbly, that did not affect his recommendations. He suggested that the majority should not be overridden, but, on the other hand, that the system should not receive formal approval, since it was more difficult to express disapprobation, if approval were ever given. And since the archbishop of Dublin seemed to think that some modifications would be allowed, some Catholic bishops should have the right according to the constitution of being members of the board, the number of inspectors and commissioners should be equally divided between Catholics and Protestants, and the archbishop of Dublin should ensure that those passages in the school books which gave offence to zealous Catholics were removed or altered. Perrone noted that even Murray admitted that some parts of the *Scripture Lessons* required an explanation during separate religious instruction to make certain that they were understood in a Catholic sense. And he singled out for special mention the absence of any reference to the divinity of Christ. The system could be useful for teaching Catholics and for helping to make the minds of Protestant children less prejudiced against the Catholic faith. If these precautions were taken, the system could be tolerated and positive approval postponed until the Holy See was convinced by experience of its advantages.[81]

Before any decision could be made on the issue in dispute, two further letters reached the congregation of Propaganda which, because of their importance, were attached to the summary of the case and the important documents which Cardinal Mai had already prepared. One was from Tobias Kirby, the vice-rector of the Irish College in Rome, and was a

[81] *Acta*, 202, ff 231r – 232r.

passionate *cri de coeur* to the pope to save Ireland from the proselytism, which the enemies of Catholicism were planning through the instrumentality of the national system. Kirby maintained that various letters from Ireland had convinced him of its evils, and among others quoted with effect from a Christian Brother, who assured him that teachers who changed to Protestantism could not be expelled from the schools and that even in a short time some of the scholars had lapsed. The enemies of the faith were merely using education as a pretext; their real purpose was proselytism.[82] At the pope's request a further letter from MacHale was also added because of its importance. In it he not only gave further examples of the violation of his jurisdiction—the punishment of a teacher for reciting the angelus at midday—but made very telling use of extracts from Whately's *Lessons on the Truth of Christianity*[83] and from his previous work the *Errors of Romanism*.[84]

Matters of major import were not decided by the officials of the congregation of Propaganda but by the plenary council or 'congregation', which consisted of the cardinal prefect and other curial cardinals who were not involved in the day to day affairs of the congregation. But the views of the permanent officials were often influential in swaying the minds of the cardinals for whom the work of Propaganda was but a part of their general responsibilities. Rumours of a generally unfavourable attitude to the national system leaked out, and Higgins and Cantwell were happy to circulate them in Ireland on their return from Rome. By the beginning of July government circles in Dublin had got wind of the reports.

A pained and angry Crolly wrote to let Murray know that he had been given the bad news by D.R. Pigot, the Solicitor-General for Ireland. Pigot, he continued, seemed to know 'that Dr Cullen has been the principal tool employed for the destruction of our System of National Education and if so, I have no language strong enough to depict his baseness'. Cullen, he maintained, had given him a false impression that only the *Scripture Lessons* would be condemned. Shattered by the disregard shown at Rome for the solemn declaration of the majority of the bishops, perturbed by the threatened loss of the schools and probably feeling that the case had been settled without a thorough and impartial

---

[82] Kirby to Pope Gregory XVI n.d. 237r – 238v.

[83] *Lessons on the Truth of Christianity* was published in 1838 for use in either separate religious instruction or for combined general instruction. MacHale quoted from it: 'What is revealed to us must be (supposing the religion to be true) but a part, and perhaps but a small part, of the whole truth'. James Keating of Ferns had already condemned this passage.

[84] MacHale to Pope Gregory XVI, 6 June 1839. ff 241v-242v. MacHale also quoted from the *Errors of Romanism*, a work which appeared in 1830 before Whately was appointed to Dublin: 'no one can know precisely when this mystery of Iniquity, the system of Roman corruptions arose'.

investigation, he suggested that 'the Catholic clergy and Laity of the three Provinces should not conceal from the Holy Father the awful consequences of the decision which is reported to have been made on this interesting subject'.[85]

Murray also had received a reliable report—from Cullen—about the likelihood of a Roman condemnation. The government had also picked up similar intelligence from the clerical grapevine. Murray traced its possession of this news to a verbal assurance which Higgins had brought back to MacHale that a condemnation was imminent, and that he himself would be directed to retire from the board.[86] Lord Ebrington, the Lord Lieutenant, alarmed at the national upheaval which a Roman condemnation would provoke, summoned the archbishop of Dublin and gave him an official letter expressing his fears about such an outcome. Enclosing it for Cullen to translate and submit to the pope, Murray, distraught at the blow he was daily expecting from Propaganda, pointed out that Ebrington was

a thinking and benevolent Man, who has not the least tincture of Religious bigotry; who has always, long before he became Viceroy, treated the Catholics on his Estates in Waterford with the kindness of a Parent, and without the least interference with their Religion, and who is still animated by the same benevolent spirit . . . Lord Ebrington has assuredly underrated the disastrous consequences which would ensue from any attempt of the Authorities of Rome to put down the Nl System. It would delight our enemies; it would degrade our Hierarchy; it would leave a soreness in the Irish heart, which would be likely to break out into more violent discontent against the Holy See than even that, which was manifested when there was question of the Veto. The Bigots would not fail to avail themselves of this occasion to brand us as Patrons of ignorance under the tyrannical influence of a foreign Power; and the very poor themselves, who find by experience the minds of their children opening under this system to useful knowledge, with perfect safety to their Religious principles, would undoubtedly look with much less reverence than heretofore on the decisions of Rome. In fact it is doubtful if even the Holy See itself could succeed against the clear convictions of the People.

Even Murray had temporarily lost his celebrated equilibrium under the pressure of defeat, and like Crolly he too, uncharacteristically, chose to lash out at Roman scapegoats, Kirby, the vice-rector of the Irish College, and the English Jesuit, who had criticized the *Scripture Lessons* and who was now accused of being anti-Irish.[87]

---

85 Crolly to Murray, 5 July 1839, DDA.
86 Lord Clifford to Murray, 18 June 1839, DDA. Clifford, writing from Rome to Murray, told him that Higgins had left that city a few days previously in the knowledge that the congregation of Propaganda disapproved of the national system and would direct him to retire from the board. Murray had received a similar indication from the secretary of Propaganda, Archbishop Cadolini, via Paul Cullen.
87 Murray to Cullen, 12 July 1839, AICR.

But the transmission of the Lord Lieutenant's letter, which so power-fully reinforced the majority view, added a new and, from the Roman point of view, disturbing dimension to the issue. It had not arrived in Rome, however, when the cardinals met on 15 July 1839 to settle the issue. The central question drawn up in accordance with the curial practice by those immediately involved in the matter was whether or not to tolerate Catholic participation in the national system. If the answer was positive a further query concerned permission for Catholics to use the books that had been denounced; if negative, whether or not the verdict could go forth in the pope's name, since the bishops had appealed to him directly. The answer was negative; and it was further decided that tactful and careful letters should be sent from Propaganda to the archbishops of Armagh, Dublin and Tuam informing them that the national system had been judged to be dangerous to the Catholic faith and telling them that steps were to be taken to ensure that boys and girls should have a purely Catholic education, that there should be a Catholic institute for training teachers in which there would be no association with Protestants, and that only Catholic books should be used and Catholic teachers employed under the direction of the bishops and parish priests.[88]

No reasons were given for this judgment either then or subsequently. The most likely factor in swaying the minds of the cardinals was probably the *Scripture Lessons* and the *Lessons on the Truths of Christianity*. Significantly, provision was made in the decision-making procedure for giving a separate ruling on the books that had been denounced to the congregation. Even Perrone had not been fully convinced by Archbishop Murray's attempts to exculpate the *Lessons*, and had noted that some passages required a special explanation to make them acceptable theologi-cally to Catholic children; and he had recommended the removal or alteration of these passages. The entry of the *Lessons on the Truths of Christianity* into the controversy may well have administered the *coup de grace* to the defence. A copy of it may have been handed in to the congregation by Higgins or Cantwell. MacHale not only deftly drew attention to an extract from it, that, if not heretical, was at least verging on the erroneous, but he followed up that successful stroke by quoting a more damning piece from Whately's earlier work, the very title of which—*Errors of Romanism*—could not have been more anathematical to the cardinals of Propaganda. And these potent references arrived in Rome shortly before the cardinals met and before any explanation or justification

---

[88] APF, *Acta*, 202, ff 207v-208r.

from the majority side could be obtained. Propaganda later told Murray that the *Lessons on the Truths of Christianity* had aroused considerable anxiety and noted that books in use were 'not only opposed to the dogmas of the Catholic church but also attacked the divinity of the Christian religion'.[89] The threat posed to the faith of children by subjection, or even the slightest possibility of subjection, to material of a perilous nature probably swayed the minds of the cardinals against the system.

However, verdicts of curial congregations are ultimately only recommendations to the pope. They do not take effect until the pontiff confirms them. But on this occasion the customary approval was withheld. The pope, on being presented with the recommendation and given at least a summary of the dispute, concluded that it was so delicate and complicated that he would like to study it more fully. He looked at some of the books, presumably the *Scripture Lessons*, and was unfavourably impressed by them. While this examination was taking place a perfervid plea reached Rome from Archbishop Murray that the pope, before making a final decision, should send a delegate to Ireland who could see for himself how the schools were conducted, or permit a bishop from Ireland to go to Rome to provide further information. The translation of the viceroy's letter also doubtless carried much weight in Rome, for it transformed a division of opinion among bishops into a possible clash between church and state which was likely to involve direct Roman intervention.

Lord Ebrington had written to Murray on 7 July that he had heard that great exertions had lately been made 'not wholly without success to prejudice the Heads of the Church of Rome against the System of National Education under the direction of that Board of which you have been from the first so valuable a member'. Excusing himself for interfering because of the bearing a mandate from Rome prohibiting Roman Catholics from sending their children to the national schools would have on the moral and social condition of Ireland, he recalled the support given to the system by the clergy, its wide acceptance by the people, and the scrupulous good faith with which its principles were maintained despite opposition in parliament from members of the established church. Asking rhetorically if the poor people to whom the system was so advantageous could be induced to withdraw their children from it without great dissatisfaction or if the clergy would not regret an order to prohibit what they had so strongly recommended, he pointed out that the Catholic poor would be left in a grievous state of moral and intellectual destitution since

[89] APF, SOCG, 958, ff 39r-40r.

they 'would have no chance of obtaining from the Legislature any aid again in terms equally favourable'.[90]

However courteous the terms in which this letter was couched, the import was clear: Dublin Castle was throwing its full weight behind the national system and inviting the Catholics to take it or leave it. No better arrangement was on offer and the consequences for Catholics of an order to withdraw from the system were extremely bleak.

Despite the rumours no official decision reached Crolly or Murray from Rome. Crolly was surprised and confused by this silence, but assuming that the communication Murray had received was fully accurate, wondered if he should call a national meeting of the hierarchy, but he deemed it more prudent to wait until Propaganda communicated the grounds for its condemnation. Still smarting from what he regarded both as a cruel rebuff and the herald of a dismal future, he could not bring himself to believe that the congregation could have reached its conclusion without the mischievous guidance of an influential Irishman:

The reports from all who have been lately at Rome are calculated to convince us that our Agent Dr Cullen has betrayed the confidence which we reposed in him, and in this particular and important case has endeavoured to injure us in the estimation of the S. Congregation. I am persuaded that the Letter which I wrote to him, for the information of the Holy Father, has not been fairly submitted to the consideration of His Holiness, which would have prevented an unfavourable decision against a System of Education so advantageous to our holy Religion. If the other Prelates will agree with me, Dr Cullen will be troubled no longer with the labours of our Agency.[91]

Promising to write at length to the pope, he invited Murray to forward suggestions for inclusion in his letter.

Murray was not disturbed by this allegation. Having recovered his balance after the initial shock and disappointment, he replied that he did not suspect Cullen of acting against them even though he did not like their 'education doings'. Believing strongly in the effectiveness of a deputation to Rome, he suggested that Crolly would be their most influential plenipotentiary. Rather than call a meeting of bishops favourable to the system and thereby give rise to 'newspaper discussions', he judged it best to settle the issue by correspondence and so had written to Archbishop Slattery of Cashel to inquire if one of his suffragans would go to Rome to represent their opinions. He felt sure that Bishop Kinsella of Ossory would go if necessary, but concluded that Crolly and one other would suffice, and assuming that Crolly might find a suffragan more

---

[90] Ebrington to Murray, 7 July 1839, SOCG, 958, ff 76r-79r.
[91] Crolly to Murray, 4 Aug. 1839, DDA.

convenient, mentioned both Cornelius Denvir of Down and Connor and Michael Blake of Dromore, a former rector of the Irish College in Rome, whose knowledge of the city and language would be useful.[92]

Crolly was not convinced by Murray's apparent attempt to exculpate Cullen. He repeated his conviction that Cullen had 'not acted honestly in this case, and I know that Dr Wiseman entertains that opinion'.[93] But he was no less critical and with much more justification of the role played by the bishops of Ardagh and Meath: 'Drs H. & C. may yet be sorry for the very unbecoming part, which they have taken in this business'. Other advocates of the majority subsequently believed that Cullen acted against them, but there is no written evidence to prove that he so acted at this stage of the dispute, and, as subsequent controversies showed, when Cullen felt strongly about an ecclesiastical problem, he was far from reluctant to put his thoughts on paper. MacHale recalled to him at an early stage of the dispute how the national board 'even in its infancy . . . met with our disapprobation'.[94] A note in the archives of Propaganda in Cullen's writing shows that at the end of 1838 his sympathies were with Murray. Having shown that he had taken the measure of MacHale by describing him as a man of ability, distinguished for his furious opposition to the national system, he went on to say that Murray in his public reply to him had succeeded wonderfully in demonstrating that MacHale's objections to the system were without foundation; nothing, he added, could be better than the manner in which he had corrected his erring brother, whose conduct had caused surprise and pain to every intelligent Catholic in Ireland—conduct which was a mystery because Murray revealed that shortly before MacHale's denunciation of the system as radically evil he had sought money for a school at Hollymount in his diocese. This action had proved that till then, at least, he had approved of the system which shortly afterwards he condemned as fully evil.

The recipient of letters from both sides, Cullen, who was generally cautious and reserved, passed on to both parties advice which undoubtedly reflected the mind of Propaganda that they should cease from arguing their case in the newspapers.[95] He translated the rules of the system at Murray's request,[96] adding a note to explain that the bible could

[92] Murray to Crolly, 19 Aug. 1839, DCDA.
[93] Crolly to Murray, 23 Aug. 1839, DDA. Nicholas Wiseman, the rector of the English College, was later praised by the Dublin priests who were defending the system for his kindness and helpfulness. Wiseman told them that he was asked by Propaganda to examine MacHale's comments on the *Scripture Lessons* but declined to do so. (Meagher to Hamilton, 24 Dec. 1839, DDA.)
[94] MacHale to Cullen, 24 Feb. 1838, AICR.   [95] Ibid., 26 Mar. 1839, AICR.
[96] Acta, 202, ff 233r-235v.

only be read in separate religious instruction, and he also, in whole or part, translated other letters of Murray for Propaganda. Murray once remarked to him that 'the opponents of the national system did not scruple to reckon you on their side, your judgement will, I am sure, be an honest one; and that is all I would desire'. This was intended as a polite hint not to stray from a position of neutrality, if he could not support Murray's side. Cullen's suspicions of government policy would have inclined him towards MacHale's views and, undoubtedly, the over-sanguine Higgins interpreted the agent's comments in a favourable light and was happy to boast of his influential support for the minority side to discourage and demoralize the majority.[97] And in the atmosphere of rumour and intrigue which the presence of Higgins and Cantwell heightened in June, it was understandable that Cullen was accused of strong partisanship. Though a translation of Crolly's lengthy letter of 4 Febuary 1839 does not survive, he may have submitted one to Propaganda or may have translated it orally in part for the secretary of the congregation. One of the agents who subsequently travelled to Rome to defend the majority side believed that Cullen's neutrality was not benevolent:

With regard to Dr Cullen's own part in the affair it seems to me certain that he never has himself studied the question & just as indubitable that he has taken no active part whatever adverse to our interests—but I *suspect* that he has been alarmed by the exaggerated—that is not the epithet—but let it stand—accounts that have been given here by bishops, priests & friars of the dangers to be apprehended & that if his opinion has chanced to be asked he did not defend us.[98]

He was probably alarmed by some of the extracts from the *Scripture Lessons*[99] and by the comparisons being made between the Irish system of education and those of France, Germany and Holland, which had allegedly been productive of much harm to the faith of Catholic children on the continent. However, on the basis of the information received in Ireland the agents remained wary of Cullen's role, though grateful for the kindness he showed them.

[97] MacHale to Cullen, 28 Oct. 1839. MacHale subsequently recognized Cullen's right not to commit himself to either side: 'From your station as agent of the Bishops of Ireland who are so divided on this momentous Controversy it is not to be expected that you would take any part nor could any of us feel jealousy at your perfect neutrality.'

[98] Meagher to Hamilton, 19 Nov. 1839, DDA. An official letter from the bishops' agent accusing Cullen of supporting MacHale's side was shown to Murray who gave him a polite if oblique warning to stay neutral: 'I need not say how galling this intelligence would be to the great majority of the Irish prelates if they could place the slighest reliance on a piece of information which for many reasons, they could not possibly anticipate'. (Murray to Cullen, 28 Feb. 1840.)

[99] It is clear from a reply of Murray that Cullen had expressed criticism and concern to him both about the *Lessons on the Truth of Christianity* and about the *Scripture Lessons*. (Murray to Cullen, 22 Aug. 1839, DDA.)

Crolly did not pursue his suggestion about dismissing Cullen from the episcopal agency. He would have required proof of Cullen's active involvement on one side—something that in the nature of the case could have been virtually impossible to obtain—and any attempt at carrying out his threat would certainly have further exacerbated the divisions in the hierarchy. Nor did he summon the bishops to a meeting in August 1839, as he had thought of doing. Perhaps, the realization that the outcome might be less than helpful changed his mind. But he did make a further impassioned appeal to the pope, contrasting starkly the opportunities afforded to the Catholics of Ireland by the national system with its predecessors, and begging him to give the system the benefit of a further examination.

Referring to the indescribable pain he felt on hearing that the Catholic poor were to be deprived of the inestimable benefit of the education they had enjoyed for seven years, he explained that he had often in the last two years discussed the system with the bishops of Ireland but especially with his own suffragans and the clergy of Ulster, and from their evidence was sure that the system had promoted morality among the poor Catholics. He suggested that, if the pope were to summon a prelate from each province to Rome, convincing evidence of the benefits of the system would emerge. And he went on to recall in strong and vivid language the powerful forces that conspired to promote proselytism not only among the children but also among their parents; the poor were both enticed by the promise of clothing and intimidated by the threats of expulsion from their homes, if they did not send their children to the proselytizing schools. God then gave them a just and impartial government which supplied them through the national system with the means of combatting those satanical machinations. Praising the four Catholic commissioners as loyal, zealous, energetic and vigilant, and repeating the safeguards of the system he observed that in parliament and the press their bitterest enemies had attacked it because it helped to propagate the Catholic faith. Should it be condemned the bishops and priests would experience new difficulties and the best government they had ever had would be antagonized and religion would suffer not only in the British Isles but also in the British colonies.[100] Murray followed up this plea with a letter with much the same content to Cardinal Fransoni. He repeated many of the arguments already used but

[100] Crolly to Pope Gregory XVI, 14 Aug 1839. APF, SOCG, 958, ff 90r–91r. Crolly gave vent to the anxiety and irritation he was feeling to Murray three weeks later: 'I cannot conceive how the System of Education could be destroyed by any decision at Rome. Surely British subjects will be permitted to cherish a social intercourse and to study together all the ordinary parts of that kind of education by which they may be useful and enlightened members of society'. (Crolly to Murray, 6 Sept. 1839 DDA.)

he added the new information that the British parliament had just voted £50,000 to the commissioners of national education and he explained that the Anglican bishops had objected to the establishment of a similar system in England because they thought it too favourable to Catholics.[101]

In the light of possible church-state confrontations and of the passionate appeals from Ireland, Pope Gregory set up a 'particular congregation' or sub-committee to advise him on the best way to proceed. This committee consisted of Cardinal Fransoni, the prefect, and Archbishop Cadolini, the secretary of Propaganda, who were concerned with the daily affairs of the congregation and would have been familiar with the issues involved. They were joined by Cardinal Lambruschini, the Secretary of State, whose participation reflected a concern about the political implications of the dispute. The other two cardinals were Mai, who had prepared the dossier for the recent decision, and Mezzofanti, the famous linguist. On 2 September[102] this sub-committee met and decided that priests should be welcomed to Rome to present the cases of both parties; bishops as delegates were, however, excluded, as it was feared that an episcopal mission would attract undesirable public expectations. The pope accepted this proposal and on 7 September Propaganda wrote to the archbishops of Dublin and Tuam, asking them each to send a trustworthy priest to Rome to explain and defend their views.[103]

VIII

Murray was immensely relieved by the papal decision. He answered immediately, promising to do as requested and outlining the major elements to be considered. He suggested that discussion should concern two questions: could the system, apart from the books edited by the commissioners, be permitted in those places where the bishops believed that it was beneficial for religion, and was there or was there not any error regarding faith or morals contained in the books? And he added that, even if he and the other bishops broke with the system, many schools erected by Catholics in each province would still continue, as their patrons had

---

[101] Murray to Propaganda, 19 Aug. 1839, ff 92r-94v.
[102] Two different dates are given in the Roman documents for this meeting. One gives 2 September and the other says it took place at the end of August and that the pope approved its recommendations on 1 September. (*Acta* 203, f 409v and SOCG, 958, ff 37r-38v)
[103] Propaganda to Murray and MacHale, 7 Sept. 1839. APF, *Acta*, 203, ff 415r-16v. The exclusion of an episcopal representation was justified by claiming 'id enim expectationi inopportunae palam communiterque commovendae, posset occasionem offerre'.

received financial assistance from the board and entered into an agreement with it.[104]

Before the invitation came from Propaganda to Murray to send a priest-delegate to Rome to explain the system, Crolly had come to the conclusion that the majority should be represented by Bishop Blake and Bishop Kinsella.[105] The exclusion of episcopal representatives ruled them out. Both Crolly and Murray were quite happy to accept that arrangement. MacHale, on the other hand, showed no enthusiasm for this plan. He was quite unwilling to invest anyone of less than episcopal rank with such an important mission. He did not reply until 20 October when he informed Cardinal Fransoni that he had discussed the request from Rome with other bishops at the episcopal ordination of Thomas Feeny, the new apostolic administrator of Killala. He explained that they were prepared to entrust the whole matter to the Roman theologians and did not feel any need to be represented at Rome. Then doing a complete volte-face in case Propaganda would not wear this reasoning, and revealing his real objective of gaining approval for an episcopal delegation, he added that, if Propaganda held that a mission was necessary, they did not think it right in a question of such importance to trust anyone but the most competent men possible and, therefore, if the cardinal prefect would permit, one or two bishops would go to discuss the issue with the pope.[106]

MacHale and his friends seem to have decided that, if bishops were not to be allowed to travel, their best bet was to prevent a delegation of priests, as the majority might find more skilful advocates. They were probably afraid that they could not find representatives who were nearly as hostile to the system as they themselves were. A few days after MacHale's letter Cantwell told Cullen that it was 'not likely that priests will be deputed to give the further information required', that there was 'an effort making to influence one of the Prelates to undertake the task of defendant' and predicted that MacHale would appear as the plaintiff.[107] Higgins, in a typically ebullient mood, claiming the support of all Ireland for their views with the exception of intriguing and 'official and officious personages', and referring to the likelihood of the government's making unexpected concessions, declared that nothing could be more unwise than the limitation of the delegations to priests: 'neither the Bishops, priests or laity would be satisfied, as they think that the discussion before the Holy

[104] Murray to Propaganda, 7 Sept. 1839, APF, SOCG, 958, ff 96r-97r. The date of this letter must be incorrect. Perhaps, it should be 17 September.
[105] Crolly to Murray, 6 Sept. 1839, DDA.
[106] MacHale to Propaganda, 20 Oct. 1839. SOCG, 958, ff 108r-109v.
[107] Cantwell to Cullen, 23 Oct. 1839, AICR.

See, of a question of such magnitude, should not, in common decency, be intrusted to any pair of priests'.[108] However, Rome stood firm and MacHale was compelled to obey.

On behalf of the majority Murray chose as his representatives John Ennis and William Meagher. Ennis had studied in Paris and Meagher in Rome and so they enjoyed the advantage of being able to communicate in French and Italian at Propaganda; Ennis, the senior, was parish priest of Booterstown, and Meagher, who was technically his secretary, was a curate at the Pro-Cathedral in Dublin. Crolly was happy with the choice of an Italian speaker and promised to obtain for him information about the system not only from his own priests but also from the dioceses of Down and Connor, Derry and Raphoe. As he was about to set off for Cork, he hoped also to persuade the bishops whom he could meet there to forward similar details on the system.[109] He himself availed of the meetings of his clergy at conferences in Dunleer, Dundalk, Armagh and Dungannon to collect information on the system. At each of these meetings the parish priests present signed a declaration recalling the pressures put on their people by threats and gifts to send their children to Protestant schools before a just and benign government made acceptable provision for the education of the poor.[110] The parish priests of the Dunleer district said they had 3,000 children in their schools, those of Dundalk had 4,000 in sixteen schools, those of Armagh had about 2,000 in sixteen schools, and those of Dungannon, who lamented the sparsity of schools in their district because anti-Catholic landlords would not grant sites, explained that nonetheless they had thirty-seven schools, which because of religious antagonisms were rarely attended by Protestants, and which numbered 2,500 pupils.[111]

Cornelius Denvir, bishop of Down and Connor, who always gave loyal support to the primate, had obviously planned with the archbishop of Armagh to adopt the same tactic. At the two conferences of the priests of Down and Connor, held in Ballymena and Downpatrick, similar statements with similar wording were prepared and signed by the parish priests. In his accompanying letter to one of the Dublin priests who was commissioned to defend the system, Denvir used uncharacteristically strong and emotive language: he predicted a new campaign of proselytism

[108] Higgins to Cullen, 4 Nov. 1839, AICR.   [109] Crolly to Murray, 29 Sept. 1839, DDA.
[110] 'filii filiaeque indigentium Catholicorum in hac parte Imperii Britannici, laqueis Ministrorum Protestantium Dominorum soli, aliorumque haereticorum, divitum, continuo expositi fuerunt; qui minis, muneribus, vestimentis, aliisque largitionibus usi sunt, ut liberos fidelium, in scholas haereticas, periculo plenas, allicerent.'
[111] APF, SOCG, 958, ff 110r-102r.

and a wild persecution in Ulster, if Catholics broke with the system. Protestants in some parts of his diocese were moving heaven and earth against the system to compel Catholic children to go to the schools of the Irish Biblical Society.[112] Some other bishops from the majority side also conveyed to Rome the approval and appreciation of the system felt by their priests. Ennis and Meagher left towards the end of October, and, presumably, at the instigation of the Lord Lieutenant, who must have kept in contact with Archbishop Murray about the vicissitudes of the dispute, called on Lord Granville, the British ambassador in Paris. He in turn gave them a letter of introduction to the papal nuncio, Archbishop Garibaldi, whose support they sought to elicit. They were disappointed by their first interview with Garibaldi, whom they found cold and reluctant to involve himself in the case, but after the nuncio had had a further meeting with the ambassador, he became more concerned and considerate. Through Granville's intervention they obtained letters of introduction to the French and Bavarian ambassadors in Rome and to 'several others of minor importance'.[113] The nuncio promptly sent a despatch to Cardinal Lambruschini, the secretary of state, in which he reported the interest of the British government in the proceedings.

Garibaldi recounted that Ennis and Meagher had asked him for letters of introduction to Roman prelates, and, though he was loathe to involve himself in a matter outside his responsibility, he gave them letters for Cardinals Brignole and Giustiniani. The British ambassador duly thanked him for this help and went on to point out his country's concern about the success of the national system in Ireland. The government believed that for the sake of the well-being and peace of Ireland the system should not encounter obstacles from the Catholic clergy. Otherwise, it would find itself caught between the Tory opposition, which regarded its educational policies as too favourable to Catholics and the Catholic clergy who would reject their benevolent intentions. Consequently, the papal decision would be of the gravest importance and could contribute to the solution of the difficulties which Ireland presented to the British cabinet.[114]

Lambruschini passed on this information to the congregation of

---

[112] Denvir to Meagher, 30 Oct. 1839, SOCG, 958, ff 106r-107r, 112r-113r, 114rv.
[113] Meagher to Hamilton, 4 Nov. 1839, DDA. Meagher and Ennis also met in Paris Thaddeus O'Malley who had completed a fact finding mission sponsored by the government to report on the education systems in Prussia and Holland. Support from O'Malley, they feared, would be the kiss of death to their cause. (Meagher to Hamilton, 27 Oct. 1839, DDA.) MacHale duly attacked O'Malley for his letters to the press contriving to associate him with the archbishop of Dublin, and Archbishop Cadolini at Propaganda was enraged by O'Malley's publications.
[114] Garibaldi to Lambruschini, 4 Nov. 1839, ASV, Nunz. Parigi, 38, ff 97r-98r.

Propaganda. As Cardinal Secretary of State he did not normally deal with Irish business but his transmission of the nuncio's report would have added some force to the majority case. At least some of the cardinals with whom the final decision rested would have been conscious of the wisdom of not offending the powerful and influential British government, unless serious religious issues dictated such a decision.

The Dublin delegates had arrived in Rome long before MacHale could bring himself to choose a representative. He continued to hope against hope that Rome would permit the minority to send a bishop or bishops to put their case. At the end of November he explained to Paul Cullen that Propaganda's insistence on the selection of a non-episcopal agent, 'embarrasses us not a little, since it is difficult to find an Ecclesiastic combining the various qualities of a full knowledge of the System in Principle and details with fluency in the French and Italian languages and who would enjoy our Confidence'. Implicitly appealing for Cullen's help in widening Propaganda's restrictive condition, he suggest that Higgins should be allowed to represent them, but, if not, 'I should wish to go myself, I would go to the ends of the earth to aid in destroying such an engine of heresy'.[115] By collusion, since MacHale was then in Athlone, Higgins wrote on the same day and on the same paper that they should be represented by a bishop and that it should be MacHale. Despite the opposition of the cardinals to episcopal visits to Rome, he was convinced that 'were the state of things emphatically explained to his Holiness, he would willingly consent'.[116]

Cullen must have let Higgins know in reply that the intervention of the British government could be significant as Rome would not wish to antagonize it. Higgins, obviously angered by the fear that their affairs should be 'decided upon, by the rules of political expediency', proposed an ingenious method for the Vatican to break the impasse without embroiling itself with the government. This was a suggestion that Rome would privately convey its views to each bishop and order them to obey as though the order resulted from their own deliberations. It could also inform the primate of its unwillingness to interfere and invite him to exhort them to terminate the controversy themselves. This personal recommendation may also have been inspired by fear of the success of the Dublin delegates. He warned Cullen that Dublin was the one part of the country which represented most imperfectly the clerical mind or feeling of Ireland. Though he conceded that the Dublin delegates were good

[115] MacHale to Cullen, 29 Nov. 1839, AICR.　　[116] Higgins to Cullen, Ibid.

priests, he implied that they represented but a small and eccentric part of the Irish clerical body.[117]

MacHale too was alarmed at the success which the Dublin deputies were reputed to be achieving, for he reported that the impression had reached Ireland that 'having failed by argument and fair means the deputies were employed in conveying as covertly and insidiously as they could hints tantamount to menaces in case of an adverse decision'. Given this situation, he dropped all pretence about his attitude towards going to Rome: 'Still I think it would be well in case of a protracted or hard pushed contest that I should have his Holiness express approval that I should go to Rome'. However, he was not given the option. On 25 December he wrote to the cardinal prefect of Propaganda excusing himself for the delay by pointing out the difficulty of finding an Italian speaker among the clergy, since the older priests educated in Rome (before the closure of colleges during the French occupation of the city) had died. Nonetheless, he promised that a delegate would set off in the following week.[118] On 12 January he identified his representative to the cardinal as Martin Loftus, the chancellor of the diocese, and a former professor of Irish at Maynooth, who did not understand Italian but who hoped to submit his case in Latin.[119]

The arrival of the delegates in Rome did not pass unnoticed by the British agent in that city. Thomas Aubin, who was technically an attaché at the British Embassy in Florence but who held a watching brief for Britain at the papal court, reported to the Foreign Office that he had told his contact at Propaganda, Monsignor Capaccini, that before making a pronouncement the Holy See should 'examine well whether their interference would run counter to any act of the British Legislature for public education in Ireland and I added that any step taken at Rome which might tend to thwart the provisions of Government on this head would give rise to consequences highly detrimental to the Roman Catholic subjects, and to the real interest of their church in the British Empire'.[120] Had MacHale known of this attempt to put pressure on the Vatican, his strictures on the baseness of British intrigue would have reached new depths of fury.

MacHale promptly followed up the announcement of Loftus' mission

[117] Higgins to Cullen, 6 Dec. 1839, AICR.
[118] MacHale to Propaganda, 25 Dec. 1839, APF, SOCG, 958, ff 141r–142v.
[119] Ibid., 12 Jan. 1840, f 145rv.
[120] Aubin to Henry Edward Fox, 7 Jan. 1840, PRO, F.O. 79/97. Aubin wrote again on 18 Jan. to inform the Foreign Office that while MacHale's delegates had not arrived the principal of the Irish College was acting for the archbishop of Tuam. Capaccini had meanwhile had an inverview with the Dublin deputy, and had undertaken to act with energy and zeal to prevent any decision being taken that would clash with the provisions of the British government in Ireland.

with a denunciation to Rome of Thaddeus O'Malley. O'Malley, *un prêtre contestataire par excellence*, had begun his career in Limerick, transferred to the United States when he found himself threatened with penalties because of his troublesome behaviour, quickly got embroiled in a dispute in Philadelphia which degenerated into a schism, whence he was again expelled. He then spent some time in Rome, sought pardon from the Vatican and at its suggestion was taken into Dublin where the archbishop allowed him to celebrate Mass in the Pro-Cathedral and live in rooms attached to it but did not enrol him among the diocesan clergy.[121] When the controversy over education broke out the smell of battle proved too strong for this doughty warrior, and he rushed headlong into the fray in defence of the national system. His was the last support that Crolly and Murray needed: his opposition would probably have been more beneficial. MacHale was not slow to spot and exploit O'Malley's potential for damaging the majority cause.

Describing him simply, and incorrectly, as a priest of the Dublin diocese, he referred to O'Malley's recent tour of Holland, Belgium, France and Germany allegedly at the behest of supporters of the national system and his defence of the forms of mixed education prevailing in Prussia and Holland. Complaining that O'Malley in his writings claimed that the pope's authority to interfere was limited to a judgement of the *Scripture Lessons*, the archbishop of Tuam referred to the painful situation created by Murray's refusal to comment on writings smacking of Jansenism and other heresies and thereby seeming by his silence to favour the author and approve of his book.[122] MacHale, in effect, was telling Rome to judge the cause by the kind of advocate it attracted, and hoping that the inevitable condemnation of the advocate would help damage the cause.

IX

The annual meeting of the bishops was due to take place on 11 February 1840, and promised to be a stormy one. And before it occurred a further development in the controversy ensured that it would live up to its promise.

On 6 February, Walter Meyler, the vicar-general of Dublin, in

---

[121] Ennis and Meagher to Propaganda, APF, SOCG, 958, 10 Feb. 1840, ff 167r-168v. Murray defended his tolerating O'Malley at the Pro-Cathedral by maintaining that 'it is hardly safe, in a Country like this to drive a Priest of some talent and strong feelings to extremities without a real necessity'. (Meagher to Cullen, 28 Jan. 1839, AICR.)

[122] MacHale to Propaganda, 14 Jan. 1840, APF, SOCG, 958, ff 147r-148v.

response to a request for information from the delegates in Rome, forwarded a questionnaire to all the parish priests of Ireland except those of the archdiocese of Tuam. His queries were mainly factual and innocuous: he wanted to find out how many national schools there were in each parish, the maximum number of pupils in attendance, and the proportion of them which was Catholic; the religious denomination of the teachers, by whom they were appointed, and whether or not they enjoyed the approbation of the parish priest, if not appointed by him; if the teachers were Protestant, whether or not they had ever interfered with the religion of the children; the religion of the patrons who were not priests and whether or not they were friendly to Catholics. In his accompanying letter Meyler, however, left himself open to criticism by ignoring the minority case completely and by referring only to the delegates from the majority; they had been provided, he asserted, with all the necessary information and 'the matter being about to be brought to a successful termination' nothing more was required.

In a letter which clearly bore the stamp of MacHale's style and was dated 10 February the ten minority prelates lambasted Meyler's communicating with their priests as they were leaving or had left their dioceses for the meeting in Dublin, thus 'adding treachery to the unprecedented and unjustifiable conduct of interfering with the Clergy and people over whom we alone, our holy and venerated Pope excepted, have canonical jurisdiction and control'. Charging that the queries did not even touch on the anti-Catholic nature of the national system, the internal construction, and the unlimited power as well as the schismatical and heretical tendencies of the board, the bishops expressed the hope that their statement would alert their people to 'such insidious and schismatical attempts as the present, and to prevent intermeddling ecclesiastics of every grade, from interfering in the religious concerns of those placed, by Divine Providence' under their spiritual care. What galled the archbishop of Tuam and his associates was the likelihood of the majority obtaining evidence from priests of their dioceses which could be used to telling effect against their own case.[123]

---

[123] D.E.P., 11 Feb. 1840. Meyler hit back at the 'many personal, most offensive and injurious accusations' contained in this letter and wondered in amazement how the bishops could have signed it. He insisted that he was acting on behalf of Archbishop Murray and that there was nothing improper in seeking the information he sought. In a postscript he remarked that he had learned that the bishops of Achonry and Elphin had not attended the meeting and wondered how their signatures could be attached to the document or how they could accuse him of tampering with their clergy in their absence. This letter was dated 14 Feb. and was published on 15 Feb. The ten bishops in their response, far from retracting their accusations against Meyler, referred to 'the captious interrogatories of this unauthorised and intermeddling ecclesiastic' and justified their use of the terms 'treachery' and 'schismatical'. (D.E.P. 20 Feb. 1840.)

Hastening, in the middle of their discussions, to send a copy of the letter to Cullen to throw light 'on the intrigues resorted to in procuring very equivocal approbations of the System', MacHale added the text of a proposition that he planned to submit to the bishops on the following day. This declared that, though they preferred a separate system, they would be willing, if the Pope approved, to tolerate a mixed system which was founded on the bishops' resolutions of 1826. Its security should be guaranteed by an act of parliament which ensured equality of membership between Catholics and Protestants on the board of commissioners, fair representation from each of the four provinces, and that among the Catholics there should be two bishops chosen from each province by their colleagues to guard both faith and morals and the just distribution of the funds.[124]

The preliminary skirmish ensured that the meeting was conducted in a very tense atmosphere. The majority subsequently reported to the pope that they had been pained by the writings of O'Malley and the letter of the minority against Meyler accusing him of deceit and schism. According to MacHale's account, the primate proposed, and Cantwell seconded his proposal, on the second day of the meeting, that a committee of three prelates who were favourable and three who were unfavourable to the system should be appointed to make 'an arrangement that would, if possible, establish unanimity in the system of combined education amongst the prelates of Ireland.' What exactly was meant by 'unanimity' is unclear and what Crolly had in mind was undoubtedly agreement on a formula that could be submitted to the government for alterations that would satisfy his opponents. There was no indication given that the majority would withdraw their support from the system, if particular conditions were not met.

The prelates chosen to represent the majority were Crolly, Bishop Ryan of Limerick and Bishop Kinsella of Ossory; the minority was represented by MacHale, Higgins and Cantwell. MacHale's side put forward as a bargaining counter a proposition that separate education was preferable and that it could be obtained, if the prelates were unanimous in requesting it. As MacHale admitted this suggestion was unlikely to win general backing and, consequently, the primate 'undertook the task of drawing up an arrangement which he prosecuted with zeal and efficiency, aided by the hearty cooperation of the entire committee'. The 'arrangement' consisted of six points which were then adopted by the meeting for

[124] MacHale to Cullen, 14 Feb. 1840, AICR.

submission to the Lord Lieutenant. These stipulated that in every national school the bishop, parish priest or curate of the parish where it was situated, should be a patron in order to prevent the appointment of any teacher whose moral and religious conduct was objectionable and, if necessary, to have such a teacher dismissed; that no book or tract for the religious or moral education of Catholic pupils should be admitted to the schools without the approbation of the four archbishops; that in every national school where the pupils were all Catholics, the bishop of the diocese or pastor of the parish, as patrons of the school, should be empowered to appoint or dismiss the teachers, and that the bishop and pastor would have access to the school at all times to give moral or religious instruction (such instruction to be given by the clergy or those appointed by them), and that every book for such instruction should be composed or selected by the bishop of the diocese; that the Lord Lieutenant should be requested to select two lay Catholics from each ecclesiastical province as commissioners and that a bishop from each province, chosen by his colleagues, should also be a member of the board; that the lecturer in the model schools appointed to instruct the Catholic teachers in religion, morals or history should be a Catholic and have satisfactory testimonials of religious and moral conduct from the bishop of the diocese where he had previously resided; and that when the funds of the national system would be sufficient, a model school should be established in each of the four provinces.[125]

Crolly and his team would certainly have known that the Lord Lieutenant would not accept most of these points. He could have agreed to the last one; he could have promised a restructured board; he could have acknowledged the right of the four archbishops to choose the books for the religious instruction of Catholic children; but the acceptance of the other terms would have involved a major upheaval, which the government would not have risked. Crolly undoubtedly knew this and went along with MacHale's demands, in the hope that, when refused, MacHale might stop shouting about the likelihood of obtaining major concessions by public pressure. The petition was not presented, therefore, as an ultimatium but rather as a means of bringing all the bishops to support the national system.

The viceroy, however, rejected all alterations in the constitution of the board or in the regulations under which it had operated. Pointing out that the diffusion of education on equal terms among all denominations was

[125] MacHale, pastoral letter and MacHale to Murray, D.E.P., 7, 19, 31 Mar. 1840.

the principle of the system, he insisted that any departure from that principal by the commissioners would be 'a violation of their duty, and a perversion of their trust'. Reiterating the rules about the selection of patrons, the appointment and dismissal of teachers, and the choice of books for common instruction, he asserted that the Catholic members of the board had been most praiseworthily assiduous in inspecting the model schools and that this involvement should be 'a sufficient security' that the lecturer in religion, morals and history would never explain them in an irreligious or offensive manner. Regretting the opposition which some Catholic prelates had shown to the system, the Lord Lieutenant concluded by stating that he would rejoice to see those attitudes changed by a closer examination.[126]

The first public inkling of these proceedings came in MacHale's Lenten pastoral two weeks after the meeting. He coolly told the people of Tuam that an 'arrangement' was unanimously adopted by the bishops to protect the faith and morals of the children and safeguard episcopal jurisdiction in education, and then submitted to the viceroy, since the public grants came from the government. The prelates had hoped that their 'arrangement' would be sanctioned by the Lord Lieutenant as he had already agreed to 'the prayers of a few Presbyterians'. Though he refused to accede to their 'proposed requisition', the unaminity of the Hierarchy had been achieved and 'that unanimity attests the wisdom, the justice, and the extreme moderation of the proposed but rejected arrangement'. MacHale then went on to state that they had done everything possible consistent with their conscientious obligations to secure a fair proportion of parliamentary funds but the viceroy had given the impression that he should have the same control over the books and teachers in the schools as he had over the public finances.[127]

Readers could draw only one conclusion from this account of the bishops' actions; they had unanimously laid down conditions on the fulfilment of which depended their continued support of the national system. The viceroy had rejected all their conditions and there was nothing further which they could do. The majority had never understood the agreement in this light at all; they had agreed to the presentation of the six demands to the viceroy in the hope of obtaining some concession which would enable MacHale to call a cease-fire.

Archbishop Murray accordingly felt obliged to correct the impression which he diplomatically claimed 'a cursory reader' might draw from

---

[126] Ibid., 31 Mar. 1840.   [127] Ibid., 7 Mar. 1840.

MacHale's assertion about the unanimity of the hierarchy. He insisted that 'the same prelates who gave their countenance and support' to the system in the previous year were its 'steady advocates, still, in its present unaltered state'. All they had done at the last meeting was to express their readiness to 'acquiesce' in the 'proposed arrangement', if it were adopted but declaring at the same time, that, if it should not meet 'his Excellency's approval, the rejection of it would not, in the least, diminish their ardour in continuing to the system in its present form, the same conscientious support to which they had hitherto considered it justly entitled'.[128]

MacHale did not take kindly to being corrected and deflated by one who, he believed, had 'become the panegyrist of the most offensive calumniators of the Catholic creed, and the Apologist of the insidious and poisonous productions that were tainting the faith' of their flocks. In an outburst of towering rage he set out to bludgeon his opponent into silence by the unscrupulous use of charges and insinuations, which were at best mere half-truths. Referring to Murray's remark about feeling pain on reading the pastoral, the archbishop of Tuam scornfully commented that his brother of Dublin seemed to have felt no pain 'in recommending strenuously erroneous books that are reprobated at Rome', and wondered if he had felt pain at the scandalous doctrines published by one of his priests, which were insulting to the Holy See, calumnious of the Catholic priesthood of Ireland and which filled the faithful people with sorrow. Had the archbishop of Dublin, he continued contemptuously, manifested more pain about the errors nearer home, he might have been spared solicitude about the flocks of other pastors, and he proceeded to advise Murray in future to confine himself to his care of his own flock. MacHale concluded by stating that, if he thought his advice would be heeded, he would counsel Murray to withdraw from the board, the system would then collapse and the education of Catholic youth would be free and flourishing, as ultimately petitions for grants to Catholic schools would have to be heeded by the government.

Murray, as was to be expected, replied to this attack but not in kind. Deliberately keeping his remarks low key, he countered MacHale's charge of publishing their proceedings by asking if the alleged substance of them had not been published in the pastoral. He then quoted a letter from Crolly referring to the pact among the bishops not to publicize details of their decisions, a pact which Crolly claimed was made precisely because they were not unanimous in their views:

[128] Murray to MacHale and MacHale to Murray, 19 Mar. 1840, Ibid.

As there was just as little unanimity among the prelates on this subject (i.e. education) at the end as there had been at the commencement of the general meeting, it was strongly recommended, and agreed to by all, that there should be no publication on either side respecting the experiment which had been tried without success to obtain certain alterations in the present system.

This quotation, as Murray noted, disposed of 'the alleged unanimity of the prelates, as far as regards the merits of the education question'. He did concede, however, that there was unanimity on a different issue: the resolution to submit the proposed arrangement to the Lord Lieutenant, but the majority of the bishops had made it clear that their continued support of the system did not depend on those changes being implemented. Murray then quoted extracts from the letters of three other bishops to show that he had accurately represented their understanding of what had happened. He concluded his letter by a gentle but effective rebuttal of MacHale's advice to confine himself to the care of his own flock and by the enunciation of what was to become the policy of the majority:

Would it be too much to express a wish that other prelates would be influenced by the same admonition, and leave every bishop in his own diocese to accept or to reject any system of education, according as he may find it useful or pernicious to his flock?[129]

Murray had written to Crolly immediately after the publication of MacHale's pastoral lamenting the interpretation placed on their deputation to the viceroy, and Crolly had replied by return of post expressing his agreement that MacHale had made 'a very unfair use of our late charitable endeavours to reconcile His Grace and the other nine Prelates to our National System of Education'. As Murray had been absent for part of the meeting, he then reminded him of what had happened. They had received a letter from Cullen (which had conveyed the pope's desire for peace and harmony) telling them that the pope believed that the system with some modifications might be accepted, and the prelates unanimously agreed with that. Overtures were then made to the minority 'and it was distinctly declared, that if the modifications which were submitted to His Excellency the Lord Lieutenant, did not meet with his approbation; then every Prelate on both sides, should be at liberty to retain the opinion which he held on the present System of Education'. The principal modification on which MacHale and his friends insisted was the admission to the board of a prelate from each of the four provinces selected by his provincial colleagues, but the Lord Lieutenant deemed this proposal likely to disrupt

[129] Murray to MacHale, 10 Mar. 1840, Ibid.

the harmony obtaining at the board. When the deputation drew a blank from the viceroy, the minority declared that it would continue its opposition, 'whilst the majority of the Prelates also openly stated that they would continue their unaltered approbation of a National System of Education which [sic] so many advantages to the poor Catholic children of this Kingdom'. In conclusion Crolly insisted that those facts could not 'be contradicted without a deviation from truth', and confided to Murray that he did not plan to publish any reply to MacHale as he feared that further controversy would only increase the scandal which was already too great.[130]

The most striking quality of Murray's and Crolly's letters is their mildness. MacHale had succeeded in conveying the impression that the hierarchy was united in demanding significant alterations to the national system to make it acceptable to them—an impression which ran contrary to the views of the majority. The majority would have been entitled to feel extremely indignant, if not enraged, by this misrepresentation of their position and by the humiliation which it inflicted on them before the Lord Lieutenant and the commissioners and officials of the national system. Public controversy between the bishops was not only highly distasteful to both archbishops personally but also, they believed, a source of scandal to their people.[131] Murray in his reply to MacHale in the newspaper was understandably circumspect but Crolly in a private letter might have been expected to give vent to the frustration and annoyance he was forced to endure in trying to preserve what he regarded as the best system of education the government was likely to offer to the Catholics of Ireland. But he refrained from manifesting such sentiments.

Before opening fire on these issues in the press MacHale sought to convey the same impressions to Rome about the unanimity of the bishops in demanding changes in the system. As soon as both sides agreed on the requests to be made to the Lord Lieutenant, he wrote to inform Cullen that they had laid a basis on which all could stand without the reproach of

---

[130] Crolly to Murray, 9 Mar. 1840, DDA.

[131] James Browne, the bishop of Kilmore, was probably expressing the fears and embarrassment of most of the prelates of both camps when he wrote: 'These letters appealing to the people must have the effect of diminishing our authority which is supported by the moral feelings of the people; and may also divide the people themselves into parties'. (Browne to Cullen, 4 Apr. 1840, AICR.) Murray detected another source of scandal in the minority bishops continuing to allow or encourage their clergy to connect their schools to the system. Cantwell was engaged in making such arrangements for a school at Athboy when the episcopal meeting took place in Dublin. Murray commented: 'This apparent double dealing of so many of our Prelates, who denounce in word what they encourage in practice, has exceedingly scandalized the intelligent portion of the Catholic body, and lowered in the minds of the Protestants to a most humiliating degree, the character of our Prelacy. To the Government their proceedings appear to be utterly factious, not having seemingly any principle of Religion to rest upon'. (Murray to Cullen, 28 Feb. 1840, AICR.)

a division and to express his hope that the pope would be happy with the
document which would be sent to him showing the vast and important
changes favourable to episcopal freedom and authority on which they had
insisted.[132] Cullen was about to convey this news to the pope, when Ennis
and Meagher let him know that the question was far from settled and that
all would depend on whether or not the government would accept the
terms which for the sake of peace the majority had agreed to.[133]

A few days later Cullen received from Crolly a letter containing the
petition submitted to the viceroy and his reply, which were to be
submitted in translation to the pope. The majority also wrote directly to
the pope to explain that they did not believe that there was any chance of
the viceroy withdrawing the power of appointing and dismissing teachers
from the patrons and giving it to the bishops and clergy as MacHale and
his supporters wanted. Anyhow, parish priests and lay Catholics already
constituted the greater percentage of patrons—some 600 of the 1200
patrons were priests—and they already enjoyed that power. If that
concession had been made, Protestants, who already bemoaned the
influence of Catholics in the system, would have protested more vigorously against it. The condition, they observed, on which the archbishop of
Tuam insisted as a *sine qua non* of his cooperation was the increase of the
board of commissioners by two lay and one episcopal representative from
the four provinces. The viceroy thought this move would produce further
discord, and the majority concluded that distance would preclude the
atendance of bishops from the provinces at the weekly meetings of the
board. The majority also sought to minimize the rejection of the plea for
altering the arrangements at the model school by pointing out that it then
numbered fifty four Catholic and only four Protestant teachers on its
rolls, and that a learned and pious Vincentian not only taught faith and
morals but also taught catechism in the boys' department and that Sisters
of Mercy taught catechism in the girls' department. They added that 250
priests in the dioceses of the bishops opposed to the system were patrons
of national schools, and again pleaded that their poor should not be
deprived of such a necessary fountain of learning and that a source of
friction with their benevolent government would not be created.[134]

The majority in interpreting the viceroy's rejection of the 'arrangement' were engaged in an exercise of damage limitation; they had to

---

[132] MacHale to Cullen, 14 Feb. 1840, AICR.   [133] Meagher to Hamilton, 29 Feb. 1840, DDA.
[134] Crolly and others to Pope Gregory XVI, 18 Feb. 1840, SOCG, 958, ff 151r-152v. The bishops ended by
    imploring the pope 'ut hic fons doctrinae tam necessarius ab iis non praescindatur; et ut cum gubernio
    nostro tam benevolo nulla dissidiui causa de hac re momentosa oriatur.'

depict his blanket refusal of all concessions as innocuously as possible. And their explanation of the rights already possessed by parish priests as patrons was fully correct and justifiable. Some of them, however, must have been disappointed that he had made no gesture towards them. And his dulcet comments about his aspirations for the removal of episcopal opposition and his view that the desired changes could not improve the operation of a system that was so successfully diffusing the blessings of moral and intellectual improvement must have stuck in the throats of the more belligerent members of the minority and contrasted rather lamely with the commissioners' response to the prolonged campaign of the Presbyterian church.

Privately, Murray assured Cullen in Rome that the majority had tried to reach the amicable settlement which he counselled them to seek, but they were never prepared to consent 'unless compelled by a higher Power, to deprive our people of the important advantages, which the system, even in its present form affords and expose our Religion to the disasters which the destruction of it would occasion'.[135] Bishop Blake summed up the contrasting position in a thoughtful analysis when he wrote of one set of speakers seeming 'to confine themselves to an abstract view of the subject, apparently unmindful of the adage that what in the abstract might be pronounced best, would, sometimes, not be even good, when in conjunction with its circumstances'. And he went on to insist that 'they substitute possible for real dangers, and although they cannot but feel that we stand better now than we were at any former period, since Ireland came under English Dominion, their imagination conjures up spectres, which, if certain combinations should ever take place, might become troublesome, and without reflecting that the more powerful our people become, the less such dangers are to be dreaded, they conclude that the shadow should make us let go the reality, and that we should oppose the friends who are most able to assist us, and set out upon a speculative venture, in which we shall be deserted by our friends and certainly favoured by our enemies'.[136]

The spectre that MacHale's imagination conjured up was that of a retreat by the majority from the concessions demanded of the Lord Lieutenant. 'Would to God' he told Cullen 'the other prelates were as practically unanimous in insisting on the conditions which their judgement has approved as they were in adopting them'. Summarizing the letter of the minority to the pope, he explained that it recalled their efforts to achieve an accommodation with the other prelates; the government's

[135] Murray to Cullen, 21 Feb. 1840, AICR.   [136] Blake to Cullen, 19 Feb. 1840, AICR.

rejection of their petition which reinforced their view that the object of the system was not to educate but to pervert the Catholic people; the sacrifice they had made in acquiescing in any conditions, convinced as they were that 'scarcely any pledges can be sufficient when on one side there is nought but prayer and on the other wealth, an arbitrary power to make new laws etc. and an undoubted disposition to destroy our faith by gradually undermining it'. The pope could insist with the goodwill of all the prelates on the conditions laid down in the petition to the viceroy as the basis of any accommodation. And he repeated the claim that, if the bishops were unanimous in petitioning for a separate grant, they would obtain it, as Catholic Emancipation had been obtained. MacHale then went on to include a suggestion—hoping doubtless that Cullen would pick up the hint and drop it in the appropriate quarter—that 'if Dr. Murray were paternally advised to retire from the Board the system would fall of itself and the Prelates whose feeble and lingering support it receives on account of a deference to him would abandon it to its fate'.[137] MacHale was certainly not naive enough to underestimate the commitment Crolly and the majority felt to the system, *faute de mieux*, and he was obviously advancing this tactic to gain a vantage point from which to mount further attacks.

X

Ennis and Meagher, the deputies of the majority, had reached Rome on 15 November. They brought with them packages from the nuncio in Paris to Cardinal Lambruschini, the secretary of state, and among the letters enclosed was one concerning themselves. Consequently, to their surprise the pope quickly got to know of their arrival, and they were pleased to realize that not only the British but also the French government was exerting itself 'effectually' on their behalf. They soon made contact with English-speaking clerical residents in Rome who would help their case, including Monsignor Charles Acton, an English official in the curia, and the rector, Nicholas Wiseman, and vice-rector, George Errington, of the English College. Paul Cullen promptly told them how their case stood and pointed out that the authorities at Rome 'detested the idea of a mixed education'. In this context they soon concluded that Crolly had made a blunder. William Meagher explained:

[137] MacHale to Cullen, 22 Feb. 1840, AICR. MacHale and others to Pope Gregory XVI, 20 Feb. 1840, SOCG, 958, ff 179r-180r.

What was indeed an injury to us & what you will greatly grieve to hear but not communicate save to those from whom nothing in the business sd be a secret, a letter from the good Dr. Crolly did us, unintentionally, of course, very considerable injury for a principal argument urged by him in favour of the system turned upon the happy results which might be expected from a mixed education in preventing the acerbities which kept Catholics & Protestants in Ireland so uncharitable towards each other—a line of reasoning very good it may be in itself, but utterly incomprehensible to the good people here.[138]

Ennis and Meagher lost no time in meeting the officials of Propaganda—Cardinal Fransoni, who enjoyed the reputation of being saintly but neither clever nor enlightened, and the secretary, Archbishop Cadolini, whom they found to be 'a man of very intellectual character, & of most polished & most amiable manners'.[139] They quickly prepared a summary of Murray's arguments in Italian and set out to overcome in conversation what they regarded as the cardinal's ignorance of the system. Their persuasive efforts soon began to bear fruit: Cardinal Giustiniani, who had been reputedly one of their adversaries, soon told them that he thought the solution was to allow each bishop to make his own decision about tolerating the system in his diocese.[140] They had an audience with the pope on 7 December and through their contacts at Rome initiated a move to get the nuncio at Brussels to write to the Holy See on their behalf.[141]

Though Ennis and Meagher were pleased with the progress of their cause as they lobbied both the cardinals and officials of Propaganda—in January they reported that Cardinals Castracane and Mai, and one of the officials felt the system would be allowed to carry on—they received a bad set-back with the arrival from Tuam of the letters which Thaddeus O'Malley had written in its favour. Meagher could scarcely contain his anger as he wrote of the body blow they had been dealt by this 'Wretch's cursed scribbling', Cadolini was shocked by O'Malley's productions and conveyed his indignation to the delegates. Meagher was extremely embarrassed and could only beg Archdeacon Hamilton, Murray's secretary, 'not to rest night or day until you have obtained the suspension & expulsion from our diocese of this ill-omened pest'.[142]

However, they acquired valuable assistance from the nuncio in Brussels. George Errington, who knew Archbishop Fornari, suggested enlisting his support and wrote to him. The government in London, when

---

[138] Meagher to Hamilton, 19 Nov. 1839. DDA. Though Crolly used this argument at home, he did not make use of it in defending his views at Rome. In his lengthy apologia for the system to Cullen he claimed that the experience of mixed schooling had not been injurious to Catholic children.
[139] Ibid., 20 and 28 Nov. 1839.   [140] Ibid., 5 Dec. 1839.   [141] Ibid., 7 Dec. 1839.
[142] Ibid., 11 and 25 Jan. 1840.

apprised of his willingness to help, decided to use his services. And Archbishop Murray, hearing about his readiness to intervene either from the agents of the majority in Rome or through London, sent one of his vicars general to Brussels to brief him on the national system. Lord Palmerston, the Foreign Secretary, had written to the British ambassador enclosing the correspondence of the bishops and the Lord Lieutenant for the nuncio and for transmission to Rome, begging him to use his best efforts to uphold the system. The nuncio duly reported the ambassador's intervention to Lambruschini, the secretary of state, explaining that the good of religion, the peace of Ireland, the possibility of re-uniting the divided clergy and the confidence which such a distinguished person as Lord Palmerston placed in him—all combined—caused him to accept the invitation to proffer his good offices. He argued that the Catholics were given all the necessary guarantees they required by the system as well as pecuniary aid and commented that it could not be supposed that the majority of the bishops were mistaken and only Tuam and his few partisans were right. Repeating the well-known arguments in favour of the system, he characterized MacHale's pretentions as useless and unreasonable, and dismissed as unattainable the demand that a Catholic bishop or priest should be a patron in each mixed school.

A month later Fornari again communicated with Lambruschini, pointing out that he was inspired to intervene not only by Palmerston's request, but also by the knowledge that the British government was prevented from having any contact, direct or indirect, with the Holy See. He again emphasized MacHale's unreasonableness, the increased dissension provoked by his articles in the newspapers[143] and the scandal caused by a small number of bishops making war on others and thereby diminishing the people's esteem for the episcopate. Again rejecting the likelihood of some of MacHale's demands being met, he concluded by declaring that he was unable to persuade himself that the majority of the bishops were so blind as to miss the danger, if it existed, or so lacking in zeal as to abandon one of their principal duties for the vile motive of winning favour with the government.[144]

The intervention of the British government in the person of Lord Palmerston undoubtedly increased the pressure on Rome to avoid any blanket condemnation of the system. While the Holy See could not tolerate the use of books containing theological errors in the schools, there

---

[143] fuocosi e quasi direi incendiarii; Meagher to Hamilton, 7 May 1840, DDA.
[144] Fornari to Lambruschini, 27 Mar. 1840 and 25 Apr. 1840, APF, SOCG, 958, ff 335r-347r.

was plenty of room for accommodation with the state in many respects of the system, and Palmerston's communication placed the Roman authorities under an additional strain to find a satisfactory compromise. Both Crolly and Murray had stressed the ramifications of the dispute where the British writ ran throughout the world, and that point was now heavily underlined by Palmerston.

Archbishop Cadolini, the secretary of Propaganda, duly requested the delegates to formulate their cases under four headings—the system in general, the religious mixing of youth in the schools, the impact of the system on the rights of the bishops, and the books used by the pupils. He arranged that each side would be allowed to read the other's submission and comment on it.

Both submitted voluminous statements which had been translated into Italian. Ennis and Meagher handed in their defence on 16 March 1840.[145] Loftus, MacHale's delegate to whom it was duly sent, was able to comment on it in his submission. On 20 June Loftus' statement was in turn sent to the Dublin deputies and after four days' perusal of it they passed on their reflections on it to Propaganda.[146] Of necessity both sides repeated most of the arguments that had already been presented and sought to explain away those advanced by their opponents.

On behalf of eighteen bishops and 600 priests, Ennis, who claimed to be dealing with facts rather than arguments, pleaded for two favours: that the bishops should be permitted to accept or reject the system according to the dictates of their consciences formed under the guidance of the Holy Spirit; and that all bishops and priests should be ordered to abstain from public debate in newspapers. And he promised full obedience to the recommendations made by Propaganda to remedy the troubles afflicting Ireland. He went on to make some points that were at once both obvious and effective, for they would help dispel possible misunderstandings about the role of the system in Ireland. He began with the basic fact that no one was obliged to avail of national education, and that other schemes could co-exist with it. The system, the gift of a government that was more sympathetic to Catholics than any other in the past three hundred years, had not claimed a single proselyte. Admittedly, aspects of it were less than desirable but had to be tolerated as had other less satisfactory restrictions on Catholic life—mixed marriages between Protestant and Catholic, and the presence of Protestant trustees on the board of management of

---

[145] Meagher to Hamilton, 21 Mar. 1840, DDA.
[146] Ibid., 9 July 1840. According to Meagher Loftus tried to get 'a peep' at their reply, but failed to do so.

Maynooth. Until the meeting of the bishops in 1839 the testimony of twenty five out of twenty seven of the bishops was favourable to the system.

Ennis, realizing the capital that had been made out of the Protestant commissioners by the MacHale camp, did his best to exonerate them or, at least, to show their unwillingness or inability to use their office to damage Catholic interests. He fully conceded the murkiness of Whately's theological writings and the former Oxford professor's intimate connection with the notorious apostate ex-priest, Joseph Blanco White,[147] but he insisted that, as archbishop of Dublin, he had never opposed the political and civil rights of Catholics. In fact, Whately's succession to the anti-Catholic Magee was regarded as a gesture of goodwill by the government, and as the beginning of an era of peace, and since his transfer to Dublin he had never attacked Catholicism, had rejected the ex-priests who had sought service under him and had prohibited some of his most fiery anti-Catholic clergy from preaching. When Carlile was a commissioner there was never any evidence that he perpetrated any injustice against the Catholic church but, since he had resigned, there was no purpose in expatiating on his behaviour. The danger of the government appointing new commissioners who might abuse their powers was non-existent: the rules by which the board operated guaranteed inalienable rights to priest-managers of schools.

The Dublin deputies devoted much comment to the *Scripture Lessons* and reference was made to the favourable reception accorded to the translation of the gospels from the original Greek by John Lingard, an orthodox English priest, in contradistinction to the hostility expressed by an English theologian to the translation of the *Lessons* from the Greek of St Luke. The *Lessons on the Truth of Christianity* were designed to resist the dechristianization of Protestant England; they did not deny Christ's miracles, and accusations had been mistakenly made that the work attacked orthodox beliefs when it was trying to show the necessity for having good reasons to defend Christianity. Not only was one of the two professors in the normal school a highly respected priest but of the 576 teachers who had been trained there all but 62 were Catholics.[148]

Loftus replied at generous length to Ennis, and, where he could not prove the malignity of the system, relied on circumstantial evidence to

---

[147] Born in Seville of Irish Catholic parents, White was ordained priest in 1800. He came to England in 1810, became an Anglican and an honorary Fellow of Oriel College, Oxford, where he associated with Whately, who was then principal of St Alban's Hall and who dedicated his *Errors of Romanism* to him. He wrote vigorously against Catholicism. Later he became tutor to Whately's children in Dublin.

[148] APF, SOCG, 958, ff 202r-323v. Shorter versions were also submitted to the congregation.

show the dangers to which children could be exposed by falling under the influence or control, however remote, of the anti-Catholic forces associated with it.

The commissioners came under heavy fire. Francis Sadleir, the provost of Trinity College, Dublin, the most Protestant university in the world and one in which many Catholics had apostatized from their faith, had publicly declared his expectation that the new system of education would be an instrument for converting Catholics to Protestantism.[149] Whately in his *Errors of Romanism* had made many malicious and poisonous references to Catholicism; he had referred to 'this system of iniquity, the system of Roman corruption', had denied that the sacrament of the Lord's Supper was, as the Romanists impiously pretended, a renewal of Christ's sacrifice and had mentioned the monstrous congeries of religious frauds in the Roman creed. Carlile had written that the Roman church had supplanted Christianity, that Roman Catholics were not really Christians—their religion being a species of paganism—and yet he was the author of the *Scripture Lessons*, which, according to the secretary of the board of national education, were read by all who were able to read. Lord Plunket, though once a supporter of the rights of Catholics, had lost their esteem because of his defence of tithes, and having a son a bishop and three others clergy in the established church, was very interested in its stability. Little was to be expected of the Catholic commissioners: Bellew, a worthy and respectable man, lived too far away from Dublin—about 40 miles—and rarely attended the board's meetings; John Corballis, who was often compelled by his legal duties to be absent, had diminished the rights of his fellow-Catholics to win the government's favour and in so doing had lost the confidence of his co-religionists; Anthony Blake, who owed his advancement in his legal career to his marriage to the Protestant relative of the viceroy, was widely distrusted by Catholics, and had gone on record before the House of Lords in 1829 as saying that he was the friend of a Protestant power, wanted the Catholic clergy paid by the state and agreed that it was not in the interests of the Catholic church to have anything to do with the pope. Murray's presence on the board, which made the system acceptable to many people, was deceptive; because of the multiplicity of his duties he could not pay attention to the details of administration and counter the duplicitous practices of the Protestant commissioners.

---

[149] He referred to a letter, which Sadleir wrote to the *Dublin Times* of 12 Jan. 1832, in which the provost remarked that, while it was not then practicable to convert Roman Catholics, the new system of education seemed to be the best means for effecting that object.

The principle of mixing children of different religions in schools was, like that of mixed marriages, wrong, and led to liberalism. The same opposition to mixed schools as to mixed marriages should prevail. To familiarize Roman officials with the inequities of the system, Loftus wondered what their reaction would be to a mixed system in Rome under the management of nine Jews and four Christians for which a rabbi had compiled a book of scripture extracts. He then took refuge in theological distinctions when dealing with the question of perversions. Though he could only point to three teachers having abandoned Catholicism, he referred to the proximate dangers of sin inherent in mixing religions and possibly leading to perversions. Quoting the six resolutions of the hierarchy in 1826, he maintained that the national system ignored the bishops' claims. The Tuam deputy made extensive use of the report of the committee of the House of Lords of 1837 and found evidence of widespread use of the *Scripture Lessons* and even of the scriptures themselves by Protestant teachers to Catholic pupils; Crolly had made no objection when present during scripture reading conducted by a Baptist teacher in a mixed school.[150]

Understandably, Loftus repeated most of MacHale's complaints about the denial or limitation of episcopal jurisdiction, the selection of school books and the power of inspectors, and he illustrated his arguments with hypothetical cases. Citing the rule that any book other than sacred scripture or the usual books of the church to which children belonged required the assent of the board for use in religious instruction as a usurpation of the bishops' rights, he also suggested that the bishop could not dismiss a teacher who was personally immoral or who disseminated pernicious doctrines; this neatly ignored the powers of the school managers, the majority of whom were priests. Not surprisingly, in view of the number of Protestants on the board, the viceroy had conceded the demands of the Presbyterians a short time before he rejected those of the bishops. Two facts were then introduced to illustrate the nefarious lengths to which supporters of the system would go: to seduce him from his opposition to the system the bishop of Galway was offered a career for his

---

[150] At the inquiry by the House of Lords into the national system, Robert Ingham, an English visitor, claimed that the Baptist teacher in the Lancasterian school in Belfast read and explained the scriptures daily to all his pupils, one third of whom were Catholics. The authorized version was normally used, but when there was a variation in the Douay translation, he pointed it out and showed how little difference there really was between the two. Crolly had raised no objections to this practice on his last visit to the school. But Maurice Cross, a former teacher in the school and latterly its secretary, maintained that the Catholic children used the Douay translation without notes, as Crolly had long allowed them to do, though he admitted that in a few schools in Antrim and Down the Catholics read the authorized bible with the other pupils. (pp 794-802, 1152-66, 1170-89, H.C. (543-II) viii, 56-64, 414-30, 432-51.)

nephew under the board, and, when the Christian Brothers had with-drawn their schools from the system, a Dublin priest invited those who had contributed funds to them to cease doing so and thereby compel them to rejoin.

Noting that the *Scripture Lessons* were compiled by Carlile, 'an inveterate enemy of the Catholic faith', with the help of a Lutheran minister as a deputy of the Protestant archbishop of Dublin, and had been already condemned at Rome by an English-speaking theologian, and repeating many of the particular objections that had already been made, he suggested that the argument that no one was compelled to use the *Lessons* was very curious; no one had been compelled to read the works of Luther, Calvin or Jansen and yet the church had condemned them. Since many schools did use the *Lessons*, it was reasonable to ask the Holy See to pronounce on their orthodoxy. He claimed that Whately's *Lessons on the Truth of Christianity* was bitterly anti-Catholic, calculated to create Deism rather than to confirm Christianity and that in any case the Catholics of Ireland did not need to have their faith confirmed by that most consum-mate opponent of it. Recalling that the bishops of Ireland had published an English translation of Leo XII's encyclical on latitudinarianism and the use of Protestant versions of scripture in the vernacular, Loftus asked which bishops were faithful to the instructions of the Holy See—those who conformed to its discipline or those who, for a fear of losing public money, would put the education of Catholic children under the control of a board composed of the bitterest enemies of their faith?

Loftus concluded his case by disclaiming any intention of making an invidious comparison between the bishops of the minority and major-ity—and then proceeded implicitly to do so. He pointed out that MacHale and Higgins had held the principal chair of theology at Maynooth, that MacNicholas had been professor of logic and Greek, that Coen and Cantwell had been deans of discipline and Feeny of Killala a professor in the seminary of Tuam. Conveniently ignoring the academic backgrounds of the opposing prelates (which were at least as impressive), he went on to claim with equal hyperbole that almost all the professors of Maynooth and almost every man who had talent and time to study the problem, were opposed to the system. Maintaining that not only all the parish priests in the dioceses of the minority (the evidence of applications for aid, notwithstanding) but some in those of the majority were opposed to the system, he insisted that Murray's withdrawal from the board would bring it down, and to illustrate the capacity of the Irish church to manage its own system he pointed to the four monastic schools opened in

Tuam in the previous eighteen months by the Brothers of St Francis and to the presence of the Presentation and Loreto nuns in almost every city, not to mention the Ursulines and the confraternities that sponsored education.

The Tuam delegate completed his dossier by enclosing translations of two documents of which Propaganda already had copies—MacHale's pastoral of 1 March, and Murray's letters of 22 October 1838 and 8 November 1839—together with a recent letter from MacHale commenting on the contents of the majority's case which he had been allowed to see. In this defence of his position MacHale denied that the proposal for modifying the system came from its opponents: the resolution to do so was proposed by the primate. The accommodation then made was not merely tolerated but adopted and he (MacHale) never claimed that the other prelates had adopted his views of the system, nor had he violated a pact by publishing false accounts of the bishops' meeting; he had been obliged to reply to a false report which had appeared in the *Monitor*.[151]

Ennis and Meagher duly responded to the arguments put forward by Loftus. Recalling the scandal caused by MacHale's letters to the press, they went on to defend the commissioners who had been so violently assailed. They did not miss the opportunity afforded by Loftus' claim that Bellew's home being forty miles distant from Dublin was too remote to permit him to attend weekly meetings of the board; they inquired sceptically how bishops from the provinces could attend weekly meetings in Dublin. They explained that Whately had not misused his position as a commissioner, however numerous his previous calumnies against Catholicism; that Bellew also had a home in Dublin; that Corballis had not lost the confidence of Catholics; and they defended Blake from the charge that he had supported the payment of the Catholic clergy by showing how that suggestion was acceptable in its pre-Emancipation context. The phrase he used about being a friend of Protestant power was to be understood as indicating a willingness to take the oath of allegiance to a Protestant sovereign. Blake had said that the Catholics, when persecuted, had sought help from the pope as a secular prince but such appeals would no longer be compatible with their religious and civil rights.

Challenging the concept of proximate danger of sin being offered by the system, they wondered if 600,000 or 700,000 children could be educated in the schools over a long period without perversions and yet suggestions about dangers of sin could be made. If three teachers out of

---

[151] Loftus to Monsignor Cadolini, SOCG, 958, ff 365r–519r.

2,000 had apostatized, three times that number of priests had done so and yet no one argued that the priesthood should be destroyed. Noting that Murray had read the draft versions of the *Scripture Lessons* they quoted the instruction of the resident secretaries of 19 April 1839 which forbade inspectors to inquire if the *Lessons* were used. If they were so Protestant, how could Protestant theologians write·books to prove that they were papist?

The Dublin deputies concluded with some telling statistics. They pointed out that 50 of the 534 parish priests who had expressed support for the system came from the dioceses of the minority and among them were the vicars general of ten dioceses and the chancellor of the cathedral at Tuam. The Christian Brothers had not yet twenty houses and all the religious orders involved in education did not have eighty, but if the Tuam deputy were to be believed these resources could cater for 500,000 children. Loftus had passed on a letter from Bishop Coen of Clonfert denying Murray's claim that his heart was not in the opposition to national education;[152] they insisted that they could produce a witness in Rome to testify that Coen had admitted the benefits of the system, and they further maintained that his admission that a worse system might replace the current one was the very reason for working it.[153]

MacHale himself wrote occasionally to Propaganda while his delegate was drawing up his arguments. The laying of the foundation stone of Longford Cathedral on 19 May afforded him an opportunity for making a point about the capacity of Irish Catholics to provide the necessary funds for separate education. No less than 40,000 were present; the collection, which had already reached £5,000, was proof of the people's great liberality and readiness to erect and promote every institution necessary for conserving and diffusing their faith.[154]

XI

In the meantime all the documentation which the congregation of Propaganda possessed on the issue was passed on to one of its consultors, the Dutch Jesuit, Cornelius Van Everbroeck. He was asked to analyse it, and suggest a solution and he duly sent to the congregation a prolix and

---

[152] Murray had made this claim in a letter to Ennis of 3 Mar. 1840, which was translated for Propaganda.
[153] *Brevi osservazioni sulla memoria presentata dal Rev. Deputato dell. Arcivescovo di Tuam*, n.d., SOCG, 958, ff 607r-620r.
[154] MacHale to Martin Loftus, 21 May 1840, SOCG, 958, ff 574r-575r.

ponderous examination of all the evidence available on the national system, larded with scholastic distinctions and ecclesiastical precedents.[155]

Having examined the background to and the nature of the system he concluded that the dangers facing Catholic children of proselytism and indifferentism were greater when funds were being provided for Protestant or proselytizing schools, before the system was funded, than under it. He investigated the role of the inspectors, patrons and commissioners and found that the safeguards to which the majority appealed were certainly adequate; of 1,574 schools only 385 were under Protestant patrons, and Loftus could only point to three Catholic teachers having abandoned their faith, something that could happen for other reasons, and, as Ennis had pointed out, was to be compared with three times that number of priests who had abandoned their priesthood over the same period of time. And if there was no case known of one child out of half a million perverting from the faith, then the system could not present any proximate danger of sin. Nor was the bishops' jurisdiction limited by the system, since the bishops voluntarily accepted money from the board and therefore had to abide by its rules. No British government was less hostile to Catholicism than the current one. Van Everbroeck asked if anything better could be hoped for and, in the light of the viceroy's reply to the bishops, answered in the negative, remarking that a bird in the hand was better than ten in the air. However, the government would not allow the rights of Catholics to be damaged by the system. In fact, the controversy had placed the government in a very difficult situation, as the reports from the nuncios in Brussels and Paris—the former in a brief but prudent intervention in favour at least of not prohibiting the system—had made clear.

Van Everbroeck then went on to state that he was unable to reconcile the views of the ten bishops as expressed in the letter to the viceroy with their previous claim that the system was radically evil.[156] And the church already substantially enjoyed the protection which the demands listed in that letter sought, for as patrons, priests could dismiss unsuitable teachers and, where they were not patrons and could not control the teachers, they could persuade the children not to attend a particular school, if it were deemed dangerous to their faith. The fear that the rules of the system could be changed to the detriment of the Catholics was unfounded. His

---

[155] Van Everbroeck complained of the Herculean labour involved in reading a huge collection of documents in the midst of other occupatons and the Roman heat.

[156] Van Everbroeck confessed to finding inexactitudes in MacHale's letters and to requiring great patience in reading them: '. . . parum exacta parum temperata, immo potius exaggerata . . . in lectione nonnullarum Epistolarum . . . aliquando indigui ferrea patientia, aliquando etiam interrumpere coactus fui in media lextione . . .'

probing into the petition to the viceroy and that dignitary's refusal to recommend changes, as with his inquiry into the actual working of the system, favoured the majority case.

Hypothesizing about the likely effects of Propaganda positively approving or positively rejecting the system, Van Everbroeck considered the disadvantages of both decisions. The possibility of a condemnation posed the greater difficulty for it was unlikely that a majority of two thirds would abandon their views to accommodate a minority of one third. All admitted that the system had its faults, and its defenders did not seek positive approbation but the right to continue making use of it as they had hitherto done. A condemnation would mean that the financial support of the state for education would go to Protestants, that there would be a resurgence of proselytism, and would also cause offence to the Protestant government. What, moreover, would the Catholic people think if their bishops and clergy condemned something which for six years they had encouraged? Fortifying himself with St Augustine's dictum that the church had to tolerate much that it did not actually like, he came to the conclusion that there was a middle way between the two positions, which did not oblige either side to accept the other's view. Both could be permitted to make their own decisions about the system, but the *Scripture Lessons* and the *Lessons on the Truth of Christianity* should be excluded. Examining some of the excerpts he accepted Murray's defence in a few cases but in others thought the notes required to be altered or enlarged. He believed that his colleague, Glover, had been too severe in his comments. The bishops could solve the problem by compiling their own excerpts from scripture for the separate instruction of their children. He also recommended that bishops and priests should be admonished to abstain from publishing articles in the newspapers on the education question.[157]

Until the summer of 1840 the congregation of Propaganda in trying to adjudge the dispute was forced to reply on the partisan statements of both parties in the episcopate and latterly on the verbal and oral submissions of their delegates. Then an opportunity occurred of obtaining evidence from a trusted emissary who could give a report at first hand on the working of the system. As rector of the Irish College in Rome and agent for the Irish bishops since 1832, Paul Cullen had got to know many of the officials of the congregation and won their regard and esteem. Cardinal Mai's subsequent characterization of him as 'an ecclesiastic endowed with great

[157] *Parere del Rmo. P. Cornelio Van Everbroeck*, undated, APF, *Acta*, 202, ff 419r-479r.

piety, learning, ability and *savoir-faire*[158] reflects the prestige he enjoyed in Rome, a prestige which was also attested by less enthusiastic observers of the Roman scene. John Ennis reported to Dublin that a Canon of the Basilica of St John Lateran, basing himself on the judgement of a cardinal attached to Propaganda, had described Cullen as the 'quasi irish [*sic*] pope' whose 'opinion & judgement contervails every other on irish [*sic*] affairs'. Ennis, who, like Crolly and other bishops, suspected Cullen of siding with MacHale, personally regarded him as 'a great puzzle' but one who might 'be converted by reasoning & instruction for he is most ignorant of Ireland & its situation etc.'[159] As it was, his visit offered the congregation an opportunity to hear an account of what it was like in practice. And since Cullen knew and understood the Roman mind and method of doing business, he could be trusted not to approach the subject solely from an Irish angle and to present the nuances of the rules and operation of the system in a clear and comprehensive manner.

Cullen wrote three letters from Ireland to Rome which were to prove of decisive importance. In his first he explained that he had hitherto been unable to make extensive observations on the system but that he had visited several schools in the dioceses of Dublin and Kildare and found that 'they could not be more Catholic, with the teachers and all the pupils Catholic and the children being principally engaged in learning Christian doctrine', and no danger to religion could be apprehended from the state of the schools. As long as they were guaranteed that no innovations would be introduced much good would derive from them.[160]

When the gist of this letter first became known in Rome, the Dublin agent, William Meagher, was delighted. He had felt that influential opinion in Propaganda was swinging his way, and he believed that Cullen's comments ensured that 'the cause of justice, of truth and of our poor people' was successful: 'Doctor Cullen has proved himself what indeed it would be impossible for anyone enjoying his acquaintance to doubt, however, he might deplore the prejudices which on the Education question so long warped his better judgement, a sterlingly & considering the embarrassments which must result to him from his magnaminity an intrepidly honest man'.[161]

Five weeks later Cullen favoured Rome with more extensive reflections. Pointing out the danger of a condemnation, he advised that the

---

[158] Ristretto of Cardinal Mai. Dec. 1840, *Acta*, 203, f 410rv.
[159] Ennis to Hamilton, 29 Nov. 1839, DDA.
[160] Cullen to Cardinal Fransoni, 7 Aug. 1840, APF, *Acta*, 203, ff 416rv.
[161] Meagher to Hamilton, 8 Sept. 1840, DDA.

situation then obtaining should be allowed to continue in the greater part of Ireland, though he admitted that there could be abuses in some schools arising from the nature of the teaching prescribed in them. Guarantees for the preservation of the faith of Catholics should be demanded. An increase in the Catholic members of the commission would not achieve this result, for the commissioner's powers were limited, parliament would not approve of bishops being *ex-officio* commissioners and anyhow the government could easily find Catholics who were hostile or indifferent to the interests of the church. Combined teaching should be rigidly restricted to literary subjects, and this the bishops could effect without the intervention of the government and thereby the controversy about the orthodoxy of the books used for common instruction would be ended.

Though the professors in the training college in Dublin, O'Sullivan and his predecessor, Carlile, said nothing against the Catholic religion, nonetheless, the practice of Catholic teachers being lectured on religion by Protestants was improper; if combined instruction on religious matters (Cullen interpreted the use of the *Scripture Lessons* as a method of teaching dogmas that were common to all Christians) were excluded from the schools, it could also be excluded from the normal school. Recommending that parish priests be the legal owners of the schools and have the right under the direction of the bishop of nominating and dismissing teachers, he concluded that the situation should be left undisturbed. However desirable separate education might be, there were very few poor Protestants around, and even they were prevented from attending the schools by the anti-Catholic denunciations of their clergy.[162]

Two and a half months later Cullen wrote to Cardinal Mai who was responsible for preparing an analysis of the problem for his colleagues. He had hoped to return sooner to Rome and give a report on the system orally, but being unable to do so, wrote to repeat and emphasize his view that the schools were in practice very Catholic, that many of those for girls were in the hands of nuns and that priests could freely teach religion and prepare the children for the sacraments in them. A condemnation of the system would cause much discontent and terrible unpleasantness. He accordingly recommended that the decision be delayed for some time since the scheme, though not without grave faults, was not doing any harm. Its supporters, while desiring a more advantageous one, were in the meantime availing of its advantages.[163]

---

[162] Cullen to Monsignor Cadolini, 13 Sept. 1840, Ibid., ff 416v–418v.
[163] Cullen to Cardinal Mai, 27 Nov. 1840. SOCG, 958, ff 588r–589v.

Cullen may have sent other letters to Rome, for Meagher referred to one written to G.B. Palma, an official of Propaganda, though he may have confused the recipients. However, the impact of the first one was enormous. What Cullen really did was confirm the consensus that was being formed in Rome about the prudence of not condemning the system and of inviting the bishops to take what steps they could to remove the dangers inherent in it. The cardinal prefect of Propaganda and some of his officials, and other curial cardinals had reached that conclusion; the consultor, Van Everbroeck, reached it independently; and Cullen, by inspecting the schools and finding them, as the majority always claimed, overwhelmingly Catholic and well suited to the catechizing of children validated that policy.

The cardinals of Propaganda met on 22 December 1840 to consider the controversy. Cardinal Angelo Mai, the Vatican librarian, prepared the documentation on the case. Explaining the course of the dispute and Van Everbroeck's recommendation, he noted that the issue was due for discussion when two significant letters reached the congregation from Paul Cullen. Quoting extensively from these letters, Mai steered his colleagues towards an acceptance of Cullen's proposals by pointing out that the precautions he suggested were precisely those which had concerned the cardinals at their previous examination of the controversy.

The cardinals decided to pronounce no judgement on the system, leaving the decision to the prudent discretion and religious conscience of individual bishops. They then added suitable counsel: all books which contained anything contrary to the biblical canon of the church or to its dogmatic or moral teaching were to be removed from the schools; efforts were to be made to ensure that none but a Catholic professor should give lectures on religious, moral or historical questions to the Catholic teacher trainees in the model school; greater security would be ensured by limiting combined instruction in mixed schools to purely literary subjects; bishops and parish priests were exhorted to be vigilant in preventing the system from causing any harm to Catholic students and were encouraged to obtain legal ownership of the schools. Finally, the congregation expressed its hope that bishops and clergy would cease pursuing the controversy in newspapers and journals so that the honour of religion, their good reputation and Christian charity would not be damaged before their people.[164]

On 10 January 1841 the pope confirmed this decision. Six days later

---

[164] APF, *Acta*, 203, ff 411v-413r.

Cardinal Fransoni forwarded the resolutions of the cardinals in the form of a rescript to the four archbishops and invited them to communicate it to their suffragans. The bishops wrote a formal reply of thanks to the pope; MacHale signed it as archbishop of Tuam and primate of Connacht, perhaps arrogating to himself a primatial title as some kind of compensation or consolation for losing the hard-fought struggle![165] Crolly, writing to the pope on 26 March in answer to a further exhortation to peace and concord on the education question, observed that after such a regrettable discussion on such a serious matter the bishops of Ireland should not only give proof of their obedience but also of that filial loyalty which traditionally bound them to the Holy See.[166]

Crolly had good grounds for gratitude. The Roman verdict was certainly not the 'non-decision' it has been accused of being:[167] it gave to the bishops of the majority all they had sought—permission to carry on as they had been doing for the past nine years. MacHale, who wanted a condemnation of the system which he had characterized as radically evil, suffered a humiliating rebuff. He too was left guarding the status quo in his own diocese. His supporters, who had not forbidden their clergy to continue receiving aid from the board, subsequently took no action against the system, and those of his suffragans who had been cowed into backing him, may have been secretly glad that their case was lost. Yet neither side was made to appear as if it had lost face; both could claim success but MacHale achieved nothing by appealing to Rome that he could not have achieved by a letter to his priests ordering them to cease their connection with the system. Even the least hostile of the Roman consultors questioned the content and suitability of books like the *Scripture Lessons* and the *Lessons on the Truth of Christianity* being used during combined instruction, and the majority had always insisted that the managers, who in the greater part of Ireland were the parish priests, could withdraw such books from the schools. The prohibition of such books was the only substantive counsel in the Roman letter and one not difficult to execute. None of the anxieties of Crolly and Murray were realized: the government was not antagonized, poor Catholics could continue to avail of state funds for education, and bishops and clergy who had supported the system were not embarrassed and humiliated by a declaration that it was evil.

Of the many ironies of the situation perhaps the greatest was that the national system was rapidly becoming *de facto* denominational as the issue

---

[165] Bishops to Pope Gregory XVI, 5 Feb. 1841, APF, SC (Irlanda), 27, f 444rv.
[166] Crolly to Pope Gregory XVI, 26 Mar. 1841, Ibid., f 463rv.
[167] Akenson, *Irish Education Experiment*, 212.

was being fought out in Rome. The Presbyterians had got what they
wanted in January 1840 and the established church was effectively
shouldering the burden of education for its own children. Even where the
population was genuinely mixed, the number of genuinely mixed schools
diminished rapidly after 1840. Both Protestant and Catholic clergy used
the system to found and operate schools that catered extensively for their
own co-religionists. Mixing, especially in Ulster, took place where one
denomination formed a small minority in a particular parish or where
Catholics had insufficient resources to found a school under the management of the parish priest. In the following decades the bishops fought a
long war of attrition with the government to enable them to transform a *de
facto* into a *de iure* denominational system.

The split in the hierarchy of 1838-41 cannot be explained in terms of
the age, background or pastoral experience of the bishops, or in terms of
Gallican or Ultramontane loyalties among them. MacHale has been
accused of Gallicanism—falsely—for no Gallican would have appealed to
Rome the way he did. The four serious opponents of the system—
MacHale, Higgins, Cantwell and Keating (since MacHale dragooned his
suffragans into supporting him)—did not differ in age or educational
background from their opponents. Murray and Higgins were trained in
seminaries on the continent and had some knowledge and experience of
the *ancien regime*. Crolly and MacHale were both trained in Maynooth,
then taught in the college and became bishops in the same year. If the
system were what MacHale claimed it was, Crolly, whose pastoral work
had made him familiar with the most Protestant parts of Ireland, should
have led the resistance to it. The Catholic children who formed minorities
in many parts of Armagh, and Down and Connor should have been the
victims who required defence by their archbishop, and not the Catholic
children of Tuam, many of whom would not have known or met
Protestants at any time. Yet it was Crolly who maintained that Catholics
should be grateful for a form of education that was free from proselytism
and MacHale who denounced any aspect of the rules of the system that
even theoretically could be interpreted as offering any opportunity to
subvert the faith of Catholic children. There were no particular circumstances obtaining in the dioceses of Ardagh, Meath or Ferns that would
explain the positions adopted by Bishops Higgins, Cantwell and Keating.

The explanation, therefore, of the policies pursued by the bishops of
both camps lies in their personalities and political attitudes. The leaders of
the majority did not distrust the Whigs but rather believed they were
trying to legislate justly for Ireland on education. Both Crolly and Murray

thought that the Whig governments of the 1830s were the best that Ireland had ever had under British rule. MacHale and his three main supporters did not believe that the leopard had changed his spots; they were deeply suspicious of the *Weltanschauung* of all British governments, which they consistently identified as anti-Catholic and anti-Irish.

Without state subvention on the scale provided by the national system the Catholic church would not have been able to create a *de facto* denominational system of education, and one that came to be recognized as the essential pastoral arm of the clergy for catechizing their youth. MacHale's successor was later to complain bitterly of the pastoral opportunities that had been neglected in the archdiocese, and of the attendance of Catholic children at proselytizing schools.[168] The dispute may have been settled without either party having to acknowledge a public defeat but the divisions and wounds opened up by a public controversy did not easily or quickly heal. As a Roman official was later to remark, the conflict over the national schools created a disposition among the bishops to quarrel over issues of government policy.[169] More than that, it created two recognizable parties in the episcopate.

A third group which was not fully committed to either party represented a floating vote which both sides later sought to attract. The two parties may be called the *zelanti* and the *politicanti* for these were the names which distinguished two recognizable parties among the cardinals in Rome. The *zelanti*, the more conservative or intransigent cardinals, strove for the full independence and rights of the church and opposed interference by governments in papal elections and ecclesiastical policy; the *politicanti* or more liberal group was prepared to cooperate with governments, where it was necessary and beneficial for the church to do so, without infringing any theological principle. For the remainder of the decade MacHale, later assisted by Archbishop Slattery, led the *zelanti* of Ireland; Crolly and Murray led the *politicanti*.

XII

In the 1840s the bishops suffered a couple of setbacks as they strove to make maximum use of the national system. The arrangement made between the commissioners and the Presbyterian church ensured that in non-vested schools managed by Presbyterians, the Catholic priest was

[168] John MacEvilly to Tobias Kirby, 20 Oct. 1879, AICR.
[169] *Voto* of Corboli-Bussi, APF, Acta, 209, f 265r.

virtually excluded from organizing any religious instruction for Catholic children in association with the school. In 1845 the commissioners decided that all schools, to the building of which they had given grants, should be vested in themselves rather than in the patrons who applied for aid; this contravened the counsel given by Propaganda in the rescript of 1841, which, deriving from Cullen's advice, was intended to safeguard Catholic children against any changes in the rules, or introduction of books that could prove damaging to the faith of the children. This regulation did not prevent parish clergy building their own schools and seeking aid in the form of books, requisites and teachers' salaries.

A change of this nature was calculated to enrage the *zelanti* and they duly brought up the issue at the bishop's meeting in November 1846. Towards the end of the meeting when Murray and several other prelates had gone, Bishop Cantwell moved and Bishop O'Higgins seconded a resolution declaring that they had received with surprise and alarm the changes recently introduced into the national system, which were at direct variance with the instructions of the pope, and that they should therefore petition parliament for a system grounded on Christian principles and subject to Catholic control; pending the success of the petition all trustees of schools were to be cautioned against the insidious transfer of their property and the clergy were to refuse their sanction to school-houses that were subsequently erected on such obnoxious terms.

As Bishop Maginn later reported, the introduction of the question 'produced a perfect hurricane'. Crolly was understandably indignant. MacHale and the *zelanti*, flushed with their success in drumming up public hostility to the Charitable Bequests Act and the Colleges, were moving in to kill the entire system of national education, which had been upheld by Rome after a prolonged struggle. The primate accordingly refused to play the game of his opponents, but he was then moved by a vote from the chair and MacHale became chairman. The resolution was then passed by a majority of nine votes to four. The four—Crolly, Denvir, Haly of Kildare and Browne of Kilmore—then entered a solemn protest against the resolution which they claimed was calculated to injure the national system, was contrary to the instruction they had received from Rome on it and was proposed in the absence of Murray and many other prelates. Cantwell maintained that he had given due notice of his resolution, but then agreement was reached on the procedure for presenting petitions to parliament: it would take place once they were passed unanimously.[170]

170 Maginn to Cullen, 3 Dec. 1846, AICR, *Minutes of bishops' meetings*, DDA.

Yet only a few months previously MacHale had swallowed (privately) his antipathy to the system to such an extent that he was prepared to regard it as tolerably innocuous. When Archbishop Slattery, his chief-of-staff in the battle against the Queen's Colleges, drew up a letter for Rome in which he attacked the argument that the Holy See should adopt the same solution in that dispute as it had done in 1841 because the two systems of education were similar, by pointing out the dissimilarities in the systems and highlighting the safeguards for religion in the schools, MacHale was happy to sign it. He explained that, though not approving of the national system, he found the arguments convincing and, though he took exception to the claim that security was afforded by the presence of a prelate and other Catholics on the board, and repeated his objection to such an uncanonical and unwarrantable invasion of episcopal authority, he praised Slattery's 'well reasoned document' for demonstrating

the utter bad faith of those who would compare the manifest and necessary evils of the Colleges with the comparatively harmless National System. There is one point which is particularly well put that, in despite of its theoretic mixture the National System is in reality and in practice a separate education. This cannot be too often repeated. In different parts of the north, they have their two national schools in the same town, one frequented exclusively by Catholics, and the other by the Protestants or Sectaries of some other denomination.[71]

Had these sentiments been publicized in the press, those who had followed the education controversy would have taken them to represent Crolly's and not MacHale's views!

The vesting of schools was again raised at the annual meeting in October 1847. Murray endeavoured to explain that the commissioners wanted to get rid of the confusion caused by the deaths of trustees and the uncertainty resulting from delays in appointments of successors. Since being incorporated, the board could assume ownership of new schools and would thereby avoid the complications that had arisen over trusteeship. But it promised not to interfere with existing schools, guaranteed the maintenance of the system as it was, and undertook to keep in repair those schools vested in it. When a discussion developed on the schools, Crolly objected on the grounds that it contravened the rescript of 1841, which limited such debate to provincial synods, and in a case of urgency and importance, ordered the prelates to refer the matter to Rome. Denvir, McGettigan and one or two others supported him but when they saw that the majority was opposed to their views, they withdrew. This left

[71] MacHale to Slattery, 2 Jan. 1846, Slattery Papers.

MacHale free to take the chair and under his guidance a resolution was passed regretting the changes introduced by the commissioners as 'most serious and dangerous' and a rejection of the pope's wishes; it was further resolved to draw up a petition to parliament for the amendment of those parts of the system which the prelates deemed incompatible with the discipline of their church, with the full and free exercise of episcopal authority and with the safety of the religious principles of Catholic children.[172] This was a more limited request than that proposed in the previous year and left room for negotiations with the *politicanti* before anything further was done. And in 1847 a further complication was added by the Stopford rule. Archdeacon Stopford of the established church succeeded in getting the commissioners to give an official interpretation of the rule that in vested schools no child should be compelled to attend or be present at religious instruction given by a teacher of another denomination. According to the new interpretation, only compulsion was excluded by the rule, and not attendance as such. The bishops regarded this decision as yet a further breach of the guarantees against proselytism which the system was supposed to afford.

Despite these further embarrassments, Crolly remained strongly committed to the national system. When Murray, on behalf of the Lord Lieutenant, sounded him out on becoming a member of the board of commissioners, he replied that he would willingly do so if his indispensable duties would so permit, but the distance from his home to Dublin and other circumstances would prevent him from attending regularly. Knowing that his letter would be shown to the viceroy, he then went on to propose that Walter Meyler, a Dublin priest whose appointment Murray himself had suggested, 'could constantly render more useful services to the interesting Institution which the British Government has liberally sanctioned for the education of the poor in Ireland'. In a later letter, presumably intended only for Murray's eyes, he remarked that he would not fear any opposition either at Rome or in Ireland to the system, if the commissioners had not attempted to get control of the schools, and he trusted that in future they would make no such attempts.[173]

Though the struggle to salvage something for the Catholic people from the funds made available for tertiary education proved too difficult for him, the primate at least had the satisfaction of knowing that he had helped save the national system for the poor.

---

[172] D.E.P., 26 Oct. 1847, Murray to Slattery, 27 Oct. 1847, Slattery Papers, F.J., 27 Oct. 1847.
[173] Crolly to Murray, 31 Mar. 1848, Clarendon Papers, and 13 Apr. 1848, DDA.

6

PASTORAL CARE AND ECCLESISTICAL
PROBLEMS, 1835–49

The archdiocese of Armagh with approximately 310,000 Catholics was twice the size of Down and Connor and the seventh largest diocese in Ireland. According to the Irish Catholic Directory of 1836 it had one hundred and fourteen priests (Down and Connor had fifty eight). The archbishops had long resided in Drogheda and had been supported by the mensal parishes of Drogheda, Termonfeckin and Ballymakenny. Archbishop Curtis had thought of moving to Armagh[1] but it was left to his successor, Archbishop Kelly, to make practical arrangements to do so. When James Byrne, the parish priest of Armagh, died in 1834, Kelly took advantage of the vacancy to apply to the pope for permission to change his mensal parishes. He wished to give up Termonfeckin and Ballymakenny in exchange for Armagh. The pope expressed his pleasure that the archbishop should return to live where St Patrick had established his see, permitted him to keep Drogheda, do as he wished about Ballymakenny but asked that Termonfeckin should not be filled while the dispute with Eugene Mulholland, the former administrator, was unsettled.[2] Kelly died before he had time to carry out these arrangements but Crolly promptly acquired houses in Armagh and in Drogheda—in the latter case in the suitably named Paradise Row—and resided alternately in both parishes.

Drogheda, however, remained the more important ecclesiastical centre and St Peter's Church was, in fact, though not in name, the cathedral of the archdiocese. A substantial building, it had been used by previous archbishops for all the great ceremonies of the liturgical year and Crolly maintained this practice. From time to time he celebrated High Mass and gave Benediction in it and always preached in it on Sundays when resident in the town. Drogheda towards the end of the eighteenth century had been one of the most important towns in Ireland and boasted a

[1] Cogan, *The Diocese of Meath, Ancient and Modern*, iii, 439.
[2] Propaganda to Kelly, APF, *Lett.*, 315, ff 616r–617v.

number of prosperous Catholic merchants. They had helped endow and
support religious orders and hence in Crolly's time the town had five
flourishing religious houses. There were two convents of nuns—the
Dominican and Presentation Sisters—and three friaries—Dominicans,
Franciscans and Augustinians. There was also a church on the southern
side of the Boyne in the diocese of Meath. Few, if any, towns in Ireland
of comparable size were as well equipped with religious institutions or
enjoyed such a vigorous religious life. Even in Archbishop Curtis' earlier
years, when Catholics still kept a low profile, there were public processions in Drogheda to celebrate the feast of Corpus Christi. And though
the mayor and corporation were not permitted to wear their robes of
office in St Peter's Church, Crolly, in the 1840s, celebrated Mass for them
to mark the beginning of each year and they then donned their robes and
processed to the tholsel, their town hall, to begin their annual business.

During Crolly's episcopate St Peter's was repaired,[3] and when the
organ was restored, a grand oratorio was held to mark the occasion.[4] Each
year at least two charity sermons were preached in St Peter's: one to
obtain funds for the school for orphans and poor girls conducted by the
Presentation Sisters and the other for the Patrician school for poor boys.
Both these schools had between four hundred and seven hundred children
on their rolls from time to time, and their buildings had to be extended to
cope with the numbers seeking admission. In 1846 the Presentation
Sisters spent £1,000 in enlarging their buildings[5] and in the same year the
Dominicans acquired ground for the establishment of a school, in which
they could give instruction to adults and factory workers on Sundays as
well as to children on weekdays, and, a few months later, they laid the
foundation stone for a new convent chapel.[6] The archbishop also lent his
patronage and support to a classical school which was conducted by a
Catholic layman.[7] Bishop Griffith, the vicar-apostolic of the Cape of Good
Hope,[8] and other missionaries, made appeals occasionally in St Peter's.
Crolly, when in Drogheda, also presided at the High Masses celebrated in
the churches of the friars to honour their special feast days.

In 1847 a new religious community entered the diocese. Crolly had
been impressed by the dedication of the Sisters of Mercy which he had
witnessed when visiting Limerick and Carlow, and, in consequence, had
supported the petition of the foundress for approval for the order,
predicting that it would 'render important services to the poor of

---

[3] D.E.P., 23 June 1838.   [4] D.A., 2 Oct. 1847.   [5] Ibid., 28 Nov. 1846.
[6] Ibid., 14 Feb. 1846; N.Ex., 8 July 1846.   [7] D.A., 7 Jan. 1837.   [8] D.A., 6 Jan. 1838.

Ireland'.[9] He certainly permitted, if he did not actively encourage, John Coyne, the parish priest of Dundalk, to bring the Sisters to the town. Coyne bought, with funds supplied by a local merchant, an ancient mansion which had been used as an excise office. This was fitted up for the Sisters and they arrived to lend much needed succour to the many who were suffering from hunger and famine fevers.[10]

The primate, however, was anxious to restore to Armagh its central role in the archdiocese, and so it was there that he decided to establish his diocesan seminary and cathedral. And he wasted little time in starting both projects. He acquired imposing sites on a hill overlooking the town for the cathedral and college, appointed Thomas Duff, a prominent architect, to design the college and it was opened on 6 August 1838. The cost was nearly double the original estimate and to make up the difference he himself advanced £600 'for which he went into debt to an amount nearly equal to all he was worth'. He had to spend a further £300 on acquiring land nearby for the use of the pupils.[11] A spacious building erected to cater for boarders and day pupils, it began with a staff of two diocesan priests and a layman and provided the usual range of courses then customarily taught in secondary schools.[12]

Crolly's biggest contribution to the religious rejuvenation of Armagh was the foundation of the cathedral. Duff, who was again appointed architect, designed a gothic building in the early perpendicular style and the foundation stone was laid on 17 March 1840. Huge crowds, estimated at between 20,000 and 30,000, turned up to witness the ceremony and afterwards the archbishop entertained some of the leading benefactors of all denominations to dinner. The task of collecting funds for the building was formidable and was not made easier by the fact that several other bishops were then collecting for similar purposes, as were very many parish priests. During the 1840s cathedrals were being built in Ennis, Longford, Killarney, Enniscorthy and Kilkenny, and substantial debts remained on some of those that had already been opened. Though Armagh could claim to be a national cathedral, it had to compete with local interests and sympathies in these dioceses. Crolly personally collected in parts of Munster and Leinster as well as in Ulster. In Down and Connor priests who had known him appealed on his behalf. Charity sermons yielded sums ranging from £20 to £50, which, however generous on the part of particular congregations, were very small contributions

[9] Crolly to Mother Catherine McAuley, 8 Nov. 1839, APF, SOCG, 957, f 320r
[10] *Reverend Mother Mary de Sales Vigne*, 3-4.   [11] G. Crolly, *Crolly*, lxxxvi.
[12] D.A., 18 Aug. 1838.

towards the final costs. Work progressed slowly, was halted completely during the famine, and was not resumed till 1854.

What made collecting for a major diocesan project really difficult was that, despite their poverty, many parishes were burdened with debts incurred in building their own churches. The two decades before the famine witnessed a truly heroic spate of church building in Ireland, and Armagh was no exception. In January 1846 Crolly could claim that he had blessed and opened seventeen new churches and that five more were nearing completion.[13] From newspaper reports it is possible to identify most of these. They include Eglish (1835), Mountjoy (1835), Coalisland (1836), Tartaraghan (1837), Portadown (1837), Moneymore (1839), Loughmacrory (1840), Ardboe (1841), Collon (1841), Dundalk (1842), Galbally (1842), Magherafelt (1842). Ballinderry (1843), Newtown-hamilton (1843), Tynan (1844) and Drumullan (1845). Other sources refer to the opening of Stonetown in 1837 and Collegeland in 1846. Churches were certainly opened at Stewartstown and Donaghmore in 1846. References in newspapers to the laying of foundation stones for churches at Walshestown (1837), Tallanstown (1839) and to the provision of a site at Sandpit (1845) would account for the others mentioned in Crolly's list.

As in Down and Connor these churches were built with substantial Protestant support and Crolly often repeated the same appeals for charity and goodwill at the solemn openings as he had done in his former diocese. This did not prevent Protestant extremists in two of the Orange heartlands in Armagh from venting their anger against them. Zealots had planned to pull down the bell and belfry in Loughgall but information was leaked to the police in advance which enabled them to place a guard and foil the attack.[14] The church at Tartaraghan, the windows of which had been broken before it was completed, was seriously damaged a year after it was consecrated. The altar was pulled down, furniture was taken out and thrown into a nearby stream and the windows and sashes were smashed to bits.[15] Minor damage was done to the churches at Termonfeckin and Tullyallen in 1837, and in the same year on 12 July a blunderbus was fired over the head of the primate and a squib thrown at his trap as he drove through Drogheda.[16] These assaults were the exceptions and the provision of Catholic churches did not normally provoke opposition.

[13] Crolly to Cullen, 26 Jan. 1846, AICR.   [14] D.E.P., 30 Sept. 1837.
[15] Ibid., 28 June 1838 and N.Ex., 4 July 1838.   [16] D.A., 18 Feb., 16 July 1837.

The primate was often called upon to preach in other dioceses at the opening of churches or to liquidate debts incurred in building them. Already as bishop of Down and Connor he had preached in Strabane in 1830 and at the dedication of the churches in Loughbrickland in 1832 and at Moy in 1834. He returned to Down and Connor to preach in his native parish at Ballykilbeg in 1836, at Carrickfergus in 1840, and he officiated at the opening of St Malachy's in Belfast in 1844. He also preached at Omagh in 1840 and at Drimard in Co. Donegal in 1841. His fame as a preacher—and the papers often reported the good impression his sermons made on Protestants—ensured that he was much in demand for special occasions. When a controversy arose in Belfast over the admonition of Bishop Mant to his people 'to touch not the unclean thing' by attending an oratorio and High Mass to mark the installation of a new organ in St Patrick's, Crolly vigorously defended the Catholic church in his sermon against the charges of idolatry and superstition, which Mant had brought against it. But then he went on to express his hope that a spirit of mutual forbearance, charity, peace and brotherly love would pervade all classes, and make men hate each other less and love each other more. The many Presbyterians in the congregation, who had been angered by Mant's outburst, were apparently impressed.[17]

Crolly's successor in Armagh later complained bitterly about the 'cathedral' he inherited, maintaining that it was 'awfully bad' and that 'the priests use only one tallow candle on the altars at Mass'. As he grew more exasperated, he described it as a 'miserable hole' and his installation in it as 'the first regularly conducted ceremony that took place there since God knows when'. His strictures were subsequently widened to embrace the whole diocese, which he characterized as 'nearly as favourable a place to commence as Oregon or California', where everything was 'primitive' and there was 'scarcely a cap or a surplice'.[18] These comments have been used to bolster a critique of the religious practices in Ireland before the famine and to support the case for a 'devotional revolution' after 1850.[19] Bearing in mind that these views were expressed by a man accustomed to the efficient bureaucracy of the church in Italy, which had enjoyed financial and political support from the state for centuries, one must still ask how much objective truth they contained. The ecclesiastical situation in Armagh parish did not in fact reflect that of the whole diocese, and Crolly was far from being the careless or incompetent prelate which such judgements would seem to imply.

[17] N.W., 6 Feb. 1840, N. Ex., 12 Feb. 1840.   [18] Cullen to Kirby, 14, 16, 28 May 1850, AICR.
[19] Larkin, 'The Devotional Revolution in Ireland, 1850-75', in *American Historical Review*, 1972, 625-52.

St Malachy's Church in Armagh was never regarded as a cathedral. It was built in 1752, enlarged and renovated in 1819, but was not suited to further extension.[20] The Catholics of Armagh who erected it were a small and impoverished body and could not afford to pay for a more elaborate structure. When the decision to replace it was taken in the 1830s, there was no point in spending scarce money embellishing it, and it later languished as a chapel of ease, when the cathedral was completed, until it was eventually demolished. The participation of the priests at ceremonies without choral dress probably derived from a prudent desire to maintain a low profile in Protestant-dominated districts, where processions in official robes would have drawn down the hostility of some Protestant zealots upon them. Had the solemn requiem for Crolly been celebrated in Drogheda, the ceremonial and vestments, at least of the celebrants, would certainly have satisfied the rubrical requirements. And while some of the churches opened in Crolly's time were not completed or fully furnished until later, one can assume that the altar equipment in them was both new and sufficient.

II

Until his death the archbishop visited each parish every third year and administered the sacrament of confirmation. The numbers confirmed were large—often six hundred or more—but in preparation for the ceremony he spent time in examining the children and often commended the clergy on the results of their catechesis as evidenced by the children's responses. According to an account of confirmation in Lower Creggan, the archbishop began Mass at 11.00 a.m., confirmed the children and then preached, and the ceremony did not end till 4.00 p.m.[21] His neighbour, Bishop Blake in Dromore was able, because of the size and compactness of the diocese, to visit every parish annually for a few days and administer both confirmation and first Holy Communion. Geography, numbers and wider commitments prevented Crolly from conducting such frequent visitations, but, when he did make them, he carried out a thorough examination of all parochial activity.

Before leaving Down and Connor he established the confraternity of Christian Doctrine, which already existed in several parishes, on a diocesan basis. Though records of confraternities are missing for the most

[20] Patterson, 'Old St Malachy's' in *St Malachy's Church, Armagh, Golden Jubilee, 1938-88*, 11-30.
[21] N. Ex., 6 Sept. 1843.

part in Armagh, one can assume that by the 1840s they were widespread. A flourishing confraternity existed in the parish of Louth from 1822, which not only met for prayers and meditation but also studied and taught religion to the local children. Such societies devoted themselves to prayer, study, religious education and the relief of the sick, poor and dying. Crolly later encouraged local temperance societies but he did not invite Fr Mathew to campaign in his diocese. A recent biographer has suggested that both the archbishop and Bishop Denvir may have been afraid of Mathew's crusade exacerbating religious tensions[22] but on at least one occasion a group of Protestants begged Crolly to permit Mathew to give the pledge in his diocese. He may also have been afraid of incurring debts as a result of Mathew's lavish distribution of medals or he may have disliked the flamboyance of Mathew's style. Crolly himself inspected the catechetical instruction in Dundalk,[23] and presumably also in Drogheda and Armagh. When he first arrived in Armagh the Catholic Book Society was widely established in very many, even in poor rural parishes in Ireland. By 1837 it had printed five million books at very cheap rates and the Catholic Book Society of Ireland supplied books gratuitously to the poor.[24] Bishop Denvir later noted that of the 47,000 copies of the Douay version of the bible or new testament printed in Belfast before 1839, 29,000 were prepared with Crolly's approval, and though it is not clear from his note how the 243,000 copies printed between 1839 and 1850 were disposed of, Crolly presumably took a large number of them for Armagh.[25]

In 1842 Dundalk acquired a prestigious church, which had cost £14,000 (and by Crolly's death was to cost a further £6,000)[26] and the Dominican church in the town acquired a new organ.[27] But Drogheda enjoyed the most flourishing religious life in the diocese. The opportunites for Lenten devotions were impressively large. In St Peter's Church there were prayers and lectures each evening, in addition of course to daily Masses. And in the Augustinian and Franciscan churches there were sermons three times weekly, and there were also special devotions in the Dominican church.[28] Feastdays were always marked by High Masses in all these churches; for the feast of St Augustine there were Masses from an early hour till High Mass at 11.00 a.m. and for three days Benediction was celebrated after Mass.[29]

[22] Kerrigan, *Fr Mathew and the Irish temperance movement*, 160.   [23] N. Ex., 22 May 1844.
[24] Keenan, *The Catholic Church in nineteenth century Ireland*, 141.   [25] Denvir papers, DCDA.
[26] *Dundalk parish – parochial meetings and chapel committee meeting minute book* (MS in St Patrick's Presbytery, Dundalk).
[27] V., 9 Mar., 30 Nov. 1842.   [28] D.A., 22 Mar. 1845.   [29] Ibid., 29 Aug. 1845.

When Cullen commented on the primitiveness of Armagh, he probably had in mind the absence of external practices in worship and of Italian clerical dress to which he was accustomed in Rome. Nicholas Wiseman, who also spent many years in Rome before returning to England and later becoming archbishop of Westminster, reacted in the same way to the situation he found in England. From the return of Pius VII to Rome in 1814 a new 'ultramontane' spirit was to spread throughout the church, a spirit which manifested itself more obviously in inessentials like devotional practices than in terms of strict relations between the pope and the bishops—and this spirit was later to develop rapidly under Pius IX. This Ultramontanism caught on more slowly in England and Ireland than on the continent but it had reached Ireland well before the famine. Cullen's comments reflect the initial disappointment of one who was accustomed to a richer liturgy than that found in Ireland, but the dress of the clergy, their attitude to precise rubrical requirements and the use of particular novenas or litanies were not of great significance and, as Wiseman's opponents told him, they did not determine people's real religious commitment.

In 1835 when Crolly was transferred to Armagh, the archdiocese had an average of one priest for every 2,175 people.[30] In 1846 he reported to Rome that there were 118 priests serving in the diocese, of whom 49 were parish priests, 65 were curates and four were administrators.[31] Both Armagh and Drogheda were served by three curates. In 1850 Bishop Denvir remarked that many Armagh priests were serving in Down and Connor,[32] so the archbishop must have believed that he had sufficient priests to satisfy the pastoral needs of the archdiocese and could afford to lend some to another bishop. Crolly in the report to Rome in 1846 also explained that he examined all his clergy four times annually at their clerical conferences and added that he only did them justice in stating that they were 'in general diligent in the study of theology', faithful in the discharge of their duties, and by no means 'prominent in political affairs'. Though brief, this account of the state of the diocese, suggests that the archbishop was not unhappy with the pastoral practice in it.

Two jubilees were held during Crolly's tenure of the primatial see: the first in 1842 to pray for the church in Spain which was then confronted by anti-clerical hostility, and the second in 1847 to pray for an end to the famine. Reports in the *Newry Examiner* of the enthusiastic response of the

---

[30] Connolly, *Priests and People in pre-Famine Ireland*, 36.   [31] Crolly to Cullen, 26 Jan. 1846, AICR.
[32] Denvir to Renehan, 5 May 1850, MCA.

people of Dromore on the former occasion could doubtless have been applied with equal force to the Catholics of Armagh. Thousands were said to have filled the cathedral at Newry without intermission from 5.00 a.m. to 10.00 p.m., with not less than 700 communicants each morning and ten or more neighbouring priests assisting the resident clergy of the town.[33] At Tullylish on the Armagh border five clergy were kept busy with confessions from 5.00 a.m. till 10.00 p.m. and administered Holy Communion to nearly 2,000 people.[34] Jubilees, during which the faithful were asked to fast, confess their sins and recite special prayers usually lasted two to three weeks, and were held in different parishes at different times within a six month or longer period. In an obituary for the parish priest of Dungannon who died in 1848, reference was made to the long hours he had spent in the confessional during the jubilee of 1847.[35]

III

The census of 1834 conducted by the commissioners of public instruction reveals a wide diversity of attendance figures for Sunday Mass. Drogheda understandably had the highest rate. If the entries are taken literally, more people attended Mass than were listed as Catholics, but if the figures for attendance at the churches of the three religious orders are taken as representing the total attendance and allowance is made for twenty five per cent who did not attend, the proportion of those present at Mass would be eighty four per cent. Assuming that those not bound by obligation to participate at Mass—children under seven years of age, the old, the sick and incapacitated, and those who cared for them—represented about a quarter of the total, the proportion who worshipped in Ardee was ninety per cent and in Termonfeckin (and Clogherhead) seventy one per cent. In the combined parishes of Dunleer and Collon the percentage of Mass-goers was fifty eight but in the Carlingford peninsula it was down to thirty nine per cent. In Carrickmore (Termonmaguirk) and Beragh the attendance rate was about fifty per cent (the numbers at one Mass are not given) but in the parishes of South Armagh it was down to thirty nine per cent. In Armagh parish, including the surrounding districts, the rate was thirty eight per cent but in the Armagh part it was forty six per cent.[36]

---

33 N. Ex., 30 Apr. 1842.   34 V., 25 May 1842.   35 D.E.P., 17 June 1848.
36 *First report of the commissioners of public instruction, Ireland, with appendix*, pp. 129-175, 1835 [45], xxxiii. i, 180-226.

Not surprisingly, the higher figures are to be found in Co. Louth where the Catholics on average were better-off than in the Ulster part of the diocese and where there were more churches. Scattered rural areas had a much lower rate than the more compact parishes based in the towns of Louth. Significantly, the great majority of the churches consecrated by Crolly were in Counties Tyrone, Armagh and Derry. And in the returns of the census of 1834 mention was made of several congregations meeting for Mass in the open air. Where the figures are low and account is taken of members of families going to church on alternate Sundays because of dress or commitments at home, they probably still indicate that there was a reasonably good attendance at Masses, either in church or at stations, even if not on a weekly basis throughout the year. Had the census been taken in 1846 when the seventeen churches to which Crolly referred had been opened—and at least one, if not two, were opened shortly before his transfer—there can be little doubt that the figures given for attendance at Sunday Masses would have been much higher.

In addition to Masses in the churches, 'stations' at which confessions were heard and Mass celebrated continued to be held throughout Crolly's time, especially in rural parishes. They had ceased to be necessary in towns like Drogheda and Dundalk, but in remote country areas they often afforded to the less mobile members of the community helpful opportunities of receiving the sacraments. A diary of the parish priest of Kilmore, which covers the years 1827 to 1829, reveals that he held sixty stations on average each year. Some of these took place on weekdays in one or other of his churches at Stonebridge or Mullavilly but most were held in the houses of parishioners. He described most of them as being 'well attended' or as having a 'good number' present, and those that were badly attended were offset by others at which 'great numbers' turned up. Actual numbers are never given but his diary indicates that in general he was satisfied with his people's response.[37]

Crolly was asked by the congregation of Propaganda in 1847 to respond to charges that had been made from Ireland that the stations were abused by priests who demanded money for the administration of the sacraments and lavish hospitality for themselves. He replied that he had heard that abuses had existed in certain parts of the country and he thought they might still exist in remote places unknown to him, but he assured Rome that the prelates of Ireland, and particularly those of the Armagh province by their statutes in 1834, had used their authority to abolish all such

[37] MS in the possession of Revd John McGrane, Cooley, Co. Louth.

malpractices. Quoting the statutes which excluded such usages as those referred to, he expressed his confidence that those laws, together with the vigilance and authority of the bishops, were a most efficacious means for countering clerical avarice. To the question about priests using portable altars merely for their own convenience, he insisted that permission to do so was necessary for places where there were no churches and landlords were refusing to make sites available.[38] Archbishop Murray pointed out in his answer to the same query that the stations were held twice yearly, around Christmas and Easter, and that because of scarcity of priests the paschal precept could be fulfilled from Ash Wednesday to Ascension Thursday, and in some dioceses even to the feast of St Peter and Paul.[39]

Crolly himself was most diligent and punctilious in carrying out all his pastoral duties. The difficulties of travel meant that the extra duties of a political nature which brought him to Dublin placed greater burdens on his shoulders. His commitment to his work impressed many who were not members of his church. Significantly, Lord Clarendon, the viceroy, who described the primate as an 'excellent man',[40] partly no doubt because of his readiness to cooperate with the government's policies, placed him at the head of the list of Irish prelates whom he commended 'for unostentatious piety & the intense zeal with which they labour for the welfare of their flocks' and whose match it would be difficult to find among the prelates of the Church of England.[41]

To Crolly's labours both at a diocesan and national level were added commissions from Rome to investigate problems that had arisen in other dioceses. He inherited a dispute in Armagh and he was invited to help end two others, one in Killala and one in Dromore.

IV

The trouble in Armagh, which was to defy all attempts at settlement, was provoked by Eugene Mulholland, the administrator of Termonfeckin. This persistent and implacable malcontent had harassed Archbishop Kelly for most of his episcopate and attempted to do the same to Crolly.

Mulholland, who had been appointed administrator of the archbishop's parish of Termonfeckin in 1826, was able, intelligent and eloquent but

[38] Crolly to Propaganda, 30 May 1847, APF, SC (Irlanda), 29, ff 152r-153v.
[39] Murray to Propaganda, 17 May 1847, Ibid., ff 128r-130v.
[40] Clarendon to Russell, 26 Oct. 1847, Clarendon Papers, Lb i, ff 97v-98v.
[41] Clarendon to Minto, 9 Feb. 1848, Ibid., ff 111r-114r.

quarrelsome, difficult and uncooperative. Ill-feeling deriving from a casual argument between himself and Thomas Trainor, a neighbouring curate, had led to a case in the court of Common Pleas in Dublin in May 1834 in which he had won the trifling and humiliating sum of one farthing. The parishioners of Termonfeckin also fell victim to his contentious and bellicose manner. In 1832 Archbishop Kelly found the parish 'in a disorderly state' and in the following year because of complaints from parishioners about 'some pecuniary exactions' felt obliged to admonish Mulholland. When the admonition fell on deaf ears, the archbishop, who believed that mental instability was at the root of Mulholland's problems, dismissed him from his post as administrator and appointed in his place Thomas Callan.[42]

Mulholland set off for Rome to seek redress from what he was ever afterwards to regard as an injustice. But the congregation of Propaganda examined his claims and upheld the decision of the archbishop.[43] By then Kelly had died. The congregation asked the vicar-capitular and later Crolly to ensure that adequate provision was made for Mulholland.[44] The congregation also furnished the unsuccessful appellant with a short testimonial bearing witness to his probity of character and educational qualifications.[45]

Crolly met Mulholland in Dublin shortly after his appointment to Armagh and promised to do all in his power to settle the problem amicably. Mulholland asked to be reinstated in Termonfeckin but Crolly refused because he believed that move would have involved injustice to the current administrator, would 'stigmatize the memory of Dr Kelly' and 'might injure religion, by exposing the faithful to a repetition of the disorders which had formerly prevailed in that Parish'. They met again on 7 August and Crolly explained that there was no parish vacant in the archdiocese and invited Mulholland to attend a conference of clergy in Armagh on 19 August, where arrangements for some provision for him could be made until a more suitable vacancy would occur. Mulholland was not satisfied, begged leave to go to work abroad and asked for an official document or *exeat* permitting him to do so, together with a reference which he could present to enable a bishop elsewhere to take him into his diocese. Crolly gave him the required *exeat* which included a declaration of his freedom from censure and a testimonial of his reputation for zeal,

[42] N. Ex., 18 June 1836.
[43] Kelly's and Mulholland's letters and pleas are to be found in APF, SOCG, 950, ff 19r-81r.
[44] Propaganda to M. McCann, 21 Feb., 2 Apr. 1835 and to Crolly 22 Sept. 1835 in APF, *Lett.*, 316, ff 108v-119v, 246v-247r, 696rv.
[45] Ibid., 2 Apr. 1835, f 306rv.

piety and learning. This was the customary procedure and Crolly probably calculated that if he were admitted to a diocese in the United States of America he would be placed at such a distance from his colleagues that he could not engage in conflicts with them. Like other Irish bishops offloading troublesome clergy onto the American church, he probably hoped that the vastness of their new mission and the difficulties of travel in it would so absorb their energies that they would have little time to cause friction with their colleagues, and might at the same time make a useful pastoral contribution to a land calling out for priests.

However, Mulholland was not going to give up so easily. He forwarded the testimonial to Rome as evidence of his good standing with an archbishop who would not make due provision for him.[46] In the meantime he attended the clerical meeting in Armagh on 19 August 1835 and there Crolly offered him the curacy of either Magherafelt or Ballinderry. He refused both. Crolly persevered and at the other clerical conferences he recommended his querulous subject to any parish priest in the diocese who would be prepared to take him on. All were happy to forego the privilege of doing so.[47]

Mulholland then claimed that Rome in response to the *exeat* and character reference had ordered his reinstatement and he wrote what Crolly regarded as an insolent letter making this request and demanding that the archbishop pay the expenses he had incurred during his two years absence from the parish. Crolly forwarded this to Rome together with the sworn statements of clergy who were present when the offers of the curacies were made.[48] He was assured in reply that Mulholland's version was untrue and Mulholland was bidden to be more docile.[49]

Balked of success both in Armagh and Rome, Mulholland then turned his attention to parliament and forwarded a petition to Lord Lyndhurst who presented it in the House of Lords. It was a highly partial statement of his case but Lyndhurst thought the details were well authenticated and won considerable sympathy for his complaint against 'injustice and oppression', but nothing further was done about it.[50] Mulholland also planned to have a petition laid before the House of Commons but O'Connell and the members whom he approached were too well acquainted with the facts of the case, and so he abandoned that project.[51]

[46] Mulholland to Propaganda, 29 Aug. 1835, APF, SC (Irlanda), 26, ff 158r-159r.
[47] N.Ex., 18 June 1836.
[48] Crolly to Propaganda, 13 Nov. 1835, APF, SC (Irlanda), 26, ff 209rv, 215r-218r.
[49] Propaganda to Mulholland and Crolly, 12 Dec. 1835, APF, Lett., 316, ff 856v-857r, 858rv.
[50] Hansard 3, xxxiv, 145-160, (7 June 1836).
[51] Crolly to Cullen, 28 June 1836, Denvir to Cullen, 28 Dec. 1836, AICR.

The priests of the archdiocese, who did not recognize Mulholland in this martyr's guise, at their conferences at Dungannon, Dunleer, Armagh and Dundalk passed resolutions promptly repudiating 'the ill-natured and irreligious charges' contained in Lyndhurst's petition. Assuring the public that Mulholland never had any canonical claim to the parish of Termonfeckin and never received from Rome an order re-instating him in his former parish, the clergy explained the trickery involved in obtaining the testimonial on the pretext of going to America. The priests at the Dungannon conference did not hesitate to publicize their relief at Mulholland's refusing the curacies in their part of the diocese, declaring that his refusal had 'saved us from much uneasiness; and, by his absence from this district, has afforded us a permanent source of unfeigned satisfaction'.[52] Crolly himself gave his account of the dispute to the press and in the course of his letter described his turbulent subject as refractory.

Mulholland promptly picked up the challenge. In a public letter he demanded that the archbishop give the instances and proofs of his misconduct and promised that he would in due course comment on them. Crolly ignored the challenge. A month later he wrote a lengthy letter to the primate in which he accused Crolly of having inspired and orchestrated the resolutions passed by the clergy of Armagh exculpating their archbishop, which he insisted were too vague and general to prove him guilty of any crime. In fact, their silence on such charges as that of swearing, turbulence, gambling and drunkenness amounted to 'a full confirmation as far as my life, conversation, and, doctrine are concerned, of the flattering testimonials of your Grace's *exeat*'. He then went on to argue that, if he had been an extortioner and had been removed for that crime by Archbishop Kelly, some record of it would exist or at least be traceable in the correspondence. He repudiated the charge of being refractory since he had never disobeyed canonical orders. He challenged the archbishop to produce the 'insolent' letter and predicted that he never would, as he must have lost or destroyed it or he would never have described it so incorrectly. Then neatly turning the tables on his opponent Mulholland claimed that the charges against him of being 'an extortioner and author of disturbance' was a libel on the memory of Archbishop Curtis, who had kept him as administrator in Termonfeckin for seven years, at a distance of only three miles from his home, and then deftly aimed a blow at the current incumbent in Armagh by declaring that 'no

[52] N.W., 23 June 1836.

more vigilant, able, learned or pious successor has followed to dim the bright fame of that great and good man.'

Mulholland then proceeded to maintain that he had been dismissed because he had taken a fellow priest to the civil courts in response to a refusal to retract the allegation that he had been encouraging insurrection in his parish by his association with the 'stickmen'. Driven to submit to slander or appeal to the laws of his country, he had been forced to choose the latter, and as a consequence had been deprived of his office by Archbishop Kelly.[53]

If the archbishop was unwilling to engage Mulholland in public about extortionate behaviour and neglect of his duties, others were less reluctant to bring these charges to the attention of Rome. Five parishioners of Termonfeckin passed on to Propaganda a statement sworn before a magistrate testifying to the exorbitant demands the ex-administrator had made for money at weddings and at a funeral. A priest also submitted statements about his neglecting to attend people who subsequently died without the sacraments, and maintained furthermore that he had done nothing to quell the outrages that had so damaged religion in the parish of Termonfeckin.[54] The archbishop duly reported Mulholland to Rome for traducing him before parliament and added that his predecessor had been harried to his death by the hostility of that intractable priest. He also forwarded a copy of a letter from himself to Archbishop Murray in which he asserted that though he believed Mulholland could not render any service to religion in Armagh, he would contribute to his expenses to a foreign mission. But Mulholland had refused to take this convenient option. Two factors, he alleged, prevented him from doing so: his mother's advanced age, helplessness and absolute dependence on him, and the impression that such a transfer to another mission would give of a sentence of transportation. Nonetheless, he still insisted that the archbishop should arrange for employment and a means of subsistence for him and claimed that his position had been made worse by the vicar apostolic of the London district refusing him permission to celebrate Mass in the churches there after Lyndhurst had presented the petition in the House of Lords.[55]

Unlike most rebel clergy, Mulholland did not succeed in surrounding himself with a band of stubborn supporters. But he did succeed in

[53] N.Ex., 20 Aug. 1836.
[54] Thomas Corrigan and others to Propaganda, 1-4 July 1836, APF, SC (Irlanda), 26, ff 310r-318v.
[55] Crolly to Propaganda, 4 July 1836, Ibid., ff 320r-321r; Crolly to Murray, 23 Nov. 1836, Ibid., f 344v; Mulholland to Crolly, 28 Nov. 1836, Ibid., ff 344v-345v.

attracting the favour of one influential admirer, Sir Henry Chester, a landlord and magistrate in Co. Louth. Chester, a Catholic, wrote a couple of derogatory letters about Crolly to Mulholland, which together with other material deemed favourable to his cause—including the *exeat*—were subsequently published as a broadsheet. In the first of his communications Chester expressed his opinion that the archbishop's conduct 'called on the court of Rome to vindicate its authority, otherwise how can she have the faithful esteem her, if she is thus treated by the primate of Ireland, who while he denounces you as a refractory priest, may himself be equally denounced as a refractory Bishop'. A month later Chester in a comment on Mulholland's open letter to the primate descended to cheap guttersnipe tactics in an attempt to wound the archbishop:

he has this advantage over you, he has his £900 as Primate—the height of his ambition. He has obtained honour and riches and, believe me, £900 a year to a man from a mud cabin, and six acres of ground in the wilds of the county of Down, is not to be despised by a worldly Bishop . . . so this will be his consolation at least in this life . . . as to the charitable feelings of Dr Crolly towards you I entertain none; he has in my mind a heart of stone, otherwise he could not ill-treat you so long as he has done.[56]

However, Chester's sympathy expressed in such a contemptuous form was counterproductive. The Irish church could do nothing for Mulholland while he persisted with such behaviour. But Cardinal Fransoni, the benign and patient prefect of Propaganda, thought of asking the vicar-apostolic of the London district to take him on, but nothing came of the proposal and Mulholland did not again hit the headlines until an opportunity for creating mischief occurred in the diocese of Cloyne.

When a dispute arose between the parish priest of Aghinagh and some of his parishioners about the provision of a church for the parish, those who wanted to repair the old church broke with their pastor and in effect started a local schism. They then searched for a priest of their own and in 1838 took the redoubtable Mulholland under their protection.[57] Having refused to consider any appointment in Armagh, other than Termonfeckin, he took up an assignment much further afield and one which swept away whatever shred of credibility he still enjoyed in Rome.

He remained for over four years in Aghinagh but gradually the

---

[56] Chester to Mulholland, 20 July, 30 Aug, Ibid., f 418rv. Crolly bore no ill-will to Chester subsequently. When unable to attend a dinner in his honour in Dundalk in 1840, he referred in his letter of apology 'to my respected friend, our late faithful representative for Co. Louth'. (N.Ex., 15 Aug. 1840.)

[57] Cullen to Propaganda, Ibid., ff 521r-524v.

relationship between himself and his flock deteriorated, and they decided to end their schism. Without any income or support he travelled to Rome and threw himself again on the mercy of Propaganda. Cardinal Fransoni, ever anxious to rehabilitate even the most uncooperative priest, wrote commending him to Crolly's charity and care, and suggesting that he be helped in his poverty and ill health. Crolly replied promptly with a gift of £10.[58] Fransoni evidently hoped for more than financial assistance and, as Mulholland continued to pester him, he again wrote to Crolly expressing the hope that the archbishop would find some work for him in Armagh, and adding that, since he had done penance for his offences, his return would not cause scandal.[59]

However, the primate was unable to comply with that request. He replied that he had consulted the clergy about the suggestion and could not find either a parish priest or curate who did not fear that the return of the prodigal would provoke scandal and schism. Recalling some of the misdeeds of the past, Crolly professed his willingness to contribute to Mulholland's upkeep annually but insisted that his return would disrupt the peace of the diocese and would not serve the interests of religion.[60] Fransoni accepted this decision but encouraged Crolly to forward as large a yearly pension as he could afford.[61] The archbishop undertook to pay the annual sum of £10 and the congregation of Propaganda assured the ill and ageing suppliant that it would add what it could to the subscription from the archbishop and the priests of Armagh.[62] Crolly kept his promise. Mulholland, whose health gradually deteriorated, moved on to Gibraltar where he insulted and abused the local bishop, and in the bishop's words opened a school and quarrelled with all those who had any dealings with him.[63] He was living there when the archbishop died. He continued to petition Propaganda for financial help and maintained the integrity of his quarrel to the end of his life. It was a quarrel which Crolly inherited and which no bishop could have settled satisfactorily. Mulholland was incorrigibly contentious and would have created trouble in whatever office he was given.

[58] Propaganda to Crolly, 11 June 1844, APF, *Lett.*, 331, f 432r and Crolly to Cullen, 13 July 1844, AICR.
[59] Propaganda to Crolly, 8 Apr. 1845, Ibid., f 208rv.
[60] Crolly to Propaganda, 30 May 1845, APF, SC (Irlanda), 28, ff 463r-464r.
[61] Propaganda to Crolly, 21 June 1845, APF, *Lett.*, 332, f 404rv.
[62] Propaganda to Mulholland, 23 Sept. 1845, Ibid., f 687r.
[63] H. Hughes to Cullen, 9 Nov. 1848, AICR.

V

Mulholland, however persistently troublesome to the archbishop, did not cause turmoil throughout the archdiocese of Armagh. But the first major non-diocesan dispute in which the primate was involved was one that threw a whole diocese into a state of turmoil. Crolly was commissioned by Rome to make a full report on the causes of a dispute in Killala and to forward his recommendations for a solution to the problems that had created bitter divisions between the bishop and his priests.

When MacHale left Killala to become archbishop of Tuam in 1834, he felt there was no candidate among the diocesan clergy of episcopal timbre fit to succeed him, and, consequently, he persuaded the parish priests to put at the top of their list a priest whom the great majority of them did not know. Francis Joseph O'Finan was a Dominican, who had spent most of his life as a priest in Portugal and Italy, and had become an adviser to the master-general of the Dominican order. Aged sixty three, this native son of the diocese, whose knowledge of it was minimal, was appointed bishop in 1835 and committed his first blunder before he even reached it: he appointed John Patrick Lyons, the parish priest of Kilmore-Erris, who had met him on his journey home, vicar general and dean of the recently restored diocesan chapter. And en route to his see he neglected to call with his metropolitan or with the bishops of Elphin and Achonry, through whose dioceses he passed.

A few days after his arrival a majority of the parish priests waited on him with a protest against Lyons' appointment and a request that the same arrangement about fees for the dispensations from the banns of marriage as applied in the other dioceses of the province be introduced into Killala. (A custom of long standing dictated that the clergy paid the bishop half a guinea from each dispensation from marriage banns, whereas in the rest of the province the clergy were obliged to pay only half that sum.) O'Finan apparently regarded this conduct as a manifestation of disobedience and insubordination, and resented it deeply. The clergy of Killala were not alone in questioning the wisdom of Lyons' appointment. Both the neighbouring bishops of Elphin and Achonry were soon convinced that it was a grave mistake. And McNicholas of Achonry grew so concerned about the reports of discontent among the priests of Killala that he advised MacHale to convene a provincial meeting to deal with them.[64]

[64] O'Reilly, MacHale, ii, 344-50.

Before that a dozen parish priests and three curates had complained to Rome about the dean and asked the pope to turn his attention to their distracted diocese. The accusations which they made against Lyons and which were to be frequently repeated in correspondence with Rome were basically threefold: he was avaricious, litigious and violent. They gave examples of his excesses in these matters: he had brought charges against parishioners in court; had scandalously pursued quarrels with his brothers; had physically struck his parishioners and was accustomed to rage against his domestic staff; had refused to pay a stipend, which had been fixed by the bishop, to an aged priest; alone among the clergy had refused to contribute to the construction of the cathedral or churches in the diocese; had often spoken contumeliously against his fellow priests in the presence of lay people, and had tried to win friends by the promise of parochial preferment in a simoniacal way.[65]

Confronted with such a litany of grievances Propaganda promptly consulted MacHale. He confirmed the truth of nearly all the accusations, added further examples of Lyons' avarice and expressed his fears that, if the dissensions were not ended, they would engulf the whole province. There could be no peace in the diocese, he insisted, as long as Lyons exercised the jurisdiction of a vicar general and the bishop was thought to be guided by his counsels. But if he were sent back to his parish and the bishop could make his own decisions, those who were alienated would after a short time put aside their hostility.[66] MacHale, who also feared that episcopal authority in general would be seriously damaged by dissensions in Killala, had a personal reason for distrusting Lyons which he made known to the rector of the Irish College in Rome but not to the congregation: he believed that one of his own opponents in Tuam had recommended Lyons to O'Finan, knowing well the dean's unsuitability and the mischief it would cause.[67]

But before Rome was thus involved in the case MacHale had already intervened. Two issues had impelled him to do so: the controversy about the fees for dispensations from banns and the appeal of John Barrett, the parish priest of Crossmolina. He had organized a meeting of the prelates of the Tuam province on 1 February 1836, a mere three and a half months after O'Finan's arrival, and there all the bishops, apart from Killala, agreed that the marriage fees in that diocese should be divided in the same

---

[65] Clergy of Killala to Propaganda, 10 Dec. 1835, APF, *Acta*, 201, ff 392r-393r.
[66] MacHale to Propaganda, 7 Feb. 1836, Ibid., ff 393r-394v.
[67] MacHale to Cullen, 10 Apr. 1836, 21 Apr. 1837, AICR.

way as in the rest of the province. He had also accepted the appeal of John Barrett to his metropolitan court.[68]

Barrett's case added a further twist to the complicated situation in Killala. The parish of Crossmolina.had been conferred on MacHale while he was still a professor in Maynooth. It was administered on his behalf and he derived no income from it. But when he became coadjutor bishop of Killala he required some of the income. In 1831, John Barrett was appointed his administrator and, when MacHale succeeded to the see in June 1834, Barrett became parish priest. There was some doubt about MacHale's right to confer the parish on Barrett, as vacancies which occurred because of promotions from Rome usually fell under the authority of the Roman congregations. MacHale had written to Rome to have the matter settled but was transferred to Tuam before this could be done and the cardinal prefect had deferred making the appointment. O'Finan took the view that the archbishop had acted *ultra vires*, transferred Barrett from Crossmolina, and replaced him by Edward Murray. The parishioners reacted angrily to this move and locked the doors of the church against Murray, when he came to take possession, and against Lyons who accompanied him to officiate at his installation. Barrett also appealed to Rome, claiming that O'Finan would have confirmed his appointment in Crossmolina, had it not been for Lyons' opposition and asking that a bishop of the province or a superior from Maynooth examine his case.[69]

MacHale, who was again consulted about this charge and who had already forwarded some material about it to Rome, confirmed the truth of Barrett's allegations. Praising Barrett's suitability and popularity in the parish, he explained that Edward Murray had been ordained a priest, despite being compelled to withdraw from Maynooth because of mental illness, and had since behaved irresponsibly in the diocese.[70]

Called upon to respond to these charges against his administration, O'Finan put all the blame for the troubles on his turbulent clergy. He maintained that radical cabals had been organizing conspiracies against him. He insisted that he needed to keep the same arrangements as his predecessors about the fees for dispensations from banns because of the poverty of the diocese, and he defended Lyons as a learned, zealous and capable priest, who had enjoyed the esteem of MacHale's predecessor in Killala. In turn he attacked MacHale for his political activities and

[68] O'Reilly, *MacHale*, ii, 351-5.   [69] Barrett to Propaganda, 16 Jan. 1836, APF, Acta, 201, f 395rv.
[70] MacHale to Propaganda, 27 Feb. 1836, Ibid., ff 395v-397r.

accused him of making appointments to parishes after he had received news of his transfer to Tuam. And he blamed Barrett and his relatives and friends for causing all the trouble in Crossmolina.[71]

Rome was not convinced by these arguments and replied by exhorting him to dismiss Lyons from the office of vicar-general. Though couched in anodyne terms, the letter declared that there could be no tranquillity or concord in the diocese while Lyons retained his office, and reminded the bishop that, though dean of the diocese, he could be sent back to his parish.[72]

Rome doubtless expected prompt compliance with what it regarded virtually as a command. But O'Finan, giving evidence of the obstinacy and obduracy that were to prove his undoing, refused to obey. But, if he thought his inaction would eventually exhaust Rome's interest in the case, he was mistaken. MacHale continued to correspond with Propaganda and, when he heard that Bishop McGettigan of Raphoe had arrived in the eternal city, he sent him a statement on the issue 'to fortify him with the truth'. In fact this letter contained further explosive material: Lyons had sought the lease of a tract of land from a landlord on the plea of expending public funds on it 'and appropriating it to public charity', and when the landlord refused him a lease as a private individual, he sued him, extracted it from him and took over the ground as private property yielding large profits, to the great loss and pain of the ejected tenants.[73] The archbishop also kept Paul Cullen, the rector of the Irish College, informed about all the moves of 'the poor deluded Bishop and his wicked Dane' (sic)[74] with a view to maximizing the knowledge of Propaganda on the affair.

Consequently, when Archbishop Murray of Dublin visited Rome in the spring of 1836, Propaganda asked his opinion on the whole issue. He suggested that a zealous and prudent bishop—he mentioned, specifically, the archbishops of Armagh and Cashel—should be sent to Killala to report fully on the disputes or be even empowered by apostolic authority to settle them.[75] Propaganda lost little time in carrying out this suggestion. It wrote to Crolly outlining the principal points of the conflict and noting that while the congregation had proposed that Lyons be stripped of his office and sent back to his parish, its request had not been carried out despite an assurance to the contrary from the bishop. Reference was also

---

[71] O'Finan to Propaganda, 3 Mar. 1836, Ibid., ff 397v-401v.
[72] Propaganda to O'Finan, 15 Mar. 1836, Ibid., f 410v.
[73] MacHale to McGettigan, 29 Feb. 1836, AICR.   [74] MacHale to Cullen, 10 Apr. 1836, Ibid.
[75] Murray to Propaganda, 4 June 1836, APF, Acta, 201, f 402r.

made to the ill-feeling between O'Finan and MacHale, to whom he owed his appointment, and Crolly, who was commended for the satisfactory contribution he had made to ending the contentions in Galway, was encouraged to heal the breaches within Killala, and those between Killala and Tuam, and submit his recommendations for the termination of the dissensions to Rome.[76]

For Crolly this commission was an invitation to enter a hornet's nest. He could have known very little about Killala, its tortuous ecclesiastical politics, and the scandalous conflicts which were daily becoming worse, and the burden of discerning the truth from the partisan pleading to which he was bound to be subjected could not have been a pleasant prospect. On the other hand his status, his independence of the factions in the diocese and his freedom from any hint of involvement in the disputes either at diocesan or provincial level, gave him a decided advantage in formulating a recommendation for their settlement.

Crolly promptly contacted the archbishop of Tuam and the bishop of Killala to make arrangements about his mission. MacHale, who was pleased with the choice of arbitrator, offered him the fullest cooperation.[77] So he opened his investigation in Ballina on 22 August but, as he had received a letter from Lyons telling him that he, the dean, had important documents in Rome which the bishop would require during the investigation, he decided to postpone it until 19 October. But a mere eight days before this date he received a letter from O'Finan asking him to put it back further until Lyons returned from Rome (whither he had gone in June to plead his cause and where, according to Paul Cullen 'his smooth insinuating talk, and his humble demeanour, made a great impression in his favour' at first) and not to admit as a witness any bishop of the Tuam province, as they were all hostile to him. The primate, however, felt obliged to adhere to his plan and on the appointed day celebrated Mass in the Cathedral at Ballina, and then, when the laity were excluded, began his inquiry with the priests about Lyons and the other controverted issues. He spent seven hours daily for four days examining witnesses in the presence of O'Finan and MacHale and of Bishop Denvir of Down and Connor, whom he brought along as his counsellor and who took extensive notes of the proceedings. Having heard many accusations about the behaviour of Lyons in his parish in Kilmore Erris, he decided to go there, despite the efforts of O'Finan to deter him from so doing by claiming that Lyons had been honourably acquitted in Rome and sworn as dean by the

[76] Propaganda to Crolly, 16 June 1836, APF, Lett., 317, ff 467v-469r.
[77] O'Reilly, MacHale, ii, 356-7.

cardinal prefect of Propaganda.[78] He spent a week in the parish examining witnesses on their oath in the presence of the same bishops and many priests. His findings, as he subsequently noted, were far from flattering to Lyons.

Crolly was convinced that the dean had taken proceedings against parishioners, twelve of whom he caused to be brought before a civil tribunal and to be incarcerated for fifteen days in Castlebar because they had made complaints to their former bishop of Killala and the former archbishop of Tuam about his avarice, ill-temper and unjust financial exactions. Lyons had persisted in restraining these parishioners from receiving the sacraments of penance and the Eucharist unless they would publicly declare that their accusations were false—something which they could not do. He refused to officiate at the wedding of one of them, and thereby compelled the man to have recourse to a Protestant minister, even though he had appealed to the bishop. His brother, Luke Lyons, with whom he had also had disputes, refused to testify, if the full and naked truth were required from him. A number of witnesses gave evidence that in a rage he had struck two men before the altar of the church at Binghamstown. His greed was evident from his possession of four farms. One of these, containing 549 acres, he acquired not without the suspicion of fraud and against the wishes of the tenants, whom he retained in great poverty as workers and whom he compelled to pay twice as much more for 90 acres than they had paid the previous landlord for 549 acres. Lyons had put the roof on a church in one of the other farms (of 120 acres) which he owned, but had so neglected it that the rain came through it and the priest and faithful were obliged to take refuge elsewhere in stormy weather. His sheep and cattle were often housed in that chapel. The parishioners of Kilmore Erris also complained of the scandalous comparison between the splendour of the house Lyons built for himself and the disgraceful condition of the chapels, for the expenses of which he exacted large sums of money, even extracting ten shillings more for marriages than the normal amount. Moreover, he had refused to pay the annual pension of £20 to his predecessor, who would have perished of want, had it not been for the help of another priest.

Crolly repeated evidence of Lyons' outbursts of ill temper. And to the accusations already made he added the very grave one of attempted seductions of women. When he asked O'Finan to prove that Barrett, the parish priest of Crossmolina, had excited disturbances in that parish, the

---

[78] MacHale to Cullen, 16 Nov. 1836, AICR.

bishop replied that he protested against further investigation in the absence of Lyons, and that he had appealed to the Holy See—which seemed a mere ruse to avoid an examination of Barrett, who, he could see, was prepared with the help of witnesses to prove his innocence. And when he asked the bishop to remove Barrett's suspension he met with a refusal. Crolly believed that the people of Crossmolina had every reason for complaining about the behaviour of O'Finan and Lyons in suspending Barrett and putting in his place Edward Murray a man who had been sent down from Maynooth because of mental instability. Consequently, he decided to postpone further inquiry into Barrett's case until he knew whether the pope was prepared to accept O'Finan's appeal.

When the investigations had been interrupted, a query had reached him from Rome as to whether Lyons should be allowed to remain in Ballina as administrator of the bishop's parish, while remaining parish priest of Kilmore Erris. He advised strongly against such a suggestion and added emphatically that Bishop Denvir, the bishops of the province of Tuam and almost all the learned and trustworthy priests of Killala shared his conviction that there could be neither justice nor peace in the diocese as long as Lyons was a counsellor of the bishop or enjoyed the most minimal authority, either direct or indirect, in diocesan administration. Crolly then went on to make two further recommendations: that the matrimonial fees should be the same in Killala as in the other dioceses, and that John Barrett should be restored to his parish in Crossmolina.[79]

Crolly certainly repaid the trust of the Roman authorities by this account of the dissensions in the tormented diocese of Killala. It was clear, comprehensive and humane. And his recommendations were couched in mild terms—the removal of Lyons, the restoration of Barrett and the adjustment of the fees connected with the banns of marriage. Cullen reported to MacHale that the primate's report had made 'a most excellent impression, and completely removed all the evil effects which had been produced by Mr Lyons' lamentable stories of oppression and bad treatment'.[80] The only complaint Crolly allowed himself to make was about the lack of hospitality and provision of accommodation which he received. In view of what he heard about Lyons and O'Finan's defence of the indefensible the archbishop of Armagh would certainly have been

[79] Crolly to Propaganda, 11 Nov. 1836, APF, Acta, 201, ff 403v–406r. Crolly sent a very similar letter to Cullen and begged him to use his influence to save Killala from Lyons. He told Cullen that the tenants on the 549 acres of rough land had paid £80 rent each year. Lyons proceeded to charge them £176.9.0 for 90 acres. (Crolly to Cullen, 16 Nov. 1836, AICR.)

[80] O'Reilly, MacHale, ii, 384.

justified in calling for O'Finan's dismissal. And, perhaps, in the longer term this tougher action might have been productive of less harm.

Crolly was not able to complete his inquiry because of personal commitments, but also because of the absence of Lyons. Not only did O'Finan try to throw all possible obstacles in his way, but the bishop made the further mistake of writing to Rome and attacking his *bona fides*. He complained that the primate, whom he designated a *Partisan prononcé* and accused of being ignorant of canon law, had not examined in depth the two really serious issues of marriage fees and MacHale's appointments, but had devoted all his energies to destroying the reputation of Dean Lyons and exalting that of John Barrett. He accused the archbishop of violating British law by citing Lyons' tenants under oath to appear before him and added in a semi-minatory way that, were this to be reported in *The Times* or the *Evening Mail*, a tremendous brouhaha against the misuse of ecclesiastical power would ensue. The dean had been strafed for vindicating his reputation in the courts, and yet both MacHale and the late Archbishop Troy had done likewise.[81] Hoping for some more pliable or credulous visitor, he requested the master-general of the Dominican Order to ask the Roman authorities to send someone else to complete the investigation. Cardinal Fransoni rejected this plea and begged Crolly to return to Ballina and resume his mission as soon as possible. Accordingly he arranged to return with the same team to Ballina on 24 January 1837.

When he arrived there he was told that O'Finan was ill and had appointed Lyons to act on his behalf. Lyons had already written two long and very insolent letters to the archbishop in which he attacked him bitterly, protesting against all he had done and would do in the affair, and claiming on oath that his case had been tried by Propaganda and that he had been found innocent of all the accusations that would be brought against them. He even maintained that the archbishop had never been given authority by Rome to inquire into his morals, though he saw copies of the original letters authorizing the visitor to do so. However, Crolly went ahead with his plans and dealt with the two issues left over from the previous inquiry: Crossmolina and the legality of MacHale's last appointments. He explained in his report that he spent four days in Crossmolina examining witnesses on oath, the principal one of whom was Lyons. He discovered that MacHale had appointed to that parish John Barrett, who had been acting as administrator for years previously and had applied to

---

[81] O'Finan to Propaganda, 27 Nov. 1836, APF, *Acta*, 201, ff 409v-411r.

Rome for confirmation of the appointment. When the document giving the bishop of Killala power to appoint whomsoever he wished to Crossmolina reached Killala, O'Finan had succeeded MacHale, and by virtue of that authorization O'Finan decided to remove Barrett, unless he withdrew his name from the list of signatories protesting against the fees for the dispensations from banns and the promotion of Lyons. Barrett refused and was told his faculties expired on 31 December. He promised to obey but on the Sunday before that date Lyons came to install Edward Murray in Crossmolina, and the parishioners reacted angrily. About thirty respectable men from the parish, and both Lyons and Murray, swore that Barrett had played no part in inciting the people to resistance, but on the contrary had strenuously endeavoured to calm them. When Barrett was summoned to Ballina and threatened with suspension as a result of these disturbances, he appealed to MacHale and was then promptly suspended by O'Finan—a censure which still afflicted him.

Crolly then betook himself to Ballina to get to the bottom of the charges against MacHale's having made appointments in Killala after he had received the bulls of his transfer to Tuam. He found that these charges were without foundation and that those whom MacHale did promote were worthy candidates. Moreover, they had been acknowledged as the legitimate pastors since the date on which the names of O'Finan and two others were submitted to Rome as possible successors in the see. Crolly also reported that he saw copies of the documents by which Murray obliged himself to pay £20 annually to Lyons or to another priest nominated by O'Finan from the revenues of Crossmolina. Two other priests had been placed in charge of parishes as administrators on the same conditions. Crolly left to Rome the responsibility of deciding whether these contracts were simoniacal or not.

In conclusion the primate repeated his previous suggestion that Killala could never enjoy peace as long as Lyons was the bishop's counsellor and abused his very extensive authority to the detriment of the diocese and of the most experienced and pious clergy. He also recommended the restoration, if possible, of Barrett to Crossmolina and the removal of Murray from that parish, the reduction of the fees for the dispensations from banns in the diocese to the same level as elsewhere in the Tuam province, and the retention of their parishes by MacHale's appointees. He pointed out that the main source of contention between MacHale and O'Finan about appointments arose from the fact that the bishop of Killala claimed the customary fees on the appointments made by MacHale after he had been translated to Tuam, even though he had not received the bull of his translation. He did not conceal from Rome the obstructions which Lyons had put in his way and he noted that the bishop had retained in office a vicar-general of whose avarice, ill-temper and impurity of life he was aware.[82]

The second visitation confirmed the findings of the first. Propaganda duly paid Crolly the best tribute in its power: his views were quoted favourably in the analysis of the whole Killala case for the cardinals who were called upon to give the pope final advice about the complex problem of O'Finan and his diocese. The cardinal who compiled the analysis obviously found Crolly's judgement just and reasonable, and quoted from it in the expectation that his colleagues would incorporate it into their conclusions. Bishop Denvir undoubtedly also reflected Crolly's opinion when he described Lyons' behaviour as incomprehensible and expressed his bewilderment at the actions of a man who could oppress the people whose pastor he was. Denvir was also nonplussed by O'Finan's inhospitality and rejection of the suggestion of the Killala clergy that they should pay the expenses of the visitation.[83]

The pope took instant action on two issues: he ordered the bishop to remove Lyons from the office of vicar-general and to lift the suspension from Barrett. Lyons was extremely annoyed by the information Crolly extracted about him and wrote to Rome threatening the congregation of Propaganda that, if it denied him justice, he might be obliged to take Crolly to the civil courts for the inquiries the prelate had made about his person and conduct.[84]

Not content with one joust against the archbishop of Armagh, O'Finan returned to the fray after the completion of the second visitation. On the second occasion he accused Crolly not only of manifest partiality but also of injustice and sent a formal appeal against his actions to the pope. He then proceeded to identify his supporters and opponents among the clergy of Killala: he claimed that of the thirty seven clergy in the diocese, twenty one backed him and only fourteen had appealed against him. He referred the cardinal to the request contained in the petition to the pope to send the archbishop of Dublin and the bishop of Limerick to institute an impartial inquiry into the Killala affair, so that the congregation of Propaganda could apply an efficacious remedy to it. He himself sought permission to visit Rome to defend himself.[85]

[82] Crolly to Propaganda, 8 Feb. 1837, APF, *Acta*, 201, ff 406v-409v.
[83] Denvir to Cullen, 27 Feb. 1837, AICR.
[84] Lyons to Propaganda, 6 Feb. 1837, *Acta*, 201, f 384v.
[85] O'Finan to Propaganda, 20 Feb. 1837, Ibid., ff 411v-412v.

A further painful chapter was added to the Killala saga when O'Finan took the editor of the *Mayo Telegraph* to court. That newspaper had carried severely critical remarks about the bishop, and one correspondent, using the *nom de plume*, *Alladensis*, had accused him of being proud, imperious and petulant, of having maltreated his clergy, of having neglected his episcopal duties and of having disturbed the peace of the diocese. The case was tried in Sligo and not only was the editor fined £500 and obliged to pay the costs but in the course of the trial one of O'Finan's leading opponents, Patrick Flannelly, confessed to the author-ship of the letters signed *Alladensis*. The editor called as witnesses Crolly, MacHale and Bishop Burke of Elphin, and the bishop later charged that MacHale caused a sensation by referring to the letter from the congrega-tion of Propaganda about the dismissal of Lyons from his offices.[86]

But if O'Finan felt he had discomfited his enemies by the outcome of the trial, he mistook a pyrrhic victory for a real one. MacHale sent a very damaging report of the whole proceedings to Rome in which he blamed the bishop for causing scandal not only by taking the case to court—others including himself had suffered such journalistic insults in silence rather than do so—but by deliberately bringing it to Sligo where it was tried before an all-Protestant jury. He had done so despite the urgent pleading of Crolly, Bishop Burke of Elphin, prominent lay Catholics from Sligo and himself. Referring to the participation of Crolly and himself at the trial, MacHale remarked:

The time chosen for the trial increased both our discomfort and the public scandal. Nothing was better fitted to provoke the laughter of our Protestant enemies, and to fill our Catholics with grief, than to behold four bishops, with a great crowd of priests, spending their time at such a trial as never had been heard of before—and spending it during Passion Week, when it is usual to be preaching to the people and ministering the sacraments.

Though Lyons was not on trial, the verdict affirmed that he had been appointed vicar-general with undue haste and without consultations with the clergy, and that he had been retained in office after the bishop had received a letter from Rome urging his dismissal. Great scandal was caused by the bishop's claim that he was not obliged to follow the advice of the prefect of Propaganda but was free to retain or dismiss his vicar general, irrespective of Roman interference. Repeating the accusations against Lyons and dubbing him the source from which all the evils of the diocese sprang, the archbishop of Tuam surmised that the only explana-

[86] Ibid., 20 Mar. 1837, ff 412v-414r.

tion for the hostility he was then showing to Crolly about whom he had once written letters 'filled with shameless adulation and excessive praise' derived from a discovery that the primate had reported his evil deeds and could not be shaken in the discharge of his duty.

However, the time was past when the removal of Lyons alone would set the diocese again on an even keel. O'Finan had seriously neglected his episcopal duties since arriving in Killala; he had never visited a single parish, never administered confirmation, and never preached to either clergy or people. Since the diocese was so torn by 'violent dissensions', 'antagonistic passions' and 'partisan strife' there was 'no hope of saving religion there, unless the Apostolic See should appoint as bishop-coadjutor some man of prudence, piety, and firmness, who will not allow himself to be deceived by flatterers or drawn by the influence of the powerful or the acts of the factions to favor one party or the other'. And even if that remedy were applied, a whole decade would be needed to repair the damage done by the O'Finan regime.[87]

Ten days later the archbishop of Tuam and all his suffragans except the bishop of Killala formally appealed for the appointment of a coadjutor and further requested that he should be chosen from the clergy of another diocese without consulting the bishop and clergy of Killala.[88] O'Finan, meanwhile, was also stirring the pot with vigour and determination. He wrote to Rome to inform Cardinal Fransoni that he was threatening to institute criminal proceedings in Dublin against Crolly, MacHale and Denvir on the grounds that they had not allowed an investigation to be conducted into whether or not a conspiracy had been mounted against the bishop's life. Fransoni, pained and embarrassed by this denouement, hastily wrote to the archbishop of Dublin to use his influence to avert this catastrophe.[89] Murray duly tried to elicit from O'Finan the reasons which induced him to take this step, and was told that a witness at Ballina had referred to a conspiracy to take the bishop's life. Thereupon Crolly and MacHale ordered all the priests, including Dean Lyons, to retire and examined this witness 'inquisitorially, with closed doors & they alone can tell the result'. O'Finan went on to complain that the visitation was ended without any reference to himself and so he wondered what could prevent him 'from summoning the three Prelates before the court of King's Bench in Dublin, to render an account of such unfair & dishonorable proceedings, and to compel them to produce the minutes of evidence taken on

---

[87] MacHale to Propaganda, 10 Apr. 1837, Ibid., ff 414r–416v and O'Reilly, *MacHale*, ii, 359–66.
[88] MacHale and others to Propaganda, 20 Apr. 1837, Ibid., f 417rv and O'Reilly, *MacHale*, ii, 391–4.
[89] Propaganda to Murray, 29 Apr. 1837, APF, *Lett.*, 318, ff 358r–360r

that occasion, and thereby have a clue to trace the conspiracy to its proper Source'. However, out of respect for Murray he was prepared to let bygones be bygones, unless Propaganda drove him to despair.[90]

O'Finan, however, on the pope's instructions was summoned to Rome to give an account of his stewardship. MacHale wanted Crolly and Denvir to be involved along with the bishops of the province in the choice of a coadjutor for Killala.[91] But, possibly because Crolly and Denvir had been accused of partisanship by the bishop of Killala, Propaganda turned for advice to Archbishop Murray, as he could not be accused of partiality. It asked his opinion about what should be done with O'Finan personally and how peace, good order and ecclesiastical discipline could be established in the diocese.[92] Murray replied that there could be no peace, if O'Finan continued to administer Killala. He therefore recommended that the bishop should, if possible, be given some honorary position and remain in Rome or elsewhere in Italy so that some other provision could be made for the governance of the diocese.[93]

In October 1837 O'Finan arrived in the eternal city to promote in person the defence of his case which had hitherto been carried on by the Dominicans, Cardinal Weld and Lord Clifford on his behalf. But by then he had an acute persecution complex, believing that not only Crolly, MacHale and the bishops of Connacht but also the cardinal and secretary of Propaganda were hostile to him. Officials of the congregation held various friendly meetings with him to try to induce him to make some concessions to the views of his opponents, but in vain. He never wavered in his estimate of Lyons, whom he described to Cardinal Fransoni as a man of wide learning, rare talent and great experience, and he insisted that from the day on which he deprived Lyons of the office of vicar-general, he never enjoyed a moment of peace or rest. He continued to reject the points put to him by Propaganda about the loss of confidence in him by the Irish episcopate and, when challenged about his hostility and bitterness towards MacHale and Crolly, he demanded proof that he ever harboured such feelings! He then in a threatening manner discoursed on the power of public opinion in British public life, juxtaposed it with the investigative methods used in Rome and accused Propaganda of interfering in the temporal affairs of Ireland. But when he attempted to defy Rome by insisting that he would never renounce his rights as bishop of Killala, and protested solemnly against any steps that might be taken to

[90] O'Finan to Murray, 18 May 1837, DDA.   [91] MacHale to Cullen, 14 Nov. 1837, AICR.
[92] Propaganda to Murray, 18 Nov. 1837, DDA.
[93] Murray to Propaganda, 12 Dec. 1837, APF, *Acta*, 201, f 418r.

violate those rights and jurisdiction,[94] he had become a sad and sorry Canute-like figure, and Rome could not indefinitely tolerate such irresponsible posturing. The pope responded to this challenge by having him formally warned that, if he left Rome without permission, he would be *ipso facto* suspended from exercising all jurisdiction. Archishop Murray was invited to make provisional arrangements for the administration of Killala.

Propaganda showed its usual patience in not hastening its verdict. The documents were all sent to Cornelius van Everbroeck, a consultor of the congregation, and he was asked to study them and submit an opinion on them. He in turn came to the same conclusion that Murray, MacHale and the five bishops of the Tuam province had reached: the restoration of peace and order depended on O'Finan being withdrawn from the diocese. At the time of his visitations Crolly may have regarded this step as too severe, but O'Finan's incorrigibility had convinced him of its necessity. Some months later he expressed the hope that the bishop would be kept in Rome and that a prudent prelate would be appointed in his place.[95]

The cardinals of Propaganda examined the Killala case at the plenary meeting of the congregation on 19 December 1838 and recommended that O'Finan should be threatened with suspension from episcopal jurisdiction if he left Rome without papal permission, and that an administrator, whom Archbishop Murray would propose, should be appointed to the diocese. The cardinals also advised that the same financial arrangements about dispensations from banns should apply in Killala as in the rest of the province, and that the parish priests appointed by MacHale were not to be disturbed.[96] The pope duly gave his approval to this proposal and Murray was commissioned to find a suitable administrator for the diocese of Killala. Thomas Feeny, a priest of the diocese of Tuam, was chosen for this office and after some time was appointed a titular bishop and apostolic administrator of Killala in July 1839. But before Feeny was endowed with full episcopal powers a further traumatic ordeal was superimposed on the tribulations of the diocese: John Barrett, the parish priest of Crossmolina, was murdered. Edward Murray, who had been appointed to that parish by O'Finan in disputed circumstances was still in possession when this outrage occurred, and the hostility and contempt for him that had previously existed were greatly compounded by this ghoulish event. MacHale instanced this tragic occurrence as evidence of

---

94 O'Finan to Propaganda, 12 Sept. 1838, Ibid., ff 418v–421v.
95 Crolly to MacHale, 15 Dec. 1837, in O'Reilly, *MacHale*, ii, 357
96 APF, *Acta*, 201, ff 390v–391r.

'the desperate lengths' to which 'a wicked factious spirit' would go. And despite an 'abortive attempt to remove the odium of the wicked deed by ascribing his death to some other cause', a jury had brought in a verdict of wilful murder.[97] O'Finan died in Rome in November 1847 and Feeny then became bishop of the diocese.

Crolly, like many of the other participants in the Killala affair, was rewarded for his pains by abuse from O'Finan, Lyons and presumably from their friends. He could have known little about the unsavoury problems of that tormented diocese until he first visited Ballina in 1836. The investigations were burdensome and distasteful. And to the pain caused by the boorish accusations of Lyons and the asinine obstinacy of O'Finan must be added the financial burden of the journey to and sojourn in Mayo in assessing the cost to Crolly of the whole operation. Like the other disinterested participants in the Killala imbroglio he must have been heartily sickened by it and immensely relieved when an apostolic administrator was appointed to take charge of the see.

VI

The other major diocesan dispute which Crolly was called on to settle occurred in Dromore. It, too, reverberated throughout the diocese, divided the clergy and involved both Catholic and Protestant laity.

John Sproule Keenan, the parish priest of Annaghlone, was ordained for the diocese of Clogher in 1809. Seven years later he moved to Dundalk where he conducted a school from 1816 to 1823. Then with the blessing and encouragement of Archbishop Curtis, he transferred to Newry and established a school, which later became St Colman's College. This school was successful and Keenan won sufficient respect and esteem from the clergy of Dromore to ensure him first place on the *terna* when the diocese became vacant in 1832. Of the fifteen votes cast, he received seven and Michael Blake, who came third, received one. However, the bishops of the province informed Rome that they regarded Keenan as most unsuitable, and he was not appointed.[98]

Blake, who became bishop, was austere and energetic, and required strict obedience from his clergy. The likelihood of clashes between him and the headstrong Keenan, who may have felt piqued at being passed over, was always strong. The first serious one occurred in 1839 when

---

[97] MacHale to O'Higgins, 2 May 1839, AICR.   [98] APF, *Acta*, 196, ff 34r-39v.

Keenan was suspended for neglecting his duties. He promptly decided to travel to Rome to appeal against the bishop but before doing so he offered to accept the mediation of Crolly and Denvir. He even wrote to O'Connell, who in turn, also sought Denvir's intervention.[99] Blake did not back down and Keenan went to Rome, where the congregation of Propaganda succeeded in persuading him to sign a deed of submission to the bishop. Furthermore, he apologized for the opposition that had been raised against the administrator, whom the bishop had appointed to replace him, and pledged full obedience to the decision of the Holy See on the issue in dispute. The suspension was then lifted and he returned to Annaghlone.[100] Blake, however, was dissatisfied with his pastoral work. He was particularly displeased by the pastor's refusal to celebrate two Masses on Sunday, by his publicly claiming that he had been robbed of £200 as a consequence of being suspended, and by his maltreatment of his curates. And he put his complaints to Keenan about these and other matters in writing.[101]

Then in the summer of 1844 Keenan was reported to the bishop for neglect of duty. He was accused both of refusing to administer the last rites to a woman who was dying, and of not leaving his house to attend a dying man. In defence Keenan argued that the woman was living in an adulterous union, which she would not promise to break, and that the sons of the dead man subsequently retracted the claim they had made about his unnecessary delay in visiting their father. The bishop later claimed that he had verified the truth of the allegations and commissioned his vicar-general to obtain an explanation and apology from Keenan before suspending him. When news of this development broke, many parishioners took their pastor's side against the bishop. Keenan immediately attempted to drag Crolly into the dispute by going to Drogheda to seek his help. The archbishop in turn visited the bishop of Dromore to hear his side of the story. A public meeting was held in the grounds of Annaghlone church to consider addressing the pope about the deplorable condition of the parish, deprived as it was of its pastor, and to discuss 'the best means of putting down the notorious and infamous SPY SYSTEM, countenanced and practised in this diocese'.[102]

At this meeting, Keenan gave an account of the various visits made to Crolly on his behalf. After the initial visit to Drogheda, a small deputation accompanied him to meet the archbishop at Armagh and begged Crolly to

---

[99] Keenan to Blake, 3 July 1839 and Denvir to Blake, 13 Aug. 1839, DrDA.
[100] The modern spelling is Annaclone. The full name of the parish was Annaghlone and Drumballyroney.
[101] Blake to Cullen, 3 Nov. 1843, AICR.   [102] B.N.L., 6 Aug. 1844.

visit Annaghlone and pass judgement on the censure which the bishop had pronounced. The primate discussed the case for four or five hours and then invited Keenan to sign an apology for omitting to attend the dying man and explain that he had no responsibility for closing the doors of the churches against the priest sent to replace him. Though he was reluctant to sign any such document, his friends agreed that he should do so and they returned to the archbishop with their account of the dispute. But since their version of events ended with a demand that Blake should make instant reparation to Keenan, Crolly stated that he would not be the medium of making an attack on the bishop of Dromore. Nothing daunted by this failure, a deputation representing 2,300 supporters of Keenan's waited on Crolly to solicit him to visit Annaghlone but, according to Keenan, not only was this request rejected but they were told 'that they knew too much of the canon law'. A further deputation went to the archbishop on 26 July to beg him to come to the parish and rectify the disorders prevailing there. Crolly did not accede to their request but, according to Keenan, who was not present, he exonerated him from all blame. The vicar-general of the diocese of Dromore, however, tried to mediate by persuading Keenan to submit to his bishop but Keenan resolutely refused to do so, insisting that the bishop had violated the canons of the church by inflicting a punishment without observing the full and proper procedures in such a case. John Constantine Magennis, who throughout the controversy acted as the chief spokesman for the Keenan camp, in his first letter to the press declared that he 'was sensibly struck with the contrast between the mild, persuasive, peace-making and fatherly conduct of that illustrious individual [Crolly], and the abrupt, testy, ungracious and overbearing manner' which characterized Blake's conduct.[103] The Protestant press quickly found juicy copy in the confrontation and exploited the dispute to publicize the obscurantism and injustice of Catholic prelates.

A new twist to the affair occurred on 25 August when John Macken, the administrator of Banbridge and neighbouring areas, who had been appointed to take charge of Annaghlone, arrived to celebrate Mass at Magheral, one of the parish churches. Keenan met him and informed him that he would be allowed to celebrate only as his nominee; Macken insisted that he would do so only on the bishop's authority, and on being refused permission to do so on those terms, drove off, but later did officiate at Annaghlone. He also publicized the bishop's pastoral instruc-

<hr>

[103] Ibid., 8, 20 Aug. 1844.

tion which stigmatized Keenan for his uncanonical behaviour. After Mass a meeting of parishioners was held and a decision was taken to send two laymen to Rome to report to the pope on the condition of the parish, and a further resolution was passed that the Catholics of Annaghlone would not rest content until they had obtained redress for the wrongs perpetrated against themselves and their pastor.[104]

On the following Sunday Macken came to celebrate Mass in Magheral, found a hostile crowd awaiting him, and was told by Keenan that Mass could not be canonically offered up 'owing to the obstinacy of the bishop in opposing the injunction' of the primate.[105]

Without specifying what the primate's injunction was, Keenan interpreted it as favourable to himself, relying exclusively on Blake's words at the conference of clergy that sooner than comply with the injunction of his metropolitan he would enter a convent. It seems unlikely that Crolly would at that stage of the quarrel have decided in favour of either party; it is more likely that he suggested some kind of examination of the issues involved or mediation between the disputants. Keenan then went on to suggest that the issue should be decided by the bishops of Raphoe, Down and Connor and Ardagh, if he were permitted to give evidence to them, or that the primate and bishops of the province should be invited to adjudicate the case in Annaghlone church, with three priests acting as advocates for both parties.[106]

Keenan's supporters not only forced the bishop's appointee to celebrate Mass in the open air by keeping the churches closed but kept up a bitter war of words with the bishop at public meetings. Not only did they attack his pastorals but in mid-September they claimed that he was guilty of disobedience to his metropolitan, for they knew 'on unquestionable authority that Dr Crolly enjoined the restoration of Dr Keenan to all his rights and privileges as pastor of Annaghlone and Drumballyroney without either apology, explanation or expression of regret, as no blame could be imputed to him'. The source of this information was prudently omitted and, since Keenan had himself confessed that Crolly had already called on him to offer some kind of explanation to his bishop, this statement reeks more of the advocate than of the judge. But when they went on to charge Blake with 'contumacy and rebellion to his lawful superior, Doctor Crolly', they were moving into a minefield of ecclesiastical law which even experienced canonists would have hesitated to enter because of the conflicting views on the application of metropolitan

<hr>

[104] Ibid., 30 Aug. 1844.　　[105] Ibid., 6 Sept. 1844.　　[106] Ibid., 13 Sept. 1844.

jurisdiction in such cases.[107] Three priest supporters of Keenan's and thirteen lay people claimed in a public letter that the primate had told them that Keenan had 'neglected nothing that the best priest in Ireland might not have omitted, under similar circumstances, without any charge of culpability'.[108]

Meanwhile, the bishop's supporters did not stand idly by. On 22 October six priests, one of whom was John Macken, the administrator of Annaghlone, went to Armagh to present Blake's side of the case and were received 'with that kindness and urbanity for which his Grace is so proverbial'. Their purpose was to rebut the argument that the priests of Dromore and people of Annaghlone would solemnly testify that Keenan had been most attentive to his duties. They maintained that Keenan's bearing towards his bishop was always of 'a contumacious and disrespectful character', and that the bishop's sentence was valid, since all that was required for validity was that the sentence be not inflicted without a cause and that it be notified in writing to the accused. A clerical member of the deputation drew Crolly's attention to the statutes of the diocese which entailed suspension for a priest who negligently failed to administer the sacraments to the dying. He went on to assert that the documents later signed by the dead man's sons, that the pastor had not been given timely notice to attend their father, was itself a condemnation of his neglect, since timely notice could never be guaranteed for sick calls. Three laymen who accompanied the clerical deputation to Armagh testified that the archbishop said that he had always regarded Keenan's suspension as valid, but that he could have freed him from it, had there been an expression of sorrow for neglecting to attend the dying man and a candid denial of all responsibility for the closure of the church doors against the administrator. The primate, furthermore, denied that he had ever decided in favour of the parish priest of Annaghlone, and expressed the view that the only tribunal competent to exercise jurisdiction on the matter was the Holy See.[109]

Keenan's allies were not intimidated by this revelation of the primate's views. On the contrary their leading spokesman, John Constantine Magennis, accused Crolly at a public meeting of having abdicated his responsibility, thereby forcing them to trouble the pope with their appeal. The primate had full power to settle the affair but he refused to act juridically. Analysing further the archbishop's inaction, Magennis recalled the catechism definition of being an accessory to sin by silence or by

---

[107] Ibid., 17 Sept. 1844.   [108] N.Ex. 23 Nov. 1844.   [109] Ibid., 4 Dec. 1844.

defence of the ill-done, and he invited the primate to examine his conscience to see whether or not he had been accessory to Blake's sin. In his address Keenan read out the 'explanation' he had already given Crolly on 22 July in which he regretted the death of his parishioners without the sacraments but in which he demanded that full reparation should be made to him by the bishop without delay. Crolly had rejected that proposal. The meeting, however, called on the primate to remove the priest whom Blake had sent to take charge of Annaghlone.[110]

Despite this admission that the archbishop had demanded a generous apology, Keenan addressed a lengthy public letter to him, when he saw how ineffective the public support of his parishioners and their Protestant friends was proving to be. Reminding Crolly that among the most exalted of his prerogatives was that of shielding the oppressed and rescuing them from the hand of the powerful, he went on to lecture him on the praiseworthy manner in which two of his predecessors had exercized their rights in the very difficult circumstances of the seventeenth and eighteenth centuries. Unlike Blake, he had always upheld the primate's right to hold a court of appeal in Dromore or to summon witnesses to a court in Armagh. And he warned the archbishop that, if he did not act, he would unthinkingly inflict a deadly injury upon the undoubted rights of his see.[111]

Crolly was doubtless less than grateful to Keenan for digging up material about his predecessors' exercise of their primatial rights. Not being of a litigious nature and unwilling to become embroiled in unpleasant quarrels for the sake of abstract rights, he could well have done without the history lessons which Keenan was determined to inflict on him. And despite his wish to steer clear of the troublesome business, he was being inexorably dragged further into it.

Eight months later, obtaining no redress from his attempts at involving the primate in his case, Keenan formally appealed to Rome. Among his arguments in defence of his conduct he repeated a statement which had been made by his advocates but which he had significantly not made in his open letter to the primate, namely, that Crolly had told his clerical friends that Blake had erred in the case of the adulteress and that any priest or prelate could allow a person to die without the reception of the last rites.[112]

The response of the congregation of Propaganda was to order Crolly to carry out an inquiry into the dispute and report back to Rome. The

[110] Ibid., 8 Jan. 1845.   [111] Ibid., 19 Mar. 1845.
[112] Keenan to Propaganda, 5 Nov. 1845, APF, SC (Irlanda), 28, ff 593r-595v.

archbishop chose to fulfil this commission by summoning both parties and witnesses to his church in Armagh to present their cases. It was a decision that drew scorn from those suffragans who were opposed to their archbishop's political views. Bishop Cantwell and Bishop MacNally regarded it as a most unprecedented way of investigating a conflict: they assumed that he should have adopted the procedure common in ecclesiastical courts of examining witnesses under oath in strict secrecy.[113] Blake was less than pleased with the means chosen by the archbishop to carry out his orders. To a request for his preference about a time and place for an inquiry, he replied tartly that he thought Crolly should have been able to formulate an answer based on what he had already heard, read, seen and known of Keenan's conduct since his suspension. He refused to suggest a time or venue, contenting himself with a prayerful wish that the Holy Spirit would guide the primate and a pledge of readiness to resign his office, if his manner of administering his duties was not what it should have been.[114]

The hearing opened in the church at Armagh on 30 December 1845. Crolly explained at the beginning that he would examine the witnesses individually in the vestry of the church. The press was allowed in, and Keenan attended to listen to all the evidence given. The bishop of Dromore refused to attend as he objected to the procedure adopted, and though not officially represented, two of the priests who had publicly defended his actions spoke in his defence. Crolly, who was later joined by Bishop Denvir of Down and Connor, sought to establish the roots of the disagreements between Blake and Keenan. The details of the grounds on which the suspension was imposed were rehearsed at length, and Crolly tried to discover if Keenan bore any responsibility for the closure of the church doors.

During the inquiry on the second day, the sons of the dead man, whom Keenan was accused of not attending until it was too late, gave evidence; they made it clear that, though summoned twice on the evening before the death, he refused to go and when he did go on the following morning their father had already died. It also emerged that fisticuffs which had taken place in Annaghlone when Keenan's opponents tried to open the churches had not stopped at the boundaries of the parish; a witness against Keenan ran into the church in Armagh complaining that he had

[113] Cantwell to Cullen, 31 Jan. 1846 and MacNally to Cullen, 26 Feb. 1846, AICR. MacNally asked indignantly: 'will it [Crolly's investigation] open their eyes to the consequences of exercising their authority through such a medium?' Cullen had already expressed his astonishment to Blake at the publication of the evidence in a newspaper (Cullen to Blake, 30 Jan. 1846, DrDA).
[114] Blake to Cullen, 15 Feb. 1846, AICR.

been assaulted with stones and mud by a crowd mainly of women and children. The investigation lasted four days, and since Crolly's aim was to get a true picture of all the circumstances surrounding the case, it terminated without any concluding statement from the archbishop.[115]

Three weeks later Crolly sent a long account of his findings to Rome. He summarized the views of priests on both sides about the validity and prudence of the suspension and then gave his own opinion: Keenan, despite a correct lifestyle, had behaved intolerably in the whole affair, especially by absenting himself from Mass and encouraging his followers to do likewise, and by bringing the priest who replaced him and his opponents to the civil courts. He therefore recommended that Keenan should be removed from the parish, which he had disturbed for too long, but given an annual pension from it. He also suggested that Bishop Blake could be admonished by the congregation to desist from rebuking his pastors in front of his people.[116]

Keenan was dissatisfied with the tribunal in Armagh, and complained disingenuously to Rome about the short time given him to prepare for it, his bad health at the time it was held and the impossibility of bringing the necessary witnesses such a long distance.[117] He then travelled to Rome, and submitted his case again at great length. Blake was then called upon to do the same,[118] but he had become so dispirited by the whole affair that he threatened to resign if all his previous statements were not deemed sufficient to vindicate his handling of the dispute.[119]

Eventually, the question was examined at a plenary session of the congregation of Propaganda on 12 July 1847. Crolly's recommendation was accepted, but the congregation also insisted that the suspension should be removed. Keenan was then to resign and receive a pension.[120] Blake was prepared to accept the first two conditions but balked at the third. He insisted that the parish would be both unable and unwilling to carry out such an order. Nevertheless, he was prepared, if Keenan evinced a proper spirit and prevailed upon his friends to open the church at Annaghlone, to try to raise an annual subscription, until the ex-pastor could support himself.[121] But Propaganda replied that a refusal to pay him a pension would be too severe and asked that an equitable arrangement should be made based on the revenues which he had formerly enjoyed.[122]

---

[115] N.T., 6, 8, 10 Jan. 1846.
[116] Crolly to Propaganda, 22 Jan. 1846, APF, *Acta*, 210, ff 438r-439v.
[117] Keenan to Propaganda, 6 Feb. 1846, APF, SC (Irlanda), 28, ff 657r-658r.
[118] Propaganda to Blake, 27 Feb. 1847, *Lett.*, 335, ff 215v-216r.
[119] Blake to Cullen (copy), 15 Mar. 1847, DrDA.   [120] APF, *Acta*, 210, f 435r.
[121] Blake to Kirby, 10 Sept. 1847, AICR.   [122] Propaganda to Blake, APF, *Lett.*, 336, ff 1216v-1217r.

However, Keenan unwittingly provided a solution to the problem. He died on 15 November 1847. His supporters kept the church doors at Annaghlone closed during the remainder of the year, whether in tribute to their fallen hero or not, but they succumbed to the demands of the other parishioners in 1848 and surrendered.

This prolonged and unsavoury struggle pained and embarrassed many Catholics both in Dromore and in neighbouring dioceses. The participation of Protestants, both lay and clerical, their financial contributions to Keenan's campaign and the extensive and hostile coverage given to the bishop in Protestant-owned newspapers greatly distressed the bishops of the northern province. The archbishop of Armagh was caught in a very difficult situation for canon law left room for argument about the rights and duties of a metropolitan in such circumstances. The decision of Rome, which confirmed his recommendation, was the best attempt to settle the invidious feud but whether it would have worked will never be known.

Of the three cases of turbulent clergy—Mulholland, Lyons and Keenan—with which Crolly as archbishop had to deal, Lyons' was the most rebarbative. Mulholland probably suffered from mental illness and Keenan's struggle derived mainly from self-righteous stubbornness, but neither of them remotely resembled Lyons in terms of blackguardly self-indulgence. No accusations of personal misbehaviour were made against Keenan, and though Mulholland was charged with greed, Lyons far surpassed him in that respect, and his extortionate demands on his parishioners and tenants can only be described as cruel and shameless. When the charges of simony, neglect of duty, litigiousness and personal immorality are added, the dean of Killala emerges as a most unpriestly man, the investigation of whose behaviour must have been a repellent experience.

7

POLITICAL PROBLEMS, 1835–49

When Crolly became archbishop of Armagh the Lichfield House compact between O'Connell and the Whigs had been in place for a couple of months. Though this arrangement with Lord Melbourne's government only obliged it to apply a share of the tithes to non-religious purposes, there was also an understanding that it would tackle the issues of parliamentary and municipal reform, and that political and legal appointments would be made on a more equitable basis. Both Whigs and Catholics were highly gratified with the choice of Lord Mulgrave as Lord Lieutenant and Thomas Drummond as under-secretary. Gradually more Catholics were admitted to magistracies and to positions of responsibility in the police—situations that had hitherto been a Tory-Orange preserve.

Crolly was highly pleased with the prospects of political reform and civil justice which this arrangement boded. He was tireless in advocating good community relations between Protestant and Catholic but he always insisted that the only firm foundation on which such relations could be built was demonstrable fairness by the government and its agencies in filling positions of public trust and responsibility. Mulgrave had not been long in office when he decided to travel throughout Ireland to acquaint himself at first hand with the country. Crolly went to meet him during his visit to Belfast and escorted him through the Donegall Street national school on the first stage of his tour. An address was then read on behalf of the bishop and clergy of Down and Connor, which expressed gratitude to the sovereign for his solicitude for the amelioration of their 'long misgoverned country' as indicated by the choice of a viceroy distinguished by his philanthropic and 'uniform practical advocacy of the great principle of civil and religious liberty'. Remarking that they had faithfully laboured under previous administrations to promote peace and charity, they looked forward to continuing that work under a government which, in accord-ance with the principles of national justice, had 'repudiated the malignant policy of governing Ireland by fomenting the divisions of the past'. Crolly, who was a guest at the receptions given to Mulgrave by the prominent Belfast liberals and later by the subscribers of the Lancasterian school, cordially commended the Lord Lieutenant for taking the pains to learn about the local circumstances of the community before taking decisions about them.[1]

A week later Mulgrave was hosted in Armagh by Archbishop Beresford. On that occasion Crolly and his clergy presented a formal address of welcome. They praised the national system of education and anticipated the extinction of party spirit through the impartial administration of even-handed justice and the execution by the legislature of wise and important measures.[2]

When, in the following year, the House of Lords rejected a bill to reform municipal corporations, O'Connell decided to apply pressure to his parliamentary partners by creating the General Association of Ireland, a mass movement on the lines of the Catholic Association, which promised to support the government and help maintain public order. He also included a satisfactory adjustment of tithes as part of his policy, but was careful to keep this measure within the realm of practical politics by not calling for total abolition. Crolly promptly joined the Association and forwarding £5 as his subscription to the rent expressed the hope in his letter that Mulgrave's equitable distribution of justice to Irishmen of all denominations, the admonitions of the Catholic pastors and the Christian patience of the people, would lead to an extinction of party spirit. Being free of the exigencies of realpolitik he could and did call for the total abolition of tithes and a thorough reform of the abuses of corporations, both of which evils he maintained had broken the peace and limited the prosperity of the country.[3] The demands of the Catholics, as he told a celebration in honour of Sharman Crawford, the Protestant liberal who was MP for Dundalk, amounted only to a claim for common justice. He foresaw that claim being realized through the work of such men as Crawford by which 'all difference of opinion between Protestant and Catholic may be abolished, and a trace of it not left to disgrace the country'.[4]

Two months later O'Connell was entertained to a public dinner in Drogheda. In reply to his toast he spoke of his five year experiment to obtain justice from England. If that goal were not achieved at the end of

---

[1] N.Ex., 28 Oct, 31 Oct. 1835.   [2] N.W., 2 Nov. 1835.   [3] N.Ex., 15 Oct. 1836.
[4] Ibid., 1 Oct. 1836.

the period, they would have to take it for themselves. Crolly, who attended, was introduced by the chairman as the friend of civil and religious liberty. And in his speech he identified that liberty as the 'equitable foundation of every institute in religion and politics', declared it to be the entitlement of every loyal and obedient citizen and regretted its sad decline in Belfast:

Liberty, civil and religious, is the birthright of all bearing the image of the Creator, as well the black as the white, and no man should assume the right of the Deity to force the opinions of his fellow-man . . . There was a period when Belfast stood pre-eminent as the friend of liberty; but that spirit is now nearly extinct—a dark cloud has passed over its horizon, and obscured the beauty in which it shone. But let this be a lesson to you, and as you rise in wealth and commerce, raise the flag of civil and religious liberty; and that you may bless and prosper under it will be the foremost wish of my heart.[5]

At a similar function in Dundalk in January 1837 honouring Patrick and R.M. Bellew, MPs for Co. Louth, Crolly developed his argument in the context of priestly duty. He used the opportunity to justify the political role played by the Catholic clergy in Ireland in advancing the temporal welfare of their people. Contending that the priest's first obligation was to explain to his people their relationship with their creator but insisting that a determination to obtain equal rights and privileges with other fellow subjects was also an indispensable duty, he went on to defend the clergy from the charge of disturbing the peace and tranquillity of society. On the contrary, he questioned whether the priests 'would deserve the name of human beings, if they stood back while it was in their power to release one single man from bondage, or to break the fetters of oppression'. They were obliged when they saw 'a man labouring to stand in the attitude of a freeman' to exert all their strength to guide him forward and help him achieve his goal 'by the light of education, honour, virtue and religion', and they had carried out their obligations faithfully. They had unceasingly inculcated the first and purest principle of religion—goodwill amongst all men of every creed and colour—and they had subdued the spirit of bigotry and intolerance. Yet it was when attempting to bind all men in the bonds of love that they had been 'blamed for taking a part with their flocks, to elevate them to that station in the land which common justice to all men declares they should occupy'. He then proceeded to paint an idealized picture of the harmony existing in that part of Ireland—an industrious and virtuous peasantry and a middle class

---

[5] Ibid., 24 Dec. 1836.

loved by the poor, with both respecting and admiring those of superior rank for the care and attention they bestowed on the humble. Had this been a general statement it would have indicated the highest of Tory sentiments, but the archbishop probably had in mind only the estates of the Bellews, and other liberal landlords. He concluded with a vigorous rejection of suggestions that had been recently mooted for state payment of the Catholic clergy.[6]

Whatever about class harmony in Co. Louth, South Armagh presented a very different picture. Agrarian outrages and homicides were sufficiently numerous to prompt demands for the introduction of coercion in the district. The parish priest of Lower Creggan, Michael Caraher, organized a meeting of local residents in Cullyhanna on 2 April 1838, which was attended by some 3,000 people of all denominations as well as by clergy of the established and Presbyterian churches. Though Caraher made a spirited defence of the general, peaceful conduct obtaining in the parish, he did admit that crimes had occurred on its borders, and others admitted that lives had been taken and homes attacked at night. Crolly attended at great personal inconvenience—he was suffering from a severe cold—but he felt obliged to make his contribution to the elimination of outrages and the promotion of good will. It was he who proposed the first and most significant resolution, that a committee of clergy and laity of different denominations be elected to prevent the recurrence of outrages and that three respectable householders in every townland be appointed to assist the committee in its work. He also paid a generous tribute to the viceroy and looked forward to a proper and permanent provision being made for the industry and comfort of the queen's loyal subjects during her forthcoming visit to Ireland.[7]

The viceroy's good reputation among non-Tories survived, even though the government did not succeed in introducing much beneficial legislation apart from giving legal and police appointments to Catholics. The tithe act was a disappointment. Consequently, O'Connell grew less sanguine about the Whigs' intentions and their ability to carry out their promises. It was with a view to stimulating them to serious action that he founded the Precursor Society in August 1838. Still holding in abeyance the threat of launching a nationwide campaign for Repeal, he served notice on the government that it would have to bring about serious reforms—the abolition of tithes and the introduction of the same system of municipal and parliamentary representation as obtained in Britain—

[6] D.A., 21 Jan. 1837.   [7] N.Ex., 7 Apr. 1838.

before the end of 1839 or he would resurrect his call for Repeal. Strangely enough his closest episcopal collaborator, MacHale, was unimpressed and showed little interest:[8] presumably he found it not full-blooded enough for his liking. Crolly, on the other hand, regarded the aims of the society as eminently worthy and deserving of support. In November a meeting was held in Drogheda (by then all reference to Repeal had been removed from the programme of the society) to discuss the establishment of a branch in the town. The leading Liberals and Catholics attended, voted unanimously in favour, and Crolly announced that he 'concurred most cordially with the objects' intended by O'Connell. Sir William Somerville, the Liberal M.P. for Drogheda, pointed out at the first meeting that both Repealers and non-Repealers could join, as one of the resolutions passed when the society was set up declared that members were not pledged to advocate Repeal.[9]

The archbishop was happy to see O'Connell chip away at the carapace of ascendancy privilege. And at the banquet given in his honour in Drogheda two months later he laid great emphasis on justice as the goal of the Precursors. Claiming that all the bishops of Ireland felt that the time had come when every man, whether wearing a clerical collar or not, 'should stand forward to demand long-retarded justice' he predicted that agitation would not cease until this goal had been achieved, and all Irishmen stood on a platform of equality. Then would Ireland be united, prosperous and happy. Voicing the hope that everyone who wanted to see that condition achieved would join O'Connell and that the Liberator would not go 'beyond the bounds of justice', Crolly declared: 'I freely recognize him as our great leader, and am ready and determined to follow him to that boundary.'[10]

Both O'Connell and Crolly were present when Thomas Redington, the Liberal M.P. for Dundalk was hosted in that town a few days later. Commending Redington for his dedicated service to the constituency and Co. Louth for eschewing sectarian influences in choosing M.P.s of distinction and ability (three of whom were Catholic and three Protestant), he added his best wishes that the movement for reform would not terminate until they had 'a pure and free representation'. Referring to parts of the north that had clung with attachment to the cause of freedom, he remarked that if O'Connell only knew the difficulties presented by the increasing persecutions of landlords and 'the machinations of great and powerful inducements', he would be astonished to find so many bright

---

[8] MacDonagh, *The Emancipist*, 176-7.   [9] D.A., 10 Nov. 1838.   [10] N.Ex., 30 Jan. 1839.

spots there. If the representation of all parts of Ireland were as honourable as theirs, the country would enjoy peace and the clergy would retire from public activities and confine themselves to the discharge of their spiritual duties. But until justice was done on the scale demanded by their wrongs, they would rally around him 'who first broke a link in our chain and . . add power and muscle to his arm, to dash from our hands the galling remnant of our fetters'.[11]

The sentiments expressed by Crolly and O'Connell were constitutionally impeccable. There was no whiff of disloyalty or sedition about them, and Crolly's tributes to the queen were at times almost lyrical. MacHale, too, who had much less confidence in the good intentions of the government, was restrained and circumspect. But his criticisms and those of other clergy, however mild, were too extreme for some of the vigilant upholders of law and order. Reports reached Rome of clergy preaching on political topics. At least one anonymous complaint (and there may well have been others) was forwarded to Rome about functions attended by MacHale and his suffragan, Browne of Galway, at which improper sentiments were allegedly aired. An extract from the *Freeman's Journal* of 9 February reporting a speech by MacHale in which he demanded the abolition of the tithe system, attacked the poor law and characterized freedom of the press as a blessing was enclosed with this charge. The writer also referred to a previous occasion when MacHale was present and Browne saluted 'the people, the true source of legitimate power'. The toast was described as revolutionary and contrary to the teaching of Pope Gregory XVI.[12]

Gregory, a stout supporter of the alliance of throne and altar, regarded such democratic declarations as the harbinger of revolutionary upheavals which would destroy both throne and altar. As used, however, in clerical circles in Ireland this salute to the source of power carried no such nuance: it was a declaration of the right of a ·Catholic people to full equality with their Protestant brothers throughout the United Kingdom.[13] However, the authorities at Rome would not have accepted the Irish application of this political affirmation and would have understood it in the sense implied by the writer as revolutionary and tending to the overthrow of legitimate governments.

---

[11] Ibid., 2 Feb. 1839.

[12] APF, SC (Irlanda) 27, f 14r-27r. A later reference to Lord Clifford, (ff 76r-80r) and an example of his handwriting suggest that he may have delated MacHale. He was a supporter of O'Finan and was strongly opposed to MacHale in the dispute about Killala.

[13] Michael Kieran, parish priest of Collon, replying in Crolly's presence to a toast to the people for whose good all governments were instituted, remarked that some claimed that the power of kings and queens derived from God and others claimed that it derived from the people, though all agreed 'it existed but for the welfare of the people'. (N.Ex., 30 Jan. 1839.)

Anyhow, Cardinal Fransoni and the congregation of Propaganda were sufficiently perturbed by these reports to decide that an appropriate admonition should be sent to the Irish church. Accordingly, Fransoni wrote to Crolly. The letter began by referring to repeated reports that MacHale and another bishop had presided at public banquets and had not hestiated to make imprudent speeches on political affairs which had disturbed and aroused their people excessively and led them away from the mildness of the gospel. Though the cardinal was persuaded that such charges were perhaps exaggerated, he felt, nonetheless, obliged to inquire whether they were true or not so that

you might suggest more prudent counsels to the archbishop and bishops, endeavour to bring the others to act in a different manner, in particular, by getting them to withdraw from political issues and controversies. It must always be remembered (and this the Supreme Pontiff especially desires) that the ministers of Christ should not forget that they have not been sent to become involved in worldly affairs or to pursue party political matters but between the vestibule and the altar to weep for the many misfortunes that afflict the church and by their prayers and acts of penance to implore the help of the Lord.

Fransoni, whose concept of the mission of the church was obviously very limited, concluded by asserting that the ball was now in Crolly's court and asking for a reply as soon as possible.[14]

This was a most troublesome and invidious request. A commission to rebuke MacHale, as Propaganda was to discover to its cost, was about as burdensome and futile a task as Rome could issue. And it could scarcely have come at a worse time. Crolly and he were at daggers drawn over the national schools and both parties to that dispute had just submitted their cases to Rome. It would have been very difficult for him to deal with one of his own suffragans about a controverted problem bordering on religious obligation and social justice, but when another archbishop was involved the task was much harder. Moreover, Crolly had committed himself and indeed the bishops and clergy of Ireland to the advocacy of social justice, and even if he had seen the incriminatory letter addressed to Fransoni, he would have found nothing to condemn in the charges brought against MacHale and Browne, in fact nothing that he himself would not have defended. To answer vague and general strictures, when the evidence on which they were based was not produced, was virtually impossible in any but the most amorphous way.

---

[14] Propaganda to Crolly, 12 Mar. 1839, APF, *Lett.*, 321, ff 220r-221r.

MacHale himself had received a warning from Rome before Crolly was entrusted with the task of correcting him. In reply to his letter invoking the pope's judgement on the national system of education, Propaganda counselled him to avoid political controversies and not to speak at any meetings or assemblies in such a way as to indicate that he was partial to political controversies. Bishops, he was reminded, should so act as to bear witness to their indifference to party political zeal.[15]

MacHale replied at length. Reminding the cardinal of the damaging rumours passed on to Rome at the time of his translation to Tuam—rumours then found to be baseless—he expressed his confidence that a similar fate lay in store for the charges recently made against him. He pointed out that he never took part in political gatherings where strife occurred and explained that the toasts to the people as the source of political power and to civil and religious liberty bore none of the pejorative associations which formerly attached to them in France. And since the civil laws in Ireland were established to foster the Protestant religion and repress the Catholic, those laws took on a religious dimension. He then gave examples: the viceroy had rebuked both Catholic and Protestant landlords for not treating as transgressors two priests who had recited the prayers for a deceased Catholic man outside the gates of a cemetery, as the law forbade Catholic clergy to enter the ancient cemeteries to officiate at funerals. Those who wished to petition the government to remove such restrictions on religious freedom were regarded by some people as being involved in politics. The other example referred to the legitimate resistance of the Catholics of Achill and their clergy to despicable means of proselytism, and to the subsequent refusal by the secular authorities to do anything about the complaints of the clergy. That case illustrated how difficult was the position of Catholic priests who were labelled as disturbers of the public peace unless they abandoned their flocks to ravenous wolves. This was an able and impressive reply and MacHale must have made the cardinal aware of some of the complexity involved in political issues in Ireland and of how the defence of basic Catholic rights could be described as an unjustified incursion into political affairs.[16]

Crolly delayed his answer for a further month and then responded much more briefly than MacHale. He had written to MacHale to obtain evidence to disprove the charges and had learned that the archbishop had himself replied fully to them. It only remained for him to say that MacHale and all

[15] Propaganda to MacHale, 26 Feb. 1839, Ibid., ff 155v-156r.
[16] MacHale to Propaganda, 25 Mar. 1839, APF, Acta, 202, ff 256r-257v.

the other prelates had always been completely loyal to the state. The bishops, he explained, were occasionally invited to meetings and dinners and were compelled to take the first place at them by their hosts; but, far from inciting their people they restrained them and directed them to claim their rights legitimately by petitioning the British parliament. Then using language harsher than was his custom, he remarked that Fransoni, if he knew the condition of Catholics in Ireland, would understand that there was in that country an intolerant, powerful and dangerous Protestant faction, which had opposed Catholic Emancipation and which wanted to put back the penal laws that had been abolished. Opposed to that faction (he obviously had the Orangemen and arch-Tories in mind) were not only the Catholics but also those liberal Protestants who wanted to concede equal rights and privileges to all subjects of the British empire, whether in Ireland or in the colonies. Their beloved queen and her viceroy had tried to establish an administration that would not discriminate between Protestant and Catholic. In consequence that evil faction had assailed the illustrious viceroy and striven with might to change the government. That intolerant body could not be withstood save by a union of the Catholic clergy and people in defence of the faith and of the peace of the state. In those politico-religious disputes, if the pastors were to abandon their flocks, the liberal Protestants would do likewise and the abandoned Catholics would be desperately oppressed by their enemies. Crolly concluded by informing the cardinal that all the bishops of his province with whom he had spoken about the subject had promised immediately to follow the pope's advice. In June he expected to meet the three archbishops and the bishops who were trustees of Maynooth and he did not doubt their readiness to cooperate on such an important issue. But the greatest prudence was necessary lest they offended their faithful people by unexpectedly cutting themselves off from them.[17]

Though couched in less combative terms, Crolly's response was essentially the same as MacHale's: the struggle for equality demanded that the bishops and clergy give a lead to their people in asserting their just claims. A refusal to do so would result in the perpetuation of injustice. The clergy were obliged by their religious obligations to encourage and participate in peaceful political activity while their people suffered from discrimination.

Fransoni's letters were probably irritants to both Crolly and MacHale. But their very general nature and absence of specific detail meant that they did not cramp the style of the bishops and priests who supported the

[17] Crolly to Propaganda, 27 Apr. 1839, Ibid., ff 255r-256r.

aims of the Precursor Society. The letter to the primate did not become public, as it would have done, had it been the result of sustained lobbying in Rome. Consequently, it caused much less embarrassment than later admonitions of a similar kind. Almost certainly it had little or no impact on most of the bishops and particularly on Crolly's two outspoken suffragans, Higgins of Ardagh and Cantwell of Meath.

If Fransoni's letter was posted within a few days of the date it bore, it should have arrived about the end of March. If so, it certainly did not deter Crolly from attending a reception for O'Connell and repeating his views on clerical participation in political issues. Significantly, the celebration was held in Newry, and therefore the archbishop of Armagh was under no obligation to attend. His presence signified his commitment to O'Connell's campaign for equality of opportunity for all citizens. O'Connell declared in his speech, that much as he desired to see a parliament in Dublin, he would not seek Repeal, if justice were done by the government. Crolly, rejecting the argument that the clergy should not meddle in politics, wondered how the moral order of society was to be maintained 'but by our associating ourselves together for the support of the principles of moral justice'. He praised O'Connell's contribution to the achievement of justice in Ireland, and commented optimistically on the diminution of party prejudcies, the increasing freedom to worship God according to the dictates of conscience alone and the peaceful development of the country. The bishops of Dromore, and Down and Connor representing the Catholics of Co. Down also spoke.[18] The presence of all three prelates certainly proved that they did not consider themselves bound by the terms of the Roman letter to abstain from advocating social justice for their people. They clearly did not believe their support for O'Connell's programme of reforms fell within the limits of the 'worldly affairs and pursuits of political matters' which Fransoni had marked off as forbidden territory for clerics.

Towards the end of 1839 Crolly joined seven other bishops from Munster and Leinster for the blessing and opening of the Dominican Church in Cork at which he delivered the special sermon. O'Connell, who had recently replaced his Precursor Society with a Reform Registry Society, designed to attract Whigs and Liberals, was chairman at the celebrations afterwards and proposed the toast to the episcopal guests. Crolly noting in reply that they could never separate their desire to promote the temporal happiness and prosperity of their brethren from

[18] N.Ex., 13 Apr. 1839.

their aspiration for their advancement in religion, went on to enthuse about the proofs of the increasing industry and benevolence of the people:

I have seen everywhere, as I passed along, specimens of useful improvement, and everything else that could lead me to indulge still stronger hopes of the approaching prosperity of my native land. This country is now in the enjoyment of many blessings . . . Formerly, the best and brightest feature of the British Constitution, the trial by jury, was brought into contempt, by the want of confidence which the mode of administering that provision of the law inspired, but now we have not only Catholic lawyers but Catholic Judges on the bench, who are working in unison for the reward of every virtue, and the punishment of every vice. . . All the apparatus for the education of the poor is now complete, and fear need no longer be entertained for any attempt to tamper with their religion. These things, gentlemen, are sources of some satisfaction to us; and there is another cause which I hope will be equally well-calculated to diffuse much happiness over the land—I mean the poor law guardians, who are being appointed in every Union in Ireland, and are selected from amongst men of every religious denomination, and amongst them will be found many men of extensive information, who have too much good sense not to keep their religious feelings aloof, or to permit them to disturb the harmony that should exist amongst them, or suffer speculative opinions to interrupt the blessing which should flow from the exertion of Christian charity. We have now bright prospects before us. It is very true we have not yet come to the point of the concession of such a full measure of justice as ought to satisfy any rational mind; but the seeds of justice are planted, the roots are already deep in the land, and we may hope soon to reap a most plenteous harvest in every department.

Having already praised extensively Lords Ebrington and Normanby, the current and previous viceroys, he concluded with a eulogy of O'Connell who established 'a people's liberty on a firm basis without shedding one drop of human blood'.[19]

The praise of past achievements and the optimism about the current state of progress at the celebrations could have been read not only as reflecting Crolly's views but also as an encouragement to O'Connell to persevere in working for reforms by constitutional means. Ironically, O'Connell was just then drawing opposite conclusions about the successes obtained during his years of collaborating with the Whigs: he had come to believe that little or nothing had been achieved, that his restraint and cooperation had not been rewarded and that the time had come to reactivate the campaign for Repeal. And it was on this issue that he and Crolly were destined to part company. By another curious coincidence the *Northern Whig*, which favoured reform but resolutely opposed Repeal, found in Crolly's speech in Cork evidence of the futility and uselessness of campaigning for a domestic parliament. It was frequently to challenge the

[19] N.Ex., 26 Oct. 1839.

wisdom of Catholics introducing a divisive policy when, according to their primate, Ireland was enjoying an ever-burgeoning measure of prosperity.[20]

II

Protestant liberals, like their Catholic counterparts, were shaken by Stanley's Registration of Voters Bill in March 1840. By calling for the annual registration of electors and the withdrawal of certificates from those who did not comply with this regulation, the bill threatened to disfranchise more Catholics than Protestants, because they were less well organized and less prepared to take the trouble to ensure that their names appeared annually on the electoral rolls. Reformers of all shades of opinion denounced these proposals. Among those in Ulster who put their names to a petition for the withdrawal of the bill were Bishop Denvir of Down and Connor and Bishop Blake of Dromore. Prominent Protestant and Catholic Liberals organized a great protest in Belfast on 30 April. Crolly signed the requisition for the meeting but was unable to attend; his brother had died and he had already arranged to attend a conference of clergy in Armagh on that day.[21] He also signed the declaration headed by the leading Irish Whigs, the duke of Leinster and Lord Charlemont, denouncing the imposition on the country of any administration which would attempt to exclude any class from political power because of its religion or prevent Catholics from obtaining their full and fair share of the honours and emoluments of the state.[22] And at a function in honour of Colonel Rawdon, the Whig MP for Armagh, he declared that he would be ashamed of his religion if he did not use his influence 'to put down all differences originating in a dissimilarity of creed, and to promote a fraternity of affection among Christians of every persuasion'. Singling out national education and the poor laws as hopeful examples of the government's concern for the country, he placed his faith in the goodwill of the Irish Whigs:

Let us follow those men whose birth, education and patriotic feeling, fit them to be our leaders; and acting under their guidance, we may hope to see the day when civil and religious liberty shall be established, not only over Ireland but over the entire habitable globe.[23]

The contretemps over Stanley's Bill further shook O'Connell's faith in the Whig alliance. He sought MacHale's views on the prudence of

---

[20] N.W., 15 Sept. 1840.   [21] V., 29 Apr., 2 May 1840.   [22] Ibid., 16 May 1840.
[23] N.W., 13 Oct. 1840.

initiating a campaign for equality of rights for Catholics; in particular he proposed to assail the privileges of the established church and to demand parity between British and Irish parliamentary and municipal reform. MacHale responded positively and accordingly O'Connell founded the National Association for full and prompt justice or Repeal. This was far from being the beginning of a single-minded campaign for Repeal: in fact, he continued to cooperate with the Liberals, and it was not until July that he established the Loyal National Repeal Association and began to devote himself determinedly to the one policy that he believed would rally the Catholic multitudes and, he hoped, Protestants of a liberal bent as well. Public rallies were again organized and a Repeal rent instituted. But by the end of the year little progress had been made and, though Bishops Cantwell and Blake had been admitted as members, O'Connell still maintained his links with the Whigs and was extremely anxious to see them remain in office.[24]

Even before the Repeal agitation started seriously political alignments in Ulster and especially in Belfast took on a more sectarian edge. Ulster Tories campaigned in favour of Stanley's Registration Bill,[25] and Henry Cooke, who was acknowledged as the leading cleric in the movement for pan-Protestant unity and resistance to Catholic advancement, challenged O'Connell to come to the north and promised him a warm reception.

Undoubtedly, fear and dislike of the sectarian passions, which he knew Repeal would arouse, were among the reasons for Crolly's consistent refusal to support the campaign. As it gathered momentum this became increasingly difficult, for pressure was put on him to attend political banquets and rallies. The primate experienced his first embarrassment in October 1840 when O'Connell paid a visit to Drogheda. His entry to the town was hailed as a triumph and 100,000 people were said to have joined the procession with him to the town centre. Amongst the prominent citizens invited to attend the dinner in his honour were Crolly, Blake, Cantwell and Denvir. None did so. But while Blake and Cantwell in their letters of apology expressed their hopes for the success of the movement, Crolly and Denvir did not mention Repeal at all. Crolly explained that he was obliged to attend a conference of clergy in Dunleer and to dine with

---

[24] MacDonagh, *The Emancipist*, 185-91.

[25] An unfortunate example of the religious polemics let loose by this bill was the remark of Robert Stewart of Broughshane that 'if a Roman Catholic committed perjury in aid of the church, it was held to be no perjury; and it was not to be doubted, when a Roman Catholic was driven by the priest to the registry or to the hustings that he would act on the same principle, particularly as he had the priest of the parish to give him absolution, at his elbow'. Daniel Curoe, the parish priest of Randalstown, challenged him to produce the evidence for this claim. (V., 9, 13 May 1840.)

them afterwards, and doubtless this was correct, as the conferences followed a long established sequence of dates but, had he wished, he could probably have shortened the proceedings and reached Drogheda in time.[26] His reluctance to jump on the Repeal bandwagon, however, did not prevent him subscribing to the O'Connell tribute in Drogheda on 8 November. He had no hesitation in contributing generously to the support of O'Connell, the reformer and liberator.[27] But his fears about the reactions of Protestants to the movement must have been greatly strengthened by their response to O'Connell's visit to Belfast in January 1841.

Even some of the veteran Protestant liberals refused to meet the Repeal leader and Cooke, as the champion of Protestantism and the union, declaring that O'Connell was 'a great bad man, engaged in a great bad cause', challenged him to a debate.[28] Cooke, a skilled orator and populist leader, thereby raised the political temperature and, though O'Connell declined his invitation, some rioting broke out and the windows of the bishop's house and of the offices of the *Vindicator*, a Repeal paper, were broken.

Bishop Denvir and Bishop McLaughlin of Derry were present at the banquet held in O'Connell's honour and letters of apology were read from Bishop Blake and Bishop Kernan of Clogher. A few Protestant liberals attended but the vast majority present were Catholics. The visit did nothing for the Repeal cause and only exacerbated sectarian ill-feeling. Protestants of nearly all shades of political opinion had come to regard the union as not-negotiable and some of them believed that their future prosperity depended on it. Repeal seemed fated to separate Ulster people politically along religious lines and indirectly to fuel sectarian rivalries in many parts of the province. The archbishop had already experienced enough strife to convince him of the ease with which it could spread and the poison it would sow.

None of Crolly's suffragans drew similar conclusions from O'Connell's experiences in Belfast: all except James Browne became Repealers. William Higgins of Ardagh in forwarding a cheque from his clergy to T.M. Ray, O'Connell's secretary, expressed his grief at the fatal credulity of some honest Irishmen who still looked to an English parliament for justice, and went on to comment that England, to the amazement of civilized Europe, had been 'too long permitted to exercise under the name of law, a cruel and barbarous sway over this ill-fated country'.[29] Crolly, however, was still prepared to back reformist measures which the Repeal Association might initiate or endorse. At a meeting of the association on 20 April in defence of the oppressed tenantry, O'Connell read a letter

[26] N.Ex., 24 Oct. 1840.   [27] Ibid., 11 Nov. 1840.   [28] V., 9 Jan. 1841.   [29] N.Ex., 6 Feb. 1841.

from the archbishop giving permission to affix his name to a requisition for a public meeting in Dublin to promote the improvement of agriculture in Ireland. He then explained his confident hopes for the happy consequences of better relations between landlord and tenant:

If those relations be impartially considered and amicably settled, I am convinced that the improvement of agriculture, the increase of honest industry, the profitable employment of the labouring classes, and the permanent prosperity of this portion of the empire, may be completely accomplished.

O'Connell, however, was much less enthusiastic than Crolly about the aims of the Agriculture Improvement Society, and explained that he would 'solicit that most reverend prelate—who is one of the wisest men I ever knew, and a man full of the most intense zeal in the performance of his duty—to pause ere he lends himself to this project'.[30]

III

With the return of the Tories to power in June 1841 any justification that O'Connell might have had for putting the brakes on Repeal vanished. Not only did a deep personal antipathy exist between himself and the new prime minister, Sir Robert Peel, but he also feared that the Tory victory would lead to a return of his Orange opponents to power in Dublin Castle and to a resumption of their unchecked sway in the law courts and on the magistrates' bench. Peel promptly confirmed these fears by his appointment of Earl De Grey as Lord Lieutenant. A right-wing Tory, he showed scant tact in his early appointments and gave the Irish arch-Tories ground to believe that the halcyon days of their untrammelled dominance had returned.[31] Peel and his government were for the most part content to ignore Catholic grievances until the Repeal campaign reached such a peak of national excitement and expectation that they were forced to think of ways of seducing the Catholics from it.

Eliot, the Chief Secretary, believed in making concessions to Catholics but found little backing in the cabinet.[32] The government supported him

---

[30] D.E.P., 22 Apr. 1841.

[31] The Catholic perception of De Grey's policy was voiced by the *Vindicator*, when it wrote that every day brought some new cause to deplore the presence of a partisan executive in Dublin Castle from its evil influence upon the mind of a violent and ignorant faction. (V., 1 Jan. 1842.)

[32] Eliot complained to Graham about De Grey's discrimination in making appointments. After two years he had appointed sixty one Protestants and nine Catholics to public offices – mainly of a legal nature – and all thirteen of his appointments in the constabulary were given to Protestants. (Eliot to Graham, 15 July 1843, Graham Papers.)

in resisting the demands of the bishops of the established church for a separate grant for their schools. It wished to avoid further conflict and to prevent the national system from degenerating into what Sir James Graham, the Home Secretary, called 'a system of pure Roman Catholic Education . . . infinitely more objectionable than the Instruction based on the Scriptures which is now in use'.[33] Graham refused to consider Eliot's scheme for increased funding to Maynooth as he was afraid it would arouse slumbering feelings and passions, and he rejected a suggestion about disarming the Protestant yeomen of the north.[34] And it was not until Peel and Graham became concerned by the strength of national feeling among Catholics that they seriously considered a policy of conciliation.

When O'Connell's year as mayor of Dublin ended on 31 October 1842, he became free to devote himself exclusively to Repeal, and shortly afterwards announced that 1843 would be the repeal year. He proposed to step up the pressure on the British government by holding more frequently ever larger 'monster meetings', and by petitions and bye-elections, should they occur, virtually to intimidate Peel by the sheer solidarity and determination of his mass demonstrations. To obtain widespread support in every county the backing of the local bishop was extremely important, because the more committed and ardent the advocacy of the bishop the greater was the likelihood of the great body of priests in his diocese lending their almost indispensable aid at local level. O'Connell's determination to net as many bishops as possible was well illustrated in his response to Patrick Kennedy of Killaloe, who was reluctant to declare himself a Repealer. Kennedy explained in the letter accompanying his subscription that he did not believe that the peaceful re-establishment of an independent parliament was practicable, for when he called to mind 'the profligate expenditure of blood and treasure and character by which . . . England, the moment she felt herself in a condition to undertake it, did not scruple to accomplish its total annihilation', he could not hope that 'she would ever quietly consent to its restoration, in its former pride and power except, perhaps, in some moment of extraordinary embarrassment'; when that embarrassment had passed, independence could only be maintained by 'a sanguinary and devastating civil war'. But since these bleak probabilities did not arise

---

[33] Graham to Peel, 24 Nov. 1841, BL Add. MS 40446, ff 140r–144r.
[34] Peel to Eliot, 13 Nov. 1842, BL Add. MS 40480, ff 145r–148v. Graham had told Peel that Eliot believed strongly that 'by an increased grant to Maynooth, coupled with some new visitatorial powers, a commanding influence might be gained over the Catholic Priesthood of Ireland and that the country might be governed by such contrivances'. (BL. Add. MS 40446, 1 Dec. 1841, ff 162r–163v.)

from a struggle for a dependent parliament, Kennedy was happy to contribute to O'Connell's fund on the grounds that such a concession would satisfy him. O'Connell chose rather disingenuously to intrepret his argument as implying support for Repeal, and maintained that he had never consented to a dependent parliament, since it would be 'a mere mockery' to send fifty or a hundred members to listen to the 'outrageous balderdash' that was to be heard in Westminster.[35]

The ham-fisted response of the Chancellor, Sugden, to the growth of Repeal activity gave O'Connell a welcome boost. In May he withdrew the commission of the peace from thirty four magistrates among whom were O'Connell, and his son, John. The furore created by this *bêtise* redounded to the advantage of the movement for not only did some Whig magistrates resign in protest but the anger provoked by this impolitic act stiffened further the backs of Repealers and pulled waverers into the fold.

By then the great majority of the bishops had declared in favour of Repeal or tacitly favoured it; only seven out of a hierarchy of twenty persevered in their refusal to support it openly,[36] but this minority included the two most influential prelates on the bench—Crolly and Murray. Their reluctance to commit themselves annoyed O'Connell but he knew that he would gain nothing by attacking them publicly. He was anxious to entice them, and let it be known that he was conscious of their silence, hoping that the pressure of their people's enthusiasm would sweep them into his arms. Crolly never stated in public his reasons for not supporting Repeal. Presumably, he regarded it as unattainable and feared that the vain pursuit of it would only increase sectarian passions and divert the government—especially a Whig one—from passing the ameliorative measures that would be of real benefit to Catholics. Murray must have begged him to make his views known for he replied:

'I have so often vexed Mr O'Connell by my opposition to his injudicious and unfortunate Repeal agitation that I am sure he would pay very little attention to anything that I could say to him on the subject. The late atrocious manifesto published by the English Protestants, the intolerant menaces of our Irish Conservatives and the indignation of the persecuted Catholics afford at present a favourable occasion for exciting the people of Ireland to call for a domestic parliament. I hope that I have succeeded in guarding my clergy against that desperate and dangerous infatuation. But I could not promise myself any further success by applying to any of the prelates who have rashly given encouragment to Mr O'Connell, contributing to support him in his deplorable undertaking. If I would venture to solicit support to stop the Repeal agitation, whilst larger contributions are received for that purpose, my

[35] N.Ex., 18 Mar. 1843.
[36] Kerr, *Peel, Priests and Politics*, 330–1.

motives might be misrepresented in such a manner as could expose me to the odium of many misguided poor Catholics'.[37]

His clergy, however, made up their own minds on the subject and some of them differed widely from him.

When John Coyne, the parish priest of Dundalk, forwarded subscriptions from himself and some of his parishioners, O'Connell was overjoyed. Describing him as a 'most learned, respectable and exemplary clergyman' he remarked that Coyne's letter was most important as the prevailing view held that 'agreeing with some high dignatories of the church' the pastor of Dundalk was not favourable to Repeal.[38] If he could not snare the archbishops of Armagh and Dublin, he was extremely happy to gain the support of their clergy, and especially of those in positions of importance in their dioceses.

The ebullient bishop of Ardagh, however, compensated at least in part for the reticence of his metropolitan. In a fiery and intemperate speech at Mullingar on 15 May, Higgins declared that he knew that every bishop in Ireland was an ardent Repealer. When the tumultuous cheers that greeted this assertion had somewhat subsided, O'Connell, who had heartily participated in the applause, interjected 'let Bobby Peel hear that'. Emboldened by the reception which this news received, Higgins went further and claimed that all the bishops had actually declared that they were Repealers. Then carried away by the response of the crowds he went on in ringing tones to defy the British authorities to set limits to their political goals and, in the process, to pour scorn on the landlords:

I for one defy all the ministers of England to put down agitation in the diocese of Ardagh. If they attempt, my friends, to rob us of the daylight, which is, I believe, common to us all, and to prevent us from assembling in the open fields, we will return to our chapels, and we will suspend all other instructions, in order to devote all our time to teaching the people to be Repealers in spite of them. If they beset our temples, and mix our people with spies, we will prepare our people for the circumstance; and if they bring us for that to the scaffold, in dying for the cause of our country, we will bequeath our wrongs to our successors. . . I am justified in saying that the bishops of Ireland and the people who cooperate with them, despite all human ingenuity and all the malignity of British councils, have within their grasp the power to countervail their designs, and to carry out Repeal in spite of every possible resistance . . . To no aristocrat on earth do I owe anything save the unbounded contempt that I have for the whole class. . . I believe that I may speak officially, and without exaggeration say, that not only are they [the bishops] Repealers, but that they participate with ardor [sic] in every sentiment that has fallen from me . . . [I] assure

[37] Crolly to Murray, 22 Aug. 1841, quoted in Kerr, *Peel, Priests and Politics*, 77.
[38] N.Ex., 13 May 1843.

you in the name of the body, that you may draw to the utmost on us until our country has not one single grievance to complain of.[39]

Not only did Crolly and Murray not participate with ardour in these sentiments but they must have been both astounded and angered by them. Higgins had not been authorized to make such a declaration and he had no evidence whatever for his claims about the unanimity of views among the bishops. The two archbishops were thus faced with a cruel dilemma: they could either keep silence and leave their views open to misinterpretation or they could repudiate Higgins' statement and bring down odium on their heads as spiritual leaders who were indifferent to the struggles of their own people for a better future. Crolly took the first option but Murray braved the wrath of the nationalists to reveal his true position. In a letter to his priests on his return to Dublin from the countryside he referred to the surprise they must have felt on seeing the statement that all the bishops were Repealers. He pointed out that he had taken no part whatever in the movement and explained that he had always acted in accordance with the resolution of the hierarchy in January 1834, which excluded clerical participation from proceedings of a merely temporal character. He was determined to continue adhering to that policy and never to give a contrary example.[40]

Repeal meetings were held shortly afterwards at Dunleer and Camlough, in the archdiocese of Armagh, but Crolly may not have been embarrassed by invitations to them. However, when a monster meeting was organized for Drogheda for 5 June he was one of the guests invited to the banquet. But he had already agreed to preach a charity sermon in Omagh and had a legitimate excuse for refusing the invitation. Even then he had to face the awkward situation created by the publication of his letter of apology alongside that of MacHale, who combined an attack on the government with a reference to Cromwell's legacy to Drogheda.[41] A misdirected letter saved him from having to turn down the invitation to the dinner after the big Louth demonstration at Dundalk on 29 June. He explained that it had been addressed to his house in Drogheda, when he was residing in Armagh, and only reached him on 28 June when he was already suffering from influenza. Some of his clergy, however, were among the forty odd priests who were present at the demonstration.[42]

[39] N.Ex., 20 May 1843.
[40] D.E.P., 23 May 1843. Higgins at a meeting in Longford five days later claimed that one of his priests heard Murray declare in the presence of a large company of clergy that he was a Repealer. (Ibid., 30 May 1843.)
[41] N.Ex., 10 June 1843.   [42] Ibid., 1 July 1843.

And yet, despite Crolly's passing over this chance of making any kind of favourable reference to Repeal and thereby clearly revealing his unwillingness to support it, the irrepressible bishop of Ardagh could inform Paul Cullen a month later that the primate was *'now a most ardent and uncompromising Repealer* in public and in private'. By immediately adding that his own speech in Mullingar 'made many a useful conversion' Higgins implied that Crolly was among those valuable converts. He then went on to affirm that the bishops had the destinies of Ireland and the Irish Church in their hands, that Rome could depend on their prudence, and ought to rejoice at the embarrassment of 'scoundrelly England' and that they had reason to believe that the queen was with them 'heart in soul' in their peaceful, legal, constitutional and moral struggle.[43] In fact, there was not a shred of evidence to support this claim. He was really concerned to mend his fences with Rome in the wake of unfavourable reaction there to his Mullingar speech, and, consequently, these ground- less assertions were advanced as self-defence and self-justification, with a dash of wishful thinking added to the melange. The queen's alleged sympathy was pure fantasy, and no one would have been more surprised than Crolly to read about the primatial enthusiasm for the cause.

The heightened excitement created by the gathering momentum of the Repeal movement generated dangerous tensions in the north of the country. Even the *Northern Whig* could only envisage a domestic legisla- ture creating nothing but sectarian animosity and 'the ascendancy of a relgious party not unnaturally exasperated by the recollection of numer- ous deep wrongs and grievous insults'.[44] Anti-Repeal meetings were held in the north, violence took place in Dungannon and in the wake of the 12 July celebrations rioting and stone-throwing between opposing factions in Belfast occurred. On 23 July more serious disturbances led to the destruction of houses belonging to both parties in the town. A large anti- Repeal meeting was scheduled to take place in the town on 7 September but in response to an appeal from Lord Londonderry it was cancelled.[45] However, the Tories and Orangemen of Lisburn went ahead with their meeting on 13 September. The ostensible purpose of the assembly was to thank the queen for the commitment she had made at the close of the parliamentary session to the maintenance of the union and to the discouragement of that 'system of pernicious agitation, which disturbs the industry, and retards the improvement of this country', and for proclaim- ing her intention of maintaining inviolate the bond between the two

---

[43] Higgins to Cullen, 28 July 1843., AICR.   [44] N.W., 4 May 1843.   [45] Ibid., 29, 31 Aug. 1843.

countries. The speakers shouted defiance at O'Connell and 'the Popish myriads who surround him', and oscillated between expressing pity for the Romanist brought up in darkness and resistance to 'the monster . . . Popery, which leads its blind votaries to the brink, eventually plunging them into the pit of destruction'. In 1829, one speaker declared, the 'pestiferous breath of Popery' had been admitted into the lungs of the constitution and in the intervening years Popery and infidelity had been fostered, the Papists had become so numerous as to threaten them with subjugation but the cloven foot had been shown in time to warn them of the danger, before the enemy had become strong enough to overthrow them.[46] The sectarian virulence of such language was calculated to intensify religious enmity and to present Repeal as the harbinger of a lurid form of persecution.

Peel's government had been watching with growing concern the intense manifestation of national feeling at the huge rallies. It had never wavered in its determination to maintain the union as it existed. A self-governing Ireland was not to be trusted, when British national security was under threat. Peel feared the possibility of war with France and the United States. An Ireland that could be used as a base by either of these powers, should hostilities break out, was unthinkable and intolerable. The government finally braced itself to act. Graham consulted with De Grey, Sugden, the Lord Chancellor, and his top-ranking legal authorities and decided to charge O'Connell with conspiracy.[47] A gigantic assembly was planned for Clontarf on 8 October. The government banned it and O'Connell hastily submitted; the meeting was cancelled. The monster rallies had ended. O'Connell's support did not immediately decline. Archbishop Slattery of Cashel soon wrote to O'Connell to explain that, though he had been reluctant to meddle in politics, he had decided to give his support to Repeal.[48]

The decision of the government to charge O'Connell and his closest allies with conspiracy, levying money for illegal purposes, trying to seduce the armed forces and assuming the royal prerogative in the courts of law was so blatantly and pathetically political that it antagonized some of O'Connell's most determined opponents. The *Northern Whig* taunted the government with having neither the wisdom to conciliate nor the judgement to control its people[49] and the decision of the attorney general to strike off the Catholic jurors who had been selected to try O'Connell

[46] B.N.L., 15 Sept. 1843.   [47] Graham to Stanley, 4 Oct. 1843, Graham Papers.
[48] N.Ex., 1 Nov. 1843.   [49] N.W., 17 Oct. 1843.

afforded both nationalists and Whigs immense scope for denouncing
the discriminatory chicanery of Dublin Castle. In February 1844 O'Connell was found guilty and on 30 May sentenced to a year's imprisonment.
He served little more than three months for the Law Lords reversed
the judgement of the Irish court. He did not attempt to hold any more
huge public meetings though the Repeal organization remained in
place and the weekly rent, if diminishing in quantity, continued to be
collected.

IV

A few months before the government decided to move against O'Connell,
the reverberations of the Repeal movement caused some anxiety as far
away as Vienna.[50] Metternich, the chancellor of the Austrian empire,
regarded himself as the policeman of continental Europe and his determination to preserve as far as possible the post-Napoleonic settlement of
1815 from being overturned by revolutionaries was enthusiastically endorsed by all the monarchical governments of Europe. Even before the
Repeal movement took off Metternich had cast a wary eye on Ireland. In
1839 he had cautiously advised Palmerston not to disdain the use of papal
power in repressing in Ireland the political movements which were all the
more terrible because of their religious dimensions.[51] He did not limit his
plans to means of repressing Irish opposition to British rule. He told the
papal nuncio in Vienna that he had counselled British ministers to
conciliate Irish Catholics and suggested that the most effective way to do
so was to restore to the clergy the temporal possessions of which they had
been despoiled. The nuncio concluded that by confiding such thoughts to
him Metternich was preparing the way for asking the pope to exhort Irish
Catholics to behave peacefully in anticipation of beneficent measures from
their government. The chancellor had also informed him that British
governments would be prepared to negotiate with the Holy See.[52] His
concern, however well-intentioned, could have afforded scant comfort to
the Whigs, for they already knew the difficulties of tinkering with the
established church; the confiscation and transfer of its property would
have been unthinkable.

But if the Austrian chancellor had grounds for disquiet in 1839 when

---

[50] Kerr, *Peel, Priests and Politics*, 98-107.
[51] Altieri to S.S., 4 Apr. 1839, ASV, Nunz. Vienna 280B, f 163rv.
[52] Ibid., 10 May 1839, ff 227v-228v.

political activity and clerical participation in it was very limited, the heady excitement and international publicity associated with the Repeal movement must have given him cause for alarm. The danger of successful popular agitations across Europe began to loom large. Accordingly, on receipt of a communication from his embassy in London about the gratitude the British government would feel towards the pope, if he got the Irish clergy who were involved in politics to moderate their zeal, he wrote a lengthy dispatch to his ambassador in Rome in June 1843, which revealed an awareness of some of the complications of the Irish political situation. Disclaiming the possibility of simple solutions to a complex problem, he stressed the importance played by religion in the conflict between the British government and Irish radicalism. Religion and revolution were closely linked. The Catholic church had lost all its property and seen it usurped by sinecurists. The Anglican church would not give up what it held, as it would lose its power, and the government's way of dealing with Ireland was to apply repression instead of remedies. The bishops were divided; some supported the dissolution of the union and the wiser or more timid opposed them. The pope could not remain passive in the crisis; he could play a role and he would have to tell the Catholics not to confuse the political and religious issues.[53]

When the Vatican sought Metternich's mediation with the British authorities to clamp down on the publication in Malta of seditious literature, which was circulating in the Papal States, the British government was given the opportunity to demand a *quid pro quo*. The nuncio in Vienna reported to Rome that as soon as the request was made, the English ambassador, a fiery Tory (Sir Robert Gordon, who was a brother of the Foreign Secretary, Lord Aberdeen) spoke as if it were already granted, and then indicated that the pope should repay this good turn by a public and severe reprimand against the Catholic clergy of Ireland forbidding them to support Repeal. The nuncio remarked that the passions ruling the British government and its agents on this score were evident from Gordon's statement that, if the pope did not rebuke the Irish Catholic clergy, his government would not feel bound to refuse aid to the Bolognese, who were agitating against Papal authority.[54] Gordon suggested the same *quid pro quo* again to Metternich[55] and Metternich duly obliged by referring the matter to Cardinal Lambruschini, the Secretary

---

53 Metternich to Ambassador Ohms, 17 June 1843, Arch SC. AA. EE. SS. (Inghilterra) 1842-5, Pos. 41-45, Fasc 16.
54 Altieri to Lambruschini, 5 Nov. 1843, ASV, Nunz. Vienna 280F, ff 198v-208v.
55 Gordon to Aberdeen, 15 Nov. 1843, PRO, F.O. 7/311, ff 239r-241r.

of State, and asking for his comments. He also told the British ambassador that not all the wrong was on the part of the oppressed but that much of it was the fault of the government which would not grant them what they were entitled to in justice and equity. To Gordon's cold reply that his government could do no more than it was doing the chancellor had answered that neither could the pope. And he had reminded Aberdeen of the pope's letter to the archbishop of Armagh, and of the commitment of the pope to the condemnation of the revolutionary tendencies of Irish Catholics.[56]

By then both Peel and Graham had come to the firm conclusion that the pope's authority over the Irish church could be exploited in the interests of British policy.[57] Peel decided that a collection of the allegedly seditious speeches and writings of Irish priests should be made and presented indirectly to the pope, or, if that proved impossible, to Metternich. Showing that insensitivity which characterized most of Britain's diplomatic contacts with the Holy See in the nineteenth century and which invariably redounded to the benefit of the Irish church, Peel pronounced himself unwilling to enter into 'any compact that we should suppress seditious publications in Malta in return for the attempt to suppress Priestly Rebellion in Ireland'. The pope and Metternich were expected to respond on the understanding that they had 'a common interest with us in discouraging the revolt of Ecclesiastics against the authority of the Sovereign . . . [and that] such conspiracies as those which we have reason to believe have been formed and are directed in Ireland by Roman Catholic priests' were disgraceful to religion and dangerous to other thrones as well as that of England.[58] Graham contacted Aberdeen, the Foreign Secretary, and arranged for De Grey to prepare either for Vienna or Rome a 'collection of the speeches of MacHale and Higgins and of other addresses from the Altar exciting to Rebellion, Treason and Bloodshed'.[59]

Aberdeen duly forwarded the collection to his brother, the ambassador in Vienna, for transmission by Metternich to Rome. To reciprocate the expected papal goodwill he explained that the Colonial Office had issued an instruction to the authorities in Malta to check as far as was consistent with the law and with the means at their disposal the publication of seditious literature and other attempts made from that island to create

---

[56] Altieri to Lambruschini, 15 Nov., 1843, ASV, Nunz. Vienna, 280F, ff 212v-214v.
[57] Graham to De Grey, and to Peel, 30 Oct. 1843 (Graham Papers), Peel to De Grey, 1 Nov. 1843 and Graham to Peel, 2 Nov. 1843, BL Add MS 40449, ff 176r-177v, 186r-187v.
[58] Peel to Graham, 27 Nov. 1843, Ibid., ff 233r-234r.
[59] Graham to Peel, 29 Nov. 1843, Ibid., ff 241r-244v.

discontent in the papal states. Metternich was invited to present that collection of outrageously seditious speeches to the papal court and to endeavour to persuade it 'to take the necessary measures for the suppression of such a flagrant abuse by their sacred functions of the Roman Catholic Priesthood in Ireland'. This could not be achieved by private pastoral letters: it required 'the publick and unequivocal reprobation of the Holy See'.[60]

Metternich in turn passed on the documents through diplomatic channels to the Secretariat of State in Rome. Since Ireland fell under the supervision of the congregation of Propaganda the intervention of the Cardinal Secretary of State in Irish affairs posed delicate problems. Roman curial departments were always sensitive about the extent of their jurisdiction, and the Cardinal Secretary of State, even when, as in this case, he had papal authority to examine the Irish question, was obliged to be extremely cautious, as he was treading on the territory of Cardinal Fransoni, who doubtless believed that his congregation alone was competent to handle Irish affairs, and who may well have resented a colleague interfering in questions concerning his bailiwick.

The bishops were not aware of this governmental *démarche*. Had MacHale and his friends known about it, they would have regarded it as yet a further example of Albion's perfidy. Crolly and Murray might not have welcomed an intervention from London but would not have objected to an examination by Rome of the more extreme statements of the bishops and clergy. Murray had already inquired from Cullen whether Rome could do anything to restrain their hotheads.[61] Crolly would not have written in this vein to Rome—his relations with Cullen were too cool to permit his doing so—and he would have been reluctant to be dragged into an interminable correspondence with the congregation. He later claimed that he wrote to some priests to tone down their language at political meetings, and he was given credit by the county inspector of constabulary of Armagh for the 'passive' attitude of the clergy of that county to Repeal[62] (those of Louth were less passive).

The Repeal question, however, may have influenced him in assessing the suitability of the candidates proposed by the clergy of Clogher for the coadjutorship of that diocese in November 1842. The leading candidate, Charles MacNally, obtained twenty four votes from the parish priests, and the other two, Francis McGinnis and Daniel Boylan, obtained four each.

[60] Aberdeen to Sir R. Gordon, 30 Dec. 1843, BL Add. MS 43156, ff 23r-24r.
[61] Murray to Cullen, 29 May 1843, AICR.
[62] Kerr, *Peel, Priests and Politics*, 84.

All three favoured Repeal. Eight bishops met to comment on the three candidates chosen. They deemed McGinnis, who had made very strong statements in support of Repeal, to be lacking in prudence. They recommended Boylan rather than MacNally, who seemed to have all the right qualifications. Higgins, who was not present, gave his preference to MacNally, and Cantwell, the other indomitable *zelante* in the Armagh province, duly changed sides and backed MacNally. Rumours blaming the primate for being prejudiced against MacNally began to circulate and letters supporting him were sent to Rome by Clogher priests and by MacHale.[63]

Personal reasons doubtless played some part in the bishops' choice— Bishop Kernan of Clogher preferred Boylan—but it seems not unreasonable to conclude that Crolly did not want another able and outspoken *zelante* in his province, one who had already taken MacHale's line on national education and who was likely to adopt intransigent attitudes on Repeal and possibly on other issues. However, MacNally was duly appointed and passionately advocated MacHale's line on the issues dividing the bishops.

As news of the increasing momentum of the Repeal movement reached Rome and Anglo-Irish landlords and others hostile to it sought to influence the papacy against it, the pope himself refused to be swayed by their arguments.[64] According to Cullen, who was an enthusiastic O'Connellite and who would have used all his persuasive powers to get Roman officials at least to remain neutral on the issue, the pope believed that one would have to be in the country and know all the circumstances of the case before pronouncing on it. He himself was familiar with the charges, which had surfaced again during the controversy over national education, about the injustices which Irish Catholics had long suffered at the hands of a Protestant government. And though his political outlook was deeply conservative, he did not regard a constitutional struggle, which directly or indirectly was demanding overdue justice, as blameworthy.

His Secretariat of State duly submitted the collection of allegedly intemperate speeches from Irish ecclesiastics to a rigorous and detailed investigation. Cardinal Lambruschini in his 'pro-memoria' or reply to Metternich of 9 February 1844 immediately went to the heart of the matter by disputing the claim that the Irish Catholics and the Italian revolutionaries in Malta were guilty of similar behaviour: the Irish agitation was constitutional and sought only a modification of the relations

---

[63] APF, *Acta*, 206, ff 4r–9r, 133r–139v.   [64] Kerr, *Peel, Priests and Politics*, 97.

of two parts of the British empire, whereas the Italians who conspired in Malta, used very different means and were motivated by anarchy. Moreover, the British could apply the full force of civil law to their problems, whereas the Holy See could only give instructions and counsel—means which had to be used with great prudence. A public rebuke to the Irish clergy for their conduct was not the appropriate response. The cardinal, while not questioning the authenticity of the statements attributed to the clergy, noted the significant differences between those published in the press and those taken down by reporters in the churches. If the few priests who were accused were really guilty, the Holy See would deal with them canonically and allow them to defend themselves rather than have the whole priesthood slurred. The printed speeches showed an abhorrence of revolution and pledged fidelity to the queen, and the speakers had often declared at public meetings that their influence had prevented their people from resorting to violence and rebellion; and were the Holy See to tell them that it was reprehensible to judge the fundamental laws of the kingdom, they could reply that it was not the role of the Holy See to tell them what was conformable or opposed to the constitution, and that the facts rather than their words proved that their presence in the movement prevented anarchy and rebellion. While refusing to issue the public rebuke Metternich had requested, the cardinal assured the chancellor that the Holy See was always ready to use its moral influence in ways that were both paternal and adapted to the circumstances to recall to their duty those ecclesiastics who seemed to be the object of complaint.[65]

The pressure of two such powerful and influential empires as the Austrian and the British could not have been easy to resist. Yet in the promemoria the Vatican skilfully dissected the English case and proved that the charges of treasonable activity levelled at the Irish priests by the government were rebutted by the very professions of loyalty and repudiation of violence made by the priests themselves. As a response to the demands of the government, backed by what it regarded as incontrovertible evidence of the morally improper behaviour of the clergy, this was magisterial. The government's claims were shown to be self-defeating, and no contrary testimony was required to disprove its case. Understandably the recipients were disappointed. Gordon reported from Vienna that the document was 'so vague and unsatisfactory' that Metternich would not give him a copy to transmit to London.[66] It seems unlikely, however,

---

[65] Pro-memoria of Cardinal Lambruschini, 9 Feb. 1844, APF, SC (Irlanda), 28, ff 203r-206r.
[66] Gordon to Aberdeen, 19 Feb. 1844, BL Add. MS 43157, ff 25v-26r.

that the chancellor, in view of his previous comments on the need for
concessions to Irish Catholics, was as surprised and disappointed as
Gordon thought.

The Vatican, following its traditional practice, did not rush out its
promised paternal exhortation to the Irish ecclesiastics who were in need
of being reminded of their sacerdotal duties. The exhortation came eight
months later in the form of a letter from the cardinal prefect of
Propaganda to the archbishop of Armagh. It fulfilled the spiritual
obligations of the Holy See by warning clerics of the necessity of avoiding
close involvement in political issues and at the same time avoided the
political repercussions to which a public letter from the pope would have
been exposed. Cardinal Fransoni's letter was private but, if it were to
become public, it could be regarded as part of the ordinary correspondence between Rome and Ireland and not a monumental rebuke issued by
an indignant pontiff to a wayward and refractory clergy. Nonetheless, it
was more solemn and formal than the previous admonition and, though
the terminology was of necessity imprecise, there was no doubting the
intention of the cardinal to put a brake on clerical political activity.

Recalling the counsel given him in 1839 to suggest wiser courses to the
bishops and clergy who were alleged to be too closely involved in political
activity, the cardinal averred that the congregation did not doubt his
assiduity. However, the desired result had not corresponded to his efforts

for, it appears from the newspapers of those parts, where sermons by clergy and even
by some bishops at meetings, banquets and in churches are reported that, if correct,
would show that they were not primarily concerned with the salvation of souls, the
good of religion, and the honour of God, and were not totally uninvolved in party
political strife. It cannot be denied that the Sacred Congregation and even the pope
were hurt by behaviour which was harmful and disgraceful to an ecclesiastical body.
The Holy See is injured by the implication that it was insufficiently interested in
giving salutary admonitions to the clergy or favoured these actions or turned a blind
eye to them. Perhaps, Your Excellency is not aware that there is scope for these
complaints or rather accusations, but the Apostolic See with its sad experience feels
hurt by these charges.

For that reason the congregation with the pope's authority had again written to
him, and reminded him of the nature and character of the ecclesiastical office, how
much it concerned the integrity of religion that those who were ministers of the King
of Peace and dispensers of the mysteries of God should not be involved in secular
matters but should concern themselves with furthering among their people quiet,
tranquillity and peace, which are the bond of Christianity. They should by word and
example inculcate due obedience to the temporal order in civil affairs and preach only
Christ crucified.

Crolly was enjoined to admonish effectively any ecclesiastic and especially any bishop who would stray from the extremely restricted line of clerical duty Fransoni had assigned them.[67]

Yet again Crolly had been given the invidious task of chastising the priests or bishops whose activity he deemed to be too political. Since most of these clerics envisaged Repeal as the herald of much needed social reform and therefore directly related to their moral and social responsibilities, his judgement in that field was bound to be resented, if his interpretation of Repeal were narrowly national or political and excluded the moral dimension. Given the passions which the movement provoked and which had been intensely exacerbated by the recent treatment and imprisonment of O'Connell, the responsibility of deciding who had transgressed the limits laid down by Rome and subsequently of reprimanding him was exceptionally delicate.

The admonition was discussed at the annual meeting of the bishops in Dublin on 13 November, when each prelate was given a copy of it, and a resolution proposed by Bishop Browne of Elphin and seconded by Charles MacNally, the newly appointed bishop of Clogher, was passed. This requested Crolly to inform Rome that the assembled prelates had received the instructions contained in the letter 'with that degree of prudence, respect, obedience and veneration that should ever be paid to any document emanating from the Apostolic See and that they all pledge themselves to carry the spirit thereof into effect'.[68] This was a masterly reply, and one that in some ways anticipated Bishop Dupanloup's famous response to the *Syllabus of Errors* twenty years later, when he made a distinction between the thesis, the ultimate and universal ideal for society, and the hypothesis, the particular state or situation at a given time. Correct, courteous and bland, it combined the proper and respectful tone of submission to the Holy See with a commitment to do nothing. It left the situation unchanged and would have been as inconsequential as the pro-memoria had not its contents been given to the press.

Details of the discussion or divisions of opinion among the prelates on the letter are not known. The resolution was proposed and seconded by the *zelanti* and represents their views. As they had a majority on Repeal and the other issue then in contention—the Charitable Bequests Act—a

---

[67] Propaganda to Crolly, 15 Oct. 1844, APF, *Lett.*, 331, ff 794r-795v. A few days earlier Cullen had been told not to hold any celebrations in honour of O'Connell's release from prison as they would greatly displease the pope who believed passionately that ecclesiastics should not take part in political affairs. (Propaganda to Cullen, 11 Oct. 1844, Ibid., f 787v.)

[68] F.J., 13 Jan. 1845. The resolution inaccurately referred to the letter from the Holy Father. In fact, it came from Cardinal Fransoni but with the pope's authority behind it.

victory on this issue was only to be expected. Those who supported it could salve their consciences by pointing to the moral dimension of their involvement in politics. Those who took Fransoni's letter literally—a minority—could act on it as circumstances permitted and conscience dictated. Crolly certainly understood it as imposing on him an obligation to admonish any priest or prelate who made an imprudent speech at a public meeting. Bishop Cantwell of Meath later revealed in a letter to Daniel O'Connell that the resolution was unanimous, though it had been preceded by a division of opinion. A few prelates interpreted it in the strictest sense, concluding that it forbade them to take any part in public meetings of a political nature or to be present at public banquets. The majority, however, took the view that the cardinal was only censuring violent and intemperate language either in churches or at public gatherings on the part of a priest or bishop on such occasions, not their mere presence. MacHale regarded the accusations against ecclesiastics of making 'intemperate Speeches' merely as 'a repetition of the Calumnies which our enemies often poured into the ears of the authorities at Rome and which more than once several of us had satisfactorily refuted'. And he believed that it was obtained by Crolly and Murray as part of their campaign to defeat the opposition of a majority of their colleagues to the Charitable Bequests Act.[69] And when the bishop of Elphin proclaimed his devotion to the fatherland at a political demonstration and the bishop of Clogher forwarded his subscription to the Repeal Association, Repealers could claim with the *Freeman's Journal* that the rescript contained nothing to threaten their liberty or repress the free expression by the clergy of their political sentiments.[70]

Crolly carried out the mandate he received from his colleagues and reported to Rome that they had all promised obedience to the orders of the Holy See and would inculcate in their flocks obedience to the temporal power in those matters which pertained to civil authority. But he also passed on personal views about the contents of the letter, which would not have met with the approval of the majority of his brethren. He described the counsel of the rescript as very opportune for all Irish ecclesiastics, and wholly necessary for several bishops. He admitted that the political addresses of some clergy and even bishops had been reported accurately in the papers and that these had been a cause of pain to the friends of the Catholic religion. He was hopeful that the advice of the

[69] MacHale to Cullen, 17 Nov. 1844, AICR. See pp. 305-26.
[70] Ibid., 16, 21 Jan. 1845.

congregation would be followed but, if not, he would admonish effica-ciously, patiently and charitably the priests, and especially the bishops, who had not been converted from their political errors.[71]

The rescript only came to light in the course of a newspaper discussion on the desirability and likelihood of a concordat being negotiated between England and the court of Rome. The *Freeman's Journal*, quoting a reliable source in Rome, warned of this danger on 26 December and pointed out that an English agent[72] was acting on behalf of the government in Rome and had already proposed the terms of a concordat which, among other conditions, gave England, directly or indirectly, the right to nominate the Irish bishops. In return Rome would prohibit the clergy from taking part in the national movement. The Holy See would gain advantages for Catholics in the British colonies at the expense of the church in Ireland. On the same day *The Times* came out in favour of a concordat and other British and Irish papers took up the theme. In the excited state of Catholic opinion resulting from the controversy over the Charitable Bequests Act conspiracy theories found a ready acceptance. O'Connell in a public letter addressed to the bishop of Meath referred to the reports, stated that he had most reliable evidence to support them and maintained that English and Austrian agents were working together to obtain an improper influence for the government over the Irish church. Commenting on the gazetting of the three episcopal members of the board of Charitable Bequests—Crolly, Murray and Denvir—he suggested that the naiveté of these prelates encouraged such nefarious designs:

The fatal facility with which some of our exemplary prelates, with pious intentions and pure designs, fall into one snare after another, encourages the ancient enemies of our faith and fidelity to augment their exertions, and to mature their plans, until they render them as they conceive and hope, irresistible.

The pope's ministers had been convinced that the government was prepared to give generous financial help to Catholics in the British colonies. The Vatican had swallowed this bait and, in consequence, had issued a letter to Crolly unfavourable to Repeal:

It is said that there was some dexterity in procuring this letter. It has, however, been some time in the hands of his Grace; But it is not a canonical document, and, at all events, as far as it may treat of matters of a temporal nature, or matters relating to the political rights and liberties of the Irish people, it is plainly void and of no effect.

---

[71] Crolly to Propaganda, 25 Nov. 1844, APF, SC (Irlanda), 28, ff 352r-353r.
[72] See p. 311.

O'Connell then deplored the existence of so much dissension among the Irish bishops, priests and laity, when so powerful a conspiracy was under foot and went on to discuss Archbishop Murray's pastoral on the Charitable Bequests Act.[73]

Crolly had every right to feel aggrieved and angry after reading this publication. Together with Murray and Denvir he was publicly accused of facilitating the government's Machiavellian designs on the Irish church by his political innocence and gullibility. And to the average reader of the *Freeman's Journal* O'Connell's claim that the letter was not canonical must have suggested that Crolly had cooperated in foisting a ukase of dubious legality on the Irish church.

The archbishop had no option but to reject this misleading and potentially explosive statement and he did so in a calm and restrained way. Having expressed his surprise and sorrow at O'Connell's action, he explained that he had received a similar canonical document from Propaganda in 1839 in which he was commissioned to admonish 'some political ecclesiastics who had made at public meetings such violent speeches as were not congenial to the mild spirit of their sacred ministry'. His best efforts to execute that order had not borne fruit:

In obedience to the injunction of the Holy See, I endeavoured to reclaim those misguided clergymen, but as my fraternal admonitions did not produce the desired effect, his Holiness desired the Sacred Congregation to send me another letter on the same subject, in order that I should more efficaciously admonish such Priests or Prelates as I might find taking a prominent or imprudent part in political proceedings.

He had laid the document before the prelates at their last meeting in Dublin, they had entered it into their minutes and had promised to regulate their own conduct by its prescriptions and to try to prevail on their clergy to follow its salutary instructions. Knowing O'Connell's honesty and fidelity to the authority of the church, Crolly felt sure that he would accept the terms of the rescript which accompanied his letter. The text of the rescript and the resolution of the bishops was then given.

Crolly concluded this lengthy riposte by adverting to the rumours about a concordat between the government and the Holy See. With a robust repudiation of such a policy, he revealed that he was far from being the tame 'castle' minion that his political and ecclesiastical opponents would increasingly accuse him of being. His hostility to a concordat, which he doubtless feared would entail arrangements about pensioning the clergy, was just as deep and instinctive as MacHale's:

[73] F.J., 11 Jan. 1845.

With regard to the concordat which has so justly excited alarming apprehensions in the minds of all the Clergy and Laity of Ireland, I can only state in the most solemn manner that I know nothing of it directly or indirectly, except by public rumour; and that I shall join the Prelacy of Ireland in using every influence in my power to prevent any such insidious scheme, which would be destructive of the independence and purity of our holy religion.[74]

O'Connell handsomely apologized to the archbishop in an open letter a few days later. He fully retracted his assertion that the document was uncanonical and explained that he had acted on misinformation: he had assumed that the rescript treated 'of matters of a temporal nature; or matters relating to the political rights and liberties of the Irish people'. He then quoted statements from various English papers about the presence in Rome of the attaché from the British embassy at Florence, which indicated the existence of an underhand agency of the government with the Holy See. He praised Crolly for producing the actual document and for adhering to the pledge of the Irish prelates to use their best endeavours to prevent the enactment of a concordat.[75]

Graham was pleased with Crolly's letter which he described as a most important document, declared that they must do all they could to support him, and authorized Heytesbury to convey to him that the government had no intention of interfering with the independence of the church.[76] Murray, who was given the same information, wrote to the *Dublin Evening Post* to publish the official note from the Lord Lieutenant explaining that he had been instructed to give to the archbishops of Dublin and Armagh the strongest assurances on the part of the government, that it had never had 'the slightest intention of entering into any negotiation with the Papal See upon the subject of the Concordat'.[77] Copies of Heytesbury's and Crolly's letters were forwarded to the agent in Rome to enable him to make an official denial of the rumour.[78]

If the contretemps with O'Connell had a felicitous ending, Crolly's encounter on the same subject with his suffragan, William Higgins (or O'Higgins, as in deference to his heightened sense of patriotism, he had begun to style himself) ended on a sadder note. O'Higgins had not been present at the bishops' meeting on 13 November and had not been privy to his colleagues' discussions on the rescript. But in a letter to the *Pilot* he described it as 'harmless' and 'hypothetical', and revealed the thinking behind the resolution of acceptance of it. Maintaining with his customary

[74] Ibid., 13 Jan. 1845.   [75] Ibid., 17 Jan. 1845.
[76] Graham to Heytesbury, 13 Jan. 1845, Graham Papers.
[77] F.J., 17 Jan. 1845.   [78] S. Canning to Petre, 22 Jan. 1845, PRO, F.O. 43/38.

vigour that the Irish clergy who actively supported Repeal were described at every soiree and political coterie in Rome as turbulent, disloyal and neglectful of their spiritual duties, when the exact opposite was the case, he regretted to have to say that some servile and mercenary Catholics in Ireland were also propagating that slander. Some effectual means should be adopted, he believed, to enlighten the pope 'as to the constitutional, legal and charitable nature of our peaceful agitation for common justice in maligned and injured Ireland'.[79]

Crolly took a more sternly realistic interpretation of the purpose of the rescript and of the obligations it imposed upon him. To his mind it was deliberately aimed at ecclesiastics who behaved like O'Higgins, and it could not be relegated to some imaginary place or time, beyond their own. Consequently, he wrote to O'Higgins to inquire on what grounds the document had been called 'purely hypothetical', and he must also have explained that Rome had been referring to imprudent speeches given by ecclesiastics on political occasions. O'Higgins was extremely angered by the innuendo and his ill-tempered reply indicates that behind the split in the hierarchy there were not only politico-ecclesiastical differences but personal antipathies as well. To Crolly's question about his reasons for describing the rescript as 'purely hypothetical' he gave no answer other than an indignant demand to know by what right he was taken to task:

May I take the liberty in return, to ask your Grace, *in what capacity* you feel justified in calling on me for an account of my public correspondence with the Editor of a Newspaper? If you take this course as my Metropolitan, I submit that you entirely outstep the bounds of your jurisdiction; and if your Grace acts in any other sense, be so kind as to let me see the powers that enable you to do so. As to what your Grace is pleased to say about *imprudent* public speeches, made by certain Prelates of this country, I really believe that the Prelates to whom your Grace seems to allude, are quite as good judges of *prudence* as any of their brother Bishops in Ireland. Surely your Grace does not mean to say, that *prudence* is a mere *negative* Virtue. If this were admitted, there is no omission of duty that might not be excused under the name of *prudence*. So far as the Holy See is concerned, you may rest assured that I shall always be found as respectful as Your Grace, and I shall deem that respect not at all diminished by endeavouring to defend myself and fellow-Repealers against the wicked calumnies which certain Irishmen would heap upon us in Rome, to please a heretical and anticatholic Government.

Promising to give his reasons when he was convinced that Crolly had a right to demand them, he ended by asking for an *authenticated* copy of the rescript.[80] What more could Crolly do? To report O'Higgins to Rome

[79] F.J., 25 Jan. 1845.   [80] O'Higgins to Crolly, 28 Jan. 1845, DCDA.

would have involved lengthy and tiresome correspondence, with interminable arguments about the prudence or imprudence of making political statements—a highly subjective and contentious area for those unfamiliar with the nuances of Irish politics—and would probably have only worsened the situation.

The archbishop may have written to other bishops suggesting that they keep a tighter rein on priests who were making extreme speeches. He certainly wrote to Charles MacNally, the bishop of Clogher, to complain of 'the imprudent and scandalous political speeches' made by Clogher clergy and by Francis McGinnis in particular at a recent meeting in Clones. The archbishop reminded MacNally that he had seconded the resolution at the bishops' meeting at which the prelates had committed themselves to carry out the spirit of the pope's letter, and called for his cooperation 'in bringing those misguided Clergymen to a proper sense of their duty'.[81] MacNally's reply was less truculent than O'Higgins' but equally unsubmissive. Neatly putting the ball back in Crolly's court, he remarked that the cardinal's letter authorized the archbishop to advise and admonish ecclesiastics, and suggested that McGinnis and the other clergy would undoubtedly 'receive with due and becoming deference such admonition as your Grace may feel it your duty to address to them'. By going on to imply that any unmeasured language used by the clergy was provoked by the Charitable Bequests Act and by recalling that the majority of the prelates had decided that that issue, far from being merely political, was bound up 'with the dearest interests of religion', he was able in turn to advise Crolly that any admonition by him which could be construed to forbid discussion on that subject would increase the existing 'painful excitement' a hundredfold. MacNally in his answer succeeded cleverly in protecting his clergy from rebukes and Crolly's only consolation was that he had attempted to do what he regarded as his duty.[82]

The anxieties about a concordat between London and Rome did not die with Heytesbury's denial of it. The *Freeman's Journal* pointed out that the Lord Lieutenant was merely forwarding an instruction from the government and explained that the head of that government was not 'distinguished for his candour', being one 'whose words frequently and designedly convey a meaning which he himself, when the occasion needs, is the first to repudiate'. Heytesbury's communication required the strictest interpretation. While it excluded consultations for a concordat it did not

---

[81] Crolly to MacNally (copy), 26 Jan. 1845, Ibid.
[82] MacNally to Crolly, 27 Jan. 1845. PRONI, Dio. (RC) 1/10B/6.

exclude the establishment of some other relationship, such as that between Rome and Prussia, which would give London some authority over the Irish church. The terms of Heytesbury's denial in fact confirmed apprehensions that some devious deal was being prepared, or otherwise he would have calmed the fears of the sensitive by declaring that the government had no desire, and was not taking any steps to obtain from the Sovereign Pontiff any authority of any nature over the Irish church.[83]

But Paul Cullen, who had been among the first to raise the alarm, soon learned that there were no grounds for believing the report and assured Murray that it was unfounded.[84] In February a letter from Bishop Blake of Dromore, quoting two Roman correspondents of the strictest veracity, whose information was derived from the highest authority, that the stories about a concordat were 'groundless fabrications' calmed the public excitement about it.[85]

There is no evidence that the government ever seriously contemplated entering into such an agreement with the Holy See. Graham, however, was angry that Murray published the assurance Heytesbury had given him lest it be later misconstrued into a guarantee that the government would never consider such an arrangement as a politic measure.[86] Concordats are a form of treaty which deal with arrangements beween church and state about property, marriage, education and other issues of conflict or possible conflict between the parties. Public opinion in Britain would scarcely have stomached a solemnly binding contract of that nature with the Vatican and apart from Irish questions which were not susceptible to that kind of treatment, there were no reasons inducing the government to enter into a legally binding agreement with Rome. British ministers certainly understood the importance of obtaining Roman support for their Irish policies and were keen to use Roman authority to make the Irish church more amenable to their wishes. And they had long realized that this could only be achieved by diplomacy. It was therefore through that channel that they sought to apply pressure to obtain these ends.

V

They also realized that merely negative policies would be insufficient to control the demand for Repeal and the discontent from which it sprang.

---

[83] F.J., 17 Jan. 1845.   [84] Cullen to Murray, 25 Jan. 1845, DDA.   [85] F.J., 11 Feb. 1845.
[86] Graham to Heytesbury, 18 Jan. 1845. Graham Papers. Graham remarked that there was a want of dignity and propriety about the publications which made official contact with Catholic prelates difficult and unsafe.

Positive and beneficent policies were needed to win over the sympathies of Irish Catholics—or at least detach the more respectable elements among them from what they regarded as dangerous agitation. Graham had advised Peel when O'Connell's monster meetings began to cause them concern that, while they could not yield to the threats or open violence of the Catholics, they should omit no opportunity 'of winning them to the state; of softening their resentments; of improving their Education; of reconciling their clergy'.[87] The first plank in this programme of palliative measures designed to wean the Catholics from Repeal was the Charitable Bequests Bill. It did anything, however, but soften resentments: it hardened them exceedingly.

In 1840 the bishops had petitioned the Lord Lieutenant to establish a new board of charitable bequests to replace the all-Protestant board that had managed all such bequests since the beginning of the century and which was empowered to decide how to apply them according to the intentions of the donor, if it deemed the actual directions of the donor 'inexpedient'.[88] The government was thereby given an opportunity to make a painless and uncontroversial concession to the Catholic community and reap some reward for its kindness. But it could scarcely have been more maladroit in its timing. O'Connell was sent to prison on 30 May and, though an appeal was lodged in the House of Lords, it seemed likely that he would spend a year in jail. The manner of his trial and sentence had exacerbated all the feelings of rage, disillusionment and contempt that had been excited by the banning of the monster meetings. Albion never appeared more perfidious to Irish Catholic eyes. Any government measure introduced at that time, however ameliorative its intent, was bound to be suspect. O'Connell himself introduced a bill in March 1844 to get around the difficulty which faced the Catholics of taking grants and conveyances in perpetuity. It would have given corporate status to the Catholic bishops and put them on the same legal footing as the bishops of the established church. But when O'Connell went to prison the bill was allowed to lapse.

The government brought in its own bill in the House of Lords in June 1844. By it a board of commissioners was to be set up, to consist of thirteen members, headed by three senior judges, and, of the ten other 'proper and discreet persons' who constituted its membership five were to be Catholics. All bequests left for charitable purposes were to come under

---

87. Graham to Peel, 18 June 1843, BL Add. MS 40448, ff 328r-331r.
88 Brady, 'Legal developments 1801-79' in N.H.I., V, 473.

its control; those which concerned Protestant charities were to be handled exclusively by the Protestant members, and those concerning Catholic charities by the Catholic members. These exclusively religious committees were also authorized to decide, in cases of legal difficulty, to which person donations or bequests should be made. Two clauses were destined to provoke intense hostility: religious orders, in accordance with the terms of the act of Catholic Emancipation were debarred from receiving any donation or bequest; and no donation or bequest for charitable purposes 'to create or convey any estate in lands, tenements or hereditaments' would be valid unless made at least three months before the testator's death. With slight amendments the bill was passed into law on 9 August 1844 and was to take effect from 1 January 1845.

O'Connell promptly denounced the bill in extravagant terms, singling out, as the clerical opponents of it were to do, the clauses relating to religious orders and to legacies of land made within three months of the testator's death. But his ultimate reason was a dislike of the possibility of the government breaking up the clerical-nationalist alliance by obtaining the cooperation of bishops for its policy.[89]

MacHale, Cantwell, and Bishop McGettigan of Raphoe, who had not sided with the *zelanti* on the national schools, met in Dublin before the end of the month to rally their colleagues against the act. They drew up a circular for the signatures of each bishop and his clergy in which they fiercely condemned the measure and pledged their full legal and constitutional opposition to it. They described the act as 'fraught with the worst consequences to Religion' and claimed that, if carried into effect, it would be certain to lead to the subjugation of the church to the temporal power. Instead of a concession it was 'a new penal law of the old leaven' forbidding the dying sinner to redeem his sins by the bequest of a single acre of landed property for any religious or charitable purpose. The act provided that Catholic commissioners, maybe even bishops, should execute the provisions of the penal clause of the Catholic Emancipation act against religious orders and that five Catholics, who might be laymen without practical religion or faith to recommend them, should judge matters vitally connected with Catholic doctrine and discipline. Should these commissioners be bishops, they would be interfering in spiritual matters belonging to the jurisdiction of other bishops and thereby flagrantly violating canon law. If the Catholic members were laymen, their nomination was to be viewed as 'a step towards the introduction of

---

[89] MacDonagh, 'Politics 1830-45' in N.H.I., V, 187.

faithless and interested politicians to tamper with the independence of our church, for the purpose of forwarding the anticatholic views of men in power and of promoting their own personal interests'. If bishops were to be appointed 'the novel project of selecting ministerial favourites from the hierarchy and honouring them with public distinctions, to the marked and offensive exclusion of others' was to be regarded as a means of creating divisions in their body and of destroying the confidence of their people by exposing them as recipients of place and patronage under the crown.[90]

The circular was eventually signed by MacHale, five bishops from the Tuam province (and by the vicar general of the diocese of Galway, which was then vacant), six other bishops—thirteen in all—and by some six hundred priests and was published in the press on 21 September. Crolly, Murray, Slattery and ten others did not sign it. Despite their reservations about the provisions of the new act, Crolly and Murray felt that it offered them much greater security than the existing arrangement and that it could be improved to give them greater satisfaction. Murray summed up this attitude when he wrote that 'the Wholly Protestant and bigotted Board of Charitable Bequests, under which we have been so long suffering . . . was most objectionable', and could alter the application of Catholic charities, whereas the new board, if the intention of the testator was clearly expressed, had no such power.[91] The *zelanti* were not prepared to tolerate the lesser of two evils. They could only see the faults of the act and they wanted nothing to do with it. To ensure its failure Rome would have to prevent bishops from acting as commissioners. O'Higgins writing from Dublin put this suggestion to Cullen:

If the Pope do not at once issue an *order* to each Bishop in Ireland forbidding him to correspond with the English Government on matters affecting directly or indirectly the Religion of the country without first obtaining the concurrence and opinions of his brother prelates the presumption, indiscretion, and dangerous weakness of a *few* will bring an open division among Bishops, priests and people, will give a barbarous triump [*sic*] to our enemies and utterly ruin Religion. Such an order cannot be issued too soon. It is the opinion of the priests even of this diocese [Dublin] and of all the priests, and vast majority of the Bishops of Ireland. Three or four stubborn or imprudent men ought not to be left the managers of a Catholic nation with such a country as England.[92]

The stubborn or imprudent men whom he particularly had in mind were Crolly and Murray.

---

[90] Copy of circular, 26 Aug. 1844, DCDA.
[91] Murray to Cullen, 7 Sept. 1844, AICR.
[92] O'Higgins to Cullen, 23 Sept 1844, Ibid.

Among those who signed the clerical protest was Paul Cullen, the rector of the Irish College in Rome. His opposition did not stop at that point: he translated the text of the bill into Italian and passed it on to Pope Gregory XVI. Gregory told him that he would never have approved of such a measure, had he been consulted about it. The cardinals to whom he showed it also regarded it as punitive. Cullen suggested to Murray that the act should be formally submitted to the pope for his consideration. His decision on it would save the church in Ireland from dissension.[93]

But before this advice reached him Murray had been contacted by the Lord Lieutenant about becoming a commissioner. The other names mentioned to him for that office were Crolly and Bishop Haly of Kildare.[94] Before committing himself to Heytesbury he wrote asking Crolly if he would also serve on the board 'as Your Grace's decision on this point would have much weight with me'.[95] But before the primate replied to him and to a request from A.R. Blake to join the board, the protest of the bishops and priests had hit the papers and he had been taken aback, not only by the intemperate language used, but also by the fear that some of its arguments would find a welcoming echo among many Catholics at home and in the congregation of Propaganda in Rome. He told Murray and Blake that he was unwilling to serve because of the imprudence of placing themselves in opposition to O'Connell and a majority of the bishops; the treatment of the regular clergy and possible Protestant interference with the bishops' authority; the danger that the act might lead on to a scheme for pensioning the clergy; the likelihood of the act being condemned at Rome on the basis of false evidence given by the protesters and of the Catholic commissioners being charged with executing a penal law against their brethren.[96] These comments were an accurate if painful forecast of the public reaction, of which he was later a victim.

The government was anxious to press on. Graham assured Heytesbury that both he and Peel were pleased with the prospect of their measure dividing the Catholics and establishing amicable relations between the state and 'the sound portion of the Roman Catholic Hierarchy and

[93] Cullen to Murray, 24 Oct. 1844, DDA. Cullen had already experienced the damaging consequences for obedience and discipline in religious orders due to the prohibition on holding property. He had passed on to Propaganda an account of a dispute among the Christian Brothers involving three Brothers who as trustees of the Institute acted independently of the superior general. (Cullen to Propaganda, 12 Feb. 1843, APF, SC (Irlanda), 28, ff 24r-27v.)

[94] Heytesbury to Graham, 20 Sept. 1844, Graham Papers.

[95] Murray to Crolly, 18 Sept. 1844, DCDA.

[96] Crolly to Murray, 23 Sept. 1844, quoted in Kerr, *Peel, Priests and Politics*, 142-3 and Heytesbury to Graham, 24 Sept. 1844, Graham Papers.

Priesthood'.[97] Both Blake and Murray advised Heytesbury to invite Crolly to Dublin, and Murray was confident that they could persuade the primate to change his mind. But Crolly, fearful of powerful episcopal opposition to the act, still refused. Accordingly, on Blake's advice, Eliot, the Chief Secretary, wrote begging him to reconsider and pointing out that the provisions to which the objections had been raised in the episcopal protest and which he presumed Crolly shared were not the malign penalties they had been depicted. He explained that the restriction on bequests of land within three months of the testator's death applied equally to Protestants, and was drawn up specifically to prevent 'an accumulation of lands in hands in which it would be inalienable' and had nothing to do with religion. No alteration had been made to the rights of religious orders and no intervention in the discipline of the church by the commissioners was envisaged. If claimants of a bequest were dissatisfied with the decision of the commissioners, they could challenge it in the court of chancery. Reminding him that the act went much further than the request of the prelates in 1840, he insisted that the willingness of the government to appoint three Catholic prelates as commissioners testified to the spirit of good will in which it was brought forward.[98]

Crolly was impressed by Eliot's arguments and answered that he was almost convinced that the objections of Rome and of his colleagues were founded on a mis-conception of the provisions of the act. He accepted the explanation about the bequests of land but thought the terms of the act would be felt more frequently by Catholics who usually bequeathed property shortly before death. Admitting that the position of the religious orders was unchanged, he still thought that Catholic commissioners would have to regard it as the continuation of a penal enactment on religious grounds and something which they could not, on conscientious grounds, carry into effect. He was also worried that bequests made with a view to promoting the Catholic religion would not meet with the approval of Protestant commissioners and that those with an anti-Catholic tendency could not be sanctioned by the Catholic commissioners. Nonetheless, he was convinced that the law was a conciliatory measure, and would be executed in a kind spirit, but he asked that appointments to the commission should not be made till after the bishops' meeting in November.[99]

97 Graham to Heytesbury, 22 Sept. 1844, Ibid.
98 Eliot to Crolly, 30 Sept. 1844, DCDA.
99 Crolly to Eliot (copy), 4 Oct. 1844, Graham Papers.

Eliot regarded Crolly's reply as far from unsatisfactory and Graham, on hearing about it, expressed his confidence that with patience and good management they would overcome the archbishop's 'coy reluctance'.[100] Eliot, accordingly, reassured the primate: a will charging lands to their full value with bequests for charitable purposes would be valid, though not made three months before the testator's death and the commissioners could not interfere with religious communities in any way, as they were not entitled to receive charitable donations or bequests. He agreed to await the bishops' meeting before appointing commissioners.[101] In doing so he had, of course, the approval of Peel and Graham, though the Home Secretary was not as hopeful as Eliot of a favourable decision from Crolly.[102]

Crolly was grateful for Eliot's agreement to his suggestions about deferring appointments, and he predicted that such 'conciliatory conduct' would make a favourable impression on the bishops so that after calm consideration of the measure they would feel the force of his kind and reasonable observations on the act. He informed Eliot that some landlords refused to grant sites to Catholic clergy for churches, cemeteries and national schools, thereby providing one of the causes of the complaints about the restrictions on the devising of lands. And he put to the Chief Secretary the difficulty facing a Catholic commissioner, if asked to take charge of a bequest made by a Protestant to induce poor Catholics to abandon their religion. He feared that that issue would be raised at the episcopal meeting and wanted to have an answer for it in advance.[103]

Eliot, too, must have been reassured by a description of Crolly that reached him from Bishop Kinsella of Ossory via Blake.[104] Kinsella had remarked that he was not surprised 'at the wavering of "our Brother at Armagh"' as that was not the first time he had done so. The implication for the government was that the archbishop could end up on the right side.

Similar criticisms of Crolly were to be made at the beginning of the dispute over the Queen's Colleges, but on both occasions they were much too sweeping. In the early stages of these disputes before he received clarification from the government he was somewhat unsure how to act, but once he received it, and made up his mind, he stuck firmly to his guns in spite of the ferocious pounding he received from his enemies.

[100] Eliot to Graham, 5 Oct., and Graham to Eliot, 10 Oct. 1844, Graham Papers.
[101] Eliot to Crolly, 12 Oct. 1844, DCDA.
[102] Graham to Peel, 8 Oct. 1844 and Peel to Graham, 9 Oct. 1844, Graham Papers.
[103] Crolly to Eliot (copy), 14 Oct. 1844, Graham Papers.
[104] Eliot to Graham, 16 Oct. 1844, Ibid.

While Heytesbury and Eliot were attempting to coax the primate into accepting office, more senior ministers were coming to the conclusion that they should be fighting their case against MacHale and his fellow-protesters at Rome. Graham was coming round to the view that they had found the right issue on which to open up communications with the papal court, one which was part temporal and part ecclesiastical and on which the bishops were divided. And since he believed that MacHale's emissaries were already on their way to Rome, he thought they should lose no time in laying the truth before the papal authorities and, perhaps, make use of a letter which Anthony Blake had promised to write in defence of the act.[105] Thomas Aubin, a secretary at the British legation at Florence, who had acted as an unofficial British agent at Rome, had died and William Petre, an English Catholic, whose religion sat lightly upon him, had offered to replace Aubin at the Holy See. Lord Aberdeen, the Foreign Secretary believed that Petre's nominal attachment to his faith would be advantageous, as he would cause little embarrassment, and Petre duly revealed his religious sentiments—or lack of them—by a remark he made to an official at the Foreign Office: 'I give you—a Protestant—perfect liberty to shoot any of my Irish Bishops'.[106] Petre's offer was accepted and he was bidden to hasten to the eternal city, and furnished with copies of letters from Graham and Heytesbury, Blake's explanations of how bequests had been previously administered and the memorial of the bishops in 1840. He was commissioned to explain the whole situation to the Cardinal Secretary of State and was further charged to liaise with Bishop Haly of Kildare, who was then in Rome and was believed to favour the act.[107]

Petre duly put his arguments to Cardinal Lambruschini, to an official at the Secrtariat of State and also to Cardinal Acton, a member of an old English Catholic family then serving in the curia, who promised to give any help in his power to the government.[108]

Lambruschini with the pope's authority then invited Acton to study the whole question and passed on to him the material which Petre had submitted about the background and details of the act as well as a generally hostile set of observations made by Cullen while the bill was going through parliament. Acton's analysis of the act, the reaction to it and its strengths and weaknesses was careful and thorough. He listed its

[105] Graham to Peel, 26 Sept. 1844, PRO, F.O. 43/38.
[106] Petre to G.L. Conyingham, 20 Oct. 1844, PRO, F.O. 43/55.
[107] Stratford Canning to Petre, 1, 7, 22 Oct. 1844, Ibid.
[108] Petre to Canning and Aberdeen, 19, 25, 28 Oct. 1844, Ibid.

shortcomings and disadvantages—those which its opponents stressed and even its supporters admitted—but he pointed out that it provided opportunities for the church to acquire property. He noted that the fourteen bishops who had protested were those who had for the most part supported political agitation, and he remarked that it was unreasonable to stir up public opinion as had been done without recognizing the improvement involved in the new law. However, he believed it was inexpedient to make a decision that could be regarded as a censure on the opinions and conduct of many people, both bishops and laity.[109]

And when a congregation of cardinals met on 24 November this was what it decided to do. The cardinals resolved not to pronounce a judgement on the issue as they had not been asked by the Irish bishops for a verdict, and to inform Petre accordingly. However, with the pope's authority a more formal response was prepared for the British agent and couched in diplomatic language to assuage his disappointment. He was assured that, though some of the regulations did not conform to canon law, the Holy See acknowledged the goodwill of the government towards the Catholics of Ireland. And it suggested that the government might make provision on two points: the position of the religious orders and the intervention of Protestant Commissioners in Catholic matters and vice versa. Reference was made to the meeting of the Catholic bishops then taking place in Ireland from which other reasons for cooperating or not with the government might emerge, but Petre was reminded that the Holy See would always give them counsels of peace.[110]

Though this document was not published as was the decision on the national schools, it favoured the views of the *politicanti*. And it meant that when the *zelanti* later called for tough measures against some of their colleagues they got no response. Petre was reasonably satisfied. He seemed to think that the Irish in Rome—presumably Cullen and his vice-rector—had anticipated a condemnation of the act, and that consequently they had lost.

By the time this verdict had been delivered the annual meeting of the bishops in Ireland had taken place. Crolly was most anxious to prevent a repetition of the struggle over national education which could not only lead to bitter acrimony among ecclesiastics but could also lead to a worsening of church-state relations, and Fransoni's letter offered him some kind of lifeline in his desire to avoid a bruising public quarrel. He probably knew that he could not close down all discussion on the subject

---

[109] Arch. SC AA. EE. SS. Pos. 46, Fasc. 18, ff 101r-120r.
[110] Ibid, ff 125r-126v and Petre to Canning and Aberdeen, 29, 30 Nov. 1844, PRO, F.O. 43/38.

by seeking to apply the letter to their immediate problem—though he was subsequently accused of attempting to do so—but he may have thought that he could use it to stop an adverse decision being publicized until the government was given time to make amendments in the act.

Twenty-two of the twenty-seven bishops were present at the meeting. Crolly produced Fransoni's letter counselling ecclesiastics to avoid inter-vention in secular affairs but, as the *zelanti* refused to accept it as a prohibition on discussing issues which, in their view, impinged on their spiritual responsiblities, they proceeded to condemn the act. Bishop Blake of Dromore, who had signed the protest, attempted to read letters which he had received from Cullen with adverse comments on the act, but Crolly, much to the annoyance of the MacHale group, ruled him out of order. MacHale proposed that the dispute be referred to Rome but claimed that the primate 'peremptorily refused', because he had already determined 'to take the fatal and obnoxious office'. His criticism of Crolly's alleged disrespect for Roman authority was scathing:

The Holy See has no right to be obliged to his Grace either for that step or for his rashness relative to the famous Rescript. His conduct was calculated to bring odium on the Holy See but the Reverence of the Irish Nation, clergy and people for the hallowed centre of Unity is too strong to be shaken by the imprudence of any individual.[111]

The angry discussions were interrupted by a visit of the four archbishops to the viceroy to beg for an increased grant for Maynooth. According to Heytesbury, Murray, after reading the official memorial from the bishops, went on to state that some alterations should be made with respect to the visitors of the college and that the trustees should be incorporated. MacHale angrily retorted that he would consent to no such changes and insisted that he spoke 'in the names of the bishops assembled in convocation', who had agreed to the petition on the express understanding that any additional money given should be granted unconditionally. He denied that a charter was necessary as the trustees already possessed sufficient powers. Crolly and Murray were obviously taken aback and annoyed at the prospect of losing much needed financial support because of what they regarded as MacHale's narrow-mindedness and unrealistic and unnecessary insistence on canonical rights, rejected his claims and an 'amusing altercation' ensued between them, with Slattery of Cashel staying silent, 'though evidently leaning in favour of' the archbishops of Armagh and Dublin. The viceroy eventually called the proceedings to a

---

[111] MacHale to Cullen, 4 Mar. 1845, AICR.

halt by agreeing to Murray's request that he present the memorial to the
government.[112]

However embarrassing the scene must have been for the archbishops of
Armagh, Dublin and Cashel, Graham saw an immediate opportunity in
the division evidenced by the 'unseemly conflict' of the hitherto united
churchmen in the presence of 'their great Protestant adversary'. He felt
that it had created an opening for the government, that it was one further
fissure in the Catholic-nationalist alliance.[113]

When the meeting resumed Crolly proposed and Bishop Egan of Kerry
seconded a resolution that each prelate should be free to make his own
decision according to his own conscience in regard to the Charitable
Bequests Act. This was the solution that Rome had found to the dispute
on the national schools, and was later to be suggested in the dispute over
the Queen's Colleges. On this occasion the motion was carried, as the
zelanti had been weakened by the departure of some of their members. It
was probably the happiest outcome that Crolly and Murray could have
expected, given the deep divisions in the episcopal body. But the press let
it be known that a majority of the prelates had opposed the Bequests Act.
The Nation listed eight bishops, headed by Crolly and Murray, who were
willing to accept it with the expectation of future amendments. Four
bishops were said to have neither signed the protest nor expressed an
opinion on it.[114] One of these was then in Rome and another was ill, but
the other two, Archbishop Slattery and Bishop McLaughlin of Derry,
were believed by the zelanti to favour their views. MacHale and fourteen
bishops opposed the act, either at the meeting or by signing the protest in
September. The zelanti who had only numbered ten in the dispute on the
national schools, had now reached seventeen. And, in fact, Bishop
Cantwell three months later claimed that all the waverers had joined them
making a total of nineteen. Of Crolly's eight suffragans, only two stood by
him. The bishops of Dromore, Derry and Raphoe had defected from the
politicanti and the zelanti had been strengthened by the adherence of the
bishop of Clogher, who had been appointed since the hierarchy had last
been split on a politico-religious issue.

The more extreme zelanti were outraged by the inconclusive result of
the meeting and the prospect of the archbishops of Armagh and Dublin
taking office as commissioners. They appealed to their Roman ally, Paul

---

[112] Heytesbury to Graham, 16 Nov. 1844, Graham Papers.
[113] Graham to Heytesbury, 19 Nov. 1844, Ibid.
[114] Nation, 23 Nov. 1844. Murray had assumed that Archbishop Slattery would rally to their side and was
surprised to discover that Slattery opposed the execution of the law. (Murray to Slattery, 30 Aug, 1, 3
Oct. 1844, Slattery Papers.)

Cullen, to use all his influence to ensure that this would not happen. MacHale contacted him immediately after their proceedings ended. He wanted Cardinal Fransoni to write a letter to every prelate forbidding him to become a member 'of such an uncanonical Board striking at the sacred rights of the Bishops and the Pope'. He then went on to accuse Crolly of inspiring the letter from Rome about ecclesiastics shunning secular affairs and of using it improperly to stifle debate at their meeting and prevent an appeal to the pope:

Such a letter would be more seasonable and useful than another document insidiously obtained for the purpose of crushing all discussion on the iniquitous act . . . On this occasion it was evidently procured nay extorted I am sure, by a malicious and calumniating importunity for the purpose of awing the Prelates. The Primate insisted that all the concerns of the bequest act were temporal concerns. The document in question recommends to the Bishops as well as all Ecclesiastics obedience to the temporal powers in civil matters. Ergo with the opinion of his Grace and were he judge we should not interfere in this concern nay nor leave it to the Pope for his decision.

He also accused Crolly of insincerity in his attitude to Rome for he forbade Blake from conveying the pope's views on the Bequests Act to the bishops, and added that throughout their meeting the primate was in close contact with Anthony Blake, 'one of the chief concoctors of this infamous Bill', whom the *zelanti* regarded as an untrustworthy and archetypal 'Castle Catholic'.[115]

Cantwell, MacHale's chief lieutenant, was equally scathing about Crolly's role, when he wrote a few days later:

Before these lines reach you, you will have read the afflicting detail of our proceedings at the meeting forwarded by the Archbishop of Tuam. He expressed the sentiments & fears of the great majority of the Irish Prelates; I am persuaded that some who in their heart abhor the Bequest act abstained from giving a full & candid expression of their just horror influenced by the working or [*sic*] Drs Crolly & Murray or from a reluctance to oppose them. Throughout the discussion both acted as if [they were] the paid advocates of the Government on the question. It was indeed painful to witness the part which they acted. The sound portion of the Clergy & Laity of all Ireland & particularly of Dublin are greatly excited and alarmed about it: you could hardly concieve [*sic*] the state of the public mind. Should one or two Prelates or Priests be so blind, as to accept a place on the Board of Commissioners, the consequences to Religion cannot fail to be most disastrous; yet I feel persuaded that the two Primates are resolved to accept office.

---

[115] MacHale to Cullen, 17 Nov. 1844, AICR.

He drew some consolation from the reports that O'Connell was again about to denounce the act, as he hoped that such an attack would frighten the two archbishops into abandoning their plans. Claiming that eight hundred acres that had been bequeathed as a charity to the diocese of Meath would be used by the Protestant board of commissioners to colonize the diocese of Meath with 'Protestants of the *right sort*', though he did not (and probably could not) explain how the board could possibly do this, he exasperatedly declared that 'it was difficult to concieve [*sic*] anything more monstrous than to have R.C. Prelates!!!! parties to such a sacrilegious confiscation'. Only the Holy See could save them from the scandal of being betrayed by the heads of their church and an order from Rome to bishops not to become members of a board and thereby assist their enemies to frustrate the benevolent intentions of pious testators was necessary to protect all their canonical rights as bishops.[116]

A few days later the archbishop of Tuam wrote directly to Cardinal Fransoni asking that the bishops be prohibited from becoming commissioners and in a letter to Cullen enclosed one addressed to the pope. This contained the same suggestion and was to be presented or substantively communicated to the pontiff at Cullen's discretion. MacHale's suspicion of the primate's intentions had become so intense that he even had the audacity to suggest that Crolly, Murray and their friends wanted to be dictators in the Irish Church:

It is rather curious and worthy of a jealous attention that the Primate and a few others who insisted that Rome has no right to adjudicate on the Bequests Bill should be so anxious to have the authority of Rome to put down public discussion. It is no wonder for then as Cobbet said they could become small political Popes in Ireland and soon alas would the Pope's authority be thrown over Board.[117]

Murray had borne the brunt of MacHale's assault on the system of national education but Crolly was given the major share of the blame for backing the government on the Bequests Act. Ironically, he was charged with having 'insidiously obtained' from Rome a letter which only brought him trouble and anxiety, and which did not at all cow the opponents of the act.

As a result of the meeting the two archbishops were free to join the board of commissioners. Both Crolly and Murray communicated their decision to do so to Heytesbury as soon as the meeting ended.[118] As Murray explained, the assurance given to the primate by the Lord

[116] Cantwell to Cullen, 20 Nov. 1844, Ibid.   [117] MacHale to Cullen, 26 Nov. 1844, Ibid.
[118] Heytesbury to Graham, 16 Nov. 1844, Graham Papers.

Lieutenant that three bishops and two laymen who enjoyed their confidence would be appointed to take charge 'of the interests of the Church and of the Poor' had eased their minds about accepting office.[119] As Haly was abroad, the bishop of Killaloe was approached to join Crolly and Murray as a third member of the board. He agreed but then bent before 'the violent storm' that was raised against him for doing so, and resigned. Crolly then asked his friend, Bishop Denvir, to join and Denvir agreed but asked that his name should not be published until after 15 December 1844, when he was due to host several prelates at the opening of St Malachy's Church in Belfast.[120] The government made a gesture to the Catholic community, and to Crolly and Murray in particular, by appointing Redmond Peter O'Carroll, a Catholic, secretary to the new board. O'Carroll was profuse in his gratitude to Crolly for helping him to obtain the post.[121] But such tokens of goodwill could not stem public anger. Murray had no doubt that reaction to the bishops becoming commissioners would be extremely hostile (the religious orders had already protested vigorously in Dublin); he was prepared for it and encouraged Crolly to brace himself to resist it with a clear conscience. Remarking that Crotty of Cloyne, who had not been present at the bishops' meeting in November, had summoned his clergy to consider the expediency of protesting against the act, he then quoted the archbishop of Cashel:

Dr Slattery trembles at the contemplation of the disunion which our acceptance of the Office of Commissioners will create. But this disunion is not our work; it began elsewhere, and the same means, which have produced it and are daily widening it more and more, will, if not checked, be had recourse to, whenever it may serve the purposes of agitation so to do.[122]

Together with the two archbishops of the established church, Sir Patrick Bellew, A.R. Blake, the dean of St Patrick's, the Presbyterian minister, P.S. Henry, and the earl of Donaghmore, their names were officially listed in the *Dublin Gazette* of 18 December. Even the manner of the Catholic bishops' designation caused controversy, for their sees were not mentioned, and nationalist papers were quick to contrast the lack of respect shown to them with the deference paid to Archbishops Beresford and

---

[119] Murray to Cullen, 20 Nov. 1844, Ibid.

[120] Crolly to Murray, 4 Dec. 1844. Kennedy to Crolly, 7 Dec. 1844, DDA. Crolly to Murray, 8 Dec. 1844, Graham Papers. Kennedy believed MacHale had intensified the storm by a 'foul insinuation' at a public meeting in Limerick. Apparently Dublin Castle had asked Crolly and Murray for their recommendations for lay Catholic representatives . They mentioned D.R. Pigot but he refused. (Pigot to Murray, 23 Nov. 1844, DDA.)

[121] Redmond O'Carroll to Crolly, 4 Dec. 1844, DCDA.

[122] Murray to Crolly, 10 Dec. 1844, DCDA.

Whately, Beresford being styled 'The Most Rev. John George, Lord Archbishop of Armagh, and Primate of All Ireland'. The *Freeman's Journal* pointed out that Crolly was simply designated 'Archbishop of— nowhere'.[123]

The ferocious criticism which the bishops had to endure for consenting to join the board took its toll of Crolly. The wife of the Liberal M.P. for Louth reported to Murray that when she met the primate he looked worried and quoted her husband as saying that he was not as accustomed to the warfare as the archbishop of Dublin.[124] Crolly complained to Murray about the 'outcry' from the friars (of whom there were three communities in Drogheda) and their claims that 'their properties and their lives were exposed to a direful persecution' by an enemy with which he was pledged to cooperate. Though he had met them with the mayor of Drogheda and felt that he had allayed their fears, 'the red-hot repealers' preferred the guidance of O'Connell.[125]

Murray duly explained his views and those of Crolly, Denvir and other defenders of the act in a pastoral which was published a few days later. Admitting that it had deplorable defects, he insisted that it was still 'a measure of substantial value'. He pointed out that the original clauses of the act had made provision for vesting property in the board for the use of 'Roman Catholic ministers of a district duly appointed thereto'. But when a general power was later granted of vesting property in the board for building any chapel or place of worship for Catholics, it was discovered that this provision would stretch the benefit of the act to religious orders 'and recourse was therefore had to the unfortunate expedient of excluding them by name'. But no new restriction was imposed on them and they were not subjected to any new disability. He hoped that since the attention of the government had been called to the unjust law by which the religious orders were penalized, it might restore them to the enjoyment of full civil rights. Though they were told how to circumvent the three months' clause, he still regretted the restrictions imposed by it. Despite conferring on the church 'advantages of the very highest value', 'denunciations of the most awful nature' had been poured out on those who had undertaken to carry it into effect and differences of opinion

[123] F.J., 19 Dec. 1844. Peel had decided in August that the archbishop of Dublin should be addressed as 'The Most Revd. *Archbishop* Murray'. Editorializing on the appointment of the commissioners the *Newry Examiner* said of Crolly: 'True, his Grace is not popular, for he has not identified himself with his countrymen, either in reference to Teetotalism, or in the grand movement for National Independence. We owe him (those of us who are his subjects) a dutiful allegiance in things lawful, and no more'. (N.Ex., 21 Dec. 1844.)
[124] Lady A. Bellew to Murray, 29 Dec. 1844, DDA.
[125] Crolly to Murray, 27 Dec. 1844, quoted in Kerr, *Peel, Priests and Politics*, 188

about it had been 'sometimes expressed in language, which charity would not sanction'.[126]

The episcopal commissioners must have been heartened by Cardinal Acton's letter to Murray at the end December 1844 which justified their presence on the board to prevent abuses of the law, and which, while reminding him of the need for Catholic members to ensure the full protection of the law for the bequests of Catholics, without infringing any bishop's individual jurisdiction, praised the decision of the prelates to allow each of them to follow the dictates of his conscience in relation to the act.[127]

The one group to which the decision of Crolly, Murray and Denvir gave pleasure was the government. Lord Eliot described their acceptance of office as 'a great step towards an alliance between the R.C. Church & the Govt'. He believed they had broken the existing party bonds thereby making the distinction between parties in Ireland as in England political and not religious. O'Connell had coaxed and menaced the most esteemed prelates of the Catholic church but Crolly and Murray had resisted 'his threats & his cajoleries'.[128] Graham hailed their success against the opposition of O'Connell and MacHale as 'a signal triumph' and was delighted with their achievement in creating 'a serious division in the Heart of the R. Catholic Church' in Ireland.[129] The cabinet instructed Petre to inform the Roman authorities that the prelates' cooperation was due in great measure 'to the wise and conciliatory counsels lately addressed by the Pope to the Roman Catholic Clergy in Ireland'. But while these prelates were undoubtedly influenced by the rescript inculcating peace and obedience to the constituted authorities of the realm, a powerful body represented by MacHale and O'Connell had rejected the advice of the pope and had repudiated all cooperation with the state, even in measures adopted for the good of the Catholic community. Petre was commissioned to let the Cardinal Secretary of State know that the party which opposed the act was not motivated by religious considerations for, if the act had damaged religious interests, the prelates would not have passed the resolution permitting each to respond to it according to the dictates of conscience. Should the democratic principle prevail over ecclesiastical authority in Ireland, the effects would spread elsewhere and Rome was asked to consider whether it would not be in its own interests

---

[126] F.J., 23 Dec. 1844.
[127] Acton to Murray, 31 Dec. 1844, DDA.
[128] Eliot to Heytesbury, 19 Dec. 1844, BL Add. MS 40479, ff 211r–214r.
[129] Graham to Stanley, 22 Dec. 1844, Graham Papers.

to give public support to the prelates who had obeyed its counsels and thereby encourage others to behave in the same way.[130]

Out of gratitude to the three bishops, and as an implicit rebuke to the opponents of its legislation, the government wanted the Holy See to address a public letter of approval to Crolly, Murray and Denvir.[131] This would have run counter to Rome's custom of minimizing division and restoring harmony where it had been broken, and Cardinal Lambruschini refused.

Archbishop Murray's attempts to restore harmony or at least to put an end to criticism being expressed 'in language that charity would not sanction' were doomed to failure. The violation of charity became much greater after the gazetting of the bishops as commissioners. In Belfast a huge meeting, attended by virtually all the prominent Catholics of the town, was held on 4 January 1845 to protest at the 'iniquitous measure'. Resolutions were passed deploring Bishop Denvir's adoption of the ill-advised course of allowing himself 'to be nominated a Commissioner, for carrying into effect the provisions of that very objectionable anti-Catholic enactment' and refusing to place confidence in any Catholic, lay or clerical, who would undertake to execute the provisions of the act. The mention of Crolly's name by the chairman was greeted with hisses and groans. A speaker regretted the primate's separation from the Catholics of Belfast, whom he had been wont to eulogize, attributed it in a humorous pun to 'a want of grace' and referred to his hopes that 'nothing would ever have occurred to mar or eclipse the splendid career of Dr Crolly—but, he had left them, and, as a necessary consequence, he had no further claim upon them'. Another speaker blamed Crolly for misleading Denvir, accused him of holding Conservative principles, charged him with taking 'the opposite side to the Liberator on every question in which the rights and liberties of Irishmen were concerned', and was greeted with cries of 'shame' when he claimed that the primate not only absented himself from the great Repeal meeting at Dundalk but arranged a clerical conference for the same day to prevent his clergy from attending.[132] Other protests were held in Down and Connor, in many other dioceses[133] and—what must

---

[130] Aberdeen to Petre, 28 Dec. 1844, PRO, F.O. 43/38.

[131] Petre to Aberdeen, 15 Jan. 1845. BL Add. MS. 43157.

[132] V., 8 Jan. 1845. N.W., 11 Jan. 1845.

[133] The priests of Derry diocese issued an address to Crolly, Murray and Denvir in which they accused them of 'most injudicious' behaviour in opposition to the conscientious convictions of a large majority of their colleagues, and of having given scandal to the pious and pleased the enemies of their faith. (N. Ex., 29 Jan. 1845.)

have been most painful to Crolly—in several parishes in Armagh.[134] A public dinner was given to Patrick Quinn, the parish priest of Kilmore, partly to express approval for his public letter against the Bequests Act and several of the Armagh clergy either attended or sent letters of support to the guest. Quinn explained that he obeyed his bishop in spiritual affairs but was not obliged to do so in temporal matters and, though he regarded Crolly's virtues as being beyond any praise he could bestow, yet when he saw his spiritual superior

willing and ready to become an unsuspecting but efficient instrument in the hands of designing men—when I saw him become a state officer, assisting to carry out the effects of a penal law levelled against another portion of the clergy—it was when I saw him a party in executing a law which says, in language not to be misunderstood, that bishops and priests tamper with the dying penitent for their own sordid purposes— when I found him officiating under a parliamentary act that goes to dry up at once the springs of charity—it was then, and not till then, that I felt called on to warn him of the impending danger through the instrumentality of my feeble pen; and that, too, when private remonstrance proved unavailing.[135]

The most brutal and wounding comments on the archbishop were made at a rally in the grounds of the church at Eglish in Co. Tyrone. Patrick Mallon, the chairman, declared that the act had been passed specifically to create division between clergy and laity. It was to be expected, he claimed, that through the influence of their hitherto respected primate the clergy and people were to be muzzled and deterred from expressing their abhorrence of their intolerable grievances. He suggested that the act was but the fore-runner of other measures such as the pensioning of the clergy, which would stifle the breath of independence and keep the people of Ireland in everlasting thraldom. Asking rhetorically who would not complain and be dissatisfied with the archbishop's opposition to O'Connell and to Fr Mathew, his suspicious acceptance of Castle honours and smiles, and government appointments, he wondered how any Catholic bishop or archbishop could associate with those who had sworn that their sacred faith was damnable and idolatrous. Then, letting his imagination rove to the heroism of the seventeenth century martyred archbishop of Armagh, and his indignation reach a climax of bewilderment and pain, he exclaimed:

---

[134] The *Drogheda Argus* declared in an editorial on 11 Jan. 1845: '. . . it is our duty to tell these exalted prelates [the commissioners] that their connection with this act has robbed them of that confidence, that love, and that respect which are essentially necessary to their usefulness as teachers and as ministers of the religion of a crucified Redeemer'.

[135] V. 11 Jan. 1845.

Oh, faithful sainted Plunkett! you who confronted the bloody persecutors of our holy principles, and yielded up your life for your faith; how must your spirit be troubled to behold one of your successors in the see of Armagh cajoled and deceived into the adoption of a course of conduct fraught with such dangerous consequence to that faith for which you endured the tortures of martyrdom (sensation).[136]

The opponents of the Bequests Act claimed that more than 1,500 priests signed protests against it. And when a call went out from a group of lay people in Dublin to the bishops to meet and repudiate the Bequests Act and other threats to the liberty of the church, most of those who replied did not mince their words in denouncing the act. Several remarked that only the primate could summon them and thereby placed the responsibility for refusing to do so on his shoulders. MacHale went further; he insisted that such a meeting was desirable, if not absolutely necessary, and went on to put the three episcopal commissioners in the dock by saying that, if they resigned office and if no bishops were connected with the government, there would be no differences among the prelates.[137] But without the primate's authorization there could be no episcopal meeting, and there was no precedent to justify calling one. The public meetings ceased after a few months but the press continued to carry hostile and hurtful comment on the three episcopal commissioners for much longer. Not untypical of this comment was the editorial in the *Newry Examiner* in September 1845. Having animadverted in a caustic manner on a favourable remark by Crolly on the government, it reminded its readers that he and two other prelates had undertaken 'the odious responsibilities of an office, in the discharge of whose functions the most learned of his brethren declare it impossible for him to avoid violating the canon law of his church'. And it inquired cynically if the destitution of the peasantry was less pinching because Murray and Crolly were styled archbishops in the *Dublin Gazette*.[138]

In private Crolly's episcopal opponents were no less searing in their criticism. Writing to Paul Cullen shortly after the names of the commissioners were published, MacHale referred to 'the grief and astonishment and indignation which this sad intelligence has spread throughout all Ireland'. Since the measure had been so widely condemned by all classes of Catholics, he could only bemoan 'the unaccountable and infatuated

---

[136] N.Ex., 22 Jan. 1845.

[137] *Battersby's Registry for the Catholic World* (1846), 408-18.

[138] N.Ex., 6 Sept. 1845. O'Connell pointed out that no meeting was held in any part of Ireland by laymen favourable to the act. He advised the laity of the dioceses where bishops had accepted office to implore them to abandon the commission. A meeting was called for the church of Dundalk without the consent of the parish priest.

wilfulness of any Prelates lending themselves to carry out such a persecuting law in defiance of the wishes of their Brethren'. If the pope did not vindicate his authority, it would soon become feeble. The resolution at their annual meeting was not interpreted by anyone as affording approval for any bishop to become a commissioner, and a notice to that effect had been recorded at some prelates' request in the minute book. If two or three of their number were to take it on themselves to disregard the feelings and sentiments of their brethren, MacHale wondered, what was to prevent others from following that terrible example and bargaining with the government about a state pension for the clergy or surrendering to whatever schemes of enslavement their enemies might put forward.[139]

The bishop of Meath maintained that Crolly, Murray and Denvir would never be reestablished in the confidence or affection of their people until they resigned office and he argued further that the evil of disharmony between bishops, priests and people existed only in the dioceses of the bishops who became commissioners or who took a prominent part in supporting them. But he hoped that the three prelates would retire since the government had made it clear that it did not intend to repeal the clauses that the bishops regarded as objectionable. But, lest they did not, he begged Cullen 'to work *incessantly*' to secure their withdrawal. He could only trust that God would open their eyes 'to a proper view of their deplorable position'. Their attitudes represented but a small minority of the Irish church: 'there is only one opinion & one feeling with 19 Prelates all the clergy & (except a *few* bad or Aristocratic Catholics) all the Laity of Ireland'.[140]

Cantwell was later believed to have instructed his priests to refuse the sacraments to those who took office under the commission, but he publicly denied this accusation in a letter to a newspaper.[141] Edmund O'Reilly, a professor in Maynooth, complaining about this alleged action in a letter to Rome reported that the secretary of the board of commissioners, a committed Catholic, had refused an invitation to spend a few weeks in the Meath diocese, rather than suffer that deprivation. O'Reilly, a moderate and detached observer of the Irish ecclesiastical scene, doubtless summed up the detrimental consequences of the dispute over

---

[139] MacHale to Cullen, 21 Dec. 1844, AICR.
[140] Cantwell to Cullen, 25 Feb. 1845, AICR. In his formal report on his diocese submitted to Rome in December, Cantwell inveighed against the unholy alliance between the successors of the Apostles and the enemies of the faith which had continued to afflict and scandalize Irish Catholics. (Cantwell to Cullen, 19 Dec. 1845, Ibid.)
[141] P., 3 Mar. 1845.

the Charitable Bequests Act and the reaction to Fransoni's rescript with accuracy when he wrote:

The bequests Bill has played the deuce with the Irish church, *i.e.* not precisely the *Bill*, but the agitation against it, which is likely I fear to do more harm than any dozen acts of Parliament. We have now the laity dictating to the clergy, & both to the Bishops. Chapels are (partially) deserted, & priests will in some places not be listened to when they attempt to *exculpate* the highest authorities of the Irish Church. . . The Church of Ireland is in a most critical position. Its bonds of union, & of subordination are much shaken. Rome requires to act at this moment with consummate *religious policy*, to keep things from getting worse, & if possible to make them better.[142]

Crolly and Murray never contemplated resignation but they did wish to meet their colleagues' objections to the act as far as they could. They therefore sought and obtained an interview with Heytesbury to lay before him suggestions made by A.R. Blake for alterations that could 'remove some of that reproach & obloquy to which they had been exposed & of enabling them to reconcile themselves with those of their co-religionists, whose opposition was really of a conscientious and not of a political nature'. They wanted the proviso which referred to religious orders excluded so that those orders would be left in the same position as they had been before the act was passed. Blake had suggested that, rather than have the commissioners decide what bishop or priest was entitled to a legacy, this should devolve on the elected visitors of Maynooth who happened to be Crolly, Murray and Lord Fingall. The prelates sought a relaxation of the rule about three months elapsing between the will and the testator's death for the bequest to be valid so that sites might be bequeathed for hospitals, schools, glebe houses or churches. Heytesbury was glad to report that the archbishops believed that opposition to the act was subsiding and would become insignificant, if their proposals were adopted. He also noted that neither showed any sign of being intimidated and that both paid tribute to the fair and liberal conduct of their Protestant fellow-commissioners.[143] Graham in a memorandum to the cabinet agreed that, while they should not yield to the importunate demands of the Catholics, nonetheless they should in the wake of their victory show magnanimity to their friends in the hierarchy. They had created a division among the bishops, 'severed from Mr O'Connell and his Repeal Party the most respectable of the Archbishops' and they ought therefore to oblige those prelates who were willing to cooperate with state

---

[142] O'Reilly to Cullen, 21 Jan. 1845, Ibid.
[143] Heytesbury to Graham, 9 Mar. 1845, Graham Papers.

policy by giving them the amendments they sought, which were neither unreasonable nor unjust.[144] But Peel was reluctant to make changes while passions in Britain were running strong about the Maynooth grant.

O'Connell caused further embarrassment to the three episcopal commissioners when he quoted them in parliament as having agreed that the act was inconsistent with the canons of the church. Murray was forced to rebuke him in a public letter and to assure him that the three prelates intended to continue in office so that they could serve the poor and protect the rights of the church.[145]

Under pressure from the *zelanti* the bishops agreed after an 'exceedingly stormy' discussion at their annual meeting in November 1846 to petition the government for changes in the act. They asked that the four archbishops should be given a right *ex officio* to serve as commissioners on the Board of Charitable Bequests. They also requested that the certificate of the bishop or his delegate should be sufficient evidence for commissioners when deciding the legitimate recipient of a will—a practice which had already been observed—and that the clause about devising lands within three months of death be repealed.[146] But it was a clause begging that the Catholic commissioners would not be compelled to carry out bequests for purely Protestant purposes that caused most division among the prelates. According to Bishop Maginn, the *zelanti* insisted on having that requirement inserted but met strong opposition from Crolly 'to the great astonishment of your humble servant, who could not conceive how any Catholic bishop could feel uneasy at the prospect of being relieved from such a painful and uncatholic obligation'. Crolly probably felt that the proposal did not need the force of law and to ask for it was superfluous. He obtained some compensation for the friction which the incident provoked by the return of McGettigan to the camp of the *politicanti* 'with all the new born zeal of a renegade'. A petition to this effect was duly presented by O'Connell.[147] However, no action was taken and at the bishops' request the same concessions were later sought by John O'Connell.[148]

These appeals for change represented a climb-down by the *zelanti*. Hitherto they had demanded that the act be opposed completely; any acceptance of it, however altered, was a defeat.

[144] Memorandum to cabinet, 23 Mar. 1845, Ibid.
[145] F.J., 4 Aug. 1845.
[146] Ibid., 16 Nov. 1846.
[147] Maginn to Cullen, 3 Dec. 1846, AICR; F.J. 13 Feb. 1847.
[148] Ibid., 3 Dec. 1847.

The intense public agitation against the act had died down before these alterations were sought. Other issues of greater significance drew attention away from the Bequests Act. But while it lasted the convulsion caused by the great and numerous protests could not but have shaken the episcopal commissioners. All they were attempting to do was to operate a system which they believed offered real benefits to the church, had few drawbacks and was much better than the previous one. But for their pains, all they got in return was public abuse deriving from misunderstanding of the true purpose and scope of the act—Murray and Kinsella both wondered if their opponents had actually read it—or from a refusal to accept that the government's attempt to meet Catholic grievances, even if not as generous as it could have been, was at least sincere and right-minded. And the government might have taken the opportunity presented by the legislation to accord to religious orders the same legal rights as the diocesan clergy enjoyed, but it was afraid of arousing atavistic fears about Jesuit power and influence. That step would at least have minimized the distrust of its intentions on which the *zelanti* fed.

Bishop Browne of Kilmore, a moderate whose sympathies lay with Crolly and Murray, summed up what their friends must have thought of the brouhaha:

I need not tell you that I have been disgusted not so much by the agitation as by its manner. Oh Sir it was shocking to see ignorant Priests mocking and ridiculing our most learned and venerable Bishops, and it was still more afflicting to witness the presumptuous arrogance of laymen without religion in Theory much less in practice passing themselves off as the only Defenders of the Faith.[149]

Edmund O'Reilly, of Maynooth, aptly described the consequences of the division there when he observed that MacHale's party appeared 'to act in a factious spirit at times' and that those who wished to promote the interests of the college were obliged to resist that 'mischievous' group and 'stand together with Dr Murray'.[150] Ironically, the increased grant to Maynooth did not exacerbate this clerical division; but the legislation for the expansion of higher education certainly did.

[149] Browne to Cullen, 10 Mar. 1845, AICR.
[150] O'Reilly to Cullen, 11 Dec. 1844, Ibid.

VI

Though Peel's government was vexed by the controversy provoked by the Charitable Bequests Act and disappointed with what it regarded as the ungrateful response of the Catholic church, it was not deterred from pushing on with other measures designed to entice Repealers away from O'Connell. The temptation to buy the silence if not the favour of the Catholic clergy, long recognized as extremely influential local leaders in O'Connell's movement, appealed to the cabinet. It may have regarded the power of the clergy with distaste and contempt but it realized that clerical authority was a force not to be ignored. Heytesbury described it as 'pernicious & almost unlimited'.[151]

The bishops afforded the government an opportunity to make a concession to the church by appealing in 1841 and subsequently for an increase to the Maynooth grant. Despite the increasing Catholic population and the pressing need for more priests, financial problems by 1840 forced a reduction of the free places available to students and a shortening of the academic course. As early as 1842 Eliot believed that the government should take steps to enable it to conciliate the Catholics by increasing the grant to Maynooth, but Peel was reluctant to arouse religious passions. Eliot, however, persisted in seeking help, passed on to Peel the arguments advanced by the trustees of Maynooth in their renewed petition of November 1842, namely, the need for more priests for an increasing population, the debt of the college and the need to reduce the courses for students, and concluded that even the civil consequences of leaving the Catholic people with uneducated pastors or without any at all suggested the need for action.[152]

However committed to letting sleeping dogs lie Peel may have been in 1842, the trauma of the Repeal year spurred him to a reconsideration and acceptance of Eliot's proposals. In a memorandum to the cabinet in February 1844 he argued that the time was ripe to detach 'from the Ranks of Agitation and Repeal' a considerable portion of moderate Roman Catholics, and he reckoned that one way to do this was to increase the Maynooth grant. The shortage of places and the poverty of the facilities there ensured that the priests who left its halls were embittered, hostile to the state and ready to campaign against the government.[153] Graham, too, took a sympathetic view of the need for a bigger grant. He explained that:

---

[151] Heytesbury to Peel, 5 Aug. 1844, BL Add. MS 40479, ff 19r-21v.
[152] Eliot to Peel, 18 Nov. 1842, Ibid. 40480, ff 149r-153r.
[153] Peel's memorandum, Feb. 1844, Ibid. 40540, ff 40r-55r.

the professors are poor and ill-paid; the scholars are ill-clothed and ill-fed; the buildings are ill-kept and ill-furnished; and so far from gratitude to the state being felt and acknowledged, the state is condemned as contributing aid with a niggard hand.

He concluded that money spent on Maynooth was a good investment:

I know not how even a large sum could be more prudently risked than in the hope of winning to the State the young priests about to be sent forth as the future guides of the great majority of the people of Ireland.[154]

As the cabinet groped its way towards an accommodation with the Catholics in the autumn of 1844, it considered the possibility of linking a better endowed Maynooth with the university colleges which it contemplated establishing. Heytesbury was instructed by Graham to communicate these intentions to the Catholic leaders Crolly and Murray and to sound them out on ways in which Protestant prejudices about the college (the objections to the constitution of the visiting body and the secrecy of the system of education) could be removed and, if possible, how it might be integrated into a new university system. He was also advised to have A.R. Blake prepare the prelates beforehand for a communication on the whole question.[155] Discussions took place between the cabinet and the Lord Lieutenant about the right of a Catholic faculty to grant degrees in divinity. Graham rejected this suggestion as too controversial but instructed Heytesbury to sound out Crolly and Murray about Maynooth students graduating in Arts at the proposed new colleges and contending for honours with lay students. He wanted to know what the two archbishops would accept and reject.[156]

Eventually, the cabinet settled for an increased endowment without any new or burdensome conditions, based on the suggestions submitted by Blake. £30,000 was put aside for capital expenditure and the annual grant was trebled to £26,360. New buildings were to be erected and older parts refurbished. The trustees were incorporated and empowered to hold property. This provided for 500 free places in addition to substantial pay rises for the professors. The system of visitation was left virtually unchanged—the crown being empowered to replace the five judges who had been visitors by any five people whom it chose. MacHale's fear about the threat of interference in the control of the college, which had led to the altercation with his colleagues in the presence of the viceroy, was not

---

[154] Graham's memorandum on Maynooth, 16 Nov. 1844, Derby Papers 37/1.
[155] Graham to Heytesbury, 30 Nov. 1844, Graham Papers.
[156] Graham to Heytesbury, 9 Dec. 1844, Ibid.

realized. Despite Protestant opposition in parliament the bill passed into law in June 1845.

Ironically, MacHale and his party, who were so quick to see evil Machiavellian designs in British legislation, did not detect any such in this grant. It was left to zealous Protestants both in Britain and Ireland to fight the case aganist the grant. Yet, the government's aim, at least in part, was the same as that of pensioning the clergy, which always drew a bitterly hostile response from the hierarchy. It was to attach the church, if possible, to the state and thereby diminish clerical sponsorship of hostile political movements. While Cantwell believed that the grant resulted from the prudent political agitation against the Charitable Bequests Act, Crolly and Murray simply regarded it as a generous and overdue gesture of conciliation, and were duly grateful. The church badly needed the money and in providing it the government was both helping the Catholic community and compensating it for its contribution to the upkeep of the established church.

VII

Two other means of controlling the clergy and of reducing their influence with their people had long been mooted from time to time in government circles: payment of the priests and some kind of understanding with Rome. At their annual meetings in 1834, 1836 and 1841 the bishops rejected any suggestion of a state pension. In 1837 Crolly adverted to this threat in uncharacteristically strong language. After defending the record of the priests in championing their peoples' rights and promoting good will, he went on to explain in detail why the threat of state payment for them was so objectionable:

This would be, perhaps, of all other species of persecution, the most unfortunate—the one most effectively calculated to disturb the peace and injure the interests of the country, and the one which would ultimately be the most fatal blow to the cause of our holy religion (hear). Is it that we are wanting in loyalty, and that it is deemed expedient to attempt the establishment of such a system? No; we are ready to shed our dearest blood in support of the throne (loud applause). Is it that we are wanting in charity to our brethren? Oh! no; the people who surround us at our altars will bear testimony to the readiness with which the clergy are ever willing to stretch forth the hand of relief to those who need their assistance (hear, hear). Is it, I ask, that we make any attempt to trample upon the religious opinions of any sect or portion of our fellow-men? No—I answer emphatically, no. Who will deny that we are ever ready to give to others—to extend to every man the right of conscience, and the freedom of that soul, which shows man there is a God he ought to adore, and to allow to every human being who differs from us on principle, the liberty of choosing the means by which he best thinks that God should be worshipped (Loud cheers).

He concluded with the assurance that the clergy were united 'in declaring their abhorrence of so michievious a measure'.[157]

Rumours that the government harboured plans to buy the silence and acquiescence of the clergy by means of payment continued to cause intense annoyance to the *zelanti* but they troubled the other bishops as well. At their annual meeting in November 1845 the prelates publicized a resolution, which Crolly had proposed four years previously, that Murray be instructed to call a special meeting of the hierarchy if he had 'clear proof or well-grounded apprehensions that the odious and alarming scheme of a state provision for the clergy . . . shall be contemplated', together with their actual resolution recording their strongest reprobation of such a move and their determination to resist a measure so fraught with mischief to the independence and purity of religion.[158]

The lull in British diplomatic activity for most of 1845 was broken by the condemnation of the Colleges Act by a majority of the bishops in November 1845, and Petre applied his skills to winning a favourable verdict from Rome for the minority which was prepared to go along with the government's plans. Before a decision was reached on this question the Tory party had lost office but their Whig successors pursued the same educational policies.

Rumours about British intrigues to secure a firmer foothold at Rome, though officially denied in 1845, continued to surface from time to time. To the *zelanti* the only purpose behind such moves was the enslavement of the Irish church. In January 1847 Slattery told Cullen about reports that had reached him 'that Diplomatic arrangements equivalent to Concordat, Veto etc are nearly arranged—that Scotch Ecclesiastics, Colonial Bishops & many others', who included members of parliament and peers, had been involved and had worked so skilfully and secretly that he (Cullen) had not heard of the intrigues.[159] While most of this was unfounded scaremongering, it was true that the government was taking diplomatic steps to persuade the pope to intervene on its behalf in Ireland. The British ambassador in Vienna told the papal nuncio that his government would be grateful for a pastoral letter or allocution from the Holy See directing the Irish clergy to exhort their people to live in peace, to forget their animosities and to confide in its good intentions to succour

[157] D.A., 21 Jan. 1837.   [158] F.J. 21 Nov. 1845.   [159] Slattery to Cullen, 31 Jan 1847, AICR.

and protect them. The nuncio was most receptive to this proposal and Lord Ponsonby, the ambassador, reported optimistically that the pope's response would encourage Catholics to be loyal to the crown, might even admonish the turbulent prelates and 'be a covert disapprobation of Repeal'.[160] The pope's exhortation, which was enclosed in the covering letter sent to the archbishops, when transmitting a copy of his appeal to the bishops of the whole church for help for Ireland during the famine, was much less extensive than the nuncio had predicted. Pius IX expressed the hope that circumstances in Ireland would permit the execution of the measures which the queen had proposed, and explained that nothing could contribute more quickly and effectively to the realization of this hope than that clergy and people would promote harmony and regulate their behaviour according to the laws of God and the church.[161]

A few months later Britain was forced to extend her diplomatic activity in Italy to embrace issues far wider than Irish ecclesiastical problems. When threats of upheavals in the Italian states in 1847 and the possibility of other European powers fishing successfully in those troubled waters arose, British concerns were awakened. In particular, the government was frightened of French ambitions to control Spain through a dynastic marriage alliance, and in its quest for allies against France and Russia directed its gaze towards Italy and Switzerland, hoping also to help guide the Italian and Swiss states towards reform and democracy. When the Austrians crossed the Po and entered the papal city of Ferrara, Pius asked Bishop Nicholas Wiseman, the pro-vicar apostolic of the London district, who was then in Rome, to return to London and seek the help of his government. Wiseman left a memorandum for Palmerston in which he urged British support for the pope and his reforms, and in which he pointed out that an accredited agent from the government could influence the situation in Italy. Palmerston acted quickly and within a week, Lord Minto, the Lord Privy Seal and son-in-law of the prime minister, was commissioned on 16 September to go as minister plenipotentiary to Italy.[162]

Minto duly contacted the governments at Florence and Turin, encouraged the foundation of a commercial league in the north of Italy and reached Rome in October 1847. Palmerston, the Foreign Secretary, who was also his cousin, wrote to advise him to persuade the pope to withdraw the Jesuits from Switzerland, and, as a mark of gratitude for Britain's

---

[160] Ponsonby to Lord John Russell, 21 Mar 1847, PRO, 30/22/6B, ff 320r-321v.
[161] Pius IX to Murray, 10 Apr. 1847, DDA.
[162] Ward, *Life and Times of Cardinal Wiseman*, i, 475-86.

forestalling Austrian intervention in his territories, to exert his authority to induce the Irish priesthood to abstain from meddling in politics, confine themselves to their spiritual duties, exhort their flocks to obedience and abstinence from acts of violence and crime and to inculcate in them the propriety of obeying the law and of carrying out their duties as citizens. He did not favour the suggestion of the Lord Lieutenant that the pope should be invited to send a confidential agent to Ireland, as he feared that such an emmissary might be influenced by MacHale and produce reports that would only add to their difficulties. Claiming that the papal condemnation of the Queen's Colleges was an ungrateful return, explained only by the supposition that it had been extorted by intrigue and false representations by the archbishop of Tuam, he told Minto to let the pope know that such behaviour created a bad impression on public opinion in England and might make it impossible for them to obtain that consent of parliament which was necessary to establish diplomatic relations between Rome and London.[163]

The Whig government had obviously come to the conclusion that the establishment of diplomatic relations with Rome could help it act as a power broker in Italy and might be exploited to enable it to use papal authority over the Irish church for its own political ends. Minto would have been appraised of this intention before his departure. Significantly, this was the first issue to which he referred in his first despatch from Rome to Palmerston in which he claimed that the pope had expressed a keen desire for the establishment of diplomatic relations. The pope, he noted, objected when he suggested that the English court might expect the Holy See to be represented by a layman. And Minto concluded that the pope would prefer not to be represented in London, unless his representative was a churchman. But Minto's claim that the pope described the rescript condemning the Colleges Act as 'an unfortunate and most ill-timed measure' seems excessive.[164] Cullen probably came much closer to the truth when he informed MacHale that Minto and his English friends had persuaded 'many of the Romans that the Pope's decision gave the greatest offence to the Irish people, and that the Pope ought to modify his Rescript in order to please Ireland'.[165] When Minto tried to get the pope to withdraw the condemnation of the Colleges, he met with 'a blunt refusal'.[166] And Minto's credibility as a diplomat was

[163] Palmerston to Minto, 29 Oct. 1847 in Curato, *Documenti della missione Minto*, i, 128-30.
[164] Minto to Palmerston, 14 Nov. 1847, Ibid., 190-94.
[165] Cullen to MacHale, 28 Jan. 1848, in O'Reilly, *MacHale* ii, 110-13.
[166] Cullen to Slattery, 27 Jan. 1848, Slattery Papers.

called into question when he joined in the shouts of the Roman mob for the independence of Italy.

The English press began to speculate on formal diplomatic relations between the courts of Rome and St James. In the House of Commons Palmerston assured Sir Robert Inglis that Minto enjoyed no official status in Rome, that he was not empowered or instructed to negotiate any agreement with the authorities there and that the legality of the exchange of diplomatic relations was unclear because of the prohibition on the Crown having communion with the Court of Rome.[167] Lord Lansdowne in the House of Lords explained that Minto had gone to offer friendly advice to Italian states which were undergoing the throes of reform and by his temperate counsel help prevent a 'disposition to excess'. He was accredited to all those states except the one which was debarred from receiving representation of that kind, and Lansdowne went on to claim that official contact with the papal states would be most helpful and useful to the government.[168] And some leading Catholics in England, especially Lord Shrewsbury, who was very critical of the nationalist bishops and clergy of Ireland, and his high ranking ecclesiastical friend, Bishop Wiseman, the pro-vicar apostolic of the London district, who believed that the church in England would gain stature by such recognition, held the same views.[169]

Minto, indeed, had not been idle and had sent back reports of his conversations with the pope and the Cardinal Secretary of State about Roman reactions to Irish ecclesiastical activities, which doubtless pleased his cabinet colleagues. He claimed to find the pope very open and well disposed to his views and anticipated 'a very energetic and effectual interposition' of papal authority, if Crolly and Murray were to reply to Roman requests for information by giving a full and frank account of the state of their church and country. During his visit on 19 December 1847 he discussed with the pope the political agitation of the Irish clergy and gave him two memoranda which he had compiled from information sent by Palmerston, including extracts from Irish newspapers. The pope, he claimed, was shocked by what he read and 'desired to manifest, as strongly as possible, his disapprobation of the political activity of the Clergy, and to do what might be in his power to check it in Ireland'. Minto did not invite the pope to try to limit the civil rights enjoyed by the

---

[167] Hansard 3, xcv, 925, (10 Dec. 1847).   [168] Ibid., 1052-1062, (14 Dec. 1847).
[169] Charles Greville noted in his diary for 7 Dec. 1847 that Wiseman had told him that the recent rescript condemning the colleges was 'all owing to there being no English ambassador at Rome, and no representative of the moderate Irish clergy'. L. Strachey and R. Fulford ed. *The Greville Memoirs, 1814-60*, v, 470-1.

clergy such as attendance at political meetings, 'involvement in factious socities' and participation in the collection of funds: but he indicated that the pope should forbid the use of churches for political meetings, that political agitation should not be associated with 'offices of devotion' and that denunciation of individuals from the altar should be discontinued. These requests were contained in a memorandum and left with the pope together with a further memorandum in which complaints were made about the clergy's membership of the Repeal association and 'other factious societies' and of a victim of clerical denunication being murdered after denunciation from the altar.[170] Attached to this was a statement of some examples of political agitation: these included cases of clergy vigorously advocating Repeal at elections, the bishop of Ardagh's plan for making every parish priest in his diocese a collector of the Repeal rent, the submission of subscriptions to Repeal by the clergy and Archdeacon Laffan's alleged declaration that 'if the English do not assassinate, it is because they have not the *courage to do anything like a man*'. Minto also left translations of documents which he had obtained about Ireland from Palmerston and Clarendon with the Secretary of State.[171]

As a result of all this political pressure and of the accusations about clerical involvement in politics and of clerical incitement to violence, yet a further letter was sent from Rome to the Irish church on these thorny questions. It was issued on 3 January 1848, signed by Cardinal Fransoni, and addressed to the archbishops of Armagh, Dublin and Cashel who were given the thankless and troublesome task of admonishing the clergy to limit their mission to spiritual matters and not implicate themselves in secular affairs. Diplomatically the letter began merely by asserting that rumours had reached Rome through the English press that some Irish ecclesiastics had allowed themselves to be carried away by party strife, that churches had been misused for the pursuit of secular affairs, and that either by imprudence, indirect encouragement from the pulpit or at least by their approval Irish priests had been involved in murders. Though the congregation of Propaganda could not believe these rumours, it felt obliged to call on the archbishops to give a true account of the situation obtaining in the country and, if necessary, to rebuke those who erred:

---

[170] Minto lamented in his first memorandum that 'a dignitary of the Roman Catholic Church has been found who, outwardly affecting to condemn the crime, stands forward as the apologist, or rather the eulogist of the assassins'. This was a reference to the murder of Major Mahon at Strokestown, Co. Roscommon on 2 Nov. 1847. The accusation was made that Mahon had previously been denounced from the altar by the local parish priest. The earl of Shrewsbury wrote to the bishop of Elphin, who replied exculpating the priest, but before he could do so Shrewsbury rashly brought his charges a step higher and attacked MacHale. MacHale duly lambasted Shrewsbury for his inaccurate and ill-informed accusation.

[171] Minto to Palmerston, 30 Dec. 1847, Curato, *Documenti della missione Minto*, i, 269-78.

This Sacred Congregation cannot bring itself to believe that such reports, so extensively noised abroad, can be true; nor can it believe that ecclesiastics have forgotten that the Church of God should be a house of prayer and not a meeting place for discussing political issues; neither can the Sacred Congregation believe that ecclesiastics have ceased to recollect that they are ministers of peace, dispensers of the mysteries of God—men who should not involve themselves in secular matters—in a word, men who should abhor blood and vengeance. Nevertheless, this Sacred Congregation deems it its duty to require satisfactory and speedy information concerning all these matters . . . and meanwhile, it exhorts you to admonish the clergy, that seeking the things which are of Jesus Christ, they sedulously apply themselves to watch over the faithful committed to their care, and that, as soldiers of God, they should not implicate themselves in worldly affairs, and should earnestly take care that from no quarter their ministry be despised, and that those who are against them have nothing wherewith to reproach them.[172]

While the letter was couched in the same style as the previous one and repeated the same advice about clergy abstaining from political matters, it contained stronger references to the misuse of churches for political activities and included the charge that priests by their imprudent or indirect language had been implicated in assassinations. And while it may have been an impeccable reiteration of the need to render to God and to Caesar the things that belonged respectively to them, it, of course, did not specify or clarify the ownership of these 'things'. No definition of secular affairs was given, nor was any reference made to their ever having a religious dimension. The letter according to Roman custom was carefully nuanced to minimize possible offence and to jog consciences if they required jogging. The prelates had already banned the use of churches for political purposes in 1834, and could defend themselves on that score. They could also easily brush aside the accusation of clerical implication in murders. Nevertheless, this brief letter aroused bitter feelings and gave rise to sharp disputes about its meaning in translation.

Crolly replied to the Roman request for information by pointing out that none of the horrendous homicides could be traced to indirect provocation by the clergy beforehand, or were afterwards given clerical approbation. Of 2,700 priests in Ireland only three or four had been accused of encouraging homicide but they had challenged their accusers to hold a full and open inquiry and no one had yet dared to bring them to court. One could therefore infer that they had been unjustly defamed. However, many priests were too closely involved in politics and frequently spoke on political matters in the churches.[173] That practice had

---

[172] Propaganda to the archbishops, 3 Jan. 1848, APF, *Lett.*, 337, ff 1r-2r.
[173] 'Equidem negari non potest multos esse ecclesiasticos viros in Hibernia rebus politics nimium addictos, qui frequenter in ecclesiis, ex altaribus, de negotiis civilibus et politicis cum gregibus suis colloquntur.'

originated with episcopal permission during the struggle for Catholic Emancipation, since that issue concerned the good of religion and Catholics had no other places for meetings, but, when that goal had been achieved, the bishops had decreed that the churches were to be no longer used for political purposes.

Then agitation began for the restoration of the Irish parliament, and drew support from many bishops, more priests and almost all Catholics, and again the churches were used for political addresses and meetings. And the people were told that they could acquire no prosperity unless the heavy rents they had to pay were reduced, and certainly the poor tenants suffering from want, hunger and poverty could not meet the heavy demands of some landlords. In some places landlords abusing their rights insisted on their rents without any leniency and evicted tenants from their farms together with their aged parents and children, and left them to perish without sustenance on the roadside. It was therefore easy to understand that the assassinations of landlords and their agents were to be ascribed not to denunciations by the priests but to the harshness of the owners of the soil, and the vengeance of their evicted tenants. Those evil deeds rarely occurred in the province of Armagh because there the rents were lighter, the landlords better and the farmers more industrious.

Nevertheless, in that as in all the other provinces of Ireland many priests and sometimes even bishops, who would have promoted the salvation of souls, the good of religion and the honour of God, if they had left political affairs to the laity, had imprudently become too closely involved in politics.[174] He himself in obedience to the orders of Propaganda had warned the bishops and through them the clergy but in some cases the anticipated result had not occurred. However, he intended to communicate the recent rescript to the bishops without delay and he hoped that political agitation in the churches would be completely ended.[175]

This balanced and temperate response must have reassured the Roman authorities and convinced them that the clergy were not culpable of the serious crime of inciting to violence within the churches. On the other hand Crolly did admit that some priests played too large a part in politics and did use their churches for political agitation. And while including bishops in this criticism, he refrained from naming those whom he had in mind—an exercise of charitable restraint which they did not reciprocate.

---

[174] '. . . multi sacerdotes et nonnumquam quidam episcopi imprudenter politicis et mundanis rebus se immiscent . . .'

[175] Crolly to Fransoni, 22 Jan. 1848, APF, SC (Irlanda), 29, ff 618r-619r.

Undoubtedly, O'Higgins and Cantwell, and probably also Maginn of Derry and MacNally of Clogher were the culprits in his province whom he did not mention and whom he thereby spared the embarrassment of having to defend themselves at Rome, had the congregation of Propaganda pursued its investigations.

Archbishop Murray leaked a copy of the letter to the *Dublin Evening Post* and the original text, together with a translation that was to provoke considerable controversy, appeared on 5 February. Why he did so and thereby brought down the wrath of his colleagues on his own head must remain something of a mystery. Perhaps he felt that sooner or later English papers would get hold of a copy of the letter in Rome; perhaps he felt that the contents merited the widest circulation possible and feared that many of the bishops would not bother to pass it on to their clergy; perhaps he felt that the clergy and laity should be appraised of the question marks Rome had placed on the behaviour of the MacHale supporters, despite their victory on the Queen's Colleges; perhaps he was encouraged by the Lord Lieutenant, to whom he communicated the contents of the letter, to publicize it for political purposes; perhaps a combination of all these motives dictated his action. MacHale himself was to sum up his own and his friends' reaction when he informed Paul Cullen that 'a most mischievous and mendacious use, as you will have seen, has been made of the Cardinal Prefect's private letter. It required much exertion to allay the odium calculated to be excited by so unwise a use of a private communication . . . it will be well to put the good and unsuspecting Cardinal on his guard regarding the sinister application to which his well meant documents are sometimes shaped'.[176]

The majority of the bishops were in a most unreceptive mood for such an exhortation. They believed that the government, instead of carrying out its responsibility to provide food and employment for the hungry, was devoting its energies to intrigues at Rome calculated to diminish the influence of the church. Bishop Cantwell spoke for this majority when he identified the accusations made against them at Rome as designed 'to give force to Lord Minto's *misrepresentations*' and 'to damage our influence in England & thereby defeat our intended deputation to the Queen in favor of our famishing flocks'.[177] As was his custom the bishop of Ardagh reacted very stormily to what he regarded as an improper exhortation from Rome, which had been wrung from it by British deceit and skulduggery. Some of this ire quite unjustly rubbed off on Crolly, who

---

[176] MacHale to Cullen, 20 Feb. 1848, AICR.   [177] Cantwell to Cullen, 17 Jan. 1848, AICR.

was but the recipient of the letter and agent in executing it. Behind this ploy, of course, lay O'Higgins' desire to punish the archbishop of Armagh for his 'collaboration' with the civil authorities; the *zelanti* believed that supporters of the Queen's Colleges had proved their general untrustworthiness by aligning themselves with a government that not only vilified the church and imposed unjust policies on her but at a time of famine and suffering turned to the Irish people a face that was harsh and cruel.

Crolly forwarded a copy of the Roman letter to all the bishops of his province and asked for their comments. O'Higgins not only replied but did so publicly—in the *Freeman's Journal*. Far from being defensive about any of his own political activities, he went on the attack, arguing that the archbishop was bound to make known to Rome 'that a most wicked and diabolical conspiracy' was being carried on by almost all the English and Irish press against the Catholic hierarchy, the Catholic priests and the Catholic people of Ireland; that Lord Minto had been sent to Rome to deceive the Holy See, and that he and his friends had used the most calumnious means to do so. The bishop of Ardagh further maintained that Cardinal Fransoni should be informed that, under the name of legal right, the body of the landlords of Ireland were literally starving the poor, and doing so without a single remonstrance from the Lord Lieutenant, or his employer, Lord John Russell. Suggesting that the primate put to Propaganda a proposal to send an Italian ecclesiastic to report on the Irish situation, he concluded by insisting that steps should be taken to acquaint Rome with all the details of the anti-national and anti-Catholic conspiracy afoot so that their enemies would be humbled and 'some little justice done to poor calumniated and persecuted Ireland'.[178]

In private O'Higgins was pleased with the reaction to his letter. He told Slattery that it had done some good, that Dublin was 'litterally [*sic*] in commotion' and with a little time they could still discomfit their enemies. He gave full rein to his combative instincts as he declared that it was time 'to be vigorous with Rome herself', that the pope ought 'to be solicited to replace poor old Cardinal Fransoni by some more circumspect and energetic Prefect' and that the sooner 'Dr Wiseman too got an Irish significant hint the better for Religion and for himself'.[179]

There was little Crolly could say in response to this aggressive posture that would not have placed him in the awkward position of discussing conspiracies and Minto's behaviour at Rome, and he wisely kept silent.

---

[178] F.J., 7 Feb. 1848.
[179] O'Higgins to Slattery, 10 Feb. 1848, Slattery Papers.

But controversy rumbled on for a few days about the implications of the correct translation of the Roman document. The *Dublin Evening Post*, a pro-Castle newspaper, had put the word '*diffamationibus*' into the original text and referred to the 'damnatory reports' about the behaviour of the clergy and had rendered '*abusu aliquarum Ecclesiarum*' 'as the desecration of some churches'; '*partium politicarum studio*' it translated as 'political party strifes'. The *Freeman's Journal* insisted that Crolly's letter to O'Higgins clearly showed that the word used was '*defamationibus*' and not '*diffamationibus*' which implied that the accusations about the misbehaviour of the priests were defamations and not 'damnatory reports' as the *Dublin Evening Post* had suggested and took issue with some of the other translations.[180] The controversy widened when a meeting was held in Dublin to protest against the slur cast on the priesthood.[181]

The *Freeman's Journal* continued to pour scorn on the *Dublin Evening Post* for its mutilation of the Roman text and especially for its translation of the word '*diffamationibus*'. However, Archbishop Murray assured his clergy that '*diffamationibus*' was in the original letter and then confirmed the correctness of the text published in the *Dublin Evening Post*. O'Higgins was quick to disclaim any responsibility for the error and informed the *Freeman's Journal*, which had used his copy from the beginning, that the word '*defamationibus*' appeared in the version he had received from the primate. Not content with correcting errors and misunderstandings, he then proceeded to land a blow on the archbishop by explaining that he had freed himself 'from the blunder or falsification, and let those who have trifled with, or insulted the Sacred Congregation settle the matter with themselves'.[182]

Crolly promptly forwarded his explanation. Remarking, not without justification, that the controversy had already occupied enough public attention, he pointed out that, until O'Higgins' letter appeared, he thought he had transcribed the Roman text correctly. Then politely taking the bishop of Ardagh to task he stated that in obedience to the pope and in the spirit of fraternal charity he had not intended the communication for publication but for the bishop's reflection 'on the pious prudent and practical directions which it contained'. He was extremely sorry if his unintentional mistake could have augmented or diminished 'the force of the salutary admonition given by the Holy See to some Ecclesiastical Politicians in this country' and he concluded by expressing the hope that

---

[180] F.J., 7 Feb, D.E.P., 8 Feb. 1848. Rome wanted to know quamam fides publicis hujusmodi diffamationibus danda sit.
[181] F.J., 12 Feb. 1848.   [182] Ibid., 16 Feb. 1848.

the pious injunction of the pope 'will be strictly attended to by all those persons for whose instruction it was intended'.[183]

To MacHale and Cantwell this reply was a 'melancholy instance of the evil' of the close association of bishops with the government. MacHale, far from being chastened by the Roman letter, declared that the clergy instead of being gagged ought to be encouraged to speak out, and remarked that unless acts were specifically interdicted, they (presumably, Crolly and Murray) ought in all prudence and decency abstain from abusing the authority of the Holy See.[184]

Bishop Maginn, the coadjutor of Derry, who was one of the most outspoken episcopal critics both of the government's policy on education and of its niggardly response to the famine, was, like O'Higgins, outraged by the implications of the Roman letter which he interpreted as but a reflection of the calumnies heaped on the Irish priesthood by British critics, and which he maintained offered Crolly a chance to warn the pope against the wiles of a British diplomacy that had stooped to such shameful proceedings. He called, in private, on the primate for an aggressive not a defensive reply:

An ardent love of country, for which our great Pope himself is so distinguished, could not be reputed an inordinate zeal for factious pursuits. A desire to promote by *peaceful* and *constitutional* means the *amelioration* of the social condition of our *unhappy country made by misrule the most wretched on earth*, could not be considered 'a political pursuit". Nor could *in fine* the praiseworthy efforts of our clergy to check the proselytiser . . . nor their earnest endeavours . . . to bring public opinion to bear on the ruthless extermination of their helpless starving hearers, through any malversion [*sic*] be deemed criminal in them.[185]

The government was naturally pleased with the pope's letter which it hoped would oblige the priests to take a less active part in politics. Minto asked Petre to let the pope know that his exhortation had given satisfaction, not only to the government, but also to the British public and especially to all the 'respectable' Catholics in England and Ireland.[186]

Crolly's actual reply to Rome would have angered the *zelanti*, had they seen it. Cullen learned of its contents from Propaganda and passed them on to Archbishop Slattery. Slattery, who had responded in a very different vein from the archbishop of Armagh, regarded it as yet another depressing example of the length to which Crolly and Murray were

[183] Ibid., 21 Feb. 1848.
[184] MacHale to Slattery, 20 Feb. 1848, Slattery Papers.
[185] Maginn to Crolly, 21 Feb. 1848, DDA.
[186] Minto to Petre, 26 Feb. 1848, PRO, F.O. 43/42.

prepared to go to ingratiate themselves with Dublin Castle at the expense of their own people:

Your second letter of the 18th conveys intelligence, which afflicts but does not surprise me with regard to the Primate's answer. I was prepared to find that he would endeavour to sustain the Government, but I scarcely expected that he would go so far as to state that the charges made of profaning the Churches, of holding political meetings in them, of having political harangues regularly delivered in them were *nimis verj*, [too true] they being as I in my conscience believe utterly unfounded & in fact ever since or at least very nearly since the time of Emancipation. I for my part have denied them as regards my own Diocese, & also as far as my knowledge goes as regards other Dioceses that I am acquainted with—but it is likely that Dr Murray & the Primate have taken counsels together & will corroborate one another, and overbalance my testimony. God help us.

Slattery went on to paint a very pessimistic picture of the condition in which Irish Catholics found themselves—stricken by poverty and affliction, enemies united strongly against them, the laity torn by contending parties and that church, which the sword of persecution could not destroy, 'a victim like Jerusalem of old to the dissension of her own High Priests.'[187] Slattery furthermore used the device of publishing a letter to MacHale to attack the publication of the Roman letter and the interpretation of it as a hostile criticism of the Irish priests. He told MacHale that he had been assured from Rome that Cardinal Fransoni did not believe the charges contained in the original letter, that the pope was satisfied with his rebuttal of them, and included a note from the secretary of Propaganda confirming that Fransoni's letter was a private one.[188] O'Higgins was delighted with this *démarche* and assured Slattery that his correspondence with Rome would give courage and hope to the clergy and people of all Ireland, 'and if they know how to blush, will bring the blood to the cheeks of certain traitorous Castle hacks'.[189]

The division among the bishops had become so deep and the *zelanti* so distrusted Crolly and Murray that they blamed them in great measure for many of the ills and problems of the church. And to add to the embarrassment which the two archbishops had to suffer because of their alleged collusion with the government came support for the *zelanti* from some of the vicars apostolic in England.

The vicars-apostolic of the Northern and Western Districts, John Briggs and Bernard Ullathorne, had become alarmed at reports of

---

[187] Slattery to Cullen, 2 Mar. 1848, AICR.
[188] Slattery to MacHale, D.E.P. 11 Mar. 1848.
[189] Higgins to Slattery, 13 Mar. 1848, Slattery Papers.

diplomatic activity in Rome and at what seemed to be a government orchestrated campaign against the Irish clergy, who were being accused of inciting their people to murder landlords. The English vicars-apostolic, like the majority of Irish prelates, concluded that the establishment of diplomatic relations between London and Rome could only redound to the detriment of the church both in England and Ireland.

Consequently, Briggs took the initiative in drawing up the draft of a memorial to be presented to the pope advising him against such a move. He sent the draft to the Irish bishops and to most of his colleagues in Britain—Wiseman significantly was excluded[190]—in December 1847. The document made reference to Minto's mission to treat of ecclesiastical affairs with the Holy See, pointed out that British diplomacy was internationally recognized as being very cunning and subtle, and was everywhere inimical to the Catholic religion. The government had long sought to establish a concordat with Rome, had previously been blocked by the bishops of Ireland or England but the danger again existed of the Holy See being deceived by it. Russell was pursuing an anti-Catholic policy and the attempts to undermine their religion were nowhere more evident than in the false and calumnious charges being made against the clergy in Ireland as abettors of murder. It was also suggested in the draft that reference could be made to Pius VII, being 'imposed upon by misrepresentations from England' with the implication that history was about to repeat itself.[191]

Crolly replied promptly but unenthusiastically. He commented on some of the points raised in the draft, explaining that he was not able to form an accurate opinion on Minto's mission but was inclined to believe that the government would not make any ecclesiastical arrangement with the Holy See without obtaining the consent of parliament, and that the pope would not conclude a concordat without ascertaining the sentiments of the prelates of the British Empire. He thought it would be imprudent to tell the pope that he might be deceived in the same way as Pius VII. Pointing out that the accusations against the clergy had been made in parliament not by the government but by such men as Lords Farnham and Beaumont, he observed that two of the accused priests had denied the charges and had called for a fair and legal investigation of their conduct. He therefore believed that Minto would not 'increase the difficulties of the Government by attempting to tarnish the character of the Catholic

---

[190] Wiseman to W.B. Ullathorne, 13 Apr. 1848, BDA.
[191] Heads of a proposed memorial . . . , LDA.

Clergy, or that the Holy Father would receive such a charge without clear proof of the facts on which it should be established'. And he concluded by suggesting that Briggs would be able to form a firm opinion on the memorial from the replies of the bishops and also decide whether 'it should be signed by the Prelates, without a general Meeting of all the Prelates of the British Empire, convened for the purpose of taking this important subject into their mature consideration'.[192]

Crolly was right in assuming that the authorization of parliament would be required before diplomatic relations or a concordat could be negotiated with the Holy See. But in thinking that Minto would not accuse the clergy of being accessory to crimes he displayed too trusting a judgement of the government, both at London and Dublin. He took the Whigs at their face value and was always inclined to believe their protestations of concern for Irish reform, but Clarendon, Palmerston, Russell and Minto blamed the clergy for inspiring and maintaining agitation that really derived from the economic conditions of the country, and were keen to use Roman authority to exclude the priests from positions of political leadership. His suggestion of a general meeting of prelates would not have been feasible because of the difficulties of travel, time, expense and the likelihood of reports about it reaching the newspapers.

As a result of the comments he received on the memorial, Briggs had it shortened and modified. The part about the danger of the pope being deceived like his predecessor was omitted but a piece was added to the charge against the clergy of abetting murder: 'as Kind Pastors they are striving to uphold & to console their deeply afflicted & perishing people & like good shepherds are in the midst of pestilence giving their lives for their flocks'. Crolly told Briggs in his reply that he saw the memorial when visiting Murray in Dublin, though he did not say, as seems certain, that they virtually coordinated their responses to it. He quoted Murray as saying that he had no evidence of Minto's intention to treat with the Holy See on their ecclesiastical affairs and that he considered the memorial to be 'neither necessary nor expedient'. Agreeing with that judgement he himself therefore declined to sign it.[193]

Not surprisingly the division among the bishops was substantially reflected in the signatures of the memorial. Crolly, Murray, Denvir, Kennedy, Browne of Kilmore and Ryan of Limerick, representing the hard core of the *politicanti* who had sought an accommodation on the

---

[192] Crolly to Briggs, 23 Dec. 1847, LDA.   [193] Ibid, 15 Jan. 1848.

Queen's Colleges refused to sign. Twenty of their colleagues headed by
MacHale and Slattery signed. O'Higgins was delighted with the proposal,
which Briggs also made, of sending a delegation from their body with the
memorial to Rome. His response typified the pleasure of the *zelanti* with
the whole project. He pointed out that he had long advocated the
necessity of sending a bishop to Rome to alert the authorities there to the
infamy of English diplomacy, wherever Catholicism was concerned, and
but for the wretchedness of his half-starved people and priests he himself
would have gone to unmask the perfidy of the British government.
Referring to Lord Shrewsbury's letter attacking MacHale, he commented
that Shrewsbury's brother had gone mad in Rome and suggested that the
same affliction might again have struck the family.[194]

The memorial signed by three or four vicars apostolic as well as by the
twenty Irish bishops was duly presented in Rome by the rector of the
English College.[195] But by then the papacy had been enabled to savour the
attitude of the government as reflected in the comments made in
parliament during the passage of the Diplomatic Relations Bill. The bill,
as Palmerston had promised, was introduced into the House of Lords in
February 1848. It sought to empower the British government to exchange
diplomatic relations with the government of the papal states at the court
of Rome. As the pope was both a temporal and spiritual ruler and as
British law forbade official contacts with him, an act of parliament was
necessary.

However, the earl of Eglintoun promptly threw a spanner in the works
when on the day after the bill was laid on the table he declared that they
would be guilty of a gross dereliction of their duty as Protestants, if they
allowed an ecclesiastic to represent the pope in London and thereby,
perhaps, allow the embassy to be 'a nucleus for Jesuits'.[196] The Anglican
bishop of Exeter pointed out that Romish ministers were not allowed in St
Petersburg and Berlin, even though Russia and Prussia sent ambassadors
to Rome.[197] Lord Stanley, a former Whig, who had served in Peel's
cabinets, refused to be constrained by diplomatic finesse and in a
comment that must have delighted MacHale he blurted out the real
purpose and value of the proposal:

You know that the Pope has influence over your Roman Catholic subjects; and you

---

[194] O'Higgins to Briggs, 14 Jan. 1848, LDA.
[195] A.S.V., Arch. Part. Pio IX, Oggetti Vari, 440, 15 Feb. 1848.
[196] Hansard 3, xcvi, 284-6, (8 Feb. 1848).
[197] Ibid., 776-8, (17 Feb. 1848).

seek to obtain an influence over the Pope, in order to prevent his interference with your Roman Catholic subjects being carried on in a mode offensive to you.[198]

Eglintoun duly moved an amendment to prevent the pope from being represented by anyone in holy orders.[199] Though it was explained that the king of Prussia was not prohibited by law from receiving an ecclesiastic as a papal ambassador and that a legal limitation of this nature would be an insult to the pope, the amendment was passed, and the bill was carried in the House of Lords.

The bill was also duly passed in the Commons and on 4 September it received the royal assent. But nothing further happened. Papal enthusiasm had by then cooled significantly, if it had not fully evaporated. Pius IX, as was to be expected, regarded the prohibition on his being represented in London by an ecclesiastic not only as an insult but as effectively putting an end to any hopes of establishing relations on an acceptable basis. While Rome did not have representatives in Berlin and St Petersburg, this situation arose not from a legal prohibition but from a practical decision to tolerate a *de facto* development, until time would permit a normalization of contacts. What could be tolerated from Prussia and Russia in the interests of the substantial Catholic minorities in those states could not be suffered in England, where there was no such pressure on the Catholic minority and where submission to a humiliation embedded in law was too high a price to pay for questionable advantages.

MacHale and O'Higgins arrived in Rome in April 1848 to lobby for a condemnation of the Queen's Colleges and there, carefully guided by Cullen, undoubtedly made their objections to British diplomacy known in the appropriate quarters. Minto, who would have been no match for them, left Rome as they arrived. When rumours from the English press again spread in Ireland about state payment for the Catholic clergy the bishops were stirred to make a public protest. They were united in their opposition to this suggestion, realizing that the proposal, far from being altruistic, was an insidious attempt to control the priesthood for political purposes, and fearing the spiritual damage it would do to the clergy and to their solidarity with the people. Among the resolutions passed at their general meeting in Dublin on 11 October 1848 was one reiterating their determination to reject all such financial support from the state. Significantly, it was proposed by Bishop Browne of Kilmore and seconded by Crolly, and it declared:

---

[198] Ibid., 780-92.

[199] Ibid., 876, (18 Feb. 1848). Cullen claimed that Minto wanted the Roman nobleman, Prince Doria, who was connected by marriage to Lord Shrewsbury, to represent the pope in London. (Cullen to MacHale, 28 Jan. 1848, in O'Reilly, *MacHale*, ii, 111-113.)

That having shared in the prosperity of their faithful flocks, the clergy of Ireland are willing to share in their privations, and are determined to resist a measure calculated to create vast discontent—to sever the people from their pastors and ultimately to endanger Catholicity in this country.[200]

This certainly sent a clear and unmistakeable message to British parliamentarians. To pursue the issue would have involved certain opposition in parliament and, if legislation were ever passed, the government would be humiliatingly rebuffed by the refusal of the church to accept state payment. Parliament's lubberly and maladroit management of the Diplomatic Relations Bill not only denied the government a valuable weapon in its struggle with the Irish church but saved Crolly and Murray from the embarrassment which would have been caused by public protests and criticisms by some of their colleagues, who would have accused them of using the Roman embassy to obtain papal approval for government policy in Ireland detrimental to the interests of the church.

The last thing they wanted to do at that time was to give their suspicious and hostile brethren another excuse for attacking them. Any slip, no matter how trivial, was grist to the mill of their opponents. In January 1849 Edward Maginn, the coadjutor bishop of Derry, died at an early age. An extreme *zelante*, he had been very critical of Crolly's handling of the jurisdictional problems in Derry, which arose from the mental illness of Bishop McLaughlin. His friends, MacNally and Cantwell, blamed the archbishop for trying to impede the vicar-capitular from summoning the parish priests to vote for a new coadjutor. They accused him of wanting to make inquiries to see if McLaughlin were capable of administrating the diocese or else of wanting to take over the administration of it himself, both of which options they regarded as evil. The imaginative Cantwell detected the malign consequences of close association with the government in Crolly's behaviour, and concluded that 'it required all the dark ingenuity of a British Diplomatist & proves the treacherous workings of intrigue to hesitate in such a case'.[201] In the event Crolly did not prevent the vicar-capitular from following the normal procedure, and so did not have to face any further show-downs with his episcopal opponents.

During the 1840s the relations of the British government with the Catholic Church in Ireland were fraught with serious difficulties, as both sides tried to come to terms with the demands of the Catholic people for

---

[200] F.J., 13 Oct. 1848. Cullen reported from Rome that Pius IX put an end to Minto's proposals for pensioning the clergy by suggesting that the state restore half of its property to the Catholic Church. (McGee, *A Life of the Rt. Rev. Edward Maginn*, 268.)

[201] MacNally to Cullen, 27 Jan. 1849; Cantwell to Cullen, 5 Feb. 1849, AICR.

what they perceived to be their civil rights.

Crolly, Murray and the *politicanti* among the bishops suffered the fate of opposition leaders who are prepared to make compromises with a state, when popular passions appeal for changes which the state regards as extreme and unacceptable. They were dismissed by the *zelanti* and by the nationalist public as weak and unreliable, as trimmers and 'Castle' bishops. Crolly supported Whiggish views and policies, not from any commitment to Whig political theory, but because he believed that the social and religious condition of his people would be best advanced through reform legislation rather than through campaigns for major constitutional change, which would be firmly resisted by Britain and would provoke sectarian strife in Ireland. His ductile approach to the government and to much of its legislation derived not from any ambition to win favour at the Castle, or from a frivolous desire to share in the entertainment at the Vice-regal Lodge. He was, however, roundly denounced for his presence at the viceroy's levees. The *Newry Examiner* expressing bewilderment at the attendance of the archbishops of Armagh and Dublin after their appointment as commissioners of Charitable Bequests among 'the crowd of parasites and tyrants who bend the knee to the delegate of alien Protestant ascendancy' believed that they did so to publicize 'their sentiments towards the minority, towards O'Connell, and towards their brother Catholics, who have hitherto grievously lamented without bitterly censuring their "compact alliance" with the inveterate foes of our creed and country'.[202] Lord Clarendon, however, regarded their presence on such occasions as a healing gesture and remarking on how strange it was to find Lords Downshire and Roden standing beside Crolly and Murray, believed that contacts of that kind were in themselves commentaries on the old English policy of creating disunion in Ireland in order to govern half the country.[203] Crolly shared Clarendon's views on the importance of such gestures since he felt that cooperation with the state rather than confrontation was ultimately more beneficial to the church. He suffered the immediate fate of those who tread such paths, when popular feelings are aroused—contempt and obloquy—but in the longer term his course may have been more judicious than that of many of his critics and opponents.

[202] N.Ex., 1 Feb. 1845.
[203] Clarendon's Lb III, 25 Jan. 1849, ff 247r–248v.

8

THE QUEEN'S COLLEGES

The national system of education established by the Whig government in 1831 was a response to the long articulated demands of the Catholic bishops and to the advice of various commissions of inquiry on the need to make some kind of provision for the children of the poor who would otherwise not have been enabled to attend school. There was nothing like the same pressure from influential sources for the establishment of colleges at tertiary level. One public figure of note did conduct a campaign for this purpose but he did not have powerful or widespread support from the leaders of public opinion.

Sir Thomas Wyse, who entered parliament in 1830, drew the attention of members from time to time to the gaps in the Irish educational system, and was eventually rewarded by being invited to chair a select committee of the House of Commons on the subject. In 1838 he produced a report which proposed, in addition to the national schools, secondary schools or academies in each county, agricultural and professional schools, four provincial colleges and other specialized educational institutions. The county academies were an attempt to cater for secondary education and the colleges for tertiary education. The colleges were to meet the needs of the middle classes and, though not quite universities, Wyse's report envisaged an examining body in Dublin which could confer degrees in subjects other than divinity on their successful students. These ideas were to materialize later in Peel's colleges.

A campaign was launched in 1838 to found a college in Munster. Some of its advocates wanted it located in Cork, but others, including Bishop Cornelius Egan of Kerry, favoured Limerick as its site. Petitions from Cork were presented to parliament, but nothing happened under the Whig administration and Wyse resumed his activity under the Tories. In 1844 he made a series of proposals in parliament for opening Trinity College to all denominations, linking it with other colleges for Catholics and Presbyterians in the University of Dublin, or failing this for the establishment of a Catholic university. But he also put forward again his ideas for provincial colleges associated with a new university on the model of London University.[1] All the requirements of the established church were met by Trinity College, Dublin. And the concerns of the Catholic church in higher education were firmly centred on the expansion and modernization of Maynooth, a goal which was achieved in 1845. The orthodox Presbyterians, who no longer trusted the Academical Institution in Belfast, were alone among the religious bodies in seeking a new college.

Initially the government, which had decided that the granting of tertiary education would be a worthwhile concession to Catholics (and Presbyterians) and would help to break up the politico-religious alliance supporting Repeal, did not exclude the idea of linking Maynooth to a new university system. But in his memorandum to the cabinet in November 1844 in which he discussed various possibilities, Sir James Graham came down in favour of a new university to which colleges would be linked and reported that Heytesbury, the Lord Lieutenant, had concluded that such a plan would be open to the least objection. Graham forwarded to the cabinet the request of the Presbyterians for the establishment of a seminary for the General Assembly and invited it to decide whether the Belfast Academical Institution should be turned into a university college with faculties of arts and law or whether a grant should be given to the Presbyterians for their student education independently of any other arrangement that might be made about colleges of education in Belfast.[2]

When he had obtained cabinet approval for the general substance of his plans, Graham instructed Heytesbury to discuss it under the seal of secrecy with P.S. Henry, the Presbyterian minister of Armagh, for the Presbyterians and Crolly, Murray and Blake for the Catholics. The Lord Lieutenant was asked to sound out the Catholic leaders about the possibility of Maynooth students graduating in arts in a new university to which it might be affiliated. The Presbyterians, Graham explained, had no authority to confer degrees, but, if they were satisfied with their own degrees, the state would not interfere. Blake, who was to be assured of the government's sincere intentions of establishing good relations with the leaders of the Catholic Church, was to be used to soften up Crolly and Murray by inducing them to be as conciliatory as possible and to make the most ample concessions out of loyalty to their church and thereby to allay

---

[1] Moody and Beckett, *Queen's, Belfast, 1845-1949*, i, lvii-lxiii; Gwynn, *O'Connell, Davis and the Colleges' Bill*, 28-33.

[2] Graham memorandum, 15-18 Nov. 1844, Stanley Papers, 37/1.

Protestant suspicions and fears.[3] For the remainder of the year Peel and
Graham continued to correspond about arrangements for staff and other
appointments in the colleges, and Blake's views on what Catholics might
accept were further solicited. Heytesbury was also encouraged to reach
amicable terms with the Presbyterians—'this powerful but unreasonable
body'—through Henry.[4]

Heytesbury showed the heads of the bill to Blake, whom he regarded as
an intermediary with Crolly and Murray, and Blake may have created a
false sense of optimism, as he may well have given misleading replies
refracted through the lens of his enthusiasm for mixed education. He did
not take Crolly and Murray directly into his confidence and his reluctance
to allow bishops to think that they had a right to be consulted proved to
be a costly error.[5] Though the government plans for a system of education
open to students of all denominations would not have met all the bishops'
requirements, confidential discussions with Crolly and Murray might
have led to alterations that could have made the bill more acceptable,
while still retaining its basic principle. And Graham, who was anxious to
maintain the division in the hierarchy, understood the importance of
keeping Crolly and Murray on their side.[6]

Graham opened the debate on the Academical Institutions in Ireland
bill on 9 May 1845. Stating that the government wished to improve the
social condition of Ireland by 'the diffusion of the benefits of education
among the middle and higher classes of society', and recalling the failures
of all schemes that interfered with conscience on religious issues, he
announced plans to set up three provincial colleges on the model of
University College, London (and to a lesser extent on that of the Scottish
universities) where the students were not subject to religious tests.
Without committing himself to their exact location, he suggested that
Cork and Belfast were the most likely sites for the Munster and Ulster
colleges, and that either Galway or Limerick would be the most suitable
place for the Connacht college. He proposed a capital sum of £100,000 for
the construction of the buildings and an annual endowment of £6,000 to
cover the incomes of the staff and prizes and exhibitions for the students
in each of the colleges. Indicating that the staff in each would consist of a
principal and ten or twelve professors, he made clear the government's
determination to vest the appointment and removal of the principal and

[3] Graham to Heytesbury, 30 Nov. 1844, Graham Papers.
[4] Graham to Heytesbury, 18 Mar.1845, Ibid.
[5] Heytesbury to Graham, 25 Apr., 13, 16 May 1845, Ibid.
[6] Graham to Heytesbury, 14 May 1845, Ibid.

professors in the crown, justifying this decision as a determination to prevent lectures from ever being 'the vehicle of any peculiar religious tenets'. Religion, though not endowed by the state, was not excluded from the colleges: facilities were to be provided for private endowment of chairs of theology and for holding theological lectures within the colleges. 'The principle', Graham insisted, on which the approval of parliament was sought, was 'the absence of all interference, positive or negative, with the conscientious scruples of the students in matters of religion'.

He then went on to refer to the Academical Institution in Belfast, which, he observed, had 'been founded originally much on the same principles for which I contend' and which received an annual grant of £2,100 from the state. Pointing out that it was attended mainly by Presbyterians, and especially by candidates for the ministry, he explained that the four professors of divinity were nominated not by the governing body of the institution, but by the General Assembly of the Presbyterian Church. Since it was his hope that the premises, buildings and library of the Academical Institution would be transferred to the government on easy terms to be transformed into one of the new colleges, he proposed that its professors, if they were not considered suitable for appointments in the new college, would be compensated and that the four professors of theology would also continue to receive their salaries.

Graham left open the university status of the colleges; a decision would be made at a later date whether each would be empowered to grant degrees or together constitute a university, possibly based in Dublin, or whether they would even be incorporated with Dublin University. However, 'neither policy, nor equity, nor justice would permit any interference with Trinity College', a Protestant foundation closely associated with the established church. Quoting with approval the opinion of Daniel O'Connell expressed in 1825 that the scholarships of Trinity College, originally intended for aspirants to the ministry, should be left to them, Graham predicted that the admission of Catholics or dissenters to the emoluments of Trinity would not be practicable, as it would outrage Protestant feeling and violate the rights of property. The establishment of the provincial colleges, he concluded, with more hope than prescience, would 'conduce to the concord, the order, the peace and the virtue of the country'.[7]

In the debate that followed the Irish members gave a generally favourable welcome to the proposals. Richard Lalor Sheil regretted the

---

[7] Hansard 3, lxxx, 345-66, (9 May 1845).

government's failure to consult the Catholic Church before submitting its proposals and suggested that some arrangements for religious instruction analogous to those obtaining in the national schools should be made.[8] Peel defended his government's behaviour by referring to the impasse which consultation with the various religious leaders would have brought about.[9] But it was Sir Robert Inglis, the Tory MP for Oxford University, who made the criticism of the Colleges that was to prove most derogatory and harmful. Bemoaning the absence of all religious education in them, something that he claimed was without precedent in any educational institution connected with the state in either Protestant or Catholic countries, he described the government's plans in a phrase that was to win instant celebrity as 'a gigantic scheme of Godless education'.[10]

Inglis found a ready echo in the O'Connellite press. O'Connell took the view that the government would yield to pressure from the hierarchy for a system of education acceptable to it, and called on the bishops to persevere in demanding what they conscientiously believed to be necessary for Catholic youth. His junior partners, however, of the *Nation*, favoured the scheme for political reasons, seeing in it a means for uniting students of diverse religious backgrounds in a common national allegiance.

Graham was pleased with the general reception accorded to his proposals in the House of Commons. In private he revealed a disdain for the Catholic priesthood and an ambition for the future success of his undertaking that, had they known about it, would have given MacHale and his lieutenants all the ammunition they needed to attack the Colleges:

I am afraid that the R. Catholic Priesthood will be jealous of the loss of power and direct control over the Education of the Youth of the Laity belonging to their Church . . . If we succeed in carrying the measure into practical operation, it will emancipate the rising generation from the thraldom of Priestly domination.[11]

Five days after the debate in the House of Commons, Crolly wrote to all the bishops to invite them to a meeting to discuss the bill, which, he maintained, seemed to be 'pregnant with danger to the faith and morals of the youth of this country'.[12] Realizing the danger of allowing MacHale to grab the headlines with a ferocious fulmination against the government and all its Machiavellian works, and thereby, to set the agenda for all subsequent negotiations on higher education, he had obviously decided that his best policy was to try to obtain some kind of balanced response

---

[8] Ibid., 380-85.   [9] Ibid., 385-91.   [10] Ibid., 377-80.
[11] Graham to Heytesbury, 10 May 1845, Graham papers.
[12] F.J., 20 Oct.1845.

from the whole hierarchy that would not preclude future bargaining. In the light of MacHale's sustained assault on the national system, based to a great extent on the dangers to the purity of the children's faith posed by the teachers and the books used in the schools—over both of which the church had, in most parts of Ireland, complete control—little foresight was required to see how implacable his hostility would be to a system of education from which all ecclesiastical, and especially episcopal, influence was being substantially excluded. And though Crolly had defended the attendance of Catholic boys at the secondary department of the Academical Institution, he must have feared opposition from some of the bishops, perhaps from some of his own suffragans, to Catholic youth sharing tertiary education in a college which had been denounced by Henry Cooke as a seminary where students imbibed Arianism from their professors and where the ethos and atmosphere were as Presbyterian as that of Trinity College was Anglican.

A few days before the bishops met, Thomas Davis informed Smith O'Brien that they were likely to disagree in their responses to the bill but stated categorically 'Crolly is for mixed education and so are others'.[13] Whether he had heard this from a reliable source or was merely drawing conclusions from Crolly's record of support for the national system and mixed schools in Belfast, is not known. On 18 May Murray wrote hastily to Crolly to let him know that he had been summoned to meet the Lord Lieutenant and shown a letter from Graham containing assurances of kindness to Catholics and emphasising that there would be no unfair tampering with their religion in the new Colleges. To guarantee such non-interference the government had reserved to itself the right of appointing and removing professors. Murray then discussed with Heytesbury the religious associations of some chairs, particularly that of history, and he added that a friend had suggested the establishment of boarding houses under the inspection of the clergy for the moral protection of the students.[14]

On 20 May, the day before the meeting, Bishop Denvir of Down and Connor, in the course of a conversation with Dominic Corrigan, a distinguished Dublin physician, mentioned the hostility of the prelates to the establishment of a non-residential form of collegiate education. Corrigan countered by outlining his experience of similar situations abroad, and Denvir was so impressed that he brought him along to discuss the matter with Crolly. Crolly in turn was so interested that he insisted that Corrigan should put his views in writing before the episcopal meeting took place.

[13] Gwynn, O'Connell, Davis and the Colleges' Bill, 52.
[14] Murray to Crolly, 18 May 1845, DCDA.

Corrigan consented, spent the night carrying out this commission, and brought along his memorandum to Crolly, Murray, Denvir and another bishop the following morning. When Crolly heard Corrigan's remarks he immediately declared that many of his objections had been removed; Denvir and the other bishop (whose name Corrigan forgot) agreed, and though Murray was non-committal, he seemed to be satisfied.[15]

Corrigan had recommended the system which he believed obtained at Eton and Cambridge, where students resided in lodging houses, which had been licensed by the college or university. The 'dames' or 'domines' in charge of the houses were held responsible for the good conduct of their lodgers and were obliged to report misbehaviour to the academic authorities. Clergymen, as deans of residences, visited the houses frequently to see that the regulations were being observed by their co-religionists, both landladies and students. Corrigan claimed that this system was preferable to residence in a college where one or two obstreperous residents could distract all the others. And he advised that students at the proposed colleges should be compelled to wear academic dress at all times and to attend class each day, leaving only at fixed times for meals. On returning home each evening they should be obliged to remain indoors until setting off for class the following morning. To avoid controversy or misunderstandings about religion, only students of the same denomination should reside together; this would furthermore exclude the temptation to sacrifice 'their respective tenets in the freemasonry of conviviality'. Corrigan, who explained that he drew both on his own experience as a student and on ten years teaching in which he lectured normally to between one and two hundred students, discouraged any suggestion of undergraduates lodging with professors, because of the danger of partiality. He was confident that the safeguards contained in his suggestions for residence provided adequate supervision for the moral and spiritual well-being of undergraduates.[16]

Twenty one of the twenty seven bishops attended the meeting on 21 May.[17] After a prolonged discussion stretching over two days the bishops resolved to withhold their approval from the Colleges' scheme as they felt it was dangerous to the faith and morals of the Catholic students, and to

---

[15] Corrigan to Thomas Redington, 7 Dec. 1847, Clarendon Papers.
[16] Corrigan's Memorandum, Ibid.
[17] The absentees were Keating (Ferns), O'Higgins (Ardagh), Egan (Kerry), McLaughlin (Derry), Coen (Clonfert), and McNicholas (Achonry). McLaughlin was incapacitated, Keating and O'Higgins had been staunch opponents of the national schools and Coen and McNicholas, whether from conviction or fear, had followed the lead of the archbishop of Tuam. Egan had supported the majority on the schools question.

present a memorial to the Lord Lieutenant containing the amendments required to make it acceptable to them. Significantly, the motion withholding approbation from the bill was proposed and seconded by MacHale and Slattery, while the one to petition the Lord Lieutenant was proposed by Crolly and seconded by the bishop of Limerick. They asked that the viceroy pass on to the government their requests that a fair proportion of the staff should be Catholic; that a board of trustees, of which the bishops of the province where the colleges were erected would be members, would appoint all office-holders; that Catholic chaplains, whom the bishops would appoint and dismiss, would be salaried by the Colleges; and that a Catholic professor would be appointed to the chairs of logic, metaphysics, moral philosophy, history, geology and anatomy.[18] This last request did not imply that the bishops were seeking to appoint half the professors. Rather they were asking for dual appointments so that Catholic undergraduates would only attend lectures in those subjects given by Catholics. One professor normally taught logic, metaphysics and moral philosophy in Catholic seminaries, and perhaps the same man would have taught history, which was added to the list as it was regarded as a potential quarry for polemicists who wanted to present a Protestant slant on the Reformation and church history in general. Geology was potentially controversial because of the claims made by some of its practitioners that it disproved divine creation of the world, and anatomy because of the possible moral connotations of its study.[19] Though details of the bishops' meeting have not survived, it is not difficult to see that this document was a compromise. That MacHale agreed to it at all may be partly explained by the absence of O'Higgins and Keating from the meeting. For, in view of the minority claims during the national school dispute, the absence of any guarantees about the role of bishops on the boards of governors, especially in connection with appointments to staff, one would have expected MacHale to insist on a veto by the bishops on the appointments of professors. He seems likely to have got his way with the request that bishops of the provinces where the Colleges were situated should be ex-officio trustees of those Colleges. And as he claimed that these were the minimum requirements of the hierarchy, he may have had in mind to elaborate on them in future negotiations.

---

[18] F.J., 24, 26 May 1845.

[19] By an act of George III establishing the school of physic at Trinity College, Dublin the three chairs of anatomy, chemistry and botany were reserved to Protestants. R.J. Bryce, an orthodox Presbyterian minister from Belfast, argued in a pamphlet on the Colleges that natural history, philosophy, geology and Greek could not be taught without reference to religion. Only Christians, he maintained, should be appointed to those chairs. (Moody and Beckett, Queen's Belfast, i, 22-24.)

The memorial was presented to the Lord Lieutenant by Crolly, Murray, MacHale and French, the bishop of Kilmacduagh, the two former representing the *politicanti* and the two latter the *zelanti*. In the interview with Lord Heytesbury, Crolly explained that the bishops' anxieties about the faith and morals of the students were related to the problems of student accommodation, and suggested that student residences should not be opened without a license from the bishop. Murray pointed out that the reference to chaplains concerned the need for clergy to be associated with the lodging houses. Heytesbury concluded that Crolly was less favourable to the bill than Murray and predicted that they would both stand by their colleagues.[20]

If these demands represented a compromise to some of the bishops, they seemed to the government to be extreme. Peel believed that they were 'wholly at variance with the principle of our measure',[21] and, if conceded, would give a wholly exclusive character to the new institutions. Graham quickly echoed this view and asked Heytesbury to find out from Murray what would satisfy 'the better portion of his Brethren'[22] and not to pay too much attention to MacHale's talk of minimal demands. He himself identified the basic requirements as 'security with regard to the Professors of History and Moral Philosophy' and religious instruction for the students 'living without the College walls'. He suggested the establishment of hostels by the state which would be under the supervision of a priest appointed by the bishop, and he added that it was MacHale's friends who had insisted on Catholics holding so many professorial appointments, with the others agreeing merely to avoid a split.[23] The government, however, rejected all the bishops' proposals. MacHale was not appeased by Heytesbury's vague promises to the deputation about making satisfactory adaptations in the charter of the Colleges and proceeded to put pressure on the government by giving the memorial to the press. And he soon delivered a vehement broadside, against the 'infidel' colleges, that boded ill for the government's plans. Resorting to his favourite image of perfidious Albion he told Peel that his 'infidel', 'slavish' and 'demoralizing scheme' only proved that Irish Catholics should be 'more apprehensive for the faith and liberties of this country during a period of political cajolery, than during one of avowed persecution'. And he went on to pay a backhanded tribute to Crolly, Murray and

[20] Heytesbury to Graham, 25, 28 May 1845, Graham Papers.
[21] Peel to Graham, 27 May 1845, Ibid.
[22] Graham to Heytesbury, 28 May 1845, Ibid.
[23] Heytesbury to Graham, 15 June 1845, Ibid.

Denvir by accusing Peel and Graham of eulogizing them for their support of the Charitable Bequests Act 'when they were but a few opposed to the great body of their brethren' and then dropping them from favour when in union with their brethren they demanded protection for Catholic education. Repudiating the suggestion that the Academical Institution could be a model for the other colleges, he characterized Peel's scheme and the rejection of the bishops' memorial as a fresh attempt to bribe Catholic youth into an abandonment of their religion, but predicted that the faith would triumph over 'the latest and deadliest of the persecutions'.[24]

At the second reading of the bill, Lord John Russell, the Whig leader, asked the Home Secretary whether the government contemplated any changes in view of the bishops' requests.[25] Graham replied that he planned to announce no alterations, but added that, at the committee stage, members could propose such alterations as were consistent with the principle of the bill; he himself, however, regarded the 'most material of the alterations' suggested by the bishops as inconsistent with that principle.[26]

In later debates Russell questioned the wisdom of reserving the appointments of principals and professors to the crown, a view that was also expressed by some Irish members. He suggested that ways should be found of making the bill more acceptable to Catholic leaders; otherwise it would not only be null, but noxious. Advantage should have been taken of the influence of the Catholic clergy to promote public instruction.[27] Lord John Manners challenged the value of all education that was not based on religion, and cited the hostility of fifty bishops in France to a similar university system imposed by the state.[28] Daniel O'Connell, warning of inevitable failure, if the opinions and advice of the bishops were ignored, quoted a letter he had received from MacHale assuring him that episcopal opposition was holding firm and describing the proposals as a 'penal and revolting . . . enactment'[29]—a description which Russell called strong phrases—but which he said had been adopted generally by the Catholic prelates; he declared that if the bill came out of committee still bearing the stigma of the Catholics of Ireland, it would have been better not to send it to that country at all.[30]

But Peel and Graham held fast.[31] They could not bring themselves to make any serious concessions, though they added regulations about

[24] F.J., 13 June 1845.   [25] Hansard 3, lxxx, 1133, (30 May 1845).   [26] Ibid., 1133.
[27] Ibid., 1237–1249, (2 June 1845).   [28] Ibid., 1137–1141, (30 May 1845).
[29] Ibid., lxxxi, 1355–58, (30 June 1845).   [30] Ibid., 1358–59 (30 June 1845).
[31] Graham felt that Archbishop Murray should have repudiated the criticisms made by his colleagues of the government's plans. He complained to Heytesbury that the archbishop's 'better judgement and feelings

residence and funding of hostels. In its final form the bill laid down strict rules about residence. Students were obliged to dwell with their parents or guardians, or with some friend selected by their parents or guardians, or with a tutor or master of a boarding house selected by the president of the College, or in a hall founded and endowed for student accommodation and recognized by the College. Halls could be founded and endowed by any individual or body—churches were therefore free to establish them— and the wardens, if the College visitor duly approved of them, could borrow money from the Board of Works to construct and extend them. The state, however, would not give grants towards the erection of denominational halls. The appointment of professors would remain a prerogative of the crown until 1848, the annual grants were increased from £6,000 to £7,000 per College, and a general provision was included to make some arrangement for ensuring that students attended divine worship. Graham insisted that lectures on religious subjects would be facilitated but never financed. And Peel, in defending the policy of religious neutrality, referred to the practice that obtained in the Belfast Academical Institution and mentioned Crolly's evidence at the commission of inquiry into it in 1825. Arguing that the Institution gave good secular education and left the parents and guardians of youth free to provide whatever religious education they chose, he quoted verbatim Crolly's answers to the question about interference by the teachers with the religious faith of Catholic children: there was no interference; Catholic parents whose sons were in attendance were obliged to send them to worship in his church, and some of the professors (who were Presbyterian ministers) far from giving offence had requested him to revise some copies of the Catholic scriptures for the use of their Catholic pupils. Concluding that this Belfast experience furnished 'facts in favour of the communions of different sects, and united education', he expressed his surprise at the claim that Catholic students could not attend lectures in geology, history or anatomy except from a Catholic professor, and argued that, if there was 'a tendency to infidelity in the study of geology or of anatomy, or in the professors of them', Protestants and Catholics stood upon the same footing in that respect.[32]

---

were overborne by the violence and animosity of his Brethren, and in public he has not the courage to give effect to the opinion and wishes, which in private he expresses and sincerely entertains'. (Graham to Heytesbury, 4 June 1845, Graham Papers.) Both Murray and Crolly subsequently showed considerable courage in resisting a powerful and clamorous public opinion.

[32] Hansard, 3, lxxx, 1279-1291, (2 June 1845).

The government was in no mood for delay and the bill was hastily passed and received the royal assent on 30 July. MacHale had sought to elicit from his colleagues another blast against the colleges when they met on business connected with Maynooth in June. Crolly, obviously determined to follow a more conciliatory approach and await clarification of the government's plans, in the hope of building on some agreement about residential accommodation, sought to stymie him by pleading the special limited nature of their assembly. Murray also took a hand in blocking other manoeuvres by the MacHale party to move against the Colleges so that any further official *prise de position* was ruled out until the annual meeting of the hierarchy in the autumn.[33]

II

The bill did not specify the location of the Colleges, and, though Belfast and Cork had been mentioned as possible sites for the Ulster and Munster Colleges, no definite decision was announced in parliament.[34] And, as the suggestion which Graham had made on introducing the bill of converting the Belfast Academical Institution into one of the Colleges had not been further pursued, the emplacement of the Ulster College was still not decided when the bill became law. Consequently, some of the leading citizens of Armagh resolved to stake their claim, as an ancient centre of ecclesiastical power and learning, to an institution that would enhance the prestige of the city, and restore some of its former eminence.

A meeting attended by Crolly, the local Presbyterian and Independent clergymen, sundry gentry, magistrates and professional and business men was held in the Market-house on 7 August to discuss and further this claim. On Crolly's motion, William Paton, a local merchant, took the chair. William Colvan, a doctor, recalled the great college which once flourished in Armagh and to which students from Scotland, England and most European countries thronged, 'when Europe was in a benighted

---

[33] Cullen to Kirby, 6 July 1845, AICR. Cullen reported that several of the bishops were said to be in favour of the bill, though they had been supposedly unanimous in condemning it.

[34] Peel and Graham had Belfast, Cork and probably Galway in mind as the sites of the colleges, and proposed to have a Presbyterian president in Belfast and Catholic presidents in the other two. Graham encouraged Heytesbury, in selecting staff, to try as far as possible not to send Presbyterians to the south of Ireland or Catholics to the north. (Graham to Heytesbury, 10 Aug. 1845, Graham Papers.)

state'. And, bewailing the dilatoriness of his fellow citizens, when other applicants from places with no comparable grounds for consideration had been busy, he went on to give a special welcome to the Catholic primate. Noting that Crolly had erected a good school and yet was not afraid of competition from the new College, he insisted that with the support of the nobility and gentry from the neighbouring counties their appeal would not be too late. Belfast 'had already got a large share of the good things of the Government' and, moreover, 'the morals of young men would by no means be so likely to be corrupted in a town the size of Armagh, as either in Belfast or Dublin'. Crolly, expressing his pleasure at seeing the respectable citizens of Armagh of every persuasion assembled on so interesting and important an occasion, observed that 'every liberal-minded man should acknowledge that the middle class of Ireland stand in great need of an impartial, enlightened system of Academical education'. The government had made good provision for the education of the poor, the commissioners of national education cooperated harmoniously, and 'from such enlightened teachers, with proper books and lessons of paternal love, it might naturally be expected that a spirit of Christian charity would be soon diffused throughout the land'.

Turning to the proposed Colleges, he predicted that, as the mixed system had so far been successful in the national schools, it would be equally so at tertiary level, if managed in the same Christian spirit. When the bill had first been published

he entertained serious apprehensions respecting the morality of the students, who appeared to be left without any moral superintendence, subject to their own inclinations and propensities, at a period of life the most critical, when the passions were most violent and dangerous. Under that impression, he called a general meeting of the Catholic Prelates, who were willing and ready to cooperate on fair and reasonable terms with the Government. They discussed the provisions of the Bill; and, after mature deliberation, went to the Lord Lieutenant and represented their objections, and the amendments they deemed advisable. The Lord Lieutenant received the memorial, and forwarded the state of the case to the government, who made such amendments as were calculated to afford general satisfaction. By the Bill, as it at present stood, no pupil could be received into any of the new colleges, unless he would lodge with his parent, a relative, a guardian, or in a house duly licensed by the President of the College for the very purpose of protecting his morality. Besides, the Bill gives full power to have chaplains of every religious persuasion duly appointed, for the purpose of superintending the moral conduct of the students, and giving them proper moral instruction, at such hours as will not interfere with their scientific studies. This being the most important point in the measure, and one to which most objection was urged, at the outset, he was determined as far as he was concerned, to give their Provincial College a fair trial, which could not be done unless it were placed in such a situation, that the students, from the nine Counties in Ulster, as far as possible, have equal access to it, and which could be evidently best accomplished, by erecting it nearly in the centre of the Province, a situation it would occupy, if situated in the ancient city of Armagh.

Crolly went on to praise Armagh's proud scholastic tradition and the fine opportunities it then offered. It boasted, he noted, a valuable library of 20,000 books, an observatory superintended by one of the best astronomers in the British empire, a hospital and infirmary attended by physicians and surgeons of the highest character, and it had been chosen by the railway builders as the most suitable terminus for all the railways of Ulster, so that, at small expense, students could commute from home, and thereby enjoy the benefits of parental supervision. Promising that, if Armagh were chosen, he would make proper provision for the Catholic students, and assuming that other religious authorities would do likewise, he concluded by moving that a committee be appointed to draw up a memorial to the Lord Lieutenant detailing the advantages of the primatial city.

When this motion was seconded the chairman put it to the meeting and it was unanimously carried. A seven member committee which included Crolly and a Presbyterian minister was chosen and retired to an adjoining room to prepare the memorial. On their return the chairman read out the draft which listed six principal grounds for selecting 'the metropolitan city of Ireland' as the seat of the Ulster college. These included its central geographical position, its public library and observatory—points which Crolly had made—as well as the claim that it enjoyed a healthy location with a pure and salubrious climate and 'having no large manufacture' was 'free from most of those inducements to immorality and vice which are to be deplored in every large manufacturing town'. The memorialists further drew attention to the denominational balance of their city which divided among 'Church Protestants, Roman Catholics and Presbyterians in nearly equal proportions', and maintained that its possession of two primatial seats should 'have much weight with her Majesty's Government, as being a guarantee to the public for the most effectual superintendence not only of the Professors and office-bearers, but of the students and all others connected with the institution'. They also suggested that this support for 'the preservation of moral rectitude and social concord', would be 'a desideratum with the government as well as with all well-disposed persons, of every religious persuasion'.

After some further discussion Crolly proposed the appointment of a deputation to present their case to the Lord Lieutenant, pointing out that personal contact would afford a better opportunity of making their plea more sucessfully than a written document. A deputation of five, including Crolly, George Robinson, the director of the observatory, and P.S. Henry, the Presbyterian minister of Armagh, who had sent his apologies for not attending the meeting, was quickly appointed. Crolly then suggested that this body wait on the primate of the established church, and invite him to accompany them to the Lord Lieutenant. When the chairman explained that the primate would not then be in Dublin but was likely to lend his support, Crolly proposed that they should obtain from him and from the prominent nobles of Armagh and the neighbouring counties, and from their members of parliament, letters indicating their approval of the project. This suggestion was readily accepted and a secretary was appointed to carry it out. The meeting concluded with two votes of thanks—one to the chairman and one to Crolly, who had replaced him before it ended.[35]

The archbishop had undoubtedly played the leading part at this meeting and his enthusiam for the location of a College in Armagh raises questions about the degree of anxiety he felt on those proposals which a short time before he had deemed to be 'pregnant with danger to the faith and morals' of Catholic students. The assumption that he was trying to make a virtue out of necessity and extract the best possible deal from an unalterable government decision does not do justice to the keenness with which he fought his corner for Armagh. Undoubtedly, he believed that Armagh was a less sectarian town than Belfast, and that a College situated there would be spared the theological polemics which had crippled the Belfast Academical Institution. And he felt strongly that the Catholics of Ulster were entitled to obtain an education in a convenient centre rather than be forced to travel to colleges in Munster or Connacht. He regarded 'the scheme of giving up the Ulster college exclusively to the Protestants, in order to get the southern and western colleges for the Catholics' as 'not only inadmissible but infamous'.[36] He wrote to a friend justifying his campaigning for Armagh:

If I had this college in Armagh, I would have the Catholic youth lodged in a house selected by myself, in which I could impart religious instruction to them, and keep

[35] A.G., 12 Aug. 1845. The leading citizens of Belfast, headed by the mayor, held a similar meeting to advocate their claims on 2 September. Henry Cooke, when commenting on the qualifications of Armagh, and referring to the advantages it enjoyed in having the advocacy of the two primates, was applauded when he said that 'in Dr Crolly, the Primate of the Roman Catholic Church, it possessed a man who needed no eulogium in Belfast, where he was not more known than appreciated'. (B.N.L., 5 Sept. 1845.)
[36] Crolly to ——, 16 Sept. 1845, G. Crolly, Crolly, xcviii.

them as perfectly under my control as the students in my own seminary. If, however, it should unfortunately be built in Belfast, I could repose very little confidence in it. It will be placed in the most Protestant place in Ireland; and you may depend that, though it may not be a proselytizing, it will infallibly be a sectarian establishment. The Protestant population preponderates so much in the town of Belfast, as well as in the adjoining counties of Down and Antrim, that any public establishment open to all, and situated in that town, will be more or less sectarian in its management. Every office in the institution in Belfast, which is also supported by government grants, is open to Catholics; and yet, not one of these, with the exception of the insignificant situation of writing—master, has ever been filled by a Catholic . . . I, therefore, think it a matter of the greatest importance to the Catholics of Ulster that the new college should be built both in a more central situation and in a place where, being more equally balanced with those of other religions, they will be less likely to be excluded from a fair share of professorships.[37]

The alterations made in the bill at the committee stage, especially with regard to accommodation, had pleased him. The government's assurance that halls of residence for students forced to live away from home could be licensed and supervised by a chaplain or dean had greatly diminished his fears about the dangers associated with the Colleges. The choice of professors and their influence over the students did not concern him to anything like the extent that it troubled his colleagues; he seems to have trusted the government's professions of fairness in making the appointments and the professors' conscientiousness in avoiding the expression of views that could give offence to their students.

At the interview with the viceroy, Crolly not only pointed out the unsuitability of the buildings and site of the Academical Institution but stressed the likelihood of Catholics not sending their sons to a locality where Unitaranism prevailed.[38] Graham saw the advantages offered by Armagh—especially their obtaining the cooperation of the two primates—but both he and Peel believed that their first duty was to conciliate the Presbyterians.[39] A deputation from Belfast which included the mayor, Cooke, Montgomery and Edgar, representing different strands of Presbyterianism, and which had the support of Bishop Denvir, also visited the Lord Lieutenant to present its case.[40] As a result a commission was appointed to visit the possible sites for the Ulster College and report on their suitability.

Crolly's public advocacy of the case for Armagh surprised and disconcerted some of his friends in the hierarchy. Archbishop Slattery obviously

[37] Crolly to ——, 5 Sept. 1845, Ibid., xcvi-xcvii.
[38] Heytesbury to Graham, 16 Aug. 1845, Graham Papers.
[39] Graham to Heytesbury, 16, 18, 20 Aug. 1845, Ibid.
[40] Heytesbury to Graham, 4 Sept. 1845, Ibid.

communicated his fears about the likely consequences to Bishop Kennedy of Killaloe, for Kennedy replied that he regretted the carelessness of the primate in stating that the changes made in the bill gave general satisfaction, and remarked that Crolly would have displayed more prudence by confining himself strictly to the presentation of his own views.[41] James Browne of Kilmore explained the archbishop's *démarche* as the fruit of his close relations with Protestants:

He has been always amongst Protestants and has been very successful in bringing many of them back into the C. Church. He has found some of them honorable and upright and in consequence has more confidence in them than is entertained by the other Bishops of Ireland. I dare say he is under the impression that if he had one of the Colleges in Armagh, he would be able to turn the balance in favour of Catholicity. ... I hope that Dr Crolly will also see the necessity of yielding to the general voice of the Bishops and people. This consummation I hope will be brought about by the Advice of the Bishops themselves who must all respect him as the successor of St Patrick.[42]

Critics of the Colleges and of Crolly were quick to point out that his contribution to this lobby for Armagh did not tally with the statement put out by the bishops on 21 May. The *Newry Examiner* claimed that parents were not free to place their children in lodgings with a friend, but were obliged to entrust them to some licensed lodging-house keeper, 'a subordinate instrument' of the president of the College, who would fashion the opinions of the rising generation and would report any manifestation of patriotic feeling by their charges. And it further reminded him that the bishops had also contemplated a more grievous danger than that which was connected with morals, namely the danger to faith arising from the absence of religious instruction and the unlimited power of the government to appoint professors without any veto by the church on persons who could be infidels.

Then, to add to Crolly's difficulties, a political complication was superimposed on the educational issues. Suspicion was cast on his association with some of the magistrates, especially Paton and Robinson, who had strongly supported him at the meeting. On the previous 12 July a young Catholic, John Boyle, had been shot dead by Orangemen in Armagh. The Catholic community had been outraged. Crolly had attended the funeral, but the magistrates, who had been remiss in tolerating the illegal march in the first place, had earned Catholic opprobrium for refusing to take stern action against the culprits. Crolly was now accused of cooperating with

[41] Kennedy to Slattery, 20 Aug. 1845, Slattery Papers.
[42] Browne to Slattery, 3 Oct. 1845, Ibid.

men who had protected the assassins of an innocent Catholic youth. The *Examiner* remarked with bitter sarcasm that when reports first appeared of Crolly's presence at a meeting at Armagh, it had concluded that he had convened his parishioners 'on the subject of the recent wanton slaughter' so that with their liberal Protestant friends they could petition the Lord Lieutenant for a full and searching inquiry into the conduct of the local magistracy, and had thought 'better late than never'. Its editorial ended on a savagely sardonic note: '"mixed education" facilitated by "mixed trains". What a happy consummation for Armagh, when Dr Crolly and Lord John Beresford, and Dr Henry (the Presbyterian primate) shall put their heads together to "mix" scriptural instruction for the rising generation.'[43]

Peel was upset by the canvas for Armagh and fearful that it would alienate the Presbyterians who strongly favoured Belfast. He told Graham that the selection of Armagh and P.S. Henry as principal would be 'fatal to the Northern College as a Presbyterian Institution' since that College had to be '*Presbyterian* or it will be worse than useless'. Crolly's intervention he regarded as unfortunate and unreasonable.[44] The solution to the difficulty lay in the appointment of a commission which would survey the opinions of leading Presyterians, consider the advantages of both locations and investigate the condition of the buildings of the Belfast Academical Institution. Despite Heytesbury's reservation about the prudence of appointing such a commission, Peel insisted, and he was happy to find his initial reaction to the postulation of the two primates for the location at Armagh borne out by Heytesbury's report of the jealousy felt by Presbyterians as a result of it. He believed that the government should not offend the Presbyterians to shield Crolly from unjust attacks.[45]

In the discussions about the Colleges, both in parliament and in the press, scarcely any reference was made to the numbers likely to frequent the Colleges. Peel on one occasion referred hypothetically to 300. And in another intervention he noted that twelve Catholics attended the tertiary or collegiate department of the Belfast Academical Institution. Almost certainly Crolly envisaged a small number of Catholic students at the northern College—perhaps twenty five but probably less than fifty. Not many Catholic parents in the north could have afforded the fees. He had a few years previously established a seminary in Armagh, and he may well have planned to extend it or to acquire adjacent or convenient property to

[43] N.Ex., 20 Aug. 1845; O'Muiri, 'Orangemen, Repealers and the shooting of John Boyle in Armagh', *Seanchas Ard Mhacha*, 11 (1985), 435-529
[44] Peel to Graham, 17 Aug. 1845, Graham Papers.
[45] Ibid., 19 Aug., 6 Sept., 28 Sept. 1845.

accommodate the small number of undergraduates he anticipated. He probably intended to appoint a priest to take charge of this house or hall and act as chaplain to the non-resident students as well.

Crolly's episcopal opponents were determined not to let the views expressed at Armagh pass unchallenged. The *Freeman's Journal*, which reminded its readers that none of the conditions contained in the memorial to the Lord Lieutenant that Crolly had first proposed had been granted, promptly published a letter of Bishop Cantwell to John O'Connell confirming his opposition to 'that hateful measure' which had been made 'worse by its amendments'.[46] And when Crolly left a meeting of prelates at Maynooth which had been held to make appointments to vacant chairs, MacHale took advantage of his absence to obtain the signatures of colleagues to a brief and pithy statement assuring their faithful flocks that the bishops' views on the danger to faith and morals contained in the Colleges Act remained unchanged. Eighteen bishops signed this declaration, and, as one was too feeble to take part and one had not expressed his opinions, the *Freeman's Journal* could claim that they represented a majority which confronted a minority of only six.[47] With this step the hierarchy had in effect been split for the third time in a decade, and Crolly and Murray found themselves faced with a large, determined and formidable opposition.

As soon as the bishops' declaration was published, Crolly called on the Lord Lieutenant to make a further plea for siting the northern College in Armagh. Heytesbury reported that the archbishop believed that his colleagues' action made it necessary for him to be more cautious 'not to expose himself to [their] just animadversions'. The establishment of a College in Belfast would place him in that predicament, for if a Presbyterian were to preside over such a College, it would become a purely sectarian institution and he could not sanction the education of Catholic youth in it.[48] Crolly went on to express his preference for a Protestant of the established church, rather than a Presbyterian, as the principal, and even suggested that such a choice would be more agreeable to the Presbyterians themselves. He himself would prefer a liberal Englishman to a native of Ulster or even of Ireland, though he was aware that O'Connell and his friends would denounce such a choice as an insult to Ireland. Referring to the bishops' meeting at which the declaration had

---

[46] F.J., 21 Aug. 1845.   [47] Ibid., 20 Sept. 1845.

[48] Cooke warned Peel that the appointment of a Catholic or a Unitarian to a chair in any of the subjects which candidates for the ministry would have to take would cause the General Assembly to prevent its students from attending the northern College. (Moody and Beckett) *Queen's, Belfast*, i, 22.

been made, he explained that it had all been done by trickery: MacHale waited until he and his friends had gone and 'then drew from the timidity of some, & the ill will of others, of those who remained, their consent' to his document. The Lord Lieutenant declined to give any assurances about the siting of the College till the commission had reported.[49] Crolly's fear of Belfast winning the prize, however, showed that he was aware how tough a fight supporters of cooperation with the government would have on their hands, and how far that town had moved from the liberal Presbyterianism which he had once extolled.

To add to his trials, Crolly was then subjected to a base personal insult by the *Pilot*. This Repeal paper, anxious to punish him for his aloofness from, if not outward hostility to, Repeal, took advantage of his seeming change of direction at the Armagh meeting to suggest that the balance of his mind had been disturbed. On the same day it published a letter addressed to the 'few and nameless Bishops who have not as yet protested against the Godless education system' and an editorial in which it claimed that the part he had played in the campaign to obtain the College for Armagh 'gave rise to strange surmises as to his Grace's state of mind; and the allusion in his speech at the meeting to the concentration of all the Northern railways at Armagh, and the facility they would afford to the entire youth of Ulster to shoot in from all quarters in the morning to take lectures, and radiate off in the evening to take shelter under the parental roof from the destructive grasp of the gigantic infidel, was so supremely ridiculous, so outrageously foolish, that those surmises were more than confirmed'. The editorial then claimed that a reliable fact had just been revealed which left *'no doubt whatever that his Grace's faculties must have undergone some disastrous change since May last'*.

The *Pilot* then went on to explain that the same person who drew up the memorial to the Lord Lieutenant had become a supporter of the Colleges and had acted in a manner 'clearly not to be accounted for in any other way but that the reports to which we have alluded are unhappily but too well founded'. Pointing out that the archbishop had been 'living rather retired for some weeks past—he has not attended the last meeting of the Prelates at Maynooth' it then compounded its unscrupulous libel with a hypocritical expression of goodwill by declaring that it sincerely hoped for 'the restoration of his Grace to mental and bodily health'.[50]

Even some of Crolly's most severe critics were incensed by this cruel attack. And the clergy of Armagh, whether or not they agreed with the

[49] Heytesbury to Graham, 21 Sept. 1845, Graham Papers.
[50] P., 29 Sept. 1845.

primate's views on education, were justifiably furious at this attempt to undermine respect for one whose zeal and integrity they admired. At the meetings of the four diocesan conferences at Dundalk, Dunleer, Armagh and Dungannon they drew up and signed statements rebutting the *Pilot's* charges in language which showed that they were scarcely able to restrain their indignation. The Dundalk declaration may be taken as representative:

That we have read, with inexpressible disgust and indignation, in the *Pilot* news paper, of the 29th ultimo, an article calculated to tarnish the high character of the Most Rev. Dr. Crolly . . . Knowing that this *slanderous and unprincipled article* is not only a vile calumny, but a *cowardly and sacrilegious* libel on the character of the pious and faithful head of the Catholic Church in Ireland, we consider it our duty to denounce it, and hold it up to the honest execration of all portions of the *Irish public* who 'love truth and hate falsehood'.[51]

The response of the *Pilot* was almost as deplorable as the original charge. After the publication by the clergy of the Dunleer district of their resolution on 7 October, it explained on the following day that 'the article complained of was neither written by the Editor of the journal nor read by him, until it appeared in print'. The author was, in fact, a distant correspondent who often transmitted valuable communications to the paper. The editor in the midst of his multitudinous duties did not have time to vet that particular contribution. Though therefore only 'technically responsible for it' he, nonetheless, had incurred responsibility and so felt obliged to apologize unequivocally for the imputation the article contained, and accordingly did so in the most unqualified manner.[52]

Crolly's Protestant friends in Armagh also insisted on publicly vindicating his character. A meeting 'pursuant to a requisition numerously and respectably signed' was held in the town on 16 October, and was attended by five magistrates and many prominent people from the district. William Paton took the chair, and, referring to the 'sort of an apology' that had been given in 'a very uncandid and shabby manner', explained that they had met to express their indignation at the malicious calumny to which the archbishop had been subjected. Resolutions were passed rejecting as 'heartless and unfounded' the allegations made in the *Pilot* and bearing testimony to 'the good feeling and kind disposition' which Crolly had always evinced to every class of inhabitant and which had 'won for him feelings of respect and regard from persons of every religious persuasion'. A short address embodying these sentiments was presented to the primate on the following day. In his reply he observed that the dignified manner

[51] N.W., 11 Oct. 1845.   [52] P., 8 Oct. 1845.

of their denunciation of his calumniator proved that the spirit of Christian concord was cherished among Irishmen of different religions and political principles, and assured them that they had conferred on him the highest honour by stating that his conduct had conformed to the great precept of doing to others what one should reasonably expect to be done to oneself.[53]

Many newspapers copied the original story from the *Pilot* and then bitterly criticized it when the truth became known. The *Nation* reminded its readers that the editor of the *Pilot*, Richard Barrett, had been guilty of forgery two years previously and contemptuously dismissed his explanation of his long delay in admitting the falsity of the accusation.[54] Riled by many adverse comments the *Pilot* carried a letter from 'a correspondent' explaining that he had written the piece from Cashel, where, on the eve of the great Repeal meeting at Thurles, he had heard many people say that the primate must have been mad to adopt the course he was pursuing. And the 'correspondent' then remarked that, though the clergy of Armagh had, in their defence of the archbishop, described him as beloved, they had not justified his stance on the Colleges and 'nothing could be more pointedly, though silently, condemnatory'.[55] The *Nation* and the *Tablet* continued to point out the inconsistencies in the *Pilot*'s defence, and then in a letter dated 21 October which appeared in the *Tablet* of 1 November, Richard Power, the parish priest of Kilrossanty in the diocese of Waterford, accused that paper of scurrilously attacking Barrett, and he vigorously defended the beleaguered editor of the *Pilot*.[56] Gavan Duffy reprinted that letter a week later in the *Nation* and revealed that persons connected with the office of the *Pilot* had reported throughout Dublin that Power had instigated Barrett 'to perpetuate the abominable libel' on the primate.[57] Power duly wrote to the *Tablet*, which had reproduced Duffy's claim, saying that Barrett was free to disclose the authorship and declaring that he was delighted with the report and that his heart 'got light at the prospect that our venerable hierarchy were relieved from the imputation of insincerity, inconsistency and tergiversation'. If Crolly were his own brother, he added, he would sooner see him raving in a madhouse and strapped down to his iron bed than that he should be open to the charges (presumably of inconsistency and betrayal of his colleagues) brought against him. The *Pilot* which reproduced this letter, also printed another, from Power to itself, fully admitting his authorship and apologizing, not for the contents of the original charge, but for the trouble he had caused to Barrett. He concluded with the brutal remark that he did not

[53] A.G., 16 Oct. and 21 Oct. 1845.   [54] N., 4, 25 Oct. 1845.   [55] P., 17 Oct. 1845.
[56] *Tablet*, 1 Nov. 1845.   [57] N., 8 Nov. 1845.

recollect 'any event in the history of the Church disastrous to religion—destructive of the liberty of the Church, and corruptive of the faith and morality of the people—that a bad Archbishop was not a principal actor in it'.[58]

While this dispute was raging the three commissioners appointed by the government to recommend the most suitable site for the northern college visited Armagh, Belfast and Derry. Though they did not interview Crolly when in Armagh, they included his submission in favour of the primatial city in their report.[59] Not surprisingly Belfast won the competition and on 29 November the Chief Secretary notified the mayor of its success.[60] The decision of this independent body, which had been known for some time, relieved the government of the fear of powerful Presbyterian hostility. Much as it would have liked to accommodate Crolly, his cooperation would have been, as Graham noted, dearly purchased at the price of surrendering Belfast and a Presbyterian head.[61] When the archbishop sent a messenger to see the Lord Lieutenant, to make a further plea for Armagh just before the bishops' meeting, hoping obviously to have some weaponry with which to defend his views, Heytesbury responded by pointing out that the numbers, weight and importance of the Presbyterians entitled them to have their interests and wishes considered.[62] If Crolly was disheartened by this decision, as he undoubtedly was, his disappointment must have been somewhat lessened by the government's choice of president for the new College. The merits of Henry Cooke had been sedulously touted in the conservative press and his selection would have given great satisfaction to the more extreme Protestants of Ulster, but Peel, who was conscious of the anti-Catholic tone in Cooke's writings, could not envisage a Catholic ever working with him as a vice-president,[63] and so the government plumped for the more complaisant Presbyterian minister of Armagh, Pooley Shuldham Henry. Henry, a commissioner of national education and of Charitable Bequests, carried none of the theologically or politically controversial baggage that weighed down Cooke, and his appointment was calaculated to mollify critics and opponents of the Colleges Act.

The government wanted to reward Thaddeus O'Malley, the controversial priest who had given it support on the national schools, Charitable

[58] P., 19 Nov. 1845.   [59] B.N.L., 26 Sept. 1845.   [60] Ibid., 2 Dec. 1845.
[61] Graham to Heytesbury, 24 Sept. 1845, Graham papers.
[62] Heytesbury to Graham, 16 Nov. 1845, Ibid.
[63] Peel to Graham, 15 Nov. 1845, Ibid. Bishop Nicholas Wiseman had been mentioned as a possible president for one of the other Colleges but Peel thought that his reputation as a controversialist and opponent of the Anglican church and his being English made him unsuitable for the position. (Peel to Graham, 14 Aug. 1845, Ibid.).

Bequests and the Colleges, and toyed with the idea of appointing him vice-president in Belfast as a sop to Crolly. It even thought of placing him in that office alongside Cooke, thereby obtaining the ablest representative of the Presbyterians and conciliating the Catholics. But apart from this being the most unlikely combination of bedfellows imaginable, O'Malley's promotion would have placed Crolly in a far worse predicament vis-a-vis MacHale than any other, with the possible exception of Cooke.[64] Graham then suggested the appointment of James Thomson, a distinguished Ulster mathematician, as vice-president to make up for Henry's lack of scholarship, but, when Thomson refused for financial reasons, Thomas Andrews, a professor of chemistry at the Academical Institution was chosen. Sir Robert Kane, an eminent scientist, and Joseph Kirwan, the parish priest of Oughterard, had already been appointed presidents of Cork and Galway. John Ryall and Edward Berwick, both of whom were graduates of Trinity College, Dublin, were named as vice-presidents, respectively.

Such crumbs of comfort as Henry's appointment bore little influence in the larger theatre of conflict whither the Colleges question had been directed. Crolly found himself fighting a war on two fronts as he sought to defend his line against hostile critics both in Rome and in Ireland.

III

Unlike the situation that had arisen over the national schools, when the Holy See was brought into the dispute by a formal appeal from one of the four archbishops, its initial involvement in the Colleges issue was brought about by the rector and vice-rector of the Irish College in Rome. Paul Cullen, the rector, chanced to be in Ireland in 1845 when the Colleges Bill was going through parliament. His reaction was instinctively hostile; he immediately feared that the worst effects of continental collegiate systems on the faith of their students would be reproduced in Ireland. Thinking not in local but in wider terms, he saw Peel's proposals not as a Machiavellian British policy to weaken Catholicism in Ireland, but rather as an extension of a secular policy that had, according to French and German episcopal critics, diminished and in some cases destroyed the religious commitment of French and German students.

---

[64] Heytesbury to Graham, 19 Oct. 1845, Graham to Heytesbury, 20 Oct. 1845, Fremantle to Graham, 11, 12 Nov. 1845, Graham to Fremantle, 14 Nov. 1845, Heytesbury to Graham, 19 Nov. 1845, Graham to Heytesbury, 26 Nov. 1845, Ibid.

Consequently, he set about stiffening the opposition of MacHale and other episcopal critics of the new scheme. On 6 July he gave his vice-rector, Tobias Kirby, an account of the bishops' meeting in Maynooth, and explained that Crolly had blocked MacHale's request for a debate on the education question by arguing that they had not met to discuss politics. The meeting then adjourned in great confusion and MacHale said he would publish the letter convoking the bishops to consider the Colleges Bill, a matter which the primate had chosen to describe as political. Archbishop Murray brought them together and it was proposed to deal with the Colleges again but nothing was done. Cullen concluded that several of the bishops were said to be favourable to the Colleges, though the hierarchy was supposed to be unanimous in condemning them. He then suggested that Crolly, Bishop Kennedy of Killaloe and Bishop Murphy of Cork would set out for Rome in September (presumably to put their case for the Charitable Bequests Act, but possibly also for the Colleges). And he also took steps to counter such a move by advising MacHale, Cantwell and another bishop to make the same journey.[65] The implication of the letter was that the weak bishops who had succumbed to government pressure on the Charitable Bequests Act would be likely to do so again.

Further investigations convinced Cullen that the majority of the bishops would oppose the Colleges but he was particularly sceptical of Crolly's role. He told Kirby that it was 'a pity [the] Primate is not to be relied much on in these matters—it is a pity that Rome s[houl]d make him the organ of her communications—were it not for him Dr Murray w[oul]d be easily managed—Dr Denvir is almost dead of terror'.[66] He also encouraged 'the orthodox prelates to address a common document to the Irish clergy and people, strongly reprobating the Infidel Colleges', and this they did a few days later.[67] Kirby passed on these apprehensions to Propaganda, and was obviously told to get Cullen to send a letter explaining the situation more fully, which he promptly did.

Outlining to Cardinal Fransoni the principal arrangements made by the government and noting the exclusion of religion from the Colleges, he explained how the whole hierarchy had declared them to be dangerous to faith and morals and how this decision was received with joy throughout Ireland. It seemed that the bishops had been again reconciled but this appearance of union did not last long. The archbishop of Armagh, who

---

[65] Cullen to Kirby, 6 July 1845, AICR.
[66] Ibid., 20 July 1845.
[67] O'Higgins to MacHale, 16 Sept. 1845 in O'Reilly, MacHale, ii, 506-7.

had declared his opposition to the scheme, had since publicly retracted his opposition and had gone with four Protestants to the viceroy the previous week to ask that one of the universities be sited in Armagh. He added that Archbishop Murray was thought likely to follow Crolly's example, expressed regret at the bad effect such episcopal inconstancy would have on the Catholic people, who were almost all opposed to the erection of schools that would produce but 'the fruits of irreligion and dissoluteness as had the Prussian universities in imitation of which they had been founded', and predicted that their Protestant government would not hesitate to take advantage of the situation it had brought about so that in a few years the church in Ireland would be reduced to the same condition as that of Prussia. He concluded this gloomy prognostication with the information that Bunsen, the former Prussian minister in Rome, was then in London influencing the government in this direction and that A.R. Blake, a commissioner of Charitable Bequests along with Crolly and Murray, had suggested a plan whereby the government could exclude the interference of the Holy See in the ecclesiastical affairs of Ireland.[68]

This was a brief but powerful broadside against the Colleges and Crolly emerged from it as the chief culprit. Cullen's high standing in Rome ensured that it was taken seriously at the highest level. From his visits to some of the bishops and his contacts with others at Maynooth, Cullen had learned that all but about six of the prelates whom he identified as Crolly, Murray, Denvir, Ryan (Limerick), Murphy (Cork) and Browne (Kilmore) were hostile to the new policy, and described Crolly as 'a decided government man'. He reported enthusiastically the rebuff Crolly received from Archbishop Slattery of Cashel when he suggested that the seminary at Thurles might become one of the Colleges, referred to the rejoinder that the bishops planned to publish against Crolly's speech at Armagh, and explained, though rather pessimistically, that he had tried to persuade the bishops to write a letter to Rome denouncing the Colleges.[69]

Fransoni, reluctantly dragged into yet a further Irish controversy, decided to write to Crolly for information. But his letter was not the traditional Roman request for full details on a particular issue: it contained an implicit rebuke for it indicated that the cardinal was confused by the archbishop's change of mind. Pointing out that he had heard how Crolly had switched to favouring and no longer regarding as dangerous a system of education which he had once denounced as perilous

---

[68] Cullen to Propaganda, 27 Aug. 1845, APF, SOCG, 968, ff 676r-677v.
[69] Cullen to Kirby, 20 Sept. 1845, AICR.

to the faith and morals of Catholics, and had even campaigned for the establishment of one of the colleges in his diocese, Fransoni sought not only an account of the whole university question but also an explanation of the archbishop's altered attitude to it.[70] Had this reproach remained secret, it would have embarrassed and pained Crolly, but, when a report of it reached Ireland from Rome, the *zelanti* were jubilant. O'Higgins, with his customary extremism, declared that the archbishop deserved to be severely punished for this further misjudgement or betrayal. He told Cullen: 'I am delighted that the Primate has received an advice from Rome. He will do mischief still unless the Pope and Cardinal are very stern and explicit. If the "odium justum populi" [the just anger of the people] be a sufficient cause for removing a Bishop, he should be either sent from Armagh or made to recant his scandalous errors'.[71] Crolly and the *politicanti* were put on the defensive.

However, the primate fought back with determination and resource. In replying to Rome he recalled the vehement opposition of several bishops to the national system of education, which had come to flourish in every diocese except MacHale's and which enjoyed the support of eight hundred parish priests as school patrons, and he pointed out that nothing had been done for the young men of a higher social class who were accustomed to frequent the Calvinist colleges of Scotland or the dangerous seminaries of France. When the government proposed to accommodate them by erecting three Colleges in which there was no instruction given in the Christian faith nor a safe residential hostel for the students, he feared that without supervision and care they would soon lose their virtue and faith. Consequently, he summoned the bishops to a meeting to discuss measures for the protection of the faith and morals of the students in the Colleges. Then deftly hitting back at those opponents whom he doubtless blamed for delating him to Fransoni, he remarked that political and ecclesiastical agitators and even some of the bishops, who had not been best pleased by the prudent admonition of the Holy See to maintain peace and tranquillity,[72] praised him for his action and called for the immediate condemnation of the system. But many bishops and the more prudent section of the people favoured an emendation rather than a rejection of the system.

The prelates then consented to petition the viceroy to have changes

[70] Fransoni to Crolly, 20 Sept. 1845, APF, *Lett.*, 332, f 654rv.
[71] O'Higgins to Cullen, 15 Oct. 1845, AICR.
[72] This was a reference to Cardinal Fransoni's letter of Oct. 1844 bidding Crolly admonish those ecclesiastics who were implicated in political and secular concerns.

made to the legislation in parliament and in response the government agreed to two significant alterations: the staff of the colleges were obliged to provide facilities to enable undergraduates to attend lectures on religion which would be given by learned clergy duly selected and appointed for that purpose, and no student would be allowed to matriculate unless he were to reside in his own home, in that of a tutor approved by his parents or in a hostel especially licensed by the president of the College. Furthermore, he added that the viceroy had told him that at least two of the presidents and many of the professors would be zealous and reliable priests, who by word and example would promote tranquillity and peace; those priests who were involved in political affairs would be excluded from office. The collegiate scheme, it was now clear, had been adapted to suit episcopal requirements and, if the bishops cooperated with the government in recommending and selecting pious and prudent priests to teach the students, the new system would not only supply much needed education but would also be a bulwark for religion. Recalling the government's generosity to Maynooth and the success of the national schools, he foresaw the same happy results from the Colleges, if the bishops cooperated in the selection of staff and the supervision of hostels. To preserve the youth of Ulster from the influence of the strong anti-Catholic prejudices of many Protestants of Belfast, he had advocated its location in Armagh where, by frequent visitations and daily inspection, he could guard the Catholic youth from any danger to their faith and morals.[73] Consequently, there was no foundation for the truth of the story about a college or university in his diocese.[74]

As a defence of his position this reply seemed comprehensive and effective. But even the more moderate of those who had signed MacHale's last salvo against the Colleges would have found serious fault with it. They would have regarded his attitude to the government as too unsuspecting; would not have accepted the claim that hostility to the Colleges derived from political attitudes; would have denied that a government which had publicly rejected appeals for various adjustments

---

[73] On 1 Oct. the F.J. quoted the demand made by the Presbyterian *Banner of Ulster* that 'the Ulster College must be Presbyterian or nothing'. The *Banner*, which repudiated any interference by Crolly 'in a seminary avowedly intended for the benefit of the candidates intended for the Presbyterian ministry' insisted that the College should be located in Belfast.

[74] Crolly to Propaganda, 10 Oct. 1845, APF, *Acta* 209, ff 288r–289r. Fransoni had written: 'additum est etiam te dare operam ut lyceum, seu Universitas ei systemati accommodata in Diocesi tua statuatur'. This was a reference to Crolly's advocacy of the claims of Armagh. But he must have interpreted it as meaning that he had campaigned from the beginning for a College in his diocese, whereas he merely sought for religious reasons to have the northern College established there rather than in Belfast.

to its plans could be trusted in private to make the right kind of appointments to chairs and would certainly have repudiated the statement that the government had amended its bill to meet the wishes of the bishops. Crolly diverged from many of his colleagues on the purely academic side of the Colleges; they wanted a guaranteed input into the method of selecting and, if necessary, dismissing staff, while he placed all his emphasis for bettering the government's plans on making residential provision for the students under the direction of chaplains who would care for their moral and religious needs. The absence of any ecclesiastical control over the staffing of the Colleges did not pass unnoticed when the opponents of the Colleges submitted their case to Rome at the end of the bishops' meeting in November.

This annual event, which was conducted without any fixed form of procedure or agenda, was bound to be devoted to this burning issue. Eighteen bishops attended the meeting in Dublin which began on 18 November in an atmosphere that was becoming ever more favourable to the views of those opposed to the Colleges. On 12 November the *Freeman's Journal* announced that it had already published protests from nearly a thousand priests in nine dioceses against the Colleges; on 13 and 14 November it added lists from Kilmacduagh and Kilfenora, and from Galway, and this opposition gathered momentum as other dioceses followed suit shortly after the meeting ended. Not only was the tide of Catholic public opinion, both political and ecclesiastical, running with the opponents of the Colleges, but they also counted in their midst the dominant and forceful personalities who were prepared to stir up elemental fears and emotions, and to resist all compromises or half-measures.

At the end of the discussions on the second day, a motion was proposed by MacHale and seconded by MacNally of Clogher, affirming that since the government had not granted the securities which the bishops had required in the university scheme to remove the dangers to the faith and morals of Catholic students, they should therefore submit the former resolutions, their application to the present act and the grounds on which they were based, to the judgement of the pope. Murray and Crolly could not support this apparently innocuous appeal to higher authority for it invited a selection of negative evidence to justify the bishops' initial reservations and did not make provision for submitting the amended version of the bill as a whole. Yet they had been cleverly boxed into a corner, for if they resisted the proposal to place a disputed issue before the Holy See they could be accused of disloyalty, if not of Gallicanism. Their counter proposal called for the submission of the bill both in its original and amended forms as well as the original resolutions.[75] In effect both sides agreed to present their own cases. Only four other bishops—Denvir of Down and Connor, Browne of Kilmore, McGettigan of Raphoe and Ryan of Limerick—supported Crolly and Murray.

Neither party lost much time in transmitting its case to Rome. On 25 November the majority headed by MacHale and Slattery forwarded a very lengthy statement bearing the signatures of seventeen bishops. Referring to the text of the act which MacHale and Slattery had already forwarded, they explained that their objections were both general and particular. They began by repudiating the right of a Protestant government to the exclusive education even in secular subjects of Catholic youth. Such a right could only be conceded when the government would be compelled under clearly defined conditions to ensure that the Catholic religion suffered no detriment, but the British government offered no such conditions and did not allow the Catholic bishops a voice, even a negative one, in the selection of staff or the framing of statutes. Even if the system were to appear good, the inveterate hostility of the British government towards Irish Catholicism made them doubt its good faith and led them to fear the Greeks when bringing gifts. The government introduced the system allegedly to make special provision for Catholics and not only neglected to consult the Catholic bishops or introduce any of the changes suggested by them but made additions to the act which left it worse than it was in its original form. It would only have been just in a country where seven eighths of the population were Catholic either to institute a Catholic system or one affording adequate protection to Catholicism—and this especially when Protestants had the University of Dublin and many schools endowed with royal munificence. The very presence of such a non-Catholic system damaged the Catholic religion both within and without the walls of the Colleges, for the bishops and clergy had erected their own colleges to provide education for both lay and clerical students and these would collapse as soon as the bishops accepted the new university Colleges.

Then descending to details the majority pointed out that no provision was made for the moral discipline of the undergraduates, that Protestants and even infidels could be professors in all literary subjects, and that the government had refused to appoint Catholic professors for Catholic students in history, metaphysics, moral philosophy, geology and anatomy, whom Catholics, for the protection of their faith, would require. The right of a Protestant queen and of her successors to approve all statutes

[75] F.J., 20, 21 Nov. 1845.

and rules for the government and discipline of the Colleges, and to appoint and dismiss all the officers of the Colleges was also reprobated, for it obliged the staff to accommodate itself to the will of the government for fear of losing tenure; furthermore, sad experience proved that a Protestant government in control of Catholic education always tried to subvert Catholicism, as the example of Belgium, when subject to Holland, and of Prussia and France verified. The additions to the original bill had made matters worse, for the texts of the act which permitted the rector and governing body to assign lecture halls for the teaching of religion to those of whom the queen and her heirs would approve, offered dangerous opportunities for mischief to Protestant authorities: they were not obliged to make the lecture halls available, and could not only reject a priest nominated by his bishop but appoint one who was suspended or excommunicated—and Protestant authorities in Ireland had on more than one occasion employed a suspended priest as a Catholic prison chaplain. The provision for residential accommodation was also open to abuses, for, without the approval of the rector the parent or tutor could not assign his son to the care of a pious priest who enjoyed the approval of his bishop for such purposes. A relative or friend chosen by a parent or tutor might not be acceptable to a rector precisely because of his commitment to the Catholic religion. Likewise the professor or lecturer with whom the Catholic youth chose to dwell could be a lax Catholic, heretic or infidel as the rector himself might be. The act permitted the foundation of halls of residence by private benefactors, but that was no guarantee of security: the regulations of such a hall depended on the will of the College visitor and its principal could be unsuited to the care of Catholic youth.

The bishops concluded by referring to their obligation not to render to Caesar what was God's. Hence they had opposed and would continue to oppose the collegiate system of education and especially because in so doing they were but conforming to the encyclicals of Pius VII and Pius VIII which exhorted the bishops of the world to guard their flocks against dangerous systems of education. Repeating the highly emotional and fantastic claim that the church was more endangered by the current offer of silver and gold in the form of concessions that were part genuine and part conterfeit than by the violence of the sword in the past, and asserting that their fears were increased by the presence of British fifth columnists within the Irish Catholic Church, Slattery, MacHale and the *zelanti* predicted that if the government prevailed against them and their faithful clergy and people the Catholic religion in Ireland would be ruined.[76]

[76] Slattery, MacHale and others to Propaganda, 25 Nov. 1845, APF, *Acta* 209, ff 289r-293r.

The bishops of Killaloe, Cork, Derry and Dromore did not sign either document. The two former supported the *politicanti*; the bishop of Derry was ill, but his coadjutor-elect was a determined *zelante*, and the bishop of Dromore, who had signed MacHale's statement in September, later expressed his anxieties about the Colleges. The final breakdown was therefore nineteen to eight.

The appeal to Rome was certainly a comprehensive account of the dissentients' case and one calculated to impress the Roman authorities. The extremely pessimistic, if not fanciful, interpretation of the rules about halls of residence together with the factual statements about the methods of appointing staff and the exclusion of significant episcopal involvement combined to produce a depressing picture of the threats to the integrity of the Catholic faith posed by the Colleges—and, fortunately, for the MacHale view—one disturbingly reminiscent of the exclusion of Catholic influence from educational systems on the continent.

Crolly and Murray must have known that the defence of the system was much more difficult than an attack upon it, as they realized that Rome could not be expected to understand the political and educational nuances in the background to the establishment of the Colleges. And, indeed, there was almost an air of defeatism about the document the six *politicanti* forwarded to Rome. Having pointed out that MacHale refused to accede to their proposal that the whole issue, together with all documents pertaining to it should be submitted to the Holy See, they then got sidetracked into a curious denunciation of Daniel O'Connell for seeking to intimidate the bishops into a unanimous condemnation of the Colleges by his public statements as their synod opened,[77] and went on to make the remarkable claim that he virtually prevented them from discussing the issue freely. Praising the newly appointed presidents of the Cork and Galway Colleges,[78] they explained that the site of the third one had not been decided but insisted that the Catholic religion would not suffer in it, and recalled the recent generosity to Maynooth and to Catholics in the British colonies which, however, did not prevent ungrateful laity, priests and several bishops from attacking it. Yet the political leaders of the people, who led the outcry against those Colleges which offered adequate protection to the Catholic faith, did not hesitate to send their sons to be

---

[77] Just before the episcopal meeting O'Connell had made an appeal to the people to rally behind their bishops and clergy in rejecting the Godless Colleges.

[78] Bishop Cantwell wrote of the appointment of Joseph Kirwan to Galway that 'while it was done for the purpose of throwing dust in the eyes of Rome, & to afford some shadow to the few Prelates who refuse to join us in denouncing the infidel scheme, has only served to strengthen the hatred & disgust which is so universal.' (Cantwell to Cullen, 19 Dec. 1845, AICR.)

trained in Trinity College, Dublin, by Protestant clergy who did their utmost to seduce them from their religion. Hitherto students of civil law, medicine and the sciences had no protection for their religion or virtue: the students at the new institutions would be obliged to lodge with their parents, tutors, friends or with people approved by the authorities and would have the pastoral supervision of chaplains appointed by the bishops.

A very curious argument was then advanced to explain why some bishops and many clergy were making a great commotion about the Colleges being infected with infidelity and falsely maintaining that they were comparable to the evil institutions of Germany: no agitator, either clerical or lay, would be appointed a professor or chaplain in them by the government. This was an attempt to win the sympathy of the congregation which had condemned the political agitation of the clergy, for the *politicanti* went on to say that the outcry of many priests and several bishops against the Colleges was difficult to reconcile with the very prudent admonition of the Holy See on the duties of civil obedience which they had promised to observe.

Enclosed with the letter was the amended version of the bill from which evidence of the government's desire to remove episcopal fears could be gleaned, the bishops' memorial to the Lord Lieutenant and the evidence of the popular enthusiasm which greeted the appointment of Kirwan to Galway which, it was hoped, would convince the cardinal prefect of the goodwill of the government.[79] Though much shorter than their opponents' brief this one did contain the essential points that could be made in favour of the Colleges and though they must have confused Rome by the reference to O'Connell, whose reputation there as a champion of Catholic rights was very high, they made the best use they could of the Roman desire for Irish churchmen to cooperate with the state rather than to agitate politically against it. Admittedly, some of the *zelanti* had charged that the government would nominate professors who had no sympathy with the Irish Catholic ethos but their general charge of infidelity was not connected with the likelihood of nationalists of whatever hue being excluded from the staff.

The majority may have heard from some source in Rome, perhaps Paul Cullen, that the minority had claimed that its presentation of the

[79] Crolly, Murray and others to Propaganda, 24 Nov. 1845, APF, *Acta,* 209, ff 298r-299v. In a postscript they noted that a distinguished Dublin priest, Daniel William Cahill, had just been appointed vice-president of the third college. A short time later Murray admitted that this information had been mistaken.

facts was the more accurate of the two. Consequently MacHale and Slattery moved quickly to quash any such impression. Writing to Cardinal Fransoni on 13 December they presented themselves as the loyal and dutiful sons of Rome ready and willing to submit the entire case fully and frankly to the judgement of the Holy See. Scornfully commenting that the dissentients from the majority view even dissented from one another and were then renouncing what they formerly proposed in opposition to the clergy and people of Ireland, they argued that the opponents of the Colleges had always been consistent and had concealed nothing from Rome. Yet those who claimed to show respect to the Holy See were the supporters of a Protestant government whose members swore that the pope had no jurisdiction in the kingdom. Supporters of the Colleges on the other hand had kept silent about matters which should have been related to the Holy See, and had not reported that Crolly and other members of his party had given a *de facto* approval of the system by their statements and actions, even though they spoke of awaiting the verdict of Rome.[80] The majority had not suspended its judgement but had submitted it to the Holy See.[81]

Three weeks later they returned to the attack. Anxious to counter any propaganda that might be circulated in favour of the Colleges as a consequence of the appointment of Catholics to their staffs (they had probably heard from Cullen that the minority had emphasized the appointments of Catholic presidents) they insisted that the whole proposed system of tertiary education was intrinsically evil and the alleged liberality behind the appointments deceived only those who wished to be deceived. They then examined the Catholic appointees. Sir Robert Kane's attitude to Catholicism, they argued, could be deduced from his refusal to have a priest as vice-rector of the Cork College and from his preference for a lay Protestant in that office. The priests, Kirwan, the president of the Galway College, and O'Toole, one of his professors, canvassed zealously for those posts and accepted them independently of the will of their bishop, who was opposed to the system. Thaddeus O'Malley, a professor in one or other of the Colleges, was as well known in Rome as in Ireland, and Henry, the head of the Belfast College, belonged to a sect, the Calvinists, which was the most hostile of all the enemies of Catholi-

---

[80] They stopped short of declaring that Crolly's party had deceived the Holy See but the tenor of their reservations was clear: 'Unde quamvis absit ut dicamus fratres nostros in Episcopatu Sanctam Sedem decipere voluisse, verumtamen de iis honorifice sentientes non possumus quin dicamus eos sibi non constare in iis quae ad Sanctam Sedem retulerunt.'

[81] Slattery and MacHale to Propaganda, 10 Dec. 1845, Ibid. ff 293v-294v.

cism. Moreover, the public approval given by the people of the country and city of Galway to the location of the College in their midst was given before the last bishops' meeting; afterwards, at least, quite a few of the Catholics of Galway expressed their support for the majority of the bishops and declared that they did not want to patronize a system opposed to the judgement of the prelates.

Afraid that the Holy See might settle the controversy in the same way as it settled the one on national education, they proceeded to reject such a solution in advance. This was supremely ironic, for while Slattery had favoured the national schools MacHale had completely rejected them. But the archbishop of Tuam now put his signature to a letter in which all the safeguards in the schools, which he had once dismissed, were stressed, and their absence in higher education lamented. In one system, pastors could exercise great authority over the faith and morals, the books, the religious instruction of the pupils and the rules of the schools; in the other, where the mixing of Catholics and Protestants was far more dangerous in youth than in childhood, they had no influence. MacHale and Slattery begged the Roman authorities, therefore, not to make the same decision as in 1841, for they realized that at least one College, and perhaps two, might come to enjoy the tolerance, if not approval of the local bishop, and those prelates—the majority—in whose dioceses Colleges did not exist, would be powerless to prevent their expansion.[82]

The *zelanti* gained a most active supporter when Edward Maginn was ordained bishop as coadjutor of Derry on 18 January 1846. Four bishops were present at the ceremony—Crolly, Denvir, MacNally and Cantwell—and, according to Cantwell 'some of those present must . . . have felt very unpleasant under the observations made by the Clergy in the afternoon speeches'.[83] Crolly and Denvir were obviously treated to anti-Colleges tirades by some of the speakers who would certainly have been reflecting the views of the new coadjutor.

The government, meanwhile, had waited anxiously to see what way the majority would go at the bishops' meeting, and was disappointed at the result. Heytesbury, the Lord Lieutenant, was critical of what he regarded

---

[82] Ibid., 30 Dec. 1845, 2 Jan. 1846, ff 295r-298v. MacHale no longer trusted any bishop who was in any way connected with the government. He told Cullen: 'the lamentable effects of the Bequest Act are now sufficiently felt in the adhesion of the Commissioners to an infidel project which they would not fail to see in the same light as their Brethren, were they not unfortunately bound up with the Government as servants dismissable at its pleasure . . . I am confident that the Holy Father will never be safe in confiding the interests of faith or morals to those who will be linked with the avowed enemies of the Catholic Church'. (MacHale to Cullen, 5 Dec. 1845, AICR.)

[83] Cantwell to Slattery, 25 Jan. 1846, Slattery Papers.

as Crolly's and Murray's supineness, telling Graham that the prelates who favoured their views had shown neither energy nor courage but had yielded much more than they should have done to the force that was made to bear against them.[84] Graham lost little time in passing on Heytesbury's comments and newspaper reports from Ireland to Aberdeen, the Foreign Secretary, and requesting him to submit the government's views to Rome. Explaining their urgent anxiety 'to conciliate, as much as possible, the goodwill and support of the heads of the Catholic church in Ireland, in favour of these new Institutions', he suggested that their chargé d'affaires explain to the Roman authorities the securities contained in the act; he mentioned particularly the visitors' power, the pledge to distribute patronage fairly, the facilities offered for the endowment of lectures in theology and the moral supervision of students in hostels. All these arrangements had been made to satisfy the scruples and meet the reasonable wishes of the heads of the church who dissented from the majority view. He concluded by stating that the influence of the chargé d'affaires should be exerted to sustain the views of Crolly and Murray in favour of an act which was calculated to confer permanent benefits on Ireland.[85] Sending a copy of the letter to Heytesbury, he anticipated a favourable Roman response, if their agent were 'adroit and possessed influence'.[86]

William Petre, the British agent in Rome, promptly called with the Cardinal Secretary of State and was redirected to Cardinal Fransoni, to whom he delivered and explained the contents of the despatch from the Foreign Office. Fransoni was non-committal and explained that the subject would be examined with great thoroughness. Petre also contacted Cardinal Acton, who professed little knowledge of the issue, but who, he alleged, agreed that in Ireland political hostility was the main source of opposition to government measures and expressed deep sorrow at the language and conduct of many of the clergy, and especially of MacHale.[87] Further inquiries from Propaganda elicited little more information than that the question would be studied by a general congregation of cardinals with the care and impartiality due to a measure proceeding from the benevolent intentions of the government. Fransoni, while claiming little knowledge of the dispute, referred to the insufficient security attached to the appointment of presidents, (which Petre ought to have regarded as an

[84] Heytesbury to Graham, 20 Nov. 1845, F.O. 43/38.
[85] Graham to Aberdeen, 24 Nov. 1845, Ibid.
[86] Graham to Heytesbury, 25 Nov. 1845, Graham Papers.
[87] Petre to Aberdeen, 9, 10 Dec. 1845, F.O. 43/38.

ominous sign) and insisted that Roman decisions would not be influenced by worldly affairs.[88]

Before the appeals of the two sides after the November meeting had reached Rome, Propaganda wrote to Archbishop Murray to inquire if the changes made by the government in its original plans had rendered them safe and suitable places for Catholic students. Murray replied that they had become safer than the universities of England, Scotland and Dublin, insisted that the government's intention in establishing them was merely to open the gates of knowledge to all who desired it and expressed his confidence that the government would respond to a bishop's request to dismiss any professor who spoke against the Catholic religion. The Colleges would be erected whether or not Catholics wanted to make use of them, hostels would be built, professors appointed and statistics published and then it would be clearer whether the emendations made to the original bill permitted Catholic youth to enrol without danger to their faith or morals; if not the bishops would warn their flocks to shun those poisoned sources.[89]

IV

With the reception of these letters the congregation of Propaganda felt it had sufficient material to form the basis of a judgement. Custom dictated that consultors would be invited to sift the submissions, summarize the arguments and draw up a balance sheet for the cardinals. The two consultors selected for this delicate task were Monsignor Giovanni Corboli-Bussi and Paul Cullen.[90] Corboli-Bussi, though of a liberal bent, had received rapid promotion in the Rome of Gregory XVI, and at the age of thirty two was Secretary of the Consistorial Congregation and also of the College of Cardinals. Entrusted with many delicate diplomatic tasks, he was regarded in the curia as exceptionally capable and as one destined for the highest promotion. In many ways Cullen was a curious choice because he had aligned himself so firmly with one faction in the Irish episcopate. On the other hand the officials at Propaganda probably did not know the extent of his involvement, and they regarded him as a skilled and prudent observer, and one whose intervention in the controversy over the national schools had been invaluable.

---

[88] Ibid., 19, 29 Dec. 1845.
[89] Murray to Propaganda, 11 Dec. 1845, APF, *Acta*, 209, ff 299v-300r.
[90] The date of their appointment is not known, but was probably towards the end of 1845. Cullen's *votum* was dated 31 Jan. 1846 but may have been submitted later. Corboli-Bussi's was undated.

Corboli-Bussi, who understood English and had some knowledge of British life and institutions, prefaced his report with a careful and balanced summary of the dispute over the national schools and of the Roman verdict on it.[91] Explaining the principal points of the Colleges Bill and the memorial of the bishops to the Lord Lieutenant he pointed out that none of their requests were translated into law. Listing the changes which the government made, he observed that the archbishops of Armagh and Dublin and four other bishops deemed them sufficient, and gave the substance of Crolly's first letter and of the submissions of both parties to Rome. Less than impressed at times with MacHale's and Slattery's charges, he concluded that the action of the government in instituting the Colleges was not disinterested—it had political interests to foster—but certainly not dictated by a desire to eliminate Catholicism. Indicating some acquaintance with British politics by explaining the views of Young England and its sympathy for the Catholic Church, he predicted that, if the bishops were to let the government see that they did not seek the separation of Ireland from Britain and were to beg unfailingly in special cases for the rights of religion, their demands would not be ineffective. But if the bishops were to condemn the new system before it had been proved by experience, there was a fear that the government's antipathy would be directed at them much more than at O'Connell's political faction, for O'Connell had already pledged himself to follow their lead. The Colleges would be established anyway and would fall into the hands of Protestants and of the less trustworthy Catholics. There would in effect be more Protestant schools and, between the education provided by the Colleges and the prohibition of the bishops, the faith would scarcely survive long intact.

Corboli-Bussi then turned to the argument advanced by MacHale and Slattery that the approval of the Colleges by the ecclesiastical authorities would spell the end of those erected by the bishops and priests. He detected flaws in it. If, he maintained, there were Catholic colleges in Ireland which taught sciences, the bishops' action would be obviously just and prudent, but MacHale and Slattery seemed to be referring to diocesan seminaries, where, apart from philosophy, sciences were not taught. Consequently, where Catholic higher institutes did not exist, the Catholics were compelled to seek scientific education in Protestant universities,

---

[91] He rightly described this issue as 'il primo seme di discordia' among the bishops and noted that, though happily settled by the Holy See, it left among them a disposition to renew the contest every time a similar occasion arose, and among the English ministers a realization that they would find in the divisions in the hierarchy a support against political dissensions.

as the archbishops of Armagh and Dublin claimed. In those circumstances the provision of mixed education from which religious teaching was excluded seemed to be an improvement rather than the opposite. The faithful should, however, not seek in mixed schools the literary instruction which they could obtain in diocesan colleges.

Turning then to the assertions of Slattery and MacHale that it was impossible to find good books in English, as all scientific works written in that language were full of calumnies against Catholicism, Corboli-Bussi found this claim excessive. He thought that natural sciences were abused to attack revealed religion rather than Catholic dogma in every country. Protestants also had to protect their youth from such abuses. The encouragement of publications by religious students of the sciences was not forbidden by the Colleges Act.

The relatives of the students enjoyed the right to make provision for their residential arrangements. And if the bishops felt they possessed so much authority that they could make the students give up the advantages of the Colleges, they could surely see that the students would not be placed by their guardians in houses not approved by them.

Corboli-Bussi concluded by recommending that, where Catholic and mixed schools offered the same courses, Catholic students should attend Catholic colleges. But where this option was not available, the solution adopted in 1841 to settle the dispute over the national schools should apply, namely, that the decision to permit Catholic students to attend the Colleges should be left to the prudent judgement and conscience of each bishop. This decision should suit both parties, for the primate's supporters had never denied that the diocesan were preferable to mixed schools, and MacHale's followers would not deny that, for those subjects not available in Catholic schools, mixed schools were less dangerous than Protestant ones.[92]

This *votum* or analysis of the problem was both shrewd and perceptive. Corboli-Bussi evinced some knowledge of the general background to the act and, though handicapped by having no first hand acquaintance of Ireland, was able to get a reasonably good grasp of the confusing statements about colleges, and the variety of concepts implied and covered by that word. In Rome, where precedents were always regarded as very important, this solution had the advantage of following in the tradition of the decision of 1841. The *politicanti* would happily have settled for it, but unfortunately for them the other consultor, fresh from a prolonged visit to

---

[92] *Votum* of Corboli-Bussi, APF, *Acta*, 209, ff 264r-270r.

Ireland, where he had immediately and wholeheartedly thrown himself into the opposition to Peel's proposals, was determined to save his native country from a form of higher education which, he believed, had ravaged the faith of students in France and Germany.

The invitation to Paul Cullen[93] to submit a detailed analysis of the case to Propaganda offered him a golden opportunity of helping to down the Colleges, and he seized it with both hands. His submission was lengthy and comprehensive, carefully compiled and ably presented. It was a far more effective attack on the Colleges than that made by the *zelanti*, precisely because it avoided the hard-hitting and extreme comments so dear to MacHale.

Beginning with an outline of British educational policy in Ireland since the sixteenth century, which he characterized as persistently proselytizing, he went on to explain how the resistance of the bishops to the Kildare Place Society led to the establishment of the national system of education. Catholics in Ireland went to schools conducted by the Jesuits or secular clergy and those who were not content with an Irish education went to English Catholic colleges. Many of these Catholic schools were recently affiliated to London University and students from these colleges could sit its exams leading to professional careers. The government, disliking this arrangement which excluded its influence from Catholic schools, decided to introduce a system which would prohibit religious teaching or at least not provide it, and would put the teaching staff directly under the secular power. Two plans were proposed to achieve this aim: to open Trinity College, Dublin to Catholics or to establish new Colleges. It was decided to leave Trinity College in the hands of Protestant clergy and to retain the usage of obliging its professors to swear to uphold Protestantism. But at the same time in the Colleges destined for the Catholics of Ireland no mention was to be made of religion in the choice of professors.

The first promoter of the Colleges project was Thomas Wyse, a great admirer of the Prussian universities and the panegyrist of the pantheistic philosopher, Cousin. Cullen then went on to quote Sir Robert Inglis, and, more tellingly, the *Oxford and Cambridge Review* to the effect that, if a stop were not put to the progress of the state of indifferentism, England

---

[93] Some of the bishops opposed to the Colleges continued to urge Cullen to keep up the fight on their behalf. O'Higgins, letting him know of the departure of two colleagues for Rome, both of whose views he feared were contrary to his own, begged Cullen 'to prepare the authorities for receiving them as they deserve' (O'Higgins to Cullen, 15 Oct. 1845, AICR) and Maginn, the coadjutor bishop of Derry, wrote of 'the infidelizing Colleges scheme' and 'of our insuperable objections to that diabolical measure'. (Maginn to Cullen, 28 Jan. 1846, AICR.)

would soon have to deal with the social and political evils that were afflicting France. The reaction of Protestants and of Catholics like Lord Shrewsbury to the proposed Colleges was strongly hostile, and, consequently, the archbishop of Armagh summoned the bishops and they pronounced against them. But later he issued a declaration in favour of them and went with the heads of the Presbyterian and Anglican churches of Armagh to the viceroy to seek the location of one of them in Armagh. The archbishop of Dublin and four others subsequently adopted his sentiments and seemed to have concluded that it was best to let them be built or by favouring them hope to derive benefits from them. Cullen then explained the attitudes of the other bishops, and suggested the advisability of a decisive response from Rome as the only means of restoring episcopal harmony and putting an end to the scandal given to the laity. Repeating the majority's criticisms of the Colleges and the bishops' requests for alterations in the bill, he pooh-poohed the concession whereby private bodies were permitted to found chairs of religion and establish hostels as unlikely to be effective, since Catholics knew from the sad example of Germany and other countries that institutes of mixed education were not suitable places for the study of Catholic theology.

The supposed advantages of the Colleges—the promotion of charity among Catholic and Protestant students, the softening of religious acerbities—had to be balanced against the evils that derived from mixed education. The experience of Catholics attending Trinity College had been distressing: many had lost their faith, or become apostates or unbelievers, and some Catholics had become Protestants and dignitaries of the Protestant church. The same things occurred in Germany, France and America. In fact English Protestants had become alarmed by the mixed system as it operated in their own country, and in Liverpool, Protestants, repelled by the mixed Mechanics Institute, had founded their own college. Apart from apostasy or unbelief, Catholic students lost the Catholic spirit by constant contact with Protestants, as they heard their religious practices, such as fasting and confession, exposed to ridicule. This problem did not arise in the national schools where the teacher was a Catholic or appointed by a priest, and which were not frequented much by Protestants, who attended their own schools, but a different situation would obtain where the religious mixture would not be so uneven. And the Protestants at the Colleges would be richer and have more powerful connections than the Catholics, and could therefore exercise a greater influence on them than vice-versa. The teachers of Catholic children in the national schools were Catholics but those in the Colleges could be of any or no religion. And the teachers in the model schools would graduate from the Colleges and their influence would permeate down to the lowest levels.

By being cheaper and offering attractive prizes the Colleges would gradually damage the Catholic schools. Significantly, they were being promoted by rich Protestants, the class which continued to despoil and evict Catholic tenants and to sponsor proselytism. Lord Brougham, one of the great defenders of the Colleges, recently denounced the Catholic Church as the enemy of civilization and progress. The professoriate could be a mixture of Anglicans, Calvinists, Rationalists and members of other sects,[94] and it enjoyed opportunities in history, metaphysics, ethics and geological and other sciences to cause grave harm or give great help to religion. The example of famous professors—Locke, Paley, Buckland, Cuvier, Whately, Ranke, Robertson, Roscoe and Hume—was mentioned and reference was made to some of the errors they taught. The president of the College was to be commissioned to ensure that professors said nothing against religion. But the famous Cousin taught pantheism in Paris when Mgr Frayssinous was the Minister of Public Instruction, and if such a zealous man could not prevent evil, what could one of the College presidents do? Weak Catholics would be appointed to chairs and if a Cousin, Michelet or Quinet could be found among Irish Catholics, he would be promoted. Priests like Hermes, Van Espen and other theologians who were in trouble with Rome would be chosen. The advantages of the new system would be of a temporal nature, but the damage would affect eternal interests, which should never be put at risk for the wretched passing things of the world.

In conclusion, Cullen declared that he would not hesitate to suggest that Propaganda should give a less than favourable reply on the colleges—a diplomatic way of recommending an unqualified condemnation—and went on to say that the bishops should be advised not to promote them or permit their clergy to have any part in them but rather to improve the existing Catholic colleges, and, where necessary, to follow the example of the bishops of Belgium who founded a Catholic university to counteract the damaging effects of the liberal universities. The Colleges would last a while, but would wither and die as other educational institutions in Ireland had done. Priests would be found who, attracted by the salaries,

[94] Cullen also found an unlikely ally in Henry Cooke, whom he quoted as having told the Irish Education Inquiry that the character of a professor inculcated his religious principles more effectively than any lectures and that youths with little education could not spend seven or eight years in the company of Arian professors without imbibing their doctrines.

would accept posts in them, but they would be few, as there would be few such posts available, few priests qualified in the sciences and few who would oppose the wishes of their bishops.

Cullen added a postscript about the situation obtaining in the Belfast Academical Institution as revealed in the inquiry into it in 1825. He pointed out that Professors Bruce, Hincks, Montgomery and others whom he did not name confessed to holding Arian views. He added that several Catholics attended Montgomery's classes and assisted at the prayers with which he began them. Crolly, who was then bishop of Down and Connor, professed satisfaction with the way the school was conducted and stated that he would have no hesitation in allowing candidates for the priesthood to study there before proceeding to Maynooth. And, furthermore, he expressed his desire that schoolteachers of all religions should be educated together in the Institution so that they would later spread abroad the spirit of virtue, learning and liberality. While a Catholic archbishop was so well disposed to this college, the head of the Presbyterians, Cooke, proclaimed his belief that the Arian professors would do a lot of harm to their students.

Montgomery also figured earlier in Cullen's text, when he was cited as an example of the apparently innocuous and liberal Protestant who could do more damage to Catholic students by subtly insinuating errors than those who were more blatantly sectarian. Before Cullen actually submitted his *votum* he had received a letter from Bishop Cantwell, which informed him that at the dinner held in Belfast after Denvir's episcopal ordination, Montgomery had declared that his friend Crolly taught doctrines which he himself 'firmly believed to be the weakest inventions of the human mind, such as the divinity of Christ'.[95] Cullen could not verify the truth of this preposterous claim, but translated it into Italian, and it must further have dented Crolly's image with the congregation of Propaganda.[96]

As an anti-Colleges brief Cullen's was highly effective for it was astutely compiled and persuasively and cogently argued. It was a serious blow to the *politicanti*, for, though Corboli-Bussi pleaded for a different solution, he did not marshal his arguments at such length or with such force, and he did not possess or claim any first-hand knowledge of the Irish ecclesiastical scene. Understandably, Crolly and Murray were aggrieved when they came to hear of some of the points raised in it.

---

[95] Cantwell had sent the letter containing this information to Cullen on 24 Feb. 1846, and it was included in the *votum* which was dated 31 Jan. 1846. The Belfast newspapers did not report the speeches given at this dinner.

[96] *Votum* of Paul Cullen, 31 Jan. 1846, APF, Acta, 209, ff 272r-284r.

V

Cullen in his analysis of the Colleges question made telling use of the inordinate fears of many of the French bishops for the survival of the faith among the young who, they believed, were exposed to strong anti-Christian influences from agnostic or atheistic professors or teachers. Both British and continental systems of education were frequently quoted in the course of the Irish dispute. In fact, that dispute was examined within the context of the dangers which state-controlled education were currently presenting to the church. The Colleges controversy and the reaction in Rome to it can only be understood against the background of other church-state clashes on education in contemporary Europe. It is important to ask, therefore, what were the obstacles or temptations posed by the educational institutions of Britain, Ireland and the continent to the religious observance of Catholic students?

VI

Oxford, Cambridge and Trinity College, Dublin were Anglican universities, where the great majority of Fellows were clergy and where the students, many of whom were candidates for the ministry of their church, were obliged to attend Anglican services. The atmosphere and ethos of the colleges of Oxford, Cambridge and Dublin were strongly ecclesiastical, and while very few Irish Catholics found their way to Oxford and Cambridge, Trinity College, Dublin undoubtedly attracted some of them, and, rightly or wrongly, was accused of causing many of these undergraduates to lose their faith. A few Irish Catholics enrolled in the Scottish universities, especially for medical studies. Their constitution was as heavily Presbyterian as that of the old English universities was Anglican, and Irish Catholics must have found the general spirit, if not positively inimical to their faith, at least not congenial to it. London University consisted of two colleges—Kings, which was Anglican, and University College, in which no regulations about religious observances obtained. It was the model which the government had in mind when legislating for Ireland, but the Irish bishops would probably have known little or nothing about it.

French education at all levels since Napoleon's time was unified and organized in a state system termed the *Université*. Apart from a few *grandes écoles* the *Université* embraced the five faculties of tertiary education, which were scattered throughout France, the *lycées* and colleges and even the *petits séminaires* (though not the limited number of secondary colleges conducted by religious orders), and the parish schools of the *communes*.

Parish clergy were involved in the administration of the primary schools, religion was taught in them and there was little church-state conflict in that area. But conflict did arise and reach a rancorous level between the passionate advocates of the *Université* and the church about the *lycées* and colleges at the secondary level, and so heated and intense were these arguments that they made the Irish debates seem restrained and genteel by comparison.

The *lycées* and colleges prepared students for the *baccalauréat*, the leaving certificate, which was conducted by the faculties of letters and sciences, and was required for entering the faculties of law and medicine and for many state appointments. The clergy could act as chaplains at these secondary schools, but there was no compulsory religious education in them and many of the teachers, including some former priests, were strongly opposed to any religious influence. Philosophy, however, was taught, and churchmen took great exception to the views of some of the leading philosophers, whose thought and teaching were then very influential. Victor Cousin, whose eclectic philosophy was particularly disliked, believed that religion was a purely subjective phenomenon, that ethics should be separate from it, and advised his students to target the Jesuits.[97] Cousin became head of the *Université* in 1840, and he and his colleagues in the *grandes écoles*, Jouffroy and Damargue, were accused of producing generations of teachers in the *lycées* who were indifferent to religion. History and literature were also deemed to be subjects affording scope for rationalist and anti-religious teaching, and the publication in 1842 of an attack on the Jesuits by the historian, Michelet, led to bitter controversy.

The liberal Catholic thinker, Montalembert, spearheaded the assault on the *Université* in the 1840s, demanding, in the name of conscience, greater freedom for the church to establish and conduct more colleges than the few tolerated by the state.[98] Many of the bishops supported him with bitter denunciations of the state's usurpation of their role, quoting in

---

[97] Dansette, *Religious History of Modern France*, 208; Moody, *French Education since Napoleon*, 37; Goutard, *L'enseignement secondaire en France*, 195.

[98] Montalembert claimed that: 'L'Université ne représente pas seulement l'orgueil du rationalisme et l'anarchie intellectuelle où conduit l'incrédulité: elle représente surtout et elle sert merveilleusement cette tendance de l'Etat à tout ployer sous l'implacable niveau d'une stérile uniformité . . . entre elle et les catholiques, la guerre doit être ouverte et sans trève, jusq'au jour où, privée du droit abusif, de nous prendre nos enfants malgré nous'. Montalembert, *Du Devoir des Catholiques dans la question de la liberté d'Enseignement*, 16, 63.

defence Christ's injunction in St Matthew's gospel 'going therefore teach ye all nations', and damning the *Université* as the source of all the pestilential errors that were sapping the faith of the nation. One of the most resolute opponents of the *Université*, the bishop of Chartres, argued that atheists, materialists, Socinians and others could be members of the *Université* without fear of censure, and claimed that the philosophy taught in it was preparing more horrifying calamities for France than those which had struck it in the previous fifty years.[99] The youth of France, he complained, was learning from its historians that Jesus Christ was only a human legislator and a myth, and was being widely exposed to sceptical ideas. Some of the other combatants in this religio-educational conflict and, in particular, Louis Veuillot, in his paper, *l'Univers*, were even more aggressive than the bishops.[100]

In fact the verbal warfare grew so intense and uncompromising that the Holy See, which wanted to reestablish the old alliance of church and state,[101] rather than have a major row with the French government, advised the bishops to lower the tone of their criticisms. The battle continued and in 1850 important concessions were made to the church, though many of the bishops remained unsatisfied.

Educational conflicts also occurred between the church and the governments of some of the German states. Disputes arose about the execution of the arrangements for *Simultanschulen* or schools with pupils of all denominations in Nassau. But the sharpest divisions occurred in Prussia, which had acquired the Catholic districts of the Rhineland and Westphalia after the defeat of Napoleon. Educational institutions in these territories, which had been under ecclesiastical or at least Catholic control, were secularized during the French occupation. Lutheran Prussia, which had decreed that education was a state responsibility, reorganized the elementary schools, colleges (*Gymnasien*) and universities in its newly acquired provinces. No serious difficulties occurred at the primary level; the church authorities were invited to cooperate with the state in managing the schools, appointing and inspecting teachers and in conducting teacher training colleges. But friction occurred between church and

---

[99] He asked rhetorically 'Pourpuoi donc ce débordement de puissance universitaire? Qui peut l'autoriser à envahir les droits des pères de famille, des évêques, surtout d'une Eglise antique et reconnue, qu'elle semble vouloir pousser pied à pied jusqu'à ce qu'elle tombe dans l'abîme. Qu'il vînt à se peupler de philosophes impies, d'hommes d'argent ou de plaisir, de sujets corrumpus sans principes et sans croyance . . .' Clausel de Montals, *Lettres et instruction pastorale de Monseigneur l'Evêque de Chartres concernant l'Université*, 11.

[100] Le monopole universitaire (et je le dis avec une conviction inébranlable) en plongeant la jeunesse dans une indifférence impie, dévore l'avenir religieux de la France . . . M. L'Abbé T. Combalot, *Mémoire adressé aux Evêques de France et aux pères de famille sur la guerre faite à l'église et à la société*, 7.

[101] Jedin, 'Liberalismo e integralismo', in *Handbuch der Kirchengeschichte*, viii, f 2, 52.

state at the secondary level. Bishops and clergy charged that the whole ethos of the *Gymnasien* was hostile to Catholicism; that books by Catholic authors were not to be found on the courses or in the libraries; that the system of appointments of teachers and of general control by state officials militated against Catholic applicants and that the time set aside for religious instruction was insufficient.

Similar accusations were made by the Catholics of Silesia. They felt that the Prussian government discriminated against them in the provision of *Gymnasien*, in the tiny representation afforded them in the administration of the educational system and in the books prescribed by the provincial authorities which, they argued, bore a distinct anti-Catholic stamp. Though the teachers of religion required the bishops' approbation, they believed that the church had little influence in other aspects of school life and complained that many of the staff of the colleges were lax Catholics and often freemasons.

The auxiliary bishop of Münster, Von Droste zu Vischering, vehemently attacked the limitations placed on the rights of the church in the secondary sector, complained less vociferously about the elementary schools and denounced the interference of the Prussian ministry with the education of seminarians, who were obliged to undergo examinations by state inspectors and to do military service. For him education was a function of the church and when he became archbishop of Cologne in 1836, in succession to the more compliant von Spiegel, the scene was set for strife between church and state.

The conflict, however, broke out over the regulations about mixed marriages. The archbishop set out to follow the Roman regulations and to reject the demands of the government that Catholic clergy would assist at such marriages without requiring the customary guarantees. Refusing to yield to the government, he was arrested and imprisoned for treason, and quickly became a Catholic hero. His example stiffened the resolve of the other bishops in Prussia. The new king, who succeeded in 1840, was anxious to settle the conflict, and at his behest the government ceased to interfere in mixed marriages, leaving the clergy to reach their own decisions. He also established a Catholic section in the ministry of religious affairs.

Von Droste zu Vischering also fell foul of the government over the teaching of theology in the University of Bonn. In 1835 Rome had condemned some of the views of the Bonn theologian, Georg Hermes. The archbishop, anxious to execute the Roman verdict on Hermes and to remove his disciples from positions of influence, forbade all but two of the professors at Bonn to lecture and withdrew his seminarians to Cologne. He argued that 'mixed' universities only led to indifferentism and false freedoms, posing threats to the faith and morals of the students. He also maintained that the faculties of law as well as those of theology should be under ecclesiastical control because of their connection with canon law. His ultimate ambition was to have Catholic universities.

Though the church-state conflict in Prussia embraced several issues other than education, nevertheless, the educational aspect was regarded by some observers, and especially those from Ireland, who did not understand the full complexity of the situation, as central to it. The argument ran that state systems of education, both in schools and universities, were conducive to indifferentism in matters of religion, and the more the church allowed the state to interfere with its rights in education, the weaker became its influence in all areas of public life. When the revolutions of 1848 led to a political crisis in Germany, both the bishops and lay Catholics, like their French brethren, predicated their demands for educational changes on the rights of the church as expressed in Christ's command to go and teach all nations. A plan to establish Catholic universites was discussed at meetings of the hierarchy in 1848, but nothing came of it.[102]

The one continental hierarchy which won praise for its initiative in university education was the Belgian. In 1830 Belgium separated from Holland, and the Liberals and Catholics, who had made common cause against Dutch rule, worked fairly harmoniously together in the first years of independence. Consequently, when the bishops decided to establish a Catholic University in 1832 they did not encounter any serious opposition. The town of Louvain put buildings at the disposal of the university, which moved there in 1835 after a year in Malines. The bishops drew up their own regulations for the university, appointed a rector as their vicar, and retained full control of the new institution.

Louvain became the model of a free Catholic university for those continental bishops who contemplated the possibility of founding their own universities, and Cullen in Rome having heard of its success, suggested that the Irish bishops also use it as model for a foundation in Ireland. He did not mention or advert to the fact that the Irish bishops did not have the resources or the buildings that the Belgian bishops had or came to possess. In taking Louvain as a model and criticizing the systems of education in France and Germany he was but expressing the widely

---

[102] Brandt, *Eine Katholische Universität in Deutschland?*, 103-13.

held and accepted views of the growing number of Ultramontanes in those countries, who viewed state forms of education at least as limitations on the mission of the church, if not pastorally damaging and downright dangerous. When the cardinals in Rome came to consider the colleges in Ireland, they were not thinking of the government's attempts to make provision for middle class Catholics in Munster, or to wean supporters away from Repeal, but of the arguments and accusations about the effects of education at state universities and colleges on the practice rate of Catholic youth.

VII

Before the opinions of Corboli-Bussi and Cullen were read by all the cardinals of Propaganda, or perhaps before they were submitted, other relevant material arrived in Rome. The archbishop of Tuam forwarded a document containing the signatures of 1,628 priests—all taken from the dioceses of bishops opposed to the Colleges and representing about seventy per cent of all the clergy of Ireland[103]—and judging from the opposition shown by some of the priests from the other six dioceses at least three quarters of the clergy of the whole country would have signed had they felt free to do so. As he continued to press his case at Rome with the same arguments Cullen did his utmost to influence Propaganda in favour of the *zelanti*.[104] Murray was able to report one minor concession which the government, faced with the threat of a papal condemnation, had made in the interest of prudence: it had expressed its willingness to include the Catholic archbishop of Dublin in a body of consultors which would be established to recommend candidates to the viceroy for appointments to chairs.[105]

A further opinion was sought from Cardinal Acton before the cardinals met to deliberate on the controversy. Acton, while counselling non-intervention on the part of the Holy See, nonetheless took a fairly hostile and pessimistic view of the Colleges. He believed that Catholics would play a small role in running the new system of education and that nearly all the books that would be used would be more or less full of errors in matters concerning faith and history. He also thought that the exposure of Catholic students to strongly Protestant or independent views, as hap-

---

[103] MacHale to Propaganda, 13 Feb. 1846, APF, SOCG 968, ff 679r-680v.
[104] Ibid, 26 Feb., 13, 14 Mar. 1846, ff 681r-684r and 687r-688v.
[105] Murray to Propaganda, 30 Mar. 1846, Ibid., f 685rv.

pened in Germany, would not be conducive to the maintenance of their faith.

There was a precedent, however, for not condemning the Colleges as the French and German systems of education had not been condemned, and he recommended that that be followed. He made the rather naive suggestion that, if the more prudent bishops agreed, a request might be made in parliament that one or two Colleges, in proportion to Catholic numbers, should be given to the Catholics; he also proposed that more Catholic colleges should be established, that suitably qualified priests as tutors should be appointed to reside in the university towns and, perhaps later, to become professors, and in the meantime that the bishops of the dioceses where the Colleges were to be established should seek to get provisions inserted into the statutes about the appointment of directors of hostels and clerical tutors.[106]

Perhaps Acton's comments arrived too late for printing with the rest of the material on which the cardinals would make their decision. Anyhow, they were not included with the letters and the *vota* of Corboli-Bussi and Cullen which were submitted to them in advance of the meeting, that was due to be held at the beginning of June 1846 but, because of the death of Gregory XVI did not take place until 13 July 1846.

The cardinals duly delivered a negative verdict. They decided that subject to papal approval a letter should go out to the four archbishops for transmission to their suffragans, informing them that the congregation of Propaganda, while acknowledging that the prelates who favoured the Colleges were motivated only by a desire to further the interests of religion, nonetheless considered them dangerous and felt obliged to advise the bishops of Ireland to have nothing to do with them. Then, in effect rebuking the minority for becoming involved in the issue before consulting the Holy See, the cardinals remarked that just as they would have wished to have been consulted before modifications were sought from the government, so they expected any bishop who had assumed any duties in connection with the Colleges to withdraw from them. Encouraging the prelates to increase the number of Catholic colleges and improve those already existing, they suggested that the bishops of Ireland be advised to work together in a spirit of harmony. By adding that the pope had himself carefully studied the whole question further weight was to be given to this decision.[107]

[106] Acton to Propaganda, undated, Ibid., ff 691r-695r.
[107] APF, *Acta*, 209, ff 259v-261r.

The influence of Cardinal Ostini, who put together the materials and prepared a summary of the case for his colleagues, in pointing them towards a condemnation of the Colleges has not been discounted.[108] But given the information available to the cardinals, any other decision was improbable. The great majority of the bishops and clergy had called for a condemnation of the government's plans and convincing evidence had been brought forward to show the resemblances between the system of tertiary education proposed for Ireland and those continental systems which were thought to have proved so deleterious to the faith of the youth of France and Germany. No matter how skilfully Crolly and Murray had handled their brief, they could scarcely have obtained even a partially favourable verdict.

VIII

The decision of the cardinals could not be promulgated until confirmed by the pope, but papal approval, which was usually given automatically in such cases, was in this instance withheld. Pius IX had been elected less than a month before the plenary congregation of Propaganda was held, and the first months of his pontificate were marked by a new spirit of openness and reform which ran counter to many of the assumptions behind the rule of Gregory XVI. Corboli-Bussi, one of his closest advisers, who had argued that in certain circumstances the judgement about the Colleges should be left to the local bishop, may well have suggested that the issue required further reflection. He told the secretary of the congregation of Propaganda that Pius IX would have wished to consult Cardinal Acton, before making a decision.[109] Probably a combination of factors—the liberal climate of the times, the pope's own pastoral experience and dislike of intransigence, and the special confidence he reposed in Corboli-Bussi,[110] whom he had appointed secretary of a new Congregation of State charged with carrying out an anmesty, reforming finances and other important tasks—may have brought about the pope's refusal to endorse the cardinals' recommendation. And, what was always an important consideration in Rome, there was a very relevant precedent which he could follow: in 1839 Gregory XVI had allowed a further examination of the controversy on national education. Reference was later

---

[108] Martina, *Pio IX (1846-50)*, 461. G.B. Palma, an official of Propaganda, told Cullen confidentially in 1848, that of the eleven cardinals who took part in the second plenary congregation, only Ostini 'avrebbe opinato di prendere una via non tanto diretta' (Palma to Cullen, 26 Sept. 1848, AICR).
[109] APF, SOCG, 968, f 550r.   [110] Martina, *Pio IX*, 462.

made to the doubt which the pope entertained about the verdict of the congregation, and this, together with his involvement in more urgent affairs, was supposed to have been responsible for his hesitation.[111]

This did not prevent the cardinals' decision from leaking out. Doubtless it was known in Rome by the *cognoscenti* after the meeting terminated, but it did not become public knowledge in Ireland until 25 August, when the *Evening Freeman* jubilantly rushed to print 'the most important intelligence we have had for some time to lay before our readers . . . the decisive condemnation of the "Godless Colleges Act" by the court of Rome'. Conceding that the official anouncement had not reached Ireland, but insisting that its sources were too reliable to admit of any uncertainty about the accuracy of the report—Cullen may well have been its informant— the *Freeman* went on to express its confidence that the government would be obliged to construct a system of education that would enjoy the support of those for whom it was intended.[112] On the other hand, William Petre, the government's watchdog in Rome, who claimed to have access to the centres of power in the curia, nonetheless assured his London masters that the rumour was 'totally without foundation'.[113] Petre's ignorance of a decision which could scarcely have been kept secret in Rome only showed that his assurances to London of friendly and familiar contacts at the Secretariat of State were, if not imaginary, at least greatly exaggerated.

By 9 November, when the bishops convened in Dublin for their annual deliberations, no official decision had reached Ireland. A further six months passed as the opponents of the Colleges waited with mounting despondency the expected papal condemnation. Then MacHale and his five suffragans decided to jog the pope's memory. Thanking him for his contribution to famine relief and exculpating the clergy from charges of involvement in violence, they drew attention to the British government's introduction of laws about mixed marriages, Charitable Bequests, and the vesting of schools in the commissioners of national education which, under the guise of liberality, sought to weaken the Catholic church.[114]

They pointed out that they awaited with anxiety his judgement on the Colleges, and remarking that they had not changed their views explained that his heavy commitments and the sufferings of their people had prevented them from pursuing the matter further. Then, taking a swipe at

[111] APF, *Acta*, 211, f 350r.   [112] F.J., 26 Aug. 1846.
[113] Petre to Palmerston, 5 Sept. 1846, PRO, F.O. 43/38.
[114] Petitions embracing the resolutions on the Bequests Act, the religious orders and freedom of religious practice for Catholic soldiers and their children were presented to Parliament in Feb. and Mar. 1847. (F.J., 13 Feb., 20 Mar. 1847.)

Crolly and Murray who served on the board of Charitable Bequests, they declared that bishops should be forbidden without the consent of the Holy See to assume offices of a political or mixed nature which involved interference in other dioceses; that proclivity to accept from the state offices which were part civil and part ecclesiastical was the fountain and source of all their evils and, if not ended by Rome, would endanger the liberty of the church and the authority of the Apostolic See.[115] In this crafty and artful letter, the six bishops situated the Colleges question neatly in the middle of a list of British misdeeds, and by making deliberately vague references to episcopal and papal rights sought to put the blame for the ills of the Irish church on Crolly and Murray.

This letter was written shortly after the death of Daniel O'Connell. His death increased the desire of the *zelanti* to have the Colleges condemned. His mighty influence had immensely benefited their cause, both at Westminster and with the Irish public, and there was no successor of stature in sight whose views could command so much respect. The tragic misunderstanding of Irish political aspirations in Whitehall was clearly revealed in the contemptuous references of William Petre to the late leader. Exulting over the refusal of the Roman authorities to allow O'Connell's heart to be carried in procession from the Irish College to the church of S. Andrea della Valle, where the funeral ceremonies were to be held, the English agent's reflection on O'Connell was as venomous as it was inaccurate: 'the greatest curse that ever fell upon Ireland'. And the lengthy panegyric by the prominent preacher, Gioachino Ventura, which praised most warmly the achievements of O'Connell, the Catholic democrat, was dismissed by Petre as very violent and unmeasured and 'a regular repeal sermon'.[116]

With or without O'Connell the *zelanti* battled on. MacHale's most influential collaborator, the archbishop of Cashel, followed up the appeal from Tuam by begging the pope in appropriately humble terms to settle the issue as soon as possible, and thereby put an end to the sad divisions in the episcopal body. The death of Daniel O'Connell, he argued, had removed their vigilant defender and, consequently, the enemies of Catholicism strove to do their utmost against the Catholic religion and proceeded more boldly because they believed that the clergy and people who were overwhelmed by famine and disease could scarcely deal with public affairs; even the Whigs and Tories buried their mutual hostility in

---

[115] MacHale and suffragans to Pius IX, 5 June 1847, APF, *Acta*, 211, ff 356r-357r.
[116] Petre to the Foreign Office, 5 July, 19 July 1847, PRO, F.O. 43/40.

a common hatred of Catholicism. The mask of Whig hypocrisy was removed a few months previously when the government refused to give the Catholics of England any part of the large sum made available by parliament for the education of the poor. Indeed, since persecution by the sword had ceased, the government had turned to a more subtle form of persecution, that of dividing bishops and priests by attracting some to its side by the offer of rewards and, under the pretext of conferring privileges, invading the rights of the church. This sad state of affairs could not be set aright, Slattery solemnly abjured the pope, until he confirmed the decision of the congregation of Propaganda against the Colleges.[117]

Though this plea was highly improper since the decision of Propaganda should not have been known officially in Ireland, it did not prove counterproductive. The letters, with their reminders to the pope of the damaging divisions the Colleges had allegedly caused within the episcopate and of their potentially harmful effects on religion in general, spurred him to take action. He had already read many of the documents connected with the dispute and he now asked the congregation to reconsider the issue. It did so on 20 September 1847, concluded that the previous decision should stand and that the bishops should be induced to found if possible a university on the model of Louvain. The pope yielded to the cardinals' decision, reflecting as it did the wishes of a large majority of the Irish bishops, and confirmed it on 3 October. He reinforced the exhortation to establish a university like Louvain, and requested that the bishops be advised to approach the congregation of Propaganda, if further questions requiring an answer arose.[118]

The official rescript from Propaganda to the four archbishops was issued on 9 October. Explaining that the delay was caused by the need to examine a dispute of such gravity with due care and deliberation, Cardinal Fransoni made clear that the congregation never thought that the bishops who seemed to be in favour of the Colleges 'had anything wrong, in mind', but had been induced 'to adopt those views solely from the hope of effecting greater good, and consulting the interests of religion in Ireland'. The congregation, however, after mature consideration, had formed a different judgement, and he went on to explain:

Nay, more, it dreads that the Catholic faith would thereby be placed in imminent danger; in one word, it is convinced that institutions of this sort prove detrimental to religion.

[117] Slattery to Pius IX, 23 July 1847, APF, *Acta* 211, ff 357r-358r.   [118] Ibid., f 359r.

For these reasons it has felt obliged to caution the Archbishops and Bishops of Ireland against taking any part in establishing them. But, as the Sacred Congregation would have wished, before some of the Prelates had entered into any negotiation with the government for amending the law regarding the aforesaid colleges, and procuring other measures in their favour, that they had taken the opinion of the Holy See; so it doubts not but that, from the profound obedience which the Prelates of Ireland invariably exhibited towards it, they will retract those things which they might have done to the contrary.[119]

The rescript then went on to exhort the bishops to enlarge their existing colleges by creating additional chairs especially in the department of philosophy and 'to procure the erection in Ireland of such a Catholic Academy as the Prelates of Belgium have founded in the city of Louvain'. To achieve these happy results the bishops were bidden 'to preserve mutual union and the greatest concord, . . . not to suffer themselves to be carried away by partisan zeal on matters which do not regard the sacred ministry entrusted to them', and assured that by so behaving they would comply with the wishes of Pope Pius IX, who had sanctioned the rescript by his supreme authority. The door, however, was not completely closed on the *politicanti*: they were told that, if they had any matters of importance to communicate to the congregation of Propaganda for its decision, they were at liberty to do so.[120]

The rescript arrived while the prelates were holding their annual meeting. Neither Murray nor Crolly alluded to it, and probably hoped that by keeping it quiet they would avoid personal embarrassment and give themselves and their friends a chance to reflect on a further submission rather than be stampeded into making a general reply. But MacHale's copy was forwarded from Tuam, and reached Dublin while some of the bishops were still in session, though after Crolly, Murray and a few of their friends had left. The *zelanti* were thereby enabled to thank the pope publicly for his decision.[121]

This long awaited verdict was a severe body-blow to Crolly and Murray. Not only had the bishops been excluded from any form of participation in the government's plans for higher education, but the

[119] In the F.J. of 25 Oct. the incorrect tense of a Latin verb and, consequently, an incorrect translation of the phrase '*ea quae in contrarium praestiterint, sint retracturi*' which was used in the original rescript, was given. The F.J. version read '*praestiterunt*' and that paper gave the translation 'those things which they have done to the contrary'. The D.E.P. accused the F.J. of having wilfully and deliberately falsified the texts to indicate that the Holy See had condemned some of the prelates for the part they had already taken in connection with the establishment of the Colleges. Paul Cooper, a Dublin priest, who was very hostile to the Colleges, accused Crolly of alerting the D.E.P. to this 'foolish distinction'. His letter was duly translated and forwarded to Propaganda. (APF, SC (Irlanda) 29, f 454v.)

[120] APF, *Acta*, 211, ff 359r-360r.

[121] D.E.P., 26 Oct. 1847 and MacHale to Slattery, 21 Oct. 1847, Slattery Papers.

minority had been taken to task for negotiating with the government before consulting the Holy See and the document could be understood to contain an implicit rebuke to Crolly for his public support for the siting of the Ulster college in Armagh. Murray and the others could bear some of the brunt for contacting the government about the regulations for student accommodation and discipline but he, the primate, had given more public support to the realization of the government's plans than any other prelate and must have felt humiliated before his brethren by the Roman reprimand.

He did not reply until 5 November and then, though promising obedience, immediately indicated that he did not regard the rescript as a final and irrevocable judgement. The statutes and rules of the Colleges, which had been composed by their presidents and sanctioned by the British government, would, he promised, be submitted to the congregation, and would show that the faith of students in the faculties of arts, law and medicine would be safeguarded. He then took issue with two of the suggestions made in the rescript—about the enlargement of the diocesan colleges and the establishment of a Catholic university—by pointing out that the education and discipline prevailing in their seminaries were geared to students preparing for the priesthood and were not of a collegiate (or university) nature, and by insisting that the church in Ireland had neither the resources to enlarge and endow them nor to fund a university on the model of Louvain. The church was completely incapable of providing the money required—the £60,000 in capital and £18,000 in running costs which the exchequer would have paid.

Crolly then went on to exculpate himself from the charge contained in Cullen's *votum* (a copy of which had been brought to Dublin by a friend of Archbishop Murray) that he had neglected to provide for the education of Catholic youth in Belfast and had not hesitated to send them to a Presbyterian college. He insisted that all the bishops of the Armagh province knew that at the beginning of his episcopate he had erected a seminary in Belfast to withdraw his students from Protestant colleges and protect their faith and morals. And, shortly after his translation to Armagh, he had done the same thing there at great expense. Cullen had seen the evidence of his interest in Catholic education and that should have sufficed to refute the malicious accusations. He then pointed out that the translation of the wrong tense of a verb used in the rescript had led to the widespread impression that the Colleges and the bishops favourable to them had been totally condemned, and predicted that much harm would result from such evil and scandalous trickery.[122]

In this response to the rescript Crolly put his finger unerringly on the basic weakness of the Roman recommendations: the confusion about the nature of the Colleges and the virtual impossibility of finding the resources among the Catholics of Ireland to build, support and staff a Catholic university. There was never any doubt in the government's mind that the Colleges were, if not in name, certainly in fact universities but the Roman authorities did not perceive the clear distinction in the British academic system between tertiary and secondary education and between seminaries and universities. The Irish bishops had secondary schools or colleges, which were principally designed as feeders to senior seminaries, but which could not have been enlarged or enhanced, as the rescript suggested, to endow them with university status; similarly the seminaries could not have provided university-style education, and Rome would not have wished to see the rules and discipline obtaining in them altered to accommodate non-clerical students. And there was a sad irony in the publication of a rescript in 1847 calling for the establishment of a Catholic university, when for so many thousands of Catholics the struggle to survive amidst famine and disease took priority over every other need. On 25 October Crolly, Murray, MacHale and Bishop Kennedy of Killaloe went to the Lord Lieutenant as a deputation from the hierarchy to present a memorial calling on the government to provide relief measures to combat the famine which was already afflicting some of the western, southern and 'several other districts of Ireland' and threatened 'a recurrence of the horrors of the last season'.[123] A university must have seemed an unimaginable luxury not only to those fighting for their lives but also to many who were closely engaged in succouring them.

The archbishop of Dublin, who had obviously coordinated his response with Crolly, replied to Rome in a similar vein two days earlier. He pointed out that the viceroy had decided to forward the statutes and rules to Rome when the rescript arrived. They would be sent, and Murray hoped that by examining the safeguards they afforded, in contrast to the dangers facing those who were compelled to seek in Protestant colleges or universities what they could not find in the Catholic colleges in Ireland, the

---

[122] Crolly to Propaganda, 5 Nov., 1847, APF, Acta, 211, ff 361r-362r. Bernard McAuley, Crolly's former curate in Belfast, wrote to Propaganda on 1 Nov. 1847 to defend the archbishop's record on Catholic education. He pointed out that Crolly had striven from the beginning of his episcopate to found a Catholic seminary and had then encouraged Catholics to attend it. Both he and John Laphen, a Dublin priest, denied that Montgomery, at the dinner after Denvir's episcopal ordination, had said anything improper about the divinity of Christ. (Ibid., SC (Irlanda) 29, ff 381r and 388rv.)

[123] F.J., 26 Oct. 1847.

congregation would judge more clearly how the Colleges were to be handled. He, too, promised obedience to the rescript.[124]

MacHale, on the contrary, was overjoyed. He wasted little time in assuring Cardinal Fransoni that the decree of Propaganda was received in Ireland with the same euphoria as the definition of the Council of Ephesus, which vindicated the dignity of the Blessed Virgin Mary, had once been received. The only people who, he believed, did not participate in this national joy were those venal Catholics who had accepted posts in the Colleges. He was able to promise on behalf of the other bishops an energetic response to the advice of the congregation, and already a few pious Catholics had contributed a not insignificant sum for the erection of a university. To impede this, the government would amend the College system, but it, in fact, was irreformable.[125]

The Catholic press for the most part bore out MacHale's enthusiastic endorsement of the papal decision. The *Freeman's Journal* could not restrain its delight on receipt of news of the Roman decision, and in its evening edition of 23 October saluted the rescript with uncontrolled hyperbole: 'Rejoice, Catholic Ireland, your dearest treasure, the treasure to preserve which your fathers abandoned home, property and life, your glorious ancient faith is safe', and declared that the question in which had originated 'the unhappy feuds which led to the disruption of our once compact and united popular party' had been settled and, it trusted, forever. When challenged by the *Dublin Evening Post*, a paper favourable to Whig policy and mixed education, the *Freeman* summed up the Catholic-national consensus by declaring that

a scheme that afforded no adequate guarantee against the corruption of faith and morals, that secured no religious instruction for any class, that took away the Catholic youth from the control of their divinely appointed guardians, that transferred the parent's natural right to a stranger, that tended to denationalize by leaving the professors dependent on the caprice of the minister of the day, and that was modelled on systems which filled France and Prussia with infidelity, was deservedly condemned by the people, priests and bishops of the Irish Catholic Church, and by the supreme head—the Sovereign Pontiff.[126]

In struggling to salvage the Colleges from the almost unanimous reprobation of the Catholic laity Crolly and Murray were indeed swimming against a strong and rising tide.

---

[124] Murray to Propaganda, 3 Nov. 1847, APF, *Acta* 211, ff 360v-361r.
[125] MacHale to Propaganda, 27 Oct. 1847, Ibid., f 360rv.
[126] F.J., 19 Nov. 1847.

IX

The Tory government which passed the Colleges Act fell in June 1846. The earl of Bessborough, who became Lord Lieutenant in the Whig administration, did not have to pay much attention to educational problems as the preparations for establishing the Colleges went slowly if steadily on, and the verdict of Rome was awaited. But his successor, the earl of Clarendon, who took office in May 1847,[127] partly out of party loyalty to the principle of mixed education and partly from personal enthusiasm for the establishment of the Colleges soon took an active interest in carrying out the policy of Peel and Graham. Like the Tories, the Whigs, thinking they knew better than Irish public figures what was good for Ireland, were not disposed to alter their policies to suit the whims of Repealers. Clarendon, who had scant sympathy for Irish Catholics and for the agitating priests who misled them, gave his immediate support to his government's decision to send Lord Minto on a diplomatic mission to Rome; he saw this as a means of correcting what he assumed were the false impressions entertained by the pope and his advisers on the encouragement given by some clergy to irresponsible forms of political behaviour, and the mistaken views held in Rome about the Colleges and the goverment's attitude to them.[128]

And the Lord Lieutenant was confirmed in his beliefs about the attitudes entertained in Rome on the Colleges question by a visit from Francis Joseph Nicholson, the Irish Carmelite who was coadjutor archbishop of Corfu. Nicholson, who was a close friend of the Irish Whig M.P., Richard More O' Farrell, and had a taste for diplomacy (or intrigue), must have given him the impression that he had been asked to report back on the Irish educational scene, for Clarendon informed the prime minister, Lord John Russell, that Nicholson was 'charged by the Pope to make general enquiries into the state of Catholic education & more particularly with respect to the vexed question of the Colleges'. He went on to explain that Nicholson, who, he claimed, was influential in Rome, had been responsible for preventing the pope from issuing a bull against the national schools and described him as 'a man of ability quite as enlightened & moderate as Archbishop Murray but with more knowledge of the world'.[129] Though there is no evidence that Nicholson had played

---

[127] One of the first commissions he received from the prime minister, Lord John Russell, was to communicate with Crolly about the Colleges as soon as the elections in Ireland were over. (Russell to Clarendon, 2 Aug. 1847, Clarendon Papers.)

[128] Clarendon to Russell, 30 Aug. 1847, Ibid., Lb i, 38rv.

[129] Ibid., 4 Sept. 1847, ff 41v–44r.

such a role in national education or been given an official commission to report back on the Colleges, he was more than happy to be involved in high level discussions about them. He subsequently claimed that he was invited by Clarendon to consult with Sir Robert Kane about the provisions necessary for the protection of the faith and morals of Catholic youth. Moreover, the prime minister had ordered that the statutes and all the documents connected with them should be sent to him and he had entered into negotiations about them and got improvements made in them with the Lord Lieutenant.[130]

Sir Robert Kane and the other presidents and vice-presidents of the Colleges, who had been drawing up the statutes, had agreed on the necessity of denominational halls of residence and on the appointment of deans or chaplains to supervise the moral and spiritual conduct of the students. Details of the method of making these appointments and of the status of the chaplains had not been finalized. Clarendon sent Kane to consult Crolly about them.

Kane duly submitted to Crolly the suggestions he intended making to his colleagues about providing satisfactory residential arrangements for the students. He proposed that those who did not stay with parents or relatives should be obliged to find accommodation in houses that had been licensed by the college authorities for that purpose; the landlords would belong to the same denomination as their students and require a certificate of good moral behaviour from the appropriate ecclesiastical authorities before obtaining recognition from the College. A chaplain or dean of residences was to be appointed with the approval of the respective religious authorities and in association with them was to make arrangements for the students to fulfill their religious duties and to supervise their moral conduct. The deans were to be recognized as College officers and to enjoy the same rank as professors. Students were to be subject to strict discipline and to be punished ultimately by expulsion for committing a wide range of offences including habitual neglect of religious duties. Professors who made any statement 'derogatory to the Truths of Revealed Religion or injurious or disrespectful to the religious convictions of any portion of His class or Hearers, or shall introduce or discuss Political or Polemical Subjects calculated to produce contention or excitement' were to be reprimanded and for a second offence suspended, and their removal from office recommended to the government. All College officers were to be obliged before assuming office to take an oath abjuring all intention of

---

[130] Nicholson to Pius IX, 26 July 1848, APF, *Acta*, 211, ff 392v-393r.

teaching anything injurious to the religious convictions of the students or of anything that could produce political friction. Kane admitted that the statutes required the sanction of the crown before taking legal effect, and that the appointment of visitors to oversee the execution of the statutes and regulations was vested in the crown, but he foresaw little opposition to the proposal made by Crolly and other prelates that the bishop of the diocese and archbishop of the province in which the College was situated should be members of the board of visitors.[131]

In forwarding an abstract of Kane's proposals to Russell, Clarendon explained that Crolly had wanted to let 'the conclave of Hierarchs' which was due to meet that week know how the educational plans were shaping up. He added that he himself favoured the payment of the deans by the state, but did not wish to see them enjoying the status of professors and thereby taking part in the College boards, as their presence would lead to denominational discord.[132]

In a memorandum for Minto to present to Rome, which the Lord Lieutenant sent to Russell, and which included the usual charges of clerical interference in politics, he claimed that the Colleges had been condemned on the basis of the false documents submitted to the Holy See and false information provided by Cullen, and but for the intervention of Archbishop Murray that condemnation would have been promulgated. In it he remarked that Crolly, Denvir and other prelates had been treated with 'the utmost insult, the payment of their dues has been refused & their chapels have been abandoned because they sold their religion, or in other words were known to be favourable to the Bequests Act or to the Establishment of the Queen's Colleges'.[133] Ironically, this was forwarded to Russell just a few days before the rescript condemning the Colleges was published.

However, the Lord Lieutenant's naive optimism was somewhat dented by the publication of the rescript.[134] Nonetheless, he believed that it but proved 'that mendacious & evil-disposed persons have authority with the Pope, & are prompting him to do mischief here'. Claiming that the Roman document was rather curious, both for its caution and latinity, he

[131] Kane to Crolly, 15 Oct. 1847, DDA.
[132] Clarendon to Russell, 18 Oct., 1847, Clarendon Papers, LB i, ff 90r-92r.
[133] Clarendon to Russell, 1 Oct 1847, Ibid, Lb i, ff 67r-70v.
[134] Petre knew nothing about the condemnation of the Colleges until reports of it appeared in the newspapers. He called to complain to Cardinal Fransoni about the discourtesy of not informing him in advance of the decision and of leaving the government ignorant of it until it was carried by the press. Fransoni, who insisted that the cardinals who came to this conclusion 'had only in view the preservation of the purity of the Catholic religion', seems to have had little trouble in fobbing him off. (Petre to Palmerston, 5 Nov. 1847, PRO, F.O. 43/40.)

consoled himself with the detection of a loophole—perhaps the omission of an order forbidding Catholic youth to attend the Colleges—and promised that Nicholson, who was very zealous and friendly, 'would insert himself' into it when he returned to Rome.[135] Clarendon did not limit himself to angry comments: he informed Minto through Lord Palmerston, the Foreign Secretary, that he had been in contact with Crolly, Murray and Nicholson, had listened carefully to their every suggestion about providing for the religious instruction and supervising the moral conduct of the students, and promised that Crolly and Murray, on whose suggestions he had acted, would be shown the statutes as soon as they were revised but before they had been finally accepted.[136] Minto's reports doubtless confirmed Clarendon's enthusiasm for pursuing the issue in Rome. He quoted the pope as having said that he had postponed giving his sanction to the cardinals' condemnation of the Colleges, but had then done so because of the views of the great majority of the Irish bishops. Moreover 'he very much regretted the effect which it was likely to produce and . . . a reconsideration of the question might perhaps be practicable'. Minto went on to claim that the condemnation had been based on false documents and misrepresentation from MacHale, the Irish College and 'other quarters unworthy of credit', and that the government might have expected some communication before such a hostile step was taken. The pope admitted that the rescript had been 'an unfortunate and most ill-timed measure', and, if he were convinced that it proceeded from false information, he could revoke or modify it.

It seems likely that Minto was gilding the lily for his colleagues in London, as the pope would scarcely have spoken so openly to him. However true it was that he felt obliged to confirm a recommendation deriving from the wishes of a large majority of bishops, Minto must have put words in his mouth when he used terms like 'unfortunate' and 'ill-timed'. But the Lord Lieutenant, as a result of the reports from Rome, became ever more convinced that the pope's mistaken decision on the Colleges derived from the unscrupulous advice he had received.[137]

Nicholson, who, Clarendon believed, would convey the right informa-

---

[135] Ibid., 23 Oct. 1847, ff 92r-94r.

[136] Ibid., 21 Nov. 1847, ff 142r-143v. Clarendon did not mince his words in describing MacHale: 'MacHale is a dangerous demagogue, whose proceeding as a citizen, and irrespective of their ecclesiastical decorum, no government in the world but ours would tolerate. Political agitations, popular elections and inflammatory publications are his favourite pursuits, his object seems to be to set the people against their rulers, and if he could have his way their ignorance and their turbulence would be perpetual. . .' (Clarendon to Minto, 26 Nov. 1847, Clarendon Papers, Lb i, ff 154r-156v).

[137] Minto to Palmerston, 14 Nov. 1847, Curato, *Documenti della missione Minto*, i, 190-4.

tion on the Colleges to the Holy See, set out for Rome in March 1848. By
then the statutes were nearly complete, though the list of visitors had not
been drawn up, but the Lord Lieutenant had promised that the archbishop of the province and bishop of the diocese in which the Colleges
were situated would be included. And Clarendon asked Nicholson to
present them to the pope as evidence that the Colleges could be regarded
as suitable centres for the education of Catholic youth.[138] The *politicanti*
among the bishops, hopeful that, on examination, the statutes would
persuade the pope to alter his previous judgement, had drafted a letter to
forward to Rome before the cabinet's approval for the greater part of them
had reached Dublin.[139] Crolly was disappointed that the viceroy's alterations did not give the bishops 'full power to *select*, and when necessary to
remove the Deans of the new Colleges'. Had that concession been made
he felt that their joint letter would have produced 'a powerful effect' at
Rome. He realized, however, that at Rome they were fighting a battle
under grave handicaps, since their 'late agent has acted so deceitfully'—
Cullen having committed himself fully to the opposite camp and having
made what Crolly regarded as untrue charges against him.[140] The Lord
Lieutenant, however, persuaded Murray not to forward the letter until
the approval arrived, and, after Nicholson's departure, Murray personally
wrote to the Pope to emphasize the significance of this development.
Expressing his confidence that the statutes would disprove the description
of the Colleges that had been relayed to Rome, Murray commended both
Nicholson's zeal and his knowledge of the number of youth who had
lapsed from their faith because there were no universities where they
could study in an atmosphere supportive of religion. And, he argued,
should Catholic youth be debarred from attending the Colleges, there was
no way of preventing them from attending Protestant universities, as
many of them had hitherto done with lamentable results.[141]

Rumours of the government's initiative in sending the statutes to Rome
with Nicholson had leaked out. The *Freeman's Journal* had already warned
of the enemies of the church energetically plying their mischievous
vocation in the eternal city, and, what was worse, with probable success.[142]

[138] Clarendon to Nicholson, 9 Mar. 1848, Clarendon Papers, LB ii, ff 153v-154v.
[139] Ten bishops signed this letter. In addition to the six who had written in support of the colleges in Nov.
1845, the bishops of Cork, Kerry, Kildare and Killaloe signed. (Draft of Crolly and others to Fransoni, 12
Nov. 1847, DDA)
[140] Crolly to Murray, 13 Apr. 1848, DDA.
[141] Murray to Pius IX, 21 Mar. 1848, APF, *Acta* 211, f 362rv.
[142] F.J., 6 Mar. 1848. MacHale was highly indignant when Sir Robert Kane, whom he met by chance,
refused to give him a copy of the statutes. Kane told him the only persons to whom copies were given
were Murray and Nicholson. MacHale was enraged that Nicholson, 'a speculator for half clerical – half
secular promotions' should have been so honoured. (MacHale to Slattery, 2 Mar. 1848. Slattery Papers.)

Though this may have referred mainly to Minto's negotiations for diplomatic relations, the *zelanti* rightly feared that his activities would encompass the educational sphere as well. Cullen, who kept a vigilant eye on developments in Rome that might militate against the *zelanti*, warned MacHale of the growing influence of England in Italy and of the consequent likelihood that the government would use papal weakness to extract concessions, and advised him to travel to Rome, accompanied by another bishop, to uphold his cause.[143] Archbishop Slattery also concluded on hearing of Nicholson's mission that 'if no one goes to oppose him our hard-earned victory will be filched from us by intrigue'[144] MacHale needed little further encouragement and with no Roman directive about ecclesiastical delegates to bar his way, as in 1839, he set off with his loyal ally, Bishop O'Higgins, who enjoyed the advantage of being able to speak Italian, and reached Rome on 16 April. Yet another agent also travelled to Rome. John Ennis, the parish priest of Booterstown, the veteran of the mission of 1839, went out at the behest of Archbishop Murray. Murray must have mentioned the high costs of maintaining a delegate there and paying for his translating and printing expenses to the viceroy, for Clarendon sought permission from Lord John Russell to offer Ennis £200 from state funds to cover his outlay. Russell, who had heard unfavourable reports about Nicholson from Lord Shrewsbury, and who probably thought it better to have two delegates in Rome representing their views, in case one of them should fail to impress the Roman authorities, readily agreed.[145]

Before MacHale and O'Higgins set off, they got fifteen other bishops to sign a letter to the pope, which they duly presented on their arrival. It was lengthy, comprehensive and aggressive. The signatories no longer regarded themselves as a party of appellants seeking Rome's verdict on a disputed issue, but rather as the faithful executors of a papal decision which had been unjustifiably and disloyally challenged and rejected by a minority of their colleagues. And what made the behaviour of that minority particularly reprehensible was its support for and encouragement of a policy designed by a hostile government to injure the interests of religion in Ireland.

Commencing on a note of high drama, the majority recalled the petition of Peter to the Lord as he sank beneath the waves, and expressed their confidence that the Lord's vicar would likewise save them from the

---

[143] Cullen to MacHale, 28 Feb. 1848, O'Reilly, *MacHale*, ii, 117-8.
[144] Slattery to MacHale, 15 Mar. 1848, Ibid., 119-20.
[145] Russell to Clarendon, 23, 26 Apr. 1848, Clarendon Papers.

waves battering against the ship of their faith. Moving quickly to attack their opponents without naming them, the *zelanti* went on to deplore the imprudent publication of the recent papal letter about clerical participation in politics.

The rumours about the profanation of churches, the incitement to murder, and their own connivance in it, were vicious lies published to serve the purposes of the government, but, nonetheless, caused anxiety until the archbishop of Cashel replied fully to each charge; they hoped the calumniators, many of whom were paid by English gold to go to Rome, or went there for other motives, would fail in their purpose. The combination of famine in Ireland, the despondency among its people and division among its bishops, the revolutions that disturbed Italy and the whole of Europe, presented the British government with the opportunity of extorting from the pope *per fas aut nefas* concessions tending to weaken not only the liberties of the church, but to destroy its independence completely.

Scarcely had the rescript condemning the Colleges been published, when not only government agents but even some bishops who were absolutely devoted to the government in that and other matters took counsel about renewing the controversy and importuning the pope to revoke his sentence; had that been achieved, a few bishops could have boasted that by their own hands they had bound the church and handed her over gagged to be under the yoke of Protestants. The government had its agents in Rome, the foremost of whom was Archbishop Nicholson, who interfered so officiously in their affairs. He possessed no more than mediocre ability; he enjoyed no authority other than that of acting as a kind of intermediary between the Protestant government and those bishops who favoured it. It was he who suggested to the government to build the Colleges and to appoint professors and other officials, by claiming that the pope could not help giving them his approbation. This pastor, who had left the vineyard assigned to him, came to stick his sickle into their harvest, and had brought to Rome a copy of the statutes which the government had compiled. The pope was respectfully advised to let Nicholson, who had come among them to seduce and destroy their flocks, go off to Corfu and leave Irish affairs to himself and them.

They then proceeded to put the statutes into context by pointing out that the act of parliament on which the establishment of the Colleges and their whole organization and administration depended still remained unchanged. The statutes did not have the authority to modify an act of parliament and could be altered at the whim of the government. And if it wanted to act with good faith, why did it not communicate the statutes to all the bishops instead of concealing them from the majority and in secrecy, and, through Nicholson, pass them on to the minority, 'the government bishops'?

To illustrate the notorious bad faith of the government they pointed out the recent change in the national system of education. Among the securities enjoyed by the bishops and parish priests which the congregation of Propaganda in 1841 deemed beneficial was the legal possession of the schoolhouses and grounds on which they were erected, but the government had set out to destroy that guarantee by trying to get legal ownership of the schools held by the bishops and parish priests. They then asked if the government could not and would not do in the case of the Colleges what they had done on national education as soon as Rome approved of them. Declaring that the government had prepared the statutes not because it loved, but rather because it wished to oppress religion and hoping to exploit the political situation in Italy to do so, the *zelanti* then hit their peak note with a plea for papal intransigence: *time igitur, Beatissime Pater, time Anglos et dona ferentes.*[146]

Bewailing the unhappy division in their body and the practice adopted by a few of their colleagues of always supporting the state, they predicted that in the unequal struggle then taking place, the anti-Catholic government would again win unless its audacity was repelled by the firmness of the pope and their colleagues were restrained by his authority. Tracing the split in the hierarchy to the Charitable Bequests Act, they contended that the government had introduced its measure of infidel university education to widen it, and the pro-government minority, instead of repudiating the vile calumnies that had recently been levelled against the church, seemed to agree with the slanderers. That same minority had refused to sign the letter composed by Bishop Briggs of York against those slanderous reports and the designs of the government based on them. There was therefore a lasting and baneful division within the hierarchy as the same prelates approved of the Charitable Bequests Board and the Colleges, and refused to sign Briggs' letter. The central question, therefore, on which all the other religious problems depended, was whether the Irish church was to be governed by the pope through the bench of bishops or by the government through a few bishops, and it could not be resolved until the pope ordered, or at least advised, the

---

[146] 'Fear, therefore, Most Holy Father, the English when they are bringing gifts.' This advice is based on Virgil, *Aeneid*, II, 49.

minority no longer to favour the government's view but to join with their brothers and priests and people of Ireland in that spirit of union recommended by the pope's letter of 18 February.[147]

This was indeed a powerfully eloquent and cleverly worded statement. By stressing both the smallness of the minority, its acceptance of British legislation against the will of the majority, and their own immediate acceptance of the rescript, the signatories cast Crolly, Murray and the *politicanti* in the role of an erastian, supine and untrustworthy clique. This would have been a most curious, if not comic, role to assign to the primate and senior archbishop, had the subject not been so complex and of such profound importance for the Catholic people of Ireland. The style of the letter bore the hallmarks of MacHale's sweeping rhetoric and the reproduction of a full English version by his biographer strengthens the likelihood that he was the author of these harsh and hostile comments on his opponents.

The bishops of Dromore and Kildare, who had previously supported the *zelanti*, did not sign this. Perhaps, they regarded it as too brutal and cruel to their colleagues or were having second thoughts about the Colleges in the light of the changes which the government might make. A few of the signatories must surely have blanched at the tirade against the two archbishops but, when presented with the document, probably felt they had either to sign or give the impression they had changed their minds.

While the representatives of both parties were sharpening their pens in Rome, the pope decided to confer an honour on their official leaders back home. He appointed Crolly and Slattery assistants at the papal throne, and, as officials of the higher ranks at the papal court were always nobles, he enrolled them among the nobility of the papal states. At that time such privileges were not often given to non-Italians, and their conferment on Crolly and Slattery was an indication from the Holy See that both sides enjoyed papal approval. Though the rescript in October 1847 had rejected the primate's plea and controversy had raged over the letter sent to the archbishops in January 1848, the bestowal of this honour, to which in their case no obligations were attached, was an expression of support for the work of both prelates and a confirmation of the esteem and respect in which both sides were held.[148]

---

[147] Slattery, MacHale and fifteen bishops to Pius IX, 27 Mar. 1848, APF, *Acta*, 211, ff 362v-366v and O'Reilly, *MacHale*, ii, 122-33.
[148] Pius IX to Crolly, 12 May 1848, APF, SC (Irlanda) 29, ff 747v-756v.

Crolly was also considered at the same time as a candidate for another honour that would have had far more controversial repercussions, had he received it. Lord John Russell, the prime minister, suggested to Clarendon that 'it could be a good thing' if Crolly were made a privy counsellor, and indicated his readiness to mention the proposal to the queen, if the Lord Lieutenant agreed. Clarendon, however, thought that Crolly's influence would be impaired by the acceptance of that honour and did not pursue the matter. Nothing further came of the idea. Murray had refused the offer and Crolly could not have entertained it. Already he and Murray were handicapped by the pejorative tag of 'castle bishops', and any further official association with the government would have limited their independence and damaged their standing with their people.[149]

Just then the case of the *zelanti* was strengthened by a practical step taken to implement the papal rescript. In May 1848 several bishops and clergy who had assembled in Dublin for the anniversary requiem for O'Connell met to discuss the establishment of a Catholic university. Bishop Cantwell took the chair, and Bishop Browne of Elphin proposed and Bishop Derry of Clonfert seconded his proposal that a committee of clergy under Cantwell's chairmanship be appointed to devise the best means of proceeding to the foundation of a Catholic university. The secretary duly reported to Cullen after their second meeting that they were confident of success.[150] This step enabled their advocates in Rome to maintain that the Irish Catholics were ready and willing to support a university, despite the claims of Crolly to the contrary.

X

Both Nicholson and Ennis brought to Rome copies of extracts from the statutes that were relevant to the moral and religious welfare of the students and also of the viceroy's letter to Nicholson requesting that they be transmitted to the pope for his consideration. Ennis, as the official agent of Archbishop Murray, had the extracts and letter translated into Italian and, together with an explanatory introduction, presented them to Propaganda.

To add authority to this viceregal letter, Ennis had the name of the

149 Russell to Clarendon, 11 Feb. and 21 May 1848, Clarendon to Grey, 6 July 1848, Clarendon Papers, and Lb iii, ff 24r-25r.
150 John O'Hanlon to Cullen, 18 May 1848, AICR.

addressee changed to Murray. Though the original bore the date 9 March, it was presented to Propaganda in an Italian translation with the dates, 19 March and 19 April. It subsequently found its way into the Irish press in an English version that had been retranslated from the Italian.

In his official letter, Clarendon, who intended his remarks for Roman consumption, observed that he was fortunate to have been able to consult the archbishop before the statutes were changed, as he was anxious that the guarantees and provisions necessary for the instruction of Catholic youth should be given 'with the most complete good faith and in the manner most satisfactory to the wishes of the Irish Prelates'. Excusing the delay, which was due to the government's endeavours to alleviate the sufferings caused by the famine, he remarked that it was not important since the Colleges could not be opened until the end of 1849. He promised that the Catholic archbishop of the province and the bishop of the diocese in which the Colleges were situated would be included in the list of visitors, which had not yet been completed, and gave an assurance that in the chairs, and in the other positions belonging to each College, the Catholic religion would be always fully and properly represented. Ingratiatingly declaring that he had a profound veneration for the character of the pope, he insisted that the statutes could 'advantageously be compared to those of any other similar institution in Europe, and that they would reflect the good faith with which they had been compiled' and 'would furnish a plain but conclusive answer to those false representations which had been so industriously spread, and which, had they been true, would have justly excited the fear and merited the reproval' of the pope.

The extracts from the statutes fleshed out the promises that the government had made about student accommodation and facilities for religious instruction and practice. They contained the provisions for ensuring that no professor could with impunity teach anything contrary to the truth of revealed religion or offensive to the religious convictions of the students (a second offence would lead to his suspension from office); they listed the offences for which students could be punished, which included habitual neglect of attending the church approved by their parents or tutors; they detailed the strict regulations about residence, laying down that students under the age of twenty one could only reside at home, in houses or lodgings of which their parents or guardians approved, and which had been licenced by the college president on the receipt of a certificate from the appropriate religious authorities, or in denominational hostels or seminaries; they assigned the moral and spiritual supervision of the students in lodgings or hostels to deans of residences, who would be appointed by the crown, but not without the approbation of their respective religious superiors, and they authorized those deans or chaplains to make rules for the students' proper observance of their religious duties, and obliged them to report to the presidents of the Colleges, at the end of each term, on the general conduct of the students and on the way in which discipline was being observed in the students' residences. No mention was made of payment for the chaplains, though Clarendon had won a promise from Lord John Russell that he would deal with that issue.[151]

In his commentary on the statutes, Ennis emphasized the security afforded Catholic youth by the virtual exclusion of all contact with members of other religions; students of different faiths would only meet in the lecture halls and, if the exclusive surveillance of their sons were not realized, the parents or teachers would be at fault. He also defended the statutes against the charges that had been made against them. To the accusation that the crown appointed the deans of residences, he replied that only one who enjoyed his bishop's approval could be eligible for that office, justified the crown's intervention by its need to exclude from that office bitter political opponents of the government and pointed to the precedent of prison and other chaplaincies where the appointments were made from among priests of whom their bishops approved. Referring to the measures which prevented the abuse of professorial power, Ennis explained that the bishops could not be entrusted with the appointments even to the chairs of history and philosophy because of the dangers of partiality or favour; in Maynooth and other university institutions all chairs were filled after a concursus or competition and sensible people would recognize the necessity for observing uniform patterns in making appointments.

Coming then to deal with the charge that the government had a hidden plan to demoralize and proselytize Catholic youth while pretending to educate them as Catholics, he maintained that the period of persecution had no longer any relevance, and argued that an examination of the legislation of successive parliaments during the previous thirty years would suffice to establish the mind and character of the government. Apart from general Emancipation, the record included the abolition of the

---

[151] Clarendon, who was confident that the pope would withdraw his rescript when he examined the statutes, believed that the arrangements made by the government would be defective, if the state did not pay the chaplains. He won from Russell a promise that consideration would be given to payment either from student fees or by a vote in parliament. (Clarendon to Russell, undated and 27 Feb. 1848, Lb ii, Clarendon Papers, ff 123v-125r, 133r-134r, and Russell to Clarendon, 25 Feb. 1848, Ibid.)

charter schools and bible schools, the establishment of Catholic chaplains
in the military and marine schools where the orphaned children of soldiers
and sailors were formerly raised as Protestants, the abolition of ten
Protestant bishoprics, the abolition of the exclusively Protestant corporations and the refusal of the government to grant a tenth of the £100,000
assigned to the education of the poor which the Protestant bishops each
year sought for their own religious schools.

The argument that nothing good could be expected from the English
government was, according to Ennis, too puerile to deserve a serious
reply. The reality was that Maynooth College received £26,600 annually,
and what government in Europe, Catholic or Protestant, he asked, granted
such a sum for ecclesiastical purposes, free from all state interference and
left entirely to the discretion of the church or college? The grant of
£100,000 annually for the education of the poor was for the most part
shared among all but one of the dioceses of Ireland, and no abuse or
complaint was attached to the system of education. Moreover, the
government had never availed of its power, under the law of Catholic
Emancipation, to register or limit the number of religious orders. Indeed,
the exercise of religious liberty was more secure than in any other nation
in Europe, and no other government would so strive to overcome the
prejudices of its people or ignore its laws to avoid persecuting dissidents
or interfering in their affairs.

Ennis then confronted the theory that by opposing the Colleges the
government would be forced to make greater and better concessions. His
riposte was brief and incisive: *cui bono?* Such opposition would be useless.
No power in England could make more generous concessions than those
contained in the improved statutes. If the influence of an English
government were ten times that of the current one, a system of education
as exclusive as that proposed could not be passed by either chamber. No
episcopal opposition or ecclesiastical or secular crusade could arrest or
keep back an act of parliament which, each day, was moving closer to
being put into operation. Opposition to the Colleges would only produce
serious deprivation to those classes for whom they were designed. That
opposition was at present unreasonable, if not unjust, and the institutions
were winning approval and support and promised to contribute to civil
and religious peace, and intellectual and moral progress, if the bishops
were permitted to keep a vigilant eye on them.

All that the bishops who favoured the Colleges sought, Ennis concluded, was permission to exercise their own judgement on the Colleges.
They had obtained the right to do so from Pope Gregory XVI on national

education, and they appealed to twenty years' success with that system to prove their vigilance and wisdom. In fact the Colleges had a greater claim on the pontiff's help for, while the rule of the national board laid down that religion could be taught in the schools, that of the Colleges insisted that religion ought to be taught, and taught under the direction of the bishops. To allow each bishop to make up his own mind as long as religion and morality were not endangered was not an unreasonable request. The three presidents were very estimable and trustworthy men: Kane, a literary figure with a European reputation and an excellent Catholic; Kirwan, a distinguished theologian and zealous pastor and preacher; and Henry, a Protestant much esteemed by many Catholic bishops and clergy whose high principles had been long in evidence as a member of the national board of education.[152]

Undoubtedly Ennis made the best use of his brief. He effectively exploded the myth of governmental Machiavellianism which the *zelanti* had so persistently touted; the list of reforms which the government had introduced was an effective answer to the suspicious dismissal of English policy which pervaded much of his opponents' case. He also milked the statutes as exhaustively as possible to convince his readers of the guarantees which they afforded to the protection of the students' faith, and his concluding request for the bishops who approved of the Colleges to be allowed to give guidance to their people according to their consciences was couched in very reasonable terms. The allusion to the precedent of 1841 on the national schools was delicately and skilfully woven into his appeal. But, while his account of the provision for student accommodation and of the moral and religious care which the chaplains were to offer was comprehensive and impressive, he did not deal effectively with the central issue of professorial freedom to convey opinions and attitudes hostile to or destructive of the undergraduates' faith. What concerned the church in France and Germany was its exclusion from any influence in the appointments of professors who could turn out to be subtle and determined enemies of the faith and exert a malign influence on the students. The regulation in the statutes which obliged the president of a College to rebuke a professor who had been delated for making comments offensive to the faith of a student and then, if necessary, to dismiss him, did not cover the situation where a professor could gradually destroy an undergraduate's faith by constant, if stealthy,

---

[152] Ennis, *Estratto dagli Statuti Corretti del nuovo Collegio della Regina in Irlanda e osservazioni*, APF, SC (Irlanda) 29, ff 590r-598r.

ridicule of religion. Both the Church of England and the Church of Scotland were determined to ensure that professors at Oxford, Cambridge and the Scottish universities did not teach anything that could corrode or damage Anglicanism and Presbyterianism.

The congregation of Propaganda followed the same pattern in 1848 as in 1840: MacHale and O'Higgins were furnished with a copy of Ennis' defence to enable them to respond to his arguments in the presentation of their case. Given an opportunity in 1848, which to their great regret had been denied them eight years previously, they determined to exploit it to the full. Their response was detailed and comprehensive; trenchantly argued, and unsparing of opponents, it allowed no scruples about overstatement to spoil the thrust and effectiveness of the various points it raised. It was carefully circulated in Rome to selected and influential officials, but Ennis was unable to obtain a copy. Several months later, after the congregation had published its decision, a copy was procured by the bishops of the minority and they were so incensed by what they (or some of them) regarded as 'the unworthy and unchristian means resorted to by these Prelates to misrepresent their brother bishops and the higher classes of Irish Roman Catholics, in order to secure the object of their journey to Rome' that they had a translation made of it for the use of those bishops whose characters were so cruelly aspersed.[153]

MacHale and O'Higgins began by tracing the origin of the Colleges to a desire of the government to introduce the Prussian system of education into Ireland—a system that had inundated Germany with the bitter fruits of Hermesianism, pantheism and irreligion. But since the established church had Trinity College for its students and the Presbyterians had their own college in the north where Arianism, Socinianism and still worse doctrines were taught, justice would have demanded that Catholics should have been given their own university, where the dogmas of their faith could be imparted and where sciences could be studied without any danger to faith. Listing the penal laws against Catholic education which had despoiled all their institutions, they maintained that the government

---

[153] This translation which was entitled *Brief remarks on the system of mixed education which is sought to be established in the co-called Queen's Colleges in Ireland* was printed in Dublin in 1849. In the following year the minority had printed in Dublin a vindication of their case, which they had already addressed to the cardinal prefect of Propaganda, entitled *Breves vindiciae contra calumnias in duobus libellis, anno 1848 Romae typis excisis, contentas, Eminentissimo ac Reverendissimo Domino D. Cardinali-Praefecto Sac. Congregationis de Propaganda Fide a subscriptis episcopis Hibernensibus suppliciter inscriptae.* This was signed by the bishops of Raphoe, Kerry, Limerick, Kilmore, Down and Connor, Killaloe, and Kildare and Leighlin. Edward Walsh of Ossory, who had opposed the Colleges, also signed it, since he believed the others had acted according to their consciences. Murray sent his own defence to the cardinal prefect in December 1849.

should not have founded Colleges which the church had not sought, or, having founded them, should have made them Catholic establishments. Recounting Crolly's summons to his colleagues to discuss the government's plans in May 1845, their memorial to the Lord Lieutenant and Crolly's support for the location of the northern College in Armagh, they observed tartly that 'the facility with which the Archbishop changed his opinions in so important a matter, and the readiness with which he departed from the unanimous decision of his brethren in the episcopacy, must have edified the Protestant viceroy'. The bishop of Down and Connor soon followed the example of his metropolitan, and shortly afterwards the archbishop of Dublin and a few other bishops privately gave their approval to the Colleges. The sturdy advocates then added an even more damning gloss than they had accorded to Crolly alone:

This vacillation, this changing of opinion, this desire of adapting themselves to the designs of a Protestant government, this departing so easily from the solemn acts of all the episcopacy, this willingness to make experiments upon the faith, could not but highly offend and scandalize the Catholic people of Ireland, who in their simplicity cannot understand how the shepherds of the flock can be so uncertain about the good pastures, and so ready to place the tender lambs under the care and protection of the rapacious wolves.

Recalling the appeal to Rome, they remarked that the decision of the Holy See was duly received with enthusiasm by the people and clergy of Ireland, who hoped that union among the bishops would be restored, but their hopes were to be disappointed for the minority in the hierarchy not only held firm to their opinions but even tried to induce Rome to withdraw its decision. The bishops and clergy who were hostile to the Colleges were abused by English agents who circulated evil reports about them even in Rome, and yet the crimes and turbulence of which these critics complained occurred in the towns and dioceses—Drogheda, Dublin, Limerick and Killaloe—of those who favoured the Colleges.[154] And Young Ireland, the faction which provoked these disturbances, supported and defended the Colleges as potential seminaries of sedition and irreligion, where their views could be propagated more easily among young men of different religions. 'Wise Prelates', MacHale and O'Higgins mused, subtly condemning their opponents by association, 'should open their eyes to the danger of such institutions, seeing that all the bad and seditious men are promoters of them, and hope to find these an easy and

---

[154] In their answer in 1850 to MacHale's and O'Higgins' charges, the seven bishops pointed out that the rebellion which had occurred had taken place in the diocese of Cashel.

opportune means for the propagating of the spirit with which they are animated'.

They then turned their attention to the three documents that Ennis had submitted—the viceroy's letter, extracts from the statutes and Ennis' brief. Dismissing the viceroy's promises as valueless, as they did not bind his successor, they scathingly rejected the pledge to have the Catholic religion fully and properly represented in the chairs and other offices as meaningless, since they maintained that the viceroy's concept of full representation was equality with some Protestant sect; for them proper representation meant the acknowledgement of the rights of the only true religion, Catholic teaching and the inculcation of a Catholic spirit among the youth. The statutes, they claimed, were compiled by the heads of the Colleges and could be changed by them or their successors. And, moreover, the impression was falsely given that they were an improvement on those which had been in force before the rescript and represented an improvement on them, and that therefore the papal condemnation did not relate to them. MacHale and O'Higgins poured scorn on Ennis' prediction that, if the condemnation of the Colleges were withdrawn, true religion and moral practice would be ingrafted on the minds of youth and future generations truly educated in Catholicism would promote prosperity and peace. And they countered it by declaring that Ennis would have prophecied more accurately had he said that 'Protestants and Catholics, mingled together in the Colleges, would begin to make each other lose every attachment to their religious principles, and there would spring from it a fine harvest of indifferentism in regard to faith'.

The two envoys then went on to illustrate and analyse this indifferentism. The professors of history, law and philosophy, they explained, would be prevented from examining or impugning the errors of heresy out of courtesy to colleagues of different faiths; the students, seeing Protestants and Catholics mount the same chair, would lose their horror of heresy and their respect for Catholicism would be diminished. Furthermore, mixed education in which the sciences were separate from religion always produced the worst effects, as the rector of Louvain and other scholars had pointed out.

Dealing with the government's appointment of superiors and professors, MacHale and O'Higgins maintained that, even if it wished to give security to the faith and morals of their youth it could not do so, as the appointments would be made from persons who professed false religions or, perhaps, none at all, and quoted approvingly the views of the bishop of Liege who had charged the government of the Netherlands with producing an education hostile to religion and morality, a spirit of independence and incredulity in youth and a deplorable licentiousness of manners. Yet the government of the Low Countries was not more hostile to Catholicism than the English government. Then, warming to the theme of the hostility of the state to Catholicism, they recalled that the predecessors of the government, who were not worse men than the current holders of office, 'made laws more cruel than those of Nero and Domitian against the Catholics, and sought every means to exterminate them'. To illustrate the antipathy of the current government to religion they cited Lord John Russell's appointment of a 'barefaced Socinian' to the bishopric of Hertford[155] in order to resist the progress of popery, and the behaviour of the Lord Lieutenant who, as ambassador in Spain, had tried to promote Protestantism and had recently made himself the panegyrist of Presbyterianism.[156] Members of the government, however liberal and enlightened, swore on oath on taking office that transubstantiation, the invocation of the Virgin Mary and the sacrifice of the Mass were superstitious and idolatrous. Maintaining that Catholics could not have confidence in educators chosen by such people, the envoys then remarked that Ennis had only discussed the three presidents of the Colleges and had made no reference to the vice-presidents. Of the six only two were Catholics, and they wondered sardonically if Ennis would have been satisfied with a situation in Rome in which four Jews and two Catholics were chosen to superintend education in a city in which the proportion of Jews to Christians was almost exactly the same as that of Protestants to Catholics in Ireland.

MacHale and O'Higgins, in commenting on the individual superiors of the Colleges, noted that not only had the Presbyterians inherited all the fury of their founders, Calvin and Knox, against the church, but that a large section of their clergy were infected with Arianism and Socinianism, and that their college in Belfast was under the direction of staff imbued with those anti-christian doctrines; and whatever about Henry's private sentiments he belonged to that 'infected school' and 'perfidious sect'. One of the vice-presidents, whom they did not name, was a Protestant barrister who did not believe in the immortality of the soul and whose moral conduct some time previously was not superior to his religious doctrines.[157] They showed the same lack of enthusiasm for Sir Robert Kane as

[155] Renn Dickson Hampden was appointed bishop of Hereford not Hertford in 1847.

[156] When Clarendon was ambassador in Madrid he obtained permission from the Spanish government for an agent of the British and Foreign Bible Society to print and sell translations of the new testament in Spain. (Maxwell, *Life and Letters of George William Frederick, Fourth Earl of Clarendon*, i, 149-52.)

[157] Presumably this was Edward Berwick, the vice-president of Galway.

in their previous letters, and they arraigned Kirwan, the president of the Galway College, for his lack of pastoral zeal, and his indifference to the starving poor during the famine. And they predicted that the professors would be either tepid Catholics, contumacious priests like Thaddeus O'Malley, who had been chosen as rector of the university of Malta, or moderate and so-called liberal Protestants, whose blandness would but mask their bitter antipathy to the church. And the professors would be able to convey their hostility to Catholicism, perhaps, by a word, a laugh, a joke, or a gesture. If students were to denounce professors before their presidents, the professor could claim that his words were misunderstood; in the case of Belfast the accuser would be faced with the impossible task of carrying his accusation against hostile Protestants.

Quoting the views of the bishop of Natchez about the indifference Catholics acquired in America through mixed education, they went on to refer to Crolly's ambition for the promotion of charity in a mixed College at Armagh and commented acidly that he should have added that, as a result of the mixed system the faith, without which charity could not subsist, would be imperilled. The deans or chaplains, they added, would be powerless in the field that counted—that of the actual teaching in the Colleges—just as the chaplains at the French universities were unable to prevent the spread of incredulity. Visitors of mixed religions who would only meet once or twice a year would be unable to interfere effectively on religious questions, and anyhow, the archbishops of Tuam and Cashel would never have any connexion with establishments they regarded as dangerous. To confirm their claims about the necessity of episcopal authority in education, they quoted Archbishop Von Droste zu Vischering of Cologne, the Athanasius of the age, who maintained that the church should have the exclusive direction of the religious part of education, and that scientific education and the moral and religious conduct of youth in educational institutions were equally subject to the superintendence of the clergy. MacHale and O'Higgins dismissed Ennis' proposal that each bishop should be allowed to make his own decision on the Colleges by arguing that such a policy would lead to the intolerable situation of bishops who approved of the Colleges taking some part in their adminis- tration and encouraging youth to attend them, and thereby annulling the authority of the local bishop, who was opposed to them. Declaring that all their ills sprang from the readiness with which some prelates opposed their colleagues and lent themselves to carrying out government measures which did not only concern their own dioceses, they recommended that bishops should not execute laws against the wishes of their colleagues, and that on issues of dispute or on matters exceeding their competency they should refer the case to Rome and, while awaiting its decision, take no step indicative of a schism among them.[158]

MacHale and O'Higgins, who had been received by the pope shortly after their arrival, forwarded a copy of their booklet to him, and, explaining that they understood that his many commitments imposed limits on the time available for studying the controversy, also presented him with a summarized version of their case. Understandably, they introduced no new arguments in it, but they went to pains to point out that the dispute was essentially an ecclesiastical one, between most of the bishops who had accepted a Roman decree and the few who had not; the government's desire for church support derived from its need to justify its policy before a Catholic people but it only offered a nominal or apparent role to the bishops in the administration of the Colleges.[159]

The case against the Colleges certainly lost nothing in the telling in these two documents. It was argued with passion, power and eloquence. The supporting evidence from continental experience and the stirring denunciations of mixed systems of education by French, Belgian, German and American prelates (which doubtless reflected Cullen's influence) were cleverly and subtly harnessed to the fears of the Irish bishops. But if the style was forceful and the pleading eager, the language in places was unnecessarily harsh and intemperate. The *politicanti* were depicted as disobedient to Rome, an embarrassment to the other bishops, and irresponsible in their enthusiastic determination to further the designs of the government at the expense of their obligations to religion. While Ennis had tried to show that the Colleges could be tolerated, and had sought permission for bishops whose consciences permitted to make use of them and had carefully abstained from challenging or questioning the *bona fides* of the majority, MacHale and O'Higgins zestfully lashed their opponents as they demolished their arguments and advanced their own. The *politicanti* and Ennis would not have been human, had they not resented the imputations so unfairly cast on their motives and their actions.

---

[158] *Brevi rilievi sopra il sistema d'insegnamento misto che si cerca di stabilire in Irlanda nei collegi così detti della regina*, APF, SC (Irlanda) 29, ff 942r-964v.

[159] ASV, Arch Part. Pio IX, Oggetti vari, 133. They also circulated another booklet entitled *Esame dei documenti presentati alla S. Congregazione dall'inviato dell'arcivescovo di Dublino, in favore dei collegi della regina in Irlanda.* Murray was later very hurt on discovering a charge made in this booklet that the bishops of the minority obtained favours for their friends from the government as a reward for their cooperation with it.

Privately, MacHale commented scathingly on 'the feeble sophistical and exceedingly offensive' defence of the Colleges made by Ennis.[160] But he reserved his most pungent and damning observations for his episcopal opponents. Though he did not name Murray, Crolly and their party, he undoubtedly had them in mind when he pointed out that it was not the heretics alone who were the enemies of the faith in every age; rather 'the *fautores* were worse and even to this very day the *fautores haereseos* [the accomplices of heresy] among Catholics nay of high Ecclesiasticy [*sic*] are the most dangerous enemies of the Catholic Church'. He went on to express pity for the pope, who was being annoyed by those who should have consoled him but were instead sending agents to support infidel colleges, and predicted that 'though they seem incorrigible truth and the Catholic faith will triumph especially in poor old Ireland'.[161]

Before taking any action on the request of the minority—for all the MacHale camp sought was the maintenance of the rescript in full force— the congregation of Propaganda with the pope's approval forwarded on 29 June 1848 to all the bishops of Ireland the excerpts from the statutes and Clarendon's letter, which Ennis had submitted, and sought their opinions on the changes which these documents allegedly made to the system of education which had been already condemned.[162]

Laurence O'Donnell, the bishop of Galway, who had signed the MacHale letter in March, was favourably impressed by the statutes. Without MacHale looking over his shoulder he obviously felt freer to express his own opinion, and the enthusiasm of people in Galway for the establishment of the College was probably not without its effects. He thought the statutes were of benefit to religion, though of little significance compared to the requirements demanded by the bishops at the beginning of the controversy. However, they did not have the force of law which prevented them from being changed. He suggested a modification to ensure that chaplains would not be appointed without the prior approval of the bishops, and in general invited the pope to suspend his assent until these suggestions were carried out.[163] Cornelius Egan, the bishop of Kerry, who had also been numbered among the *zelanti* in March, replied that, if the statutes were once given the force of law by

---

[160] MacHale to Bishop French, 20 May 1848, GDA. O'Higgins was even more robust in his criticisms of the advocates for the colleges: 'You can scarcely conceive the unjustifiable means resorted to by our blind and unprincipled opponents. Everything that systematic lying, or British intrigue could effect, was called unscrupulously into requisition, but the justice of the cause and the prayers of the faithful have, so far, baffled our enemies and left us in the ascendant'. (O'Higgins to Maginn, Aug. or Sept. 1848 quoted in MacNamee, *History of the Diocese of Ardagh*, 445.)

[161] MacHale to French, 24 May 1848, GDA..   [162] APF, *Lett.*, 337, ff 466v–467r.

[163] O'Donnell to Propaganda, 20 July 1848, APF, *Acta* 211, ff 366v–367r.

parliament, there would be no reason to fear that Catholic youth would come to any harm in the Colleges.[164] Michael Blake, the bishop of Dromore, in general commented favourably on the statutes, and, though noting that the act of parliament from which all power derived had been condemned by the bishops, limited himself to saying that Ireland badly needed the Colleges, and expressed confidence that the British government would make greater improvements at the behest of the Holy See and that all would turn out well in the end.[165]

These were the only members of the majority to shift to a more tolerant and benign stance. The rest held firm and insisted that no compromise was possible. They argued that the concessions supposedly made by the statutes were useless unless confirmed by legislation in parliament and they refused to consider the possibility that the government was prepared to treat them in a fair and considerate manner. Edward Maginn, the coadjutor bishop of Derry, even succeeded in matching the violence of MacHale's polemics against the policies of the government and Ennis' vindication of the Colleges.

Crolly's reply was briefer, and more factual and unemotional. Maintaining that a careful perusal of the viceroy's letter and of the College statutes which enjoyed the approval of the government revealed that the genuine character of the institutions had not been accurately explained to the congregation of Propaganda, he went on to list the guarantees which afforded ample protection to the faith of the students. Of necessity, he repeated Ennis' assurances about the value and significance of the visitational role assigned to some of the bishops, the promise of an adequate number of professorial appointments for Catholics, the pledge of non-interference by the teaching staff with the religion of the undergraduates and the authority conferred on the chaplain to bring about the expulsion of those who offended against religion or morals. Emphasizing again the dangers to which Catholic youths were exposed in Scottish and French universities, and in Trinity College, Dublin, where many, succumbing to financial inducements, abandoned their faith, he referred to the fear that Catholics would not obey an episcopal injunction to stay away from institutions that were safer, especially as they were aware that the Colleges were founded on the same principles as the national system of education, which had proved to be a bulwark of their faith and morals.

---

[164] Egan to Propaganda, 28 July 1848, Ibid., f 380v.
[165] Blake to Propaganda, 16 Aug. 1848, Ibid., ff 384v-385r. Blake told Cullen that were it not for the strong desire of the middle classes to have the Colleges, he would prefer to see them rejected, but he hoped for more concessions from the government. (Blake to Cullen, 19 July 1848, AICR.)

He concluded by reminding the cardinal prefect that the Irish bishops could scarcely support junior seminaries and were completely incapable of building and endowing suitable colleges for the laity.[166] The bishops of Raphoe[167] and of Down and Connor wrote in such a similar vein that it seems likely they had coordinated their responses with Crolly before forwarding them. Bishop Denvir of Down and Connor wrote at greater length than Crolly and, in fact, developed some of the points which the archbishop had made. He explained how the lure of free accommodation and bursaries tempted Catholic pensioners and sizars at Trinity College to join the ranks of scholars, to whom alone the offices of the College were open, often at the price of their faith. He also pointed out the unlikelihood of any medical or law student attending colleges, if by any chance they were provided by the bishops, since at the end of his course he would not be licensed to practice.[168]

Of the original group of six who defended the Colleges in November 1845, the bishop of Kilmore did not reply till late September, and his letter arrived too late to be printed among the documents on which the cardinals would make their decision. He wrote in English, asked how Catholics could be censured for attending the new Colleges when they were not censured for attending Trinity College, where their faith and morals were exposed to imminent danger, and expressed the hope that with the careful attention of the clergy, students would be as safe at the Colleges as in the national schools of which he had a hundred in his diocese and from which not a single case of perversion had occurred.[169] The bishop of Kildare and Leighlin changed sides, and the bishops of Galway and Kerry wavered in a direction which the minority would have regarded as favourable.

The final line-up in response to the Roman request for further information did not appear as unequal as it would have, had all the bishops adhered to their initial responses. The intransigent opponents of the colleges numbered fifteen out of a hierarchy of twenty seven. But the determination of that majority to pursue its goals unflinchingly and the depth of hostility some of them felt towards Crolly and Murray was strikingly illustrated by the comments of John Cantwell, bishop of Meath, in a letter to Paul Cullen:

---

[166] Crolly to Propaganda, 1 Aug. 1848, Ibid., ff 380v-381v.
[167] MacGettigan to Propaganda, 3 Aug. 1848, Ibid., f 382rv.
[168] Denvir to Propaganda, undated, Ibid, ff 385v-387v.
[169] Browne to Propaganda, 21 Sept. 1848, APF, SC (Irlanda) 29, ff 924r-925v. Corboli-Bussi read this letter and in a note to the congregation praised Browne as one of the best of the bishops. (Corboli-Bussi to Propaganda, 4 Oct. 1848, Ibid., f 920r.)

That Bishops & Priests have been found not only to tolerate but even to advocate such Institutions was sufficient to provoke the vengeance of Heaven to ingulph (sic) us in a depth of misery still greater than that with which Providence has visited our unhappy country. In my letter to the Cardinal Prefect I thought it unnecessary to advert to the misrepresentations & falsehoods of Dr Ennis. The presence of the Archbishop of Tuam & the Bishop of Ardagh, who were so well disposed & so much more competent to do ample justice to this pensioned hireling, relieved me from the painful task. . . . I have just received a Circular from Dr Flanagan [the secretary of the bishops] saying '*that his Grace Dr Crolly & Dr Murray think it expedient in the present state of the times to put off the general meeting of the Bishops until after Christmas*'. What is to become of a people abandoned at such a crisis? What influence the smiles of the court & the favours of the Castle!!! Until Providence relieves us of them or the Pope cut the unnatural & unholy official chain which links them to the bitter enemies of the Faith, there is no security for religion; there is no protection for our people. What will become of us. They are either mad or corrupt in adopting such a course in existing circumstances.[170]

The *zelanti* also had the advantage of having their case pressed in Rome by three heavyweights—MacHale, O'Higgins and Cullen. Cullen's high standing with the curia and his wide knowledge and experience of Roman procedures and acquaintance with influential figures attached to the congregation of Propaganda gave the opponents of the Colleges a decided lead. The political situation in Rome also worked in their favour, as many of the pope's advisers believed that at the root of much of the anti-clericalism of his political enemies was the absence of an education properly grounded in religion. To make matters worse for the *politicanti* their two representatives did not even present a united front. Francis Joseph Nicholson, the coadjutor archbishop of Corfu, was delayed by illnesss from reaching Rome until the latter half of July. By then, much to his chagrin, Ennis had stolen his thunder. He had removed Nicholson's name from the letter Clarendon had written about the statutes and substituted that of Archbishop Murray, 'Dr Nicholson being with me, a nobody'. And though he claimed that Clarendon had agreed to this alteration at their meeting in Dublin before his departure, both Clarendon and Murray were embarrassed and annoyed by this contretemps.[171] The archbishop, who seems to have been on friendly terms with Corboli-Bussi,

---

[170] Cantwell to Cullen, 24 Sept 1848, AICR. Some of the *zelanti* assumed that Crolly and Murray were intriguing with Dublin Castle to prevent them from having an opportunity to express their views. The *politicanti* may not have wished to give their opponents an opportunity of forwarding a solemn document to MacHale in Rome, but when Slattery insisted on holding the meeting, Murray gave his and Crolly's consent.

[171] Ennis to Clarendon, 24 July 1848, Murray to Clarendon, 26 Aug. 1848, Clarendon to Nicholson, 30 Aug. 1848, Clarendon Papers, Lb iii. The F.J. of 13 June 1848 carried a report on Ennis' presentation to the pope and Propaganda of the statutes, Clarendon's letter (allegedly) to Murray and Ennis comments on them.

promptly contacted him to complain that Ennis had submitted an inexact copy of Clarendon's letter, and accompanying papers which gave an imperfect knowledge of the arrangements made by the government; to insist that he alone was authorized to pass on the statutes to the Holy See; and to suggest that the pope should appoint a special congregation to examine the whole university question before a general congregation pronounced judgement on it.[172]

Nicholson also wrote a lengthy letter enclosing the statutes to the cardinals attached to the congregation of Propaganda. His explanations and clarifications added little to those of Ennis, but he emphasized the importance of the gesture made by the government in communicating with Rome, which he interpreted as a national retraction of all the calumnies made against the Catholic religion by England and an act of homage by a Protestant government to the spirit of Catholicism. He insisted that Clarendon, whom he had often met, was a man of honour and foresight, and was very anxious to promote the good of Ireland and, in particular, of the Catholics. And he stated further that Clarendon had assured him that the prime minister had promised to lay before parliament a proposal to pay the chaplains a salary equal to that of professors and not less than £200 per year. The controverted subject of history, he added, would be dropped from the curriculum of the Colleges.[173]

Both Ennis and Nicholson were optimistic about the success of their mission, which, given the task they had to achieve and the knowledge Paul Cullen possessed of Roman procedures and attitudes, indicates a degree of naïveté on their part.[174] Ennis, who was inclined to be fulsome in his reports to Clarendon, later told him that he was 'tolerably sanguine' that the justice of his cause and 'the moderation of the Prayer or object sought' would triumph over his two formidable antagonists.[175] And later he declared that he had not the most distant doubt that the Roman decision would be sufficiently satisfactory, and he attributed that favourable outcome to the happy coincidence of views between Clarendon and the pope on Irish ecclesiastical and political affairs.[176] Nicholson apparently

---

[172] Nicholson to Corboli-Bussi, 25 July 1848 and undated letter, Arch. SC AA. EE. SS., Inghilterra 1847-50, Pos. 55-57, Fasc. 25, ff 8r-9r, 22r-23r.

[173] Nicholson to Propaganda, 30 Aug. 1848, APF, Acta, 211, ff 387v-392v. History, a subject which attracted a lot of controversy, was eventually united to the chair of English, when the Colleges opened.

[174] They both believed that Corboli-Bussi was very well disposed to the British government. Ennis later told Cullen that when Pius IX stated that Ireland was too poor to support a 'Louvain' he expected a favourable result on the colleges. (Ennis to Cullen, 23 Nov. 1848, AICR.)

[175] Ennis to Clarendon, 6 July 1848, Clarendon Papers.

[176] Ibid., 4 Sept. 1848. An experienced observer of the Roman scene later blamed Ennis' imprudent zeal for increasing the opposition to his cause. (Thomas Redington to Clarendon, 21 Oct. 1848, quoting a priest from Rome, Ibid.)

sent back a report to Ireland that he had succeeded in getting the authorities at Rome to set up a special committee of cardinals or a 'particular congregation' to study the whole question before it would come before the general congregation.[177] But his success in this field was illusory.

This further documentation was then passed to the two consultors—Corboli-Bussi and Cullen—who had submitted *vota* on the question more than two years earlier. Corboli-Bussi returned a sober and thoughtful answer, and one that reflected much of Crolly's and Murray's thinking on the subject. He first disposed of the confusion surrounding the word 'colleges' by making clear that Irish Catholics did not have university colleges of the kind proposed by the government, and then ruled out the possibility of the foundation of a university on the model of Louvain, as the Catholics of Ireland lacked the resources enjoyed by the Catholics of Belgium. Irish Catholic youth desirous of obtaining a university education were left with three choices: to attend Protestant universities, to go to Catholic universities on the continent which would involve heavy expenditure and a not insubstantial danger of losing their faith at such a great distance from their parental homes, or not to seek entrance to the learned professions. These two latter possibilities he regarded as too severe to be prudently imposed on the consciences of the faithful. The likelihood was that the children of the middle classes would succumb to the temptation to send their sons to the mixed Colleges, despite an episcopal prohibition; and once having stilled the voice of conscience the practice of their religion would become lukewarm and they would find no spiritual support in the Colleges—the Colleges being, of necessity, in the hands of Protestants or bad Catholics. If the danger of perversion existed, Catholics could not attend mixed Colleges; but if it were neither certain nor proximate, if on the contrary greater evils were to be feared from a prohibition of attendance at the Colleges 'then it would seem conformable to ecclesiastical prudence to make an effort to improve the institution so as to render it as innocuous as possible rather than to keep obedient sons as far removed as possible from it'.

Corboli-Bussi then noted that the bishops had not condemned the bill outright in 1845 but had demanded alterations. He concluded that the government had made substantial and significant concessions and that others could be obtained. He thought the requirement that the professors of logic, geology and anatomy should be Catholics was of little impor-

[177] Murray to Clarendon, 3 Sept. 1848, Ibid.

tance, since the errors that could give offence in those areas affected not only the Catholic religion but revealed religion in general. He felt the same might be said of metaphysics, but he agreed fully that the professors of moral philosophy and history should be Catholics, since Protestant theology had introduced many errors into moral philosophy and since religious and general history were inseparable.

He concluded a penetrating analysis of the problem by recommending that a very secret negotiation be conducted with Lord Clarendon, whose keenness to know the mind of the Holy See was both novel in the context of British history and highly commendable. In thanking him for his initiative the points which required attention to permit Catholics in good conscience to attend the Colleges could be indicated to him.[178]

The other consultor, Paul Cullen, stuck firmly to his guns. Remarking that he had found nothing important in the documentation presented in favour of the Colleges, he took advantage of the opportunity offered him to rebut some of the factual statements in Nicholson's memorial which did not have any significant bearing on the issue in dispute. He did, however, go on to challenge the argument that Ireland was too poor to establish and maintain a Catholic university by arguing that three thousand churches had been built since 1800 and by listing some of the impressive expenditure on the cathedrals, churches, colleges and religious houses that had been erected since the beginning of the century.[179]

When all the relevant papers on which the cardinals were to be asked to make a judgement had been printed, a letter reached the cardinal prefect from Luigi Gentili, a well-known member of the Institute of Charity, who had been conducting missions in Ireland and had taken advantage of his travels through the country to discuss the university question with some of the bishops. Though his sojourn only lasted five months and his understanding of the nuances of the problem was probably a good deal more limited than he imagined, his evidence was probably regarded as valuable in Rome, since it represented the views of an independent observer. And it was unfortunate for Crolly and the supporters of the Colleges that Gentili's reactions were decidedly negative. Not only did he criticize very adversely the arrangements whereby Protestant visitors could inquire into the discipline of Maynooth College and thereby cast doubts on the good faith of the government, but he also emphasized the damage done to Catholic students in Trinity College, Dublin, by consorting with others of the Protestant faith or of none at all, and by the

---

[178] Corboli-Bussi to Propaganda, 9 Sept. 1848, APF, *Acta*, 211, ff 403r-406r.
[179] Cullen to Propaganda, 15 Sept. 1848, Ibid., ff 406r-407r.

deleterious effects of Locke's philosophy, which, he claimed, had done more to spread scepticism and incredulity than Luther. The good party in the episcopate, he added, intended to follow the advice of the pope and found a Catholic university and the bishop of Meath had already £10,000 in hands for that project. Consequently he hoped Rome would stand firm and resist the insidious proposals of the government.[180]

And this was exactly what the cardinals decided to do when they met on 25 September 1848. The previous decision was maintained intact, and the bishops were again exhorted to put aside their divisions, and to do their utmost to establish a Catholic university.[181] The pope duly confirmed the decision and a rescript clothed with his authority and dated 11 October, embodying the recommendations of the cardinals, was sent to the four archbishops to be transmitted to their suffragans. The bishops were further enjoined to hold their meetings according to canonical regulations and advised to forward their decisions to the Holy See. Despite the fears expressed by the *zelanti*, the likelihood of a different outcome must have been remote. The *politicanti* would have had to prove that the whole system of higher education, which had been condemned in 1847, had in the meantime been so radically altered as to merit the reversal of a judgement that had been reached after prolonged study and inquiry. This they could not do. All they could claim was that the charters provided certain securities for the Catholic youth at the Colleges and made some provision for episcopal involvement in ensuring that the rules were observed, but, as the *zelanti* correctly insisted, the charters did not have the force of law and could be easily changed. Evidence of a transformation of the system of sufficient magnitude to justify the cardinals in setting aside the rescript of 1847 was not produced. MacHale forwarded the rescript and an explanatory pastoral letter to the *Freeman's Journal* and, hailing the papal decision as 'the triumph of truth over error, the triumph of faith over the powers of the world—the triumph of Christ over his enemies', he predicted that never again would 'the enemy prevail over the Irish faithful portion of the Catholic church'. The *Freeman's Journal*, reflecting the views of the Tuam party, saluted the Roman document as 'the charter of religion, of liberty, and of independence in this country'.[182] If the *zelanti* were cock-a-hoop, the *politicanti* were

---

[180] Gentili to Propaganda, 7 Sept. 1848, Ibid., ff 409r-410v.
[181] Ibid., ff 354v-355r.
[182] F.J., 26 Oct. 1848; Cantwell was delighted that the rescript 'silences forever the treacherous whisperings of any feeble or false member of our body with the enemies of our faith and the murderers of our people' (McGee, *A Life of the Rt. Rev. Edward Maginn*, 172).

understandably downcast by the papal verdict. The bishops' meeting had taken place before the rescript arrived. Slattery suggested at it that some steps should be taken towards founding the Catholic university, but when some bishops, doubtless the supporters of Crolly and Murray but perhaps also one or two others, objected, he did not push the matter. He was aware of the enormous problems involved and felt that there was little enthusiasm among those whose help was essential.[183]

Redington, the under-secretary at Dublin Castle (and a Catholic), who met Murray on 5 November, reported that he found him in very low spirits, much afflicted by the Roman decision.[184] Crolly undoubtedly shared this despondency. They obviously combined their views in their responses to Rome. Murray wrote on 20 November promising full obedience and explaining that, though invited by the viceroy to be a member of the council entrusted with the appointment of the professors, he had deferred giving his assent till the mind of Rome was known. Crolly, too, promised full submission to the rescript but went on to point out that in the midst of food shortages and the destitution of the poor, circumstances were not propitious, though in the course of time they could become so.[185] Maginn, the coadjutor bishop of Derry, and one of Crolly's severest critics, wrote to him enthusing about the opportunities afforded the bishops by the rescript to put their bitter discussions behind them and drink copiously from 'Lethe's oblivious stream'. He suggested that they should at once set about building their Catholic university for, despite their poverty, the Catholic world was wide and God was a good provider. Consequently, there were grounds for optimism and

Were your Grace to consent to bless and lay its foundation stone, amid the assembled prelacy, priests and people, on Tara Hills, I would not have the least doubt of its Success. Your own Cathedral might go hand in hand with it, and the great Apostle of our Country, worthy of this double honour, would have his name hallowed in both these splendid memorials of knowledge and Sanctity.[186]

Crolly was doubtless in no mood to pursue such romantic dreams. But he told Maginn that he would in due course lay the foundation stone, and

---

[183] Slattery to MacHale, 16 Dec. 1848 in O'Reilly, *MacHale*, ii, 157-9. Slattery explained: 'In the first place, we ourselves are not, like the bishops of Belgium, who are proposed as our model – of one heart and one mind. Our high Catholics are rotten to the core, and our middle classes are fast-corrupting in the same manner by the love of self and of place. There does not exist that pure Catholic feeling, that lively and Irish faith, which distinguished our people even a short time ago. . .'

[184] Redington to Clarendon, 5 Nov. 1848. Clarendon Papers.

[185] Murray to Propaganda, APF, SC (Irlanda) 29, ff 907r-909v and Crolly to Propaganda, 21 Nov. 1848, Ibid., f 969rv. Crolly's reference to the foundation of a Catholic university was less than enthusiastic: de erigenda universitate desperandum non est.

[186] Maginn to Crolly, 17 Nov. 1848, DDA; McGee, *A Life of the Rt. Rev. Edward Maginn*, 131.

this answer led Cantwell to remark that he had given 'some shadow of hope that the Holy Spirit has enlightened him as to the dangers of his course'.[187]

MacHale and his suffragans held a provincial synod in January 1849 and issued decrees against the Colleges which went beyond the terms of the rescript and for which they were duly rebuked by Rome. But they were not published during Crolly's lifetime. The primate was also probably spared the pain of reading the booklet which MacHale and O'Higgins had produced in Rome. Reports about its contents had reached Ireland as early as October 1848 when Redington commented that Murray, Crolly, Denvir and Kennedy of Killaloe had been 'grossly abused' in it, but though he explained that he wanted to obtain a copy,[188] it seems that a copy did not become available until much later. The normally placid Murray could scarcely contain his indignation when he read it. He told Clarendon:

I cannot but feel the deepest humiliation in being obliged to avow that a more disingenuous document I never read. Circulated secretly and left uncontradicted to fasten its misrepresentations on the mind of the Pope and on all the Cardinals, I am not surprized at the effect which followed.[189]

By then Crolly was dead and so probably never knew the full details of this, one of the last distressing episodes, of a sad and harrowing chapter in the history of the Irish church.

Of the three great disputes of the 1840s the one on the Colleges was the most lasting and must have been the most painful. The controversy over the Charitable Bequests Act engaged the public in a passionate way, coming as it did so soon after the banning of the Repeal meeting at Clontarf and O'Connell's trial. But the issue of collegiate education touched a deeper and more sensitive nerve in the bishops because of the fears and anxieties aroused by it in other countries and the sharpness of the response to it by members of other hierarchies. And the accusations made in nationalist papers that the Colleges would reflect an anti-national ethos, together with O'Connell's vigorous denunciation of them, ensured that most of those who shared his political views were hostile to them. Because of the depth of feeling, the arguments of those opposed to the Colleges were expressed in language that became more extreme and intemperate, and though their adversaries did not know what was being

---

[187] Cantwell to Slattery, 30 Nov. 1848, Slattery Papers.
[188] Redington to Clarendon, 27 Oct. 1848, Clarendon Papers.
[189] Murray to Clarendon, 3 Sept 1849, Ibid.

said about them they could assume that the case against them would not suffer from understatement! Three and a half years passed from Crolly's first summons of the hierarchy to discuss the bill until his letter of acceptance of the second rescript. The debate about the Colleges, under any circumstances, would have been bitter and stressful, but coming as it did when Ireland was undergoing the traumatic suffering of the famine, it must have taxed the patience of Crolly and Murray to the limit.

9

FAMINE AND DEATH

The potato blight which had crossed the Atlantic and seriously diminished the crop in Belgium in 1844 made its dreaded appearance in Ireland in the following year. In August the premature withering of the leaves was observed in different parts of the country. By October the tubers in the ground had rotted so extensively that when dug they quickly disintegrated. The exclusive dependence of so many small farmers and labourers on the potato for their sustenance and survival was so great that the disease boded serious ill; even tenants who could afford some modest variety of food relied ultimately on the potato to pay their rents.

Aware of the threat of ecological and nutritional disaster, Peel's government appointed a committee of scientists in October 1845 to investigate the phenomenon and to suggest ways of preserving the potato and countering the blight. The experts were baffled and could offer no solution. A committee was set up at the Mansion House in Dublin at the end of October to offer advice and help. On his own initiative Peel ordered £100,000 worth of maize from North America and appointed a Relief Commission for Ireland to which were named prominent government officials in association with Sir Randolph Routh of the commissariat for purchasing food for the army. This body, which was empowered to appoint local committees representative of the landlords and their agents, gentry, magistrates, clergy and other prominent figures, would raise funds and bring food that could be resold to the distressed, or if necessary, distribute it free of charge, and initiate schemes to provide employment. The central committee could give aid to the local committees on receipt of a warrant from the Lord Lieutenant. Early in 1846 some reorganization took place: Routh became chairman of the central commission and the practice was established of this body adding a half or two-thirds to the sums subscribed to the local committees, which by August 1846 came to number six hundred and forty eight.

By December 1845 the prices of potatoes in the shops had doubled and the prices of grain had greatly increased. Complaints began to reach the Mansion House Committee from clergy and others of the spread of disease and of the scarcity of potatoes in some of the poorer parts of Ireland. Want was increased by the export of corn and the rate of protection on imported foreign corn. Though the bishops realized that the loss of part of the potato crop was serious, they could not foresee its extent and duration and at their annual meeting in October did not make arrangements to contact the Lord Lieutenant about it. At that stage there were still sufficient supplies available and prices had not yet begun to rocket.

In January 1846 a bill was passed to make provision for public works— the construction and improvement of roads, harbours and piers and drainage—which were to be financed equally by the Board of Works and by local landlords. Local committees were authorized to distribute tickets to those they deemed deserving of employment on these projects.

Though the government passed a coercion bill for the protection of life which enabled the Lord Lieutenant to place particular districts under martial law, it also continued its efforts to cope with the consequences of want. Among those, fever, which was destined to be by far the most fatal accompaniment of the distress, had already appeared. In March a Board of Health was established in Dublin and was given the power to require Boards of Guardians to establish fever hospitals in every union. Also in March a bill was passed which allowed five people in any barony to meet and submit to the Lord Lieutenant proposals for local works.

Bishops and clergy of all denominations threw themselves into the work of the local relief committees. Much of what they did went of necessity unrecorded. Their collections and distributions of alms were often done on the understanding that they would not be publicized.

The archdiocese of Armagh did not suffer as heavily as other parts of Ireland but reports from some poor law unions indicate that conditions were very bad. Before the end of 1845 several bad cases of fever were reported in Drogheda and the board of guardians arranged to rent a house as a temporary fever hospital. In January 1846 the clerk of the Armagh Union claimed that two-thirds of the potato crop in the union was unfit for human consumption and predicted a scarcity of three months. The guardians at Magherafelt believed that half of the local crop was lost to human consumption and foresaw 20,000 people having no potatoes by the beginning of May.[1] By March accounts of famine and fever become more

[1] D.E.P., 15 Jan. 1846.

frequent even in the more prosperous counties of Antrim and Armagh, which were supposed to be among the most prosperous counties of the province.[2] Prices had by then doubled, and food riots occurred in Donegal and Tipperary. Bishop Blake and his clergy at the cathedral feared that some 500 in Newry and the surrounding area could no longer survive without relief. The bishop at a public meeting referred to a death from starvation that had already occurred in the town.[3] And near Belfast want and fever were particularly prevalent at Ballymacarrett and despite generous help from Belfast and elsewhere the situation did not improve.[4]

Crolly was due to pay his *ad limina* visit to Rome in 1846. He sent a summary of his report to Cullen to pass on to the Roman authorities and begged to be excused from travelling because of his commitments with the cathedral and his wish to be of help to the poor as famine threatened.[5]

In May a meeting was organized in Dundalk to counter the local distress and in June a deputation from the Drogheda Relief Committee waited on the Lord Lieutenant to solicit aid for funds raised by private subscription for the employment of the poor. Crolly, who took an active part in promoting this move, was unable to accompany the delegation because of ill-health. The vicar of Drogheda explained that they had collected nearly £750, were improving the lanes and alleys of the town and had three hundred and seventy people employed, on whom nearly 1,500 depended for support. The Lord Lieutenant directed the delegation to the Relief commissioners who gave it a sympathetic hearing.[6] In a letter to the congregation of Propaganda the primate bewailed the condition of the poor and explained that they could scarcely be saved from famine even by a more frequent distribution of alms. He did not, however, ask for financial assistance.[7]

II

In June 1846 the Tory government fell and was replaced by the Whigs under Lord John Russell. By then all the healthy potatoes had been consumed and hunger threatened until the new crop could be harvested in October. Widespread distress had become evident in parts of the western seaboard—Belmullet had been an early casualty—but during the year 1845-46 very few deaths from hunger occurred. Side by side with the

---

[2] Ibid., 17 Mar. 1846.   [3] N. Ex., 22 Apr. 1846.   [4] V., 15 Apr. 1846.
[5] Crolly to Cullen, 26 Jan. 1846, AICR. On 8 Mar. 1846 the pope acceded to this request.
[6] D.A., 20 June 1846.   [7] Crolly to Propaganda, 28 May 1846, APF, SC (Irlanda), 28, f 717rv.

official machinery set up to cope with the emergency, religious bodies which derived help from abroad, most notably the Society of Friends, established their own networks for distributing relief.

The Whigs introduced new methods of dealing with the crisis in August 1846. The entire burden of public works was now placed on the men of property in each barony. The Board of Works was empowered to carry out all the schemes of public relief and to respond as it saw fit to the requests made at presentment sessions. And it was also obliged to repay all loans made to it for this purpose. Furthermore, the government decided not to buy food or establish depots to sell it at low cost; it was forced, however, to modify this plan for the west of the country where the poverty of the people and the dearth of merchants compelled it to set up depots for the sale of Indian corn which it bought in America. This power was quickly removed and transferred to official inspectors, who were commissioned to employ only those who had no other means of subsistence. The government also decided to appoint the local committees which would liaise with the central one and furnish lists of men eligible for employment; but to add to the general inconvenience which their lavish adherence to a policy of *laissez-faire* was creating, it refused to nominate curates to these local committees: only local men of substance and the senior clergy of the districts were eligible for appointment. This exclusion of curates at once deprived the committees of many young men with youthful energy and of the clergy who had intimate knowledge of the remoter parts of many parishes.

By September the terrifying fact had again to be faced. The potato crop had failed a second time. An almost all-time high acreage had been planted but the yield per acre was a mere twelfth or fourteenth part of the average one.[8] Only extraordinary measures could have prevented widespread distress and starvation but governments wedded to the doctrinaire and sacrosanct economics of the time were incapable of envisaging such schemes. The potato failure and consequent loss of basic food was immediately felt in the poorer parts of the country, especially along the western and south-western seaboards. Reports began to appear in the press of numbers of people starving to death. In October the government permitted work of a productive nature, such as drainage, to be carried out. But to prevent unfair competition with ordinary wages, those offered for relief work were kept lower, and the wages of ten pence or one shilling per day were insufficient to feed a worker and average-sized family. And

---

[8] O'Grada, *The Great Irish Famine*, 41.

depending on insufficient food the worker was often physically unable to last a full day of strenuous work.

To add to the suffering generated by food shortages the weather turned bitterly cold. The winter of 1846-47 was one of the longest and worst in living memory. Snow fell in November and the ravages of cold, added to those of hunger, soon began to take a deadly toll. The dismal plight and even bleaker prospects of so many victims of hunger and destitution prompted a wave of sympathy both in Britain and Ireland, and this was translated into the foundation of more charitable and relief organizations.

Catholic communities, especially in North America and Australia, began to collect and forward money to Ireland. Donations began to arrive before Christmas 1846. The pope ordered a triduum of prayers to be held in one of the principal churches of Rome in January 1847 at which sermons were preached about the Irish situation and collections taken up. Then in March he addressed an appeal for prayers and financial assistance to all the bishops of the world and this led to church collections in many dioceses on the continent. Bishops in Italy, France and Germany responded generously; but the papal nuncio in Lucerne, forwarding money from Fribourg, remarked that some cantons forbade the bishop of Basle to publish the pope's appeal.[9]

From the early autumn of 1846 distress was very evident in Armagh and its neighbourhood. At a meeting in the city on 30 September a magistrate described a deputation of labourers coming to him for work, some of whom had not had any breakfast. A memorial was forwarded to the Lord Lieutenant calling for a presentment session. At the sessions held for the barony of Upper Dundalk, the clergy of Dundalk and South Armagh appealed for large sums of of money for local needs.[10] A few days later it was reported that thousands of families in the barony of O'Neilland were starving. At a session in the barony of Lower Dundalk, the rector of Carlingford claimed that more than 250 people were in distress and needed employment, and Bernard McKeown, the parish priest of Lordship in Co. Louth, pointed out that one third of his 5,000 parishioners were in a state of destitution. In Armagh arrangements were made to buy Indian meal for sale to the poor at less than market value, and a sum of £10,500 was sought for drainage and other works. But William Paton was told that this practice contravened government regulations which permitted gratuitous aid to be given only to the infirm, when the workhouse was already full. Relief inspectors reported that a

9 APF, SC (Irlanda), 29, f 166rv.
10 D.E.P., 3 Oct. 1846.

state approaching starvation obtained among the poorer farmers and cottiers in the baronies of Upper Fews and Upper Orier, and among the working people of Portadown.[11] Three of the local landlords announced reductions in rent,[12] and Lord Caledon offered employment at one shilling per day to all who wanted work, and provided coal and meal at half price and even less. The Caledon family also subscribed very generously to funds for buying clothes for the poor.[13]

In Dundalk hunger drove people to demand bread free from a local baker.[14] By the beginning of December the Armagh workhouse was full and £700 had been raised in the parish and barony for the poor who could not support themselves.[15] In Dundalk and Louth the Catholic clergy headed appeals for funds to raise £500 for the distressed. By the end of the year a death from starvation was reported from Tartaraghan, a few miles from Armagh; a man, aged forty five, with his wife and three children had been subsisting for several days on kale and turnips and he died begging for a cup of water with meal in it.[16] Deaths from starvation in the poorer parts of Ireland became common.

By January 1847 the poorhouses had been mostly filled, and local committees had to care for those who were left without any support. Accounts of distress within the archdiocese of Armagh continued to appear in the papers. In January 1847 the rector of Stewartstown reported that the majority of his six thousand parishioners were in a state of the greatest destitution and many of them at starvation level.[17]

Francis Clements, the rector of Tartaraghan, noted that both weavers and labourers were becoming daily less fit for work and 'starvation is pictured in their countenances'. Numbers were subsisting on less than one meal per day and upon raw turnips and nuts. John Keating, the parish priest of Loughgall, and other members of the local committee, informed Routh that one half of their community of 5,000 was in extremely distressed circumstances and at least one quarter was in a state bordering on starvation. In Moneymore the local committee, which had supplied soup three days weekly to 948 people, decided to supply it daily and anticipated an increase of 250 supplicants for it. From Ballinderry Revd John Jackson explained to the commissioners in Dublin that a Protestant and a Catholic had listed those requiring relief and found they had 204 families or 1,022 people, but because of their shortage of funds could only

---

[11] Paton to Routh, 2 Dec. 1846, Hornsby to Stanley, 8 Dec. 1846, Woodhouse to Stanley, 12 Dec. 1846, N.A., Rel. Comm. II/2/2/441/30.
[12] D.E.P., 13, 15, 20 Oct. 1846.   [13] Ibid., 14 Nov. 1846.   [14] Ibid., 14 Oct. 1846.
[15] Ibid., 1 Dec. 1846.   [16] Ibid., 29 Dec. 1846.   [17] Ibid., 21 Jan. 1847.

help those in the greatest need. Sixty nine families or 399 people were turned away. In Castledawson one half of the population—over 2,000—was in a state of destitution, but supplies of meal were insufficient for 200 of them.[18]

The news that 95 deaths had occurred in a week in the workhouse at Lurgan, a town regarded as one of the centres of the linen industry, that 1,200 people were in want near Belfast and that three-quarters of the people of Ballymacarrett of whom between 1,100 and 1,200 were receiving relief were 'in a state of sickening poverty', confirmed the view that the consequences of the potato blight had reached into every part of the land.[19] The *Banner of Ulster* reported that in the first seven weeks of 1847 some 400 people had died in the townland of Derrymacash in Co. Armagh and in approximately the same period 400 paupers had died in the workhouse in Lurgan.[20]

On 8 December 1846 a public meeting was called by the Mayor of Drogheda to discuss possible measures that could be taken to employ the poor until the public works which had been suggested for that area a few days earlier would be started. Crolly proposed the first resolution to this effect and it was seconded by the local vicar. Paying tribute to the zealous few who invariably bore the burdens of committee work despite the criticisms they got for their pains, he thanked particularly the committee at Drogheda which had negotiated on behalf of the unemployed during the previous year. That committee had received no help from the Board of Works or the railway companies, but from the government grant and local collections, several of the narrow streets and lanes of the town had been improved, the houses of the poor had been whitewashed and filth removed. Insisting that the poor would have to be employed and fed before the Board of Works could commence the schemes for which they had applied, and emphasizing that a far greater calamity had befallen the country than could have been foreseen, he stressed the urgency of obtaining contributions of all sizes to enable them to relieve the distressed. The vicar, in supporting Crolly's case, praised the good order maintained by those who had suffered the most severe destitution during the past year. Another resolution called for the provision of employment by task work: by this was meant payment for work done rather than by time, and this method, which was often employed throughout the famine years, was

---

[18] Clements to Routh, 7 Jan. 1847, Keating and others to Routh, 21 Jan. 1847, Hewitt to Stanley, 30 Jan. 1847, Jackson to Routh, 2, 24 Mar. 1847, Pepper to Routh, 4 Mar. 1847. N.A. Rel. Comm. II/2/2/441/30.
[19] D.E.P., 16 Feb. 1847 and N.W., 30 Jan 1847.   [20] D.E.P., 6 Mar. 1847.

chosen to circumvent the refusal (for whatever reason) of men to do a fair amount for their wages. On this occasion the response was very negative. The primate intervened to say that generous payment of task work was to be commended; for those who could not work, other provision would have to be made. This clarification met with the consent of the meeting. A committee was appointed for each district of the town and given the task both of raising funds and of finding those to whom employment should be given. The meeting ended with a collection which raised £306, with sums ranging from £50 to £1.10.0. Crolly gave £10 and expressing his regret that he could not give more referred to a similar obligation he had in Armagh. He observed that his income was small and that 'there were many imperative demands on it'.[21]

At the annual new year's dinner given by the mayor of Drogheda in 1847 a tribute was paid to the archbishop's 'untiring and increasing exertions' to relieve the destitution of the town. He replied to the toast by emphasizing one of his favourite themes: the praiseworthiness of Christians of all denominations cooperating in the cause of charity. Commending the union of Protestant, Presbyterian and Catholic in Drogheda as a foretaste of that union of all the children of Ireland which would bring greatness and prosperity to the country, he expressed his hope that the cooperation which their care of the needy evoked would be lasting:

I trust the extensive demands upon property caused by the destitution of the poor will be more than compensated by the union of all classes in the exertions of Christian charity; and when the sufferings have been removed that this feeling will not pass away, but will remain as the standard by which our country will be distinguished among the nations—I am sure everyone must be delighted with the exertions of the clergy of all creeds. No language can express the respect which I entertain for my Protestant and Presbyterian friends who have come forward so nobly in the cause of charity; all seemed to be actuated by the one desire; that the law of charity shall prevail—that no fellow creature shall perish; no matter what shall be the cost the shield of charity shall be thrown over him to preserve him.[22]

The spread of typhus and other fevers accelerated the deaths both in the workhouses and elsewhere. As 1846 ended the workhouses were nearly full. The Armagh workhouse, which had been built for 1,000 with an upper limit of 1,200, had reached its quota, despite the grim conditions in it. In March the guardians had decided that only the sick and children under nine years of age would have three meals per day; others were

[21] D.A., 12 Dec. 1846.   [22] Ibid., 9 Jan. 1847.

limited to two. Dinner for those over twelve years of age was to consist of six ounces of rice or eight ounces of bread and a quart of soup; working men and women received seven ounces of rice or nine ounces of bread and a quart of soup.[23] On 7 January 1847 Drogheda workhouse, which had been built to house 800 inmates, had still 80 spare places; five weeks later the number of inmates had risen to 886.[24] Dundalk workhouse, built for a similar number, held 935 on 10 February 1847; three weeks later that number had grown to 958.[25] Fever, which did not ease until the summer, carried off more than twenty victims per week. Ardee, though built for 600, held as many as 1,012 as late as 3 July when the Drogheda and Dundalk workhouses had begun to empty.[26]

At the peak of the fever epidemic Belfast had over 2,000 patients in the hospital and workhouse infirmaries.[27] In Co. Armagh temporary fever hospitals were erected in Keady, Loughgall, Markethill and Middletown in addition to the sheds for 200 patients in the Armagh workhouse grounds. Fever reached its peak in May in Armagh when the workhouse alone had 400 patients but in Dungannon the number of patients increased till June.[28] O'Connell's death on 15 May, when Ireland was near the nadir of her misfortunes, symbolized the bleakness of the country's prospects. Crolly, who respected and admired his work for justice, and equality but parted company with him on the advocacy of Repeal, wrote to assure his son, John, that on receiving the news of his father's decease he himself and his clergy had offered public prayers for him in Drogheda had offered Mass for him in Armagh and that he would pass on John O'Connell's request for prayers to his clergy.[29]

In January 1847 the government brought in a 'soup kitchen act' by which commissioners were authorized to distribute soup to the hungry. Public works were virtually ended by June 1847, when two and three quarter millions were being relieved by soup.[30] The soup kitchens ceased to operate in September. From then onwards the infirm, aged, and those who could not work were given relief either inside the workhouse or outside it, as the boards of guardians decided. They were also empowered to give temporary help to the able-bodied unemployed, who were destitute. But by the Gregory clause of August 1847, all those who held as little as a quarter acre of land were refused relief.

---

[23] PRONI, BG2/A/3, 4.   [24] D.A., 20 Feb. 1847.   [25] N.Ex., 6 Mar. 1847.   [26] Ibid., 3 July 1847.
[27] N.W., 1 May, 20 July 1847.
[28] Grant, 'The Great Famine in the Province of Ulster—The Mechanisms of Relief' (PhD dissertation, Q.U.B. 1986), 277.
[29] F.J., 9 June 1847.
[30] Donnelly, 'The Soup Kitchens' in N.H.I., V, 309-10.

Belfast, like several other towns, had had an active soup kitchen committee which predated the government schemes, and which was increasingly importuned for help by residents of and migrants to the town. By April it was claiming that 15,000 people were depending on public charity and that at least 1,000 families in Belfast had no beds other than heaps of filthy straw.[31] Armagh county was reported to be suffering more than any other in the north with the exception of Fermanagh and Donegal.[32]

Money began arriving from Rome in 1847. Archbishop Murray received £730 on 11 February with instructions to consult the other archbishops about its allocation. MacHale insisted that such donations should be distributed exclusively by the bishops but Murray, claiming that some clergy thought that method of apportionment too exclusive and 'having but little of the spirit of the good Samaritan in it', consulted Crolly and Slattery. Crolly, in turn, having counselled his suffragans strongly favoured Murray's wish of channelling it into the central relief funds:

I am still of opinion that any mode of *exclusive distribution* by the Bishops and other Clergy will be attended with bad consequences as the dangerous and uncharitable principle of exclusive distribution will be adopted by other influential Persons who will refuse to give Relief to the Catholic Poor. If therefore His Grace of Cashel will join us, I think that 3/4 of the Roman money may be given to the Central Committee with a request that it should be distributed in the poorest localities of Munster, Leinster and Ulster.[33]

Slattery's support for MacHale's plan put an end to Crolly's and Murray's proposals.

The money collected in response to the pope's encyclical letter to the bishops was forwarded to Ireland from the congregation of Propaganda and began arriving about June 1847. Crolly replied to the first instalment of £50 in July, thanking the cardinal and informing him that the alms they had received from Rome and from many people in Europe and America had sufficed to relieve the wants of the sick and destitute, and paid tribute to the contributions made by the government and the rich Catholics and Protestants of England and Ireland. He predicted an abundant harvest and remarked that the awful famine was nearly over and its accompanying fevers declining.[34] Thanking the cardinal a month later for a further £50,

[31] N.W., 10 Apr. 1847.
[32] D.E.P., 1 June 1847.   [33] Murray to Slattery, 11, 20 Feb. 1847, Slattery Papers.
[34] Crolly to Propaganda, 21 July 1847, APF, SC (Irlanda), 29, f 208rv.

the primate was even more optimistic: he foresaw the harvest yielding an abundance of food and the poor no longer requiring such alms.[35] He received another sum of £50 from Rome in August bringing his share of the funds to £150. Other dioceses received larger subventions. A correspondent writing from Rome to the *Freeman's Journal* on 18 September estimated the Roman disbursement at £4,000[36] and this may well have been an underestimate. When money sent later in the year is included, at least £5,000 must have come from Rome in 1847.

Crolly was also called upon to distribute the money raised in America. When it began arriving he tried to organize a meeting of the archbishops to make arrangements about dividing it, but as it was inconvenient for them to leave their dioceses, he decided to apportion it among them so that they could forward it to their suffragans in accordance with local needs.[37] In March he passed on to all the bishops their share of the funds sent from Boston, New York and Rhode Island.[38] The Boston share, to which Protestants had also contributed, amounted to over 4,000 dollars. Crolly assured the bishop of Boston in reply that it would be distributed without regard to religion. Three months later he received a further £800 from Boston.[39]

In thanking Cardinal Fransoni in July, Crolly also pointed out that the jubilee had been faithfully performed in Armagh, and as far as he knew, throughout the whole country. He was referring to the specially indulgenced religious exercises, which Pius IX had proclaimed to mark the beginning of his pontificate. The jubilee had been used in Ireland as a means of intercession to halt the ravages of the famine, and had been enthusiastically carried out. Some churchmen in all denominations regarded the famine as an affliction sent by God to punish the sins of the Irish people, though they did feel obliged as a consequence to let it take its natural course: they combined this view with a strong desire to use all natural means to end the suffering associated with it. Crolly does not seem to have reflected theologically on the causes of the disaster but to have contented himself with doing what he could to alleviate the suffering it brought in its train.

---

[35] Ibid., 23 Aug. 1847, f 267r.   [36] F.J., 1 Oct. 1847.
[37] Crolly to Slattery, 18 Mar. and Slattery to Crolly (copy), 21 Mar. 1847, Slattery Papers.
[38] Blake papers, DrDA.
[39] Bishop Fitzpatrick to Crolly, 27 Feb. 1847 and Crolly to Fitzpatrick, 22 Mar. 1847 and 21 May 1847 in O'Toole, *Guide to the Archives of the Archdiocese of Boston*, 174.

III

Most of the charitable work done by religious groups during the famine transcended denominational lines. Clergy of the established church in parts of Ireland where their congregations were small, helped the destitute Catholics in their districts, and the Society of Friends won particular esteem for its selfless dedication to relief of the needy. However, there was another element involved in relief work, which has passed into forklore as souperism, namely, the distribution of food and alms by Protestant missionaries to those who would embrace their faith. Though not extensive, this form of proselytism gave serious offence, not only to Catholics, but also to many Protestants. A typical example of this kind of denominational aggrandisement was to be found in an appeal in the *Belfast News Letter* to the members of the established church:

in numberless cases an opening has been made for conveying the light of the Gospel into the darkened minds of the Roman Catholic peasantry thus severely suffering: they have listened with the deepest attention to the ministers of the church proclaiming the way of salvation while humanely engaged in efforts to rescue their bodies from famine and disease. A wide and effectual door is thus thrown open to our brethren in the hitherto benighted parts of Ireland. In order that advantage be taken of these providential circumstances, in the hope and belief that their spiritual as well as temporal necessities may with God's blessing, be in great measure alleviated, a fund has been commenced for the relief of the temporal sufferings of our fellow countrymen of all denominations.[40]

This robust attitude to Irish Catholicism later manifested itself in opposition to schemes for assisted emigration to Canada. The *News Letter* feared that such projects would be too favourable to Romish propagandism and rejoiced when these proposals were abandoned.[41]

The religious consequences of emigration continued to trouble some zealots. James Morgan, the Moderator of the General Assembly of the Presbyterian Church in Ireland, bemoaned the failure of his church to enlighten the Catholics who were about to carry their false faith abroad:

These people are blinded and bigoted children of a fallen church. They hold their errors and cleave to their superstitions with a tenacity altogether remarkable. Wherever they go they carry their principles and habits with them. They are filled with the spirit of proselytism . . . The settlement of these people through other lands is therefore a solemn consideration. . . Have we not reason to fear that God is visiting us with this punishment for our neglect? We did not send the gospel to them. They were abandoned to their Sabbath desecrations and they have now become a host

---

[40] B.N.L., 8 Jan. 1847. [41] Ibid., 16 Apr. 1847.

which we are unable to withstand. A mighty torrent of impure water has been allowed to send forth its streams and overflow the lands.[42]

The helpless and disheartened refugees fleeing the famine would not have recognized themselves in the guise of active and enthusiastic proselytizers.

Some Protestant missionaries had been working in Kerry and Connacht before the famine. The Presbyterian Church also had a mission to Connacht, for which £5,000 had been subscribed, and during the famine some of their clergy certainly attracted converts by offering food and clothing. Elsewhere there were Catholics who passed over to Protestant churches for material reasons, but, fortunately, most religiously-inspired aid was untainted by these motives. Crolly did not have to face a problem which greatly concerned the archbishop of Tuam and the bishop of Kerry. But he did have several Irish schools in his diocese, in which Presbyterian teachers taught Catholic children with special emphasis on scripture through the medium of Irish. In 1848 the home mission claimed to have seventy such schools between Tyrone and Galway—and these were designed to serve the same purpose.[43] But probably many of those in Tyrone, like those in the Glens of Antrim, often existed only in the imaginations of the 'teachers', when they went to collect their pay packets.

The contemptuous dislike of some Ulster Protestants for poor Catholic peasants was increased by official policy during the famine. To alleviate the pressures on the heavily indebted poor law unions in the most distressed parts of the country, proposals were mooted early in 1849 for the institution of a rate-in-aid, or an increase in the rates in all unions to help out those which had borne the brunt of famine relief.

This suggestion was decidedly unpopular especially in the unions of the north of Ireland. The *Belfast News Letter* asked impatiently why a rate-in-aid should be raised only in Ireland and not throughout the whole United Kingdom, and, referring disdainfully to the reports of collections which Irish dioceses were organizing for the pope, insisted that there was no excuse 'for the robbery of generous and industrious Ulster to mitigate the burden of pauperism in districts which can afford to subscribe their thousands as a "rate-in-aid" to a fugitive Italian priest'. In view of the funds being gathered for the pope it wondered how Lord John Russell could plead the shadow of a necessity for plundering the enterprizing, benevolent and improving Protestants of Ulster.[44] Even some of the more

---

[42] Ibid., 9 July 1847.   [43] Ibid., 11 July 1848.
[44] Ibid., 23 Feb, 2 Mar. 1849.

liberally-minded Protestants of Belfast united with their conservative co-religionists in calling for a rejection of this proposal.[45] Their resistance, however, was unavailing.

IV

Crolly's predictions in July 1847 about the abundance of the harvest proved wildly optimistic. The shortage of seed due to the losses of the previous crop meant that the acreage of potatoes sown in 1847 was greatly reduced; in fact it was only one seventh of that of 1846 and one ninth of the acreage of 1845. Though raised again in the spring of 1848 to three times the 1847 level, the wet summer and the blight cut the yield of 1848 to about half of that of 1847.[46] The same problems of hunger and unemployment arose in the autumn. The Armagh guardians resolved in October to increase workhouse accommodation by 500 places to enable them to apply the workhouse test strictly and avoid the heavy and increasing expense of outdoor relief.[47] The workhouse in Lurgan which had less than 800 inmates in September had nearly 1,300 by the end of the year, and by March 1848 the number had risen to 1,350.[48] At the same time the numbers in Magherafelt workhouse climbed from 600 to 1,000.[49] The coadjutor bishop of Derry claimed in January that there was not 'in the North of Ireland a diocese or a parish in which the half of the Catholic population is not starving'[50]

The impatience of the government with the duration of the famine and the donor fatigue of the British public was met by increasing frustration and anxiety by the bishops and other leaders of public opinion in Ireland. At their meeting in October 1847 the hierarchy drew up a memorial to the Lord Lieutenant protesting at the inadequacy of the official remedies and asking for the provision of employment. Explaining that there were insufficient resources available to prevent 'an extensive destruction of human life', the bishops claimed that the distress derived not from any idleness or indolence on the part of the people but from the violation of the principles of justice and Christian morality inherent in the penal enactments that deprived them of the rights of property in other days. Defending their people's respect for law and order under 'unheard of

[45] N.W., 1 Mar. 1849.   [46] Donnelly, 'Production Prices and Exports 1846–51' in N.H.I., V, 288.
[47] PRONI, BG/2/A/5.   [48] Ibid., BG 22/A/6.   [49] Ibid., BG 23/A/1-2.
[50] Maginn to Cullen, 27 Jan. 1848, AICR.

privations', the prelates pointed out that the right to life was more sacred than the rights of property, and argued that, if that scale of values had not been frequently reversed, they would not have witnessed such heartrending scenes of evictions. Recalling the Christian axioms of the labourer being worthy of his hire and of doing to others what one should like done to oneself, they maintained that it was a violation of those maxims to appropriate the entire crops of the husbandman without compensating him for the seed or the labour expended on the cultivation of the soil. Describing the current arrangements for relief as totally insufficient, they begged the viceroy to use his influence to procure measures commensurate with the magnitude of the calamity, and expressed their preference for employment of a productive nature. They remarked that gratuitous relief had a demoralizing tendency and had been 'perverted by many into a means of proselytism, thus abusing what was destined for saving the lives of the starving into most annoying and vexatious aggression on the faith as well as on the morals of the poor'. They concluded by referring to the necessity of an equitable arrangement of the relations between landlords and tenants as the only guarantee of employment and protection for the poor.

The memorial was presented to the Lord Lieutenant on 25 October by Crolly, Murray and MacHale and the bishop of Killaloe, representing the archbishop of Cashel. Lord Clarendon in his reply made favourable reference to some of the points raised by the bishops and promised that the government would fulfill its duty to preserve human life but gave no specific commitments. He pointed out that the maxims quoted by the bishops were not more applicable in any country in the world than in Ireland. He agreed that the axioms were violated if an exorbitant or disproportionate rent were charged, but insisted that a similar infringement occurred if the owner could not obtain rent or the surrender of his land. If necessary, more workhouses would be provided, outdoor relief made available and the government would ensure that the laws regulating those matters would be carried out. He asked if men who would not make sacrifices themselves should insist that others put the precepts of religion into practice. In those districts where dreadful misery existed and local exertion was incapable of relieving it, the government would ensure that its first duty, the preservation of human life, was performed. He trusted that parliament would place the relations of landlord and tenant on a sounder footing and, in conclusion, told the prelates that he was pleased to meet them and would be anxious at all times to communicate with them and their colleagues when they came to Dublin, convinced as he was of their enormous influence with the majority of the people of Ireland.[51]

However, Clarendon's honeyed words belied his real sentiments. He described the memorial in private as 'about as mischievous a document as could have been devised at the present moment'. He explained that in asnwering he attempted 'to speak the truth without giving offence'. He said he was agreeably surprized by MacHale, who read the document and was the chief spokesman, and he was happy to note that Crolly, whom he described as 'an excellent man', was complimentary about his response and said that 'it ought to induce every man in Ireland to make exertions'.[52]

After the presentation of the memorial, some of the bishops—mainly the *politicanti*—did not resume their meeting. That of the *zelanti* reassembled and among the resolutions they passed was one expressing regret at the viceroy's ignoring their comment about gratuitous relief being pressed into the service of proselytism and another arranging for a deputation to the queen to lay their petition before her, if the Lord Lieutenant were unable to carry his humane wishes into effect.[53]

Paul Cullen, who was visiting Ireland at that time, reported that 'it was with difficulty' the bishops could be got to represent the great destitution of the country to the Lord Lieutenant. He went on to explain that Bishop McGettigan of Raphoe had stated that things were going so well in his diocese that they had sent back to the government £1,500, which had been given to them for relief, but that on the following day 'when there was question of the Pope, he said the distress indeed was tremendous and that he could not obtain or give anything'. Cullen noted that Crolly had spoken in the same way, and then added the gloss: 'see how hard it is to get anything done when people are connected with government. They were afraid to embarrass the ministry . . .'[54]

It is difficult to gauge the accuracy of this story. Cullen's information doubtless came from his friends in the hierarchy, who were staunch opponents of both Crolly and McGettigan, and whose version of events may not be fully reliable.[55] Crolly's connection with the government did not subsequently prevent him from opposing state payment of the clergy, and there seems no reason to suspect that he would have objected to a temperate plea for gainful employment for the poor.

[51] F.J., 26 Oct. 1847.
[52] Clarendon to Lansdowne and Russell, 26 Oct. 1847, Clarendon Papers, Lb i, ff 94v-98v.
[53] D.E.P., 28 Oct. 1847.
[54] Cullen to Kirby, 1 Nov. 1847, AICR.
[55] Bishop Maginn, the coadjutor of Derry, later denounced a northern bishop for returning the money sent to him by Cardinal Fransoni. But he based this charge on information he had received from MacHale and not from the cardinal. (Maginn to Cullen, 27 Jan 1848, AICR.)

Since the outbreak of famine MacHale had been writing strongly-worded letters to the prime minister, and his complaints had become more vigorous with time. Others, especially O'Higgins and Maginn of Derry, joined him in berating the government for its inaction. O'Higgins denounced 'the privileged class' which 'in defiance of the law of nature, and the revealed law of our common Creator, has the legal right of starving to death the people of these islands . . . and, whilst many of that class daily practise the most hideous forms of murder, they have at their command, to carry on their abominations, that noble soldiery of England, Ireland and Scotland . . .' He regretted the power of the 'absolute dictator' on whose mercy and caprice their lives and liberties depended and, remarked that while he kept 'the law for the relief of the poor in very charitable and becoming abeyance', his Irish fellow subjects 'for want of the application of that law, were dying of hunger by hundreds, by the day'.[56]

O'Higgins had some of the poorest parishes of Ireland in Longford and Leitrim and he witnessed the ravages of the famine at their worst. On another occasion he lamented to Rome the loss of very many of his best priests, 'victims to pestilence caught in the faithful discharge of their Sacred duties', and the death from hunger and disease during the previous season of 711 people in Gortleitra, in one of his 'ordinary country parishes', most of whom 'were buried by night in bogs, cabbage plots and in the cabins where they departed'.[57]

In general the bishops who supported the government on the Charitable Bequests and Colleges acts tended to assume it was doing what it could in the famine, while some of the *zelanti* (or 'orthodox' as Bishops Maginn and Cantwell described themselves) denounced it vigorously for its cruel and callous indifference to the sufferings of the poor. Cantwell declared that England 'will now, as she has ever done, do only what she is compelled to' and 'will give us nothing which she is not afraid to withhold'. Though the markets were cheap, the poor throughout Ireland were 'dying of hunger in the midst of plenty tho' subjects of the most wealthy & powerful Kingdom'. Maginn describing the terrible condition of the country where 'starvation & death the constant companions of our poor people—despair—disaffection, bordering on madness in the breasts of many' were everywhere, argued that the controlling influence of the Catholic clergy was never more necessary to bridle the impetuousity of

[56] N.W., 27 Jan. 1848.
[57] O'Higgins to Kirby, 4 Dec. 1847. AICR.

young blood and to preserve the country from the worst of scourges, civil war.

Both of them raged against the connection of their brethren, especially Crolly and Murray, with a government that was so unconcerned with the awful sufferings of its subjects. And both of them quite unfairly used this supposed connection with a heartless government to justify their own opposition to its policies on higher education. Cantwell remarked that 'the official connection of some of our Prelates with a Government acting such a part towards our poor was a great encouragement to them heretofore & is now an aggravated scandal in the face of the whole Kingdom'. He insisted that this 'unnatural & unholy alliance ought to be broken up', and that Rome alone could achieve that goal; and Maginn wrote bitterly of 'not a few [of their colleagues] who seem inclined to consider the smile of a Viceroy of much more importance than the symbol of their faith, the independence of their church or the salvation of their people'.[58]

Crolly never indulged in public denounciations of this nature but strove to relieve suffering at the local level and encouraged his clergy to do everything possible for the hungry and destitute. Some of his priests threw themselves into campaigns for tenant right and in particular for the legal recognition of the Ulster custom. At a meeting in Portadown, Eugene Crolly, the local parish priest, advocated the need for security for tenants who made improvements on their holdings, and pleaded for them to have a permanent interest in their farms.[59] And at the general meeting of the tenant right associations of Ulster, Patrick Quinn, the parish priest of Beragh, proposed the resolution attributing the social, economic and political evils of Ireland to the unjust and unsettled state of relations between landlord and tenant.[60] Catholic clergy also participated in meetings at Cookstown and Lurgan. An insight into the hectic activity of clerical life during the famine is afforded by the obituary of John Montague, the parish priest of Dungannon, who died in 1848. He was said to have spent hours daily on relief committees 'or in helping to carry out arrangements adopted for mitigating the privations of the distressed', by assisting them financially to obtain food from the soup kitchens. And during the jubilee of 1847, he was to be found in his church each day from 4.00 a.m.[61] One of Crolly's curates, Patrick Hart, died of fever in the house they shared in Armagh.[62] At least one other priest of the archdiocese, Peter Crilly, is listed in the obituary of the clerical directory as

[58] Cantwell to Cullen, 17 Jan., 10 Mar. 1848, and Maginn to Cullen 27 Jan., 7 Apr. 1848, AICR.
[59] N.W., 11 Apr. 1848.   [60] Ibid., 27 May 1848.   [61] D.E.P., 17 June 1848.
[62] N.Ex., 14 Feb. 1849.

having died of fever in 1847, and some of the others for whom no cause of death is assigned may also have died of famine-related fevers.

The 'rebellion' or skirmish between a few rebels and police at Ballingarry in Co. Tipperary in July 1848, while of little immediate political significance, helped further diminish sympathy in Britain for the famine-stricken Irish. The Catholic church gained credit with local magistrates and officials for its discouragement of all violence, whether it was politically motivated or was a reaction to social and economic oppression at local level. The *Northern Whig*, while very critical of the 'rebellion', praised the clergy for the zeal they showed for restraining strife-prone men in the disturbed districts.[63]

But if the bishops and clergy insisted on peaceful means of dealing with the catastrophe they faced, they demanded more effective intervention by the state. At their meeting in October the prelates passed a resolution expressing the grief and alarm they felt at the impending famine and the likelihood of many perishng from it, unless comprehensive measures were adopted. Reminding the government of the viceroy's declaration about its paramount duty being the preservation of human life, the bishops implored it to employ all the resources at its disposal for the immediate relief of the poor, and 'to use all its influence to effect such an equitable adjustment of the relations between landlords and tenants as shall stimulate an outlay of capital, ensure the employment of the able-bodied, and increase the agricultural products of the soil'.[64]

During the famine the bishops relaxed the observance of penitential practices during Lent, and some, including Crolly, withdrew the prohibition on working during holydays of obligation. Surprisingly, the hierarchy did not divert the money collected for the Propagation of the Faith during those years to local needs; though these collections declined significantly they continued to be taken up. And after the pope's exile to Gaeta in November 1848, some dioceses arranged collections to help him in his financial need, though they knew these would be small. Crolly made provision for one such in Drogheda a short time before he died.[65]

When the famine eventually ended it had claimed about one million lives and well over a million had emigrated. It was the greatest natural catastrophe in Europe in the nineteenth century, and given the constraining principles within which British economic thought operated, would have required intervention of a kind that the government was not prepared to make. Clergy of all denominations were overwhelmed by the

[63] N.W., 5, 8, Aug. 1848.   [64] Ibid., 14 Oct. 1848.   [65] D.E.P., 13 Mar. 1849.

sheer magnitude and duration of the catastrophe. All they could do was to organize and sponsor relief measures within the means at their disposal and cooperate at local level with the official schemes approved by the government. And as the toll of victims among them indicates, they did their best in very trying circumstances.

*   *   *

Typhus and relapsing fever, the products of famine conditions, carried off far more victims during the famine than actual hunger. While those weakened by hunger were obviously very vulnerable, these infectious diseases spared no class or age group. Towards the end of 1848 the Asiatic cholera, a pandemic which had swept through the continent during the year, finally hit Ireland. By the end of February 1849 nearly 3,000 cases of fever alone were reported in Belfast. Crolly fell victim to this dread disease on 5 April 1849 and died the next day, Good Friday, in Drogheda. His remains were brought to Armagh on the following day and he was interred in the sanctuary of the unfinished Cathedral,—itself a victim of the terrible upheavals, as building had been stopped when the walls were but a few feet above ground. Lord John Beresford, archbishop of Armagh, clergy of the established and Presbyterian churches, and gentry of the county joined Catholic bishops, clergy and laity in one of the largest funeral processions ever seen in the north of Ireland.

Newspapers with a mainly Catholic readership paid the conventional tributes to the deceased and commented on his pastoral zeal and tireless activity on behalf of his people. The *Northern Whig* remarked that he 'was distinguished by a combination of talent, prudence, independence and affability rarely found united in the same individual. He was a man of liberal principles, regulated and directed by a sound discretion, and a wise regard for the good of his country and those of his own denomination'. Describing his death as a national loss, the paper claimed that his influence and example were of great value in calming the passions of a large body of the Catholic people and promoting the enlightenment and liberties of his church, and recalled that the deceased prelate had been held in the highest respect in Belfast.[66] Participating in the sympathy expressed by all shades of opinion, the *Belfast News Letter* declared that the late archbishop had been 'greatly esteemed and respected by all with whom he had any connexion or acquaintance' and described him as 'a man of charitable, philanthropic and conciliatory disposition; moderate in his political opinions—simple and unostentatious in his manner'.[67]

[66] N.W., 10 Apr. 1849.   [67] B.N.L., 10 Apr. 1849.

These two notices testified in a striking way to the standing which Crolly had won and held in the Protestant community even among those who were increasingly reluctant to apportion praise to Catholic prelates. And, significantly, the papers of nationalist sympathies which had differed so strenuously from his political stance on Repeal, the Charitable Bequests Act and the Queen's Colleges, dismissing him somewhat disdainfully as a Whig, acknowledged his personal integrity and the uncompromising sincerity with which he reached his decisions on political issues. If Bishop Cantwell's terse and tearless comment, 'May God forgive him & have mercy on his soul',[68] represented the attitudes of the most intransigent of the *zelanti*, it seems likely that Bishop James Browne spoke for the less committed among the bishops as well as for the *politicanti*, when he wrote:

The poor Church of Ireland has suffered many severe calamities but in my Heart, I believe the most distressing of all has fallen on her by the death of our dear Friend the Primate. Where shall we find such rational firmness of Soul, such honest Candour united with an happy facility of getting through difficulties in a sweet inoffensive Manner. I really feel solitary after him, and never again expect to enjoy much comfort or satisfaction on the occasion of our Meeting. You have lost a Father, indeed one nearer, and poor Dr Murray's heart will be scarcely able to bear the shock.[69]

The manner and timing of the archbishop's decease poignantly reflected the death and distress which had so grievously afflicted millions of his fellow countrymen and co-religionists. It was indeed fitting that the primate should have suffered the same fate as so many hapless and unknown victims of the fevers that had so brutally and swiftly decimated Ireland and that his death should have occurred on the day which commemorated that of the Lord, whom he had ever struggled to serve with fidelity and fortitude.

---

[68] Cantwell to Cullen, 7 Apr. 1849, AICR.   [69] Browne to Denvir, 9 Apr. 1849, DCDA.

BIBLIOGRAPHY

MANUSCRIPT SOURCES

ARMAGH

Armagh Diocesan Archives
Papers of Archbishop Crolly

BELFAST

Down and Connor Diocesan Archives
Papers of Bishops Crolly and Denvir
Papers of William MacMullan
Evidence given at the Coleraine inquiry
Minute Book of the Belfast Chapel Committee, 1804-13
Minute Book of the Parish Committee of Drummaul, 1826-81 (copy)

Public Record Office of Northern Ireland
Applications for aid for national schools
Clogher Diocesan Papers
Minutes of Boards of Guardians
Tithe Applotment Books
Johnston Papers
Pilsen Papers

Linen Hall Library
Minutes of the General & Committee Meetings of the Belfast Society for
    Promoting Knowledge

St Patrick's Presbytery
Baptismal Registers

BIRMINGHAM

Papers of Bishop W.B. Ullathorne, Vicar-Apostolic of the Central District

DUBLIN

Dublin Diocesan Archives
Papers of Archbishop Murray

459

Papers of Archdeacon Hamilton
Papers of Francis Joseph Nicholson, Coadjutor Archbishop of Corfu
Minutes of Bishops' meetings

National Library of Ireland
Papers of Sir James Graham (on microfilm)
Papers of Archbishop Michael Slattery (on microfilm)

National Archives
Papers of the Famine Relief Commission

DUNDALK

Dundalk Parish: Parochial Meetings and Chapel Meeting Minute Book

GALWAY

Galway Diocesan Archives
Papers of Bishop Nicholas French

LEEDS

Leeds Diocesan Archives
Papers of Bishop John Briggs, Vicar Apostolic of the Northern District

LIVERPOOL

Liverpool Public Library
Papers of Edward George Geoffrey Smith Stanley, Fourteenth Earl of Derby

LONDON

Public Record Office
Correspondence of the Foreign Office with Diplomatic Representatives in Rome
    and Vienna
Home Office Papers relating to the Queen's Colleges

British Library
Papers of Sir Robert Peel
Papers of George Hamilton-Gordon, Fourth Earl of Aberdeen
Papers of Richard Wellesley, First Marquis Wellesley

MAYNOOTH

Archives of St Patrick's College
Minutes of the Meetings of the Trustees

NEWRY

Dromore Diocesan Archives
Papers of Bishop Michael Blake

OXFORD

Bodleian Library
Papers of Sir James Graham (on microfilm)
Papers of George William Frederick Villiers, Fourth Earl of Clarendon

ROME

Vatican Archives
Papers of the Secretariat of State relating to Ireland

Archives of the Sacred Congregation for the Evangelization of Peoples (formerly the
    Sacred Congregation de Propaganda Fide)
Correspondence and Recommendations of the Congregation relating to Ireland.

Archivio Storico della Congregazione degli Affari Ecclesiastici Straordinari
Papers relating to the Charitable Bequests and Queen's Colleges Acts.

Irish College
Correspondence of Paul Cullen and Tobias Kirby, Rectors of the College

NEWSPAPERS

Armagh Guardian	*Newry Examiner and Louth Advertiser*
Belfast Monthly Magazine	*Newry Telegraph*
Belfast News Letter	*Northern Herald*
Drogheda Argus	*Northern Whig*
Dublin Evening Post	*Pilot*
Freeman's Journal	*Tablet*
Irishman	*Vindicator*
Nation	*Weekly Vindicator*

PARLIAMENTARY DEBATES AND PAPERS

(i)   Hansard's parliamentary debates, 3rd series
(ii) Reports of the commissioners of national education, and of Irish education
      inquiry, and other parliamentary papers.

*First report of the commissioners appointed by the lord lieutenant to administer funds
    voted by parliament for the education of the poor of Ireland*, H.C. 1834 [70], xl.
*Second report of the commissioners of national education in Ireland, for the year
    ending 31st March 1835*, H.C. 1835 [300], xxxv.
Third report . . . , for the year ending 31 March 1836, [44], H.C. 1836, xxxvi.
Fourth report . . . , for the year ending 31st March 1837 [110], H.C. 1837-8, xxviii.
Fifth report . . . , for the year ending 31st March 1838 [160], H.C. 1839, xvi.
Sixth report . . . , for the year 1839, [246], H.C. 1840, xxviii.
Seventh report . . . , for the year 1840, [353], H.C. 1842, xxiii.
Eighth report . . . , for the year 1841, [398], H.C. 1842, xxiii.
Ninth report . . . , for the year 1842, [471], H.C. 1843, xxviii.
Tenth report . . . , for the year 1843, [569], H.C. 1844, xxx.
Eleventh report . . . , for the year 1844, [629], H.C. 1845, xxvi.
Appendix to the eleventh report . . . , for the year 1844, [650], H.C. 1845, xxvi.
Twelfth report . . . , for the year 1845, [711], H.C. 1846, xxii.
Thirteenth report . . . , for the year 1846, [832], H.C. 1847, xvii.
Fourteenth report . . . , for the year 1847, [981], H.C. 1847-48, xxix.
Fifteenth report . . . , for the year 1848, [1066], H.C. 1849, xxiii.
First report of the commissioners of Irish education inquiry, H.C. 1825 (400), xii.

Second report . . . , H.C. 1826-7 (12), xii.

Third report . . . , H.C. 1826-7 (13), xiii.

Fourth report . . . , H.C. 1826-7, (89), xiii.

Eighth report . . . , H.C. 1826-7 (509), xiii.

Ninth report . . . , H.C. 1826-7 (516), xiii.

Report from the select committee to whom the reports on the subject of education in Ireland were referred, H.C. 1828 (341), iv; reprinted H.C. 1829 (80), iv.

Report from the select committee appointed to take into consideration the state of the poorer classes in Ireland, H.C 1830 (667), vii.

First report of the commissioners of public instruction, Ireland, (45 and 46), H.C. 1835, xxxiii.

Second report of the commissioners of public instruction, Ireland, (47), H.C. 1835, xxxiv.

A report of the select committee of the House of Lords on the plan of education in Ireland; with minutes of evidence, H.C. 1837 (543-I), viii, pt i.

Minutes of evidence taken before the select committee of the House of Lords on the plan of education in Ireland, H.C. 1837 (543-II), viii, pt ii.

Report from the select committee appointed to inquire into the progress and operation of the new plan of education in Ireland, H.C. 1837 (485), ix.

Copies of any applications made by clergymen of the synod of Ulster to the board of education in Ireland, for aid to schools connected with the synod, since the recent conference between the deputation from the synod and the board, in presence of the lord lieutenant of Ireland; and, of any answers returned to such applications, or of any minutes made or resolutions entered into by the board in relation thereto, H.C. 1840 (110), xl.

A copy of the charter of incorporaton lately granted by her majesty to the board of national education in Ireland, H.C. 1846 (193), xlii.

Report from the select committee of the House of Lords appointed to inquire into the practical working of the system of national education in Ireland, 2 pts. H.C. 1854 (525), xv.

Royal commission of inquiry into primary education (Ireland), vol. i, pt i; *Report of the commissioners* [C6], H.C. 1870, xxviii, pt i.

Minutes of evidence taken before the select committee appointed to examine into the nature and extent of the disturbances which have prevailed in those districts of Ireland which are now subject to the provisions of the Insurrection Act, H.C. 1825 (20), vii.

Minutes of evidence taken before the select committee of the House of Lords appointed (in 1824) to examine into the nature and extent of the disturbances which have prevailed in those districts of Ireland which are now subject to the provisions of the Insurrection Act, H.C. 1825 (200), vii.

Report from the select committee appointed to inquire into the State of Ireland, more particularly with reference to the circumstances which may have led to disturbances in that part of the United Kingdom, H.C. 1825 (129),viii.

Minutes of evidence taken before the select committee of the House of Lords appointed to inquire into the State of Ireland, more particularly with reference to the circumstances which may have led to disturbances in that part of the United Kingdom, H.C. 1825 (181, 521), ix.

Evidence taken before Her Majesty's commissioners of inquiry into the state of the law and practice in respect to the occupation of land in Ireland, parts i, ii, and iii, H.C. 1845 [606,616,657], xix, xx, xxi.

Appendix to the minutes of evidence taken before Her Majesty's commissioners of inquiry into the state of the law and practice in respect to the occupation of land in Ireland, part iv, H.C. 1845 [672], xxii.

DISSERTATIONS

Acheson, A.R., *The evangelicals in the Church of Ireland, 1784-1859* (Queen's University, Belfast, Ph.D. thesis, 1968)

Grant, J., *The Great Famine in the Province of Ulster - the Mechanisms of Relief*, (Queen's University, Belfast, Ph.D. thesis, 1986)

Hill, M., *Evangelicalism and the churches in Ulster society, 1770-1850* (Queen's University, Belfast, Ph.D. thesis, 1987)

Jamieson, J., *The influence of the Reverend Henry Cooke on the political life of Ulster* (Queen's University, Belfast, MA thesis, 1950)

Rodgers, R.J., *Presbyterian missionary activity among Irish Roman Catholics in the nineteenth century.* (Queen's University, Belfast, MA thesis, 1969)

—, *James Carlile 1784-1854* (Queen's University, Belfast, Ph.D. thesis, 1973)

PRINTED WORKS

Ahern, J., 'The Plenary Synod of Thurles', *Irish Ecclesiastical Record*, lxxxv (1951) 385-403; lxxviii (1952), 1-20

Akenson, D.H., *The Irish Education Experiment: the National System of Education in the Nineteenth Century* (London, 1970)

—, *The Church of Ireland: Ecclesiastical Reform and Revolution, 1800-1885* (New Haven, 1971)

—, *A Protestant in Purgatory: Richard Whately, Archbishop of Dublin* (Archon Books, 1981)

An Authentic Report of the Discussion which took place at Downpatrick on the 22nd, 23rd, 24th, 28th, 29th, 30th April 1828 between Rev. E. Hincks, Rev. H.S. Cumming, Rev. R.W. Kyle and Rev. B. McAuley, Rev. C. Denvir, Rev. D. Curoe on six of the points of controversy between the Church of England and the Church of Rome (Belfast, 1828)

Anglesey, [7th] Marquess of, *One-leg: the Life and Letters of Henry William Paget, First Marquess of Anglesey, K.G. 1768-1854* (London, 1961)

Aubert, R., *Le Pontificat de Pie IX* (Paris, 1963)

Auchmuty, J.J., *Sir Thomas Wyse, 1791-1862: the Life and Career of an Educator and Diplomat* (London, 1939)

Authenticated Report of the Controversial Discussion upon the Supremacy of St. Peter which took place between the Rev. Bernard McAuley, P.P. and the Rev. Robert Stewart, A.M., Minister of the Gospel at Broughshane, on the 24th, 25th, and 26th July 1827 at Ballymena: Reported specially by L. Sheridan, and Joseph H. Leech, of Dublin (Belfast, 1827).

Baker, S.E., 'Orange and Green: Belfast, 1832-1912' in *The Victorian City: Images and Realities*, eds., H.J. Dyos and M. Wolff, 2 vols. (London, 1973), ii, 789-814

Balfour, G., *The Educational Systems of Great Britain and Ireland* (Oxford, 1903)

Bardon, J., *A History of Ulster* (Belfast, 1992)

Barkley, J.M., *A Short History of the Presbyterian Church in Ireland* (Belfast, 1959)

Barry, P.C. 'The Holy See and the Irish National Schools', *Irish Ecclesiastical Record*, series 5, xcii(1959), 90-105

Bartlett, T., *The Fall and Rise of the Irish Nation: The Catholic Question 1690-1830* (Dublin, 1992)

Battersby, W.J., *The Complete Catholic Directory, Almanac and Registry* (Dublin, 1836)

Beames, M., *Peasants and Power: The Whiteboy Movements and their Control in Pre-Famine Ireland* (Brighton, 1983)

Beckett, J.C., *The Making of Modern Ireland, 1603-1922* (London, 1966)

Beckett, J.C. and Glascock, R.E., *Belfast, The Origin and Growth of an Industrial City* (London, 1967)

Berens, E., *A Memoir of the Life of Bishop Mant* (London, 1849)

Bossy, J., *The English Catholic Community, 1570-1850* (London, 1975)

Bourke, U.J., *The Life and Times of the Most Rev. John MacHale, Archbishop of Tuam* (Dublin, 1882)

Bowen, D., *Souperism: Myth or reality? a Study of Catholics and Protestants during the Great Famine* (Cork, 1970)

—, *The Protestant Crusade in Ireland, 1800-70; A Study of Protestant-Catholic Relations between the Act of Union and Disestablishment* (Dublin, 1978)

Brady, J.C., 'Legal Developments 1801-79' in N.H.I., v, 51-80

Brant, H.J., *Eine Katholische Universität in Deutschland?* (Cologne, 1981)

Brett, C.E.B., *Buildings of Belfast* (Belfast, 1967)

Broderick, J.F., *The Holy See and the Irish Movement for the Repeal of the Union with England 1829-1847* (Rome 1951)

Brooke, P., *Ulster Presbyterianism: the Historical Perspective 1610-1970* (Dublin, 1987)

Budge, I. and O'Leary, C., *Belfast: Approach to Crisis: A Study of Belfast Politics 1613-1970* (London, 1973)

Cahill, G.A., 'Irish Catholicism and English Toryism', *Review of politics*, xix (1957), 62-76,

Cannon, S., *Irish Episcopal Meetings, 1788-1882: a juridico-historical study* (Rome, 1979)

Castlereagh, Viscount, (Robert-Stewart), *Memoirs and Correspondence*, 4 vols. (London, 1848-9)

Clarke, S. and Donnelly, J.S. (eds.), *Irish Peasants, Violence and Political Unrest 1780-1914* (Manchester, 1983)

Clausel de Montals, C.H., *Lettres et instruction pastorale de Monseigneur l'Evêque de Chartres concernant l'Université* (Avignon, 1843)

Coen, M., *The Wardenship of Galway* (Galway, 1984)

Cogan, A., *The Diocese of Meath, Ancient and Modern*, 3 vols. (Dublin 1870)

Combalot, T., *Memoire adressé aux Evêques de France et aux pères de famille sur la guerre faite à l'église et à la société par le monopole universitaire* (Paris, 1843)

Comerford, R.V. et al., *Religion, Conflict and Coexistence in Ireland: Essays presented to Monsignor Patrick J. Corish* (Dublin, 1990)

Connell, K.H., *Irish Peasant Society* (Oxford, 1968)

Connolly, S.J., *Priests and People in Pre-Famine Ireland 1780-1845* (Dublin, 1982)

—, 'Catholicism in Ulster, 1800-1850', in *Plantation to Partition: Essays in Ulster History in honour of J.L. McCracken*, ed. P. Roebuck (Belfast 1981)

—, *Religion and Society in Nineteenth Century Ireland* (Dundalk, 1985)

—, 'Mass politics and sectarian conflict, 1823-30' in *N.H.I.*, V, 74-107

Corish, P.J., *The Irish Catholic Experience* (Dublin, 1985)

Corish, P.J. ed. *A history of Irish Catholicism*, V, 6-10, (Dublin, 1970-71)

Coulter, J.A., 'Dr Edward Maginn (1802-1849), Priest or Politician', *Derriana, Journal of the Derry Diocesan Historical Society* (1981-2), 9-29

Cramsie, J., *The Life and Times of the Rev. Hugh O'Donnell, Founder of St Mary's Church, and First Parish Priest of Belfast* (Belfast, 1868)

Crolly, G., *The Life of the Most Rev. Doctor Crolly, Archbishop of Armagh, and Primate of Ireland, which are appended some letters in defence of his character* (Dublin, 1851)

Crone, H.A., Moody, T.W., and Quinn, D.B., (eds.), *Essays in British and Irish history in honour of James Eadie Todd* (London, 1949)

Crozier, J.A., *The Life of the Rev. Henry Montgomery, LLD., Dunmurry, Belfast* (London, 1875)

Curato, F., *Gran Bretagna e Italia nei documenti della missione Minto*, 2 vols. (Rome, 1970)

Dallat M., 'In the Beginning'. *St. Malachy's College Sesquicentennial* (1984), 36-40

D'Alton, E.A., *History of the Archdiocese of Tuam*, 2 vols. (Dublin 1928)

Daly, M., *The Famine in Ireland* (Dundalk, 1986)

—, 'The Development of the National School System, 1831-40' in *Studies in Irish History presented to R. Dudley Edwards*, eds., A. Cosgrove and D. McCartney (Dublin, 1979), 150-63

Dansette, A., *Religious History of Modern France* (Edinburgh and London, 1961)

Donnelly, J.S., 'Pastorini and Captain Rock: Millenarianism and Sectarianism in the Rockite Movements of 1821-4' in *Irish Peasants, Violence and Political Unrest 1780-1914*, ed. S. Clark and J.S. Donnelly Jr. (Manchester, 1983), 102-39

—, 'Famine and government response, 1845-6', in *N.H.I.*, V, 273-49

—, 'Production, prices and exports, 1846-51, in *N.H.I.*, V, 273-49

—, 'The administration of relief, 1846-7, in *N.H.I.*, V, 273-49

—, 'The soup kitchens', in *N.H.I.*, V, 273-49

—, 'The administration of relief, 1847-51', in *N.H.I.*, V, 273-49

—, 'Landlords and tenants', in *N.H.I.*, V, 272-49

Duffy, C.G., *Young Ireland: a Fragment of Irish History, 1840-1845* (2nd ed. Dublin, 1880)

—, *Four years of Irish history 1845-1849: a sequel to 'Young Ireland'* (London, 1883)

—, *My Life in two Hemispheres*, 2 vols. (London, 1903)

Dyos, H.J. and Wolff M., (eds) *The Victorian City: Images and Realities*, 2 vols. (London, 1973)

Edwards, R.D. and Williams T.D., *The Great Famine: Studies in Irish History 1845-52* (Dublin, 1962)

Fitzpatrick, W.J., *The Life, Times, and Correspondence of the Right Rev. Dr Doyle*, 2 vols. (Dublin, 1861)

Foster, R.F., *Modern Ireland 1600-1972* (London, 1988)

Friedrich, J., *Ignaz von Döllinger*, 3 vols. (Munich, 1899-1901)

Garvin, T., *The Evolution of Irish Nationalist Politics* (Dublin, 1981)

—, 'Defenders, Ribbonmen and others: Underground political networks in pre-Famine Ireland', *Past and Present*, 96 (1982), 133-55

Gash, N., *Politics in the age of Peel: a study in the techniques of parliamentary representation 1830-50* (London), 1953)

—, *Mr Secretary Peel: the Life and Times of Sir Robert Peel to 1830* (London, 1961)

—, *Sir Robert Peel: the life of Sir Robert Peel after 1830* (London, 1972)

Gerbod, P., *La condition universitaire en France au XIXe Siècle* (Paris, 1965)

Gibbon, P., *The Origins of Ulster Unionism: The Formation of popular Protestant Politics and Ideology in Nineteenth Century Ireland* (Manchester, 1975)

Goutard, M., *L'enseignement secondaire en France de la fin de l'Ancien Regime à la loi Falloux 1750-1850* (Aix-en-Provence, 1984)

Graham, R., *Vatican Diplomacy: A Study of Church and State on the International Plane* (Princeton, 1959)

Gwynn, D., *Daniel O'Connell, the Irish Liberator* (London, 1929)

—, *O'Connell, Davis and the Colleges Bill* (Cork, 1948)

Haire, J.L.M. et al., *Challenge and Conflict: Essays in Irish Presbyterian History and Doctrine* (Antrim, 1981)

Hänsel-Hohenhausen, M., *Clemens August Freiherr Droste zu Vischering, Erzbischof von Köln, 1773-1845: Die Moderne Kirchenfreiheit im Konflikt mit dem Nationalstaat* (Egelsbach bei Frankfurt/M., 1991)

Harkness, D. and O'Dowd, M., (eds), *The Town in Ireland* (Belfast, 1981)

Healy, J., *Maynooth College: its Centenary History 1795-1895* (Dublin, 1895)

Heatley, F., *The Story of St Patrick's, Belfast 1815-1977* (Portglenone, 1977)

Hempton, D. and Hill M., *Evangelical Protestantism in Ulster Society, 1740-1890* (London and New York, 1992)

Hill, J., 'The Protestant response to Repeal: The case of the Dublin working class' in *Ireland under the Union: Varieties of tension: Essays in honour of T.W. Moody*, ed. F.S.L. Lyons and R.A.J. Hawkins (Oxford, 1980), 35-68

—, 'The Meaning and Significance of "Protestant Ascendancy" 1787-1840' in British Academy/Royal Irish Academy (ed.), *Ireland after the Union* (London, 1987), 1-22

Holmes, R.F., *Henry Cooke* (Belfast, 1981)

—, *Our Presbyterian Heritage* (Belfast, 1985)

Hoppen, K.T., *Elections, Politics, and Society in Ireland 1832-1885* (Oxford, 1984)

—,. *Ireland since 1800: Conflict and Conformity* (London and New York, 1989)

Jamieson, J., *The History of the Royal Belfast Academical Institution, 1810-1960* (Belfast, 1959)

Keenan, D., *The Catholic Church in Nineteenth Century Ireland: A Sociological Study* (Dublin, 1983)

Kennedy, L. and Ollerenshaw, P. (eds) *An Economic History of Ulster 1820-1939* (Manchester, 1985)

Kerr, D.A., *Peel, Priests and Politics: Sir Robert Peel's Administration and the Roman Catholic Church in Ireland, 1841-46* (Oxford, 1982)

—, 'England, Ireland, and Rome' in *The Churches, Ireland and the Irish*, ed. W.J. Sheils and D. Wood (Oxford, 1989)

Kerrigan, C., *Fr Mathew and the Irish Temperance Movement 1838-1849* (Cork, 1992)

Klöcker, M., 'Kirche, Staat und Schule im 19. Jahrhundert' in *Lehrer-studium, Festschrift für Heinrich Kronen* (Cologne, 1991), 13-27

Larkin, E., 'Church and State in Modern Ireland in the Nineteenth Century', *Church History*, xxxi (1962), 294-306

—, 'The Devotional Revolution in Ireland', *American Historical Review*, lxxvii (1972), 625-52

—, ed., *Alexis de Tocqueville's Journey in Ireland* (Dublin, 1990)

Latreille, A., and Rémond, R., *Histoire du Catholicisme en France*, 3 vols. (Paris, 1962)

Lee, J., 'The Ribbonmen' in *Secret Societies in Ireland*, ed. T.D. Williams (Dublin, 1973), 26-35

Lessons on the Truth of Christianity being an appendix to the Fourth Book of Lessons, for the use of schools (Dublin, 1838)

Lill, R., *Die Beilegung der Kölner Wirren* (Düsseldorf, 1962)

Lipgens, W., 'Staat und Kirche in den rheinischen Volksschulen und Gymnasien 1820-35' in *Annalen des Historischen Vereins für den Niederrhein, Heft 163*, (1961), 96-127

Macaulay, A., *Patrick Dorrian: Bishop of Down and Connor 1865-85* (Dublin, 1987)

MacDonagh, O., 'The politicization of the Irish Catholic Bishops, 1800-1850', *Historical Journal*, xviii (1975), 37-53

—, *The Hereditary Bondsman, Daniel O'Connell, 1775-1829* (London, 1988)

—, *The Emancipist, Daniel O'Connell 1830-1847* (London, 1989)

—, 'The Age of O'Connell, 1830-45';

—, 'Politics 1830-45'; 'Ideas and institutions, 1830-45'; 'The economy and society, 1830-45', in *N.H.I.*, V, 158-241

Machin, G.I.T., 'The Maynooth Grant, the Dissenters and Disestablishment 1845-1847', *English Historical Review*, lxxxii(1967), 61-85

MacIntyre, A.D., *The Liberator: Daniel O'Connell and the Irish party, 1830-1847* (London, 1965)

MacNamee, J.J., *History of the Diocese of Ardagh* (Dublin, 1954)

Maguire, W.A., *Belfast* (Keele, 1993)

Malcolm, E., *Ireland sober, Ireland free: Drink and Temperance in Nineteenth Century Ireland* (Dublin, 1986)

Mant R., *History of the Church of Ireland* (London, 1840)

—, *Horae Ecclesiasticae. The Position of the Church with regard to Romish Error considered in a charge delivered to the clergy of his diocese, in July 1845* (London, 1845)

Mant, W.B., *Memoirs of the Right Reverend Richard Mant, DD, MRIA, Lord Bishop of Down and Connor, and of Dromore with an introductory sketch of the History of those Dioceses from the beginning of the seventeenth century* (Dublin, 1857)

Manzini, L.M., Il *Cardinale Luigi Lambruschini* (Vatican City, 1960)

Martina, G., *Pio IX, 1846-1850* (Rome, 1974)

Mathes, R., *Löwen und Rom: zur Gründung der Katholischen Universität Löwen unter besonderer Berücksichtigung der Kirchen und Bildungspolitik Papst Gregors XVI* (Essen, 1975)

Maxwell, H., *The Life and Letters of George William Frederick, Fourth Earl of Clarendon*, 2 vols. (London, 1913)

Mayeur, F., *De la Révolution à l'Ecole républicaine; Tome iii — Histoire générale de l'enseignement et de l'éducation en France, sous la direction de L.H. Parias* (Nouvelle Librairie de France, 1981)

McClelland, A. 'The Early History of Brown Street School', *Ulster Folklife*, xvii, (1971). 52-9

—, *William Johnston of Ballykilbeg* (Lurgan, 1990)

McClelland, V.A., *English Roman Catholics and Higher Education, 1830-1966* (Oxford, 1973)

McErlain, J., *A Statement of Accounts and of a few Facts of Local Interest presented to the Catholics of Ballymoney & Derrykeighan* (Ballymoney, 1881)

McGee, T.D., *A Life of the Rt. Rev. Edward Maginn - Coadjutor Bishop of Derry with Selections from his Correspondence* (New York, 1857)

McGrath, F., *Newman's University: Idea and Reality* (Dublin, 1951)

—, 'The University Question' in *A History of Irish Catholicism*, ed. P.J. Corish, v, Fasc. 6, (Dublin, 1971)

Miller, D.W., 'Irish Catholicism and the Great Famine', *Journal of Social History*, ix (1975), 81-98

—, 'Presbyterianism and "Modernization" in Ulster', *Past and Present*, No.80 (1978), 66-90

Mokyr, J., *Why Ireland starved: A Quantitative and Analytical History of the Irish Economy, 1800-1850* (London, 1983)

Montalembert, J.C., *Du Devoir des Catholiques dans la question de la liberté d'Enseignement* (Paris, 1843)

Moody, J.N., *French Education since Napoleon* (Syracuse, 1978)

Moody, T.W., *Thomas Davis, 1814-45* (Dublin, 1945)

—, (ed.) *Ulster since 1800: a Political and Economic Survey* (London 1955; corrected impression, 1957)

—, *Ulster since 1800: A Social Survey* (London 1957; corrected impression 1958)

Moody, T.W. and Beckett, J.C., *Queen's, Belfast, 1845-1949: the History of a University*, 2 vols. (London, 1959)

Moran, P.F., *Spicilegium Ossoriense: being a collection of original letters and papers illustrative of the History of the Irish Church from the Reformation to the year 1800*, 3rd series (Dublin, 1884)

Murphy, I., 'Primary Education' in *A History of Irish Catholicism*, ed. P.J. Corish, v, Fasc. 6 (Dublin, 1971)

Murphy, J.A., 'The support of the Catholic Clergy in Ireland 1750-1850', *Historical Studies*, v (1965), 103-21

—, 'Priests and people in modern Irish history', *Christus Rex.*, xxiii (1969), 235-59

Norman, E.R., *Anti-catholicism in Victorian England* (Cambridge, 1968)

Nowlan, K.B., *The Politics of Repeal: a Study in the Relations between Great*

Britain and Ireland, 1841-50 (London, 1965)

—, 'The Catholic Clergy and Irish Politics in the Eighteen Thirties and Forties', *Historical Studies*, ix (1974), 119-36

O'Connell, M.R., *The Correspondence of Daniel O'Connell*, 8 vols.(Dublin, 1972-80)

O'Connell, M.R., ed. *Daniel O'Connell: Political Pioneer* (Dublin, 1991)

—, *O'Connell: Education, Church and State* (Dublin, 1992)

O'Doibhlin, E., *Domhnach Mór (Donaghmore) : An Outline of Parish History* (Omagh, 1969)

O'Ferrall, F., *Catholic Emancipation: Daniel O'Connell and the Birth of Irish Democracy 1820-30* (Dublin, 1985)

O'Grada, C., *The Great Irish Famine* (Houndmills and London, 1989)

—, 'Poverty, population and agriculture, 1801-45'

—, 'Industry and communications, 1801-45' in *N.H.I.*, V, 108-57

O'Laverty, J., *An Historical Account of the Diocese of Down and Connor, ancient and modern*, 5 vols. (Dublin 1878-95)

O'Muiri, R., 'Orangemen, Repealers and the shooting of John Boyle in Armagh 12 July 1845' *Seanchas Ard Mhacha* 11, no.2, (1985), 435-529

O'Neill, T.P., 'The Catholic Church and Relief of the Poor, 1815-45', *Archivium Hibernicum*, xxxi (1973), 132-45

Ordnance Survey Memoirs of Ireland, I-XXXIV (Belfast and Dublin, 1990, in progress)

O'Reilly, B., *John MacHale, Archbishop of Tuam; his Life, Times and Correspondence*, 2 vols. (New York and Cincinnati, 1890)

O'Toole, J.M., *Guide to the Archives of the Archdiocese of Boston* (New York and London, 1982)

Patterson, T.F.G., 'Old St Malachy's',*St Malachy's Church, Armagh, Golden Jubilee 1938-88* (Monaghan, 1988)

Phillips, W.A., ed., *History of the Church of Ireland from the Earliest Times to the Present Day*, 3 vols.(Oxford, 1933)

Ponteil, F., *Histoire de l'énseignement en France*, (Paris, 1964)

Porter, J.L., *The Life and Times of Henry Cooke* (Belfast 1875)

Records of the General Synod of Ulster from 1691 to 1820, iii, (Belfast, 1848)

Reeves, W., *Ecclesiastical Antiquities of Down, Connor, and Dromore consisting of a Taxation of those Dioceses compiled in the year MCCCVI* (Dublin, 1847)

Reynolds, J.A., *The Catholic Emancipation Crisis in Ireland, 1823-1829* (New Haven, 1954)

Rogers, P., 'St Malachy's College, Belfast, 1833-1933', *The Collegian*, ix (1933), 13-29

—, *Father Theobald Mathew: Apostle of Temperance* (Dublin, 1943)

—, 'The Minute Book of the Belfast Rosarian Society', *Down and Connor Historical Society's Journal*, viii (1937), 17-24

Sacred Poetry adapted to the understanding of children and youth for the use of schools (Dublin, 1845)

St Alphonsus de Liguori, *Opera Moralia Sancti Alphonsi Mariae de Ligorio, theologia Moralis*, Tomus Primus cura et studio P. Leonardi Gandé (Romae, MDCCCV)

Schaaf, E., *Die niedere Schule im Raum Trier-Saarbrücken von der späten Aufklärung bis zur Restauration. 1780-1825* (Trier, 1966)

—, 'Lehrerbildung in der Zeit der preußischen Reformnbewegung und Restauration (1814-1840)' in H.A. Höhnen und E. Schaaf, *Lehrerbildung in Koblenz: Geschichte und heutiger Stand* (Trier, 1976), 307-28

—, 'Das Schulwesen in Koblenz von 1794 bis heute' in *Geschichte der Stadt Koblenz: Von der französischen Stadt bis zur Gegenwart* (Stuttgart, 1993), 517-30

Schatz, K., *Geschichte des Bistums Limburg* (Mainz, 1983)

Schwedt, H.H., 'Das Römische Urteil über Georg Hermes (1775-1831)' in *Römische Quartalschrift*, 37. Supplementheft, 1-372

Scripture Lessons, adapted for the use of schools: Old Testament, No. I (Dublin, 1832)

Scripture Lessons, for the use of schools: Old Testament, No. II (Dublin, 1846)

Scripture Lessons: New Testament, No. I, for the use of Irish National Schools (Dublin, 1834)

Scripture Lessons: New Testament, No. II, for the use of Irish National Schools (Dublin, 1835)

Seng, U., *Die Schulpolitik des Bistums Breslau im 19. Jahrhundert*, (Wiesbaden, 1989)

Senior, H., *Orangeism in Britain and Ireland, 1795-1836* (London, 1966)

Sharp, J., *Reapers of the Harvest: The Redemptorists in Great Britain and Ireland 1843-1898* (Dublin, 1989)

Silke, J.J., 'The Roman Catholic church in Ireland 1800-1922': a Survey of Recent Historiography, *Studia Hibernica*, xv (1975), 61-104

Statuta Diocesana in Episcopo [sic] Dunensi et Connoriensi [sic] observanda, et a RRmo. Guilelmo Crolly, Episcopo Dunensi et Connoriensi in sua Synodo Diocesana Edita et Promulgata (Dublinii, 1834)

Stewart, A.T.Q., *The Narrow Ground: Aspects of Ulster, 1609-1969* (London, 1977)

—, *Belfast Royal Academy: The First Hundred Years* (Belfast, 1985)

—, *A Deeper Silence: The Hidden Roots of the United Irish Movement* (London, 1993)

Strachey, L. and Fulford R. (eds.), *The Greville Memoirs, 1814-60*, 8 vols., (London, 1938)

Vaughan, W.E., ed., *A New History of Ireland 1801-70*, V (Oxford, 1989)

Walpole, S., *The Life of Lord John Russell*, 2 vols. (London, 1889)

Walsh, W.J., 'The Board of Charitable Donations and Bequests', *Irish Ecclesiastical Record* 3rd series, xvi (1895), 875-94,971-96,1071-99

—, *O'Connell, Archbishop Murray and the Board of Charitable Bequests* (Dublin, 1916)

Ward, J.T., *Sir James Graham* (London, 1967)

Ward, W., *The Life and Times of Cardinal Wiseman*, 2 vols. (London, 1897)

Whately, R., *Essays on the Errors of Romanism, having their Origin in Human Nature* (5th ed. London, 1861)

Whyte, J.H., 'Daniel O'Connell and the Repeal party', *Irish Historical Studies*, xi (1959), 297-316

—, 'The Appointment of Catholic Bishops in nineteenth century Ireland', *Catholic Historical Review*, xlviii (1962), 12-32.

INDEX